Date Due	
MAR 0 8 2002	
APR 0 3 2002	
NOV 1 5 2005	
NOV 1 5 2005	
FEB 1 0 2006	

Studies in Victorian Life and Literature

Charles Dickens c. 1850, Age Thirty-Eight

From a daguerreotype by Henri Claudet. Huntington Library, San Marino, California.

The Night Side of Dickens
Cannibalism, Passion, Necessity

Harry Stone

with 145 illustrations

Ohio State University Press
Columbus

Library of Congress Cataloging-in-Publication Data
Stone, Harry, 1926–
    The night side of Dickens : cannibalism, passion, necessity / Harry Stone
        p.   cm.—(Studies in Victorian life and literature)
    Includes bibliographical references and index.
    ISBN 0–8142–0547–X
    1. Dickens, Charles, 1812–1870—Criticism and interpretation. 2. Necessity (Philoso-
phy) in literature. 3. Light and darkness in literature. 4. Cannibalism in literature. 5. Emotions in literature. 6. Death in literature.   I. Title.   II. Series.
PR4588.S76   1994
823'.8—dc20   92–26043
                                                                       CIP

Type set in ITC Galliard by Graphic Composition, Athens, GA.
Printed by Bookcrafters, Chelsea, MI.

9 8 7 6 5 4 3 2 1

This book is Dedicated

to my son,

Jonathan

and my daughter,

Ann

with Love

Contents

Illustrations

All illustrations, unless otherwise specified, are from the author's collection.

Preface

The Night Side of Dickens concentrates on a profoundly important element in Dickens' life and writings, what I call the "night side" of Dickens, and examines the ways in which that shaded element—a dark, slowly accreting cluster of emotions and ideas—germinated, grew, and then entered and shaped Dickens' art. The night side of Dickens has many forms and colorations—and many disguises. In "Dickens and Necessity," Part 3 of this book, one aspect of that somber, and often veiled, side of Dickens emerges in sharp focus:

> [This is] the hidden, diseased night side—the wounded George Sil-
> verman side—of Dickens, a side that had its origins (again as with George
> Silverman) in a series of repeated and reinforcing experiences that go
> back to Dickens' earliest days. Many years after those earliest days, long
> after Dickens had become rich and famous, Thomas Carlyle had glimpses
> of this region of darkness that lay so deeply buried beneath the burnished
> surface of Dickens' intense life-affirming engagement with the outer
> world. Beneath Dickens' "bright and joyful sympathy with everything
> around him," Carlyle wrote, there were "deeper than all, if one has the
> eye to see deep enough, dark, fateful, silent elements, tragical to look
> upon, and hiding, amid dazzling radiances as of the sun, the elements of
> death itself."

The Night Side of Dickens tracks this hidden and death-environed night side in three crucial areas of Dickens' concern—cannibalism, passion, and necessity. These areas, which seem at first glance to be independent and distinct, are in reality deeply intertwined. There are hosts of connections, reciprocities, overlaps, and reinforcements—entanglements of origins, ideas, events, reticences, responses, and results. What emerges from studying these night-side areas and manifestations are patterns of great significance not only for those interested in Dickens and his art but for those interested in the mysteries of artistic creation.

The realization that Dickens' genius was compounded of dark as well as dazzling elements did not begin with Thomas Carlyle, nor was he the sole early witness to the "tragical" elements that lay beneath Dickens' "bright and joyful sympathy." In fact, Carlyle's comment, made in a letter to John Forster, had been provoked by some of Forster's own comments and revelations. In his biography of Dickens, Forster had revealed (often quoting Dickens' own impassioned testimony) some of the early wounds and humiliations Dickens had suffered, some of the secret shame and morbid sensitivities those early experiences had engendered, and some of the ways those experiences had shaped his subsequent work and had bred his need to transcend the sad imperfections of intractable reality through the ever-responsive fulfillments of creation. Forster had also gone on to reveal Dickens' later restlessness and unhappiness, connecting those symptoms, and the breakup of his marriage (another product of that unhappiness), to Dickens' frustrated yearning for an unattainable ideal or, more exactly, to his search for the ideal in the actual (his dream world, that is, his creative world, in those latter years no longer sufficing as it had in the past); "but what he would have sought there [in the actual], it supplies to none; and to get the infinite out of anything so finite, has broken many a stout heart."

For the next sixty or seventy years after Forster's biography these darker elements in Dickens' life and character, and more especially in his writings, were largely ignored; certainly they were never seriously explored. Then this long neglect, which had been only partially mitigated by the writings of Gissing, Shaw, and one or two others, and only partially breached by the disclosures (in the 1930s) of Wright and Storey, came to an end. In "Dickens: The Two Scrooges," an essay first published in the *New Republic* in 1940, and then in the following year, in revised and enlarged form, in *The Wound and the Bow,* Edmund Wilson emphasized the divided character of Dickens' sensibility, the undercurrent of darkness that runs through his writings, the importance of the gloomier later novels, and the transcendent stature of his genius. In the following years the floodgates opened. A host of works—biographical, sociological, Marxist, psychological, new critical, mythic, and more—examined the darker strain in Dickens' life and writings.

Four representative early studies with this new emphasis, two long works, and two short ones (dozens could be cited), each quite different in its "dark" outlook, and each an important witness to the changed conception of Dickens and his art, are: Lionel Stevenson's "Dickens's Dark Novels, 1851–1857" (1943), Jack Lindsay's *Charles Dickens: A Biographical and Critical Study* (1950), Edgar Johnson's *Charles Dickens: His Tragedy and Triumph* (1952), and Lionel Trilling's "Little Dorrit" (1953). Johnson's two-volume work, by far the most important of these four, immediately became the influential standard modern biography of Dickens. Its subtitle, which gives "tragedy" equal billing with "triumph," reflects the new emphasis on a darker Dickens. Such a title would have been inconceivable a generation earlier. But the winds of critical interest and the tides of critical perception fluctuate. In the last twenty years or so the emphasis on the darkness in Dickens has subsided; other orthodoxies have taken center stage.

The Night Side of Dickens draws upon this checkered and fluctuating interest in a darker, more concealed Dickens, going back to Forster's (and Dickens') original revelations and insights in this area, and then drawing upon the scholarship and criticism of the last fifty years and more. But these insights, and other very different ones have been applied here in new ways, and abundant use has been made of Dickens' lesser-known works as well as his major works to bring fresh perspectives to his writings and to highlight dimensions in his thought and art that have gone largely unnoticed or unappreciated. Many of the writings examined in these pages have never been used before in the context used here; in fact, many of these writings have never been used before in any context or any criticism.

One result of this unconventional casting of nets is a whole range of insights and discoveries, some major, some minor, but all incorporated into the text without fanfare (that is, without calling attention to their status as discoveries). Many of these revelations emerge from unknown, or virtually unknown, works. For example, after visiting Hampton Court with Ellen Ternan (this in the early perfervid days of their relationship), Dickens wrote "Please to Leave Your Umbrella," a strangely conflicted confessional essay, but neither the visit nor the essay nor the import of the essay, despite its indiscreet, half-hidden, half-flaunted revelations, has been noticed before. Other fresh insights emerge from examining Dickens' original manuscripts. A study of the manuscript of *George Silverman's Explanation,* for example, allows one to trace (among many other matters) the origins and evolution of the title of that remarkable but neglected work, an evolution that casts crucial light on the meaning of that story, a haunting and enigmatic creation—really a novel in miniature—Dickens' last completed work of fiction.

By the same token, much original background research has been incorporated throughout the book, again without fanfare. Take, for example, Dickens' visit to Hoghton Towers, a visit that helped engender and then shape *George Silverman's Explanation.* A close inspection of the Hoghton Towers buildings and grounds makes clear that the topography, spatial relationships, architecture, empty courtyards, gaping stairwells, green growth, foraging rats, as well as many other details of the manor house and its environs, played crucial roles in determining the theme and meaning of the story—a fact to which Dickens himself testified in a letter, but without giving any clues as to how or why those engenderings came about. The implications of these casual (or seemingly casual) engenderings and their momentous fulfillments—implications that range far beyond house or visit or story, and that shed light on dark nooks and crannies of Dickens' life and art—are explored here for the first time.

Or take one other example, Dickens' visit to Lancaster in 1857. That brief visit, not only to the city, but to the King's Arms, Lancaster, Lancaster Lunatic Asylum, and Lancaster Castle, and the haunting significance for Dickens of Edward Hardman's monstrous Lancaster-linked crime and Lancaster Castle hanging—all hitherto unexplored subjects (the Hardman case an unknown subject)—became deeply entwined with Dickens' life and art. That tangled web of settings, events, associations, and emotions, in turn, is important not only for understanding the genesis and eventual unfolding of "The Bride's Chamber" and *Great Expectations,* but for understanding Dickens' innermost psychological state as he determined to end his marriage. These intertwined matters and the new insights they evoke are fully explored in this study. Every part of the book—the section on cannibalism is especially rich in this respect—contains many similar unremarked discoveries and explorations.

The book also contains explorations of a different sort. It utilizes a wide range of eighteenth- and nineteenth-century literary, journalistic, graphic, medical, ethnographic, historical, and other ancillary sources, most of them unfamiliar, many of them obscure, all of them pertinent to the central focus of the book, in order to give a larger context to the exotic and sometimes forbidden pathways being pursued.

Also important in distinguishing what is presented here from what has gone before is what I mean by "night side" and what is included under that rubric. Night side is not used in these pages as a simple synonym for dark; that is, it is not used as a picturesque way of talking about the darker view of life that Dickens held in his later years and conveyed in his later writings. Though such matters are included in the term *night side* as used here, and though they are dealt with throughout this study, what this book chiefly pursues is a number of the most hidden and disturbing dimensions in Dickens' art, deep but often unregarded dimensions that pervaded his thought and writings, sometimes willy-nilly, and that helped shape the nature and often the very meaning of his art. These night-side aspects of his thought and art were sometimes hidden from Dickens' own full consciousness as well as from the direct and open gaze of the world. But whether conscious or unconscious (and by far the greater part of what is discussed here was conscious), this special use of night side to signify the most hidden and secret dimensions of a subject or concern was sanctioned by Dickens himself. In 1848, reviewing Catherine Crowe's *The Night Side of Nature; or, Ghosts and Ghost Seers* for the *Examiner*, Dickens defined what the term *night side* meant in its original, astronomical signification. "Night side," he wrote, is "that side of a planet which is turned from the sun." He then went on to explain that the term had soon taken on larger, more metaphorical meanings, and it is in this enlarged metaphorical sense that the term is used here. *The Night Side of Dickens* concentrates on that side of the planet Dickens which is turned from the sun.

More particularly, the book concentrates on three profoundly important areas of Dickens' thought and creativity that were turned from the sun, a turning away that shrouded in darkness their deepest and most revealing significances. It concentrates on such obsessive and meaningful Dickensian concerns as cannibalism, a nightmare concern at once strangely attractive and profoundly revolting to Dickens, a necessitous concern that appears everywhere in his writings, but that appears there in such secret, disguised, effaced, or transformed ways that it has scarcely been remarked upon in a hundred and fifty years of criticism. The book also concentrates on passion, not the passion of noble sentiments and high romance, but blind, malignant, uncontrollable passion, consuming passion that leads inexorably and compulsively to misery and self-destruction. Though much has been written about love and women in Dickens, little has been written about this wild, raging, titanic force (a force observable primarily in Dickens' men), and little has been done to trace the inmost nature of this passion, its genesis in Dickens' life and its development in his writings. Finally, the book concentrates on necessity and the bleak impositions of compulsion and determinism, a subject that is largely unaddressed in Dickens criticism. This silence is surprising, for the subject increasingly perplexed Dickens, increasingly engrossed him, increasingly informed his writings (those concerning cannibalism and passion as well as those focused more directly on necessity), and increasingly darkened his outlook.

In each of these three areas—intertwined, deeply troubled areas that tormented and drove Dickens—this study sets forth what Dickens had to say on the subject and then goes on to trace the origins of its sway over his life and to show its importance for understanding his art. In order to provide this comprehensive in-depth treatment, each area is studied in turn, and each is given a separate part of the book: Part 1, "Dickens and Cannibalism: The Unpardonable Sin," Part 2, "Dickens and Passion: The Tangled Web," and Part 3, "Dickens and Necessity: The Long Chain." Each part endeavors to survey the entire realm of Dickens' connection with the subject and also seeks to show how the subject in question, or rather, Dickens' special version of that subject, emerges in his writings and helps form the inmost nature of what he creates. Finally, each part surveys the chief works that exemplify this process.

In the last two parts of the book, in addition to such surveys and analyses, I have selected a short, little-known, little-explored, but crucial work ("The Bride's Chamber" in "Dickens and Passion," and *George Silverman's Explanation* in "Dickens and Necessity") and examined it in detail, seeking by such examination to explore in much greater depth and nuance matters that had to be treated more selectively everywhere else. These more intensive demonstrations give a better sense of how the strand being traced weaves in and out of the overall pattern, contributes to it, and becomes—or rather is—the essence and simulacrum of the pattern itself, part of the beating heart of the work. At the same time, these more intensive readings make it possible to do justice to "The Bride's Chamber" and *George Silverman's Explanation* as independent works, to place each in its full and profoundly meaningful context, and to assess the central and ramifying importance of each in Dickens' life and writings.

The tripartite structure of *The Night Side of Dickens* also makes it possible to deal with divergencies as well as connections. The three parts of the book are interconnected by a complex web of shared origins and developments and by an intricate network of entanglements and recurrences. But Dickens was myriad-minded; his works are full of diversities and contradictions, and though one can find patterns and interests and interconnections that emerge over and over again in his writings, one can also find everywhere a plenitude that refuses to be comprehended in fixed categories. This study seeks to convey that richness and complexity by occasionally viewing a particular work through different but related lenses—the lenses of cannibalism, passion, and necessity—sometimes viewing not simply the same work through those refracting and reflecting lenses but the same character or the same scene. Thus, to give just two or three examples, *A Tale of Two Cities* looms large in "Dickens and Cannibalism" and "Dickens and Passion," while *Great Expectations* looms large in those two parts and in "Dickens and Necessity" as well. (*A Tale of Two Cities* also enters "Dickens and Necessity," but in a different way from that just alluded to.) By the same token, we meet John Jasper as cannibal and as lover (also as cannibal-lover), Bradley Headstone as passion's slave and necessity's pawn (the two are often one), and so on. Sometimes these scenes and roles merge, sometimes they diverge. Dickens rarely wrote with formulas, categories, or theories in mind, and he was not doctrinaire. Accordingly, this book does not seek to impose artificial rigidities on his protean richness but rather to follow him in his diverse, multivisioned yet distinctive ways, dwelling on one pattern of recurrences in the first part, on other (usually interconnected) patterns in the second and third parts, but pointing out anomalies as well.

One should keep in mind, then, that though the patterns being traced in this book are fundamental and profoundly important, they are not all-inclusive: Dickens created aggressive adults who are not cannibals, smitten lovers who are not passion-driven self-destroyers, struggling humans who are not blind thralls of necessity. Furthermore, he often created scenes and characters and actions that hint and whisper rather than shout, that softly, often intermittently, convey their cannibalistic, or passion-freighted, or darkly necessitous, or intermingled messages. This study attempts to keep this diversity and commingling in view, and to keep in view also the wider worlds in which these elements exist, keep those worlds in view and reflect them in these pages.

The Night Side of Dickens is not confined to one body of information or to one critical stance. Rather, it utilizes whatever sources and approaches seem most helpful in elucidating the particular subject in hand. Each section of the book, therefore, contains a diversity of materials (not simply literary materials) and a variety of perspectives, but only insofar as those materials and perspectives are crucial aspects of the central subject, and only insofar as they help to focus, balance, and illuminate that central subject and make it fully comprehensible. As a consequence, the book incorporates, where pertinent, biographical, psychological, sociological, historical, linguistic, structural, textual, archetypal, genderal, and still other approaches, and in addition it often depends upon (what I hope is) a sensitive and revealing *explication de texte*. My purpose in drawing upon this diversity of disciplines and approaches was to provide a coherent, well-rounded, illuminating assessment of the three profound and interrelated Dickensian concerns that are the focus of this study. My purpose was also to convey that assessment in a lucid, jargon-free way that is not parochial, single-minded, or reductive—a way that I hope will bring the reader back to Dickens' writings with a greater awareness of their richness and a greater understanding of their complex meaning.

Finally, I felt that there was something fresh, something surprising, and at times something startling, to say about fundamental and seemingly settled aspects of Dickens' life and craft. I hope that this multiapproach study, which attempts to track the ways of the imagination, ways that are so astonishing and so mysterious, will shed new light on the nature of Dickens' art and the magnitude of his achievement.

Los Angeles   HARRY STONE

1990

Acknowledgments

I am indebted to the officers and staffs of the following institutions and collections for allowing me to consult (and in many instances to reproduce) important manuscript, rare-book, and graphic materials in their collections, and for many additional courtesies: Arts Library, Manchester Central Library (Manchester); Beinecke Rare Book and Manuscript Library, Yale University (New Haven, Conn.); Henry W. and Albert A. Berg Collection, New York Public Library (New York); Bibliothèque Historique de la Ville de Paris (Paris); British Library (London); British Museum (London); Carnegie Museum of Art (Pittsburgh); William Andrews Clark Memorial Library (Los Angeles); Dickens Fellowship (London); Dickens House Museum (London); Enthoven Theatre Collection, National Arts Library, Victoria and Albert Museum (London); Fitzwilliam Museum, Cambridge University (Cambridge, Eng.); Forster Collection, National Arts Library, Victoria and Albert Museum (London); Richard Gimbel Collection, Yale University Library (New Haven, Conn.); Hampton Court Palace (Hampton, Greater London); Hoghton Tower (Hoghton near Preston, Eng.); Houghton Library, Harvard University (Cambridge, Mass.); Henry E. Huntington Library and Art Gallery (San Marino, Calif.); Library of

Congress (Washington, D.C.); Lancaster Central Library (Lancaster, Eng.); Lancaster City Museum (Lancaster, Eng.); Lancaster Moor Hospital (Lancaster, Eng.); Manchester Central Library (Manchester); National Portrait Gallery (London); Newspaper Library, British Library (London); Parrish Collection, Princeton University Library (Princeton, N.J.); Pierpont Morgan Library (New York); New York Public Library (New York); Bancroft Library, University of California at Berkeley (Berkeley); Research Library, University of California at Los Angeles (Los Angeles); President and Council of the Royal College of Surgeons of England (London); John Rylands Library (Manchester); Tate Gallery (London); Harry Elkins Widener Memorial Collection, Harvard University Library (Cambridge, Mass.); University Libraries, California State University, Northridge (Northridge, Calif.); Wellcome Institute of the History of Medicine (London); Yale Center for British Art, Yale University (New Haven, Conn.).

I am grateful to Mr. Neville Harrison, Keeper of Monuments, County Hall, Preston, for granting me special permission to visit the whole of Lancaster Castle, and to Miss Dorothy Atherton, Resident Curator of Lancaster Castle, her staff, and the authorities of Lancaster Castle Prison, for conducting me on an exhaustive tour of the castle, the courtrooms, and the prison, for allowing me to photograph restricted areas of all three, and for providing me with copies of nineteenth-century documents and records.

I am also much indebted to Mr. Stephen J. Brook, Chief Administrator, Lancaster Moor Hospital, who took several hours from his busy schedule to conduct me through the wards, courtyards, chapels, museums, grounds, and other facilities of Lancaster Moor Hospital, who allowed me to photograph the buildings and wards that Dickens had visited, who patiently answered my torrents of questions about every aspect of the hospital, who provided me with documents, plans, and historical summaries concerning the hospital, and who accorded me many other exceptional courtesies.

I also wish to thank Sir Richard Bernard Cuthbert de Hoghton, 14th Baronet, for granting me special permission for a private visit to Hoghton Tower, and Mrs. Margaret Hutton, Chief Administrator and Resident Curator, for taking me through every nook and cranny of that fascinating estate, for allowing me to photograph its odd corners and remote precincts, and for providing me with memorable hospitality and many hours of her time. I am grateful also to Dr. David Parker, curator of the Dickens House Museum, London, for giving generously of his time to satisfy a long series of queries and requests. I am indebted as well to Mr. Emmanuel Pernaud and Mr. Hubert Prouté of Paul Prouté (Paris) and to the staff of Roger-Viollet (Paris) for their aid in searching out French graphic materials.

I would also like to acknowledge the help of Brita F. Mack, Jacqueline Dugas, and Aldo R. Perdomo (Huntington Library and Art Gallery), Rishona Zimring and Vincent Giroud (Beinecke Rare Book and Manuscript Library, Yale University), A. J. White and Susan Ashworth (Lancaster City Museum), S. J. Eccles and Miss Gaddes (Manchester Central Library), Melissa Dalziel (Fitzwilliam Museum), John Jenkins (Hoghton Tower Preservation Trust), C. M. Craig (Royal College of Surgeons of England), H. H. Mathews (British Museum), Helen Foster (Arts Library, Manchester Central Library), Rodney G. Dennis and Vicki Denby (Manuscript Department, Houghton Library, Harvard University), Marilyn Hunt (Yale Center for British Art), Lisa Miriello (Carnegie Museum of Art), and J. Chester and Julie Phillips (Newspaper Library, British Library).

I would like to thank Jerome Richfield, Dean Emeritus of the School of Humanities, California State University, Northridge, who has encouraged my research and writing not only for *The Night Side of Dickens,* but for many other projects, and has done so in countless tangible and intangible ways. I would also like to thank my colleague Harry Finestone who read this book in manuscript (some portions more than once) and offered many valuable suggestions. I am much indebted to Mary Alvarez, secretary of the English department, who typed (or rather computer-set and printed) this book too many times for me to remember or her to forget, and always did so with unfailing good humor and devotion. I am also indebted to my assistants, Catherine Kilkes, Lori Carroll, Patricia Hackl, Anetta Stark, and Paula Foster, and to the former secretary of the English department, Carol Nadler. I wish to thank as well Peggy Laird, Supervisor of Photography, Instructional Media Center, California State University, Northridge.

In the course of researching and writing this book, I have utilized some of my findings (usually in a very different form and on a much smaller scale) in a number of papers, public lectures, and introductions. These include a paper at the annual meeting of the Modern Language Association of America (New York, December 1983); the Introduction to *George Silverman's Explanation* (Santa Susana Press, 1984); a public lecture at the University of California, Santa Cruz (August 1985); the Sixth Annual David L. Kubal Memorial Lecture at California State University, Los Angeles (January 1988); the Faculty Research Lecture at California State University, Northridge (February 1988); public lectures in Tokyo (August 1990) and Sendai (June 1991) before the Dickens Fellowship of Japan, and lectures at Seijo University, Tokyo (June 1991), and the Centre for English Studies, University of London (June 1992).

This book has been aided by grants from the School of Humanities, California State University, Northridge, the Research and Grants Committee, California State University, Northridge, and the Department of English, California State University, Northridge. I deeply appreciate this support.

Part 1
Dickens and Cannibalism

3. Charles Dickens in 1830, Age Eighteen

Engraving after a miniature by Dickens' aunt, Janet Ross Barrow.

Dickens and Cannibalism
The Unpardonable Sin

I shall never see that sea-beach
on the wall or in the fire,
without him, solitary monster,
eating [human flesh] as he prowls along,
while the sea rages and rises at him.

—from Dickens' "The Long Voyage"

I

"I am rather strong on Voyages and Cannibalism," Dickens wrote in 1854 to his subeditor, W. H. Wills, "and might do an interesting little paper for next No. [of *Household Words*] on that [subject]" (20 November 1854).[1] Dickens was right. He was not simply strong on, he was obsessed by the subject of cannibalism—the unpardonable sin, that "dreadful," "horrible," "wolfish" "last resource," as he later called it (*HW* 10: 361, 364)—and he wrote not one but three articles on the subject in an attempt to refute the charges that Sir John Franklin's final ill-fated Arctic expedition had resorted to cannibalism, arguing, with much evidence of wide reading on the subject, that no well-bred Englishman, no matter what the extremity, would ever succumb to that frightful feasting. Dickens' attitude toward cannibalism and the Franklin expedition is well summarized

| PART OF FLANNEL SHIRT. | PIECE OF PLATE. | PART OF COMPASS. | CERTIFICATE CASE. | BUTTONS, LINKED WITH CORD |

| COOK'S KNIFE | KNIFE HANDLE. | BUTTON. | GOLD-LACE BAND. |

4. Relics of the Franklin Expedition

These relics were brought back to England by Dr. John Rae. *Illustrated London News* (4 November 1854).

by a letter he wrote to Mrs. Richard Watson some three weeks before he broached the possibility that he might write something on the subject for *Household Words*. The letter shows both the intensity of his interest in the subject and the focus of his concern:

> Dr. Rae's account of Franklin's unfortunate party is deeply interesting; but I think hasty in its acceptance of the details, particularly in the statement that they had eaten the dead bodies of their companions, which I don't believe. Franklin, on a former occasion, was almost starved to death, had gone through all the pains of that sad end, and lain down to die, and no such thought had presented itself to any of them. In famous cases of shipwreck, it is very rare indeed that any person of any humanising education or refinement resorts to this dreadful means of prolonging life. In open boats, the coarsest and commonest men of the shipwrecked party have done such things; but I don't remember more than one instance in which an officer had overcome the loathing that the idea had inspired. Dr. Rae talks about their *cooking* these remains too. I should like to know where the fuel came from. (1 November 1854)

As the days went by, Dickens found he could not dismiss the lost polar party and images of cannibalistic feeding from his mind. As a matter of fact, his interest in the Franklin controversy and all its implications waxed rather than waned. He was now desperately busy with writing, organizing, and editing *The Seven Poor Travellers*, the Extra Christmas Number of *Household Words* for 1854; but despite the pressure of this unpostponable labor, he found he could not contain or put off the impulse to speak out on Franklin and cannibalism. He soon gave way to the impulse and went feverishly to work. About a week after he had completed his task, he described his earlier state and his present predicament: "I took it into my head to be violently interested in writing two papers on Dr. Rae's report concerning Franklin; wherein you will see strung together some of the most extraordinary cases of shipwreck I know. This has helped to drive me up into the corner in which I at present stand at bay—with this Christmas Bull trying to toss me" (1 December 1854).

The articles that Dickens wrote for *Household Words* (ultimately there were three articles entitled "The Lost Arctic Voyagers") dem-

Spanish infantry, till then invincible. As strong and as closely united as the celebrated ancient phalanx, it opened itself with an agility which the phalanx had not, and thus suddenly made way for the discharge of eighteen pieces of cannon that were placed in the midst of it. The Prince of Condé surrounded and attacked it three times; and at length victory decided in his favour.

In the attack on the camp of Merci at Fribourg, the following year, which was renewed three successive days, the prince threw his staff of command into the enemy's trenches, and marched, sword in hand, to regain it, at the head of the regiment of Conti. This bold action inspired the troops with redoubled ardour, and the battle of Fribourg was gained.

SHIPWRECKS AND DISASTERS AT SEA.

—

WRECK OF THE MEDUSA FRIGATE.

THE French possessions on the west coast of Africa, extending from Cape Blanco to the mouth of the Gambia, having been restored at the general peace, an expedition, consisting of a frigate and three other vessels, was sent, in the month of June, 1816, to take possession of them. It was complete in all its parts, as the French expeditions usually are, including men of science, artisans, agriculturists, gardeners, miners, &c. amounting, with the troops, to nearly two hundred persons, exclusive of the crews. The naval part was entrusted to M. de Chaumareys, who had the command of the frigate, La Méduse, of forty-four guns.

Owing to a very relaxed state of discipline, and an ignorance of the common principles of navigation which would have disgraced a private merchant ship, this frigate was suffered to run aground on the bank of Arguin. Attempts were made to get her off, attempts, however, which, according to the narrative before us, were as inefficient and discreditable to the naval

5. Shipwreck of the *Medusa*

Dickens first encountered the cannibalistic horrors of the *Medusa* when reading the *Terrific Register* and the *Portfolio* as a boy. "Wreck Of The Medusa Frigate." From the *Terrific Register* (1824–25).

onstrate that he was a skillful, self-aware polemicist, well grounded in the literature of human predation.[2] In his defense of Franklin and his crew he quotes Franklin's accounts of fortitude and moral rectitude in the face of earlier strandings, and he marshals similar examples from the writings of Parry, Richardson, Back, Bligh, Barrow, Bruce, Mungo Park, and Prescott. He invokes literary support from Byron, Smollett, Coleridge, Albert Smith, Defoe, and the *Arabian Nights*. He ranges through the harrowing literature of shipwrecks and disasters at sea. He summons the histories of such ships as the *Pandora, Centaur, Don Juan, Juno, Peggy, Nautilus, Thomas, Wager, Jacques, Tyrel, Philip Aubin, New Horn, Nottingham Galley, St. Lawrence, Dido*, and *Medusa*. He paints heroic accounts of human self-denial; he sketches horrific vignettes of human weakness and savagery. We learn how the mate of the shipwrecked *Philip Aubin* "exhorted the rest [of the survivors] to cut a piece out of his thigh, and quench their thirst"; how the men in a drifting whaleboat drew lots as to which "should bleed himself to death, to support life in the rest"; how three survivors of the *Tyrel* cut pieces from the thigh of a dead cabin boy but sickened when they tried to swallow his flesh; and how the crew of the *Medusa* "fell upon the dead bodies with which the raft was covered, and cut off pieces, which some instantly devoured" (*HW*, X, 389, 390, 387).

Accounts such as these, hundreds of additional accounts, and multitudes of cannibalistic associations had long since sunk deep into Dickens' consciousness. Their reconstituted shapes—sometimes disguised, sometimes blatant, sometimes effaced, sometimes enlarged—are astonishingly diverse and protean. Now heroic, now horrific, now humorous, now blended and combined in startling permutations, they emerge in extraordinary abundance in the flux and flow of Dickens' everyday living. All life long the subject of cannibalism would well up from the depths of Dickens' consciousness, fused, through the multitudinous associations of infancy, childhood, and youth with his most primordial creative impulses.

In "The Lost Arctic Voyagers," however, Dickens was writing a lawyer's brief. He was bent on defending the reputation of Franklin and his men.[3] His evidence given, his arguments made, he honored the memory of that small band of intrepid Englishmen, free, as far as he was concerned, from any defilement of indulging in unspeakable feasting, absolved by training and character, and absolved also, by the evidence (as Dickens read the evidence), of succumbing to that "last resource" of the weak, the benighted, and the depraved. He was stirred and relieved by their story—or rather by his ennobling version of their story. Compelled and revolted by the thought of men eating men (we will return to these compulsions and revulsions later), he was stirred and relieved in a like fashion by all stories of brave men triumphing in similar straits.

Dickens was also stirred by the fortitude of men confronted by the utter desolation and extremity of the frozen regions, extremes that test men's souls. At the end of his first Arctic voyagers essay, he invokes a desolate polar image of the lost Franklin party, their scanty remains strewn pitifully, but also sacredly—did these men not pass the test?—across the Arctic solitudes. "We think," Dickens writes, "of the specks, once ardent men, 'scattered about in different directions' on the waste of ice and snow, and plead for their lightest ashes" (*HW* 10: 365).

That fervent plea did not end with "The Lost Arctic Voyagers." Less than two years later, at Dickens' suggestion, he and Wilkie Collins wrote, and he staged and acted the lead in, *The Frozen Deep*, a play set in the frozen Arctic solitudes, and a play that tested the moral fiber of men stripped of all but their innate humanity.[4] *The Frozen Deep* was written in 1856 and staged in January 1857. Also in 1856, Dickens wrote *The Wreck of the "Golden Mary,"* a tale he had conceived a year earlier—that is, in 1855, less than a year after "The Lost Arctic Voyagers"—a tale of icebergs, shipwreck, open boats, famine, and fortitude, and of "terrific"—the word is Dickens'—cannibalistic obsessions (*WGM*, 9).[5]

Dickens' preoccupation with cannibalism had other, less formalized and self-conscious manifestations. A casual task or a train of everyday thoughts could set his mind thronging with cannibalistic associations. When, in 1851, he drew up lists of humorous titles to place on the dummy bookbacks he was having custom-made to conceal the library door at Tavistock House (and when later—and then later still, for Gad's Hill Place—he drew up additional lists), jokes, puns, and satiric allusions, many rife with cannibalistic implications, sprang unbidden into his consciousness. These lists of imaginary book titles (their full import will emerge later) included such gems as *Blue Beard in Search of a Wife* by More, *Burke (of Edinburgh) on the Sublime and Beautiful* (two volumes), *Captain Cook's Life of Savage* (two volumes), *The Cook's Oracle, Butcher's Suetonius, Drouet's Farming* (five volumes), *Malthus' Nursery Songs, Swallows on Emigration* (two volumes), and *Captain Parry. Virtues of Cold Tar*. All but the first title were actually used (V&A MSS; Gad's Hill Place library).

But we do not need Dickens' overt avowals, or his articles devoted to man-eating, or his allusive lists of fictitious book titles to convince us of his interest in cannibalism. His reading on the subject and his fascination with the lore of man-eating emerge over and over again in his writings. Take, for instance, an earlier example of his preoccupation with this subject (earlier, that is, than the three impassioned articles just mentioned). Dickens wrote the earlier piece, "The Long Voyage," in December 1853 for the New Year's Eve issue of *Household Words*. The brief opening paragraph of this essay, just two sentences long, seems relaxed and offhand, but woven into that disarming commencement are somber strands that foreshadow the darkness to come.

"The Long Voyage" is an account of human fortitude and human depravity. It chronicles the ordeals of real-life voyagers in the face of extremity and disaster. But "The Long Voyage" is also a New Year's meditation. Its harrowing histories are metaphors for the ultimate long voyage, the long voyage of life, the perilous journey that each reader of "The Long Voyage," like all human travelers, must pursue to its unknown end. Yet every journey, no matter what its length or its destination, has stages. Dickens' readers, like Dickens himself, were poised at an unmistakable stage; they had traveled to the end of one year and were about to embark upon a new one. What would that new year and the years beyond (if there were years beyond for

reader and writer) bring? And how would each traveler acquit himself as he sailed his chartless journey? Would he fall prey to some
man-turned-beast, or, worse yet, would he become that beast?
These are the themes and the musings of "The Long Voyage," an
essay in which cannibalism (as so often in Dickens) becomes a
quintessential emblem of all that is depraved and predatory in man.
But here is the brief comfortable cannibal-haunted opening of the
essay:

> When the wind is blowing and the sleet or rain is driving against the
> dark windows, I love to sit by the fire, thinking of what I have read in
> books of voyage and travel. Such books have had a strong fascination for
> my mind from my earliest childhood; and I wonder it should have come
> to pass that I never have been round the world, never have been ship-
> wrecked, ice-environed, tomahawked, or eaten. (*HW* 8: 409; later in *RP*)

This brief overture, so revealing concerning Dickens' "strong fascinations" and equally strong fears, ends with the word *eaten,* with
the nightmare horror (albeit here only implied in passing) of becoming fodder for some human beast. As a matter of fact, the horror here is deliberately effaced. The passage, especially toward the
end, adopts an insouciant, tongue-in-cheek tone; it also distances
the writer—and the reader—from the enormity of being "eaten,"
that is, from the enormity of being butchered, torn asunder,
chewed, and swallowed by some ravening man-turned-monster. A
counterpoint of palliation is a frequent strategy in Dickens' evocations of cannibalism, but in this instance the palliation does not last
for long: the essay goes on to detail other, less mitigated and less
glancing accounts of depraved cannibalistic appetites.

The essay also goes on to evoke the consciousness of the predator
as well as the preyed-upon. In the third paragraph of "The Long
Voyage," Dickens draws upon his reading in parliamentary blue
books to help him in this evocation, surely an unlikely and unpromising source for cannibalistic lore, but, in this instance, one that goes
back to his boyhood reading (to his early horrified perusal, in a sensational weekly periodical called the *Terrific Register,* of the very episode later encountered in the blue book). This parliamentary (and

boyhood) source, unlikely and unpromising though its blue-book antecedents seem to be, demonstrates Dickens' preternatural and early-bred sensitivity to any mention—early or late—of such specially conditioned fare.

Drawing, then, on a parliamentary report and the horrific reading of his boyhood, Dickens conjures up a vision, at once factual and colored by imagination, of one such fiendish predator. The predator in question, a convict in an island penal settlement, embarks with a group of fellow convicts on a hopeless escape attempt. The route these despairing men take, the only one possible, preordains their failure and recapture, but they set forth nevertheless. They steal a boat, get to the mainland, and toil doggedly along a rugged and precipitous seacoast, their narrow way to nowhere. The weaker members of the band begin to fail, and then to die; and the remainder, driven by desperation and famine, feed on their former companions. At last this horrible resource is exhausted too, and the depraved remnant begin to murder each other in a savage scramble to survive. Finally, only the predator-convict is left. "This one awful creature," writes Dickens, "eats his fill, and sustains his strength, and lives on to be recaptured and taken back" (*HW* 8: 409).

But the gruesome story does not end here. In the course of his terrifying ordeal—Dickens calls that ordeal "so tremendous" as to be "unrelateable"—the man-eating convict develops such an "inappeasable relish for his dreadful food," that he subsequently lures a fellow prisoner into another foredoomed escape attempt with the sole purpose of killing his companion and eating him (*HW* 8: 409). The predator-convict accomplishes his purpose. He murders his companion, eats his fill, stuffs his clothing with choice portions of his victim's butchered body, and then travels on, following a river to the sea. The scene haunts Dickens; it echoes and reverberates in his mind. Among other far-off consequences, it will help shape the conception and the destiny of *Great Expectations,* especially of Magwitch. (Magwitch was created seven years after "The Long Voyage" and thirty-five years after Dickens' initial boyhood encounter with the grisly story of the man-eating convict.)

Dickens' conception of Magwitch re-creates that boyhood and

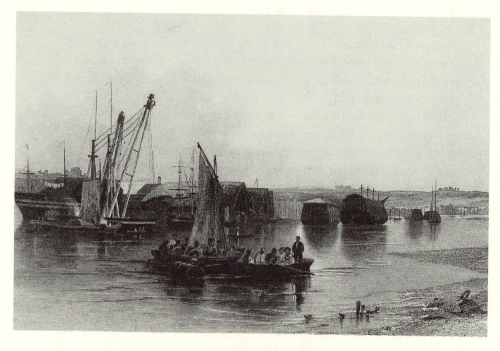

6. Chatham and Its Convict Hulks: The Fearful Hulks of Dickens' Childhood Looming like "Wicked Noah's Arks"

Notice, in the central and right mid-distance, the great lowering Chatham convict hulks festering malignantly on the watery verge of the dockyard and the town. The ravenous and bestial Magwitch escaped from a convict hulk based upon those shown here, the hulks of Dickens' Chatham childhood. Dickens, as a child, lived hard by the river Medway and these hulks. Dwelling in the quiet Eden of Chatham's gentle hills, green fields, and flowing river, Dickens viewed the rotting convict hulks, so somber, so secret, so forbidding, as dark, fearful, embodiments—hellish embodiments—of nascent wickedness, wickedness that soon became entwined, in Dickens' associating mind, with the escaped cannibal-convict of the *Terrific Register,* a convict clothed and fettered like the convicts of the Chatham hulks, a convict who foraged ravenously along river banks and beaches—shades of Medway banks and beaches—and gorged greedily and voraciously on the flesh of his fellow men. *Chatham.* Engraving after a drawing (c. 1825) by Charles Warren. See also figure 7.

manhood reading and imagining and blends it with his Chatham childhood. The fearsome escaped predator and the fearsome escaped Magwitch have much in common. They both escape wearing irons on their legs; with the aid of accomplices, they both free themselves of their fetters. Magwitch, to dwell for a moment on his Chatham heritage, has escaped from one of the wicked prison ships of Dickens' childhood—that is, from one of the lowering old convict hulks that festered malignantly, like a "wicked Noah's Ark," just offshore from Chatham's serene fields, neat houses, sleepy churches, and bustling dockyard. Magwitch, in short, emerges— both imaginatively and physically—from the old hulks that were familiar yet disturbing presences for Dickens during his Chatham years, hulks that were part "of the terror of childhood," dark, rotting embodiments—ever-present and ever-threatening embodiments in Dickens' impressionable childhood eyes—of sin and its fearful garnerings (*AYR* 4: *GE*, 28:558).

These diverse and time-distanced worlds, the childhood world of Chatham impressions, the boyhood world of *Terrific Register* reading, and the manhood world of blue-book reports—worlds so outwardly remote from one another in time and in character—were, over the years, rooted deep in the recesses of Dickens' imagination, coalescing, recombining, and finally engendering new but deeply rooted and predetermined (or at least deeply influenced) creation. Slowly, gathering power and significance, these worlds—or, to be more exact, special bits and pieces of them—fused now, and recreated, were becoming potent correlatives, in the cannibal-convict instance a somber correlative, of dark resonances in Dickens' fabling consciousness.

It is easy to see how such conjunctions, in the cannibal-convict case conjunctions of Dickens' boyhood *Terrific Register* reading and manhood blue-book sources, became fused forever in Dickens' consciousness with their childhood counterparts—with childhood convicts, childhood convict hulks, childhood rivers, childhood fantasies, childhood cannibal lore, and "the terror of childhood." It is also easy to see how such sources made their shaping contributions to their metamorphosed, yet in many ways unchanged, latter-day offspring: first, to the veritable cannibal-convict of "The Long Voyage," a monster who kills and eats his companions with eager relish; then to the fierce, cheek-eating, heart-eating, and liver-eating Magwitch of the opening chapters of *Great Expectations,* a terrifying creature who tells Pip he is sorely tempted to cut his throat and devour him then and there. Those nightmare offspring, part created from within, part recalled from without (part recalled from the boyhood *Terrific Register* and part from the manhood blue book) share other telltale features, features that whisper insistently of secret consanguinities, of shared horrors and depravities, features that go back in their earliest engenderings to Chatham's "wicked" convict hulks, "the terror of childhood," and ultimately, to the cannibal-haunted mists of infancy.

Those shared features continue to emerge over and over again in the account (part real and part imagined, as Dickens purveys his version of the account) of the cannibal-convict, and in the still later, much more complex role that Dickens creates, of the cannibal-convict's refashioned avatar, the fictional Magwitch. Yet however refashioned and transformed, the old engendering consanguinities persist. The ravenous man-eater, like Magwitch after him—Magwitch, we recall, is so ravenous that he threatens to eat Pip on the spot—is soon retaken and, again like Magwitch after him, is retaken in the coastal margin between land and sea. The bonds that link these two bestial and ravenous escaped convicts (Magwitch snaps up each mouthful of food with "strong sharp sudden bites, just like [a] dog" [*AYR* 4: *GE,* 3:194]) are strong, numerous, and striking, but also circumscribed: the island predator is only a depraved prefigurement, an emotionally charged monster precursor, of the sinning but also sinned against Magwitch.

Nevertheless, since the island predator is a generative prototype of Magwitch, the links and similitudes continue. In "The Long Voyage" the pursuers of the escaped man-eater discover when they capture him that he has not touched his ample supply of stolen prison pork (the escaped Magwitch "gobbles" his stolen pork [*AYR* 4: *GE,*

3:194]) but instead has stuffed his "coarse convict-dress" with food (Magwitch also stuffs his "coarse" convict dress with food) (*HW* 8: 409; *AYR* 4: *GE*, 1:169; 3:194). In the man-eater's case, this food—to use Dickens' no longer reticent language—consists of "portions of the man's body, on which he is regaling" (*HW* 8: 409). But now the savage boyhood and blue-book tale is almost told; the "inappeasable" man-eater will butcher and regale no more. The ravenous monster, on this, his second, retaking, like Magwitch on his second retaking, is sentenced to death.

Later we will focus in greater breadth and depth on the cannibal-savior Magwitch and on the interrelated networks of cannibalistic motifs that help define and unify *Great Expectations,* but to return for one last moment to "The Long Voyage," Dickens concludes his account of the fearful convict-predator with the following unforgettable image, an image that reifies the fascination and horror that Dickens invariably felt when trafficking with cannibalism. "I shall never," writes Dickens, haunted by what he himself has summoned forth, an image half imposed from without, half created from within, "I shall never see that sea-beach on the wall or in the fire, without him, solitary monster, eating [human flesh] as he prowls along, while the sea rages and rises at him" (*HW* 8: 409).

II

Dickens' fascination with cannibalism and his profound anxieties concerning it were rooted, as he himself proclaimed, in his earliest days. His recollections of those infant days include stories and events that focus recurrently on that horrendous theme. His nurse-maid, a macabre Scheherazade (there were several female caretakers and storytellers in Dickens' childhood, hence my use of the generic "Scheherazade"), used to tell him nightly of a monstrous Captain Murderer, who married innocent young girls for the express purpose of cutting off their heads, chopping them up, baking them in giant meat pies, feasting on them, and picking their bones. This ferocious captain had his teeth filed and refiled into sharp razorlike

7. Chatham Dockyard During Dickens' Childhood

As a child Dickens knew this government dockyard well: his father was attached to the Navy Pay Office there from 1817 to 1822, and during the last year of that stay, the Dickens family lived hard by the dockyard. "Chips and the Devil," according to Dickens' nursemaid, was set at this dockyard or a very similar government yard—an added terror for Dickens. *Chatham Dockyard*. Wood engraving (1820s–30s) by John Jackson. See also figure 6.

points and told his prospective meals savage cannibalistic jokes. His mode of murdering his victims was invariable and fiendishly sadistic. He caused each "tender bride" to prepare a piecrust and line an immense silver pie dish (["Nurse's Stories"], *AYR* 3: 518; later in *UT*). After the obedient "house-lamb"—calling his bride a house-lamb was one of his little jokes—had rolled out the piecrust, she would innocently ask her dear lord where the meat for the pie was (*AYR* 3: 518). Then Captain Murderer would tell his lovely bride to look in the mirror, and he would roar with laughter. A few moments later, while his victim was again looking at herself in the glass at her dear lord's behest, he would inform her that she was to be the meat in his fearful pie. In the next instant, as she stared in horror at her nightmare reflection in the mirror, she saw her demon husband cutting off her head.

Dickens, faint with terror, would beg to be spared his nightly ordeal with Captain Murderer, but the implacable Scheherazade derived a "fiendish enjoyment" from terrorizing the little boy. "Clawing the air with both hands, and uttering a long low hollow groan," she would ignore his pleas (*AYR* 3: 519). Then, after a suitable interval of direful gestures and ghastly sounds, she would commence her dreadful narrative. "She never spared me one word of it," Dickens writes, but "commended the awful chalice to my lips as the only preservative known to science against 'The Black Cat'—a weird and glaring-eyed supernatural Tom" that sucked "the breath of infancy" and had a special thirst, Scheherazade assured Dickens, for his frail life (*AYR* 3: 519).

Another favorite tale of this redoubtable storyteller concerned a ship's carpenter named Chips who worked at a government dockyard—Dickens' father at this time worked at a government dockyard. The Devil appeared to the wretched Chips in the form of a speaking rat, and the benighted carpenter sold his soul to that worthy for an iron pot, a bushel of tenpenny nails, half a ton of copper, and a rat that could speak. Scheherazade's version of this Faustian tale (heightened and reshaped by Dickens, no doubt) contains vivid pictures of rats nibbling at larders, sniffing hungrily at sleeping infants, and gnawing on corpses in graveyards. These allusions to feeding on human flesh have their horrible fulfillment. Chips, his compact sealed, his destruction certain, tries to escape that fulfillment. He tries to outwit the speaking rat and his hungry minions, but his efforts are futile. Rat-haunted and rat-besieged from the moment of his infernal compact, communing with rats, babbling about rats, he is finally certified mad, dismissed from the yard, and pressed as a seaman. He sails on a rotting ship swarming with ravenous rats. He hears the rats nibbling and gnawing and talking in the dark hold of the doomed vessel, but no one will heed his warnings of dreadful danger. The story ends when the ship goes down and the Devil—in the form of an immense, overgrown, laughing rat that has become fat and bloated from feasting on Chip's half-eaten body—fulfills (by means of this loathsome gorging) the rhyming threat that he had uttered and reuttered throughout the story, a threat that conceals, until the very end, its gruesome cannibalistic implications. The threat had seemed straightforward enough at first:

> A Lemon has pips,
> And a Yard has ships,
> And *I*'ll have Chips!
> (*AYR* 3: 519–20)

But for Dickens (after his first fateful introduction to the story) that simple rhyming refrain magnified rather than concealed the menace of its message. As he himself put it, "For this Refrain I had waited since its last appearance, with inexpressible horror, which now culminated" (*AYR* 3: 520). Impressionable and imaginative, listening to this rhyming refrain over and over again, he repeatedly experienced, indeed in his imagination he repeatedly underwent, that revolting, rat-filled violation.

This early conditioning was often reinforced by subsequent events. To cite just one instance, but one so important that it can scarcely be overemphasized, Dickens later associated—merged is perhaps a better word—the fearful, rat-infested, cannibal-haunted nightmare of his childhood (a distillation of his darkest childhood terrors and imaginings) with the most desolate time of his subsequent life. That desolate time, the blacking-warehouse period, a period of several months—probably a good deal longer—in his twelfth year when he felt that he had been cast forever into the pit of hell, was for him then, and ever after, a phantasmagoria of rats, rottenness, servitude, and dire peril.[6] But this harrowing interval, sufficiently devastating in its own right, was shaped and magnified by the past, most particularly by images traumatized by the past. Those powerful images helped to accrete and generate meaning for Dickens; they gave emotion physical form. One such image we have just met. In the nightmare storytelling of his early childhood and then in the blacking-warehouse reality of his adolescence, rats became visible incarnations of his misery and fear—incarnations that were now, in the blacking warehouse, waking nightmare itself. Storytelling horrors had somehow become actualities of daily living. The swarming subterranean cannibal-rats of "Chips and the Devil," scuffling and squeaking and talking in the dark hold of Chips' doomed ship, had, in the course of Dickens' blacking-warehouse servitude, unaccountably become horrifyingly real: they had metamorphosed into the swarming rats that actually squeaked and scuffled in the dark cellars of the tomblike blacking warehouse, dreadful harbingers—indeed, dreadful witnesses and agents (so it must have seemed to Dickens)—of his tomblike and Chips-like fate.

The blacking warehouse, especially its rotting cellars, teemed with rats. Significantly, in describing the warehouse, Dickens focused more on the rats swarming and scuffling in the cellar depths than on the house. The warehouse abutted the river (shades of the shipyard and Chips), and the building, a crazy, tumbledown old house, was "literally overrun with rats" (F, 25). More than twenty years after he had left the blacking warehouse forever, Dickens could still see and hear (so he tells us) "the old grey rats swarming down in the cellars, and the sound of their squeaking and scuffling coming up the stairs at all times" (F, 25). That inferno-like vision of swarming subterranean rats, with its subliminal suggestions for Dickens of being buried alive and devoured, for that is how he felt about his blacking-warehouse banishment (the busy blacking-warehouse rats perhaps laughing like the Devil-rat in "Chips and the Devil" as they hungrily scuffled and voraciously waited in the cellar darkness below), haunted his consciousness. Voracious, swarming, murderous rats, scuffling and squeaking in nether depths, waiting to devour their human prey, became a permanent part of his Boschian vision of hell.[7] But this is to glance forward and catch a glimpse of how one seed, sown in infancy, sprouted in childhood and grew in youth. Its far-off harvest was still deeply shrouded in the mists of distant time.[8]

Dickens listened, and Scheherazade pursued her baleful campaign. She continued to regale her reluctant but rapt victim with her virtuoso renderings of terrifying tales. "Captain Murderer," "Chips and the Devil," and other savage stories scarred the boy permanently. They also produced in him a strange craving for similar terrors, a craving he indulged amply. From an early age he forged a fearful bond with the ravenous marauders of the monstrous world of man-eaters: with Sawney Beane and his infernal band of depraved Scottish cannibals; with Bluebeard and his Captain Murderer-like propensity (in cannibalistic versions of the story) for disposing of wives; with Sweeney Todd, the voracious demon barber of Fleet Street; with sinister innkeepers who butchered unsuspecting guests in order to stock their larders; and with a host of similar fiends.

In addition, Dickens was an early devotee of the wonder-filled realms of fairy tales, folklore, and mythology, realms that contained nightmare as well as reassuring histories, and that bristled with ravening ogres, man-consuming beasts, child-eating witches, and hungry giants. *Jack the Giant Killer*, for example, reminded him, from childhood on, of "those dreadfully interesting, double-headed giants, with their clubs over their shoulders . . . dragging knights and ladies home for dinner by the hair of their heads," while *Little Red Ridinghood* made him think, again from childhood on, of "the cruelty and treachery of that dissembling Wolf who ate [Little Red Ridinghood's] grandmother, without making any impression on his appetite, and then ate [Little Red Ridinghood], after making that

POLLOCK'S CHARACTERS IN JACK THE GIANT KILLER. *Plate 3.*

London. Published by B. Pollock, 73. Hoxton Street, Hoxton

Indian Juggler.

Giant Blunderbore
with Villagers.

Fig 1.

Giant Blunderbore with Villagers.   Jack.   Dazzelbright.

8. Succulent Villagers Led Home by the Giant Blunderbore

Characters from a toy-theater pantomime version of *Jack the Giant Killer* being led home by Blunderbore to stock his larder. As a boy Dickens delighted in his own toy-theater productions, including flamboyant spectacles similar to this. *Pollock's Characters in "Jack the Giant Killer,"* Plate 3. Early nineteenth-century sheet of characters reissued by Benjamin Pollock. This sheet is hand-colored in bright, primary hues.

9. *Little Red Ridinghood:* "The Cruelty and Treachery of that Dissembling Wolf"

When Dickens thought of *Little Red Ridinghood*, he thought of "the cruelty and treachery of that dissembling Wolf who ate [Little Red Ridinghood's] grandmother, without making any impression on his appetite, and then ate [Little Red Ridinghood], after making that ferocious joke about his teeth." "The Disguised Wolf." Wood engraving after a drawing by Gustave Doré. From *The Fairy Realm* (1862).

ferocious joke about his teeth" ("A Christmas Tree," *HW* 2: 290–91). As these and many other allusions attest, Dickens never forgot his equivocal childhood responses to these fearsome creatures—to the giant Thunderdel in *Jack the Giant Killer,* for example (the most famous and most open of the rhyming cannibalistic threateners), a hungry monster who intones his dire warning:

> Fee, fie, fo, fum,
> I smell the blood of an Englishman.
> Be he alive, or be he dead,
> I'll grind his bones to make my bread.

Like countless generations of English children, Dickens reveled in this fierce, inflated threatening, but, unlike most English children, he was preternaturally sensitive to any hints of cannibalistic feeding. For Dickens, Thunderdel's threats, like the Wolf's "ferocious joke," and like the multitudes of similar threats and jokes that thronged his childhood, in addition to their usual childhood associations contained deeper and darker resonances, profound personal resonances of special vulnerability and aggression. These dark reverberations, unconsciously generated in infancy and earliest childhood (long before Scheherazade's ministrations), eventually grew to be major chords and motifs in his writings.

Those reverberations also echoed and reechoed down the years, sounding again and again in Dickens' daily life, often in half-comic, half-ferocious ways. To cite for the moment a single brief example, on one occasion while holidaying at Broadstairs (this many years after his introduction to Thunderdel and his threats), Dickens attended a theatrical entertainment. Forster, using a letter from Dickens as a guide, paraphrases Dickens' description of the high point of this event: "With this [an account of attending a provincial circus] I will couple another theatrical experience of this holiday, when he saw a Giant played by a village comedian with a quite Gargantuesque felicity, and singled out for admiration his fine manner of sitting down to a hot supper (of children), with the self-lauding exalting remark, by way of grace, 'How pleasant is a quiet conscience

Said Giles, " who be you ?" said the ghost, " I be I,
A coming to punish your *par-ju-ry !*"

KITTY MAGGS AND JOLTER GILES;
OR, THE APPLE-PUDDING GHOST.

KITTY MAGGS was a servant to Farmer Styles,
  And a buxom wench was she ;
And her true *lovier* was Jolter Giles,
  A ploughman so bold was he ;
Giles had wages, five pounds, due at Candlemas-
    tide,
And then he told Kitty he'd make her his bride.
        Ding dong, bo!

Betty Blossom she wore a high-cauled cap,
  Which caught fickle Jolter's eye ;
And poor Kitty Maggs, O, dire mishap!
  Mourned his incon-stan-cy!
And high on the bough of an apple tree,
When they married, Kate finished her misery.
        Ding dong, bo!

At the supper Giles gave for Betty his bride,
  An apple-pudding had they,
And from the same bough on which poor Kitty died
  The apples were plucked they say ;
The pudding, *pies* on it, grew deadly cold !
The death-watch ticked, and the church-bell tolled !
        Ding dong, bo!

To carve the pudding was Giles's post,
  He cut, and from the gap
Popped the head of poor dear Kitty Maggs's ghost,
  All in a new fashioned *shroud* cap :
Said Giles, " who be you ?" said the ghost, " I
  be I,
A coming to punish your *par-ju-ry !*"
        Ding dong, bo!

" O Kitty," said Jolter, " pray alter your note !"
  " *I vo'n't !*" the ghost replied ;
When plump flew the pudding down Giles's throat,
  And on the spot he died.
Now his ghost, once a year, bolting pudding is seen,
While blue devils sing, every mouthful between,
        Ding dong, bo!

ADIEU, MARINETTE, THOU PRETTY COQUETTE.
A RONDO.
(Kenney.)

ADIEU, Marinette,
  Thou pretty coquette,
My folly ne'er hope to renew ;
  In vain all thy pains,
  They have broken my chains,
And gaily I bid thee adieu.

  Seek early, seek late,
  In vain you may wait,
For a heart that's as honest as mine ;
  And wherever I fly,
  Your sweet sex can supply
Ten thousand such trifles as thine.
        Adieu, Marinette, &c.

There's a time in our youth,
  To be all love and truth,
There's a time when we sigh and adore ;
  But, beware, lest you learn,
  From each lover in turn,
There's a time to be wise and give o'er.
        Adieu, Marinette, &c.

THE FIREMAN'S HOLIDAY;
OR, LIFE IN WATER-COLOURS.

Air—" *The merry old Maid.*"—(Jesse Hammond.

SIX firemen ply'd on the river Thames,
  All dressed in their jackets so gay,
And though I can't tell you all their names,
  Stout lads from the *Eagle* were they ;
The *Globe* you might search to find such a set,
  For each was a *Phœnix* at fun ;
But the fact is, these firemen were apt to get
  A little too much in the *Sun ;*

---

10. Comic Songs: Jilted Love, Cannibalism, and Death

As a child and as an adult, Dickens was renowned for his renditions of comic songs. Some of those songs were more macabre than comic, as the cannibalistic ballad of "Kitty Maggs and Jolter Giles" (and its accompanying illustration) demonstrate. Wood engraving after a drawing by Robert Cruikshank. From Vol. II of *The Universal Songster* (1825–26).

and an approving mind!'" (F, 385n; [19 August 1845]). It is not surprising that this self-congratulatory scene of eating children piping hot impressed Dickens, nor is it surprising that he "singled [it] out for admiration." Eating children, whether such eating is conceived as unalloyed nightmare or is tempered by mitigating humor, had a profound and special significance for him.

Images as well as words sank into Dickens' consciousness. Grotesque picture books, frightening songster graphics, gruesome illustrations, horrific prints, nightmare cartoons, macabre squibs, savage caricatures—to concentrate for a moment on the darker range of these images—inundated and surrounded Dickens from his earliest childhood and helped shape his way of seeing and thinking. This is hardly surprising. A rich tradition of grotesque art had long held sway in Britain. It had come to the fore at the time of Hogarth's ascendency in the 1730s and 1740s, and had continued to flourish for a century or more thereafter, waxing strong throughout Dickens' childhood, youth, and early manhood. The tradition had gathered momentum in the mid-eighteenth century and the years immediately following, had burgeoned throughout the period of the French Revolution and the Napoleonic Wars, had continued strongly through the whole of the Regency, and then had evolved in the early Victorian period into a less savage and political, more moderate, even genial, satire and caricature, an enormously vital movement that had finally found its chief home, no longer in prints, but in comic periodicals (such as *Punch*) and in the great flourishing of book, especially novel, illustration from the 1830s onward. This graphic tradition, to mention only the chief luminaries who helped shape and convey it, began with Hogarth and continued with Gillray, Rowlandson, the Cruikshanks, Seymour, Browne ("Phiz"), and Leech. Dickens became intimately connected with this vital tradition in its early Victorian evolution. His first three illustrators were George Cruikshank, Robert Seymour (both older than he and both already famous at this time—he was unknown), and Hablot Knight Browne, who subsequently illustrated most of his novels. Cruikshank and Browne, like John Leech, became Dickens' friends.

JACK THE GIANT KILLER.

Kind Reader, Jack makes you a bow,
 The hero of giants the dread;
Whom king and the princes applaud
 For valour, whence tyranny fled.

In Cornwall, on Saint Michael's Mount,
 A giant full eighteen feet high,
Nine feet round, in cavern did dwell,
 For food cleared the fields and the sty.

And, glutton, would feast on poor souls,
 Whom chance might have led in his way;
Or gentleman, lady, or child,
 Or what on his hands he could lay.

He went over to the main land, in search of food, when he would throw oxen or cows on his back, and several sheep and pigs, and with them wade to his abode in the cavern.

3

Till Jack's famed career made him quake,
 Blew his horn, took mattock and spade;
Dug twenty feet deep near his den,
 And covered the pit he had made.

The giant declared he'd devour
 For breakfast who dared to come near;
And leizurely did Blunderbore
 Walk heavily into the snare.

11. The Ogres of Dickens' Childhood: The Gluttonous Chapbook Giant Who Feasted on "Gentleman, Lady, or Child"

The woodcut shows brave Jack killing the "glutton" Blunderbore after "The giant declared he'd devour / For breakfast who dared to come near." As a child, Dickens delighted in and trembled over chapbooks such as this; their graphic images and dire threats haunted his imagination. From *Jack the Giant Killer, A Hero Celebrated by Ancient Historians* (Banbury, c. 1830).

Leech, for his part, also worked with Dickens; he illustrated *A Christmas Carol* and contributed to three additional Christmas Books by Dickens.

But long before Dickens began writing, he had become a devotee of this rich graphic tradition, including its many flourishing rivulets and tributaries. As a small child he had reveled in the fantastic world of Regency picture books, chapbooks, dreamers, songsters, confessions, criminal lives, fairy tales, ballads, broadsides, squibs, toy-theater scenes, toy-theater characters, and Gothic tales. Most of these cheap popular works were illustrated; many of them were garishly colored in bright blues, reds, yellows, browns, and greens. Dickens delighted in these bright, kaleidoscopic, often fantastic, images. They provoked his imagination. He found them intriguing and irresistible.

As a child Dickens had also gazed with wonder-filled excitement at the painted booths of London fairs and shows. What marvels and what monstrosities, glimpsed so graphically and so enticingly from without, dwelt in even greater profusion (and even greater intensity) in the hidden recesses of the magical dominions within! He had also gazed with rapt attentiveness at the shop windows of toy-theater merchants, print sellers, chapbook vendors, sheet-music purveyors, ballad mongers, booksellers, and the like. There, crowded onto display platforms, easels, and stands, hung from ceilings or affixed to windows (often covering large street windows from floor to ceiling and wall to wall), he would see giants marching their human meals to their castle dungeons, murderers hacking their victims to death amidst pools of blood, politicians with bloated bellies and enormous mouths ravenously devouring their opponents and their constituents, highwaymen roasting secrets out of their tormented captives, Ali Baba and his forty thieves quartering their opponents and hoisting their remains to the cavern ceiling, survivors of shipwrecks butchering each other in mad efforts to eat and live, and ferocious cannibals, wild and gleeful, dancing up a ghastly appetite, circling round their hapless prey. All this and much more enthralled and provoked him, and all this and much more registered indelibly on his consciousness.

MILES MENAGERIE   SAUNDERS's TRAGIC THEATRE   GYNGLES GRAND MEDLEY.

12. Bartholomew Fair: Cannibalism in the Heart of London

Dickens loved the entertainments of the people, including the London fairs and shows, and he often wrote about them. Such entertainments, along with the allied worlds that Dickens early reveled in—popular graphics, toy theaters, chapbooks, comic songs, and the like—often featured horrors and sensations, including cannibalism, as here in Gyngell's booth at Bartholomew Fair, which depicted a giant, aided by Punch, devouring human beings. Dickens owned a large collection of memorabilia of Bartholomew Fair (covering the period 1703–1850), including many handbills, playbills, drawings, engravings, portraits, cuttings, manuscripts, etc., perhaps intending to use the collection in his writings. Dickens also owned three copies of the 1859 edition of Henry Morley's book on Bartholomew Fair, the book from which the above illustration is taken. (Morley was employed by Dickens as a staff member of *Household Words* and *All the Year Round*.) Detail of a print (1799) by Thomas Rowlandson from a drawing ascribed to John Nixon. From Morley, *Memoirs of Bartholomew Fair* (1859, 1880).

There were also less gruesome delights in these enticing shop windows. Dickens gazed with wonder at both extremes of this inexhaustible world of portentous images, at nightmare images of revolting horror and at supernal images of heavenly bliss. Some of those images—the terrifying woodcuts featured on the front of the weekly *Terrific Register* (see, for example, figure 30) or the charming illustrations (by Robert Cruikshank) in the delightful *The Dandies' Ball; or, High Life in the City* (see figure 141)—became not simply icons to stare at but his own treasured possessions to shudder over or to dream on at leisure.[9] Dickens describes his childhood enchantment with these shop windows (see figures 13 and 14) and their brightly colored wonders:

> Here, Dr. Faustus was still going down to very red and yellow perdition, under the superintendence of three green personages of a scaly humour, with excrescential serpents growing out of their blade-bones. Here, the Golden Dreamer, and the Norwood Fortune Teller, were still on sale at sixpence each, with instructions for making the dumb cake, and reading destinies in tea-cups, and with a picture of a young woman with a high waist lying on a sofa in an attitude so uncomfortable as almost to account for her dreaming at one and the same time of a conflagration, a shipwreck, an earthquake, a skeleton, a church-porch, lightning, funerals performed, and a young man in a bright blue coat and canary pantaloons. Here, were Little Warblers and Fairburn's Comic Songsters. Here, too, were ballads on the old ballad paper and in the old confusion of types; with an old man in a cocked hat, and an arm-chair, for the illustration to Will Watch the bold Smuggler; and the Friar of Orders Grey, represented by a little girl in a hoop, with a ship in a distance. All these as of yore, when they were infinite delights to me! ("Out of the Season," *HW* 13: 556)

These "infinite delights," in those early childhood years, were only that: supernal wonders or infernal horrors that stimulated Dickens' imagination. Such intensities were not yet part of the dim, half-formed, inchoate designs that were even then, all unconsciously, of course, slowly emerging from the limbo of nothingness. This passive (or seemingly passive) receptivity was the preeminent province of the most frightening horrors—wild cannibalistic hor-

13. The Shop Windows of Print Sellers

Graphic realizations of some of Dickens' nightmare imaginings, imaginings often brimming with gruesome cannibalistic horrors, confronted Dickens from his earliest days: in picture books, chapbooks, song illustrations, and—as here—in shop windows. This print, which would have evoked some of Dickens' earliest memories and associations, was in the volume of Gillray that he later owned. *Very Slippy-Weather* (1808) by James Gillray. Department of Prints and Drawings, British Museum, London. See also figure 14.

rors and the like—for such horrors were apparently too terrifying and yet somehow too appealing to be anything other than what they were: intractable (or seemingly intractable) nightmares that haunted his consciousness.

So, for now, the young boy was (or at least seemed to be) experiencing and accumulating rather than creating—unconsciously sifting out the multitudinous motes of cannibalistic lore and images, and any other highly charged lore and images (comforting or disturbing) that engrossed and repelled him. In fact, this seemingly passive absorption was far from passive. Those elemental intensities helped shape his vision of the world, and they helped shape his innermost yearnings and fears. Much of this lore and many of these images, usually modulated, deepened, or otherwise transformed, entered Dickens' novels, stories, articles, and essays, coloring their very nature.

There were other realms to explore, realms of adventure, fear, and wonder. He early became, as he tells us in "The Long Voyage" and elsewhere, an avid reader of volumes of voyages and travels. He read and reread innumerable accounts of visits to the Cannibal Islands; he soon became a queasy connoisseur of the many dismal legends of those alarming lands. At the same time he became an expert in worldwide disasters and depravities. He pored over calamitous accounts of shipwrecks, famines, and sacrifices, dire catastrophes and afflictions that often culminated in unnatural feasts. As he put it in "The Long Voyage," such accounts were "familiar to me from my early boyhood" (*HW* 8: 410). In another work, *David Copperfield,* Dickens' surrogate, David, in a passage that is literal autobiography (so Forster assures us), exhibits the same inappeasable fascination in his early boyhood that Dickens exhibited in his early years. "I had a greedy relish," David confesses, "for a few volumes of Voyages and Travels—I forget what, now—that were on those shelves; and for days and days I can remember to have gone about my region of our house, armed with the centre-piece out of an old set of boot-trees—the perfect realisation of Captain Somebody, of the Royal British Navy, in danger of being beset by savages, and resolved to sell his

14. The Shop Windows of Print Sellers: Another View

Another view of Hannah Humphrey's print shop in St. James' Street (see figure 13). For many years, "Mrs." Humphrey (who had a special relationship with Gillray) was the exclusive purveyor of his prints. Dickens returned to London in 1822, age ten, a year after the time depicted in this print. *Honi Soit Qui Mal Y Pense*. Caricature (1821) by Theodore Lane. Department of Prints and Drawings, British Museum, London.

life at a great price" (*DC*, 4:41). Note the reference to "savages," and note also the suggestive phrase "greedy relish." For Dickens, the inordinate desire to devour (and to act out) accounts of shipwreck and arduous travel, accounts that often contained harrowing descriptions of cannibalism narrowly forgone or horribly indulged in, continued all his life. In *David Copperfield*, Steerforth dies in a shipwreck, and Ham dies trying to save him. In *Dombey and Son*, Walter, a great devotee (with his uncle) of shipwreck literature, also is shipwrecked; and *Dombey and Son* has a picture of a shipwreck (with an apparently dead body cast upon the shore) on its monthly wrappers and a different picture of a shipwreck on its engraved frontispiece. Many of Dickens' minor works focus on shipwreck and its dire, sometimes cannibalistic consequences.

Forster, using the phrase "insatiable relish" in place of Dickens' phrase "greedy relish," tells us that during one season at the seashore, probably in the late 1840s, Dickens, as was his custom, read "a surprising number of books of African and other travel for which he had insatiable relish" (F, 505). Forster was hardly exaggerating. Dickens was constantly reading and rereading the works—both delightful and horrific—that had early fascinated and shaped him. During the Christmas of 1850 he was a houseguest at the Watsons' estate at Rockingham (the prototype for Chesney Wold in *Bleak House*) and brought with him some books to read. "I believe," he wrote Mrs. Watson after returning home, "I may lay claim to the mysterious inkstand, also to a volume lettered on the back, Shipwrecks and Disasters at Sea, II., which I left when I came down at Christmas" (28 January 1851). As a matter of fact, Dickens' library was replete with volumes about shipwrecks and disasters at sea, and he later filled *Household Words* and *All the Year Round* with similar fare (see figure 17).[10]

III

Dickens' childhood-engendered "greedy relish" for accounts of terrible deprivations, heroic fortitude, and terrifying—often cannibal-

THE

NEW UNIVERSAL

DREAM-BOOK;

OR, THE

DREAMER'S SURE GUIDE

TO THE

Hidden Mysteries of Futurity:

TO WHICH ARE ADDED,

SEVERAL REMARKABLE DREAMS,

AND

UNDENIABLE PROOFS

OF THE

Real Importance of Interpreting Dreams

BY MOTHER SHIPTON.

DERBY:

PUBLISHED BY THOMAS RICHARDSON

THE DREAMER.

15. "All These [Chapbook Illustrations] as of Yore, When They Were Infinite Delights to Me!"

Like the chapbook Dreamer Dickens describes (see p. 29), this chapbook Dreamer, "still on sale at sixpence," contains an illustration of "a young woman . . . on a sofa in an attitude so uncomfortable" as to make her dream, amongst other things, of "a shipwreck" and "a skeleton." Again like Dickens' Dream Book, this one is boldly colored in red, yellow, green, and blue. But this Dreamer depicts scenes not mentioned by Dickens: a headless woman in the background (a "good woman") being ushered toward heaven, and (amidst many other warning signs) three offerings being brought to the serpent-menaced and death-menaced young woman dreaming on the sofa. The first offering is a flaming heart; the second, an emplattered hand and wrist; and the third, an emplattered man's head and neck. (In connection with the latter images, see figure 20, "Hogarth's 'Noon': Profane Feasting," illustrated and analyzed below.) "The Dreamer." From *The New Universal Dream-Book* (c. 1825).

istic—disasters was not confined to his reading about shipwrecks and arduous travels, nor was it confined to the gruesome illustrations that often accompanied those tales of heroic suffering. He found many other sources from which to cull graphic depictions of monumental suffering and brutality. As a child he gazed and gazed again at the horrendous illustrations in Fox's *Book of Martyrs,* raptly viewing ghastly pictures of men and women being boiled, roasted, seared, flayed, and otherwise butchered. He never forgot those gruesome images, and he never forgot the impact they had upon his dawning imagination. Many years later, he made those harrowing illustrations help shape David Copperfield's emerging consciousness (see figures 45 and 46; see also Part 1, note 51).

Also in these childhood days, or perhaps a little later, Dickens became acquainted with the engravings of William Hogarth. In the crowded, tumultuous, brawling world of those engravings, he found once again—now in a more intellectual, sophisticated, satiric context, and in a more social and symbolic context as well—images that had long haunted his imagination, images of leering ogrelike predators, wriggling infants spitted by besotted parents, corpselike humans gnawing on bones, voracious animals devouring human fare, oblivious mothers murdering (in effect) their infants, hanged bodies decomposing amidst rotting rafters, and grotesque corpses being dismembered, dissected, and devoured.

This last image, a nightmare vision from "The Reward of Cruelty," the fourth and final engraving of *The Four Stages of Cruelty,* Dickens found especially harrowing. This ghastly image, the inevitable culmination of what Dickens later called "the detestable advances in the Stages of Cruelty" (*MP,* 1: 40), shows the murderer Tom Nero, or rather his hanged corpse (Nero is the chief exemplar in *The Four Stages of Cruelty* of this dreadful downward progress), being grossly violated and butchered. Hoisted up by a huge screw driven through his skull, Nero's hideous body can now be more efficiently and more gruesomely butchered, a butchering that recapitulates his own brutal exploits. While one "butcher"—that is, doctor—gouges out his eye, another disembowels him, and a third

Socivizca roasting two Turkish prisoners.

approached it, publicly called upon the Turk to defend himself. Smaich advancing, instantly fired his carbine at Socivizca; and aimed so well, that the ball grazed the upper part of his head: fortunately for him, he had turned himself, to see that the enemy did not surround him while he was engaged with his adversary, and in this position the ball passed obliquely, and only gave him a slight wound; but it rendered him desperate, and with amazing rapidity he fired his carbine, and with a second shot, killed Smaich on the spot. His companions instantly fled; but five of them were overtaken in the pursuit, and put to death by Socivizca's companions.

After they had plundered the caravan, and divided the spoils, they disguised themselves, and took different roads, the better to avoid the researches of the Turks, who generally go in search of troops of robbers, and pay little or no attention to single persons on the road. For some time after this event, Socivizca lived so quiet and retired, that it was generally believed he was dead; but when it was least expected, he suddenly appeared again, at the head of a formidable banditti, consisting of twenty-five stout young men, with whom he marched to attack a very considerable caravan, that was going from Ragusa into Turkey, with a prodigious quantity of visclini, a silver coin of base alloy, worth about fourpence of our money. At the first onset, they killed seventeen of the Turks, and took three prisoners; which so terrified the rest of the guards, that they fled with the utmost precipitation, and left him in quiet possession of the treasure. Socivizca was no sooner arrived at a neighbouring wood, than he ordered two of his prisoners to be impaled alive, and assigned to the third, the dreadful office of turning the stake, which was passed through their bodies, before a slow fire. His companions advised him to put the third to death: but, instead of this, when the two victims were half roasted, he ordered their heads to be cut off, which he delivered to the surviving prisoner with this commission: ' Carry these to the bashaw of Traw-

16. Cannibalistic Enormities: Dickens Becomes an Expert in Worldwide Disasters and Depravities

"Socivizca roasting two Turkish prisoners." From the *Terrific Register* (1824–25). As a boy, Dickens read each weekly issue of this sensational periodical.

begins to cut up his limbs. (The disembowler, his mouth wide open, thrusts his hand into the gaping corpse.) Meanwhile, an attendant collects Nero's entrails (swine and other beasts will feed upon them), and a dog eats his heart. But this grisly desecration and consumption only presage what is to come. Nero's butchered bones, riven skull, and clinging flesh will be rendered in the great iron cauldron that flames and bubbles and smokes in the foreground, a miniature inferno that serves as a graphic reminder of the everlasting fires that will torment Tom's soul throughout eternity. As for the remaining bits and scraps of Tom's butchered body, rats and other vermin will eventually feast on the greasy scum, vile and thick and gelatinous, that will coat the horrible cauldron. And what will become of Tom Nero's boiled bones? Those unhallowed bones, reassembled like the bones of the two pointing skeletons that preside over the scene (skeletons of two earlier murderers), will be pawed over by medical students, gaped at by doctors, desecrated by attendants, and hungrily devoured by ghoulish visitors. To cite just one gruesome afterglow in Dickens' writings of these ghastly images, in "The Bride's Chamber," a wild Gothic story that Dickens wrote in 1857 (see Part 2, "Dickens and Passion"), the narrator-murderer (an avatar of Dickens) says: " 'I had been anatomised, but had not yet had my skeleton put together and re-hung on an iron hook' " (*HW* 16: BC, 392; see figure 18, also Part 1, note 40).

The charnel-house images of "The Reward of Cruelty," though gruesome and "detestable" (to use Dickens' word, the same word he will later use to describe the Morgue), and though provocative, even sensational, cannot be equated with the lurid simplicities of chapbook horrors and broadside sensations. Like all Hogarth's images, these images are intellectual; they are also rich with covert meanings. As Dickens put it many years after his introduction to Hogarth, speaking of Hogarth's figures, buildings, gestures, and juxtapositions, his smallest details and largest effects (Dickens is talking now about *Gin Lane*), "we take all this to have a meaning" (*MP*, 1: 41). The grisly details and monitory meanings in *The Four Stages of Cruelty* (details and meanings that recur and evolve from

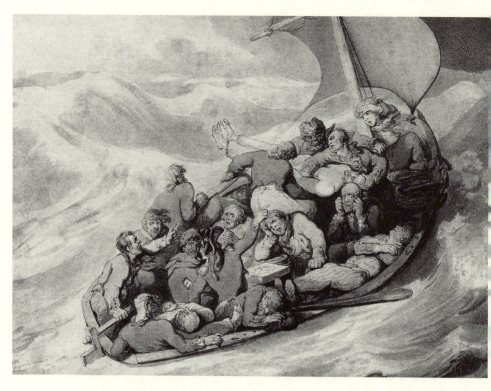

17. Dickens Had a "Greedy Relish" for Voyages and Travels and for Shipwrecks and Disasters at Sea

In this drawing, based upon accounts of the wreck of the *Centaur* (1782)—Dickens knew the story of this wreck well; he cited it by name and drew upon its harrowing history in his writings—note that a dead body is about to be thrown overboard, while some of the survivors seem close to death, and the remainder exhibit emotions that range from terror to desolation to ravening ferocity. *Distress.* Drawing and watercolor (c. 1795) by Thomas Rowlandson. An engraving from this drawing was published c. 1799. Paul Mellon Collection, Yale Center for British Art, New Haven, Connecticut.

plate to plate) are, like those in all Hogarth's engravings, calculated parts of larger artistic designs, powerful devices for achieving loftier social purposes, and therefore, for Dickens, impressive and powerful. Such expressive elements, really ways of seeing and of bearing witness, are admirable, worth studying, and worth emulating—or so Dickens thought.

Hogarth's way of representing and conveying meaning sank deep into Dickens' consciousness, though his immediate appeal for Dickens, that is, the attraction Dickens felt on first viewing Hogarth's works, was probably far less intellectual: the young Dickens was probably entranced and then mesmerized by the grotesque beings, horrific actions, and ghastly images that swarmed through Hogarth's engravings. It is worth looking ahead for a moment (since Hogarth's art helped shape Dickens' art) to see how Dickens assimilated some of Hogarth's images and methods, and some of his visions as well. In part, this assimilation was accretive: Dickens absorbed graphic representations that amplified or intensified his already established obsessions and fears. In part, the assimilation was formative: Dickens found in Hogarth purposes and techniques that he wished to emulate or advance.

As early as *Oliver Twist*, we find Dickens comparing his writings to Hogarth's engravings and publicly proclaiming his kinship with Hogarth. The criticisms that were leveled at *Oliver Twist*, Dickens tells us, were also leveled at Hogarth's works:

Hogarth, the moralist, and censor of his age—in whose great works the times in which he lived, and the characters of every time, will never cease to be reflected—did the like [brought upon the scene the very scum and refuse of the land], without the compromise of a hair's breadth; with a power and depth of thought which belonged to few men before him, and will probably appertain to fewer still in time to come. Where does this giant stand now in the estimation of his countrymen? and yet, if I turn back to the days in which he or any of these men flourished, I find the same reproach levelled against them every one, each in his turn, by the insects of the hour, who raised their little hum, and died, and were forgotten. (*OT*: The Author's Introduction to the Third Edition, viii-ix)

18. Hogarth's "The Reward of Cruelty":
Tom Nero Being Butchered and Eaten

Plate IV of *The Four Stages of Cruelty* (1751) by William Hogarth.

This impassioned manifesto, in which Dickens goes on to proclaim *Oliver Twist* a work in the Hogarthian tradition (and in the tradition of Fielding, Defoe, Goldsmith, Smollett, Richardson, Mackenzie, and Cervantes, as well), was written in 1841. Seven years later, in an essay on Cruikshank's new series of cautionary etchings, *The Drunkard's Children,* a sequel to his earlier series, *The Bottle,* Dickens compared Cruikshank to Hogarth—to Cruikshank's great disadvantage. Dickens explained that when Hogarth depicted drunkenness or any vice, he made it part of the tangled and interconnected social attitudes and conditions of the entire society. Every detail in a Hogarth engraving—the clothing, the houses, the atmosphere, the gestures, the expressions—every line and every suggestion, the outward form and the inward conception, the inmost essence of the entire design, is part of a profound criticism of the social order. Hogarth never depicted a particular vice, however degrading or horrific, as the root of all degeneracy and evil; rather, as in *Gin Lane,* he indicted all the multifarious forces, hidden and open, high and low, that contribute to that vice. Cruikshank, on the other hand, in a series such as *The Drunkard's Children,* made drunkenness the beginning and end of all evil. In his work vices are isolated and inflated into primal causes rather than marshalled as pathological symptoms. Cruikshank's art is deficient. Brilliant and powerful though it is, it is narrow, shallow, and misdirected ("Cruikshank's 'The Drunkard's Children,'" *The Examiner,* 8 July 1848: *MP,* 1: 39–43).

As in the Preface to *Oliver Twist,* one sees that here again Dickens is allying himself with Hogarth and his method; furthermore, one sees that his analysis of Hogarth's art could stand as an exemplification of his own vision and method. In the course of his essay, Dickens demonstrates that he has an easy familiarity with Hogarth's works. He mentions minute details and overall designs, fleeting nuances and profound social concerns. He reads the works adroitly, easily, and he uses his reading to make his telling points. As he makes those points, he refers naturally and incisively to a multitude of works: *The Rake's Progress* (an eight-plate series), *Marriage à la*

Mode (a six-plate series), *The Four Stages of Cruelty* (a four-plate series), *A Midnight Modern Conversation* (one plate), *The Election* (a
four-plate series), *Industry and Idleness* (a twelve-plate series), and
Gin Lane (from a two-plate series). He shows a knowledge and understanding of Hogarth's methods and *œuvre* that could only come
from long study and thought. (Dickens' essay, remember, is not
about Hogarth, to whom he refers only by way of comparison, but
about one series of cautionary Cruikshank plates; it is about, in Hogarthian nomenclature, Cruikshank's *The Drunkard's Progress*.)

As a matter of fact, Dickens' writings are filled with allusions to
specific Hogarth characters, places, and props. These visual allusions
were effortless; they flashed into Dickens' mind as he conjured up a
person, a building, or an item of clothing. Hogarth's world, it is
clear, had become part of Dickens' world, part of the way he perceived and visualized the universe. Dickens will refer to a flabby,
raw-boned, untidy nurse in a workhouse "Itch Ward" as "a woman
such as HOGARTH has often drawn"; or he will tell us that looking
down Cheapside at a Lord Mayor's Show makes him think of "Hogarth's idle and industrious apprentice"; or he will affirm that an old
pensioner in an almshouse "wore a long coat, such as we see Hogarth's Chairmen represented with"; or he will insist that the
"heavy-framed windows" and the "panelled walls" in the Foundling
Hospital "are such windows and such walls as pervade Hogarth's
pictures"; or he will discover that a church he has stumbled upon is
"the exact counterpart of the church in the Rake's Progress where
the hero is being married to the horrible old lady"; or he will assert,
speaking of a "stout old lady" in a dreadful waterside slum, that
"HOGARTH drew her exact likeness more than once"; or he will analyze the "fascination" surrounding a hanging, describing that fascination and then describing the scene in which "Hogarth's idle
apprentice is hanged," a scene of "quarrelling, blasphemy, lewdness,
and uproar," a scene that shows us the "unmistakeable stout lady,
drunk and pious" (what is "unmistakeable" is that the stout lady is
a bawd), and a scene that depicts "Tiddy Doll vending his gingerbread, and the boys picking his pocket."[11] (See figure 19.)

In this final example, a recollection of the crowded, tumultuous, penultimate engraving in *Industry and Idleness* ("The Idle Apprentice Executed at Tyburn"), Dickens remembers (or chooses to emphasize) a curious collocation of details—the hanged person (his soon-dead body and its accompanying coffin the occasion for the gathering), the eating and guzzling by the infernal but festive crowd, the "pious" stout lady, well-fed and well-content, replete with drink (in the engraving she is downing another glass), and Tiddy Doll providing something to munch on while the hungry crowd indulges its parallel but more savage appetite—all these suggestions tell us that Dickens' cannibalistic obsessions have amplified Hogarth's anger and disgust (and his milder, less focused hints of cannibalism) and turned the saturnalia into a public spectacle of obscene cannibalistic feasting. Dickens' revulsion, in other words, has transformed Hogarth's engraving into a particularly Dickensian version of "blasphemy" and "lewdness": the guzzling and munching English public, degraded by what they are called upon to witness and participate in, have become bestial savages, publicly feasting on a dead body with infernal appetite. (In the engraving, the doomed man and his coffin constitute a single visual entity—Thomas Idle is already, in effect, a dead man, an uncoffined corpse, his initialed coffin accompanying him and waiting for him—and that central image of a living corpse is one primary focus of Hogarth's design, a focus that is made literal and unmistakable when we notice that one enterprising hawker in the central foreground is already selling a broadside entitled *The Last dying Speech & Confession of Tho. Idle.* Idle, then, though living is already a veritable corpse. Only the day before, in the prison chapel, the waiting coffin at his side, he had listened as the burial service was read over his still living but already dead body, a horror that Dickens, identifying with Idle, visualized and then underwent vicariously, and a horror that haunted and scarified his imagination.[12] The eager crowd waiting impatiently for Idle's hanging participates in this barbaric horror. For Dickens, the hungry crowd is literally feeding upon, taking its sustenance from, Idle's dead body. The crowd, in other words, is a crowd of

19. Hogarth's "The Idle Apprentice Executed at Tyburn":
The English Public Feasting on a Dead Body

Plate XI of *Industry and Idleness* (1747) by William Hogarth.

debauched corpse eaters. Corpse eating, in turn, is a recurrent Dickensian nightmare, one that will emerge over and over again in his writings, a nightmare that has special horrors, special attractions, and special connotations for him.)

Dickens' knowledge of Hogarth's engravings was not confined to those he directly named or explicated. Some of his earliest sketches appear to have been inspired by Hogarthian scenes and series. For example, Hogarth's famous four-plate series *The Four Times of the Day*, with its satiric engravings of "Morning," "Noon," "Evening," and "Night"—each scene taking place in London streets or lanes—is almost certainly recollected by Dickens in "The Streets—Morning" and "The Streets—Night." (As a matter of fact, Dickens' "Morning" covers the period from dawn to noon, and his "Night" from early evening to late night, thus comprehending the activities delineated in all four Hogarth engravings.) Dickens' "Morning" was published in July 1835, his "Night" in January 1836; both pieces were subsequently collected (with some changes) in *Sketches by Boz*.

This indebtedness to Hogarth's depiction of the streets of London at different times of the day and night (and year) is not confined to using Hogarth's general idea but emerges in many scattered touches—including details of place, atmosphere, attitude, and observation—as even a cursory comparison of the two series will disclose. One striking and localized grouping of conjoined images in "Noon" that must surely have impressed and fascinated Dickens, though he did not bring it directly into "The Streets—Morning" or "The Streets—Night"—he did bring it into other early works, however—is a grouping that is crucial to Hogarth's noontime design. In "Noon," in the middle distance, Hogarth depicts the sign of a vendor of spirits, a strange sign that features a woman without a head (the ironic image of "The Good Woman"). He also depicts a public house in the foreground bearing a sign that is even more prominent and more ironic, and that is allied to the sign of the headless woman. The more prominent sign shows a bearded head—the head only—very dead and very gruesome, displayed on a serving platter, as a choice dish would be displayed. (The head is probably that of John the Baptist; the public house would then be known as "The Baptist's Head.") At the bottom of this grisly sign, in large, distinct, and very visible letters (with a mutton chop on either side of the legend) is the rubric: "Good Eating."

Hogarth places further emphasis on profane feasting by depicting—still in that localized left portion of the engraving—a platter of food being fought over by an angry couple and thrown out the window by the irate woman (this, just above the headless "Good Woman" sign). To further relate and comment on these conjoined images, Hogarth uses another device. He arranges his perspective so that the spear supporting the sign with the decapitated head and its assurance of "Good Eating" ends in another head, in the head of the violent, food-throwing woman, the spear point in her cheek. Hard by these scenes, but closer to the viewer, two additional platters of food have been spilled and one platter broken (in two additional incidents that have their origins in animal appetites), the latter incidents taking place just below the cannibalistic "Good Eating" sign and characterized by it. There are also unmistakable hints, quite bawdy and suggestive, that the lustful black man who is fondling the partially bared breasts and mouthing the turned cheek of a pretty serving girl, and thus causing her to spill the juices from a meat pie she is carrying—all this directly below the "Good Eating" sign—is a hungry cannibal displaying his ancestral appetites. Meanwhile, a famished little street urchin, a girl, ragged and unkempt, takes advantage of the accidents by greedily lapping up the spilled food that cascades from the meat pie and the broken platter and puddles on the cobblestones. This exemplary scene of debauched "Good Eating" takes place in Hog Lane.

Permutations of beastlike eating and cannibalistic feeding, and nightmare (or macabre) visions of ogreish aggressors devouring human heads ("Good Eating" indeed!), will recur in Dickens' writings. To glance forward for a moment, one later reflection, a grotesque and transformed reflex of this repeated imprinting—for Hogarth's "Noon" reinforced for Dickens many earlier visions of

20. Hogarth's "Noon": Profane Feasting

Plate II of *The Four Times of the Day* (1738) by William Hogarth.

devoured heads and other cannibalistic enormities—occurs in *Oliver Twist,* a novel begun just a year or so after the "Morning" and "Night" sketches. In *Oliver Twist* Dickens created the grim and irascible (yet ultimately golden-hearted) Mr. Grimwig, a kind of surly, melancholy-mad giant who is always declaring ferociously, "I'll eat my own head." This reiterated threat evokes (among other associations) echoes of Hogarth's emplattered and bearded head in "Noon" and its grisly promise of "Good Eating," echoes that are simultaneously mitigated and magnified in Dickens' rendering of the notion; for Dickens makes the idea of eating one's head—or any head—both comic and graphically real. He does this by translating the comic threat from the realm of the merely fanciful to the realm of realistic dining. At the same moment that we are introduced to Mr. Grimwig and his half-comic half-ogreish set phrase, we are also introduced to what that utterance, if put into effect, would entail. Dickens tells us that "Mr. Grimwig's head was such a particularly large one, that the most sanguine man alive could hardly entertain a hope of being able to get through it at a sitting, to put entirely out of the question a very thick coating of powder" (*BM,* 2: *OT,* [1]: 14:219). We are still in the realm of the comic, but with an uncomfortable, not to say queasy, sense of the actual.

It is clear from Dickens' allusions to and transformations of Hogarth cited above, and from many other allusions and transformations scattered throughout his works (including his very early works), that when Dickens sat down to write "Cruikshank's 'The Drunkard's Children,'" he already had an easy mastery of Hogarth's *œuvre,* a mastery he could call upon effortlessly. On the other hand, his allusions to Hogarth's engravings in his essay on Cruikshank are often so detailed or specific that it seems likely that he had a volume or collection of Hogarth beside him.[13] This collection (if it was one) was probably not the same as the superb collection he later owned, which he seems to have bought some ten years or so after writing the Cruikshank piece. Furthermore, the later collection did not have *The Election* or *The Four Stages of Cruelty* in it, though Dickens, of course, when writing the Cruikshank piece, could have been referring to those two series, or to other Hogarth works for that matter, from memory. In any case, Dickens later owned forty-eight fine Hogarth engravings, all early impressions and most first impressions, and all framed ([Dickens], *Catalogue of the Library*, 58–59). He seems to have bought these engravings (unframed, and possibly over several years) around the period when he moved to Gad's Hill Place. By the time he was well established at Gad's Hill, the collection had pride of place in his home. He hung the engravings in the entrance hall, down the central hallway, along the main staircase ascending to the second floor, and in his bedroom. For the last ten or twelve years of his life, perhaps longer, therefore, Hogarth's images were daily before his eyes. We occasionally get some corroboratory external glimpses of how important those images were to Dickens. James T. Fields, latterly Dickens' chief American publisher and, in the 1850s and 1860s, his close friend, was a house guest at Gad's Hill Place during the summer of 1869. In *Yesterdays with Authors*, Fields writes about Dickens and Hogarth:

Dickens's admiration of Hogarth was unbounded, and he had hung the staircase leading up from the hall of his house with fine old impressions of the great master's best works. Observing our immediate interest in these pictures, he seemed greatly pleased, and proceeded at once to point out in his graphic way what had struck his own fancy most in Hogarth's genius. He had made a study of the painter's *thought* as displayed in these works, and his talk about the artist was delightful. He used to say he never came down the stairs without pausing with new wonder over the fertility of the mind that had conceived and the hand that had executed these powerful pictures of human life; and I cannot forget with what fervid energy and feeling he repeated one day, as we were standing together on the stairs in front of the Hogarth pictures, Dr. Johnson's epitaph, on the painter:—

"The hand of him here torpid lies,
    That drew the essential form of grace;
Here closed in death the attentive eyes
    That saw the manners in the face."
(Fields, 209)

Dickens also owned an atlas folio edition of Gillray's works. This superb edition, entitled *Celebrated Caricatures*, contained six hundred large, brilliant engravings, all fine impressions, and all from the original plates. Most of Gillray's work was grotesque, much of it savage. Many of his caricatures showed monstrously bestial humans, gross and bloated from ravenous feeding, gorging on their fellowmen. Some of these ferocious engravings, which Dickens could now study in the comfort of his library, he had shuddered over when viewing them in shop windows as a child. These fierce childhood images, together with their boyhood and teenhood counterparts, also burned into Dickens' consciousness; they later entered his writings (as Hogarth's images did) in multitudes of striking ways.

What we see here (Hogarth is our primary example) is a pattern that will emerge over and over again later in this section and then throughout the book—namely, that some of the early forces already touched upon (such as Dickens' reading and rereading of the literature of shipwrecks, voyages, travels, disasters, and the like), and some of the similar forces to be touched upon shortly, continued to impinge upon Dickens in later years and continued to evolve and expand in his consciousness, both in the way he thought about them and in the way he used them. With Hogarth, as with many other early influences, there is initial fascination, continuing exposure, gestation, and ultimate transformation. The latter phase or development is the most crucial, for here Dickens fully internalizes and reformulates an idea, image, or emotion and transforms it into his own vision of meaning and significance. The meaning is indebted to its source, but it also usually transcends its source.

With Hogarth (to continue with him as our chief example for now) we can see Dickens utilizing and reformulating in multitudes of ways. We can see him using Hogarthian symbolism, parallelism, foreshadowing, redundancy, repetition, horror, grotesquerie, exaggeration, distortion, predation, and more, and we can see, from the Preface to *Oliver Twist*, that from early on Dickens was conscious that he was drawing upon Hogarth and emulating him. To cite one brief example, the election scenes in *The Pickwick Papers* are, among other things, rethought and reworked versions of the four satiric scenes in *The Election* (a series that Dickens referred to in his essay on Cruikshank). Dickens' use of *The Election* in *Pickwick* thus parallels his use of *The Four Times of the Day* in *Sketches by Boz*. To cite another, more profound and complex example, think for a moment of the Dombey-Edith marriage in *Dombey and Son*. We see at once that this sad progress—which wends its inevitable way from exploitation to impropriety to degradation to death to ruin to destruction, is a thoroughly updated, thoroughly transformed, and thoroughly Dickensian version of *Marriage à la Mode*. Dombey's mercenary and loveless marriage, and in particular the significance of his and Carker's cannibalistic contributions to that marriage, will be explored later.

Meanwhile, one should recall that *Marriage à la Mode* begins with the formal signing of the marriage contract (on both sides, as in *Dombey*, a mere matter of calculated business) and ends with the just-dead countess, self-condemned and self-murdered, sprawled in her chair, her mouth slightly open, her small crippled child, held by a servant, clutching her mother's lifeless head and pressing her mouth to it, while an emaciated dog, in a virtually identical pose, hind legs on a chair, tears with its mouth at the human food at the center of the table (the only substantial food present), that food being the grotesque head of a repulsive and very dead piglike animal, its mouth slightly open. The counterpart images of daughter and dog, countess and pig, instruct us. The ravenous dog, through parallel structure, shows us what the countess has come to: like Carker at his end, she is disgraced and degraded, mere human fodder, useless to her daughter or to any human creature, food for curs. In both Hogarth and Dickens, the latter phrase—"food for curs"—is more than a metaphor; it is a Biblical allusion and a Biblical judgment (see figure 21).

Dickens found in Hogarth many other moral fables and many other images that blended with his most sensitive and shaping awarenesses. Profound lessons and speaking images, Dickens discovered, were scattered broadcast in Hogarth's works, broadcast in-

21. Hogarth's "Death of the Countess": Devouring the Sinful Dead

The ravenous dog devouring the grotesque head that garnishes the center of the dining table is an exact imagistic parallel (in posture, activity, and other details) to the small child who eagerly grasps and mouths her mother's death-distorted head. This parallel, which evokes similar devourings in the Bible, tells us that modern-day Jezebels (like modern-day Carkers after them) will come at last to the old disgraceful end: their bodies will be eaten by dogs. Plate VI of *Marriage à la Mode* (1745) by William Hogarth.

deed in individual plates. To cite just one more instance, he found ghastly home truths in *Gin Lane*. In this plate, about which Dickens said, "we take all this ['this' signifying every detail in the plate] to have a meaning," Dickens found several unforgettable images, including a number of ferocious cannibalistic ones, that not only had "a meaning," but a special meaning—special for him, at least. These monitory images magnified a terrible transgression that had been committed against him and that had long festered darkly in his consciousness. This terrible transgression was his parents' transgression, especially his mother's. His parents (so Dickens felt) had neglected him and then cast him out; they had left him to perish alive. (For what unpardonable sin, he wondered, had he become a "small Cain," a mere "labouring hind"? [F, 27, 23].) His parents had sold him into the slavery of the blacking warehouse for the sake of a few shillings, sold him so that they and the rest of the family could better eat and drink. In a real sense (so Dickens' anguish and resentment told him at the time), it was his life and being they were consuming; day after day, month after month, they were eating him alive. Hogarth gave visible form—intensified, harrowing form—to this transgression, a transgression that Dickens soon found was all too frequent and commonplace in the world at large. In other words, in *Gin Lane,* among other monster wrongs, Hogarth gave magnified expressionistic form to the sins of fathers and mothers against their innocent children and, more particularly, gave nightmare form to the crimes that Dickens' father and mother, all unaccountably, Dickens thought (yet somehow deservedly as well), had committed against him.

In *Gin Lane* four infants are the victims of grievously neglectful parents: three, of neglectful mothers; one, of a neglectful father. In the first instance, a dazed mother (dazed from too much gin?) pours gin down her infant's throat; in the second, another mother, cold and inert, half-naked, just dead from gin, is put into her coffin while her bereft infant, unattended and naked, wails at the coffin's side; in the third instance, a third mother, half-naked and syphilitic, gin-soaked and preoccupied, oblivious of the world around her, allows

22. Hogarth's *Gin Lane:* "We Take
All This to Have a Meaning"

Part of *Gin Lane's* meaning for Dickens concerned the sins—including the
cannibalistic sins (see text)—of fathers and mothers against their innocent
children. Plate II of *Beer Street and Gin Lane* (1751) by William Hogarth.

her infant to slip from her arms and fall toward a great open black portal—a dark mawlike portal—fall to its inevitable death and the waiting maw of hell (directly above that yawning maw, a skeleton-headed man and a sharp-toothed dog, two gruesome embodiments of what that maw portends, gnaw ravenously on a bone); and finally, in the fourth instance, a gin-crazed father, pursued by his horrified wife, has impaled their naked child on a monster spit, and with the wriggling infant held aloft (and a bellows in his other hand), parades in besotted triumph through the street. Some of these images, especially the last three, and preeminently the last two, will emerge in Dickens' writings fully refashioned—for the most part consciously, but also unconsciously—reshaped to express his own emotions and convey his own insights, unique emotions and insights, but universal as well.

Gin Lane is only one plate out of scores of Hogarth plates, and Hogarth is only one influence out of innumerable influences. In the remainder of this book, and especially in the next few score pages, we shall see many examples of Dickens' conscious and unconscious transformation of these and other seminal sources, mostly dark, secret, disturbing sources—literary sources and lived sources— sources of great power and potency, sources that Dickens drew upon and struggled with and ultimately reshaped, sources that, together with his profound reaction to them, helped fashion the nature of much of his art.

IV

But in his childhood and early youth Dickens was absorbing and responding rather than actively creating. Part of that absorption took place in a magical dominion. He immersed himself in the protean world of fiction, a world that was, as he later affirmed (in a passage in *David Copperfield* that Forster assures us was literal autobiography [F, 5–6]), crucial to his survival. As Dickens himself put it (speaking through David), the world of fiction, a world so freeing, so limitless, and so transcendent, was "my only and my constant comfort" (*DC,* 4: 42). From his imaginative reading and rereading in this all-important realm he culled (along with much else) his special harvest. One moiety of that special harvest came from the writings of Jonathan Swift. As Dickens' many later references to Swift indicate, he early shuddered at, but also gloried in, such savagely cool and convincing baby-eating satires as Swift's "A Modest Proposal," a devastating fiction that seemed to advocate the fattening, butchering, and eating of children, and a fiction, moreover, that advocated this ferocious enormity in the dry, matter-of-fact guise of a most deliberate and reasonable proposal, a strategy of presentation that accentuated the horror, not simply of the cannibalistic "remedy" being advocated, but (and more to the point) of the dire social evils being attacked.[14]

Dickens also knew and delighted in, but shuddered at as well, more adventure-filled and more wonder-provoking fare. As his many later references and testimonials again show, he never forgot the plentiful wonders and savageries of *Gulliver's Travels*. Reading *Gulliver* as a very young boy, immersing himself in its adventures over and over again, he not only perused but in his usual fashion he underwent Lemuel Gulliver's dire predicaments and terrifying experiences. Scattered through Dickens' writings are the transformed offspring of that impassioned reading. Those offspring include (to mention no other aftereffects) scores of later references to Gulliver and his adventures, not simply in Lilliput and Brobdingnag, but in Laputa, Lagado, Luggnagg, Balnibarbi, and Glubdubdrib, and in the patrician domain of the exalted Houyhnhnms as well.[15]

Swift's imagination was contradictory; it was both robust and fastidious. In *Gulliver's Travels* he dwelt obsessively on the gross physicality of the human body (a physicality that fascinated and disgusted him), and especially on the animal functions of ingestion and elimination. *Gulliver's Travels* is filled with horrible visions of being mauled, chewed, eaten, digested, disgorged, and defecated. These scenes of gross animality and terrifying cannibalism—though animality and cannibalism made, as in Hogarth, to serve the purposes

23. The Rats of Dickens' Childhood: Gulliver Almost Devoured by Gigantic Rats

This illustration by Grandville (and the one below) are from a two-volume 1838 French edition of *Gulliver's Travels* that Dickens owned. Such illustrations, encountered in manhood, gave visible form to Dickens' old childhood nightmare.

24. The Rats of Dickens' Childhood: Monstrous Ratlike Yahoos Devouring Wild Rats

From *Gulliver's Travels* (1838), illustrated by Grandville.

of brilliant satire and engrossing art—early entered Dickens' consciousness. He read and reread those terrifying cannibal-tinged adventures; he lived and relived the experiences of being sniffed, stalked, mouthed, dismembered, and cooked. In Brobdingnag, Dickens, like Gulliver, experienced the terrors of encountering, close at hand, without bars or other impediments, fierce-visaged cats three times the size of an ox, or looming farmhouse mastiffs four times the size of an elephant. He also, like Gulliver, endured being sniffed at and then attacked by ravenous monster rats (a special terror for Dickens), being thrown at dinnertime, like a delectable tidbit, into a silver bowl filled with rich cream, or being stuffed into a marrow bone and then set on a serving dish on the dining table, a succulent morsel.

He underwent (so vivid was his imagination) other frightening nightmares of being eaten alive, or almost eaten alive. Like Gulliver, he was snatched up and then carried about in the deadly, sharp-toothed jaws of a giant spaniel, attacked and almost dragged off in the talons of an enormous kite, and beleaguered by frogs, monkeys, and other creatures that hungered to devour him. In the land of the Houyhnhnms, again like Gulliver, he was attacked, naked, by an enamored female Yahoo, also naked, a filthy creature with a devouring appetite for his body, but an appetite more libidinous than cannibalistic (by way of animalistic parallel, Yahoos "greedily devour" wild rats); while in Laputa he meditated on other depraved practices, on the practice, for example, of sawing the skulls of contending individuals in half, then switching the halves—both halves still living and still contending—and joining them with their butchered and opposed counterparts. (Dickens owned an 1838 two-volume French edition of *Gulliver's Travels*, profusely illustrated by Grandville, that graphically highlighted many of these enormities; see figures 23–26; see also Part 1, note 14.)

Perhaps the most frightening cannibalistic experience of all for Dickens (certainly one of the most emotional) occurred in Brobdingnag. In the episode in question, a one-year-old Brobdingnagian child begins to play with a new bauble, the toylike Gulliver himself.

25. Gulliver Becomes a Tidbit in a Bowl of Cream

Dickens owned the two-volume French edition of *Gulliver's Travels* from which this illustration (and the one below) were taken. *Gulliver's Travels* (1838), illustrated by Grandville.

26. Gulliver Almost Eaten by a Brobdingnagian Infant

"This child . . . presently seized me by the middle, and got my head into his mouth." *Gulliver's Travels* (1838), illustrated by Grandville.

Then, in a twinkling, the gargantuan infant picks Gulliver up and
thrusts him, headfirst, into his mouth. Gulliver, terrified, roars so
loudly that the frightened infant drops him. Now it is the infant's
turn to roar. The mother, to quiet the screaming infant, finally decides to nurse him. When this hungry infant, who had almost swallowed Gulliver, began to suck and gulp at his mother's mountainous
breast (the coarse nipple, all spotted and pitted, is half the size of
Gulliver's head), Gulliver tells us that he found the sight of this ravenous child feasting greedily on its mother's gigantic body disgusting beyond anything he had ever seen.[16]

Dickens lived all these experiences in his own imagination.[17] He
never forgot these narrow escapes—nightmare escapes—from the
horrors of being eaten alive, of being attacked by gigantic, ravenous
rats and being thrust into the mouth of a monster child. Nor did he
forget other cannibal encounters in the imaginative reading of his
childhood. There were multitudes of such encounters, and he remembered them and that rapt reading and rereading as he remembered the veritable experiences of his own life. As a consequence,
when he thought of *Robinson Crusoe*, he thought of scenes and incidents that were part of his own being, scenes he had visited for as
long as he could remember, incidents he had experienced over and
over again. The cannibals of *Robinson Crusoe* loomed large in those
memories, in fact, out of all proportion to their presence in the original text. When Dickens summons up the shadows of *Robinson
Crusoe*, often and often he summons up cannibalistic scenes and
cannibalistic rites. In one typical flood of *Robinson Crusoe* memories, he tells us of "the little creek which Friday swam across when
pursued by his two brother cannibals with sharpened stomachs";
and then, a few moments later, he refers to "the sandy beach . . .
where the savages hauled up their canoes when they came ashore
for those dreadful public dinners, which led to a dancing worse than
speech-making" ("Nurse's Stories," *AYR* 3:517; later in *UT*.).[18] In
both of these references the cannibalistic horrors are mitigated by
humor, a frequent strategy with Dickens. The thing to note here,
however, is that for Dickens *Robinson Crusoe* and cannibalism were

intertwined. The cannibals of *Robinson Crusoe* trooped into his consciousness and into his writings, testimonials, whether veiled by humor or intensified by horror, to their abiding significance.

Many of the cannibalistic creatures that Dickens encountered in his childhood reading were more fearsome and fantastic than the dusky cannibals of *Robinson Crusoe*. He never forgot the man-eaters and ghouls of *The Arabian Nights*, the loathsome predators of *The Tales of the Genii*, and the hungry dragons of legend and romance. These creatures became his daily companions; they haunted his sleeping and waking dreams. They remained in his consciousness all life long, potent forces, troubling and generative; they remained there as did the swarming grotesques of Hogarth's London, part of his shaping heritage. And, as with Hogarth, whose works he turned back to all his life, he turned back to *Gulliver's Travels*, *Robinson Crusoe*, *The Arabian Nights*, and other early fictions over and over again, reading them on railway journeys, delving into them for an apt allusion or a neat confirmation, going back to them for solace or reassurance or delight, returning to them to experience once more the still fresh wonder and fear of a vanished childhood.[19]

There were other childhood literary works that shaped Dickens' cannibalistic imaginings. Some of those works and some of those cannibalistic phantasms were less threatening than the savages and monsters who peopled the world of adventure and romance. As a matter of fact, some of the cannibalism that Dickens encountered in his early reading was comic and delightful, though even in that delight darker realities, obscured by laughter, lurked. One lesser-known work that he read with enormous enjoyment and unencumbered empathy (he was ten or eleven at the time) was *Broad Grins* by George Colman the younger (F, 12). Colman's book, a small volume of comic narrative poems (and the illustrations that accompanied them), helped to lighten a difficult time for Dickens. That trying time was the miserable London year when Dickens watched the family fortunes disintegrate and the family library dwindle, when his father descended into debtor's prison and he descended into the blacking warehouse. In that stressful year, before the final

our ship, who was a fat, stout, broad-shouldered man; a person of
strength and vigour: so he pleased him, and he seized him as
the butcher seizeth the animal that he is about to slaughter, and,
having thrown him on the ground, put his foot upon his neck,
which he thus broke. Then he brought a long spit, and thrust it
into his throat, and spitted him; after which he lighted a fierce fire,
and placed over it that spit upon which the master was spitted, and
ceased not to turn him round over the burning coals until his flesh
was thoroughly roasted; when he took him off from the fire, put
him before him, and separated his joints as a man separates the
joints of a chicken, and proceeded to tear in pieces his flesh
with his nails, and to eat of it. Thus he continued to do until he
had eaten his flesh, and gnawed his bones, and there remained
of him nothing but some bones, which he threw by the side of the
pavilion. He then sat a little, and threw himself down, and slept
upon that maṣṭabah, making a noise with his throat like that which
is made by a lamb or other beast when slaughtered; and he
slept uninterruptedly until the morning, when he went his way.

As soon, therefore, as we were sure that he was far from us, we

27. The Voracious Giants of Fable and Romance

This hungry giant from *The Arabian Nights*, a creature familiar to Dickens
from childhood on, spitted his plump victim, roasted him, tore him to pieces,
ate his flesh, and "gnawed his bones." Wood engraving (1841) after a drawing
by William Harvey. From Vol. III of *The Thousand and One Nights* (London,
1841).

descent, *Broad Grins* was a succoring part of the fast-fading world of amusement and relief.

One of the poems in *Broad Grins,* a short piece entitled "Lodgings for Single Gentlemen," tells the story of Will Waddle, a fat, Pickwickian sort of gentleman who rents a room from a landlord who dwells on the premises. From Will's very first night in his new lodgings his life becomes a misery. He is in a fever. Hot and distraught, he languishes in his ovenlike bed. Doctors and potions are to no avail: he sweats and roasts and dwindles and bakes. This goes on for six months; he becomes a gaunt shadow of his former self. At last he makes a discovery. His landlord is a baker; his suffocating inferno of a bed is directly over the bakery oven:

> "The Oven!!!" says Will—says the host, "Why
>   this passion?
> In that excellent bed died three people of
>   fashion.
> Why so crusty, good Sir?"—"Zounds!" cries Will,
>   in a taking,
> "Who would'nt be crusty, with half a year's
>   baking?"
>   (Colman, 38)

The next stanza concludes "Lodgings for Single Gentlemen." The last line in the poem, spoken as Will leaves the premises, emphasizes, not only that Will has been transformed by the baker into one of his crusty loaves of bread, but that he has been (as a tenant) consumed by the baker. In phrases that can be read several ways, Will tells the baker: "'But I'd rather not *perish,* while you *make your bread*'" (Colman, 39). Here cannibalism is witty and amusing, even succoring—but it is cannibalism nevertheless.

Dickens' vanished childhood had many phases and many tributaries. His early cannibalistic conditioning was not confined to listening to stories, or poring over pictures, or reading and rereading favorite books. There were memorable excursions as well. Scheherazade, or one of her earlier or occasional counterparts (the embryo artist was blessed—or cursed—in his nursemaids), would drag the little child to local lyings-in or layings-out, there to felicitate or commiserate as the occasion demanded. One such visit Dickens recalled with special clarity:

> At one little greengrocer's shop, down certain steps from the street, I remembered to have waited on a lady who had had four children (I am afraid to write five, though I fully believe it was five) at a birth. This meritorious woman held quite a Reception in her room on the morning when I was introduced there, and the sight of the house [on a recent visit to Chatham] brought vividly to my mind how the four (five) deceased young people lay, side by side, on a clean cloth on a chest of drawers: reminding me by a homely association, which I suspect their complexion to have assisted, of pigs' feet as they are usually displayed at a neat tripe-shop. Hot caudle was handed round on the occasion. (["Dullborough Town"], *AYR* 3: 275; later in *UT*)

The child Dickens contemplates this bizarre scene. He is duly impressed. Nevertheless, he refuses his nursemaid's injunction to donate his pocket money to a subscription being solicited from those assembled, whereupon his conductress and her friends inform him that he "must dismiss all expectations of going to Heaven" (*AYR* 3: 275). This extraordinary image—of corpses laid out like meat in a neighborhood butcher shop while an assembled company, gathered at a greengrocer's shop (another food shop), eats and drinks, and Dickens is consigned by his nursemaid to hell—this bizarre image and the defensive humor that surrounds it will recur over and over again in Dickens' writings (see below in Part 1).

This early cannibalistic conditioning and association—the nurses' stories, the picture books, the reading, the visits, the engravings, and the like—was supplemented by constant later reinforcement. One could supply abundant examples of this reinforcement, but perhaps one instance—or, rather, one series of instances—will suffice. At the age of twelve we find Dickens eagerly reading each week's bloodcurdling issue of the *Terrific Register,* an aptly named periodical that specialized in gore and sensationalism and purveyed many histories of debased appetites. Of this lurid weekly Dickens

HORRIBLE MURDER OF A CHILD.

THE annals of crime scarcely furnish a more diabolical instance of cruelty than the one we are about to record; but the circumstances of the murder are eclipsed, in point of hardened depravity, by the means taken to conceal it.

In July, 1762, Sarah Metyard and Sarah Morgan Metyard, mother and daughter, were placed at the bar of the Old Bailey for the murder of Ann Nayler, a girl, 13 years of age, by shutting up and confining her, and starving her to death. There was also a second indictment for the murder of Mary Nayler, her sister, aged eight years. The unfortunate child (Ann) it appeared, had been apprenticed to the elder prisoner, and it was principally on the evidence of her own apprentices that she and her daughter were convicted. They deposed that about Michaelmas, 1758, Ann Nayler attempted to escape, she was used so ill; being frequently beaten with a thick walking stick and a hearth-broom, and made to go without her victuals. The day she endeavoured to run away, a milkman who served the family, stopped her, as she was running from the door, and brought her back to the prisoners. The daughter dragged her up stairs, and while the mother held her head, beat her cruelly with a broomstick. She was then tied up with a rope round her waist, and her hands fastened behind, so that she could neither sit nor lie, and in this position she remained for three days without food. During this period she never spoke, but used to stand and groan. At the end of the three days, the witness observed she did not move; she hung double; and when this was mentioned to the daughter, she said, she'd make her move. She ran up stairs, and struck her with a shoe, but there was no animation in her. The mother came up, laid the child across her lap, and sent one of the girls for some drops. The girls were ordered down stairs, and the unhappy victim was never afterwards seen by them. In order to remove the suspicion of her death from the minds of the apprentices, by leading them to imagine she had made her escape, the

VOL. I.   2

28. Dickens and the "Attraction of Repulsion"

"I used [as a boy] to take in the *Terrific Register,* making myself unspeakably miserable, and frightening my very wits out of my head, for the small charge of a penny weekly; which considering that there was an illustration to every number, in which there was always a pool of blood, and at least one body, was cheap." Note that this particular atrocity—the "horrible murder of a child"— was committed by a mother and daughter. Note, also, that the illustration contains not just a body and a pool of blood, but a dismembered body and a bucket of blood. "Horrible Murder Of A Child." From the *Terrific Register* (1824–25).

later wrote: "I used, when I was [twelve or so], to take in the *Terrific Register*, making myself unspeakably miserable, and frightening my very wits out of my head, for the small charge of a penny weekly; which considering that there was an illustration to every number, in which there was always a pool of blood, and at least one body, was cheap" (F, 43–44). The *Terrific Register* contained many accounts of cannibalism (often replete with horribly explicit woodcuts); it also contained tales of travel, shipwreck, famine, strange appetites, and the like.

One can imagine Dickens reading the *pièce de résistance* of one memorable issue, a front-page article headed in great black capital letters, "THE DEAD DEVOURED BY THE LIVING!" This grisly case history told the story of one Antoine Langulet of Paris, a man who gradually developed an appetite, to use the polite language of the periodical, for "animal substances in the highest state of putrefaction" (*TR* 2: 737). This appetite eventually drew the unfortunate creature to a nearby graveyard where he disinterred recently buried bodies and feasted ravenously on them on the spot, all the while stuffing his pockets with choice morsels for later dining in his hayloft den. The *Terrific Register* account goes on—sometimes clinically, sometimes provocatively—to dwell upon gruesome details of this repulsive feeding (how Langulet conveyed "his darling article of food to his lodging," how "he had always been fond of . . . loathsome food," how he would feast upon "intestines in preference to any other part of the body [and] would fill his pockets with . . . this horrible material," how "he sometimes felt the greatest inclination to devour children of a tender age" [*TR* 2: 738]), details that Dickens, we may be sure, devoured with horrified appetite.

The impact on Dickens of this revolting narrative of depraved cannibalism, plus the impact of later allied narratives, sensational narratives that described the grave-despoiling, and the body-snatching and body-slaughtering depredations of Burke, Hare, Bishop, Williams, and other ghoulish traffickers in bodies (Burkers and Resurrection Men, primarily from the 1820s and early 1830s, who lived on bodies, who made bodies, in effect, their meat and

THE TRIAL, SENTENCE, FULL CONFESSION, AND EXECUTION OF
BISHOP & WILLIAMS,
THE BURKERS.

BURKING AND BURKERS.

The month of November, 1831, will be recorded in the annals of crimes and cruelties as particularly pre-eminent, for it will prove to posterity that other wretches could be found base enough to follow the horrid example of Burke and his accomplice Hare, to entice the unprotected and friendless to the den of death for sordid gain.

The horrible crime of "Burking," or murdering the unwary with the intention of selling their bodies at a high price to the anatomical schools, for the purpose of dissection, has unfortunately obtained a notoriety which will not be soon or easily forgotten. It took its horrify-ing appellation from the circumstances which were disclosed on the trial of the inhuman wretch Burke, who was executed at Edinburgh in 1829, for having wilfully and deliberately murdered several persons for the sole purpose of profiting by the sale of their dead bodies.

APPREHENSION OF THE BURKERS.

On Tuesday, November 8th, four persons, viz., John

Bishop, Thomas Williams, James May, and Michael Shield, were examined at Bow Street Police Office on the charge of being concerned in the wilful murder of an unknown Italian boy. From the evidence adduced, it appeared that May, *alias* Jack Stirabout, a known resurrection-man, and Bishop, a body-snatcher, offered at King's College a subject for sale, Shield and Williams having charge of the body in a hamper, for which they demanded twelve guineas. Mr Partridge, demonstrator of anatomy, who, although not in absolute want of a subject, offered nine guineas, but being struck with its freshness sent a messenger to the police station, and the fellows were then taken into custody, examined before the magistrates, when Shield was discharged and the others ultimately committed for trial.

THE TRIAL.

Friday, December 2nd, having been fixed for the trial of the prisoners charged with the murder of the Italian boy, the Court was crowded to excess so early as eight o'clock in the morning.

At nine o'clock the Deputy Recorder, Mr Serjeant

29. Burkers (Often Erstwhile Resurrectionists or Resurrection Men) Garnering Fresh Bodies for Sale

Dickens, nineteen in 1831, was working in the very streets where John Bishop and Thomas Williams, greedy and rapacious Resurrection Men turned Burkers, committed their crimes, were tried, and hanged (see Part 1, note 40). In *A Tale of Two Cities*, Jerry Cruncher is a Resurrection Man. His grave-yard "fishing," like Bishop and Williams' (or Burke and Hare's) more murderous predations, puts meat and drink on the family dining table. In Dickens' view, such ghoulish scavengers and predators were veritable eaters of corpses, mercantile versions of the corpse-eating Antoine Langulet. Broadside (1831). From [Hindley], *Curiosities of Street Literature* (1871).

drink—see Part 1, note 40)—these two converging streams of horror, one stream from his boyhood, the other from his youth—comprise two sources for Jerry Cruncher's nighttime occupation in *A Tale of Two Cities*. (Note, in this connection, the name "Cruncher"; remember Jerry's oft-repeated avowal that his nocturnal "fishing" [read: graveyard body-snatching] brings "wittles and drink" and "a jinte of meat or two" to his family's dining table, and recall his suggestive habit of sucking the rust from his corpse-contaminated fingers, ingesting on one occasion, as Dickens puts it, "quite a lunch of rust"—the occasion in question being when Darnay, in danger of being "butchered and torn asunder" by order of the court, is regarded by Cruncher and the other courtroom spectators with "Ogreish" relish [*AYR* 1: *TTC*, 2: 14:290–91; 3:124; 2:101]. That this "Ogreish" relish, that Jerry Cruncher's graveyard foragings and body-snatching depredations in quest of "meat" for his dining table, and that the other examples of eager cannibalistic hungerings and devourings we have just noted in *A Tale of Two Cities* are much more than passing allusions becomes clear when Dickens begins the subsequent chapter, which immediately follows the two chapters that contain the "lunch" and "butchering" and "Ogreish" references. The new chapter began a new weekly segment of *A Tale of Two Cities* in *All the Year Round;* that is, it, like the other two chapters, came after a week's hiatus. Here is the recapitulative opening sentence of that new chapter and new segment: "From the dimly-lighted passages of the court, the last sediment of the human stew that had been boiling there all day, was straining off, when Doctor Manette, Lucie Manette his daughter, Mr. Lorry, the solicitor for the defence, and its counsel Mr. Stryver, stood gathered around Mr. Charles Darnay—just released—congratulating him on his escape from death" [*AYR* 1: *TTC*, 2: 4:145]. The boiling human stew drains off. Charles Darnay, the hungrily anticipated chief ingredient of that boiling human stew, is saved from death, saved from being publicly slaughtered, turned into the stock of a crowd-pleasing stew, and then eagerly devoured, saved by Sydney Carton—saved for now, for the first time.)[20]

But to return to the *Terrific Register*, and more particularly, to Antoine Langulet and his graveyard foraging. The ghoulish Antoine eventually began to convey whole sections of bodies and then entire bodies from the graveyard to his hayloft garret, there to feast on his ghastly bounty in a more leisurely fashion, and was thus discovered "regaling" on his "horrible repast" (*TR* 2: 738). Taken prisoner, Antoine's full depredations are revealed. His years of ghoulish feeding, of eager burial-ground burrowings and gluttonous midnight feastings, are finally at an end. The hungry rifler of graveyards (a graveyard forager whose ravenous dining strips the softening evasions from Jerry Cruncher's much later graveyard foraging) will rifle and forage no more. Now, taken from his charnel-house loft and confined in prison, the ravenous Antoine can only dream of vanished graveyard feasts, dream longingly, hungrily, swooningly, of putrefying arms, legs, thighs, and choice intestines. The insatiable devourer of corpses—so the thirteen-year-old Dickens discovered as he avidly pored over his read and reread copy of the *Terrific Register*—was languishing at that very moment (one can imagine the intense attracting and repelling visions that this stunning information conjured up in Dickens' receptive mind), was languishing hungrily in his dour Paris prison, the grim and notorious Bicêtre, languishing in his wretched prison cell, deprived—deprived forever—of his "darling" human fare.

This horrifying *Terrific Register* account is adorned with a crude but riveting woodcut of a scene described in the text, a woodcut that shows the wildly ravenous Antoine in his hayloft den gnawing furiously on the severed arm of a young female, while sundry other pieces of her decaying body—legs, thighs, arm, and head—lie strewn about the floor (see figure 30).

The story of Sawney Beane, "the Monster of Scotland," also appeared in the *Terrific Register*, also accompanied by a gruesomely graphic woodcut, but a woodcut, ferocious as it was, that hardly did justice to the savage account it illustrated. That account describes how, in the reign of James VI of Scotland, the destitute Sawney Beane and his wife "resolved to live upon human flesh." They soon

THE DEAD DEVOURED BY THE LIVING!

Instances of extraordinary and depraved appetites may be found in the writings both of ancient and modern authors; and there are also many cases on record, in which it will be seen that this horrible disease has reached to a most astonishing height; but not one of them can parallel the following disgusting narrative. We have some recollection of reading an account of a brutal Englishman, whose depraved and unnatural appetite could only be appeased by human flesh; but even this case was not attended with such diabolical circumstances of depravity and horror as will be found on perusal of the following :—

The police of Paris a short time since apprehended and lodged in the Bicetre, a man named Antoine Langulet, who, they were given to understand, had been for a long time past in the habit of satisfying an unnatural appetite with food of the most repulsive and disgusting description. It appeared that animal substances in the highest state of putrefaction, and even the human body itself were regarded by this miserable wretch as very delicate morceaux. He usually staid within doors the whole of the day till sunset, when he would walk forth, and parade up and down the dirtiest lanes and alleys of Paris ; and noting where a piece of stinking carrion lay floating in the kennel, he would return at midnight, and, seizing it, convey it to his lodgings, and feast on it for the next day's meal. In this manner he kept up his wretched existence for years, until, by a refinement in his appetite, he at length found his way to the burial grounds ; and after many attempts, (with some rude instrument his ingenuity had formed for that purpose) he at length succeeded in pulling out of the graves several of the bodies recently interred. His appetite was so ravenous that he would feast upon them on the spot, and covering the remains with mould, would return for several successive evenings to finish the repast, as he states he was at first fearful of being seen carrying any thing from such a place as a cemetery. What is still more extraordinary he would feast himself upon

30. "The Dead Devoured By The Living!"

Antoine Langulet "regaling" on "the body of a young female which had been entombed a week before." "The Dead Devoured By The Living!" From the *Terrific Register* (1824–25).

acted upon their resolve, and they went about their work in an industrious, provident, sensible manner. "When they had murdered any man, woman, or child, they carried them to their den, quartered them, salted and pickled the members, and dried them for food." In the course of time Sawney Beane and his children and grandchildren (the latter "the offspring of incest") became so numerous and prosperous that they sometimes had a superabundance of their horrible fare. Then they would "throw legs and arms of dried human bodies into the sea by night." This ghastly debris would often be washed ashore "to the great consternation and dismay of all the surrounding inhabitants." The inhabitants, country people, were terrified. Friends, relatives, and neighbors were constantly disappearing. But who could imagine the monstrous nature of their peril? Who could imagine that they were the chosen prey of a hungry band of "merciless cannibals"? (*TR* 1: 161–62).

At last some clues turned up, and finally a search party, led by the king and accompanied by bloodhounds, set forth. After much searching, guided by the dogs, the king and his men, four hundred strong, came upon the "dark and dismal" cave, a hellish place of "utter darkness," an "infernal den," "the habitation of horrid cruelty," in which "these horrible cannibals" lived. Upon entering the cave the search party was "shocked to behold a sight unequalled in Scotland, if not in any part of the universe":

> Legs, arms, thighs, hands, and feet, of men, women, and children, were suspended in rows like dried beef. Some limbs and other members were soaked in pickle; while a great mass of money, both of gold and silver, watches, rings, pistols, cloths, both woolen and linen, with an inconceivable quantity of other articles, were either thrown together in heaps, or suspended on the sides of the cave. (*TR* 1: 163; see figure 31)

The "whole cruel brutal family" (after twenty-five years of marauding and reproducing, they now numbered forty-eight) was seized and marched to Edinburgh. As the wretched prisoners—men, women, and children—passed through the streets of the city, great crowds flocked to see the voracious monsters of Scotland.

treason. "The words, traitor and treason," said Blount, "belong to thee and the infamous Rutland, by whom the flower of English chivalry is this day destroyed. I summon you both before the face of Jesus Christ, for your great treason against our sovereign lord, the noble King Richard." The executioner then knelt down before him, and kissed him in a very humble manner, and soon after his head was cut off, and he was quartered.

THE MONSTER OF SCOTLAND.

SAWNEY BEANE was born in the county of East Lothian, about eight miles east of Edinburgh, in the reign of James VI. His father was a hedger and ditcher, and brought up his son to the same laborious employment. Naturally idle and vicious, he abandoned that place, along with a young woman equally idle and profligate, and they retired to the deserts of Galloway, and took up their habitation by the sea side. The place which Sawney and his wife selected for their dwelling, was a cave of about a mile in length, and of considerable breadth; so near the sea that the tide often penetrated into the cave above two hundred yards. The entry had many intricate windings and turnings which led to the extremity of the subterraneous dwelling, which was literally "the habitation of horrid cruelty."

Sawney and his wife took shelter in this cave, and commenced their depredations. To prevent the possibility of detection, they murdered every person that they robbed. Destitute also of the means of obtaining any other food, they resolved to live upon human flesh. Accordingly, when they had murdered any man, woman, or child, they carried them to their den, quartered them, salted and pickled the members, and dried them for food. In this manner they lived, carrying on their depredations and murder, until they had eight

VOL. I.   11

---

31. Sawney Beane and His Band of Cannibals Butchering Their Prey

"The Monster Of Scotland." From the *Terrific Register* (1824–25).

Sawney Beane and his entire cannibal family were executed—slaughtered is perhaps a better word—in a manner as barbarous as their own ghastly predations:

> The men had their privy-members thrown into the fire, their hands and legs were severed from their bodies, and they were permitted to bleed to death. The wretched mother of the whole crew, the daughters and grandchildren, after being spectators of the death of the men, were cast into three separate fires, and consumed to ashes. (*TR* 1: 163)

Dickens' writings, some produced ten years after the *Terrific Register* days, some twenty years, thirty years, or a lifetime later, show us in retrospect how he reacted at the time to this and similar accounts. Impressionable, retentive, imaginative, unusually sensitive to cannibalistic fantasies and aggressions, he transformed each gruesome detail from matter-of-fact narrative to palpable reality, a reality that haunted his consciousness and became a generative part of his shaping night side. Dickens himself tells us as much. He was simply stating the unadorned truth (but not the whole truth) when he wrote that the *Terrific Register* touched his vulnerabilities and evoked his most profound fears. Yet something is surely missing here. If the *Terrific Register* was so disturbing and terrifying—nightmarish and nothing more—why did he continue to buy the periodical week after week, and why did he choose, week in and week out, to gaze at the woodcuts and pore over the articles that made him "unspeakably miserable" and "frightened" his "very wits" out of his head? Why, in other words, this irresistible compulsion to indulge his revulsion? Moreover, what did that indulgence—especially that cannibalistic indulgence—signify? We shall return to these matters later.

The *Terrific Register,* and to a lesser degree the *Portfolio* (another weekly twopenny periodical with lurid woodcuts that Dickens read at this time), contained an endless stream of cannibalistic stories: stories about the modern "Anthropophagi, or Men-Eaters" who "subsisted on human flesh" (*TR* 1: 287); stories about the famished multitudes of India who often "devoured their own children!" (*TR* 1: 315); stories about "the men [of the shipwrecked *Medusa,* who], driven to desperation [by hunger], at length tore off the flesh from the dead bodies that covered the raft, and devoured it" (*P* 1: 371); stories about the ferocious Christian Crusaders who "broke open the tombs of the Musselmans; ripped up the bellies of the dead for gold, and then dressed and eat the fragments of flesh" (*TR* 1: 674); stories about Morat, who so hated his uncle Ramadan, cruel Bey of Tunis, that after his uncle had been strangled and burnt, he mixed his very ashes into his wine and literally drank his hated uncle (*TR* 1: 223); stories about the miser who locked himself into his treasure room by mistake and then "gnawed the flesh off both his arms and shoulders" in a futile effort to survive (this monitory account accompanied by a lurid woodcut) (*TR* 2: 369–370); and stories about the Parisian *perruquier* and barber who killed and robbed his customers and then gave their bodies to his next-door neighbor and accomplice, a *pâtissier* in the Rue de la Harpe famous for his "savory patties" (and grown rich by selling them)—the savory patties made, of course, from the bodies of the victims (*TR* 2: 310–12).[21] Dickens read these accounts, and many similar *Terrific Register* and *Portfolio* accounts—"Dreadful Account of Cannibalism," "Diabolical Cannibalism," "Barbarous Custom of Eating Human Flesh" (*TR* 2: 84–86; 297; 603–4)—with undiminished appetite.

"Dreadful Account of Cannibalism" (to examine this piece for the moment) is, for the most part, the gruesome, first-person, prison-house confession of Alexander Pierce, a confession dated 20th June 1824 in Van Dieman's Land (the evening before Pierce's execution), and thus fresh and newsworthy when the twelve-year-old Dickens read it in London some months later. The confession tells the very story that Dickens retold almost thirty years later in "The Long Voyage" (and then retold—or rather transformed—later still in the character of Magwitch and the opening of *Great Expectations*), but the confession tells that "dreadful" story with unemotional exactitude, a telling made all the more horrifying by the contrast between the savagery of the atrocities being depicted and the matter-of-factness of the style in which they are recounted. The effect on the adolescent Dickens was profound. The unadorned, la-

EXTRAORDINARY DEATH OF M. FOSCUE, A MISER.

AVARICE is a vice of all others the most detestable. The avaricious man knows no bounds to his ambition, no summit to his grasping wishes; his life is one continued line of misery and wretchedness—he is the slave of suspicion, always mistrustful, always discontented; he obtains but to desire more; his wishes succeed each other as billow succeeds billow, and lead him on from possession to expectation, until the grasp of death seizes him, and his hopes and his desires lay buried together in the sepulchre. It appears to us that a truly sordid mind is devoid of all religion—his only god is pelf—and is therefore not only an object of the most pitiable scorn, but also of disgust and detestation. The miser is unworthy of the land he lives in, he is unworthy to mix in the society of other men—he is unworthy to live, and unfit to die. A perusal of the lives of the most noted misers present us with such a picture of the debasement of the human mind, that we feel ourselves nauseated at the view; and we shall generally find that their last hours have been visited by the judgment of the Almighty, in some shape or other. The late noted Mr. Elves, who carried this strange passion almost to madness, died in a state of utter starvation, although he was possessed of thousands! The author of the beautiful romance of ' Kenilworth' has also noticed the horrible death of Antony Foster, the miser, and the following instance of the just judgment of God upon avarice, which occurred in late years, does not yield to any former circumstances of the kind, in point of frightful interest.

Monsieur Foscue, one of the farmers-general of the province of Languedoc, in France, who had amassed considerable wealth in grinding the faces of the poor within his province, by which he rendered himself universally hated, was one day ordered by the government to raise a considerable sum; upon

32. The Miser Who Cannibalized Himself

Dickens was fascinated by misers, had books on misers in his library, and included the lore and history of misers in his writings, most notably in *Our Mutual Friend*. Given his fascinations and sensibilities, we can be sure that this edifying *Terrific Register* conjunction of misers and cannibalism (with its culminating catastrophe made apocalyptic by a flamboyant woodcut) would have left its macabre imprint on the specially sensitized boy. Note, in this connection, the miser's gnawed wrist, forearm, biceps, and shoulder. "Extraordinary Death Of M. Foscue, A Miser." From the *Terrific Register* (1824–25).

conic narrative allowed him, indeed forced him, to re-create the scene for himself. In his usual way, he endowed it with an intensity and a reality more real (for him) than any lurid account could be. "I killed Cox with the axe," the convict relates in his flat, straightforward narrative. "I ate part of him that night, and cut the greatest part of his flesh up, in order to take on with me" (*TR* 2:86). Again with matter-of-fact detachment, Pierce says that he killed Cox on the bank of a river and then journeyed down the river and along the coast with his burden of human flesh. In "The Long Voyage," Dickens translates this brief scene, encountered in his boyhood and manhood reading in the most meager and compressed form ("I swam the river with the intention of keeping the coast round to Port Dalrymple" [*TR* 2:86]), into his own unforgettable image, an image filled with a lifetime's intensity and horror: "I shall never see that sea-beach . . . without him, solitary monster, eating [human flesh] as he prowls along, while the sea rages and rises at him."

Dickens' imagination invested with horror (or at times with humor and horror) the briefest factual cannibalistic accounts, whether such accounts are found in the dry parliamentary blue books of his manhood or in the cheap popular periodicals of his boyhood. The childhood and boyhood accounts, however, are the most crucial and the most influential. When, as a boy, he read the following didactic report in the *Terrific Register,* a report clothed in the protective mantle of "useful knowledge," one wonders what thrills of horror and what dawnings of the absurd revolted and delighted him:

> [There are] in South America, and in the interior of Africa . . . people who feed upon human flesh merely on account of its delicacy, and as the height of gourmandize. These nations not only eat the prisoners they take in war, but their own wives and children; they even buy and sell human flesh publicly. To them we are indebted for the information that white men are finer flavored than negroes, and that Englishmen are preferable to Frenchmen. Farther, the flesh of young girls and women, particularly of new-born children, far exceeds in delicacy that of the finest youths, or grown men. Finally, they tell us that the inside of the hand and the sole of the foot are the nicest parts of the human body. (*TR* 2: 603)[22]

Whether Dickens' vivid memories of the bizarre and sensational lore of cannibalism were products of his earliest conditioning, or whether his innate sensibilities made him preternaturally sensitive to all such accounts and associations, we can never know. Probably both factors were involved: his innate temperament made him thrill with horror at each faint suggestion of eating human flesh and caused him to dwell on and retain such suggestions, while his earliest experiences and then his special childhood exposure to such lore enlarged and shaped the very things it fed upon. In any case, the two influences complemented and magnified one another. But whatever the generative process, the end results are clear: by the time he was twelve or thirteen Dickens' complicated feelings about cannibalism—an emotional nexus of fears, fascinations, revulsions, and obsessions—had been definitively formed. Cannibalism had become for him a preeminent example of what he was later to call the "attraction of repulsion."[23]

V

Our chief concern at the moment, however, is how this particular attraction of repulsion entered Dickens' art. Another concern—it is a related but subsidiary theme—is why Dickens used the comic mode (or rather, why he used it so often) when writing about cannibalism. One can hardly miss the reiterated comic note. A memorable example appears in his very first novel: I refer to the Fat Boy of *Pickwick*.

We all recall that this great favorite of the public—witness the *Punch* cartoons, Royal Doulton figurines, Kyd portraits, Player cigarette cards, and the like—is fat and is always falling asleep. We also recall that when he is not sleeping he is eating—or at least thinking about eating. But we may forget that his eating proclivities are not confined to food. He makes no distinction between food and sex, and his sexual appetite is conveyed in alimentary terms: his way of making love is to ingest the loved object. By the same token, eating for him is an act of love. When he unpacks a picnic hamper Dickens tells us that he "leered horribly upon the food" (*PP*, 4:40). His ardor does not cool as the unpacking continues: "the fat boy was hanging fondly over a capon, which he seemed wholly unable to part with. The boy sighed deeply, and, bestowing an ardent gaze upon its plumpness, unwillingly consigned it to his master" (*PP*, 4:40). This is suggestive enough, but the cannibalistic passion of the Fat Boy is not limited to hanging fondly over capons and gazing ardently at their plumpness. He conflates eating animal flesh, or even thinking about eating animal flesh, with eating human flesh. When Sam Weller remarks approvingly to Emma (one of Mr. Wardle's servants) that Mr. Wardle is a "'reg'lar gen'l'm'n,'" the Fat Boy agrees: "'Oh, that he is!' said the fat boy, joining in the conversation; 'don't he breed nice pork!' and the fat youth gave a semi-cannibalistic leer at Mr. Weller, as he thought of roast legs and gravy" (*PP*, 28:294).

When the Fat Boy becomes enamored of Mary, and they go down to the "eating room" together, it is difficult to tell when he is complimenting her and when the food (*PP*, 53:579—54 in later editions). "'Oh, my eye, how prime!'" he says with "rapture," addressing Mary and swooning over the food (*PP*, 53:579). When they sit down together, the Fat Boy's rapture increases. Looking simultaneously at Mary and the food he says ravenously, "'I am *so* hungry,'" and the next instant he plunges his knife and fork "up to the very ferules" in a meat pie (*PP*, 53:579). Then, just as he is about to begin eating, he pauses, leans toward Mary with knife and fork in hand, and exclaims slowly, "'I say, how nice you do look!'" (*PP*, 53:579). Lest a careless reader mistake what has been going on throughout this scene, Dickens adds, "there was enough of the cannibal in the young gentleman's eyes to render the compliment a doubtful one" (*PP*, 53:579). We are delighted by Dickens' insightful humor; we concentrate on the comic hits. In our enjoyment we banish any *Terrific Register*-type vision of a compulsive demon lover gnawing hungrily on his loved one's bloody flesh.

The theme of cannibalism in *Pickwick* is not confined to the hungry passion of the Fat Boy. It emerges elsewhere in the novel in quite different contexts and with quite different characters. In the

following scene, for example, cannibalism emerges as a more gruesome and threatening business than in the Fat Boy scenes, yet the
occasion is still convivial and still rich with an irresistible, if macabre,
humor. The scene takes place at the groaning breakfast table at
Dingley Dell on Christmas Day. Mr. Wardle has just introduced Mr.
Pickwick to two young medical students, Mr. Benjamin Allen and
Mr. Bob Sawyer. The two gregarious surgeons-to-be are eating
with relish:

> "Nothing like dissecting, to give one an appetite," said Mr. Bob Saw-
> yer, looking round the table.
> Mr. Pickwick slightly shuddered.
> "By the bye, Bob," said Mr. Allen, "have you finished that leg yet?"
> "Nearly," replied Sawyer, helping himself to half a fowl as he spoke.
> "It's a very muscular one for a child's."
> "Is it?" inquired Mr. Allen, carelessly.
> "Very," said Bob Sawyer, with his mouth full.
> "I've put my name down for an arm, at our place," said Mr. Allen.
> "We're clubbing for a subject, and the list is nearly full, only we can't get
> hold of any fellow that wants a head. I wish you'd take it."
> "No," replied Bob Sawyer; "can't afford expensive luxuries."
> "Nonsense!" said Allen.
> "Can't indeed," rejoined Bob Sawyer. "I wouldn't mind a brain, but I
> couldn't stand a whole head."
> "Hush, hush, gentlemen, pray," said Mr. Pickwick, "I hear the ladies."
> (*PP*, 29:309)

We are amused, even delighted, by this nonchalant cannibalistic
gorging, but like Mr. Pickwick (and like Dickens) we also shudder.
The scene and its juxtapositions linger. We have met this commingling of dining and corpses and young children before in Dickens
and we shall meet this bizarre conjunction—in both humorous and
nightmare guise—often again.[24]

The pattern that emerges in *Pickwick,* Dickens' first novel, re-
emerges with darker overtones and with more submerged hints in
his second novel, the much more somber and autobiographical
(emotionally autobiographical) *Oliver Twist*. The most famous

33. Medical Men Dissecting

Dickens was not the first to dwell on the ghoulish proclivities of medical men. The medical men depicted here, like Benjamin Allen and Bob Sawyer in *The Pickwick Papers,* seem to dissect with an appetite. Note that the gentleman on the right (the one dissecting a leg) has his hand up to his nose and mouth, and note that the two intent gentlemen on the extreme left are concentrating on a dead woman's leg and pudendum with a relish that is not entirely scientific. (The dead woman and her alluring attributes—alluring for the engrossed gentlemen—are sketched very lightly and tentatively in pencil.) Compare with Hogarth's "The Reward of Cruelty" (figure 18), discussed and illustrated above; see also Part 1, note 40. *The Dissection.* An unfinished drawing (c. 1780) by Thomas Rowlandson. Huntington Library, San Marino, California.

scene in that often disturbing novel—the scene in which Oliver asks for more—is generated by a bizarre and laughable fear. Everyone is familiar with the scene itself, but how many remember the fear that generates the scene? That fear flows directly from a terrifying cannibalistic threat, but this threat—a threat made by one workhouse boy that he will devour another—is cauterized by its outlandishness and by its humor: we chuckle rather than shudder, and we dismiss the threat as a bit of humorous Dickensian grotesquerie; the threat, we feel, has no abiding importance. But Dickens does not dismiss the threat, nor does he discount it or forget it.

The threat is not a random phenomenon; it is generated by deliberate and methodical institutionalized starvation. The workhouse boys, barely surviving on their daily bowl of thin starvation gruel, have grown "voracious and wild with hunger"; they seem able to "devour the very bricks" that surround the workhouse copper. But these ravenous boys, who are constantly "sucking their fingers most assiduously" (they seem reduced to devouring their own members), have also become gaunt, weak, and submissive. One of Oliver's more robust fellow inmates, however, had been well fed prior to his workhouse incarceration. This boy, "who was tall for his age" and had "a wild, hungry eye," "hinted darkly to his companions, that unless he had another basin of gruel *per diem,* he was afraid he should some night eat the boy who slept next him, . . . a weakly youth of tender age" (*BM* 1: *OT,* [1]: 2:114).

This bizarre threat, comic to us but terrifying to his companions—they take it seriously—leads at once to a fearful council of the famished boys and to nine-year-old Oliver being delegated to ask for more. Oliver's fear-inspired cannibal-goaded temerity in asking for more, in turn, is the immediate cause of all his subsequent troubles. (Most significantly, almost twenty-five years later, Dickens repeated this humorous but also fearful and portentous genesis. He caused the chain of fateful actions that surrounds the seven-year-old orphaned Pip and that dominates what follows in *Great Expectations* to be generated by terrifying cannibalistic threats. See below in Part 1.) But though a cannibalistic threat is the immediate cause of Oli-

ver's appeal for more and his subsequent troubles, the original cause
(though Oliver does not consciously acknowledge this truth) lies
elsewhere. It lies with his sainted—so Oliver regards her—but sinning mother. "She was weak and erring"; she sinned and then she
died (*BM* 5: *OT,* 3: 15: 425—Chapter 53 in modern editions).[25] In
other words, though sainted in Oliver's wishful apotheosis of her,
his mother sinned and then abandoned him. She cast him forth, an
innocent, vulnerable child, into a cruel, uncaring cannibalistic
world. His years and years of suffering, then, all stem from her. (The
autobiographical components—and the cannibalistic dimensions—
in these opposed versions of motherly sainthood and motherly
abandonment, contending extremes of motherhood that appear frequently in Dickens, are treated at length below.)

Dickens continues to sound his cannibalistic theme in what follows. As a result of Oliver's effrontery in asking for more, the workhouse board, headed by Mr. Limbkins (note the name), apprentices
the greedy, ungrateful boy to a chimney sweep—a virtual guarantee
of injury or death—and this particular chimney sweep, moreover,
savors the fact that his apprentices' feet are often roasted in the
course of their duties. In honor of Oliver's sale to the brutal chimney sweep—a sale beneficial to parish and chimney sweep alike
(though not to Oliver)—that great bumbler of a beadle, the officious Mr. Bumble, brings Oliver a basin of gruel and the holiday
allowance of two ounces and a quarter of bread. At the unaccustomed sight of so much food, "Oliver began to cry very piteously,
thinking, not unnaturally, that the board must have determined to
kill him for some useful purpose, or they never would have begun
to fatten him up in this way" (*BM* 1: *OT,* [1]: 3:221).

But Oliver is saved from a roasted or a fatted (and then slaughtered) death and is apprenticed instead to an undertaker and coffin maker, a ghoulish predator with an even more ghoulish wife.
This ghoulish couple bear the appropriate name of Sowerberry, a
name that combines something unpleasant to eat (sour berry) with
its darker, less obvious homonyms: with sower, that is, planter or
burier, of corpses (sower bury). In fact, Mr. and Mrs. Sowerberry
are sowers and buriers of corpses. Mr. and Mrs. Sowerberry, in

short, feed upon corpses; they quite literally make their living from, take their very nourishment from, sowing the dead in the earth.

The more rapacious of these two ghouls is Mrs. Sowerberry (Mr. Sowerberry has long since been bullied into submissiveness by his harpy wife), and it is Mrs. Sowerberry, a harsh vindictive surrogate mother to Oliver—in this section a mother of unredeemed wickedness—who quite literally pushes Oliver into the nether world of the cellar, "a stone cell, damp and dark" that is also called the "kitchen" (*BM* 1: *OT,* [1]: 4:229). Like the helpless captive of a hungry ogre and ogress, Oliver now dwells in a prison-kitchen, fresh provender in a deadly larder. Mrs. Sowerberry tells Oliver he must sleep under the counter amidst the coffins, an area "tainted with the smell of coffins" and looking "like a grave" (*BM* 1: *OT,* [1]: 5:326). She calls him "little bag o' bones" (*BM* 1: *OT,* [1]: 4:229). Poor "bag o' bones" Oliver, the thrall of corpse-traffickers and a fierce ogress surrogate mother, is now lodged in hell, surrounded by death and coffins. The cannibalistic workhouse threat that had seemed so fanciful and amusing to the reader (but so terrifying to the workhouse boys) now lowers nightmarishly over all Oliver's dawning encounters with the voracious outer world: it lowers over the ogreish Mr. Limbkins, over the sadistic foot-roasting master chimney sweep, over the corpse-devouring Sowerberrys (especially over boy-devouring and boy-burying Mrs. Sowerberry), and it also lowers over poor "bag o' bones" Oliver himself in his charnel-house hell down amongst the coffins, dreaming of food and fearful of being fattened for the slaughter.

The crucial opening pages of *Oliver Twist* are thus filled (as are many subsequent pages) with scenes and images of cannibalistic ferocity, but ferocity leavened, at times virtually effaced, by reassuring humor. Of course, there is much more in *Oliver Twist* (or in *Pickwick,* or any Dickens novel, for that matter) than cannibalistic imagery and cannibalistic motifs, but such imagery and motifs combine with other crucial elements (sometimes other obsessive elements) to form a core of meaning in many of Dickens works; they also combine to shape his writings in countless additional ways.

If we turn from *The Pickwick Papers* and *Oliver Twist* to Dickens'

third novel, *Nicholas Nickleby,* we see the same pattern of portentous but equivocal cannibalistic horrors, horrors made palatable,
even engaging, by genial or disarming laughter. Take, for instance,
the following vignette. Mrs. Nickleby, nominally addressing her
daughter, Kate, is in the midst of one of her rambling free-
association monologues. (Mrs. Nickleby was based, in part, on
Dickens' own mother; see Part 1, note 32):

> "Roast pig—let me see. On the day five weeks after you were christened,
> we had a roast—no that couldn't have been a pig, either, because I recol
> lect there were a pair of them to carve, and your poor papa and I could
> never have thought of sitting down to two pigs—they must have been
> partridges. Roast pig! I hardly think we ever could have had one, now I
> come to remember, for your papa could never bear the sight of them in
> the shops, and used to say that they always put him in mind of very little
> babies, only the pigs had much fairer complexions." (*NN,* 41:399)

Obviously we have here a recrudescence of the childhood episode
in which Dickens, accompanied by his nursemaid, was taken to view
five very little dead babies laid out side by side like pigs' feet in a
butcher shop. We recall that then, too, it was their complexions that
triggered the association. In the early episode it is stillborn infants
laid out at a greengrocer's that produce the pork-in-a-butcher-shop
association; in the later fictional transformation it is suckling pigs
laid out in a butcher shop that produce the "very little babies" association. In both instances the occasion is connected with birth and
with eating (note, in addition to the references to newborn infants,
very little babies, and eating, the christening allusion in the *Nickleby*
passage, and note that the christened infant, Kate, who bears the
name of Dickens' wife, is the protagonist's sister); furthermore, in
both passages the result is identical: we are forced to regard the human body—in these cases the corpses of infants—as food, as something to be devoured and incorporated, though in both examples
this ghastly idea is screened by beguiling humor.

These macabre fantasies, in which the corpses of infants (or the
infants themselves) are regarded as food, are not unique. In a let-

ter to Angela Burdett Coutts written more than eight years after the *Nickleby* passage, Dickens offers another, more impromptu, commingling of corpses, butcher shops, infants, and eating. Upon receiving a Christmas turkey from Miss Coutts, Dickens wrote the following extraordinary response: "A thousand thanks for the noble turkey. I thought it was an infant, sent here by mistake, when it was brought in. It looked so like a fine baby" [24 December 1847]. This bizarre conjoining of infants with ogreish feasting is no mere freak of this particular Christmas occasion. In *A Christmas Carol*, written four years earlier, Dickens had twice associated the large Christmas turkey Scrooge had seen "hanging up" in the local poulterer's with children, in this case with young boys: Scrooge tells us that the big prize turkey carcass hanging in the butcher shop— Scrooge envisions the roasted carcass on the Cratchits' dining table—is "twice the size of Tiny Tim," and the boy hired to fetch the turkey, when asked by Scrooge if he knows which turkey Scrooge is referring to, says, " 'What, the one as big as me?' " (*CC*, 5:156). Nor were those similar conjoinings mentioned earlier freaks of their particular occasions—that is, they were not idiosyncratic or random responses to the *Nickleby* moment, or to the babies-cum-pigs in butcher-shop moments.

How profound and abiding this grotesque association of children, and especially of babies, with cannibalistic fantasies was for Dickens may be seen when one notices that the conjunction appears—to cite, for the time being, only one more example—in yet another outwardly amusing letter. This letter to John Pritt Harley, written more than a year after the *Nickleby* passage and more than seven years before the Coutts letter, had its origins, like the humorous *Nickleby* vignette, in a christening. Like an unconscious reflex or an unwitting obsession, the strange unerring association emerges once more out of the elemental depths: "A babby [Kate Macready Dickens—named after Dickens' wife] is to be christened and a fatted calf killed on these premises on Tuesday the 25th. Instant. It (the calf; not the babby) is to be taken off the spit at 6. *Can* you come" (17 August 1840). (See, in connection with babies and spits, figures 22 and 57.) Dickens' conflation of babies—and mothers, and wives—with cannibalistic feasting, whether that cannibalism is blatant or screened or effaced, seems to emerge willy-nilly; it seems to emerge, moreover, out of a hidden tangle, an untoward but profoundly meaningful tangle, of strangely compelling and strangely recurring associations. We shall meet those compelling associations again; we shall also meet their primordial and engendering sources. In the case of the *Nickleby* passage, the humor that informs the vignette is wonderfully functional. It helps to characterize Mrs. Nickleby, her world, and her values. On the other hand, the savage implications latent in the comic cannibalistic allusions are deeply submerged and disguised. Who would ever accuse Mrs. Nickleby— a real feeder on the largess of others—of cannibalistic proclivities? And who would ever think of an interloping infant as something to be devoured?

Another, more overt, less comic, series of cannibalistic images, a series that emerges ultimately from the same sources and moves inexorably toward the same destinations, occurs many years later in "Travelling Abroad," a piece Dickens wrote in 1860 for his magazine, *All the Year Round*. In that essay he recalls one of his many visits to the Paris Morgue, a fearful yet enticing place to which he always found himself "dragged by invisible force" (*AYR* 2: 558; later in *UT*).[26] On a prior occasion when he found himself dragged to the Morgue by invisible force, a visit described four years earlier in a *Household Words* essay entitled "Railway Dreaming," he had gazed musingly at the dead bodies, many of them fished, all bloated and disfigured, from the nearby Seine. The bodies, displayed as usual without sentiment or ceremony, laid out side by side on inclined slabs behind large plate-glass windows (see figure 39), had caused him to imagine a new scene from a childhood favorite of his, Holbein's *Dance of Death*. "As though," Dickens writes, "Holbein should represent Death, in his grim Dance, keeping a shop, and displaying his goods" (*HW* 13: 387).

The disquieting implications of this bizarre butcher-shop image are subtly accentuated and extended a few moments later when

Melior est Mors quam Vita. Eccle. 7.

34. Holbein's *Dance of Death:* "Death, in His Grim Dance"

"Death, in his grim Dance," was a macabre image that haunted Dickens' consciousness from childhood on. "The Old Woman." From *The Dance of Death . . . of . . . Holbein* (London: J. Coxhead, 1816). The Coxhead edition, or a very similar contemporary edition, was the one that Dickens pored over when he was ten or eleven.

Medice cura te ipsum.

35. Holbein's *Dance of Death:* Dickens' Death's Butcher Shop

Viewing bodies in the Morgue, Dickens imagines that Holbein's slaying skeleton (shown here in a physician's chambers) has become the keeper of a butcher shop "displaying his goods." "The Physician." From *The Dance of Death . . . of . . . Holbein* (London: J. Coxhead, 1816). See figure 39.

Dickens again connects the Morgue with shops and food, now with everyday shops and food (and with everyday feeding), and also with mothers and children. The Morgue, he tells us, is frequented by "Cheery married women, basket in hand, strolling in, on their way to or from the buying of the day's dinner," and by their appealing infant offspring: "children in arms with little pointing fingers" (*HW* 13: 387). We are disarmed at first by this engaging domestic scene, just as we were delighted at first by the imaginative presiding image—but only at first. We soon begin to feel the frightening undertow of the sinister suggestions that lurk beneath the smiling surface of Dickens' matter-of-fact and often amusing description. There is a dark humor in the presiding butcher-shop image, for example, but it does little to mitigate the stark reminder that all men are grass— or, in this version, meat. This macabre cannibalistic image of Death's butcher shop, a shop frequented by dinner-bound mothers and pointing infants-in-arms (contemplating what ghastly provender and anticipating what revolting feasts?), and its earlier counterparts—the childhood image of the five stillborn babies displayed like pig's feet in a butcher shop and the subsequent butcher-shop image of tiny fair-complexioned suckling pigs-cum-babies—lie behind what Dickens details in "Travelling Abroad" and a host of similar works.

For instance, in an essay written three years after "Travelling Abroad," "Some Recollections of Mortality" (1863), the old butcher-shop association, an association that conjoins corpses on display and loathsome cannibalistic feeding, rises up once more in Dickens' consciousness. It rises up unbidden; it rises up like an unquiet ghost, but like an unquiet ghost that no longer deigns to mask or mitigate its sinister implications. At the opening of "Some Recollections of Mortality," Dickens has just arrived in Paris on one of his frequent visits. He goes out for a stroll and soon finds himself— where else?—near Death's macabre butcher shop—that is, near what Dickens now calls the "obscene little Morgue" (*AYR* 9: 276; later in *UT*). The squat, unlovely building, already sentenced to be demolished, looks "mortally ashamed of itself, and supremely

36. The Morgue from the Street

The "obscene little Morgue . . . mortally ashamed of itself, and supremely wicked." Notre Dame is a few hundred yards away, straight ahead and just to the left. The Seine is immediately adjacent on the right. *La Morgue*. Engraving (c. 1848).

wicked" (*AYR* 9: 276). As Dickens, drawn to the Morgue by some deep, unfathomed inner necessity, stands halfway between the soaring towers of Notre Dame and the small grim lodestone mass of the grisly charnel house (a scabrous house that hugs the Seine and casts its dark shadow on the fast-flowing river), he sees a swirling, high-spirited crowd coming round the cathedral and crossing in front of it. At the center of this debonair crowd is a litter "with fluttering striped curtains" (*AYR* 9: 276). Dickens is entranced. He soon discovers, however, that the blithe procession is not a wedding or a christening or a similar celebration but "a Body coming to the Morgue" (*AYR* 9: 276).

Dickens joins the festive crowd as it mills and pushes toward the Morgue, but when the throng reaches the Morgue the body is taken in and the crowd is kept out—kept out, that is, until the body can be prepared and displayed. Dickens notices that as the body is being brought into the Morgue the custodians pull off their coats and tuck up their shirt-sleeves, preparations suggesting some unspeakable "business" that "excited" the crowd (and Dickens) in the "highest degree" (*AYR* 9: 277). "Shut out in the muddy street," Dickens continues, "we now became quite ravenous to know all about it" (*AYR* 9: 277). The "ravenous" crowd, wild with anticipation, presses and surges at the gates. "People made a start forward at a slight sound, and an unholy fire kindled in the public eye, and those next the gates beat at them impatiently, as if they were of the cannibal species and hungry" (*AYR* 9: 278).

Dickens, a part of the crowd, is also of the cannibal species and hungry. He, and they, can hardly contain their appetite; he, and they, are ravenous for the fresh new body that will soon rest, like a great succulent delicacy, on its butcher-shop slab. Some in the throng wipe their mouths on their sleeves; others bite at their coat collars "with an appetite" (*AYR* 9: 277). One pretty young mother, "pretending to bite the forefinger of her baby-boy, kept it between her rosy lips" (*AYR* 9: 277). When Dickens finally gazes at the near-naked body—the body, as it turns out, of a "poor spare white-haired old man, so quiet for evermore"—he is "sated at a glance"—or so

37. The Morgue from the River, with Notre Dame

Note the bodies, still unidentified after their three-day display in the Morgue, being brought to the pinnace that will carry them to burial (or to other disposition). *La Morgue*. Engraving (c. 1830).

he says (*AYR* 9: 278). Others are not sated at a glance. They look at the body with a "wolfish stare" (*AYR* 9: 278).

As Dickens re-created this Parisian episode and limned his picture of a ravenous corpse-hungry crowd, another experience, "also of the Morgue kind" (*AYR* 9: 279)—the word *Morgue* here emphasizes his association—an experience that he had undergone in London twenty-three years earlier, reemerged out of the past. On the earlier occasion he had sat as a juror in a coroner's inquest. The inquest, a local affair, concerned the death of a newborn male infant. The jury had to determine whether the death was a case of concealment (the child having been stillborn and then hidden) or of murder. The miserable mother stood nearby. Agonized and distraught, she uttered a "terrible low wail" throughout the proceedings (*AYR* 9: 280). The inquest took place in the Marylebone Workhouse, and in the course of the proceedings the jury went downstairs to view the body in the "crypt," a dim, subterranean chamber to which the infant's body had been brought. This desolate region, a nether world devoted to "warehousing" coffins, contained a "perfect Panorama of coffins of all sizes" (*AYR* 9: 279). The tiny corpse lay stretched out on a box—the young mother had put her newborn son into that selfsame box—but subsequently the body had been cut open for autopsy and then "neatly sewn up," so that now "it looked like a stuffed creature" (*AYR* 9: 279). The corpse—turned by Dickens' imagination into a stuffed *pièce de résistance*—"rested on a clean white cloth, with a surgical instrument or so at hand, and regarded from that point of view, it looked as if the cloth were 'laid,' and the Giant were coming to dinner" (*AYR* 9: 279). Dickens tells us that "there was nothing repellant about the poor piece of innocence, and it demanded a mere form of looking at" (*AYR* 9: 279). But Dickens' imagery of butchering, stuffing, cooking, and dining tells us that—for him, at least—that "looking" was no "mere form."

This episode of mothers, corpses, and dining concludes "Some Recollections of Mortality." The Morgue episode and the jury episode—so different and yet so similar—are the entire substance of this essay. Dickens recounts both experiences in rich detail, but he

38. The Morgue from the River, with a Watching Crowd

Note the drowned body being carried into the Morgue, and note the watching crowd. The low structure on the river itself is a laundry barge. *La Morgue*. Etching (1854) by Charles Meryon. Carnegie Museum of Art, Pittsburgh, Pennsylvania.

39. The Interior of the Morgue: "Death . . . Keeping a Shop, and Displaying His Goods"

Note the inclined slabs, the hanging clothes, the plate-glass windows, the water taps dripping above the near-naked bodies, and the casual visitors—all as Dickens described them. (See Part 1, notes 26 and 33.) *Vue Intérieure de la Morgue*. Engraving (c. 1845) after a painting by Carrie.

fails to tell us something crucial about the second experience "of the Morgue kind," that is, about the jury experience of twenty-three years earlier. (The description of this experience as a "Morgue" experience is a retrospective label given at the moment of writing in 1863. At the time of the inquest, 14 January 1840, Dickens had never laid eyes on the Morgue.)[27] What Dickens fails to tell us in "Some Recollections of Mortality" is that on the night of the inquest he had suffered a terrible attack, an attack which at the time he could not comprehend. The next day he wrote to Forster:

> Whether it was the poor baby, or its poor mother, or the coffin, or my fellow-jurymen, or what not, I can't say, but last night I had a most violent attack of sickness and indigestion which not only prevented me from sleeping, but even from lying down. Accordingly Kate and I sat up through the dreary watches. (F, 158)

Dickens' intense responses, his "violent . . . sickness and indigestion," and his inability even to lie down, tell us that fearful forces are at work. Viewing the infant corpse, butchered and stuffed and trussed on its cloth-laid table in that ghastly coffin-strewn dining room, Dickens sees and responds and partakes willy-nilly. "From that day to this," he tells us, "the poor little figure . . . has lain in the same place, and with the same surroundings, to my thinking" (*AYR* 9: 279). It is not a hungry Giant who is coming to dinner, but Dickens himself.

Dickens creates—he has no choice but to create—the vision that he perceives, a dark, insistent vision, a necessity-driven vision, the vision that haunts and torments him. He cannot banish the dread cannibalistic associations that well up unbidden from the primordial depths. He is always compelled and hungry—and always compelled and revolted—when gazing at the ghastly wares (to use his graphic Morgue images) of Death's gruesome butcher shop.[28]

Dickens gazed at those ghastly wares often. On an earlier occasion when he visited the Morgue, an occasion already alluded to, and described in "Travelling Abroad," Dickens saw displayed in Death's grim shop window "a large dark man whose disfigurement by water was in a frightful manner, comic, and whose expression was that of a prize-fighter who has closed his eyelids under a heavy blow, but was going immediately to open them, shake his head, and 'come up smiling'" (*AYR* 2: 558). The comic here does not diminish but accentuates the dread reality; on viewing the drowned body of the grimacing dark man, Dickens immediately becomes faint and leaves the Morgue. A similar faintness does not overcome the only other viewers then in the Morgue. They consist of a mother, "a very neat and pleasant little woman," and "her little girl" (*AYR* 2: 558). As the mother, "with the key of her lodging on her forefinger," shows the large dark disfigured body to her little child—here the mother is like the pointing Morgue-entranced children in "Railway Dreaming," or like the pretty young mother in "Some Recollections of Mortality" who, wild to get into the Morgue and view the freshly found corpse, bites the forefinger of her little baby and then keeps that pointing finger between her rosy lips, or like the pointing death-purveying summoner in Holbein's *Dance of Death*—as the pleasant Morgue-lingering mother with the key on her pointing finger shows the large, dark, disfigured body to her little child, "she and the child," munching as they look, devour "sweetmeats" (*AYR* 2: 558). It is at this point that Dickens, sickened, hurries out of the Morgue. The munching mother and munching child are leaving too, and the mother, seeing that Dickens looks "poorly," asks him, "with her wondering little eyebrows prettily raised, if there were anything the matter" (*AYR* 2: 559). Faintly replying in the negative, Dickens crosses the road to a wineshop and drinks some brandy.

Dickens does not say so here, but profound cannibalistic associations have festered and then combined to sicken him. This becomes clear a little later when he decides to enjoy a Seine bathing establishment.[29] He enters a nearby bathing palace, undresses, dons striped bathing drawers, joins the festive crowd, and soon immerses himself in the soothing waters of the Seine. The unspoken association of the Morgue as a butcher shop displaying Death's gruesome viands, a subliminal association that was suddenly given reality and horribly

40. A Mother and Her Children Visiting the Morgue: The Shock of Recognition

Here the Morgue and its "butcher-shop" display serve their intended pur-pose—to provide a means of identifying unidentified bodies. For most Parisians and most visitors, however, the attraction of the Morgue was darkly psychological rather than functional, an attraction that was, to use Dick-ens' phrase, the "attraction of repulsion"—in Dickens' case, an attraction and a repulsion of a most intense and dread sort. *A la Morgue*. Engraving (1868) after a drawing by G. Séguin showing the new Morgue (see Part 1, note 26).

intensified when the engrossed mother and child daintily munched and swallowed, munched and swallowed, as they gazed at the bloated body—that revolting but still unacknowledged and unspoken association now begins to exert a more overt force. In the midst of his delightful bathing, Dickens is seized by the irrational idea that the large dark body of the drowned man from the Morgue is floating straight at him. In his panic-stricken haste to leave the river, he involuntarily ingests some of its water. He is instantly sick. "I fancied," he tells us, "that the contamination of the creature was in it" (*AYR* 2: 559). Dickens, in other words, has now eaten of the dead man's body in deed as well as in subliminal seeming. The unacknowledged night-side fear that had sickened him an hour earlier has suddenly metamorphosed into hideous nightmare fulfillment. He is ill; he is in a panic. "Dressing instantly," he rushes out of the bathing establishment, too nauseated and too horrified to pause or think (*AYR* 2: 559). He manages to get back to his cool, dark apartment and to lie down upon the sofa. Only then, secluded and protected, can he begin to reason with himself.[30]

But the taste of the dead man, now in his mouth as well as in his imagination, is not so easily exorcised. That evening at dinner, "some morsel on my plate," as Dickens puts it, "looked like a piece of him"; Dickens gets up and leaves (*AYR* 2: 559). Later that evening he attends a boxing match, watches as one of the boxers is struck between the eyes, immediately sees the drowned man's frightful grimace, and is "finished"—Dickens' vague euphemism—for the night (*AYR* 2: 559). The haunting continues for days. He begins to associate smells as well as sights and tastes with the dark man's dead body. The dead man seems ubiquitous. Dickens confronts him in hotels, shops, theaters, and streets, and each new association, fraught with cannibalistic implications, sickens him. "O," Dickens writes, "what this large dark man cost me in that bright city!" (*AYR* 2: 558). But despite this emotional cost, Dickens perseveres. Gradually, after a week or so, the episodes of sickening "possession" grow less frequent, and then finally stop (*AYR* 2: 559).

The possession stops, but its imprint does not disappear from

41. A Seine Bathing Establishment: Dickens, Bathing Blithely, Sups on a Dead Man

"The bath was crowded in the usual airy manner, by a male population in striped drawers of various gay colours, who walked up and down arm in arm, drank coffee, smoked cigars, sat at little tables, conversed politely with the damsels who dispensed the towels, and every now and then pitched themselves into the river head foremost . . . I . . . was in the full enjoyment of a delightful bath, when all in a moment . . . the large dark body was floating straight at me. . . . In the shock I had taken some water into my mouth, and it turned me sick, for I fancied that the contamination of the creature was in it." *Vue intérieure des bains Deligny.* Wood engraving (c. 1845) after a drawing by Grandville.

Dickens' imagination. It gestates in his consciousness, emerging from time to time in new configurations and new permutations. When it does emerge, it is transformed; yet it is also always the same. We see this fixity in the midst of change over and over again in Dickens. We see it, for example, with the dark bloated body (forever cannibal-fraught for Dickens) fished from the flowing Seine. We notice it again with Dickens' Seine bathing and Seine swallowing—bathing and swallowing that remain eternally alive in Dickens' transforming consciousness, and that become, in time, generative forces, forces fueled somehow by his revolting complicity (an involuntary, secret, seemingly unaccountable complicity) in loathsome cannibalistic foragings. These Seine scenes and their implications recur, to cite just one instance, in *Our Mutual Friend,* not as far-off echoes or as faded shadows of what once had been—the scenes and their implications are both more direct and more transformed than echoes or shadows—but as shaping imaginative conceptions at the heart of the novel (see below in Part 1).

Long before the reemergence of the Seine episodes and their hidden antecedents in *Our Mutual Friend,* however, Dickens pondered the significance of such powerful unreasoning recurrences. In "Travelling Abroad," he puzzled over the mystery of his cannibal-fraught haunting by the dark water-logged body from the Morgue. Why had that body, fished from the Seine all bloated and grimacing, unmanned and sickened him? Why had it pursued and haunted him in crowds and solitudes, in rivers, gardens, and streets, in hotels, shops, theaters, clubs, and restaurants? Commenting on this "possession" and on similar possessions—"possession" is Dickens' word for these unreasoning hallucinative obsessions—he relates them to childhood, and to the "intensity and accuracy of an intelligent child's observation" during this, the most formative period in his emerging life (*AYR* 2: 559).

(In *David Copperfield,* in an analogous comment about formative impressions—most of David's earliest impressions are versions of irrational fears—Dickens again relates such shaping sensations to childhood and to a child's special acuity and impressibility. "I

believe" writes David, speaking of his receptivity to the innocuous—
or seemingly innocuous—but often fear-filled childhood experiences that shaped and burdened him, "I believe the power of
observation in numbers of very young children to be quite wonderful for its closeness and accuracy" [*DC,* 2:10]. And then he adds:
"If it should appear from anything I may set down in this narrative
that I was a child of close observation, or that as a man I have a
strong memory of my childhood, I undoubtedly lay claim to both
of these characteristics" [*DC,* 2:10].)

If a child is traumatically conditioned at "that impressible time of
life," continues Dickens in "Travelling Abroad," nothing that a parent or a mentor might try to do at that juncture can eradicate the
dread impression (*AYR* 2: 559). If a parent (or nurse or teacher)
tries to force a child to confront or abjure such unreasoning fear—
Dickens insists that such childhood fear is unreasoning—"you had
better murder it" (*AYR* 2: 559). Dickens would soon make a similar
observation in "Nurse's Stories," except there he not only warns the
rearers of children of the dangers they run of enlarging and intensifying such traumas but accuses them—many nursemaids, at any
rate—of causing the traumas. In "Nurse's Stories" he speaks of the
"dark corners" of the mind—corners of fear and loathing—that
"we are forced to go back to, against our wills," forced to go back
to all life long, owing to the maleficent influence of nursemaids
(*AYR* 3: 518). Dickens, presumably, was basing such observations
on his own experiences. In "Nurse's Stories," an essay replete with
wild cannibalistic terrors—one recalls that those two ferocious
nightmares, "Captain Murderer" and "Chips and the Devil," appeared in "Nurse's Stories"—we need not simply presume such
connections. In that essay Dickens makes the connections with his
own childhood explicit. In "Travelling Abroad," he was also, one
assumes, giving an account of some of his own unreasoning
childhood-generated fears (again cannibalistic fears), and he was
again relating them to childhood trauma—why else the conflation
of the Seine corpse, cannibalism, and childhood, and why else the
suddenly intruded disquisition on ineradicable childhood terrors?—

though he does not directly say that he is speaking about his own childhood conditioning in that piece. But though he does not directly say so, the subject, the imagery, the associations, the analogies, the interjections, the repetitions, and the usages, speak for him.

The six accounts just surveyed are not unique, nor are such accounts, as the last two in particular might suggest, special fantasies that have their genesis in the Morgue or in dead bodies, although in the next vignette, dead bodies, though nowhere in sight at first, like Banquo's ghost or King Charles' head, soon intrude upon the scene, and then, transformed willy-nilly by Dickens' shaping imagination, become dread caches of cannibalistic fodder. The vignette in question occurs in "Night Walks," another piece written in 1860, but written more than three months after "Travelling Abroad" (and almost three years before "Some Recollections of Mortality"). In this somber essay, Dickens tells us of an even more revealing encounter, again a chance encounter, but one that occurred not in Paris during the day but in London at night. The episode, in fact, took place in the course of two of his insomnia-provoked all-night London wanderings, and it happened in this unexpected manner. After wandering the cold, desolate streets of London for most of the night, Dickens felt the need for human companionship (and for warmth), and he took shelter before dawn in a coffee shop near Bow Street, Covent Garden. There he sat for a while eating hot toast and drinking hot coffee, and there he watched the little world about him: the still half-asleep cook-waiter of the establishment and an occasional customer from nearby Covent Garden Market, then just opening. As he watched, a strange, cadaverous, horse-faced man, clad only in coat, hat, and shoes, came into the small refuge. This strangely clad man, his ways and needs apparently familiar to the cook, was not only eerie in appearance but in the mode (or what Dickens presumes to be the mode) of his life. "I should say," Dickens surmises, that he was "just out of bed, and presently going back to bed" (*AYR* 3: 351; later in *UT*). Dickens finds other peculiarities noteworthy. Despite the "cadaverousness" of this creature, or rather, despite the cadaverousness of his figure, the man is not (as

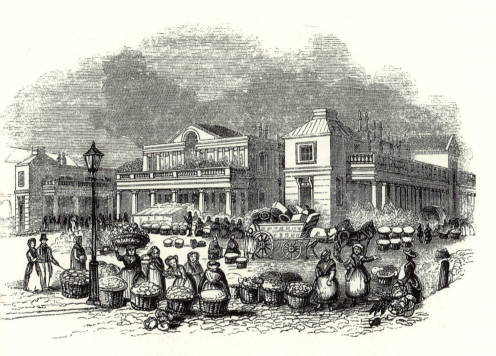

42. Covent Garden Market: The Precincts of the Red-Faced Man

Covent Garden. Engraving (c. 1830) after a drawing by Thomas H. Shepherd.

his clothing and bearing seem to betoken) pale and ashen visaged (*AYR* 3: 351). On the contrary, this "mysterious" and "spectral" creature had, Dickens writes, dwelling on the startling and incongruous feature, "an excessively red face" (*AYR* 3: 351).

Dickens took shelter in the coffee shop twice, and both times he watched as the cadaverous red-faced man came into the shop and went through his nightly ritual of eating a huge meat pudding that he himself had brought—under his hat, no less—to the establishment. The "large cold meat pudding," as Dickens makes clear, is a surrogate for the corpse of the man's dead mother—there are even hints that the pudding is made from his mother's body—and each night the cadaverous man, who is "known by his pudding," murders and consumes his mother in the guise of the totemic pudding. Here is Dickens' description of the excessively red-faced man, his strange meat pudding, and his even stranger actions: "Left to himself in his box, he stood the pudding on the bare table, and, instead of cutting it, stabbed it, over-hand, with the knife, like a mortal enemy; then took the knife out, wiped it on his sleeve, tore the pudding asunder with his fingers, and ate it all up" (*AYR* 3: 351). In describing his second witnessing of this murderous and ravenous performance, Dickens calls the man's knife a "dagger," and he concludes the episode with these words:

> On the second occasion of my seeing him, [the red-faced man] said, huskily, to the man of sleep [that is, to the cook], "Am I red to-night?" "You are," [the cook] uncompromisingly answered. "My mother," said the spectre, "was a red-faced woman that liked drink, and I looked at her hard when she laid in her coffin, and I took the complexion." Somehow, the pudding seemed an unwholesome pudding after that, and I put myself in its way no more. (*AYR* 3: 351)

These recurrent episodes, so ranging in time, scattered in setting, and varied in occasion, yet all so full of death and fantasies of ghoulish dining, show that beneath the selfsame cannibalistic images that had appeared so benign and laughable in *Pickwick* and *Nickleby* lay powerful forces of the utmost potency and dread.

43. A Working-Class Victorian Coffee Shop

The red-faced man, alone in his coffee-shop booth, "stood the [meat] pudding on the bare table, and, instead of cutting it, stabbed it, over-hand, with the knife, like a mortal enemy." "Coffee Shop—Petticoat Lane." Wood engraving after a drawing by Gustave Doré. From Doré and Jerrold, *London: A Pilgrimage* (1872).

VI

Some of those dread forces, as seven of these cannibalistic vignettes seem to suggest (eight, if we count the two episodes of "Some Recollections of Mortality" separately), are rooted in Dickens' earliest feelings toward his mother.[31] The first and third vignettes focus on babies and birth and the eating of infants; the second, on cannibal-haunted engenderings and culpable mothers. In the first, the vignette from "Dullborough Town," in which five babies are laid out like pig's feet in a butcher shop while the assembled guests view the wares and eat, the protagonists are Dickens' nursemaid and a mother; in the second, the opening episodes from *Oliver Twist*, the chief originators of Oliver's cannibal-fraught sufferings are two mothers: a sainted but sinning mother who abandons him, and a harsh, vindictive surrogate mother who pushes him into a dark, encoffining hell; in the third, the vignette from *Nicholas Nickleby* in which a dinner of roast pig is associated with small pigs in butcher shops, pigs that look like "very little babies," the protagonists are a father and a mother, with the mother, Mrs. Nickleby, being an avowed portrait of certain traits in Dickens' own mother.[32] The fourth vignette, from "Railway Dreaming," again mentions mothers (many with children in arms), cheery mothers who buy food for dinner and on their way pause to regale themselves and their children with savoring dead bodies in Death's butcher shop.

Two similar scenes emerge from "Some Recollections of Mortality," the source of the double-imaged fifth vignette. There a mother eats her "baby-boy" as she "ravenously" waits for a fresh male corpse to be displayed in Death's grim butcher shop; and there also, but a world away, another mother, under suspicion of murder, looks upon her dead infant son who is stuffed and trussed on a clean white tablecloth, ready to be eaten. In the sixth vignette, again in Death's butcher shop, but this time taken from "Travelling Abroad," a mother and her little girl feast on "sweetmeats" as they gaze at the large, dark body of a grotesquely disfigured man. The last of these vignettes (I should add that these vignettes are representative rather than exhaustive),[33] taken from "Night Walks," is nightmarish and profoundly chilling. This fearsome vignette is of a son who over and over again murders and devours his mother, stabbing her with his "dagger," tearing her "asunder with his fingers," and eating her "all up." Keeping these seven (eight) vignettes in mind, let us turn to two much better-known scenes in Dickens' writings, scenes which seem at first to have no overt cannibalistic elements, but which are, nevertheless, central to our purposes.

The two scenes occur in *David Copperfield,* a novel that is often minutely autobiographical and wildly wish-fulfilling, and both scenes tell us much about David's—and Dickens'—most hidden yearnings and resentments. When the banished and disgraced David arrives home from school for the holidays, he hears his mother singing a song similar to one she had sung to him when she nursed him as an infant, and he moves timidly to the parlor door through which the singing issues and opens it softly, unannounced. His mother is suckling his unheralded and unexpected supplanter, the usurping son of the usurping Murdstone (see figure 44). When David speaks, his mother starts, then, seeing him, calls him her dear Davy, her own boy, comes across the room to meet him, kneels down upon the floor, kisses him, and lays his head down on her bosom next to the baby nestling there. Of this moment—pressed against his mother's bare breast—David writes: "I wish I had died. I wish I had died then, with that feeling in my heart! I should have been more fit for Heaven than I ever have been since" (*DC,* 8:80). But this moment of felicity, union, and restored grace is only a moment. Murdstone and reality intervene, and in any case, David soon returns to school. The next time he sees his mother she is in her coffin, his dead brother once more nestled on her breast. David concludes this second homecoming with this extraordinary passage:

> From the moment of my knowing of the death of my mother, the idea of her as she had been of late had vanished from me. I remembered her, from that instant, only as the young mother of my earliest impressions . . . In her death she winged her way back to her calm untroubled youth, and cancelled all the rest.

44. David Makes a Discovery: An Interloper at His Mother's Breast

Note the subtext conveyed by some of the ancillary elements in this illustration. The small wall-picture on the left depicts the Prodigal Son's return, while that on the right depicts the infant Moses found amidst the bulrushes. These pictures are separated by the much larger portrait of the bountifully breasted young female in the center, her eyes turned not toward the Prodigal Son but toward the newly discovered infant. This subtext confirms the main text: in the Eden-like realms of undivided motherly attention and motherly affection, it is the newborn infant, not the interloper David, who dwells in the heaven of primary—in effect, exclusive—maternal love. "Changes at Home." Etching by Hablot Knight Browne ("Phiz") for Number III, Chapter VIII (July 1849) of *David Copperfield*.

The mother who lay in the grave, was the mother of my infancy; the little creature in her arms, was myself, as I had once been, hushed for ever on her bosom. (*DC,* 9:96)

The central burden of these deep and exquisite scenes is clear. David has been cast out from his mother's breast, partly as a normal process of maturation, partly owing to the foolishness and weakness of his mother, partly at the behest of the cold and murderous Murdstone. David yearns to return to his mother's breast; that is, he yearns to return to the idyllic days before the fall, before his mother abandoned him, before the advent of Murdstone, his infant brother, and the intrusive outside world. When he comes home from school, he does momentarily return, and not simply figuratively, to his mother's breast. In that instant of union and love he feels purged of all sin, corruption, and guilt (read: hidden anger, resentment, and self-accusation), and he wishes he could preserve that blessed moment by fixing it forever in the eternity of death. When he goes on living and his mother dies, dies and goes to the grave clasping her second son in an eternal and unchanging embrace, David, banishing his long-smoldering resentment and repressing any new-fledged feelings of guilt, in his mind becomes that second son. He now rests forever on his mother's breast in prelapsarian bliss. As David remarks, he "cancelled all the rest."

It is worth recalling at this point that seven of the eight cannibalistic vignettes discussed earlier, vignettes which focused on human beings as meat in butcher shops or as provender in ogresses' larders, concerned mothers and newborn infants or mothers and very young children, just as this scene from *Copperfield* concerns a mother and a newborn infant. But the vignette infants (with the exception of Oliver—like David, another "hero") will not metamorphose into purged and guiltless protagonists and then be apotheosized, they will be devoured as food or, more rarely, as with one little girl, will join their mothers in cannibalistic feasting. The eighth vignette, the least disguised in its anger and in its incorporative vengeance, concerns murdering and devouring the mother herself—the "mortal enemy," as the vignette has it. Newborn infants and mothers in Dickens are frequently in special danger, it seems. David's newborn brother and his mother are more fortunate. They are spared the butcher-shop or the meat-pudding fate. They are not destined to be eaten, they are simply consigned to death. Obviously Dickens did not cancel all the rest.

David cannot cancel all the rest either. He cannot cancel the pain and suffering that his mother unwittingly brought into his life, nor can he cancel his unacknowledged anger and resentment. He must recognize and confront what he does not recognize and confront here: that in many ways his mother was a bad mother, that she brought much misery into his life, and that he has been shaped in part by her weaknesses and blindness. One of the central themes of *David Copperfield*, as the working notes and the novel itself make clear, concerns bad mothers and the havoc they wreak. In his working notes Dickens wrote, "Shew the faults of mothers, and their consequences" (Stone, *Working Notes*, 170–71).

Another theme, as Betsey Trotwood constantly reminds us, centers on David's blindness. David pays dearly for both his bad mother and his blindness. Dora, his weak, immature wife, is another version of his weak, immature mother. David does not see this. He seeks through Dora to recapture a lost world of rosy ideality, but he only succeeds in reenacting the bitter lessons of a misconstrued reality. David's early passion for Dora is as romanticized and unsustainable as his prelapsarian bliss at his mother's breast, and his later marriage to Dora is as unsatisfactory and unfulfilling (so remote is it from his ideal dream of felicity) as his postlapsarian desolation when banished from his mother's bosom. To use a phrase that recurs throughout the novel, David has not yet learned to discipline his "undisciplined heart." It is not till the end of the book, long after weak mother and childish wife have been punished by death, that David begins to see and act upon what he has been blind to all his life.

But what does all this have to do with cannibalism? Most assuredly, a great deal. The image of a child suckling at its mother's

breast could hardly be more primal and benign—or more unexpectedly cannibalistic. The latter implication, of aggressive cannibalistic
feeding, lurks subversively in the benign image itself. An infant
suckling at its mother's breast is a preeminent emblem of closeness,
nurturing, and love. But an infant suckling at its mother's breast is
also, quite literally, consuming its mother, incorporating her into
itself. The resentment Dickens felt and expressed toward his mother
is amply documented. That resentment (and the anger and guilt
which accompanied it) undoubtedly had its roots in, indeed built
upon, his earliest feelings, whether justified or not, of being rejected
and neglected by her, a primordial rejection that was reinforced by
her subsequent treatment of him.

The "labouring hind," the "small Cain" (F, 23–24, 27), as Dickens later called his fallen childhood self, had many opportunities
from the time he was a year or so old to see his mother suckling his
supplanters, lavishing upon them the love and attention that she
had unaccountably withdrawn (or so he felt) from him. This early
turning away of the central figure in his dawning existence was his
first, and perhaps his most inconsolable, experience of rejection and
neglect, the prototype of all his later perceptions of betrayal and
abandonment. It is notable that the anger he later expressed over
his blacking-warehouse servitude, a servitude occasioned largely by
his father, is directed primarily toward his mother. Listen to the
chilling words, written almost twenty-five years after the event, that
climax his indictment. These long-pondered words, seething with
undiminished fury, ignore his father's central guilt and dwell instead
upon his mother's lesser sin: "I never afterwards forgot, I never shall
forget, I never can forget, that my mother was warm for my being
sent back [to the blacking warehouse]" (F, 35).

In *Copperfield* the voiced anger of son toward mother is almost
totally suppressed in David himself, though it comes out, of course,
in parallel or contrasting relationships: in Steerforth's treatment of
his indulgent and possessive mother, in the depiction of several
other bad or absent mothers, and in many other ways, some of
which have already been suggested. In "Night Walks," the anger of

son toward mother—note that this mother drank too much, in other words, that she too was a bad mother—is acted out in a nightly ritual of murder and consumption. It is no coincidence that both scenes center on consumption—namely, on the equivocal act of incorporating the mother into the self: the *Copperfield* scene, on consuming a good mother (that is, the prelapsarian mother) in love by nursing at her breast; the "Night Walks" scene, on consuming a bad mother (that is, the postlapsarian mother) in hate by murdering and eating her. Nor is it a coincidence that in both scenes the crucial understanding flows from the guilty son (guilty of what unknown transgression, of what unpardonable sin?) acknowledging the dead mother and affirming his consanguinity with her while she is lying in her coffin.

What I am suggesting is that some of Dickens' obsession with cannibalism—some of its attraction and repulsion for him (some of his conflicted and complicitous engagement in its revolting horrors)—can be traced back to his dawning love for his mother and his guilty anger toward her: to his being cherished and nurtured by her, taken to her breast, and then (as he saw it) being betrayed and rejected by her, banished from her breast. Yet his profoundly disturbing and deeply ambivalent feelings toward his mother, later imaged in their most elemental form as suckling a mother in love or devouring her in hate, were only the foundation for what came thereafter. A multitude of other influences from within and without—storytelling, reading, visiting, poring over illustrations, gazing through shop windows, singing comic songs, fantasizing, and the like—enlarged and elaborated this foundation, enlarged and elaborated, in other words, the original, emotion-charged, mother-engendered origins. The boyhood phases of this development—all part of a dynamic, deepening, accreting process, all part of what cannibalism eventually came to mean to Dickens—continued to evolve. The later boyhood years—the years of penny periodicals, Wellington House toy-theater productions, sensational Resurrectionist revelations, and the like—entangled additional emotions and associations, usually allied emotions and associations, and made them, too, a part of this growing foundation. This steadily developing foundation, in turn, further reinforced by related events and kindred increments in his youth and early manhood (yet always shaped by the rage and guilt of his early years), this long-forming and long-evolving foundation—so mazelike and involuted and interconnected—at last, in manhood, found astonishing expression in the unlikely motif of cannibalism as it finally emerged, diverse and transformed (yet also uncannily constant), in his writings.

VII

That night-side motif, so fraught with dangerous emotion for Dickens, both conscious emotion and unconscious emotion, appears over and over again in his work, but it appears there (especially in the middle and later writings) wonderfully transfigured. The motif becomes, in time, a primary imaginative resource that helps Dickens convey whispering nuances and profound themes. It also becomes (but now for us) a window into his mind and craft. Through the perspective of cannibalism, sensitive to its shaping presence—a presence at once so powerful, protean, and disturbing—we can often better understand, at times we can newly discover, what Dickens was seeking to say in his ever-surprising and richly reverberant art.

Take, for example—to continue, for the moment, with *David Copperfield*—that unforgettable scene, at once delightful and terrifying, in which poor David, fleeing from Murdstone sadism, goes from one brutal fleecing to another as he makes his way on his first solo pilgrimage through the great, fearsome outer world. At last, faint, hungry, footsore, and virtually penniless, he limps into Chatham (significantly, Dickens' own boyhood home) and approaches a used-clothing dealer with the thought of selling his jacket for some food. The dealer—another frightening incarnation of the savage adult world—is both a ferocious cannibal, ready to eat David alive, and a daft old man, ludicrous in his eccentricity. Dickens achieves this double vision in the most artful way: the crazy old man, his eyes starting out of his head, talks incoherently of lungs and livers and eyes and limbs and hearts on fire, and he keeps crying out the strange refrain, "Oh, goroo, goroo! Oh, goroo!" (*DC*, 13:132–33).

The "Oh, goroo" man intrigues and delights us with his wild, fairy-tale strangeness; but he also disturbs us. We recall that he thrust "his trembling hands, which were like the claws of a great bird," into David's hair (*DC*, 13:132). We note that he lived in a "dirty den" behind his shop; we also note that he rushed at David "mouthing as if he were going to tear [him] in pieces" (*DC*, 13:132, 133). We realize that his strange chant has to do with organs and appendages of the body: with lungs and livers and eyes and limbs and hearts on fire. And then we understand. The "Oh, goroo" man is a ravening ogre; his chant is simply a version of the word *ogre* itself—"Oh, goroo, oh, goroo" is his telltale and appropriate cry. The lungs and livers and hearts he constantly invokes are nothing more nor less than the things upon which he feeds.

The scene is conveyed from within and without. On the one hand, we see with David's fearful eyes. The child David apprehends his peril in the most terrifying terms he can imagine. He is in the nightmare world of folklore and fairy tales, the world of his childhood storybooks and childhood fears, a world where young children are eaten by monstrous ogres who chant their terrible intentions ("Fee, fie, fo, fum"). On the other hand, we see with adult eyes and assess the everyday reality. The responsive child in us feels the fullness of the terror; the experienced adult in us discounts that magnified response and substitutes a more rational interpretation. Dickens reveals and conceals. We are meant to smile but we are also meant to understand—fully understand, with a child's unreasoning terror—the soul-destroying vulnerability of an innocent child cast out on an uncaring world.

David's terror and vulnerability (a special terror and vulnerability) had many sources and many components. Long before he was cast out on that uncaring world, a world teeming with fierce ogres and ravening predators, he—like Dickens—had come to savor unspeakable horrors, to think and visualize and imagine in wild cannibalistic tropes. We have already traced some of Dickens' strange appetites

Flaying *them alive*.

Cutting out the Tongues of CHRISTIANS.

Roasting a Christian, *pouring* Vinegar *and* Salt *on* his Members.

Published as the Act directs, for H. Trapp Pater-noster Row.

J. Smith sculp.

45. Fox's *Book of Martyrs:* Flaying, Cutting, and Roasting Christians

Dickens' first acquaintance with Fox's *Martyrs* was probably, like David Copperfield's childhood introduction to the work, through a "precious" late-eighteenth-century "large quarto edition" such as this. Engraving for Fox, *The Book of Martyrs* (London: H. Trapp, 1776).

115

and strange proclivities. As a child, he was drawn irresistibly by the "attraction of repulsion"; he dwelt upon savage accounts and gruesome pictures, making them a fearful part of his secret soul. We can be sure that David's childhood fascination with Fox's *Book of Martyrs,* set forth in a notable passage in *David Copperfield,* is based upon Dickens' own childhood fascination. Dickens' allusions in *Copperfield* are not unique. In his writings, he scatters many references to Fox's *Book of Martyrs,* especially to the horrific illustrations in the book, references that usually bespeak childhood fears and fantasies. The passage just alluded to in *David Copperfield* concerning Fox's *Martyrs* is a good example of Dickens' typical stance. David tells us that his favorite object in Peggotty's new home concealed a "precious" treasure:

> Of all the moveables in [Peggotty's little house], I must have been most impressed by a certain old bureau of some dark wood . . . with a retreating top which opened, let down, and became a desk, within which, was a large quarto edition of Fox's Book of Martyrs. This precious volume, of which I do not recollect one word, I immediately discovered and immediately applied myself to; and I never visited the house afterwards, but I kneeled on a chair, opened the casket where this gem was enshrined, spread my arms over the desk, and fell to devouring the book afresh. I was chiefly edified, I am afraid, by the pictures, which were numerous, and represented all kinds of dismal horrors; but Martyrs and Peggotty's house have been inseparable in my mind ever since, and are now. (*DC,* 10:107)

Think of the strange conjunctions in David's childhood reminiscence. Even Peggotty, David's good mother, is associated, it seems, with barbarous horrors and cannibalistic fantasies. There can be no doubt about that association and its cannibalistic implications. The "dismal horrors" that David pores over—the horrors that are inseparable from Peggotty and her home—are of men and women being flayed, dismembered, boiled, roasted, and otherwise butchered and cooked. This is the "precious . . . gem . . . enshrined" in Peggotty's parlor "casket" that David kneels before. And this book, or rather the book's gruesome pictures—"terrific pictures" David calls them

Engraved
for the
PRIMITIVE MARTYRS.

S.^T LAURENCE *laid on the* Gridiron *by* Decius *or* Gallienus.

Christians *put into a* Copper *of* Boiling Oil.

Published as the Act directs, for H. Trapp, Pater- noster Row

T. Smith sculp.

46. David, Like Dickens, Devours Dismal Horrors: Roasting and Boiling Human Beings

"I . . . fell to devouring [Fox's *Book of Martyrs*]. . . . I was chiefly edified, I am afraid . . . by . . . pictures . . . of dismal horrors."—*David Copperfield*. For Dickens' adult reaction to one of the "dismal horrors" in Fox's *Book of Martyrs*—the horror depicted here, a graphic picture of St. Laurence being roasted on a gridiron—see Part 1, note 51. Engraving for Fox, *The Book of Martyrs* (London: H. Trapp, 1776).

years later (*DC*, 21:219)—are what David, on every visit, always "fell to devouring . . . afresh." Peggotty provides, and David worshipfully devours, and the feasts consist of flayed and butchered human bodies. This early mother-haunted cannibalism is direct and savage, but it is also, as Dickens makes clear, unconscious on David's part, safely disguised and displaced.

But the cannibalistic motifs of *David Copperfield* are not confined to David's innocence or his childhood; they hover over his manhood, and they hover over other protagonists and other realms as well. When David falls in love, he, like the Fat Boy, expresses his adoration in cannibalistic terms. Unlike the Fat Boy, however, David falls in love at first sight—or, perhaps I should say, at first bite. "I don't remember," David declares, "who was there, except Dora. I have not the least idea what we had for dinner, besides Dora. My impression is, that I dined off Dora, entirely, and sent away half-a-dozen plates untouched" (*DC*, 26:275). Later that evening David tells us how Dora smiled upon him and gave him her "delicious hand" (*DC*, 26:277). That this oral and incorporative response to Dora is not simply a reflex of the moment of meeting (or eating) is made clear a few chapters later when David tells us that in the days and weeks after meeting her, "I lived principally on Dora and coffee" (*DC*, 28:289).

David's devouring preoccupation with Dora (devouring in more ways than one) is charming and humorous; we understand how to interpret his perfervid cannibalistic imagery; we know that those images are simply David's way of expressing his head-over-heels infatuation with Dora. But there is also an undercurrent of egotistical aggressiveness here, a foretaste (if one may be permitted that word) of David's post-married attempts to incorporate Dora into himself, to possess her very soul by making her over into his own image of what she should be, an impulse that rejects even as it seeks to remake and incorporate. David decrees, in effect, that Dora's Dora will cease to exist; only David's Dora, wholly absorbed into his being and then re-created as an avatar of his needs and fantasies, will flourish.

David is reenacting with Dora his fantasy with his mother. With his mother he banished from his mind—or so he thought—all her damaging post-Murdstone weaknesses and foolishness and nestled forever, in prelapsarian bliss, at her nurturing breast; with Dora he cancels—is blind to—all her immaturity and incapacity and feeds rapturously on his self-created image of her as bountiful woman incarnate, as adored playmate and nurturing helpmate. As David puts it, he "dined off Dora, entirely," "lived principally on Dora"—a blind, heedless, self-indulgent feeding. Dora cannot live up to David's image of her, nor can she supply what he wants and needs. After marriage his disillusionment and his yearning grow. We watch that sad progress. Child-wife Dora, who is incapable of maturation or even of change, is slowly eaten alive by her doting yet increasingly dissatisfied and increasingly critical husband. Inevitably, inexorably, she droops and dwindles, and then gradually disappears.

But this sad end, so sweetly pitiful, has sinister antecedents. Dickens has rendered afresh, through Dora and David, the nightmare tale that haunted his Chatham childhood: house-lamb Dora has finally been totally consumed by her Captain Murderer husband. David's lovesick confession that he "dined off Dora, entirely" now reverberates with darker meanings. We begin to read those darker meanings. We see, for example, that it is no coincidence that the first quarrel between the newly married couple—a quarrel that begins this ingestive process—concerns food and eating: it focuses on Dora's incapacity to serve, that is, adapt herself to, David's most basic alimentary needs. She cannot provide him—so runs David's complaint—with the food he wants at the times he wants in the manner he wants at the price he wants with the servants he wants in the amounts he wants or with the degree of doneness he wants. She has failed in her principal role; she has failed as divine nurturer. Or, to put the matter in less transcendental terms, she has failed as a provider of food and nourishment for her ogre husband.

David is indeed an ogre. We recognize this not only because of his attitude toward his helpless bride, not only because of his food-centered demands on her, not only because of his cannibalistic treatment of her (in a later chapter, speaking of Dora, he acknowledges

47. Bluebeard at Home, or, How to Devour a Wife

David attacks the raw meat while his helpless and incompetent bride, discomfited, looks on. Notice the disarray of the room; notice also the resemblance of this illustration to Hogarth's "The Reward of Cruelty" (see figure 18). Both works have a prominent table (and tablecloth) upon which an operation is proceeding, a central carver carving with knife in hand, a conspicuous waste receptacle in the foreground into which waste and food are tumbling, and an intrusive dog intent upon—and succeeding in—joining the feast. "Our Housekeeping." Etching by Hablot Knight Browne ("Phiz") for Number XV, Chapter XLIV (July 1850) of *David Copperfield*.

that unless he restrains himself, "I must degenerate into the spider again, and be for ever lying in wait" [*DC,* 48:494]), not only because of his cognomen (in the midst of their quarrel Dora calls him "Blue Beard" [*DC,* 44:450]), but because of his overwhelming post-quarrel guilt. David's guilt, unexamined but fully acknowledged, stems from his essential decency: on some intuitive level he senses that his indictment of Dora is profoundly destructive—indeed, soul-crushing. As a consequence, though his grievances are real, he feels depraved, like some monstrous Bluebeard or bride-devouring Captain Murderer. "I had," David writes, "the conscience of an assassin, and was haunted by a vague sense of enormous wickedness" (*DC,* 44:451).

That Dickens did not idly use the figure of David feeding upon his beloved and that he was very much aware of the aggressive and incorporative elements that lurked in that deceptive figure is made even clearer when Uriah Heep, one of David's alter egos, a dark embodiment of some of David's most hidden appetites, proclaims his love for Agnes (later to be David's wife) in images that mirror David's own hidden hungers, hungers hidden from himself no less than from others. David reacts outrageously to the aggressive sexual appetites and stratagems of his dark double (on earlier occasions when Uriah had expressed his sexual interest in Agnes, David almost fainted, felt he knew all that Uriah would say and do, called him a red-headed animal, dreamt of him all night, and referred to him as the Devil); but David does not understand the reasons for his excessive reactions. He does not see that in many ways he and Uriah are counterparts, that what he hates and fears in Uriah, he hates and fears in himself. He does not see that Uriah's desire to devour Agnes (David's true love) is an aggravated version of David's desire to devour Dora (who is an imperfect prefigurement—a sexual prefigurement—of Agnes). In both instances the urge to possess the loved one and the images expressing that urge are identical, though Uriah's images are more graphic and alarming—that is, more openly aggressive—than David's. In a wonderfully suggestive and menacing scene, Uriah informs David of his lip-smacking intention: he will devour Agnes alive.

The scene occurs when David, who has been visiting the Wickfields in Canterbury, is about to take the early morning coach back to London. The evening before, Uriah had publicly proclaimed that he adores Agnes, "'my Agnes,'" he calls her, "'the divinest of her sex,'" and that he intends to make her his wife—sentiments that produce such a fit in Mr. Wickfield that Uriah is obliged to equivocate and, by way of apology, to acknowledge that perhaps his declaration was a bit premature (*DC*, 39:407–9). But early the next morning, as David boards the London coach, thinking about Agnes, Uriah's head—his head only—looms suddenly out of the "mingled day and night" (*DC*, 39:410). Uriah accosts David, propitiates him, and after some additional conversation, conveys his central message. The scene and chapter end as David, full of fear and loathing, contemplates that message:

> "I say! I suppose," with a jerk, "you have sometimes plucked a pear before it was ripe, Master Copperfield?"
> "I suppose I have," I replied.
> "*I* did that last night," said Uriah; "but it'll ripen yet! It only wants attending to. I can wait!"
> Profuse in his farewells, he got down again as the coachman got up. For anything I know, he was eating something to keep the raw morning air out; but, he made motions with his mouth as if the pear were ripe already, and he were smacking his lips over it. (*DC*, 39:410)

That Agnes is a ripe pear which Uriah intends to devour, there can be no doubt. That Dora is a dainty dish which David dines upon, there can be no doubt either. David's lovesick assertion that he "dined off Dora, entirely"—especially since Dora and Agnes, as well as David and Uriah, are counterparts—now takes on its full significance. David's milder hegemony and milder cannibalistic images are stripped of their charm and humor when they are transformed by his dark counterpart into naked lubricity and lip-smacking threat. David senses this. His unacknowledged consan-

HOW TO COOK A WIFE.

While MEN spare no pains in obtaining the BEST MATERIALS for this superlative DISH, they are often totally regardless after the first MOUTHFUL, of the necessary precautions to render it permanently SWEET, and if through neglect it turn sour they invariably slander the Dish, while the fault is in themselves. To MAKE the wife a sweet companion, but to keep her so, this may be accomplished in the following manner: —Obtain an adequate supply of the pure water of affection, and gently immerse her therein: should the water during this process become ruffled, a little of the original balm of courtship will soon restore it to its usual smoothness. The fire should be composed of true love, with a few sighs to increase the flame, which should not be too warm, nor yet suffered to abate entirely, as that would spoil the dish. Coolness is often the ruin of this dish, erroneously asserted by some cooks to be necessary, which cooks add also sprigs of indifference, but this is a very dangerous practice, as a good wife is exquisitely delicate and susceptible. A few evergreens, such as industry, sobriety, and fondness, are necessary, and a moderate quantity of the spirit of coaxing and oil of kisses may be added, giving the whole a most delectable flavour. Garnish with flowers of endearment and kindness, and you will then fully appreciate the delights of a dish, compared with which all others sink into insignificance; namely

A GOOD WIFE.

47

48. How to Cook a Wife: Undercurrents of Cannibalism and Wife-Eating in Nineteenth-Century Popular Literature

Though this "recipe" for cooking and eating a wife is supposedly witty and benign, the outrageous title, murderous woodcut, and cannibalistic associations—"mouthful," "fire," "flame," "cooks," "flavour," "delights of a dish," and so forth—convey (as Dickens conveys more consciously and artfully in *Copperfield*) a hidden and more devouring message concerning husband and wife. *How To Cook A Wife.* Broadside (c. 1850). From [Hindley], *Curiosities of Street Literature* (1871).

guinity with Uriah feeds his fury against him. In turning upon
Uriah, David is turning upon the answering darkness within himself.
David, unlike Uriah, saves himself—or, perhaps it would be more
accurate to say, he is saved. His sexual aggrandizement is ultimately
redeemed by Agnes' spirituality (Agnes is David's soul or better
self), a redemption that Uriah, who is all materiality, can never
experience.

Cannibalism helps Dickens express these deep but often figurative
or subliminal meanings. But Dickens does not confine Uriah's (or
David's) cannibalistic impulses to scenes of Captain Murderer-like
love. Uriah's desire to devour Agnes is but one instance of a more
omnivorous feeding. Much later in the book, at Uriah's downfall,
Traddles tells him, "'You must prepare to disgorge all that your rapacity has become possessed of,'" thus showing us that Uriah's battening is all of a piece: the cannibalistic impulse that makes him long
to devour his prospective bride also makes him a hungry feeder on
everything he envies or covets (*DC*, 52:537). He feeds upon his
"betters," especially his weak and vulnerable "betters," the castoffs
of the middle class, poor wounded derelicts such as Mr. Wickfield
or his hostage daughter. As we gradually come to perceive, Uriah's
feeding is profoundly predetermined; he preys vindictively upon the
social order that created and humiliated him, vengefully gorging
himself in mock "umbleness" on the middle class that degraded
him. By such and similar means—by Uriah's lip-smacking relish for
Agnes, by David's lovelorn dining on Dora, by the "Oh, goroo"
man's fierce appetite for lungs and livers and hearts on fire, by David's dream of displacing his usurping brother and feeding forever
at his mother's breast, by Mr. Murdstone's role-reversing transformation of David from bitten into biter, a savage creature who must
wear the dire warning: "Take care of him. He bites."—by such
means, by scenes and signs and characters and figures of speech and
transformations and recurrences, Dickens enlarges and integrates
his cannibalistic motifs, weaving them, now subtly, now boldly, into
his central design until they become not simply one with the design
but inextricable from it, coterminous with theme and meaning.

VIII

Yet some themes are more powerful than others. The vulnerable child, parent-bedevilled or parent-bereft, cast out on an uncaring world, provokes Dickens' most recurrent nightmare visions. And no wonder: the theme is a moving paradigm for him of his own early plight. That archetypal (and autobiographical) theme and its cannibalistic (read "life-threatening") implications haunted Dickens. Think, for a moment, of the opening of *Great Expectations*. All is new, yet all is somehow recognizable. When Magwitch, Pip's dark father, rises out of the grave to seize and threaten the orphaned and put-upon Pip (put-upon, it will be remembered, by his mother-sister, Mrs. Joe), one of his most frightening threats takes a familiar form: "'You young dog,' said the man, licking his lips, 'what fat cheeks you ha' got.'" And then, with a threatening shake of his head, he adds, "'Darn Me if I couldn't eat 'em . . . and if I han't half a mind to't!'" (*AYR* 4: *GE*, 1:169). Pip pleads to be spared and is barely able to keep from crying.

We recall with something of a shock that this is simply an exaggerated version (in a much different context, of course) of the Fat Boy's desire for Mary. In *Pickwick* the threat—or rather compliment—strikes us as primarily humorous. In *Great Expectations* the threat, coming from this "fearful man, all in coarse grey, with a great iron on his leg" and with "an old rag tied round his head," who seizes Pip and turns him upside down, is much more credible (to Pip, at least) and much more frightening (*AYR* 4: *GE*, 1:169). Indeed, this cannibalistic threat, dark affliction from his dark father (Joe is his good father), is soon followed by a series of similar threats that are even more terrifying. Magwitch commands Pip to bring him food and a file. "'You bring 'em both to me,'" he says. "'Or I'll have your heart and liver out'" (*AYR* 4: *GE*, 1:170). Magwitch, escaped marsh-prowling convict, despoiler of hearts and livers, reminds us of his ravening kin. We think of another seaside despoiler of hearts and livers, the fearsome "Oh, goroo" man, and of his ogreish interest in those vital organs; we think also of another escaped coast-hugging convict, the escaped convict of "The Long Voyage," and of his insatiable appetite for human flesh. All the while Magwitch is tilting Pip back or turning him upside down to emphasize his threats. After a tremendous dip and roll, he grips Pip tightly by the arms and goes on as follows:

> "You bring me, to-morrow morning early, that file and them wittles. You bring the lot to me, at that old Battery over yonder. You do it, and you never dare to say a word or dare to make a sign concerning your having seen such a person as me, or any person sumever, and you shall be let to live. You fail, or you go from my words in any partickler, no matter how small it is, and your heart and your liver shall be tore out, roasted, and ate. Now, I ain't alone, as you may think I am. There's a young man hid with me, in comparison with which young man I am a Angel. That young man hears the words I speak. That young man has a secret way pecooliar to himself, of getting at a boy, and at his heart, and at his liver. It is in wain for a boy to attempt to hide himself from that young man. A boy may lock his door, may be warm in bed, may tuck himself up, may draw the clothes over his head, may think himself comfortable and safe, but that young man will softly creep and creep his way to him and tear him open. I am a keeping that young man from harming of you at the present moment, with great difficulty. I find it wery hard to hold that young man off of your inside. Now, what do you say?" (*AYR* 4: *GE*, 1:170)

Pip says he will comply.

We are still, *Pickwick*-like, amused by this cannibalistic bullying. Unlike the child Pip, we know that Magwitch will not eat the boy's fat cheeks, and we understand that he knows no young man who will, like the ogreish "Oh, goroo" man, roast and eat his heart and liver. In the security of our knowledge, we can savor the rich inventiveness and the shrewd psychological acuity of Magwitch's outlandish threatening. But to the seven-year-old Pip, orphaned, alienated, and abused, alone on Christmas Eve on the darkening marshes and in the clutches of this "fearful man," the threats are unimaginably terrifying. Again Dickens has it both ways: we can experience Pip's unreasoning terror (a terror that helps mitigate his subsequent crimes)[34] but we are also distanced from that terror; we are amused by his groundless fears. But it is only the fear of cannibalism, not the life-threatening danger, that is groundless. Indeed, this is the moment of Pip's fall, the moment that sets him groping in his poor labyrinth. That Dickens connects this primal scene with cannibalism, however mitigated by humor, again attests to the potency that dread feeding (and his own nightmarish fall) held for him.

As a matter of fact, the cannibalistic motifs in *Great Expectations* do not end with Pip's fall or his painful groping. Those motifs, and the events they help color and convey, are reinforced by scores upon scores of scenes and touches, some fleeting, some lingering, some deftly recurring. Here, for example, is another scene, a comic yet threatening episode that harks back not only to Pip's fall but to the previously discussed scenes from Dickens' Chatham childhood, the nursemaid-haunted and mother-haunted lying-in and laying-out scenes, scenes that conflate children as pigs (or pigs as children), and then turn the slaughtered victims into butcher-shop fare. Sinful Pip, a far-off fictional afterglow of Dickens' Chatham childhood, is one such victim.

There can be no doubt that Pip is sinful. His sister, who has brought him up from infancy, and thus serves also as nursemaid and as mother, has long dinned into the browbeaten and physically beaten boy that he is innately wicked. This harsh judgment of his moral nature is echoed on every hand. The whole adult world (except for the childlike Joe) inveighs against Pip's depravity and savors his predestined doom. When, at the Gargerys' Christmas dinner, the fatuous Pumblechook tells Pip he should be very grateful for having been born a boy, for he might have been born "'a four-footed Squeaker'"—that is, a pig—and "'what is detestable in a pig, is more detestable in a boy,'" and when Mr. Pumblechook then goes on to ask Pip if he *had* been born a pig where would he be now, Mr. Wopsle interrupts, gestures knowingly towards the plump, juicy leg of pork they are eating, and indicates that Pip would be present "'in that form'" (*AYR* 4: *GE*, 4:197). Mr. Pumblechook, disconcerted momentarily by being so offhandedly anticipated, soon recovers himself and, warming once more to his moral discourse, describes how poor, swinish, fallen Pip, before becoming a leg of pork at a Christmas dinner, would have been slaughtered:

> "You would have been disposed of for so many shillings according to the market price of the article, and Dunstable the butcher would have come up to you as you lay in your straw, and he would have whipped you under his left arm, and with his right he would have tucked up his frock to get a penknife from out of his waistcoat-pocket, and he would have shed your blood and had your life." (*AYR* 4: *GE*, 4:197)

Much later in the novel, in a faint echo of this half-terrifying half-farcical scene, Pip describes how "that ass, Pumblechook" is always "putting me before the fire as if I were going to be cooked" (*AYR* 4: *GE*, 12:338).

Later still, these hints that Pip is destined to be put before the fire and cooked become stronger; they also become more threatening and more sinister. Yet Dickens still manages to lull and reassure the reader. He does this by softening the true import of what he is saying, a sleight of hand, or rather a sleight of language, brought about by the apparent—but only apparent—nonchalance of his narrator, and by the narrator's tone of amused retrospective irony. (Pip is looking back at his naive childish self and at his blind youthful self many years after the events, and many years after he has survived and learned from the events.) Nevertheless, the darker implications lurk menacingly in the depths, and they emerge unmistakably despite the disarming play of distance and humor. How this works can be seen very clearly with Orlick. The threat that Pip will be put before the fire and cooked (to invoke once more Pip's description of the aggressive and destructive blunderings of "that ass, Pumblechook") emerges yet again as soon as Orlick slouches into the novel, but now in a new and more devastating guise.

When we first meet Orlick, we are told that he slouches in, and slouches out, and slouches about "like Cain or the Wandering Jew," and a moment later we learn that he has terrified Pip—a "very small and timid" Pip—with the terrific information that the Devil lives "in a black corner of the forge"—Joe's forge and Pip's forge but also Orlick's forge—and that he (Orlick) knows "the fiend very well." Then Pip learns his fate. It is no longer the Pumblechookian fate of being put before the fire and cooked, but the far more horrible fate of being put into the fire and consumed. Furthermore, his tormentor will no longer be "that ass, Pumblechook," but a more formidable creature, at once a cohort (a fellow blacksmith and a dark double) and a foe. Pip will be fed to the fire, fed to the Devil, fed by Orlick himself, the Devil's "swarthy . . . slouching" surrogate. Orlick tells Pip all this. Orlick tells Pip he will be fed alive to the fire in that very forge, the forge where the Devil lives and Pip works; he will be roasted and consumed in the fierce, hot flames of the Devil's own fire, a hellish fire. (Orlick's strange name helps enforce these fearful meanings. The name "Or lick" is cognate with "Old Nick," the Devil's nickname—Or lick–Old Nick; furthermore, Orlick, though young, frequently refers to himself as "Old Orlick"—the "Old" capitalized as the "Old" in "Old Nick" is capitalized. Orlick, apparently, is old as evil, old as the Devil.) Pip's immutable destiny, then, is to be consigned by the Devil to the fires of hell. Orlick tells Pip (but notice in the following retrospective telling, and especially in the last phrase of what follows, how Dickens, through Pip, distances and mitigates the telling) "that it was necessary to make up the fire once in every seven years, with a live boy, and that I might consider myself fuel" (*AYR* 4: *GE*, 15:363).

These hints and more than hints, and their many analogues—sometimes sinister, sometimes frightening, sometimes humorous, sometimes engaging, sometimes all four (or sometimes yet other combinations or permutations of the fear of being devoured or the impulse to devour)—recur throughout the novel. For example, still later in Pip's career, in a totally different and sympathetic environment (Pip has just been translated to London in his new gentleman's clothes), Pip's very name—now a gentlemanly "Philip" in place of the plebian "Pip"—serves to suggest that his destiny is to be eaten, this time without the nice preliminaries of being cooked or roasted. On this momentous occasion, which is also the occasion of his reunion with Herbert Pocket and the beginning of his close friendship with him, Herbert tells Pip that he does not like Pip's real given name—"'I don't take to Philip,'" he says—and then he explains why: "'For it sounds like a moral boy out of the spelling-book, who was . . . so determined to go birds'-nesting that he got himself eaten by bears who lived handy in the neighbourhood'" (*AYR* 4: *GE*, 22:482). This is amusing enough (and a well-deserved passing jab at relentlessly improving children's literature), but Herbert is not spoofing when he tells us he doesn't "take" to "Philip": he loses no time in rechristening Pip "Handel" (in honor of Handel's *Harmonious Blacksmith*—a dubious name and association for Pip, who wants to forget his lowly blacksmith past). "Philip," alias "Pip," now redubbed "Handel," will be protected, presumably, by that magical sobriquet. So protected, he will not "[get] himself eaten by bears," or by Pumblechook, or by Orlick, or by the Devil, or by any of the other threatening monsters that gird him round—or so at least Pip thinks. But poor Pip by any other name is poor Pip still; he will have to undergo much more than he has already undergone, and he will have to learn much more than he has already learned, before he can escape the Devil, before he can escape being consumed by the everlasting bonfire.

The type of mitigated cannibalism we have been surveying in the last few examples, which mixes levity and terror in varying combinations and varying degrees, and which recalls the opening of the novel and Pip's fateful, but also humorous, confrontation with Magwitch, is dispensed with in some of Pip's later confrontations with his more demonic tormentors. When Orlick captures Pip and prepares to kill him, Dickens does not soften Orlick's ferocious cannibalism with the disarming leaven of humor. Orlick is now a real-life ogre pure and simple, a fearsome tiger thirsting for Pip's blood and ready to drink it drop by lingering drop. Dickens suggests his ferocity and voraciousness in the most artful yet graphic ways. Orlick, "his mouth snarling like a tiger's," his heavy fist hammering the table, tells Pip in a spasm of furious hatred, "'I'm a going to have your life!'" Then, leaning toward Pip and staring at him, he "slowly unclenched his hand and drew it across his mouth as if his mouth watered for me" (*AYR* 5: *GE*, 53:338; see figure 49).

Orlick's tiger mouth does water for the captive Pip. His rapacious mouth, snarling like a tiger's, waters with sadistic relish. Orlick savors his dominion over Pip. He taunts and torments him, and all the while he drinks. We soon come to see that he is literally drinking—that is, consuming—the last drops of Pip's life; in a few more moments Pip will cease to exist. Dickens evokes Orlick's thirsty rapacity with startling explicitness: "He drank again, and became more ferocious. I saw by his tilting of the bottle that there was no great quantity left in it. I distinctly understood that he was working himself up with its contents to make an end of me. I knew that every drop it held, was a drop of my life" (*AYR* 5: *GE*, 53:339). Orlick goes on drinking the drops of Pip's life, and he goes on tormenting his victim. Dickens presents the final act of predation with wonderful intensity. The act is totally realistic and brilliantly metaphoric:

> Of a sudden, he stopped, took the cork out of his bottle, and tossed it away. Light as it was, I heard it fall like a plummet. He swallowed slowly, tilting up the bottle by little and little, and now he looked at me no more. The last few drops of liquor he poured into the palm of his hand, and licked up. Then with a sudden hurry of violence and swearing horribly, he threw the bottle from him, and stooped, and I saw in his hand a stone-hammer with a long heavy handle. (*AYR* 5: *GE*, 53:340)

In the next instant Pip is saved, but we have already watched ogre Orlick at his fearsome, tigerish feeding licking up "the last few drops" of Pip's life, a life he literally and figuratively holds in "the palm of his hand." (At this point we note with a sudden shock of recognition that one of the components in devil Orlick's name is "lick." Dickens' linguistic virtuosity never ceases to astonish us.)

A different sort of cannibalism, less savage but more relentless and perhaps more terrible—certainly more universal, more passionate, and more haunting—appears elsewhere in *Great Expectations*. It appears strongly in the weird, disordered Miss Havisham focus of the novel, a focus that integrates a crucial array of meanings in the story.

THE PORTFOLIO

OF

ENTERTAINING AND INSTRUCTIVE VARIETIES

IN

History, Science, Literature, the Fine Arts, &c.

VOL. I.]   PRICE TWO-PENCE.   [No. 22

HORRID DEATH OF MR. MONRO BY THE ATTACK OF A TIGER.

THIS ferocious and savage animal, which is the terror of the east, not only partakes of the noxious qualities of the lion, but shares none of his generosity. The lion very seldom approaches the haunts of man, nor even then except when he is excited to do so by excessive hunger; whilst the tiger, though glutted by the slaughter of his victims, still continues the carnage, for whether he meets with flocks or herds, tame or wild beasts, he goes on destroying one after another, and swallowing the blood of each, as if it increased, rather than satiated his voracious appetite. This terrific creature is an inhabitant of hot countries, and is often met with in the East-Indies, where it frequently commits depredations of the most horrid nature. Although the natives are considered to meet tigers with great courage, and often succeed in their efforts to destroy them, yet men, women, and children very commonly fall a sacrifice to their dreadful ferocity. They frequently quit the woods, and enter villages, seeking whom they can devour, when they carry off their victims

VOL. I.   No. 22.   Z

49. The Voracious Man-Eating Tigers of Dickens' Boyhood

Dickens' boyhood reading taught him that the tiger (unlike the lion and other animals) was a "terrific creature" that had a "voracious appetite" for blood and that fed on "men, women, and children" with "dreadful ferocity" and for the pure joy of killing—a conception that later led him to associate tigers and tigerish humans (as with Orlick and his snarling tiger's mouth) with fierce, inappeasable cannibalistic voraciousness. In this connection, see also the cannibalistic tiger imagery of *A Tale of Two Cities* (discussed below). "Horrid Death Of Mr. Monro By The Attack Of A Tiger." From the *Portfolio* (1823–24), a weekly periodical that Dickens had "a great fancy for," and that he bought and read as a boy.

132

Miss Havisham has wasted her life. She is surrounded by the tokens of her folly: ruin, decay, darkness, and death. Wounded as a young woman, she seeks to wound; but she wounds no one more than herself. To use Dickens' metaphor for her embittered reflexive destructiveness, she eats, and she is eaten:

> "On this day of the year, long before you [Pip] were born, this heap of decay," stabbing with her crutched stick at the pile of cobwebs on the table but not touching it, "was brought here. It and I have worn away together. The mice have gnawed at it, and sharper teeth than teeth of mice have gnawed at me." (*AYR* 4: *GE,* 11:316)

The "gnawed" "heap of decay" festering on the dining table is Miss Havisham's bridecake. As Miss Havisham puts it, "It and I have worn away together"—that is, "It and I" are one. When Miss Havisham has decayed still further, has decayed into death, she will become that gnawed bridecake: she will be placed—so she has decreed—on that selfsame dining table where her gnawed bridecake now rots. She will then become the fully corrupted and gruesomely gnawed centerpiece of her own corrupted life. She will rest where the great "black fungus" wedding cake, festooned with cobwebs, now moulders; she will fester—that is, she will be gnawed and nibbled and chewed—on the very spot where "speckle-legged spiders with blotchy bodies," "black-beetles," squeaking mice, and other "crawling things" have long fed (*AYR* 4: *GE,* 11:315). Pip, looking at the desolation all about him and listening to Miss Havisham's words, is aghast. When Miss Havisham tells him of her grisly plan to enshrine the last remnants of her time-gnawed body on the dining table, he shrinks from her very touch. He has horrible visions "that she might get upon the table then and there and die at once" (*AYR* 4: *GE,* 11:315). But Miss Havisham does not get upon the table then and there, and she does not die—yet; she eats, and she is eaten.

Very early in the book, Miss Havisham makes it clear to Pip that her relatives, the parasitic Pockets, whom she has called together for their yearly visitation, are only waiting for her to die. When she is

50. Miss Havisham Tells Pip How Her Gnawed Corpse—A Final Feast for Hangers-On—Will One Day Replace the Vermin-Gnawed Bridecake on the Dining Table

"'It's A Great Cake. A Bride-Cake. Mine!'" Wood engraving (1860) after a drawing by John McLenan for Chapter XI of *Great Expectations.* This illustration (one of thirty-four) first appeared in *Harper's Weekly,* which (by arrangement with Dickens) serialized the novel (1860–61) from early proof sheets of the English serialization. In 1861 Harper & Brothers (New York) and T. B. Peterson & Brothers (Philadelphia) published book editions of *Great Expectations* with the McLenan illustrations. The authorized English illustrations by Marcus Stone (only eight, all told) did not appear until 1862.

dead, Miss Havisham tells her assembled relatives (repeating for their benefit—and for ours—what she had earlier told Pip), her corpse will be laid upon the dining table where the gnawed bride-cake presently rots. But then she reveals an additional provision of her macabre plan: when her body is set on the dining table, her relatives will encircle her corpse. She tells them what their positions will be when they take their places round her lifeless body. " 'Now,' " says Miss Havisham, " 'You all know where to take your stations when you come to feast upon me' " (*AYR* 4: *GE*, 11:316). Isolated in this manner the cannibalistic implications of "feast" and of the entire scene are obvious, but in context the sinister import of what Dickens is saying can easily slip past one's notice. Lest the reader miss the full significance of what he is implying here, Dickens later has Mrs. Camilla, one of the relatives, say, " 'It's very hard to be told one wants to feast on one's relations—as if one was a Giant.' " And then she adds, compounding the cannibalistic implications and the humor, " 'The bare idea!' " (*AYR* 4: *GE*, 11:316). The original image and its promise of gruesome feasting are both accentuated and softened by this humorous coda, but it is the original image, not the humorous coda, that prevails.

Dickens' art is intricate and centripetal; it echoes and reverberates, it combines and recombines, and it does so in countless meaningful counterpointings and harmonies. We are astonished to discover, for example, that the macabre coupling of corpses and dining—a coupling made central when we are introduced to Miss Havisham—is both re-sounded and its promise of culminating feasting prefigured much later in the novel (but long before Miss Havisham's entabled death) when Pip's abusive sister dies. Pip, who is already on his self-centered (but also guilty) way to becoming an exalted London gentleman, goes dutifully but perfunctorily down to the humble Gargery house to attend his sister's funeral. When he enters the parlor of his old home, his train of thought evokes yet again the once and future series of images, a series fraught with thematic (and cannibalistic) significance. At this crucial moment, when Pip returns to his earliest origins and confronts the death of his sister-mother (his only relative and lifelong tormentor), Dickens takes us into Pip's mind. He causes Pip to think and to associate—a process, in this instance, both random (seemingly) and portentous—and he causes us to ponder (at least we should ponder) the unmistakable import of Pip's casual and quite ordinary, yet extraordinary, associations. When we do ponder those associations, we are confounded by what we discover. We have met these strange interminglings before—and so has the unaware unconsciously self-revealing Pip. Pip thinks, all unwittingly (yet wittingly too), of the old bizarre collocation of images; he thinks, but now in a new and personal context, of corpses, cakes, and dining tables—and of feasting on one's relations: "I . . . began to wonder in what part of the house it—she—my sister— was. The air of the parlour being faint with the smell of sweet cake, I looked about for the table of refreshments" (*AYR* 5: *GE*, 35:76).

This unexpected reemergence of corpses, cakes, and dining tables—this new-old association of corpses with feasting (with "refreshments," no less)—here evoked through the agency of Pip's freely associating inner consciousness (Pip, remember, has ample reason to hate his sister-mother, to become a vengeful biter—a refreshed but also guilty biter—after being so long bitten), this astonishing reemergence is only one of many virtuoso contrapuntal re-soundings, in this instance a re-sounding removed from Miss Havisham, that is, removed from what elsewhere in the novel is the most spectacular and ghastly embodiment of this central theme.

That central theme, the sin of feasting on others (Pip, too, once he is deformed by his great expectations, is an egregious feeder on the largess of others), that cannibalistic theme and its most striking images are reinvoked throughout the story. We are told that no one has ever seen Miss Havisham eat, yet she feeds incessantly. Dickens shows us this over and over again. Like an obscene vampire or an unclean ghoul (the similes are Dickens'), Miss Havisham feeds passionately, ravenously, remorselessly on Estella, Pip, and others, but most of all upon herself. She consumes, but she is not nourished. We see the wasting effects of her sick, impious feeding. Her grotesque bridal finery, withered like her withered body and her withered dreams, hangs loosely on her shrunken form like a ghastly shroud. Devouring, witchlike, she has become the gaunt, skeletal *memento mori* of her insatiable appetite for revenge. At times Dickens makes her profane feeding daringly explicit. In one such scene, which takes place immediately before dinner, Miss Havisham places her withered hand upon the dining table (a collocation of actions and images that suggests her sin and prefigures her end), and then, while Estella, standing in the doorway, turns to look back over her shoulder at her weird white mentor before leaving the room to "prepare herself" for dinner (another meaningful collocation of actions and images), "Miss Havisham kissed that hand to her, with a ravenous intensity that was of its kind quite dreadful" (*AYR* 5: *GE*, 29:4). "Ravenous" and "dreadful" are the key words here. Wan and weird in her ancient bridal dress, Miss Havisham ravenously devours her own hand and her handiwork. In fashioning Estella to be a poison princess, in gloatingly feeding day after day on her growing beauty and burgeoning allure, so deceptive, so sterile, so deadly, Miss Havisham has devoured not only her ward (she has long since consumed Estella's heart, left her heartless) but her own life and spirit.

This rendering of Miss Havisham as an insatiable devourer—a passionate, obsessive, aggressive devourer—is Dickens' way, all through the novel, of giving dramatic outward form to Miss Havisham's inward (that is to say, psychological) destructiveness. Miss Havisham is now a fitting emblem of her fierce, impious feeding: she sits day after day, night after night, in her dim hermetic world, a shriveled wraith, a grotesque shade, gaunt, emaciated, ghastly. In yet another scene, Dickens (again using hand imagery) has Miss Havisham, monstrous child-eating sire, devour herself even as she devours Estella. In her "witch-like eagerness," Dickens writes, "she hung upon Estella's beauty, hung upon her words, hung upon her gestures, and sat mumbling her own trembling fingers while she looked at her, as though she were devouring the beautiful creature she had reared" (*AYR* 5: *GE*, 38:122).

Miss Havisham eats her fingers as she devours Estella. The two actions are not separate but one. Estella is merely an extension of

Miss Havisham, an unfeeling monster Miss Havisham has fashioned to wreak her vengeance on all men. When Dickens shows us Miss Havisham greedily gazing at Estella and all the while "mumbling her own trembling fingers . . . as though she were devouring the beautiful creature she had reared," he is showing us yet again (this time most graphically) that in devouring Estella, Miss Havisham eats herself. He is also showing us the archetypal bad mother, the mother who devours her offspring, the mother who is a veritable witch. For weird entombed time-stopped Miss Havisham is most certainly a mother and most certainly a witch. She is a mother of sorts, a luring, entrapping mother, to Pip; and she is a mother in fact, a heartless parasitic mother, to Estella. She feeds upon her offspring, a foul unnatural dam. (Pip's other mother, the child-quelling Mrs. Gargery, who is really Pip's sister, is smashed over the head and done in by Orlick, Pip's tigerish double, an act for which Pip, who had often wished to annihilate his abusive mother-sister, feels somehow responsible.)

But now Miss Havisham's profane feeding is almost done. The novel circles back to its opening, and Miss Havisham circles as well. The portents that surrounded her entrance and then accompanied her ghoulish feeding now reinforce her departure. Her gruesome vision of her relatives gathering after her death to feast, cannibal-like, upon her entabled corpse is fulfilled at the end of the book when her seared body, still dressed in white, but now the metamorphosing white of cocoonlike cotton wool—Miss Havisham is in the process of transformation and translation—is indeed placed upon the dining table where the nibbled and gnawed and corrupted bridecake once stood, a fitting and symbolic end for one who has dined so relentlessly on others. Miss Havisham's rapacious relatives, indeed the world, can now gather round her dining table and her burned, time-seared corpse and feast on her as she feasted on herself and others. Dickens underlines but does not belabor this momentous fulfillment. "She lay indeed," he has Pip write, "where I had seen her strike her stick, and had heard her say that she would lie one day" (*AYR* 5: *GE*, 49:292). That is all. But this brief reminder of Miss Havisham's scornful injunction (and the vision it evokes of that final, funereal, cannibalistic feast) is enough to cue our understanding. By this time we can interpret and fully respond to Dickens' gruesome symbolism. Like Pip, we too have learned a good deal about the deadly wages of feasting on the substance of others—a lesson that is conveyed and reconveyed throughout the novel not only by Miss Havisham, but by Pip, Magwitch, Orlick, Estella, the Pockets, and others, and by scene, image, and action.

IX

This richly integrated and articulated use of cannibalistic motifs is a hallmark of many of Dickens' middle and late works. But one must draw distinctions here. In these mature works the cannibalistic motifs are frequently, as with the more general instances in *Great Expectations,* utterly transformed. They become so intertwined with the innermost themes and structures of the novels, so colored and shaped by Dickens' unifying imagination, that one often fails to recognize them for what they are. The more obvious instances do not function in this unobtrusive way. They are the unmistakable outcroppings of the larger submerged mass. Dickens wants us to recognize the outcroppings; they help guide us to the submerged mass. The outcroppings are usually presented to us as egregious examples of fundamental social pathologies, cannibalistic pathologies that reemerge in more subtle and unexpected cannibalistic configurations elsewhere in the novel. An outcropping helps us to see a pathology stripped of its protective and socially accepted veneer, and this, in turn, helps us to strip the veneer from more cunningly disguised examples.

Take Mr. Vholes of *Bleak House,* for instance, an outcropping if ever there was one. Mr. Vholes, the most flagrant man-eater in *Bleak House,* is an additional example of how Dickens, in his maturity, weaves, interweaves, and then enlarges and generalizes his obsessive vision of profane feeding. There can be no doubt that deathlike Mr. Vholes—part reptile, part bird of prey, part scavenging rat, part harbinger of doom—is all cannibal. (The word *vole,* incidentally, means rodent or rat, and we already know, from "Chips and the Devil" and from the hungry rats scuffling in the depths of the blacking warehouse, that Dickens had long since come to associate rats with revolting cannibalistic voraciousness.) Dickens takes pains to show us that ratlike Mr. Vholes, despite his three dependent daughters, despite his aged father in the Vale of Taunton (supported, as Mr. Vholes never fails to remind us, entirely by him), despite his politeness, gentility, and legalistic scruples, feeds gluttonously and unremittingly on the substance of others. We watch Mr. Vholes as we might watch some unclean animal or ghoul, and yet we are assured that he is the epitome of "common sense, responsibility, and respectability, all united," a model of the "exemplary man" (*BH*, 37:374).

Mr. Vholes may be exemplary, but he is exemplary of a society that can throw the mantle of altruism and respectability over the most relentless exploitation of others, or, to use Dickens' metaphor, over the most relentless cannibalistic feeding. Mr. Vholes, gaunt, stooped, and lifeless, buttoned up and buttoned in, dressed entirely in black, gazes steadily at Richard Carstone "as if he were looking at his prey" (*BH*, 37:376). Or yet again, he gazes at Richard "as if he were making a lingering meal of him" (*BH*, 39:387). When Mr. Vholes removes his "close black gloves," it is as if "he were skinning his hands"; when he lifts his "tight hat," it is as though "he were scalping himself" (*BH*, 39:387). His black chambers smell of mutton fat and of the "fretting of . . . skins in greasy drawers" (*BH*, 39:385). Mr. Vholes' digestion is impaired—and no wonder!—for he has, as Dickens puts it, been "making hay of the grass which is flesh" (*BH*, 39:385).

This kind of imagery and these figures of speech build our awareness of the sinister feeding of Mr. Vholes and his tribe. Very soon we come to watch him with the same rapt attention he exhibits when he watches his wretched victims. But at times Dickens becomes so concerned that we apprehend the full import of what he is saying, and so outraged by the abuses he is depicting, that he conveys his message through outright statement rather than image and action. At times he even argues like a Chancery lawyer in a brief, as in the following passage: "As though, Mr. Vholes and his relations being minor cannibal chiefs, and it being proposed to abolish cannibalism, indignant champions were to put the case thus: Make man-eating unlawful, and you starve the Vholeses!" (*BH*, 39:386).

But for the most part the imagery of loathsome, single-minded cannibalistic feeding is developed in the course of many chapters and in many hundreds of subtle touches, some fleeting, some barely perceptible, others fully orchestrated. The effect in context is richer, more compelling, and more complex than the brief quotations presented here can suggest. The portrait grows and deepens. Its end confirms its beginning. Our final glimpse of Mr. Vholes occurs as the news arrives that Jarndyce and Jarndyce has at last consumed itself in costs. Richard, weak and wasted, on the verge of death, lingers in the high court of Chancery. And what of Mr. Vholes? Mr. Vholes, with "that slowly devouring look of his," gives "one gasp as if he had swallowed the last morsel of this client," and glides out of the ancient hall like an unclean creature (*BH*, 65:616).

Mr. Vholes is not the only cannibal in *Bleak House*. Other denizens of legal London exhibit man-eating and woman-eating proclivities. The Inns of Court and of Chancery, the lanes and warrens and dingy courtyards abutting Chancery Lane, Fetter Lane, Fleet Street, and their environs—the London focus of *Bleak House*—swarm with voracious predators. These predators are busy, persistent, and omnivorous. They scavenge for fat carcasses, choice morsels, or, if nothing better can be found, scurvy scraps. Old Krook, disreputable and secretive, crafty and crazy, looking out at the labyrinthine legal world through an alcoholic daze, accumulates the last leavings of lawyer and client, suitor and defendant, persecutor and victim. He sits like a slovenly ogre amidst the dirt and detritus of the legal universe he feeds on. His shop is filled with old rags, bottles, law books, and bones, with crackled parchment scrolls, dog-eared law papers, and rusty keys, with cat skins, torn law gowns, and broken scales. Krook himself is bent and crooked. His hair, beard, and eyebrows are frosted, his veins gnarled, his skin puckered. "With his head sunk sideways between his shoulders, and the breath issuing in visible smoke from his mouth, as if he were on fire within," he is a frightening storybook monster, hoary and threatening (*BH*, 5:36). Krook, of course, is called the "Lord Chancellor" and his shop is called the "Court of Chancery."

Given his appearance and his occupation, it is no wonder that Krook's junk shop, full of legal trophies, also contains great sacks of ladies' hair, cropped—scalped is perhaps a better word—primarily from Chancery clients (so one gathers) who have been well-fleeced in the course of time. (In this connection, we recall that Krook fondles Ada's hair—she, too, is in Chancery; while Vholes, who later represents Richard and Ada in their Chancery suit, is, as Dickens specifically informs us, a scalper [*BH*, 5:37; 39:387].) And given Krook's proclivities and his appetites, it is no wonder that he views the litigants who are enmeshed in Chancery as something to eat, as grain "being ground to bits in a slow mill," or meat "being roasted at a slow fire" (*BH*, 5:38). It is no wonder, too, that his shop is filled with the unmistakable trophies of his dismal legal trafficking, that it contains "bones . . . piled together and picked very clean," like "the bones of clients" (*BH*, 5:36). Krook, ogre and Lord Chancellor, presides over this charnel house of the law, final resting place for the flayed skins and picked-clean bones of Chancery and its clients. He thus presides over a mirror image of the High Court of Chancery itself, which is also—and truly—like its charnel-house counterpart, a court of death and cannibalistic annihilation.

Given his attributes and his appetites, it is only fitting that Krook at last should become food for other feeders on the largess of the law and should be devoured by those cannibalistic feeders. This happens quite literally in the course of Krook's slow, smoldering death by spontaneous combustion. Mr. Snagsby, a law stationer, Mr. Weevle (alias Tony Jobling), a law writer, and later Mr. Guppy, a law clerk, enter Krook's domain (that is, enter the precincts surrounding his charnel-house shop) as Krook's body combusts into smoke and grease and wafting fatty residues—a combustion that finally, in the course of several hours, leaves behind only a few charred remnants and a sprinkling of white ashes. (Krook's transformation into residues of grease and fat recalls the final scene in Hogarth's *The Four Stages of Cruelty,* in which Tom Nero's entrails are consumed by a dog while a giant rendering pot, filled with dissected human skulls and bones, billows forth its thick, greasy smoke [see figure 18]. It also recalls the greasy end of Cornelia Bandi, Countess Cesena, one of several reputed cases of spontaneous combustion that Dickens drew upon for *Bleak House,* and one of several cases detailed in the *Terrific Register.*)[35]

There is no doubt that Snagsby and Weevle (and later Guppy) ingest the greasy residues of Krook's burnt body, residues that fall in great sooty flakes that cannot be blown off when they land on one's skin or clothing but smear "like black fat" (*BH,* 32:316). In the following passage, such words as *flavor, greasy, taste* (repeated three times), and *tainting,* words associated with eating chops and the concomitant acts of spitting and mouth wiping, guide our awareness. Also guiding our awareness are the insistence upon "the horrors" and the subsequent discovery (not quoted here) of the charred fragments of Krook's remains and their "sickening" residue, a "thick nauseous pool" of "offensive" smelling "yellow liquor." That nauseating combination of taste and smell and smoke and "oil" that "defiles" everything its odor engulfs, its grease contaminates, and its liquid touches, has, we are told, "some natural repulsion in it" that makes one "shudder" (*BH,* 32:319). But before that shudder, before the discovery of the charred remains and the pools of grease, Mr. Snagsby and Mr. Weevle meet in the courtyard just in front of Mr. Krook's shop (Mr. Weevle rents a room from Mr. Krook). It is night; the air is damp, cold, and misty but also close:

"Don't you observe," says Mr. Snagsby, pausing to sniff and taste the air a little; "don't you observe, Mr. Weevle, that you're—not to put too fine a point upon it—that you're rather greasy here, sir?"

"Why, I have noticed myself that there is a queer kind of flavor in the place to-night," Mr. Weevle rejoins. "I suppose it's chops at the Sol's Arms."

"Chops, do you think? Oh!—Chops, eh?" Mr. Snagsby sniffs and tastes again. "Well, sir, I suppose it is. But I should say their cook at the

51. Mr. Snagsby and Mr. Weevle Discover
What It Is They Have Been Tasting

"The appointed time." Etching by Hablot Knight Browne ("Phiz") for Number X, Chapter XXXII (December 1852) of *Bleak House*.

Sol wanted a little looking after. She has been burning 'em, sir! And I don't think;" Mr. Snagsby sniffs and tastes again, and then spits and wipes his mouth; "I don't think—not to put too fine a point upon it—that they were quite fresh, when they were shown the gridiron."

"That's very likely. It's a tainting sort of weather."

"It *is* a tainting sort of weather," says Mr. Snagsby; "and I find it sinking to the spirits."

"By George! *I* find it gives me the horrors," returns Mr. Weevle. (*BH*, 32:313)

This association of a dead body with public eating, more particularly, the thought of a group of individuals, even a community of individuals, unknowingly consuming a dead body, had emerged earlier in *Bleak House*. The earlier association, or rather the earlier occasion, foreshadows Krook's macabre end: in each instance we get a solitary, unexpected, Chancery-encompassed death, a bizarre cannibal-haunted aftermath, and a ravenous public at a coroner's inquest devouring each grisly tidbit. The earlier occasion is the death of Nemo the law writer. In fact, Nemo's death occurs on the very premises that later become the scene of Krook's death. The literal basis for this symbolic connection is simple: Nemo, like a number of other wretched victims of Chancery (Miss Flite is yet another example), had rented a room from Krook. Law writer Nemo is a stark, anonymous casualty of Chancery. Like Bartleby after him (in Melville's "Bartleby the Scrivener"), Nemo (his real name is Captain Hawdon) has become in truth a "Nemo"—he has become, as his name implies, a no one, a nobody—a mere instrument or machine for mindlessly copying mindless texts. Nemo is gradually eaten up by the system he serves. A no one and a commodity when he begins his law-writing career, he becomes, quite literally, a no one and a commodity when he ends that career in death: his body and his identity (more interest-provoking and therefore more valuable in death than in life) is sold for food and drink. Law writer Nemo's cannibal-environed death on Krook's Chancery-enmeshed premises, in turn, foreshadows "Lord Chancellor" Krook's later death on those same premises, and revolting corpse-eating—Chancery corpse-eating—to come.

When Nemo's body is discovered, Dickens immediately associates that discovery—the body still lying in its coffinlike room—with thoughts of eating bodies, though here the thoughts (unlike those that will surround Krook's corpse) are introduced in tangential and parodic ways. The means of association is a bungling beadle. Dickens depicts this outmoded and fast-disappearing functionary, an archaic holdover from an earlier age, as floundering about in the preliminary inquiry concerning Nemo's death. This officious, or would-be officious, beadle is so incompetent and "imbecile," so obviously a befuddled remnant of a "barbarous" past, that the public, especially the youthful public, gathered in anticipation outside the quarters where Nemo's newfound body rests, "taunts the beadle, in shrill youthful voices, with having boiled a boy; choruses fragments of a popular song to that effect, and importing that the boy was made into soup for the workhouse" (*BH*, 11:102).

Dickens' sardonic humor and deadpan reporting mitigate the horror of what is being chorused here, but the "popular song," as Dickens well knew is more graphic and more grisly concerning the workhouse boy and the workhouse soup than Dickens' passing references suggest. (The grisly details of the song and what those details signified to Dickens were part of what made the song memorable for him.) Here is the concluding stanza of "The Workhouse Boy":

> At length the soup copper repairs did need,
> The Coppersmith came, and there he seed,
> A dollop of bones lay a grizzling there,
> In the leg of the breeches the poor boy did vear!
> To gain his fill the boy did stoop,
> And, dreadful to tell, he vos boil'd in the soup!
> And ve all of us say, and ve say it sincere,
> That he vos push'd in there by an overseer.
>   Oh the Poor Vorkhouse Boy, etc.

By means of the inept beadle of the preliminary inquiry and the ogreish folklore of beadledom, Dickens quickly proceeds from Nemo's corpse to a corpse-based broth—a corpse and a broth (in the song version) that is consumed by the workhouse populace.

That tainted workhouse broth, moreover, is associated in *Bleak House* with a bumbling and corrupt social order and its bumbling and corrupt officials (personified here by the bumbling beadle and the wicked overseer). Dickens rings changes on this theme (reminiscent of *Oliver Twist*) and on its cannibalistic overtones. Those overtones are again sounded when the benighted beadle, maintaining in his own private entrepreneurship the beadlish connection between corpses and liquid nourishment, shows Nemo's body to a favored few for "a glass of ale or so" (*BH*, 11:102). In other words, the beadle subsists, in part, on Nemo's body; he sells Nemo's body for drink. This atmosphere of corruption and debasement, this association of public corpses with public eating and drinking—the whole sanctioned, abetted, and sometimes even presided over, by the High Court of Chancery—does not come to a close with the allusions to boiled boys, loathsome workhouse soups, and corpse-generated glasses of ale; it continues at the coroner's inquest.

The inquest takes place at the Sol's Arms, and Dickens makes a point of telling us that on the day of the inquest, with the dead body hard by and at the center of everyone's consciousness, "the Sol's Arms does a brisk stroke of business all the morning." "Even children," Dickens continues, "so require sustaining, under the general excitement, that a pieman, who established himself for the occasion at the corner of the court, says his brandy-balls go off like smoke" (*BH*, 11:102). (We are reminded of Tiddy Doll the pieman, who does a brisk business selling his gingerbread to the excited crowd at the execution of Thomas Idle [see figure 19 above], a Hogarthian conflation of death and appetite that Dickens had emphasized six years earlier in his second letter to the *Daily News* on capital punishment; see, also, in this connection, Part 1, note 12 and the pastry merchants in *Pictures from Italy*: the latter merchants, vendors of food to a hungry crowd, do a brisk business at an Italian execution.)

The coroner, like the enterprising beadle or the thirsty frequenters of the Sol's Arms, associates dead bodies with another form of ingestion, convivial public drinking: "The smell of sawdust, beer, tobacco-smoke, and spirits, is inseparable in [the coroner's] vocation from death in its most awful shapes" (*BH*, 11:102). But the association of corpses with eating and drinking does not end when the inquest ends. Afterward, the jurymen, reluctant to leave, lounge about the Sol's Arms, smoking and drinking. A group of them, their ghoulish appetites whetted by what they have seen and heard, soon engage to get together that night and have a feast. In celebration of their corpse-viewing and corpse-examining, they will go to the theater and "top up with oysters" (*BH*, 11:105).

Nemo's solitary opium-induced death in Krook's quarters prepares us for what is to come; prepares us, that is, for Krook's solitary alcohol-induced death in those same quarters. By the same token, the communal corpse-eating, real but distanced, that surrounds Nemo's death prepares us for the communal corpse-eating, real and graphically dwelt upon, that surrounds Krook's death. In *Bleak House* the horrors of predation in all its ghoulish guises (however muted or intensified those protean guises are), are never far distant. It is always, to extend the meaning of Mr. Weevle's comment as he unknowingly tastes the remains of Mr. Krook's tainted body, "a tainting sort of weather" in *Bleak House*. But Mr. Weevle does not leave the matter here. He goes on to tell us how that vague, undefined taint, in reality a corpse-cooking and corpse-eating taint, affects him. "*I* find," he says, "it gives me the horrors." We may be sure that it gave Dickens the horrors as well.

Mr. Vholes' remorseless cannibalism, Mr. Krook's pile of picked-clean clients' bones as well as his own rendered and ingested corpse, and Mr. Nemo's corpse, a corpse associated with a body being boiled in a soup and devoured by famished workhouse inmates, are only the most overt examples of Chancery's true effect: Chancery is an institution that consumes all those who approach its voracious maw. Chancery, in turn, is simply the most flagrant feeder in a ravenous legal system. The business of law is not justice (we recall that Krook's scales are broken) but consumption—consumption, that is, for those who take their nourishment from the law. The functionaries of the legal system, the lawyers, judges, clerks, law writers, stationers, wigmakers, robemakers, beadles, jurymen, junk dealers, and the like, must busily consume that which they are meant to serve and represent. Jarndyce and Jarndyce, in typical fashion, eventually consumes its entire substance in costs. Yet the legal system, as Dickens takes great pains to show us, is only a microcosm of the world at large.

The aristocratic Dedlocks, for example, decaying scions of a decaying breed, so high above ordinary scufflers for survival, batten even more unremittingly than the Vholeses and the Krooks on their neighbors. In life the Dedlocks feed dronelike on their long-departed ancestors and on their fellowmen; in death their fellowmen, like the haughty Dedlocks themselves, feed on the dusty Dedlocks. Dickens presents this consumption with subtle directness. In the Dedlock church the very atmosphere is redolent of decaying Dedlocks. This image and its untoward ramifications are impressed upon us when we first meet the Dedlocks: "On Sundays, the little church in the park is mouldy; the oaken pulpit breaks out into a cold sweat; and there is a general smell and taste as of the ancient Dedlocks in their graves" (*BH*, 2:6). This is revealing enough. The word *taste* tells us (if we are alert to its full implications) that the churchgoing gentry of this world, Dedlocks included, devour the dead in genteel brotherhood with the most depraved human beasts, with such repulsive monsters as the ravenous, grave-rifling ghoul of the *Terrific Register* or the murderous man-eating fiend of "The Long Voyage." The nicety and sanctity of the gentry's feeding (note that it takes place in church) disguise and sanction its cannibalistic essence. Society connives at this deception. In fact, society's unwillingness to see cannibalism as cannibalism when it is clothed in goodly garb is part of Dickens' arraignment.[36]

In subsequent episodes, Dickens does not abate his charge or his imagery, though he handles this dangerous onslaught on received respectability with adroit delicacy. Much later in the book, for example, he returns to his image of sanctified cannibalism—that is, genteel cannibalism—and also modulates it: "On Sunday, the chill little church is almost warmed by so much gallant company, and the general flavor of the Dedlock dust is quenched in delicate perfumes"

(*BH*, 12:112). The language here—"general flavor of the Dedlock dust" and "quenched in delicate perfumes" (the words *flavor, dust, quenched,* and *perfumes* are critical)—tells us once more that the living, despite their perfumes and their pretensions, are not simply in the presence of the dead but ingest the dead with every breath they draw. They batten on their brothers, quench and perfume that truth as they will.

Dickens is also making a statement about equality and inequality. All men—Dedlocks included—Dickens is saying, echoing the resonances of the burial service, are dust. The Dedlocks reject this commonality in life but bow to it in death. That this is so becomes even clearer when, still later in the book, Dickens modulates his image once more and extends it from Dedlock church to Dedlock house. Now living and dead Dedlocks are mingled in a new way: "On all the [Dedlock] house there is a cold, blank smell, like the smell of the little church, though something dryer: suggesting that the dead and buried Dedlocks walk there, in the long nights, and leave the flavor of their graves behind them" (*BH*, 29:282). The word *flavor* again guides our awareness: the living Dedlocks feed on their dead and buried ancestors not simply in church but in their homes and in their daily lives. In truth, living or dead, the Dedlocks are no better than the Vholeses or the Krooks—or the Weevles or the Snagsbys or the Guppys or the Nemos or the Skimpoles or the Chadbands or the Smallweeds. They all obey society's golden rule: eat or be eaten—or, more exactly, eat *and* be eaten.[37] We consume our neighbors, we even batten on our progeny and our progenitors, Dickens is saying, instead of loving them. Mr. Vholes' cannibalism is only the most unadorned representation of this grim truth and of society's law.[38]

X

Dickens works variations on this cannibalistic theme over and over again. He weaves the theme into his short fictions and he looms it into his novels, but he surrounds each new appearance with fresh contexts, contexts that enlarge our awareness and provide us with fresh insights as well. This pattern of innovation in the midst of continuity can be seen in *Our Mutual Friend*, Dickens' last completed novel. The novel begins with Gaffer Hexam, that unclean fisher of lost bodies rather than lost souls, plying his ghoulish trade. That Gaffer Hexam, miserable Thames scavenger, feeds on dead bodies there can be no doubt, and this whether he steals, as he often does, the valuables from such bodies, or whether he simply claims the bounty for bringing a body in. As usual, Dickens does not allow us to linger indefinitely in the comforting displacement of metaphor; from the very beginning he scatters hints and declarations and reactions that force us to confront the sickening reality and loathsome significance that lurk behind the veil of analogy. The opening chapter is entitled "Birds of Prey," a keynote that recurs, and the chapter is replete with phrases and images that suggest the unspeakable rites that are enacted on London's dark river.

Lizzie Hexam, who rows her father's boat, watches her father's face as he scans the darkening river. She looks at him, as she always does when they are so occupied, with a look of "dread or horror" (*OMF,* 1: 1:2). The setting sun touches a rotten stain in the bottom of the boat so that it resembles "a muffled human form, coloured . . . as though with diluted blood" (*OMF,* 1: 1:2). The girl shudders. Gaffer scans and scans the swift-flowing river, his eyes watching every break and anomaly in the current. He looks at each strange ripple, each drift of debris, with "a hungry look" (*OMF,* 1: 1:2). When fisherman Gaffer hooks the body he has been fishing for, Lizzie shivers in revulsion and can hardly bear it. Her father quickly reproves her. " 'As if,' " he says, " '[the river] wasn't meat and drink to you!' " "At these latter words," Dickens continues, "the girl shivered again, and for a moment paused in her rowing, seeming to turn deadly faint" (*OMF,* 1: 1:3). (A few years earlier, in *A Tale of Two Cities*, Dickens had used virtually identical imagery: Jerry Cruncher calls his nocturnal body snatching "fishing," and he claims that this sinister "fishing" is meat and drink to his family—much to the dismay of his wife [*AYR* 1: *TTC,* 2: 14:290–91].)

52. Gaffer Hexam, Fishing for Bodies, Scans the River with "A Hungry Look"

"The Bird Of Prey." Wood engraving after a drawing by Marcus Stone for Number I, Book I, Chapter I (May 1864) of *Our Mutual Friend*. The illustration was designed to serve as a frontispiece for Volume I.

We know what to make of Gaffer's fishing and Lizzie's reactions. We know how Dickens, much earlier, diverting himself in a great urban river, had turned deadly faint when he imagined that the drowned body of the dark man of the Morgue, fished swollen from the Seine, but now somehow floating insistently toward him, had become his meat and drink. This cannibalistic obsession, sickening him for days, had sprung from one involuntary, panic-stricken swallow of the river water. The hallucination—"possession," Dickens called it (["Travelling Abroad"], *AYR* 2: 559)—had gradually faded, but obviously it had not vanished from his innermost consciousness. In *Our Mutual Friend* the vision of dead bodies fished like obscene harvests from a polluted river emerges once more from the deep, now wonderfully transformed and exquisitely fashioned to serve his larger purposes.

Indeed, the close blood ties between the Thames fiction and the Seine episode do not end with the water-logged body fished from the Thames, Gaffer's meat-and-drink remark, and Lizzie's deadly faintness. Some time later, when Gaffer Hexam is once more garnering his meat and drink from the river, Eugene Wrayburn, Mortimer Lightwood, and a police inspector commence a long night vigil in order to take the bodyfisher into custody for questioning. The three watchers begin by drinking delicious burnt sherry at a waterside tavern, the Six Jolly Fellowship-Porters. They chat in their snug quarters and savor the aromatic brew. After a while they go down to the black river, linger there, then return to the tavern, where the following exchange occurs:

> "Give me some more of that stuff" [said Eugene].
> Lightwood helped him to some more of that stuff, but it had been cooling, and didn't answer now.
> "Pooh," said Eugene, spitting it out among the ashes. "Tastes like the wash of the river."
> "Are you so familiar with the flavor of the wash of the river?"
> "I seem to be to-night. I feel as if I had been half drowned, and swallowing a gallon of it." (*OMF*, 1: 13:125)

53. Fishing Two Bodies from the Seine: Thirty Francs for Meat and Drink

As Dickens well knew, many of the bodies in the Morgue—the body of the "large dark man," for example—were fished from the Seine. Some men, like the two illustrated here, and like Gaffer Hexam in *Our Mutual Friend,* earned their meat and drink from such ghastly fishing—a means of putting food on the table that fascinated and horrified Dickens, for he regarded such scavenging as a form of cannibalism, as a way of feeding on dead bodies. Jerry Cruncher in *A Tale of Two Cities* also earns his (and his family's) meat and drink, as he tells his distraught wife, by "fishing"—the word is his—fishing in graveyards rather than rivers, but fishing still for corpses and food. *Les Pêcheurs De Morts.* Wood engraving (c. 1875) after a drawing by P. Kauffmann.

"Taste," "flavor," "drowned," and "swallowing" are the key associations here. Eugene, unlike Dickens, does not flee to his chambers with the corpse-contaminated wash of the river in his mouth, but he is profoundly disturbed. Like Dickens when he swallowed the river water, Eugene feels polluted, as though he has committed some terrible crime, partaken of some profane communion. And, indeed, though he does not yet realize how deep his involvement is, he is already caught up in—has drunk of—the dark ebb and flow of Gaffer's watery world.

A little while later, in verification of his prescient reaction and as a further token of his involvement with the watery world, Eugene, along with his companion watchers, discovers Gaffer's drowned body awash in the midnight river. Gaffer, the eater of corpses, has become a corpse to be eaten, and Eugene, like Dickens before him, has somehow become a sickened participant. Eugene's waking nightmare of swallowing a gallon of the river and half drowning in its turbid waters now takes on its full significance. On some deep intuitive level he perceives that he has, metaphorically, not simply eaten of the dead Gaffer (that is, drunk the water in which Gaffer is awash) but has become his drowned counterpart, a perception that is fulfilled toward the end of the book when he too is dragged half dead from the selfsame river.

These central cannibalistic motifs have many contrapuntal variations. To cite one striking variation, a grotesque example, Dickens parodies and elaborates the Hexam-Wrayburn corpse-eating motifs in the unlikely person of Mr. Venus. Mr. Venus is a taxidermist and articulator of skeletons. But he is no ordinary preserver of animal remains. He deals in much more than the stuffed parrots, canaries, robins, ducks, dogs, cats, frogs, and alligators that jam every passage and corner of his shop. He also crams his shop with human skulls, human bones, human teeth, even dried human cuticles; he collects whole human arms, whole human legs, whole human ribs, and whole human hands; he fills great baskets, hampers, trunks, and shelves with human skulls "warious," human bones "warious," and human bones miscellaneous and assorted (*OMF*, 1: 7:62). But this is not all. He adorns his shop with huge glass jars of preserved babies—Indian babies, African babies, "Hindoo" babies, British babies, and more. He owns and displays other choice specimens: Belgian legs, English legs, complete French gentlemen, and "human warious" (*OMF*, 1: 7:64). The shop smells "musty, leathery, feathery, cellary, gluey, gummy," and bellowsy (*OMF*, 1: 7:59). It is no wonder that a visitor to this grisly cannibal-like abode receives a greasy induction. He goes into this reeking fat-encrusted charnel house through a series of greasy chambers and portals. He proceeds down a "dark greasy entry, pushes a little greasy dark reluctant side-door, and follows the door into the little dark greasy shop" (*OMF*, 1: 7:59).

Mr. Venus, quite clearly, traffics in human bodies just as surely as Gaffer Hexam does. Human bodies are "meat and drink" to him no less than to the disreputable fisher and despoiler of corpses. As Mr. Venus himself puts it, " 'I . . . live by my calling' " (*OMF*, 3: 14:122). Mr. Venus' calling is sanctioned by society, but it is also frowned upon by society. His ladylove, Pleasant Riderhood (the daughter of another disreputable fisher of corpses), will not marry him, for, as she puts it, she does not want to be regarded "in that boney light" (*OMF*, 1: 7:63).

Though Dickens casts a comic aura over Mr. Venus' sayings and doings, he also evokes the more sinister associations—cannibalistic associations—that lurk in Mr. Venus' grisly shop and grisly occupation. In addition to the greasy shop and its musty smell of bones and skins and cellar damps, Dickens provides us with more open hints that profane death and predation are the baleful businesses so matter-of-factly pursued in this quiet corner of London. When Mr. Venus drinks tea with the predatory Mr. Wegg, "a pretty little dead bird" lies with "its head drooping" against the rim of Mr. Venus' saucer (*OMF*, 1: 7:60). This association of corpses and eating—a central motif in other phases of *Our Mutual Friend*—is not accidental, nor is it confined to one Venus-Wegg scene. Much later in the novel, for example, we are told that Mr. Venus, preparing for another feast with Mr. Wegg, "produced from among his skeleton hands, his tea-tray and tea-cups, and put the kettle on" (*OMF,* 3: 7:59). As a matter of fact, at the very beginning of the book, right after the association of "the pretty little dead bird" with Mr. Venus' tea drinking, we are given other juxtapositions of corpses and eating. When Mr. Venus toasts a muffin for the arch predator, Mr. Wegg (through much of the novel his coconspirator and voracious copredator), he takes out the long stiff wire that pierces a small dead robin's breast (Dickens associates this dead robin with the murdered Cock Robin) and, thrusting the wire through a muffin, uses that "cruel instrument" to toast the tasty morsel for his greedy partner (*OMF,* 1: 7:60). As Mr. Wegg eats his toasted muffins (now no longer impaled but swathed in greasy butter), he gazes at the Hindoo baby in the bottle. The baby is "curved up with his big head tucked under him" (*OMF,* 1: 7:60). Mr. Wegg looks and eats. A few moments later, Mr. Venus informs us that two teeth—both "molars"—dropped into the coffeepot at breakfast that morning. " 'They drop into everything,' " he says (*OMF,* 1: 7:61).

These cannibalistic hints are soon magnified to nightmare proportions, though the ghoulish implications continue to be veiled (as the earlier hints were veiled) in disguising subtleties or softening humor. For example, while Venus and Wegg are still drinking their tea and savoring their toasted muffins, a boy comes into the dark greasy den to collect his stuffed canary. The boy soon becomes prey for the irritable, love-crossed Venus, a grotesque deity, feeder on death, a frustrated lover who bears the name of the goddess of love. Mr. Venus tells the boy not to "sauce" him (the word *sauce,* used twice, guides our awareness) and then, shaking his shock of dusty hair, and winking his weak eyes at the intimidated youth, he utters the following threat: " 'You've no idea how small you'd come out, if I had the articulating of you' "—which has the calculated effect on the cowed boy (*OMF,* 1: 7:62). The boy, cringing under this threat, has nightmare visions, one presumes, of being impaled, flayed, dismembered, dried, and reconstituted—articulated—of being turned by Mr. Venus into a commodity, into (eventually) the steaming tea he greedily gulps and the hot buttered muffins he noisily devours. (Later in the novel, Venus makes similar threats—with similar effects—against the bullying Wegg.)

Mr. Venus' role as a potent cannibalistic deity surrounded by his greasy trophies (one incarnation—a threatening incarnation—of the haggard corpse-begirt bone merchant) is accentuated by Dickens' artful imagery. As Mr. Venus gulps countless cups of hot tea in his dimly lighted lair, he is engulfed by clouds of steam from the burning tea, the boiling kettle, and the "smoking saucer" (*OMF*, 1: 7:62, 63). Often only his head or his face looms eerily out of the steam-filled darkness. Cloud-begirt, he broods in solemn splendor over his domain. He sits in the shadows, a grotesque deity, "blowing his tea: his head and face peering out of the darkness, over the smoke of it" (*OMF*, 1: 7:62). Mr. Venus, reduced—or enlarged—at such times to a disembodied face peering through billowing clouds of steam, swallows his burning tea as though he were swallowing the grisly contents of his greasy shop. He gulps and swallows and gulps again. He is all mouth and eyes. The tea is "so hot that it makes him choke" and makes his eyes water as he gulps and swallows, blinking and shutting his eyes as he does so (*OMF*, 1: 7:62). But he perseveres. He again takes "gulps of hot tea, shutting his eyes at every gulp, and opening them again in a spasmodic manner" (*OMF*, 1: 7:62). Mr. Venus, like a great ingestive deity, or a giant lizard or snake that gulps its prey entire—the two incarnations are really one—sits enshrined in billowing steam and blinks and gulps and swallows and chokes amidst his greasy trophies.

The effect of this part macabre, part humorous, part sinister cannibalistic counterpoint is twofold. It throws into starker relief the more serious and threatening cannibalistic motifs of the novel, and it helps to unify seemingly disparate movements of the story. Guided by that omnipresent cannibalism, we see the similarity in occupations, behaviors, attitudes, and values that at first sight seemed diverse or even opposed. One touch of cannibalism makes the whole world kin.

Elsewhere in *Our Mutual Friend* the cannibalistic motifs are echoed and varied in old-new permutations. We catch those echoes

54. Mr. Venus in His Element: Human Skulls, Bones, Teeth, and Bottled Babies

Note, amidst other *memento mori*—skulls, skeletons, bones, decapitated heads, bottled babies, and the like—the naked figure of a child hanging in the upper right-hand corner. Note also, in the background, just above Mr. Venus' head, a duelling frog slaying its hapless opponent. This latter embodiment of death and of the taxidermist's art had a special meaning for Dickens: he kept two stuffed duelling frogs on his writing desk. "Mr. Venus Surrounded By The Trophies Of His Art." Wood engraving after a drawing by Marcus Stone for Number II, Book I, Chapter VII (June 1864) of *Our Mutual Friend*.

in the glittering realm of polite society as well as in the squalid domain of the unwholesome river scavengers or in the exotic dominion of the dismal traffickers in human bones. In the second chapter of *Our Mutual Friend,* the news of the drowned body Gaffer has fished from the deep is introduced dramatically and climactically to the Veneerings, the Podsnaps, the Lady Tippinses, and the Twemlows, to Boots, Brewer, and all the others, at the dinner table. This unsavory association of a dead water-logged body with dining—another conjunction of corpses and eating—and many similar associations, some strong, some muted, some direct, some inverted, reverberate through the remainder of the novel. Dickens makes sure that we do not forget the "awful sort of fishing" that brings meat and drink to the Mortimer Lightwoods (the "dead"—presumably drowned—man's hungry solicitor, whose Christian name, appropriately, incorporates the French words for "dead" and "sea") as well as to the Gaffer Hexams of this world (*OMF,* 1: 14:131). And we are not allowed to forget that such meat and drink is tainted. Gaffer dies a victim of his own unclean fishing. Leaning over to gaff his prey, he becomes the dreadful catch of his own line and boat. (In his number plans, Dickens reminds himself to "Kill Gaffer retributively" [Stone, *Working Notes,* 340–41].)

Dickens makes much of these parallels and of the many ironies they generate. Toward the end of the novel, in a reprise of her old occupation, Lizzie fishes Eugene's battered body out of the Stygian river. The skills she had learned while fishing for corpses—that trolling which had clothed, fed, and sickened her—now saves her loved one's life. She, too, has become a fisher for life. Her father had fished for dead men so that he—and she—might eat; she fishes for a near-dead man so that he might live and she might love. Dickens consciously orchestrates this rich counterpoint and all its implications. In his working notes for the seventeenth number, and then for the sixth chapter of Book 4, the number and chapter in which Lizzie saves Eugene, Dickens twice wrote, both times with underlining and other emphasis: "Back to the opening chapter of the story," and then, later, "Back to the/ opening chapter/ of the book,/ strongly" (Stone, *Working Notes,* 366–67). And what he emphasizes in that recursive chapter is Lizzie's dreadful, but now, in a new sense, life-sustaining, fishing.

In *Our Mutual Friend* the cannibalistic motif is less overt and satiric than it is in *Bleak House,* but it is no less central, and it is just as wedded to the great counterpart themes that structure and integrate the novel. Gaffer Hexam and his tribe (and Lizzie, Charley, and Rogue Riderhood, too, for that matter) are not alone in feeding on the detritus of their fellowmen. The great treasure-trove dust heaps of the Golden Dustman, piled high with offal, refuse, and human waste, remind us once more that the rich and fashionable as well as the dispossessed and the humbly employed are scuffling scavengers who take sustenance from the dead remains of human life. The Lammles, the Veneerings, Fledgeby, Silas Wegg, Mr. Dolls, Mr. Venus, and many others help to refine and enlarge this theme. All humankind is compromised by a social order that must sustain itself by feeding each one on the other.

This bleak view of the social order, a view conveyed throughout the novel by multitudes of scenes, metaphors, characters, and actions, is made explicit at the very end of the book in a brief but definitive interchange. The interchange, a moment of comic repartee, allows Dickens to be stunningly direct; it also allows him to make the most categorical indictment of modern civilization in the entire novel. Civilization and cannibalism, he declares through Mortimer Lightwood, are one: civilization is just another name for cannibalism. Here is how Dickens confronts us with this devastating equation:

> "Say, how did you leave the savages?" asks Lady Tippins.
> "They were becoming civilized when I left Juan Fernandez," says Lightwood. "At least they were eating one another, which looked like it." (*OMF,* 4: 17:303)

This exchange occurs in "Chapter the Last," "The Voice of Society." We laugh at this satiric thrust, delivered here as we close the book, but the laughter fades and the indictment lingers.[39]

XI

The examples chosen so far are neither special nor isolated. Dickens can present the dark shadow of cannibalism directly or he can lighten it by laughter or soften it by indirection, but he cannot expunge it; it grips and compels him; it is part of his puissant night side, part of his shaping blackness, part of his generative power; it emerges like an indelible stain everywhere in his writings. A few additional examples, wider-ranging and more varied than those already marshaled, will show that this is so, and will also show how the stain seeps into the great open places and the small hidden crannies of Dickens' writings.

We have already seen how the stain of cannibalism appears openly and repeatedly in *A Tale of Two Cities* in conjunction with Jerry Cruncher, his "Resurrectionist" predations and his graveyard foragings.[40] However, Jerry's ghoulish foragings, conveyed with humor as well as loathing, are not presented to us simply as a macabre garnish for the central dish of epic history and high-flown romance that Dickens seems to be serving up. Jerry's predations are a grisly parody of one of the great recurring themes of the novel—resurrection— or, to use the words and the form of resurrection that constitute the title of Book 1 of *A Tale of Two Cities*, "Recalled to Life," a title which is also a metaphorical version of Jerry's more earthy and utilitarian exploits in revivalism. But cannibalism in *A Tale of Two Cities* is not confined to Jerry Cruncher's Resurrectionist graveyard "fishing" and dining, however thematic or parodic those activities may be, nor is it confined to the "Ogreish" relish with which that "boiling" "human stew," that is, the courtroom spectators—respectable prerevolutionary London spectators, not the blood-maddened courtroom spectators of Paris during the Terror—gaze at the chief ingredient in that boiling human stew, the mortally endangered Darnay (*AYR* 1: *TTC*, 2: 2:101; 4:145). Cannibalism in *A Tale of Two Cities* is part of the way Dickens expressed the deep flow of history, the inevitable working of cause and effect, the dire calculus of ghastly sin and ghastly retribution.

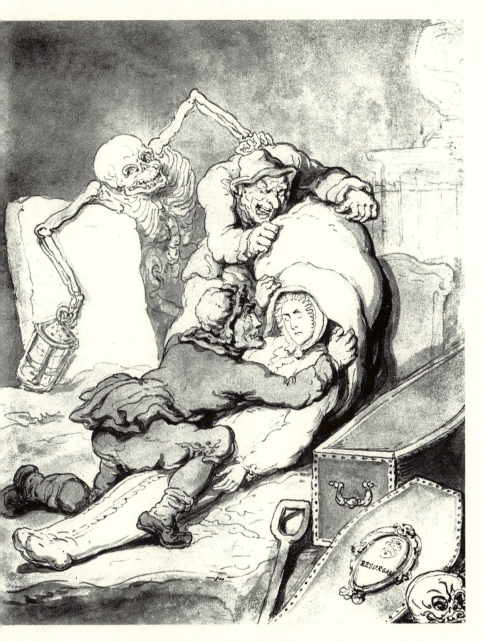

55. Rapacious Resurrectionists: Selling Bodies for Food and Drink

Note the eager and predatory expressions of the foraging Resurrection Men. In *A Tale of Two Cities* Jerry Cruncher, another eager Resurrection Man, tells his wife that his graveyard foraging, which he calls "fishing," brings "meat" to the family dining table—a conflation of corpses with domestic dining that sickens her (and that obsesses and revolts Dickens). *The Resurrectionists.* Drawing and watercolor (c. 1815) by Thomas Rowlandson. Royal College of Surgeons of England, London.

Dickens saw the sleek French aristocracy as murdering and devouring the famished French populace; then he saw the famished populace, goaded and exploited beyond endurance, as butchering and devouring the aristocracy. He renders this savaging and devouring quite literally. We learn, for example, shortly after meeting Monsieur the Marquis, the chief representative of the aristocracy in the novel, that it requires four men to serve him his dainty chocolate. Dickens makes much of this scene, and he describes it in great detail. He shows us that Monseigneur's swallowing—even here, even on so slight an occasion—is an intricate, self-centered celebration of ostentatious and aggrandizing ingestion. Monseigneur, it seems, is always swallowing, and he swallows more than his chocolate and more than the hosts of cringing human creatures who serve and propitiate him. "Monseigneur could swallow a great many things with ease, and was by some few sullen minds supposed to be rather rapidly swallowing France" (*AYR* 1: *TTC*, 2: 7:193).

Shortly after this scene of dainty and then gargantuan swallowing, Dickens shows us Monseigneur in the very act of swallowing France; but well before this crucial scene, much earlier in the novel, Dickens prepares us for Monseigneur's depredations on the starving populace and for the retributory devouring ferocity of the starving populace as well, for, strange to tell, that hunted and hounded populace harbors "some wild-beast thought of the possibility of turning at bay" (*AYR* 1: *TTC*, 1: 5:50). The earlier scene is the famous episode in which a large cask of red wine breaks open upon the street pavement of the impoverished Saint Antoine district of Paris, the wine running in red rivulets that ensanguine the stones of the street, trickle rapidly hither and thither, and then gather in little pools and puddles. The men and women of the neighborhood, in a frenzy of hunger and anticipation, swarm into the street to drink, lap, sip, and gulp the dark red wine. Some go further, devoting "themselves to the sodden and lee-dyed pieces of the cask, licking, and even champing the moister wine-rotted fragments with eager relish" (*AYR* 1: *TTC*, 1: 5:49). The men and women of Saint Antoine soon bear the savage signs of their hungry ferocity:

[The wine] had stained many hands, too, and many faces, and many naked feet, and many wooden shoes. The hands of the man who sawed the
wood, left red marks on the billets; and the forehead of the woman who
nursed her baby, was stained with the stain of the old rag she wound
about her head again. Those who had been greedy with the staves of the
cask, had acquired a tigerish smear about the mouth; and one tall joker
so besmirched, his head more out of a long squalid bag of a nightcap
than in it, scrawled upon a wall with his finger dipped in muddy wine
lees—BLOOD. (*AYR* 1: *TTC,* 1: 5:49)

Dickens immediately follows this infernolike scene of bloody chewing, licking, and drinking—a savage nightmare vision of frenzied
men and women with tigerish smears about their mouths—with a
concluding single-sentence paragraph: "The time was to come,
when that wine too [that is, the wine that is blood] would be spilled
on the street-stones, and when the stain of it would be red upon
many there."

It is in the context of this famished ferocity, this sudden frenzy of
symbolic bloodletting and blood drinking (bloody similitudes that
will one day metamorphose into bloody realities), that Monseigneur, years later, on the occasion of his having finished swallowing his chocolate, goes driving recklessly through the narrow
streets of Paris. Careening through Saint Antoine, Monseigneur's
carriage kills a child. Monseigneur, delayed momentarily by this trifling incident, watches with impatient annoyance as the dead child,
now a mere "motionless bundle," is carried by its father to the
nearby fountain and laid on the fountain's base. The father offends
Monseigneur; he makes, Monseigneur complains, an " 'abominable
noise!' " The father does indeed make a noise. He is down in the
mud and the wet by the body of his dead child, "howling over it
like a wild animal" (*AYR* 1: *TTC,* 2: 7:195). Monseigneur runs his
eyes over the "wild animal"—the "wild animal" will soon become
a wild animal in truth: a savage bloodstained tiger—and Monseigneur also runs his eyes over the gathering residents of Saint Antoine "as if they had been mere rats come out of their holes." (We
know the ferocious—and loathsome—cannibalistic attributes that

Dickens associated with rats, and with tigers.) Monseigneur throws a gold coin to the howling animal-father, admonishing him to take better care of his children in future and not to endanger his (the Marquis') horses, and he throws another coin to a masterful "philosophic" man (it is Defarge) who is comforting the sobbing father.

While the Marquis is looking elsewhere, a coin is flung back at him. Furious, he turns and tries to determine who committed this offense, but he sees only the watching crowd, cowed and submissive, and Madame Defarge, in Defarge's place, staring at him steadily. (One should note that the Defarges, stalwarts of Saint Antoine, are proprietors of the corner wineshop [bloodshop]; the broken cask of red wine had been intended for their shop—indeed, the chapter is titled "The Wine-Shop.") The Marquis, more furious still, addresses the famished populace of Saint Antoine: "'You dogs! . . . I would ride over any of you very willingly, and exterminate you from the earth'" (*AYR* 1: *TTC*, 2: 7:196). He gazes in contempt at Madame Defarge and "all the other rats" and then drives off.

As the day wears on, other carriages of other dignitaries drive through Saint Antoine—all part of the elegant Fancy Ball that is being exquisitely danced by the self-absorbed aristocratic devourers of France—while the residents of Saint Antoine, who years earlier had lapped and chewed and swallowed in a tigerish frenzy, sullenly watch the resplendent ball and its heedless celebrants (the latter so blithe, well-fed, and debonair) with hungry eyes: "The rats had crept out of their holes to look on, and they remained looking on for hours." Meanwhile, the fountain runs on, time runs on, and night falls. And what of the watching rats? "The rats were sleeping close together in their dark holes again, the Fancy Ball was lighted up at supper, all things ran their course" (*AYR* 1: *TTC*, 2: 7:196).

Slowly, bit by bit, Dickens weaves his unfolding pattern of elegant supping and famished repression, and slowly, bit by bit, he enlarges the meaning—a coherent, continuing, expanding meaning—of cannibalistic feasting and cannibalistic retribution, of lapped up blood, sacrificed children, heedless supping, ratlike watching, and growing wild-animal cravings, tigerish cravings, to devour the devourers. These cannibalistic images, carefully orchestrated and counterpointed, are summoned up again and again. By means of these and hundreds of similar images (and by means of other central galaxies of images) Dickens generates and enforces the emotional core of his meaning.

Dickens develops his cannibalistic structuring and detailing scene by scene and touch by touch. While the somber depths seem to slumber, all things, as Dickens puts it, ran their course. The rats were sleeping in their dark holes, and the Fancy Ball was lighted up at supper. The rats were sleeping and the Marquis was supping; but when the rats were not sleeping, some of them at least were preparing for another form of supping. One of those preparers is Defarge. We see him training one small rat, a rustic mender of roads, to know, rend, and devour his prey. The naive road mender, fresh from the country, would like to see the King, Queen, and Court. Defarge's confederates are aghast, but Defarge, who plans to use the road mender in his revolutionary plans, tells his companions that they should grant this country road mender his wish: " 'Judiciously show a cat, milk, if you wish her to thirst for it. Judiciously show a dog his natural prey, if you wish him to bring it down one day'" (*AYR* 1: *TTC*, 2: 15:316). Defarge, with the help of his wife, puts his plan into effect. The following Sunday he and Madame Defarge take the road mender to Versailles and show him the King, Queen, and Court. The road mender, all unknowingly, begins to learn his predatory role. Defarge "held him by the collar, as if to restrain him from flying at the objects of his brief devotion and tearing them to pieces" (*AYR* 1: *TTC*, 2: 15:317).

While the road mender and his many counterparts are being trained all over France—later in the novel we shall meet the road mender again, but then he will be butchering and devouring— Monsieur the Marquis, one of the chief suppers at the Fancy Ball, after the annoying delay with the slaughtered child, continues on his way to his country estate. This arrogant devourer of chocolate and children, contemptuous swallower of France, arrives at sunset on his second day of travel at the verge of a small, poverty-pinched village hard by his château. It is now many hours since he left the tiny square of Saint Antoine, that wretched square, hardly more than a widened street, with its corner wineshop, its steadily flowing fountain, and its slaughtered child—precincts that years earlier had been splashed and stained with the ruddy hue of red, red wine. As the Marquis approaches this wracked and taxed and toiling country village (he is its lord), the setting sun encrimsons his face, engulfs his entourage, and strikes so brilliantly into his carriage "that its occupant was steeped in crimson." "'It will die out,' said Monsieur the Marquis, glancing at his hands, 'directly'" (*AYR* 1: *TTC*, 2: 8:196). We know better; we know that it is he and his blood-stained race that will die out "directly."

It is growing dark as the Marquis passes through his little village, past its central fountain, past its gaunt inhabitants foraging for leaves and grasses and "any such small yieldings of the earth that could be eaten"—a village so poor that "the wonder was, that there was any village left unswallowed" (*AYR* 1: *TTC*, 2: 8:196). The Marquis has swallowed this village but his swallowing is not a special case; that is, he is not the only aristocrat who devours his villages and their inhabitants. All landed aristocrats are cannibals: they exploit and hunt their human charges as though they were hunting game. Dickens says this explicitly. He tells us (this long after the Marquis' death) that the aristocracy—here given the generic title "Monseigneur" (which Dickens had earlier reserved for the Marquis)—is callous and rapacious: "For scores of years gone by, Monseigneur had squeezed [the village] and wrung it, and had seldom graced it with his presence except for the pleasures of the chase—now, found in hunting the people; now, found in hunting the beasts" (*AYR* 1: *TTC*, 2: 23:435).

The Marquis, an elegant but ruthless hunter (he has preyed upon "his" peasants, "his" province, "his" France all his life), has finished his hunting for the time being. After two days of journeying through Saint Antoine and France, he has arrived at his château. It is night now, but though his hunting is done for the time being, he continues his voracious swallowing. He eats his "sumptuous and choice supper," luxuriously presented and splendidly served, alone (*AYR* 1: *TTC*, 2: 9:217). Later still, he prepares to go to bed. He moves "like a refined tiger . . . like some enchanted marquis of the impenitently wicked sort . . . whose periodical change into tiger form was either just going off, or just coming on" (*AYR* 1: *TTC*, 2: 9:220). This tigerish Marquis, so smooth and fastidious and well-fed (his head and hands fresh-stained with new-spilled blood), is a counterpart of the tigerish residents of Saint Antoine, so haggard and unkempt and starving (their mouths long-stained with metaphorical blood). Soon the well-fed tiger of St. Evrémonde will be swallowed up in a bloody frenzy by the starving tiger of Saint Antoine. (We recall that old premonitory half-human, half-bestial embodiment of Saint Antoine as a famished creature with "a tigerish smear about the mouth"; we also recall the voracious man-eating tigers that haunted Dickens' boyhood [see figure 49 and the accompanying letterpress from the *Portfolio*, reproduced above].) But now the "refined" tiger of St. Evrémonde, pacing "to and fro" in his "softly-slippered feet" that make "no noise on the floor," is satisfied for the moment and ready for sleep (*AYR* 1: *TTC*, 2: 9:220).

Relaxed, the tiger-Marquis thinks over the events of the day: the setting sun encrimsoning him and his surroundings, the little village, the peasants at the village fountain. "That fountain suggested the Paris fountain, the little bundle lying on the step, the women bending over it, and the tall man with his arms up, crying, 'Dead!'" (*AYR* 1: *TTC*, 2: 9:220). The Marquis falls asleep. That night he is murdered in his bed. Round the hilt of the knife that is plunged into his heart are the words, "*Drive him fast to his tomb*" (*AYR* 1: *TTC*, 2: 9:221). He has been murdered by Gaspard, the father of the little "bundle," the man who had written "BLOOD" upon the wall, the man (or rather, one of many) with "a tigerish smear about the mouth," the tall man with his arms up, crying, "'Dead!'"

As the new day begins to dawn, the château fountain and the village fountain are flowing still. Slowly the dark waters of both turn grey and ghostly and then red. "In the glow, the water of the château fountain seemed to turn to blood, and the stone faces crimsoned" (*AYR* 1: *TTC*, 2: 9:220). The spilled wine that was so savagely lapped from the unfeeling stones by the famished residents of Saint Antoine (residents turned into tigers and rats by the contemptuous Marquis and his tribe) has metamorphosed into the blood of that selfsame tigerish Marquis, swallower of France. This retributive butchering is the first sign of the butchering and devouring to come. The famished residents of all the squeezed and wracked Saint Antoines and all the squeezed and wracked little villages of France will soon indulge in an orgy of savage feasting.

Dickens prepares for that orgy slowly, carefully, meticulously. He adds touch to touch, echo to echo, foreshadowing to foreshadowing. He shows us the ineluctable dawning of that wild cannibalistic frenzy of famished feasting. But until that orgy begins, the aristocracy, with all the ranged might of the state, continues to hunt and devour its miserable prey, persisting in the fierce tigerish rapacity that makes that retributive orgy inevitable. We see this with Gaspard. Gaspard, the avenger of his child's wanton death, becomes, for the aristocracy (and thus for the state), an object lesson in official vengeance. For his murder of the Marquis, Gaspard—he of the tigerish smear—is placed, all bloody and encrusted with dust, in an iron cage and displayed to all the village. Then he is hanged forty feet high over the village fountain, poisoning its waters and forcing the thirsty villagers to become complicitous ghouls and drink the tainted draught of death.

Gaspard is a human sacrifice; he is caged and then butchered by the cruel and rapacious state as an animal would be caged and butchered. This fierce tiger sacrifice by a tiger state of the lesser tiger antagonist (lesser for now) confirms the omnipotence of that tiger state. The tiger metaphors and similar metaphors help Dickens convey the inner meaning (as Dickens perceives that meaning) of what he is depicting. Such fierce cannibalistic metaphors, and their many analogues, continue throughout this scene and throughout the novel. That Gaspard has been eaten alive by the savage governors of France is made clear, for example, by the manner of his arrest and incarceration. A witness to the scene describes how Gaspard, goaded and tormented, battered and bleeding, was brought to the prison, a prison on the verge of the Marquis' village and the Marquis' château:

> "They bring him into the village; all the village runs to look; they take him past the mill, and up to the prison; all the village sees the prison gate open in the darkness of the night, and swallow him—like this!"
>
> He opened his mouth as wide as he could, and shut it with a sounding snap of his teeth. (*AYR* 1: *TTC*, 2: 15:314)

The brutish swallowing of Gaspard, a swallowing ritualized and glorified by the state, provokes on the part of the people more brutish swallowing yet. When that orgy of retributive feasting begins, Dickens continues to suggest its cannibalistic ferocity: the pent-up thirst for blood (a thirst exhibited when the men, women, and children of Saint Antoine, long parched and famished, lapped up the blood-red wine and chewed up the crimson cask—ferocious harbingers of savageries yet to come), that thirst for blood can no longer be contained. When Saint Antoine rises up and then hears that Old Foulon has been taken—Old Foulon "who told the famished people that they might eat grass"—a mob of ravening revenge seekers soon forms and rapidly grows (*AYR* 1: *TTC*, 2: 22:433).

This rapidly growing and rapidly escalating mob is, as Dickens fashions it, both nightmarishly terrifying and wildly exhilarating. This paradoxical rendering is not surprising. Mobs were always frightening to Dickens—but they were (as they were to Carlyle, one of Dickens' chief sources for *A Tale of Two Cities*) fascinating and liberating as well. Dickens' evocations of mobs usually exhibit this polarity and ambivalence. Think for a moment of the three mobs in *Oliver Twist*. Think, to begin with, of the first mob, a tigerish mob, "tearing, yelling, and screaming," yet at the same time a mob of good citizens doing their civic duty, a mob that shouts "Stop thief!" and pursues poor innocent Oliver (an avatar of Dickens as a boy), "terror in his looks, agony in his eye," through the unfeeling streets of London. Or think of the second mob, another tigerish mob, and yet at the same time another mob of good citizens, outraged citizens, eager that justice should prevail, ravenous to tear Fagin, "all muddy and bleeding," away from the officers who have him in charge, a mob that is, as one "horror-stricken" eyewitness puts it, "'snarling with their teeth, and making at him like wild beasts; I can see the blood upon his hair and beard, and hear the dreadful cries with which the women worked themselves into the centre of the crowd at the street corner, and swore they'd tear his heart out!'" Or think, finally, of the third mob, again a tigerish mob, a mob with the "ecstasy of madmen," "panting with impatience," lashed into "ferocity," and yet once more a mob of good citizens hungry to see justice done, a mob that roars with eager relish as brutish Sikes is cornered and then slaughtered (*BM* 2: *OT*, 1: 10:9; *BM* 5: *OT*, 3: 12:159; 163–64—in subsequent one-volume editions, chapter 50).

Or, if one were to argue that the mobs in *Oliver Twist* are atypical, think of the many mobs in *Barnaby Rudge*, mobs composed of multitudes of the befuddled, the dispossessed, and the malignant (of innocent victims such as Barnaby and Hugh—Hugh an innocent victim turned beast—and of vile, vindictive predators such as Simon and Dennis), but all, righteous and depraved alike, caught up in the contagion of the moment, in wild animalistic frenzies of pillage and destruction. The mobs of *Barnaby Rudge*, like those of *Oliver Twist*, evoke fear and fascination, empathy and revulsion in Dickens. What he sees in the mob he sees in himself, and that insight excites and disturbs him. He is the hunter, and he is the hunted. In *Oliver Twist*, in the midst of the first mob scene (with the mob in wild pursuit of Oliver), Dickens tells us directly that mobs, even mobs that are acting to uphold and enforce the law, contain dark, fearful, bestial elements. "There is," he writes, "a passion *for hunting something* deeply implanted in the human breast" (*BM* 2: *OT*, 1: 10:9).

Dickens empathized with the real grievances of raggle-taggle mobs, especially with the desperation and frustration of the downtrodden and the dispossessed. He also abandoned himself to the wild, explosive savagery, contagious savagery, that the many-headed but headless mob unlooses and also sanctions. The mob, Dickens felt, can evoke the primitive savage in man. It can also, by virtue of its many-headed headlessness, dissolve those bonds of individual responsibility that ordinarily control such tigerish impulses. (A letter that Dickens wrote while working on the riot scenes of *Barnaby Rudge* shows us how much a part of a mob—a mob he did not intellectually sympathize with—he could become. "I have just burnt into Newgate," he wrote, "and am going . . . to tear the prisoners out by the hair of their heads. . . . I feel quite smoky when I am at work" [F, 169].) But Dickens was frightened by the mob as well. It was anarchic and animalistic. It threatened the very foundations of humanity, of civilized behavior and civilized intercourse. It also threatened Dickens' precarious belief in the human and the rational (as against the bestial and the irrational) in the individual soul.

In *A Tale of Two Cities* the mob of ravening revenge-seekers thirsting for Old Foulon's blood and Old Foulon's body rapidly grows. The men in that mob are "terrible" in their "bloody-minded anger"; but "the women," like the women in *Oliver Twist,* "were a sight to chill the boldest." They poured into the streets. "They ran out with streaming hair, urging one another, and themselves, to madness with the wildest cries and actions." Other women, equally possessed, rushed to join them, "beating their breasts, tearing their hair, and screaming." These wild harpies, spinning about in a blood-thirsty frenzy, cried out, "Give us the blood of Foulon, Give us the head of Foulon, Give us the heart of Foulon, Give us the body and soul of Foulon, Rend Foulon to pieces! . . . With these cries, numbers of the women, lashed into blind frenzy, whirled about, striking and tearing at their own friends until they dropped in a passionate swoon" (*AYR* 1: *TTC*, 2: 22:433–34). This passionate cannibalistic desire to butcher and devour, this savage female appetite for blood, is not an isolated instance; that is, it is not simply a female reaction to Foulon's monstrous predations and flagrant callousness. Earlier, before the news of Foulon's capture had raced through Saint Antoine, the starving women of the district had hungered for flesh and thirsted for blood. "'To me, women!'" cries Madame Defarge. "'We can kill as well as the men' . . . And to her, with a shrill thirsty

56. The Women Cry, "Give Us the Blood of Foulon, Give Us the Head of Foulon, Give Us the Heart of Foulon, Give Us the Body and Soul of Foulon"

Note how, in this illustration, true to Dickens' conception of the scene, the bestial mob, frenzied and bloodthirsty, is urged on by wild rapacious women who dominate the foreground: Madame Defarge on the left, knife in hand; the three Harpies at the center, the foremost like a gaunt, famished death's-head; the wild Fury "with streaming hair" featured at the front (probably The Vengeance), exhorting the mob, knife in one hand, sword in the other; and the formidable drummer rounding out the right, meat cleaver raised on high. "The Sea Rises." Etching by Hablot Knight Browne ("Phiz") for Part V, Book II, Chapter XXII (October 1859) of *A Tale of Two Cities*.

cry, trooping women variously armed, but all armed alike in hunger and revenge" (*AYR* 1: *TTC*, 2: 21:411).

The thirstiest and hungriest of these thirsty and hungry women, the most vengeful and the most bloodthirsty as well, is Madame Defarge. (Remember, she keeps a wineshop—in the iconography of the book, a bloodshop. One of Madame Defarge's leading female lieutenants, mirroring her commander's ferocity, is known only as "The Vengeance." Later, in the time of the Terror, Madame Defarge and The Vengeance sit every day in their accustomed, choice seats to feast upon and to participate in the daily blood-drinking of that thirsty female saint—to continue with Dickens' imagery—Sainte Guillotine.) Madame Defarge's ferocity, relentless and bloodthirsty, has been growing and maturing for many years. She is the product of unendurable grievances. She has good reasons for being what she is and doing what she does. She embodies in her person what mobs—or at least most Dickensian mobs—embody in their corporate being. Like the mobs of *Oliver Twist* and *Barnaby Rudge,* like the mobs she leads but also follows, Madame Defarge is righteous as well as savage, aggrieved as well as wantonly destructive. However disordered her vision, however distorted her actions, she is still a rough embodiment of perceived justice in pursuit of perceived evil. She is an embodiment, in short, of human and righteous impulses become wild and savage. Dickens fully empathizes with her wounded beginnings, he can savor, even glory in, her fierce flourishings; but at the same time he views her with horror as a monstrous harpy, and he revels in her destruction.

There is no doubt that Madame Defarge's grievances are real. When she was a young girl, her sister was raped, brutalized, and finally (in effect) murdered by the Marquis (Darnay's uncle). But this is not all. In those same days her brother was killed, her brokenhearted father driven to death, her brother-in-law intentionally worked to death, and her sister's unborn child deprived of life—that is, murdered—by the selfsame Marquis. Madame Defarge proclaims this last atrocity equal to the others, an atrocity demanding, along with the others, bloody vengeance: "'That sister of the mortally wounded boy upon the ground was my sister, that husband was my sister's husband, that unborn child was their child, that brother was my brother, that father was my father, those dead are my dead, and that summons to answer for those things descends to me!'" (*AYR* 2: *TTC*, 3: 12:23).

Madame Defarge, another mother, a fierce frightening mother of the revolution, who has seen her whole family, including an innocent mother and a more than innocent child, swallowed up—mere momentary morsels to sate the Marquis' passing appetite—Madame Defarge, that fierce barren matriarch, will now devour, in turn, another innocent mother and child. Dickens points up this retributive and replicate ferocity. Lucie Manette—now Lucie Darnay—appeals to Madame Defarge as sister, wife, and mother: "'O sister-woman, think of me. As a wife and mother!'" Madame Defarge, unrelenting, contrasts Lucie's radiant conception of sanctified wifehood and beatific motherhood, their burden and their destiny, with the jungle wifehood and motherhood that she has known. "'The wives and mothers we have been used to see,'" she tells Lucie, "'since we were as little as this child [little Lucie], and much less, have not been greatly considered. . . . Is it likely that the trouble of one wife and mother would be much to us now?'" (*AYR* 1: *TTC*, 3: 3:509).

This answer, argumentative and exculpatory, is not typical of Madame Defarge. She rarely offers explanations, and she is totally unmoved by "womanly" appeals. By the time we meet her, she has nursed her wounds and grievances into furious tigerish ferocity. Indeed, she has become a tigress—the female counterpart of the tigerish Gaspard and the tigerish Marquis (other devourers and other devoured)—a calm, pitiless, bloodthirsty creature that tears, kills, mutilates, and devours. She, like her victims, is caught up in the bloody web of fate, a web she knits for an entire class, but also for herself. Dickens sees Madame Defarge as an implacable knitting Fate, a bloody, tigerish Doomstress. He tells us that "the fingers of the knitting women [Madame Defarge, The Vengeance, and others] were vicious, with the experience that they could tear" (*AYR* 1:

TTC, 2: 22:433). But most often he fashions Madame Defarge as a tigress (a creature that "could tear"), and he explains her actions in tigress terms: "Imbued from her childhood with a brooding sense of wrong, and an inveterate hatred of a class, opportunity had developed her into a tigress. She was absolutely without pity. If she had ever had the virtue in her, it had quite gone out of her." She now kills and devours, Dickens tells us, as a tigress kills and devours. She regards those she kills and feeds upon as "her natural enemies and her prey, and as such [they] had no right to live" (*AYR* 2: *TTC*, 3: 14:70). In other words, she feeds upon her chosen victims as naturally as a tiger feeds upon its prey.

We see Madame Defarge hunting, running down, and bloodily killing her prey. We see her, for example, sharp knife in hand, as part of the pride of sharp-toothed tigers that hunts down the grim old governor of the Bastille. In truth, she is the most ferocious and at the same time the most calmly calculating of that bloody band. She is, as Dickens puts it, the "one quite steady figure" in all that "passion and contention." She, too, is driven by passion, but in her the passion to love (she loved her sister, brother, father, brother-in-law, and unborn niece or nephew all too passionately) has been transformed into its nightmare opposite, into the ravening passion to kill. She remains close to her quarry, close to the torn and bleeding governor of the Bastille, "immovable close to him"—Dickens repeats this phrase five times in a single sentence—as she and her quarry progress through the streets accompanied by a howling pack that hits, beats, and stabs the hapless old officer. Finally, she pounces. At the kill, "suddenly animated," she "put her foot upon his neck, and with her cruel knife—long ready—hewed off his head" (*AYR* 1: *TTC*, 2: 21:412–13).

Madame Defarge's final predatory expedition and her death are equally tigerish. She goes off on that expedition with a "loaded pistol" in her bosom and a "sharpened dagger" at her waist. (In her hunting expeditions she always carries, often flashing in her hand, cruel and rending, a sharpened knife or sharpened dagger, sometimes an axe as well.) Deadly as a sharp-toothed sharp-clawed tigress, she moves with the supple grace of a tigress also. She makes her quiet way along the streets to hunt her prey. She moves freely, boldly, lithesomely. She moves "with the confident tread" and the "supple freedom of a woman who had habitually walked in her girl-hood, bare-foot and bare-legged" (*AYR* 2: *TTC*, 3: 14:70). In her final death-struggle with Miss Pross she is unable to use her pistol or her sharp dagger. Her struggle, instead, is more tigerlike and more primitive than her usual dagger-toothed tiger attacks. Her clawlike hands rip and mutilate her victim. Madame Defarge's "two hands . . . buffeted and tore at [Miss Pross'] face." Indeed, Madame Defarge mauls and rends Miss Pross' entire body. Her hair is torn, her dress "clutched and dragged a hundred ways," her countenance a bleeding mask: "for the marks of griping fingers were deep in her face" (*AYR* 2: *TTC*, 3: 14:73).

This is only one tigerish encounter, albeit the last, in Madame Defarge's long, fierce predatory career. Throughout the novel we see her biding her time, waiting for her chance, and then springing into deadly action. She has an insatiable appetite for bodies and for blood. Toward the end of the novel even Defarge, stalwart husband to his tigerish mate, is not savage and vindictive enough for her bloodthirsty cravings. He is willing to let the innocent Dr. Manette go. She is not, and she contrives (at the last minute and behind his back) to assure that all the Manettes and all the Darnays will be fed to the insatiable guillotine. This greedy desire for blood and more blood leads directly to her death. But for Madame Defarge, shed-ding the blood of her sworn enemies (ravagers of her kith and kin) is more important than preserving her own life. She is fearless. She is also iron-willed and implacable. Her vengeful mission in life—it is her sole mission and her sole obsession—is to atone for blood with blood. However, an eye for an eye and a tooth for a tooth is not enough for Madame Defarge: only many eyes for one eye and many teeth for one tooth will sate her appetite for revenge. When she expresses her dismay at the thought that even one Ma-nette or one Darnay—even one small Darnay child—might escape the monstrous maw of the guillotine, Jacques Three, her counterpart in vengeful savagery, and another greedy devotee of the guillotine, proves his allegiance to her and the guillotine (Madame Defarge is an embodiment of the guillotine—Sainte Guillotine is a female devourer), by echoing her bloodthirsty resolve.[41] "'That must never be'" he says; "'no one must escape. We have not half enough [guillotined each day] as it is. We ought to have six score a day'" (*AYR* 2: *TTC*, 3: 14:69).

But this is much later, at the height of the Terror. Now, with Old Foulon at bay, the mob is just beginning to feel its power, whet its appetite, and gain its prey. When the mob finally takes Foulon, it tears him and batters him and mauls him. Then, all the roaring creatures of the mob, men and women alike, prepare to kill their quarry and feast upon the grisly remnants. These frenzied men and women, sensing the end, attracted by the thought of fresh-killed carrion, sweep down upon Foulon "like birds of prey." Then Madame Defarge, taking charge for a short interval, lets Foulon go for a moment, "as a cat might have done to a mouse." Finally the savage crowd, men and women alike, kill him, cut off his head, place it on a pike, stuff his mouth with grass, and dance like frenzied cannibals about the bloody remains (*AYR* 1: *TTC*, 2: 22:434). As for Foulon's son-in-law, another arrogant feeder on the poor, Saint Antoine "set his head and heart on pikes, and carried the three spoils of the day, in Wolf-procession through the streets" (*AYR* 1: *TTC*, 2: 22:434). This savage "Wolf-procession" proceeds in raucous triumph. Then these ravenous creatures, downtrodden men and subjugated women, displaying their grisly trophies, their "stomachs faint and empty" from their long frenzy of pent-up killing and butchering, embrace and prepare for their repast: "Slender fires were made in the streets, at which neighbours cooked in common, afterwards supping at their doors" (*AYR* 1: *TTC*, 2: 22:435).

In boyhood, in the *Terrific Register*, in "The Furies of the Guillotine," Dickens had read about wild cannibalistic female revolutionaries, fierce and depraved, who paraded with their grisly trophies through the bloody streets of Paris. These frenzied women, violent and dangerous, "headed processions where the bleeding heads of butchered innocence were carried in triumph; they assisted at the savage feasts where the hearts of victims of loyalty and honour were served up roasted, and were devoured as the most delicious morsels" (*TR* 1: 772). Given Dickens' sensitivities—given his deep emotional obsession with cannibalism, given his cannibalistic fantasies concerning fierce, empowered women (especially fierce, empowered mothers), given the way the *Terrific Register* purveyed to these and similar sensitivities (conflicted sensitivities) over and over again—it is no wonder that Dickens bought and avidly read each weekly issue of the magazine, and this despite the fact that it made him "unspeakably miserable," "frightening" his "very wits out of [his] head." Finally, it is no wonder that the *Terrific Register* creeps into his writings so often, so darkly, and so powerfully.

In many of the scenes depicted here and in many of the passages quoted, the cannibalistic suggestions are strong and fierce; in others they are more muted and oblique; and in still others they are barely perceptible, hidden and subliminal murmurings. One may wonder at times how conscious Dickens was of his cannibalistic orchestrations. But this question is answered—and answered largely on the side of consciousness—not only by his intricate use of such images and allusions, not only by his artful repetition, development, and counterpointing of them, not only by his strong structural and integrative deployment of them, but by his frequent habit of signaling the reader: hinting, suggesting, alluding, and then finally revealing—openly stating and confirming—that ferocious cannibalism is being and has been depicted.

A good example in *A Tale of Two Cities* is Jacques Three. One of the more frightening revolutionary leaders of Saint Antoine, a confederate and subordinate of Defarge, Jacques Three is introduced to us on the occasion of the broken cask of wine. He enters the novel, therefore, when the Defarges and the populace of France do, and he makes his contribution to the meaning of Saint Antoine—that is, to the meaning of the spilled wine and the devouring crowd, and to the meaning of the developing appetite for revolution, the growing thirst for revenge, the growing hunger for tiger remedies (these are Dickens' metaphors) and all that follows.

Un petit Souper, a la Parisiènne:—or—A Family of Sans-Culotts refreshing, after the fatigues of the day

57. A French Family Refreshing Itself in a Cannibalistic Frenzy—The Retribution of "The Terror"

Note how the child being basted as it roasts on the fire resembles adults being basted as they roast on the fire in Fox's *Book of Martyrs,* and note how the children on the floor in the foreground gorging on human entrails resemble the dog on the floor in the foreground gorging on human entrails in Hogarth's "The Reward of Cruelty," works that had impressed Dickens mightily from childhood on (see text and figures 45, 46, and 18). Dickens also knew this ferocious Gillray caricature; it was in his folio volume of Gillray's collected works. These and still other graphic renditions of bestial cannibalistic feeding (French and non-French) contributed to *A Tale of Two Cities.* "Un petit Soupèr, a la Parisiènne:—or—A Family of Sans-Culotts refreshing, after the fatigues of the day." Caricature (1792) by James Gillray.

181

At first Jacques Three seems innocuous enough. In his initial flourish on the stage we barely glimpse him: he appears only briefly; he is not described; and he makes one short comment. But just before he makes this comment, he drinks the last drops of his wine. Then, "he put down his empty drinking vessel and smacked his lips." "'Ah!'" he says, speaking of the broken cask and the unaccustomed taste of wine that the "miserable beasts" of Saint Antoine have just had, "'A bitter taste it is that such poor cattle always have in their mouths'" (*AYR* 1: *TTC*, 1: 5:51). This is all, and we are likely to take this brief appearance as little more than a passing embodiment of picturesque local color and simple social concern. But, unknown to us (though carefully calculated by Dickens), Jacques Three's fierce lust for human blood has just been revealed to us: he finishes off his vessel of wine (blood), smacks his lips, and talks of mouths, taste, and beasts. In subsequent appearances these stigmata recur in ever more sinister guise. The next time we see Jacques Three— much later in the novel—we notice that his "agitated hand" is "always gliding over the network of fine nerves about his mouth and nose" (*AYR* 1: *TTC*, 2: 15:315), and this gesture, or rather variations and incremental repetitions of this gesture, begin to define our awareness of the man and to guide our appraisal of his significance.

We soon notice that Jacques Three has other attributes besides the hand that wanders about and into his mouth. He has sinister yearnings. He has "a strikingly greedy air, as if he hungered for something—that was neither food nor drink." He also has a "craving air"; indeed, he is now "the man with the restless hand and the craving air." Dickens emphasizes "greedy" Jacques Three's "restless hand" and "craving air" at the very time that he has Jacques Three, intense and vindictive, describe how, years before, in the streets of Paris, the aristocrats (or rather their agents) slowly and ceremoniously tore two legs and an arm off a condemned prisoner while a vast concourse of people—including, most particularly, a "crowd of ladies of quality and fashion . . . full of eager attention to the last"— looked on hour after hour (*AYR* 1: *TTC*, 2: 15:315).

That Dickens should imbue this scene with the cannibalistic cravings of Jacques Three, and more particularly with the depraved appetites of "ladies of quality and fashion," is most significant, for his earliest source for the scene, and undoubtedly his most emotionally memorable and influential source, was the *Terrific Register,* yet the *Terrific Register* version contains neither cannibalistic implications nor ladies "full of eager attention" watching as the prisoner is tortured and then slowly torn limb from limb. (A later source, Louis-Sébastien Mercier, does mention that some women watched the spectacle avidly.) In other words, Dickens imposes the cannibalistic hungerings and cravings upon the scene—partly to suit the particular propensities of Jacques Three, partly to accord with the larger weavings of *A Tale of Two Cities* (institutionalized butcherings, pent-up retributions, bloodthirsty women, and so on), partly owing to his own lifelong proclivities, partly on a hint from Mercier, and partly in obeisance to old associations—to the savage dismemberments and the equally savage cannibalism (the two often combined) of the *Terrific Register,* his compelling childhood source.

In *A Tale of Two Cities* the account of the butchered prisoner—an account of Robert-François Damiens' execution in 1757—is introduced when the road mender tells Defarge, Jacques Three, and the other Jacques what he heard whispered by Monseigneur's villagers concerning the captured Gaspard and his fate:

"They even whisper that because he has slain Monseigneur, and because Monseigneur was the father of his tenants—serfs—what you will—he will be executed as a parricide. One old man says at the fountain, that his right hand, armed with the knife, will be burnt off before his face; that, into wounds which will be made in his arms, his breast, and his legs, there will be poured boiling oil, melted lead, hot resin, wax, and sulphur; finally, that he will be torn limb from limb by four strong horses. That old man says, all this was actually done to a prisoner who made an attempt on the life of the last King, Louis Fifteen. But how do I know if he lies? I am not a scholar."

"Listen once again then, Jacques!" said [Jacques Three] the man with the restless hand and the craving air. "The name of that prisoner was Damiens, and it was all done in open day, in the open streets of this city of Paris; and nothing was more noticed in the vast concourse that saw it done, than the crowd of ladies of quality and fashion, who were full of eager attention to the last—to the last, Jacques, prolonged until night-fall, when he had lost two legs and an arm, and still breathed!" (*AYR* 1: *TTC*, 2: 15:315)

The story of Damiens was the first article and the first woodcut (a front-page woodcut) in the first issue of the *Terrific Register.* Al-though the text in the *Terrific Register* does not say that Damiens' right hand when it was burned off was "armed with the knife" (the weapon of attack in his case, as in Gaspard's), the woodcut does show Damiens, as Dickens describes him, knife in hand. The other details (with the exceptions already noted) are in the *Terrific Regis-ter* version; indeed, they are in that version in more explicit and re-volting form than in *A Tale of Two Cities.* Here (shorn of Damiens' horrifying self-perusals of his wounds and a few other grotesque details) is Damiens' execution as recounted in the *Terrific Register:*

> The executioner burnt his right hand (with which the villanous stab had been given) in flames of brimstone; during which operation Damiens gave a very loud and continued cry . . . The executioner then proceeded to pinch him in the arms, thighs, and breast, with red-hot pinchers; and Damiens, at every pinch, shrieked in the same manner as he had done when his hand was scorched with the brimstone . . . Then boiling oil, melted wax and rosin, and melted lead, were poured into all the wounds, except those on the breast: which made him give as loud shrieks and cries, as he had done before when his hand was burnt with sulphur, and his breast, arms, and thighs, torn with hot pinchers. (*TR* 1: 2)

The first part of Damiens' torment (stipulated in his sentencing) concludes with these shrieks and these barbarities; the second part (also stipulated) now commences. The *Terrific Register* describes the slow, agonizing process of fixing ropes around Damiens' muti-lated and harrowed arms and legs so that those limbs could be torn from his body. Then, for over an hour, "four stout, young, and vig-orous horses" strained against Damiens' limbs, "stretching his joints to a prodigious length," but the horses were unable to rip the

THE

TERRIFIC REGISTER;

Or, Record

OF CRIMES, JUDGMENTS, PROVIDENCES, AND CALAMITIES.

DREADFUL EXECUTION OF DAMIENS FOR ATTEMPTING TO
ASSASSINATE LOUIS XV. KING OF FRANCE.

THIS unhappy man, who fell a victim to his fanatical spirit, or the temporary influence of insanity, for it is doubtful which instigated him to the commission of the crime, was a native of St. Pol, a village in France. He had for some months meditated the assassination of the king, and was only prevented by circumstances from putting it into execution before. On the afternoon of the 5th of January, 1757, his majesty was stepping into his coach at Versailles, when Damiens, who had concealed himself at the bottom of the stairs, rushed forwards and stabbed him at the fifth rib. Damiens, instead of endeavouring to escape, which he might have done in the confusion, remained with his hat on, which the king observing, gave him into custody. He soon underwent the most agonizing tortures to induce him to confess his accomplices, and he handed over a list, which he afterwards owned to be false. He was tried on the 25th of March, and the following day being Sunday, he was ordered to be executed on the 28th.

VOL. I.   1

---

58. Images from Boyhood: Damiens Is
Butchered Before an Attentive Crowd

With the exception of two innovations, both with cannibalistic overtones (see text), Dickens' account (in *A Tale of Two Cities*) of Damiens' frightful execution is a faithful recapitulation of the *Terrific Register* account. "Dreadful Execution Of Damiens For Attempting To Assassinate Louis XV. King Of France." First page of the first issue of the *Terrific Register* (1824).

arms and legs from the body. Hereupon the officials ordered that
Damiens' "principal sinews" be cut "as night was coming on, and
it was desirable that the execution should be accomplished before
the day was over." The *Terrific Register* concludes its account of the
"dreadful execution" as follows:

> The sinews being cut, the horses began to draw anew, and after several
> pulls, a thigh and arm were torn from the body. Damiens looked at his
> several members, and had some remains of sense after the other thigh
> was pulled; nor did he expire, till the other arm was likewise torn away.
> As soon as there was no appearance of life left, the trunk and dismem-
> bered quarters were thrown into a large blazing pile of wood, erected for
> that purpose near the scaffold, where they continued burning till seven
> o'clock the next morning, and afterwards his ashes were, according to
> the sentence of the court of parliament, scattered in the air. (*TR* 1: 3)

This is the sickening account that Dickens read and reread as a
horrified boy. This is the unimaginable spectacle that Dickens,
thirty-five years later, had the "crowd of ladies of quality and fashion
. . . full of eager attention to the last," gaze at hour after hour. And
this is the gruesome story (in Dickens' version) that the road
mender (later transformed into a wood sawyer) tells and that
Jacques Three confirms. It is Jacques Three who adds the detail
about the eager ladies, and it is he who throughout the telling exhibits a growing excitement, beginning with "his agitated hand always gliding over the network of fine nerves about his mouth and
nose," continuing with "his fingers ever wandering over and over
those fine nerves, with a strikingly greedy air, as if he hungered for
something," and culminating when "the hungry man gnawed one
of his fingers . . . and his finger quivered with the craving that was
on him" (*AYR* 1: *TTC*, 2: 15:315–16).

Jacques Three begins to gnaw his finger after the account of Damiens' execution is concluded and the account of Gaspard's execution is begun. This is Dickens' way of linking the distant past
(Damiens) with the recent past (Gaspard) and with cannibalistic
atrocities yet to come. In this linking, Jacques Three, with his rest-

less hand, his craving air, and his greedy hunger for vengeful butcherings yet to be, plays a crucial and terrifying role. As the linking
continues, Dickens' cannibalistic sketching and Jacques Three's
meaning grow more and more distinct. When the road mender tells
Defarge and his lieutenants (including Jacques Three) how Gaspard
was hanged forty feet high above the village fountain and left to
rot there, poisoning the water, "The hungry man [Jacques Three]
gnawed one of his fingers as he looked at the other three [compan-
ions], and his finger quivered with the craving that was on him"
(*AYR* 1: *TTC,* 2: 15: 315–16). After hearing the road mender's
ghastly tale, Defarge declares that the St. Evrémondes are "doomed
to destruction." " 'Magnificent!' croaked the man with the craving."
Then Defarge amplifies. He explains that the St. Evrémonde "château, and all the race," are to be wiped out. "Extermination" is the
decree. Upon hearing this, "The hungry man repeated, in a raptur-
ous croak, 'Magnificent!' and began gnawing another finger" (*AYR*
1: *TTC,* 2: 15:316).

Much later, Jacques Three begins gnawing in good earnest.
Toward the end of the novel, the Reign of Terror in full swing, he
sits on the jury that is trying Charles Darnay. At this point Dickens
makes Jacques Three's cannibalism, which has been emerging ever
more prominently as the novel unfolds, adding meaning and definition to the other depictions and suggestions of cannibalism that
abound in the novel—the thirsty blood-drinking of Saint Antoine,
the tigerish predations of the Marquis, the frenzied butcherings of
the mob, and all the rest—at this late point in the novel, Dickens
makes Jacques Three's cannibalism explicit. When Dickens describes
Jacques Three sitting in the midst of his fellow jurymen, it is hard
to miss his hungry cannibalism—indeed, Dickens now names it cannibalism outright—and it is hard to miss the immediate and the
larger significance of his long-abetted (socially abetted) and long-
whetted (socially whetted) appetite for human fare. Even the random spectators, diverse products of the same conditioning (and varied exhibitors of the same hunger), recognize and savor Jacques
Three's cannibalistic cravings: "Eager and prominent among [the

jurymen], one man with a craving face, and his fingers perpetually hovering about his lips, whose appearance gave great satisfaction to the spectators. A life-thirsting, cannibal-looking, bloody-minded juryman, the Jacques Three of Saint Antoine." Jacques Three may be life-thirsting and cannibal-looking, but he is not unique, and he is not an aberration; he is one of many, and he, like the many, has been created by the abominations of the past, by the Damiens, the Gaspards, and the Monseigneurs. All Jacques Three's fellow jurymen, for example, lust as he lusts. Dickens depicts "the whole jury, as a jury of dogs empannelled to try the deer" (*AYR* 1: *TTC*, 3: 9:604–5).

After this outright identification, Jacques Three's insatiable hunger for human flesh and human blood is unmitigated and undisguised. When we next see him, once more "with his cruel fingers at his hungry mouth," we know what to expect, and we are not disappointed. A few moments later Jacques Three is envisioning (and savoring) the guillotining of Lucie: "'She has a fine head for it,' croaked Jacques Three. 'I have seen blue eyes and golden hair there, and they looked charming when Samson held them up.' Ogre that he was, he spoke like an epicure." This vision of Henri Samson, the executioner, displaying Lucie's bloody head whets Jacques Three's ogreish and epicurean appetite: "'The child also,' observed Jacques Three, with a meditative enjoyment of his words, 'has golden hair and blue eyes. And we seldom have a child there. It is a pretty sight!'" (*AYR* 2: *TTC*, 3: 14:69).

With these scenes of Jacques Three, "Ogre that he was," reveling in his epicure's taste for blue-eyed, golden-haired female flesh and blue-eyed, golden-haired children's blood, his role in *A Tale of Two Cities* comes to an end. We see now that his smacking his lips over a vessel of wine (vessel of blood) and his talk of mouths and taste and miserable beasts—the unobtrusive and seemingly innocent appetites and commendable social concerns that accompanied him when he first entered the novel—are all of a piece with his development and with this ferocious exit from the novel smacking his lips over severed heads and children's blood.

In such instances, Dickens is both attracted and repelled by what he is creating. He hovers close and he pulls away; but he does not desist—he cannot desist. He is drawn over and over again to conjure up these cannibalistic nightmares, nightmares filled with the equivocal yet engendering energy of attraction and repulsion, an energy that had its formative shaping in his earliest days. Elsewhere in the novel, compelled by the same engendering energy, we find other ogres who exhibit strange cannibalistic appetites, and who, like Jacques Three, seem to have a special relish for young mothers and their young children—a favorite dish (a childhood-engendered dish) on the Dickens menu.

The road mender is such an ogre, fierce and threatening, and he too has a well-developed craving for young mothers and their children. Trained by Monsieur and Madame Defarge to hunger for and then to savor his prey, he has learned his lesson well. He is now a wood sawyer, and thus metamorphosed from bent-back laborer to sharp-toothed ripper and cutter, he keeps a miserable little shop hard by La Force Prison, the prison in which Darnay is incarcerated. One day the wood sawyer sees Lucie accompanied by little Lucie loitering nearby, a loitering that soon becomes a daily ritual. She loiters there so that Darnay may occasionally catch a glimpse of her (and whoever accompanies her). The wood sawyer is delighted. After enquiring if Lucie and little Lucie are mother and daughter (the wood sawyer is in league with Madame Defarge and knows more than he lets on), he tells them:

> "Ah! But it's not my business. My work is my business. See my saw! I call it my Little Guillotine. La, la, la; La, la, la! And off his head comes!"
> The billet fell as he spoke, and he threw it into a basket.

This sadistic little gnome, crooning "La, la, la!" before mother and child, and tossing metaphoric heads into a basket—giving the two Lucies a graphic glimpse of how Darnay's severed head will soon be tossed into a similar basket—this bloodthirsty gnome can hardly contain his anticipation and his glee. A moment later, like some jocose cannibal-demon in a terrifying fairy tale, he outdoes his sadism and his gleeful anticipation:

> "I call myself the Samson of the firewood guillotine. See here again! Loo, loo, loo; Loo, loo, loo! And off *her* head comes! Now, a child. Tickle, tickle; Pickle, pickle! And off *its* head comes. All the family!"
>
> Lucie shuddered as he threw two more billets into his basket. (*AYR* 1: *TTC,* 3: 5:532)

Thenceforth Lucie propitiates this savage gnome with drink money, an offering he readily accepts, thus turning his appetite for severed heads and butchered bodies into welcome drink. This thirsty and bloodthirsty wood sawyer is propitiated momentarily by this offering, but there is no doubt as to the true nature of his thirst and the true import of his allegiance. Just as he formerly paid worshipful, even fearful, homage to that implacable and insatiable goddess, Madame Defarge (he still does), he now pays worshipful homage to a new goddess—or rather a new embodiment of the old goddess—the guillotine. He stations his saw (yet another avatar of his new-old goddess and patron saint) in his miserable little shop window, and he inscribes that sharp-toothed provider "his 'Little Sainte Guillotine,'" for, as Dickens goes on to explain, "the great sharp female was by that time popularly canonised" (*AYR* 1: *TTC,* 3: 5:532).

Humor (in this case macabre humor) and the grotesque allowed Dickens, as here with the wood sawyer and his Little Sainte Guillotine, to give full vent to his darker emotions. There are innumerable examples in his writings of how this works. Take, for instance—take yet again—that recurrent icon, his emotion-engendered image of mother and child. Without the screen of humor or the grotesque (or other screening techniques), he can, and does, present us with saintly mothers and angelic children—with Lucie and her daughter, for instance—and he surrounds such pictures with a warm halo of glowing sentiment and idealization. Here all is sweetness and perfection. Love reigns supreme, good feelings are unalloyed, emotions are undivided. Through such idealized icons he could indulge his need for worshipful adoration, ministering angels, and unending bliss to his heart's content.[42] By employing humor and/or the grotesque (or still other disarming techniques or combinations of techniques) he could effect far different indulgences. He could vent his anger and rage; he could kill and dismember and devour that mother and child (to continue with our example), and do so with demonic gusto and glee. These brutal actions and emotions are not Dickens'—or so, at least on the surface, it may appear to the author and to the reader—they are Jacques Three's or the wood sawyer's or the mob's. So screened, Dickens was able to savor the full indulgence of such emotions even while he disapproved of them and arraigned them. He is doing here with mother and child, using two different modes, what he does elsewhere in the novel with other divided responses using a single mode (he uses similar techniques in many other works): he segregates the two responses—the approved response and the forbidden one—and thus segregated, he indulges them both.

To cite just one example (elaborated and analyzed in "Dickens and Passion," Part 2 of this book), Dickens segregates using a single mode—that is, eschewing humor or the grotesque—with Charles Darnay and Sydney Carton, both of whom love the angelic Lucie. Darnay is an evocation of approved, decorous, sanctified married love; Carton, his dark double, an evocation of forbidden, dangerous, unmarried love, but cleansed finally of its wickedness and dross by heroism, renunciation, and self-immolation. Through such dualities, whether achieved by employing different modes or other segregating or regenerating techniques, Dickens can indulge his ideal dream of felicity, and he can also indulge (safely indulge) his forbidden, guilt-laden, self-condemned longings and aggressions.

In *A Tale of Two Cities,* as so often in Dickens, cannibalism becomes a supreme evocation of aggression and depravity. The chief personifications of cannibalism in *A Tale of Two Cities,* all so different yet so similar, are Madame Defarge, the Marquis, Jacques Three, the wood sawyer, the mob, and the guillotine. As with so many of Dickens' cannibalistic portraits—Jacques Three, for example—it may seem at first that the gleeful wood sawyer (our present illustration) is simply aggressive or sadistic, that Dickens did not conceive him as a cannibal and did not connect him to the thronging cannibalistic motifs of the novel. But as the metaphors, associations, and connotations accumulate, and as they become more pointed, we are forced at last (as we were with Jacques Three) into full realization: with the wood sawyer Dickens is bringing us face to face once more with fiendish cannibalism; that is, he is confronting us once more with his most succinct and emotion-fraught embodiment of childhood fear and childhood rage, but also, enlarged now and generalized, with his most condensed embodiment of profound societal savagery and fierce, devouring hegemony.

The wood sawyer's cannibalism (like society's) was long in the making. Born a mere laboring hind, a lowly, slaving road mender, he is taught at mid-life to recognize and crave his true prey. Years later, reincarnated as an industrious wood sawyer, a disciple of Madame Defarge (his erstwhile trainer) and a worshipper of his sharp-toothed saw (Madame Defarge and sharp-toothed saw are two evocations of Sainte Guillotine), he gleefully cuts off metaphorical heads, the wooden billets tossed into his basket, that bring him—that are—his food and drink. All this can be traced back, traced back ineluctably, to the time before the wood sawyer (or at least to the time before *this* wood sawyer), before even the naive road mender (or at least before *this* naive road mender, so strangely and so meaningfully transformed), was brought upon the scene, to the time at the very outset of the novel, years before the revolution, when we were first introduced to France and to Saint Antoine, the time when red wine (red blood) first ran in the streets of that quarter and when its famished residents greedily lapped it up and then chewed and licked the wine-soaked staves. We realize with something of a shock that one of those famished drinkers of blood so long ago was also a wood sawyer, a wood sawyer whose hands, when he went back to his sawing, "left red marks on the billets." And we realize with even more of a shock that another famished drinker in those long-vanished days was a nursing mother who pulled a ragged handkerchief from her head, dipped it into the wine, squeezed the ruddy drops into her infant's mouth, and then anointed her own forehead with the selfsame bloody sign: "the forehead of the woman who nursed her baby, was stained with the stain of the old rag she wound about her head again" (*AYR* 1: *TTC*, 1: 5:49).

Now, years later, in the grim shadow of La Force, in the presence of another mother and child, Lucie and her child (blood-engulfed and threatened with a bloody end), in the presence of another wood sawyer, but somehow the same wood sawyer, a fierce, frightening, gleeful wood sawyer (the billets with the "red marks" now horribly transformed into severed heads being merrily tossed into a waiting basket), at this late point in the novel, in a chapter titled "The Wood-Sawyer," the wood sawyer's long-growing and increasingly open appetite for human fare—he has been well trained by the blood-aggrieved and blood-hungry Defarges—at this climactic point in the novel the wood sawyer's cannibalistic appetite (like the cannibalistic appetite of the nation) culminates. This culmination occurs (in narrative sequence but not in time) immediately after we hear the wood sawyer crooning joyfully over his sharp-toothed saw, his firewood guillotine, and his obscene basket of billet-heads.

The occasion of this culmination is the wild, frenzied singing and dancing of the Carmagnole. We catch sight of that tumultuous dance as it spills into the area between the prison and the wood sawyer's shop; Lucie, and later her father, witness the terrifying spectacle from the doorway of that sinister, guillotine-haunted shop. The dance is danced by five hundred people who are pouring through the streets "dancing like five thousand demons" to no other music than their own singing. They dance like some wild tribe of celebrants; they dance a dance "gone raving mad." They dance around Lucie; they dance "with their heads low down and their hands high up." They spin, swoop, and scream; they "struck, clutched, and tore." They dance as though "delivered over to all devilry"; they dance in a "slough of blood and dirt." They dance and dance, and still they dance; they dance until they drop (*AYR* 1: *TTC*, 3: 5:532).

This infernal dance has no leaders; indeed, we recognize only two persons in all this devilish throng—The Vengeance and the wood sawyer, "hand in hand." Dickens is describing a primitive rite: a group of frenzied savages, of demonic cannibals, dancing with bestial abandon, some dancing in hungry anticipation of ferocious cannibal feasting yet to come, others dancing in surfeited conclusion to bloody cannibal feasting just indulged in. There is no doubt of this. "They danced," Dickens tells us, conjuring up a nightmare vision of ravening ferocity incarnate, "They danced . . . keeping a ferocious time that was like a gnashing of teeth in unison" (*AYR* 1: *TTC*, 3: 5:532).

The germ of this scene probably goes back to Dickens' boyhood reading in the *Terrific Register*, for there, in "The Furies of the Guillotine," an article that also seems to have contributed much to Dickens' conception of Madame Defarge and The Vengeance and to his depiction of frenzied bands of bloodthirsty revolutionary women, we find the following passage: "The Furies of the Guillotine finished the labour of the day by forming a ring round the scaffold, dancing in the blood, and forcing every woman who happened to pass to join in the dance for half an hour or longer, to the tune of the 'Carmagnole,' of 'Ca Ira,' of the 'Marseillois Hymn,' or other cannibal and revolutionary airs" (*TR* 1: 773). Dickens, always sensitive to cannibalistic associations, and preternaturally sensitive to powerful cannibalistic women, would not have forgotten this infernal vision of ferocious women "dancing in . . . blood" to wild "cannibal . . . airs."

Creations such as Jacques Three, the wood sawyer, the dancing mob, and their many counterparts (and especially the early hints and subtleties and the later growths and flowerings in such creations) should alert us once more to the intricate and conflicted refinement of Dickens' art. Dickens was sensitive to the most subliminal nuances of his carefully crafted language, and he was supersensitive to the resonant and often contending nuances of his cannibalistic imaginings. Given these sensitivities and the emotions they generated and reflected, given the fact that cannibalistic images

and motifs were part of his innermost being from his earliest days—
part of his deepest fascinations and his deepest fears—it is not
surprising that he used such images and motifs to create, suggest,
emphasize, convey, and unify, and that he did so, often, in conflicted
and ambivalent ways. It is not surprising either that Madame Defarge, the archetypal female devourer in *A Tale of Two Cities* and a
mother of the revolution—a mother who is both deeply aggrieved
and brutally aggressive—is slaughtered in the end, a slaughtering
that satisfied Dickens emotionally (it fulfilled deep, forbidden childhood fantasies) and also served his fictional purposes.

Jacques Three, Madame Defarge, and the wood sawyer help us
see how calculated and self-conscious Dickens' peripheral and central uses of cannibalism were, but they also help us assess—more
vividly and graphically assess—some of the central meanings of *A
Tale of Two Cities*. The ferocious delight that these three and others
take in the gory depredations of the bloody guillotine remind us
that by the end of the novel a terrible transformation has convulsed
and engulfed France. What might have been an abstraction has become a nightmare reality. The gruesome appetite such characters
exhibit, a depraved appetite for bloody heads, particularly for
bloody heads of people we have come to know—heads of angelic
young mothers and innocent young children, heads with golden
hair and pure blue eyes, heads butchered now (if Madame Defarge's
will is done), brutally severed, and held up all horrible with dripping
blood—their relish for such obscenities, and Madame Defarge's insistence upon them, make the terrible transformation that has engulfed France personal and savage and real.

But Jacques Three and the wood-sawyer are only two notes in
Dickens' orchestration of cannibalism, and Madame Defarge is only
a third. Dickens did not want us to view such cannibalism as the
sickening province of one crazed man or one vengeful woman, or
even as the province of a group of bloody-minded conspirators.
With the coming of the Terror, the savage butchering and devouring that had begun as a kind of symbolic miming at the outset
of the novel has not only become real in such men as Jacques Three

and such women as Madame Defarge (the latter character Dickens' embodiment of retributive fate, and his would-be surrogate killer of mother and child), but has become institutionalized in a new and terrible way; it has turned into an ever-present nightmare horror, a murderous monster—the sharp-toothed Guillotine—glorified, sanctified, even deified, by the new state and devouring its daily dinner of human lives. The terrors of the past have sired the terrors of the present; the terrible afflictions of the old state have generated the terrible afflictions of the new one. The bloody gallows forty feet high that poisoned the waters and forced the thirsty peasants to sup on death has turned into the thirsty maw of death itself, the bloody guillotine, glutting on the old order, the voracious aristocrats and oppressors—but glutting also on the wretched and the poor. The blood-red wine that flowed so long ago in the stony streets of Saint Antoine, the blood-red wine that was lapped up so thirstily by the famished residents of that impoverished quarter has now become a deeper color and flows more copiously and widely yet. The thirsty residents of Saint Antoine, the hungry peasants of the Marquis' little village, and the thirsty and hungry residents of all the other city quarters and village precincts of France have fashioned a thirsty monster, a savage female monster (sharp-toothed avatar of sharp-daggered Madame Defarge), more terrible and more insatiable than their own gaunt selves, however hungry for butchering and however thirsty for blood:

> Every day, through the stony streets, the tumbrils now jolted heavily, filled with Condemned. Lovely girls; bright women, brown-haired, black-haired, and grey; youths; stalwart men and old; gentle born and peasant born; all red wine for La Guillotine, all daily brought into light from the dark cellars of the loathsome prisons, and carried to her through the streets to slake her devouring thirst. Liberty, equality, fraternity, or death;—the last, much the easiest to bestow, O Guillotine! (*AYR* 1: *TTC*, 3: 5:531)

With the guillotine's "devouring thirst" for "red wine," spilled once more in the "stony street," we have come full circle. Cannibal-

HORRORS OF THE FRENCH REVOLUTION.

The following narrative of the atrocious massacres in the prisons in Paris, planned by Danton and his associates, on the night of the 30th and 31st of August, 1793, and known as the work of the Septemberizers, is extracted from "The History of the French Revolution," lately written by M. Thiers and M. Bodin:—

Three years before, a person named Maillard figured at the head of the band of women who marched to Versailles on the famous 5th of October. This Maillard was a bailiff by occupation; in mind intelligent; in disposition, sanguinary; and, since the unquiet times of the revolution, had left every man at large to exert his own influence, without any control or impediment, he had collected together a band of ignorant and low-born associates, who were prepared for every desperate undertaking. He himself was captain of this band: and, if we may credit a discovery which transpired so long a time after the event it refers to, he was employed by Danton and his party in the execution of the most atrocious cruelties. He was ordered to place himself in a situation best calculated to effect his dire intention; to prepare instruments of death; to take every precaution to stifle the cries of his victims · and to have vinegar, holly-brooms, lime, and covered carriages in readiness for all those purposes.

On the 3rd of September, the ministers assembled at the hotel of the marine department only waited for Danton, to hold their Council. The whole city was on tiptoe. Terror reigned in the prisons. The Royal Family, to whom every noise seemed menace, anxiously demanded the cause of so much agitation. The gaolers of the several prisons appeared struck with consternation. He who had the care of the Abbaye sent away his wife and children in the morning. Dinner was served to the prisoners two hours before the accustomed time; and all the knives were taken from their plates. Alarmed at these circumstances, the victims demanded the cause with importunity, but

VOL. II. 9J

59. Drinking the Wine That Is Blood

As a boy Dickens read this account of how savage French mobs, drinking wine and "panting" for blood, led by "the blood-thirsty butcher," Maillard, slaughtered and butchered in wild frenzies, swirling triumphantly through the streets with their grisly trophies—gory heads and bloody hearts—raised on high. The accompanying illustration, which undoubtedly horrified and engrossed Dickens, depicts one such orgy of drinking and butchering. It also depicts an allied episode (also recounted in the article) that showed how a loving, Lucie-like daughter saved her father from the cannibal mob by drinking the red wine of the revolution, "a goblet full of blood." "'Drink,' said they, 'drink the blood of the aristocrats!'" In *A Tale of Two Cities* Dickens makes this theme of blood drinking—figurative blood drinking and literal blood drinking—central to the revolution. "Horrors Of The French Revolution." From the *Terrific Register* (1824–25).

ism, once hardly a whisper of things to come, now reigns supreme in France. It reigns deified and frightful. It reigns as a bloody female saint, devouring embodiment of France, the ravenous Sainte Guillotine. In scenes such as these, cannibalism flourishes boldly and openly at the glaring center of the novel; elsewhere it lingers obscurely at the dark edges and drear margins of the work. This is Dickens' way. Cannibalism emerges in the great open reaches and in the tiny, hidden crannies of *A Tale of Two Cities*. It emerges there as it emerges in so many of Dickens' works, sometimes summoned up to bear witness and enforce meaning; sometimes rising up willy-nilly, with the old unplumbed and unassuaged rage, fear, and fascination of childhood; sometimes emerging partly summoned, partly unbidden. *A Tale of Two Cities* is filled with that rage, fear, and fascination, with that dark new-old stain, the ever-emerging stain (ever-emerging for Dickens) of cannibalism—with tigerish matriarchs, dismembered parents, butchered children, hungry corpse fishers, ravenous corpse eaters, and the like. These nightmare visions, cannibalistic visions, are conflicted and emotion-fraught, yet in this novel Dickens usually uses them in ways that are controlled and self-aware, ways that accord with his sense of history and that serve his perceived moral and fictional purposes.[43]

In *A Tale of Two Cities* cannibalism helped Dickens structure, convey, and then profoundly realize—imaginatively realize—his central vision of social depravity and social retribution, of refined tigerish exploitation and fierce tigerish revenge.

XII

In *Dombey and Son,* the stain of cannibalism also emerges in open places and hidden crannies. What place could be more transparently open and yet more covertly hidden than the very commencement of the book? Here is the entire opening paragraph, a single-sentence paragraph, that heralds the onset of this vast novel about Mr. Dombey—and Son—and daughter:

> Dombey sat in the corner of the darkened room in the great arm-chair by the bedside, and Son lay tucked up warm in a little basket bedstead, carefully disposed on a low settee immediately in front of the fire and close to it, as if his constitution were analogous to that of a muffin, and it was essential to toast him brown while he was very new. (*DS*, 1:1)

We are amused and delighted by this disarming commencement and by the outlandish figure of speech with which it concludes. On reading these lines for the first time we cannot know how artfully they are constructed or how fraught with hidden significance. We cannot know, for example, the deadly menace that lurks beneath the smiling surface of the outlandish final figure. But the dread meaning is there nevertheless. For, as we eventually come to perceive, little Paul, here only a few minutes old, is already—unhappily—a commodity, the predestined and preordained Son of Dombey and Son. In truth, he *is* nothing more than a muffin, an object to be toasted—that is, to be brought into perfection (into the Sonhood of Dombey and Son) and thus to serve his barren purpose in life, to be utilized, subsumed, and incorporated.

Mr. Dombey is the ogre of this instructive vignette, though of course he will feel—in the blindness of his overweening pride and the arrogance of his dehumanizing materialism—that he is nurturing rather than consuming his child. When we read this disarming opening for the first time we cannot know that the stiff and stately Mr. Dombey is really a base savage, a ghastly cannibal who battens most unnaturally on his own coveted son. On looking back from the vantage of the completed novel, however, we can see why Dickens chose to compare the newborn Paul (we remember Dickens' early association of newborn babies with butcher-shop meat) to food that will be toasted and browned and then devoured.

The cannibalistic overture of *Dombey and Son* is no isolated phenomenon. Other man-eaters, woman-eaters, and child-eaters prowl the pages of the book and other human victims become their fodder. In this novel of genteel and not-so-genteel predation, Mr. Dombey's subordinate, Carker the Manager, is the chief hunter and consumer of human prey. Dickens conveys Carker's predation through cat, snake, wolf, and devil imagery; but at the core of all such imagery is Carker's devouring ferocity. His feline softness cannot disguise his appetite or his savagery. His gestures, actions, and attributes, his very bearing and demeanor, betray him. We feel his murderous power; we track his patient hunting. We watch with fascinated horror as he singles out a quarry, the neglected and vulnerable Florence, for example. "Ready for a spring, or for a tear, or for a scratch, or for a velvet touch," the predatory manager turns his pitiless gaze upon the newly nubile heiress, that tempting "bird in a cage," as Carker has it, whom he now longs to possess or, rather, to devour; for to possess in Carker's lexicon is to bite and to devour (*DS*, 22:221).

Carker is perpetually menacing. Even in his most fawning smile, Dickens tells us, "there was something . . . like the snarl of a cat" (*DS*, 13:122). (We recall that Dickens' nursemaid nightly threatened her terrified charge with "The Black Cat," a deadly, "glaring-eyed supernatural Tom" that "sucked the breath of infancy" [*AYR* 3: 519]. We also recall—among many later offspring of that potent childhood threatening—the ferocious ogre-cum-cat of *Great Expectations:* how Orlick, "his mouth snarling like a tiger's," drew his hand "across his mouth as if his mouth watered for me" [*AYR* 5: *GE*, 53:338].) The devil Carker—now a watching cat, now a hypnotizing snake, now a ravening wolf, now simply two rows of glistening teeth—is always a rapacious predator. He stalks his human prey with the intent watchfulness of a coiled snake, a hungry wolf, a murderous cat. Before he kills, he toys with his victim or coils and coils around him. (These are Dickens' images.) We watch Carker ready himself to pounce upon Edith and Florence (depicted as poor fluttering birds), and we have no doubt how he will deal with them once he catches them.

Dickens' conception of Carker as a voracious predator menacing, stalking, and then consuming his vulnerable prey runs strongly through the novel. Carker is "sly of manner, sharp of tooth, soft of foot, watchful of eye, oily of tongue, cruel of heart, nice of habit" (*DS*, 22:211). He bides his time. He sits "with a dainty stedfastness and patience at his work, as if he were waiting at a mouse's hole" (*DS*, 22:211). Each touch tells, and, touch by telling touch, Dickens limns Carker's portrait. Carker is smooth and soft and fastidious, but his ferocity constantly bursts through his polite dissimulation. When he confronts his broken brother, for example, he confronts him not with the feigned solicitude he shows to the busy world but "with his two rows of teeth bristling as if he would have bitten him" (*DS*, 13:125).

Carker the Manager must manage. He is a mine of manipulative hostility. He vents his disguised savagery upon the high and powerful (upon Mr. Dombey, for example) as well as upon the lowly (upon his brother or Rob the Grinder). Through such savagery he achieves ascendency: he subdues and he possesses. A primary target of Carker's ferocity is Mr. Dombey, his social superior, his nominal master, and his business cohort. That Carker the ruthless manager should turn upon Dombey the aggrandizing owner is a fitting culmination to the ethic they both profess: they are business counterparts, twin exemplars of the new, soulless business world. The savage ethic they share, shorn of its social trappings, is nothing more nor less than blatant cannibalism. They blindly obey the dictates of their deadly creed. They feed remorselessly on all within their circle, on wives, children, lovers, friends, servants, employees, business associates. Carker often overtly demonstrates this cannibalistic instinct, this urgent need to bite and to devour. "For a moment," Dickens writes, as Carker hovers about the lofty Mr. Dombey, "one might have thought that the white teeth were prone to bite the hand they fawned upon" (*DS*, 26:268). Or yet again, as Mr. Dombey lies insensible after his horse has thrown him, the ostentatiously solicitous Carker "bent over his prostrate chief with every tooth disclosed" (*DS*, 42:426).

Carker's tendency to bite and rend, the unmistakable prelude to killing and consuming, is not confined to enemies or rivals (patrician or plebian), nor is it simply a function of his catlike attributes. When Carker conveys Florence's love to Mr. Dombey, the manager can hardly contain his hot rapaciousness at the thought of loving (that is, devouring) such a dainty morsel. Dickens describes the manager's countenance at that moment: "Wolf's face that it was then, with even the hot tongue revealing itself through the stretched mouth" (*DS*, 26:259). Florence's danger is palpable; she will be eaten alive by this dissembling wolf. We think of poor, wolf-threatened Little Red Ridinghood and her ferocious fate.

But it is a more formidable object, Edith, who soon becomes Carker's foremost quarry. He stalks her slowly, craftily. He gradually imposes his person and his menace upon her inmost being. We see this guileful process unfolding in hundreds of hints and touches. After Edith's marriage to Mr. Dombey, for instance, Carker, like all the other members of the wedding party, salutes the voluptuous bride with a kiss, but he does so with a difference, a difference that only Edith understands: "Lastly, Mr. Carker, with his white teeth glistening, approaches Edith, more as if he meant to bite her, than to taste the sweets that linger on her lips" (*DS*, 31:315).

Carker's impulse to bite Edith rather than "to taste" her (he will taste her to begin with) culminates toward the end of the novel when, having run off with her, he triumphantly enters the assignation suite in the hotel in Dijon to greet the delectable creature he now denominates his "wife" (*DS*, 54:538). Dickens imbues this culminating scene with the unmistakable attributes of Carker's cannibalistic depravity. Carker is all appetite, anticipation, and smooth, incorporative ferocity. At the moment of his triumph, or rather his supposed triumph, he approaches his "wife" not as an ardent man, though he is eager and lustful enough, but as a frightening, sharp-toothed maw. Carker comes to his beloved's chamber with "gleaming teeth" (*DS*, 54:538). He comes "through the dark rooms" to his waiting "bride"—the moment appointed, the banquet ordered, the table set—he comes through the dark rooms, as Dickens brilliantly epitomizes it, "like a mouth" (*DS*, 54:538). (At such moments we recall the sharp-toothed Captain Murderer, his delectable wives, his horrible chamber, his terrifying tooth-filled maw, and his unspeakable "house-lambs" banqueting.)

Dickens' Bosch-like images seem clear enough. Carker, in the

The MONSTER *going to take his Afternoons Luncheon.*

60. The Toothy Devourer of Women, Knife and Fork in Hand

The Captain Murderer-like ogre-libertine, offspring of the traditional ogres of fable and folklore, appears dramatically in the graphics of the late eighteenth and early nineteenth centuries (graphics that Dickens knew from childhood on). Here the figure appears in the memorable guise of a hungry, Carker-like devourer with a terrifying, tooth-filled maw. Dickens knew this ferocious image firsthand; it was in the large folio volume of Gillray's caricatures that he owned. "The Monster going to take his Afternoons Luncheon." Caricature (1790) by James Gillray.

shorthand of metaphor, is nothing more than a mouth, a savage creature of teeth and appetite, a stealthy but ferocious man-eater and woman-eater. But at times even such compelling tropes and figures, profoundly directive and powerfully expressionistic though they are—they are also, of course, camouflaged and rendered less visible when met in context—fail to satisfy Dickens, and he informs us in so many words of Carker's dread nature and loathsome feeding. Carker, for all his stealth and polished cunning, is a modern-day Captain Murderer, a savage cannibal with an insatiable appetite for human prey. Dickens tells us this outright. Carker, Dickens informs us, rides his horse and comports himself "as if he hunted men and women" (*DS*, 42:426).

Carker, all mouth, who lives by biting and devouring, is finally devoured himself. Earlier we noticed the affinity (quite self-conscious, in its larger aspects, on Dickens' part) between Hogarth's *Marriage à la Mode* and Dickens' marriage à la Dombey. Hogarth's mercenary and loveless marriage ends with the symbolic image of a ravenous dog devouring the grotesque head that garnishes the center of the dining table, as exact imagistic parallel (in posture, activity, and other details) to the small child who eagerly grasps and mouths her dead mother's death-distorted head (see, above, figure 21). These duplicate images tell us that the sold and bought countess, tool of a mercenary parent, faithless spouse to her vain, self-absorbed, debauched husband, unwitting agent of his death, has met her just fate: it is now her turn (as it will be Carker's turn after her) to become carrion for devouring dogs.

And as with *Dombey and Son,* so with *Marriage à la Mode*: cannibalism threads through the entire work, weaving its grim import into scene, image, object, action, and structure, a recurrent motif that Dickens responded to, we may be sure, over and over again. The cannibalistic motifs of *Marriage à la Mode* are strongest, or perhaps most obvious, in the third plate of the series, "Scene with the Quack," for the quack doctor's chamber, like Mr. Venus' shop in *Our Mutual Friend,* abounds in grisly mementos of predation, death, dissection, and consumption. It contains mummies, skele-

61. The Devourers and the Devoured: Hogarth, "The Moralist, and Censor of His Age," Limns the Quack Doctor's Ghastly Chamber

All of the protagonists here, like the earl's diseased little daughter in the final plate (doomed to a wretched death by the debauchery of her neglectful father—see figure 21), are being eaten alive by syphilis, a gruesome end grimly foreshadowed by the grisly props in this grisly chamber. "Scene With The Quack." Plate III of *Marriage à la Mode* (1745) by William Hogarth. Compare this illustration with the two illustrations entitled "Cannibals and Quacks" (see figures 143 and 144).

tons, bones, stuffed animals, dried human bodies, giant tooth-filled maws, grotesque heads, gaping human skulls, and an anthropopha-gus or cannibal.[44] Other grisly signs and hints are strewn about: piercing instruments, tearing instruments, pressing instruments, rendering instruments, and cutting instruments (the quack doctor's giant female cohort, a syphilitic bawd, holds and tests an open knife or razor). Given such symbols and suggestions, here (where they serve as a gloss on the dissolute, syphilitic, soon-dead Earl-to-be) and throughout the series, we are not surprised at the suggestion in the final plate ("Death of the Countess") that the dead countess (fulfilling her predatory and preyed-upon role in a predatory mar-riage and predatory world) has, again like Carker after her, become fodder for ravenous dogs (and ravenous doglike humans) in death.

There are also many noncannibalistic parallels between *Marriage à la Mode* and the Dombey-Edith marriage that attest to a strong indebtedness. In *Marriage à la Mode* the mercenary parent is the father of the bride, the mother is absent and presumably dead. In *Dombey and Son,* the mercenary parent is the mother of the bride, the father is absent and dead. In both works the wife is faithless, though Dickens, in a last-minute change, saved Edith from the actu-ality, but not from the symbolic effect, of committing adultery and dying; in both works an assignation is the pivot of the discovery; in both the death occurs when the husband confronts the lover (or would-be lover); in *Marriage* the husband is killed, in *Dombey* the would-be lover; in both works the loveless marriage brings desola-tion and destruction; in both a female child is left bereaved and dou-bly orphaned—Florence calls herself "orphaned" (*DS*, 47:472).

There are many additional parallels and iconographic links be-tween these two works, but one of the most unexpected parallels—or rather series of parallels—emerges at Carker's death. *Marriage à la Mode* ends with the self-inflicted death of the countess and with her body being devoured (symbolically) by a dog. So also with Carker. Carker's odyssey ends with his self-inflicted death (in a guilty panic, pursued by Dombey, he backs in front of an onrushing loco-motive, an iron embodiment of the "remorseless monster, Death"

[*DS*, 20:200], a monster with "red eyes, bleared and dim," a monster that "spun him round and round, and struck him limb from limb, and licked his stream of life up with its fiery heat, and cast his mutilated fragments in the air" [*DS*, 55:553]); and then, final indignity, savage and degrading, Carker's body, like the countess' body, is devoured (symbolically) by dogs. Carker's death is double. First he is devoured by the monster locomotive that "licked his stream of life up," then he is devoured by the predatory dogs that "sniffed upon the road" where his blood and mutilated flesh lay, hungry dogs that had to be driven off by the grim attendants who gathered up his remains (*DS*, 55:553). His death is fitting. Carker the mouth, the insatiable devourer, is savagely devoured—then savagely devoured again.

The death of Carker owes something to Hogarth, something to Cruikshank and his devouring locomotives (see figure 62), something to Dickens' obsession with cannibalism, something to the integrating function of the cannibalistic imagery that runs all through Carker's role and all through the novel, and something to still other sources. Surely both Dickens, in his depiction of Carker's final end, and Hogarth, in his depiction of the countess' monitory death, owe much to the Bible. The Bible contains many allusions to dogs eating the bodies and licking the blood of dissolute or disgraced or grasping or wicked men—and women: "So the King died . . . and the dogs licked up his blood"; "Him that dieth of Ahab in the city the dogs shall eat"; "The dogs shall eat Jezebel by the wall of Jezreel" (1 Kings 22:37–38; 21:24; 21:23). Doubtless these warnings and predictions—the countess, remember, was a Jezebel—add depth and resonance to the related messages Dickens and Hogarth are purveying. But beyond such Biblical sharings, *Dombey and Son* and *Marriage à la Mode* reinforce what we have already seen: Dickens' lifelong links to Hogarth and to cannibalism, and to cannibalism in Hogarth, are abundant, striking, and strong.

Carker and Mr. Dombey are not the only cannibals in *Dombey and Son*. Other man-eaters and other cannibalistic motifs, less important and less sustained than those just surveyed, combine mo-

62. "I Come to Dine, I Come to Sup. I Come.
I Come. – – To Eat You Up!!"

Cruikshank's ferocious "Monster" locomotive, a cannibalistic embodiment of the railway panic of 1845, devours "beef" and "babbies" alike. Dickens, who had special fantasies concerning cannibalism (and super-special fantasies concerning baby-cooking and baby-eating cannibalism), knew this striking engraving by his friend George Cruikshank, an engraving of a fierce devouring "Railway Dragon," an image of ravening railway ferocity that appeared shortly before Dickens began *Dombey and Son* and created his own version of a devouring railway dragon. *The Railway Dragon*. Steel engraving (1845) by George Cruikshank. From *George Cruikshank's Table-Book* (1845).

mentarily with Carker's central menace and Dombey's socially sanctioned predations to extend and generalize their threats. Mrs.
Pipchin, for example, that witchlike quencher of young children and
young sensibilities, is introduced to the reader as an "ogress and
child-queller," and imagery of child-quelling and child-eating surrounds all her acts and attributes (*DS*, 8:72). She is thus like Mr.
Tackleton, the toy-maker and toy merchant of *The Cricket on the
Hearth,* a child-queller Dickens had created several months before
beginning *Dombey and Son,* and a child-queller who is introduced
to the reader as "a domestic Ogre, who had been living on children
all his life, and was their implacable enemy" (*CH,* 1: 37)—though,
in good Christmas Book fashion, Mr. Tackleton, unlike Mrs. Pipchin, is ultimately transformed and redeemed.

Mrs. Pipchin is Mr. Dombey's proxy. She acts as his deputy while
Paul is away at school. She was based, in part, as Dickens himself
averred, on a Mrs. Roylance, an old lady who served for an interval
as Dickens' surrogate mother while he was living away from home
and toiling at the blacking warehouse (F, 27). Her transformation
into a child-eating witch reflects Dickens' blacking-warehouse anguish and anger. Her very abode—Dickens' lodgings for a portion
of those despairing days—takes on in *Dombey and Son* the nightmare coloration of Dickens' childhood fear and desperation. In
Paul's disapproving eyes, Mrs. Pipchin's lodgings are as dismaying as
their witchlike mistress. The fortress "Castle" of this ogress and
child-queller—a dim, dour, frightening fastness complete with a
torture chamber called the "Castle Dungeon"—is where this redoubtable "dragon" torments her dispirited charges and sups in
"greasy" glory (*DS*, 8:72–74, 78). But Mrs. Pipchin is more than a
child-quelling ogress. She is a harbinger of death and destruction;
she hovers over the dying Paul and she attends upon the doomed
Dombey. Her final exit from the novel (after the crash of the Dombey empire) evokes, in one last summing up, her cannibalistic appetites and incorporative satisfactions: "Mrs. Pipchin herself is next
handed in [to the fly van], and grimly takes her seat. There is a snaky
gleam in her hard grey eye, as of anticipated rounds of buttered

toast, relays of hot chops, worryings and quellings of young children, sharp snappings at poor Berry, and all the other delights of her Ogress's castle. Mrs. Pipchin almost laughs as the Fly Van drives off, and she composes her black bombazeen skirts, and settles herself among the cushions of her easy chair" (*DS*, 59:594).

Other *Dombey* mothers, fierce and implacable, also take on cannibalistic dimensions. Good Mrs. Brown, a rapacious, exploitive mother, a mother even more witchlike and despoiling than the child-quelling Mrs. Pipchin (Good Mrs. Brown has sold her daughter for money, literally for food and drink), hobbles through *Dombey and Son* like a malignant plague. Her cannibalistic attributes help make her child-devouring sins nightmarishly palpable. Good Mrs. Brown is not only a terrifying intensification of the ogress Mrs. Pipchin, she is an expressionistic version, low and disreputable, of the lofty Mr. Dombey.[45] When Good Mrs. Brown abducts the lost and unloved Florence, she takes the elegantly clad child to her shabby little house, a frightening dwelling, an isolated black den set off by itself on a back road. Once in the house, Good Mrs. Brown leads Florence into a bare back room that contains no furniture, a room with black walls, a black ceiling, a heap of rags, and a pile of bones and cinders.

Good Mrs. Brown, an ugly old woman who carries animal skins over her arms (she later strips Florence and gives her a skin to carry), has red rims round her eyes, a shrivelled yellow face and throat that twists in spasmodic contortions, and a mouth that constantly mumbles and chatters and mows "of itself," an "industrious" mouth that works and works even "when she is not speaking" (*DS*, 6:51). Good Mrs. Brown, sitting down on the pile of bones, threatens the lost child. "'I'll kill you,'" she tells Florence. (Like the ogreish Magwitch, who threatens to pursue Pip into his home and into his bed, the ogreish Good Mrs. Brown tells Florence, "'I could have you killed at any time—even if you was in your own bed at home'" [*DS*, 6:51–52].) A few moments later Good Mrs. Brown "whipped out a large pair of scissors," "fell into an unaccountable state of excitement," and, brandishing those fearful scissors, hovered round the terrified girl (*DS*, 6:52).

Florence, looking at this red-eyed creature, gazing at her working mouth and contorting throat, is petrified with fear. She had felt that fear the moment she entered the bare black room with its unaccountable cinders (from what profane fires?) and its unaccountable bones (from what profane feasts?). At the first sight of the room, Dickens tells us, "the child became so terrified that she was stricken speechless, and looked as though about to swoon" (*DS*, 6:51). That terror is understandable. After all, what does Florence know, poor little rich girl that she is, about grubbing rag and bone scavengers? In Good Mrs. Brown and her black, bone-strewn den Florence has seen a different reality, a more fearful reality, a reality that reflects her parlous, unloved state. She has caught a nightmare glimpse of her final end. She is destined to be slaughtered by this repulsive ogress; her bones will be cast upon that charnel-house heap.

But Florence does not swoon, and Good Mrs. Brown, a more frightening ogress and child-queller than Mrs. Pipchin, does not serve Florence as her threats and the mementos that fill her grisly house suggest that she will. That is, she does not kill Florence, skin her, and devour her (devour her with that horrible working mouth), nor does she add Florence's skin to her other skins or Florence's bones to her other bones in that ghastly black chamber. She does, however, strip Florence of her clothes, inflicting a symbolic flaying. Then, "Mrs. Brown resumed her seat on the bones, and smoked a very short black pipe, mowing and mumbling all the time, as if she were eating the stem" (*DS*, 6:53).

Other mentors of the young in *Dombey and Son*, though more subdued and genteel in their cannibalism than Mrs. Pipchin or Good Mrs. Brown, are no less members of the child-quelling and child-eating tribe. Miss Blimber, for instance, one of Paul's teachers, and thus another, though more remote, surrogate mother—more remote, that is, than Mrs. Pipchin—soon exhibits her ghoulish nature. Though essentially goodhearted (and redeemed in the course of the novel), Miss Blimber has been desiccated by her avid feeding in the sterile realms of classical knowledge. Her ghoulish trafficking with dead learning has sapped her very life; and now, in turn, she saps the life of the young neophytes she must induct into those

selfsame mysteries. In truth, she feeds upon those neophytes, drain-
ing, by the very nature of what she professes, their intellectual curiosity and vigor. Her livelihood comes from her teaching, but (so
dusty, Dickens is saying, is the world of classical learning and genteel
education) her teaching is coincident with aridity and death. As a
result, she inevitably brings the chill shadow of the yawning grave
into the lives of her young charges. Her appearance and her appetites proclaim her deadly nature: "There was no light nonsense
about Miss Blimber. She kept her hair short and crisp, and wore
spectacles. She was dry and sandy with working in the graves of deceased languages. None of your live languages for Miss Blimber.
They must be dead—stone dead—and then Miss Blimber dug
them up like a Ghoule" (*DS*, 11:101).

But it is not simply ghoulish Miss Blimber, it is the entire Blimber
Academy—that is, the entire middle-class educational system—that
is arraigned here. In view of that system, a system Dickens felt devoured its young, and in view of his metaphors for depicting and
condemning that system, it is not surprising that the only other in-
structor at Dr. Blimber's Academy that Dickens chose to develop,
he named "Mr. Feeder." Mr. Feeder—or to use his full title, Mr.
Feeder, B. A.—is far from being an ogre; nevertheless, he feeds just
as inevitably as dry ghoulish Miss Blimber does on his young
charges—hence his name. Given this unremitting institutionalized
feeding, it is fitting that Mr. Feeder eventually marries Miss Blimber
and becomes proprietor of the Blimber establishment, now in name
as well as in function the Feeder establishment. (Elsewhere in his
writings Dickens also uses names to hint at the cannibalistic proclivities of characters who feed on their fellows. In *Nicholas Nickleby*, for
example, that voracious predator, Sir Mulberry Hawk, who hawk-
ishly devours, that is, mercilessly feeds upon and finally kills,
Sir Frederick Verisopht, one of his many victims, is accompanied
in his predations by two rapacious subalterns—Mr. Pluck and Mr.
Pyke—whose names are as expressive of their predatory roles as Sir
Mulberry Hawk's name is expressive of his. To mention only two
additional instances of cannibalistic naming, earlier we met the

"Oh, goroo" man, a fierce feeder whose ogreish cry soon comes to serve as his name; later we shall meet Mr. Pecksniff, another avid feeder—this time an unctuous and dissembling one—a feeder with cannibalistic proclivities and a cannibalistic name. Compared to these hungry feeders, Mr. Feeder, though appropriately named, is a genteel diner indeed.)

The educational system—of which Miss Blimber and Mr. Feeder are victims as well as a purveyors—devours the children it is supposed to nurture. Dickens makes this clear in multitudes of additional ways. Poor, good-hearted Mr. Toots is one hapless victim of this cannibalistic system; he has been eaten up, left a mere stalk, by the Blimber forcing academy. Paul Dombey is another victim. On Sunday nights, when Paul must return to Doctor Blimber's Academy after his weekend respite, it seems to him as though the "Doctor's dark door stood agape to swallow him up for another week" (*DS*, 12:116). The Doctor's dark door—the gaping door of genteel education and of death (the two are coincident)—"swallows" Paul up week after week, indeed, it swallows up the last precious months of his fast-ebbing life. But though that dark gaping Blimber door swallows up Paul's waning life, he does not die at school. He returns to the source of his undoing: he comes home to die in his father's funereal mansion. There, where he started life as a mere muffin to be toasted, browned, and consumed, he is finally swallowed up entirely. While his father broods—indeed presides—over his dissolution in mute incomprehension, he is swallowed into eternity.

In the portrait of Mrs. Pipchin and her Castle there is a grim humor; in the portraits of Miss Blimber, Mr. Feeder, and the Blimber Academy, a more genial, less personal, though no less devastating, indictment. Such portraits, while extending and reinforcing the central cannibalistic motifs of the novel, also manage, by virtue of their nicely discriminated humor, to mitigate (each in its own measure and carefully calculated degree) the menace they also purvey. Good Mrs. Brown's continually working mouth is frightening; Carker's feline and lupine ferocity is life-threatening; on the other hand, Mrs. Pipchin's or Miss Blimber's or Mr. Feeder's menace, tinged with humor and circumscribed by limits, is (for the reader at least) delightful as well as menacing.

Still other cannibalistic images and other minor characters with cannibalistic overtones, characters such as Mrs. MacStinger and Susan Nipper, also delight and menace. Susan Nipper, for example—note her biting name—like Dickens' own nursemaid, enforces her cannibalistic bullying by telling Florence that she, Susan, will have a goblin come from a nearby loft and " 'eat you up alive!' " (*DS*, 5:38). Then, again like Dickens' nursemaid, this nursery-room harpy (who later in the novel becomes a much more benign character) claws the air angrily and utters a "horrible lowing" sound (*DS*, 5:38). We are amused by Susan's familiarity with the abodes and habits of goblins, and we admire the effectiveness, if not the humanity, of her terrorizing histrionics. Florence, we may be sure, like Dickens with his Scheherazade, had a far different view of such matters. Susan evolves and softens, but she does not forget her heritage. Even when she becomes a defender of Florence, she remains true to her cannibalistic antecedents. Years after the goblin episode, she speaks of being "torn to pieces," even "though I may not be a Fox's Martyr" (*DS*, 44:436)—an allusion to a book that had, as David Copperfield's "devouring" addiction to the work's "precious" (and gruesome) illustrations demonstrates (*DC*, 10:107), strong cannibalistic associations for Dickens, associations conjoined with childhood and nursemaids, with savage butcherings and ghastly roastings.

As Scheherazade, Dickens' archetypal nursemaid, demonstrated in many of her evocations, as *Copperfield* and Dickens' frequent Morgue visits also demonstrated, and as we have just seen here with Mrs. Pipchin, Good Mrs. Brown, Miss Blimber, and Susan Nipper, Dickens often associated cannibalism with nursemaids and with other warders of the young—that is, with surrogate mothers as well as real mothers—and with birth and death. Dickens, though infinitely varied, is also remarkably consistent. The just-mentioned goblin scene, for example, in which nursemaid Susan threatens to have Florence eaten alive, occurs immediately before the motherless but many-mothered infant Paul undergoes another rite of birth, his cold and comfortless christening. Baby Paul's christening, in turn, is followed by a christening feast in which the celebrants dine, cannibal-like, upon "a dead dinner lying in state" (*DS*, 5:42). The cannibal-haunted *Dombey* christening calls to mind still other cannibalistic christenings in Dickens (cannibalistic christenings are, in fact, a Dickensian speciality), fictional christenings and real-life christenings, bizarre, baby-eating christenings such as those we surveyed earlier: the fictional christening, for instance, in which Mrs. Nickelby (a character based upon Dickens' mother) associates her daughter Kate's christening with dining on butcher-shop babies-cum-pigs, or the real-life christening (by way of contrast and confirmation) in which Dickens associates his own daughter Kate's christening (baby, wife, and mother all bore the name of Kate) with dining on a baby-cum-calf roasting on a christening-feast spit.

The more things change, it seems, the more they remain the same.

XIII

The frequency with which Dickens introduces these cannibal-haunted rites of passage and their presiding cannibal familiars, and the virtuosity with which he varies and modulates them, are truly astonishing. In *Martin Chuzzlewit* Mrs. Gamp, another nurse and proxy mother, though of a different kind, goes "to a lying-in or a laying-out with equal zest and relish" (*MC*, 19:236). "Zest and relish" are the operative words here. Mrs. Gamp's appetite for work can hardly be distinguished from her appetite for food. As we see in scene after scene, eating and drinking are her true occupations. She eats and drinks as she watches over her charges, an insatiable deity feeding on her helpless devotees. Her devotees sustain her life; she takes her nourishment from their abject dependency, and eating, eating, eating as she tends them (or rather neglects them), she speeds them on their way. As midwife-mother she ushers infants into life (and often death); as nurse to the ill and aged she hastens them to their final end; as washer of corpses she prepares them for their last long journey. But all the while she feasts with "zest and relish," taking her ample sustenance from man's frail flesh. After laying out Anthony Chuzzlewit's body, she eats and drinks with gusto. As Dickens puts it, she "feasted like a Ghoule" (*MC,* 19:241).

Ghoulish Mrs. Gamp, eating and boozing her way through life, sups on man's mortality—on birth and death—with equal appetite: birth and death are her meat and drink. But this statement needs to be qualified. Like a hungry, thirsty goddess of the rites of passage, who feeds most satisfyingly on grief-filled occasions, Mrs. Gamp has a special relish for death. Indeed, she often turns birth into death, a lying-in into a laying-out. She proclaims her love of death and of all those it embraces. "'Don't name the charge,'" she says, "'for if I could afford to lay all my feller creeturs out for nothink, I would gladly do it; sich is the love I bear 'em'" (*MC,* 19:237). But Mrs. Gamp can't afford such altruism, so she exacts her toll in wages— and in meat and drink. She feasts, sometimes quite literally, on the very bodies of the dead and dying, and she is in league with that other greedy feeder on dead bodies, the undertaker Mr. Mould.

In *The Old Curiosity Shop* we find a very different appetite for human bodies. The irrepressible Quilp delights in calling himself an ogre ("'How dare you approach the ogre's castle,'" he calls out, [*MHC* 2: *OCS,* 67:182]); and we, like his wife, who is alternately terrorized and charmed by him, soon come to agree with his self-designation. In one episode, Quilp, unobserved, "greedily" watches Nell and her grandfather, his greedy watching a lubricious anticipation of depraved feasting to come. Following in the Fat Boy's gourmandizing footsteps, Quilp regards Nell, as the Fat Boy regarded Mary, as a succulent morsel. "Fantastic and monkey-like," Quilp gazes at Nell, his great ogre head "turned a little on one side." Nell suddenly catches a glimpse of Quilp hungrily watching her; in a nightmare flash, she sees his "ugly features" and his ogre head "twisted into a complacent grimace." She utters "a suppressed shriek . . . and half doubting [Quilp's] reality, looked shrinkingly" at the apparition, but she soon discovers that the nightmare head, the greedy gaze, and the twisted grimace are all too real (*MHC* 1: *OCS,* 9:136–37).

63. Quilp at the Window: Man or Beast?

Note the disembodied head of a queen at the lower right. Note, also, just above the decapitated head, the word "Man," and then, in bolder letters, another word, the word that dominates and lingers and that truly defines the fanged, yellow-clawed, ogreish Quilp: "Beast." Wood engraving after a drawing by Hablot Knight Browne ("Phiz") for Number 38 (19 December 1840) of *Master Humphrey's Clock,* incorporating Chapter 60 of *The Old Curiosity Shop.*

The reason for that greedy gaze soon becomes apparent. When, a few moments after Quilp's materialization, Nell's grandfather kisses her cheek, Quilp is in ecstasy; the action whets his appetite: "'Ah!' said the dwarf, smacking his lips, 'what a nice kiss that was—just upon the rosy part. What a capital kiss!'" (*MHC* 1: *OCS*, 9:137). Quilp, smacking his lips over Nell's rosy cheeks, reminds us not only of the Fat Boy but of Magwitch "licking his lips" and threatening to eat Pip's "fat cheeks" (*AYR* 4: *GE*, 1:169). A moment later Quilp continues with his lip-smacking rhapsody: "'Such a fresh, blooming, modest little bud . . . such a chubby, rosy, cosy, little Nell! . . . She's so . . . so small, so compact, so beautifully modelled, so fair, with such blue veins and such a transparent skin, and such little feet, and such winning ways—but bless me, you're nervous. Why neighbour, what's the matter?'" (*MHC* 1: *OCS*, 9:137). We know what the matter is.

What the "matter" is, is only suggested in the foregoing vignette, albeit in mouthwatering tropes. Elsewhere Quilp's predatory ravenousness is labeled more directly. This irresistible monster-dwarf, who feeds so gleefully and exuberantly on his fellow men and women, betrays his cannibalistic nature in the most prosaic details of his everyday life. He prepares his food as a cannibal would his repast. We are told that a beefsteak he has just dined upon he had "cooked himself in somewhat of a savage and cannibal-like manner" (*MHC* 2: *OCS*, 67:182). Even his denials betray his inmost nature. "'Don't be frightened, mistress,'" he reassures Kit's mother as she clutches her infant to her breast, "'I don't eat babies; I don't like 'em'" (*MHC* 1: *OCS*, 21:207). As Quilp approaches his death, Dickens continues the cannibalistic imagery, but with a difference. Now the biter is bitten. The dark mystery of death is depicted as a great mouth waiting to devour the devourer: "He darted forward for a few paces, as if into the mouth of some dim, yawning cavern; then, thinking he had gone wrong, changed the direction of his steps; then stood still, not knowing where to turn" (*MHC* 2: *OCS*, 67:186).

The motif of cannibalism in *The Old Curiosity Shop* does not end with Quilp; it recurs throughout the book, and it emerges in grotesque as well as in comic and sinister ways. In one outlandish scene we find Mr. Vuffin, the itinerant showman, reminiscing matter-of-factly about his and Mr. Maunders' entourages of giants and dwarfs. In a reversal of the roles of giants and dwarfs as usually depicted in fable and romance, Mr. Vuffin's and Mr. Maunders' giants, as they grow old, become weak, put-upon servants, while their dwarfs move from strength to strength and become ever more savage and dominating. This bizarre reversal mirrors the serious central reversal of the novel: Little Nell, the wise, steadfast, parenting child guides and comforts her grandfather, the foolish, errant, childlike adult. The latter reversal, in turn, grows out of Dickens' own early experiences. (See Part 3, "Dickens and Necessity"; see also figure 132, "The Child as Responsible Parent, the Parent as 'Wicked Child.'")

The mild giants in *The Old Curiosity Shop* serve their voracious and vindictive dwarfs. "'There was one dwarf,'" Mr. Vuffin tells us, "'as had grown elderly and wicious who whenever his giant wasn't quick enough to please him, used to stick pins in his legs, not being able to reach up any higher'" (*MHC* 1: *OCS*, 19:194). The bondage of these old, weak-legged giants is most marked at mealtimes, for then they wait directly upon their hungry tormentors, bringing them, amidst kicks and pinches and imprecations, the provender upon which they glut themselves.

Hablot Browne, illustrating this memorable scene under Dickens' guidance and supervision, has caught the wild aggressive spirit of Dickens' fantastic imagining. The peaceful giants feed the unruly dwarfs. The dwarfs, in Browne's rendition, are a frightening lot: three brandish their knives and forks (one seems about to stab a nearby giant); two others greedily gobble or guzzle; while yet another opens wide his maw and reveals two sharp rows of Captain Murderer-like teeth. The frightening import of all this devouring activity becomes clear when one notices the central feature of this voracious feeding: a half-headless giant brings in upon a platter a startling *pièce de résistance*, a grotesque main dish that gives the appearance of being the giant's own cooked head, a delicacy that comes complete with eyes, eyebrows, hair, nose, and grimacing mouth.

Such half-comic, half-frightening reversals of conventional cannibalistic mythology appear less frequently in Dickens' writings than do their straightforward counterparts. The latter, more ordinary, cannibalistic motifs occur over and over again, and they occur at the very center of Dickens' conceptions. They also usually occur as integral aspects of the everyday. To cite just one instance, twenty years after creating the scene of the weak-legged giants and the voracious dwarfs, Dickens created another scene—or really a series of scenes—of communal banqueting. This latter-day banqueting is as ordinary and matter-of-fact as the giant-dwarf banqueting had been bizarre and extraordinary, but in both episodes Dickens used cannibalism as a potent means of conveying his central meaning. In the later, matter-of-fact example of communal dining, found in an 1860 essay entitled "Refreshments for Travellers," Dickens attacks the wretched fare provided for travelers in Britain. He gives substance to his grievance by conducting the reader on a graphic tour of dismal, traveler-frequented eating establishments, allowing the reader to sample with him the delights of dining in railway refreshment rooms, or, in desperate but vain attempts to avoid the inedible fare purveyed by those desolate institutions, the delights of dining in nearby hotels, inns, restaurants, and the like. (Dickens returned to the horrors of dining in railway refreshment rooms in "Main Line. The Boy at Mugby," one of his contributions to *Mugby Junction*, the Extra Christmas Number of *All the Year Round* for 1866.)

There is no way, Dickens tells us, of escaping the gustatory horrors of traveling; "Refreshments for Travellers," we discover, is a mockingly ironic title. We soon come to understand what we can expect in the way of refreshments while on the road, an understanding that Dickens makes real for us in two culminating episodes. The first takes place in the coffee room of a hotel hard by a railway terminus. Dickens, soon to catch a train, orders a quick dinner; and slowly, disastrously, excruciatingly, it arrives. When he looks at the pretentious meal that has been set before him, he sees a most singu-

64. The Mild Giants Feed the Voracious Dwarfs

Note the grotesque, headlike entrée, hot and steaming, being brought in on a platter. Wood engraving by Hablot Knight Browne ("Phiz") for Number 17 (25 July 1840) of *Master Humphrey's Clock*, incorporating Chapter 19 of *The Old Curiosity Shop*.

lar feast. The veal cutlet has "a sort of fur" on its surface, a strange accoutrement that somehow accords with the peculiar sauce that accompanies the cutlet—"a cutaneous kind of sauce, of brown pimples and pickled cucumber" (*AYR* 2: 515). Given this auspicious beginning, we are not surprised to find that other components of this feast have peculiar properties as well. Hard on the heels of the furry cutlet and the pimply sauce come "three flinty-hearted potatoes and two grim head of broccoli . . . badly boiled" (*AYR* 2: 515).

That Dickens was very much aware of the cannibalistic nature of his imagery, and that he intended the reader to regard the meal, as he did, as an abomination, as an obscene cannibalistic rite, is made clear in the next paragraph; for there Dickens continues his imagery but also translates it from hints and figures of speech to direct statements. Now we are in another dining place for travelers, an old establishment called the Bull's Head. At the Bull's Head one is served "ailing sweet-breads in white poultices" and "stringy fowls, with lower extremities like wooden legs, sticking up out of the dish" (*AYR* 2: 515). This directive imagery culminates with the succulent main dish of the meal. That featured dish, tender and juicy, is a "cannibalic boiled mutton, gushing horribly among its capers, when carved" (*AYR* 2: 515). For Dickens no imagery could better express his outrage and disgust at the food customarily offered to travelers in the British Isles than the imagery he had just fashioned, imagery that is oblique and insinuating at first but then grows increasingly explicit. That imagery tells us that the food travelers in Britain are compelled to eat is gruesome, corpselike, obscene. It is under a baleful spell. It has been transformed by the docility of the public, the malice of the purveyors, and the cupidity of the owners into ghastly provender, sickening sustenance. The whole system is at fault. Under such a system, held thrall by its dominion, boiled mutton turns into a gruesome body "gushing horribly" when cut, and a traveler turns into a revolting cannibal feasting on brown pimples, flinty hearts, and grim heads.

The imagery is brilliant; it is wonderfully creative and effective.

65. Dickens' Hungry Traveller, Presented With "Cannibalic
Boiled Mutton, Gushing Horribly
. . . When Carved," Is Not Refreshed

This sketch by Phiz, delineating a scene in "Refreshments for Travellers," was
drawn after Phiz had ceased to work with Dickens. The sketch was not published until 1915. Drawing (1860 or after) by Hablot Knight Browne
("Phiz"). Dickens House Museum, London.

It is also quintessentially Dickensian. The old childhood obsession, compelling and sickening, of devouring dead bodies, the old childhood feeling, freeing and fettering, of being an innocent yet somehow guilty participant in forbidden rites—that dual imposition, old yet ever new, unchanged yet ever changing—fills his imagination once more, controlling how he sees the scene and empowering him to realize and convey it.

In *The Old Curiosity Shop,* in the scene in which the mild giants and the savage dwarfs dine, Dickens uses cannibalism to accentuate his potent vision of the grotesque vitality and menace of the bizarre and the exotic; in "Refreshments for Travellers," he uses cannibalism to convey his extraordinary vision of the ordinary, to enforce his special perception of the routine and the everyday. After all, what could be more commonplace, more boringly and depressingly familiar, than the bad food—dreary, sad, run-of-the-mill bad food—purveyed day in and day out by innumerable coffee rooms, pastry shops, refreshment rooms, restaurants, chop houses, inns, and hotels? But that, of course, is the point. For Dickens, cannibalism was—or at least could be—both exotic and ordinary. He used it in myriads of contexts (often opposite, or seemingly opposite) and in myriads of ways.

XIV

One such context and one such way we have met before. As Quilp's lip-smacking relish for "chubby" Little Nell and the Fat Boy's mouthwatering appetite for the delectable Mary suggest, Dickens seems to have had a penchant for edible young females, though his appetite is not quite of the Captain Murderer order. (We recall that David Copperfield "dined off Dora, entirely," while Uriah Heep "made motions with his mouth as if the pear [Agnes] were ripe already, and he were smacking his lips over it" [*DC,* 26:275; 39:410].) The arch, provocative girl-woman, demure but coyly sexual, is the most likely candidate to bring forth Dickens' lip-smacking relish.

Dolly Varden in *Barnaby Rudge* is another tempting morsel of the lip-smacking variety. During the rioting, Dolly, along with her less flirtatious counterpart, Emma Haredale, is captured by the animalistic Hugh. Hugh is smitten by Dolly's beauty and then further aroused—really brought to fever pitch—by her voluptuous resistance to his aggressive lovemaking. Dickens builds towards those lovemaking scenes with imagery of hungry animality, imagery that soon escalates into undisguised ogreish relish. The scenes take place at night. Hugh, fresh from the rioting, emerges from the midnight woods and rejoins some companions who are guarding a curtained post chaise that stands nearby. After downing, without pause, three flasks of wine—the wine "gurgling down his throat"—Hugh's first words are: "'Have you got anything to eat, any of you? I'm as ravenous as a hungry wolf'" (*MHC* 3: *BR*, 59: 278).

A few moments later, still "ravenous as a hungry wolf," Hugh approaches the post chaise in which Dolly and Emma are confined, steps up to Simon Tappertit, who is guarding the two young beauties, and slaps the strutting little peacock on the back:

> "Now then," he cried, "I'm ready. There are brave birds inside this cage, eh? Delicate birds,—tender, loving, little doves. I caged 'em—I caged 'em—one more peep!"
>
> He thrust the little man aside as he spoke, and mounting on the steps which were half let down, pulled down the blind by force, and stared into the chaise like an ogre into his larder. (*MHC* 3: *BR*, 59:278–79)

But ogre Hugh's larder seems to be ogre Dickens' larder as well. A moment later Dickens, using Hugh's voice, tells us that Dolly, one of the "tender, loving, little doves" struggling in that prison-"larder," is delectable. Hugh is enamored—and apparently so is Dickens. As this animalistic animal-tender (ostler), his "great head" bending over Dolly, holds the caged and struggling girl, she tempts him (and Dickens) more and more; she is, as Hugh puts it, "'so bright-eyed, and cherry-lipped, and daintily made'" *MHC* 3: *BR*, 59:279). (The imagery Dickens uses here—of a great ogreish head looming greedily over a young, daintily made female "morsel"—

recalls the imagery Dickens had used a year earlier in depicting Quilp and Little Nell.) Grasping Dolly's "little hand" and refusing to let go of it, Hugh brings his "great head" ever closer to her face, till at last she thrusts the looming head away with all her force and pulls the blind up.

Hugh, thwarted for the moment, climbs up to the front windows of the carriage, taps at them, bends his tousled head against the panes, and leers inside. He continues to eye his prey, to struggle toward the caged birds fluttering in his larder, and as he concentrates on his quarry, Dickens, like Hugh, grows more and more excited. A few moments later, Dickens, now in the guise of narrator, continuing his mouth-watering description of the "cherry-lipped . . . daintily made" Dolly, tells us how "Dolly—beautiful, bewitching, captivating little Dolly—her hair dishevelled, her dress torn, her dark eyelashes wet with tears, her bosom heaving—her face, now pale with fear, now crimson with indignation" is "her whole self a hundred times more beautiful in this heightened aspect than ever she had been before" (*MHC* 3: *BR*, 59:280).

The more ogre Hugh abuses Dolly, the more "heightened" her "aspect" grows, and the more tempting and delicious she becomes ("a hundred times more beautiful," as Dickens puts it). When the carriage stops momentarily in a "lonely spot," Hugh, ravished by Dolly's beauty and seeing his opportunity, jumps in beside her. The struggle now becomes more and more physical. Once more Dolly thrusts Hugh's looming face away "with all her force." But Hugh persists. After he hugs her, Dickens, also ravished, writes: "Poor Dolly! Do what she would, she only looked the better for it, and tempted them the more. When her eyes flashed angrily, and her ripe lips slightly parted, to give her rapid breathing vent, who could resist it?" (*MHC* 3: *BR*, 59:281–82).

Certainly not Dickens. Dickens seems to delight even more than the ogreish Hugh as the "tender . . . little dove" with her "ripe lips" and her "rapid breathing" flutters appetizingly in the "larder." Salivating ever more copiously, sorely "tempted," Dickens runs on, conjuring up vision after vision of appetizing physicality and delicious

66. "Ogre" Hugh in His "Larder" Works Up an Appetite

Hugh, his ogreish appetite whetted by the flutterings of his prey's distress, is shown here enjoying the resistance of one of his "tender, loving, little doves," the "bright-eyed, and cherry-lipped, and daintily made" Dolly Varden. Wood engraving after a drawing by Hablot Knight Browne ("Phiz") for Number 76 (11 September 1841) of *Master Humphrey's Clock*, incorporating Chapter 59 of *Barnaby Rudge*.

distress: "What mortal eyes could have avoided wandering to the delicate boddice, the streaming hair, the neglected dress, the perfect abandonment and unconsciousness of the blooming little beauty?" (*MHC* 3: *BR*, 59:282). What mortal eyes indeed! Dickens' strong condemnation of Hugh and his overt conduct—Hugh is presented here and throughout the book as a savage, society-created man-beast—sanctions Dickens' parallel but more covert fantasies. By condemning Hugh and his ogreish sexual aggressiveness, Dickens (in a strategy he frequently adopted) disassociates himself—seemingly, at least—from the very emotion he is indulging.[46]

Martin Chuzzlewit also has its lusting ogres, ogres who can hardly contain their greedy appetite for luscious young girl-women, especially those who are distressed, trapped, endangered, embarrassed, or otherwise disconcerted. These virginal girl-women are creatures of spotless virtue and surpassing beauty, but their unsullied virtue and their spirited defense of it when it is threatened (as Dolly Varden demonstrates) only whet the ogreish appetite: the more passionate their resistance to ogreish advances, the more appetizing they become to the ogreish palate. Fortyish Mr. Pecksniff, amorous arch-hypocrite, is one such hungry ogre; seventeen-year-old Mary Graham, budding young innocent, is one such tempting dish. (For Dickens, the name "Mary" would have vibrated with special resonances. He would have associated the name, in profoundly emotional ways, with his beloved "angel" sister-in-law, Mary Hogarth, who had died in his arms some five years earlier at the age of seventeen.)[47] Pecksniff's name, on the other hand, hints at his ogreish appetites. That odd name, composed as it is of two easily recognized components, "peck" and "sniff," carries clear connotations of Pecksniff's ogreish proclivities: he smells and eats his prey; that is, he sniffs and pecks at (pecks at "peckishly," to use a popular British colloquialism) his human victims.[48] When Mr. Pecksniff captures and threatens Mary, Dickens conveys that threat through imagery that combines ogreish appetite with reptilian cunning and rapacity.

The scene takes place in a primeval woods, a shady and sensuous domain. The woods contain "deep green vistas where the boughs arched over-head," "dewy fern from which the startled hares leaped up, and fled at [Mr. Pecksniff's] approach," and "mantled pools, and fallen trees, and . . . hollow places . . . whose scent was Memory" (*MC*, 30:360). Into this ancient Eden, oily Mr. Pecksniff glides, or rather stumbles, for he trips over "the spreading root of an old tree." At that moment, alone in the deep woods (the woods where frightened animals leap up and flee from him), at the base of an old tree, wily old Pecksniff, ancient devouring snake, sees Mary. He approaches her and begins his seductive advances, which she, "turning her glowing cheek indignantly upon him," rejects (*MC*, 30:361). (Dickens tells us a little later that Mary's "mind was so strangely constituted that she would have preferred the caresses of a toad, an adder, or a serpent: nay, the hug of a bear: to the endearments of Mr. Pecksniff" [*MC*, 30:363].) But Mr. Pecksniff perseveres. Pressing her arm with one hand and then encircling her waist, he begins to force her. "His disengaged hand, catching hers," he "employed himself in separating the fingers with his own, and sometimes kissing them, as he pursued the conversation." He says, "'My soul! I love you!'" Mary shudders. As Dolly with Hugh, so Mary with Mr. Pecksniff: she tries and tries again to free her hand "but might as well have tried to free herself from the embrace of an affectionate boa constrictor" (*MC*, 30:361–62). Boa constrictor or not—as boa constrictor Mr. Pecksniff would squeeze Mary to death and then swallow her whole—Mr. Pecksniff volunteers the information that he is not "a monster," thereby reminding us that he *is* a veritable monster. Then, saying, "'Ah, naughty Hand!'" he "slapped the hand to punish it" for taking him prisoner, "but relenting, folded it in his waistcoat, to comfort it again." With a "greasy smile," ignoring Mary's vehement protests, Mr. Pecksniff walks on through the woods with her, "his arm round her waist, and her hand in his" (*MC*, 30:362).

Finally, "with a playful tightening of his grasp"—a boa constrictor after all?—he begins to threaten her. Vowing to destroy the future of young Martin Chuzzlewit (whom she loves), he terrifies and subdues her. Mary begins to cry. Still grasping her hand, he tells her that she will eventually, despite anything she may say or think or feel, consent to be his wife. Then, as they emerge from the woods, he pauses playfully and gives us a fleeting glimpse of his inmost nature:

> Holding up her little finger, [he] said in playful accents, as a parting fancy:
>   "Shall I bite it?" (*MC,* 30:364)

Mary does not reply. Mr. Pecksniff kisses the little finger instead of biting it. Then, "stooping down," the monster who proclaims he is no monster, "inclined his flabby face to hers," blessed her, released her hand at last, and let her go. We sense at once that Mr. Pecksniff's outrageous "blessing" has little to do with Mary's welfare; on the contrary, in context it takes on the unmistakable resonances of grace before meals.

Again Dickens has it both ways. The scene is superbly crafted. He casts over this aggressive and frightening episode a humor so engaging and a hypocrisy (here primarily a sexual hypocrisy) so co-lossal and so incipiently perverse (among other things, Mr. Pecksniff has two daughters, Mercy and Charity, who are Mary's age and are struggling in analogous toils), that we follow Mr. Pecksniff's con-founding exploits as we would follow the perverse sexual exploits of some lesser god who is not bound by the moral laws of mere mor-tals. (In analyzing this scene the cannibalistic elements have been emphasized rather than the brilliance of the humor and the felicities of the characterization.) Dickens, in short, could savor every nuance of Mr. Pecksniff's violation of Mary—his enforced fondling of her, and his threats to crush, bite, and devour her—while also separating himself from that violation and condemning it. But here, unlike with Hugh and Dolly, Dickens is artistically successful; he does not intrude himself, that is, he does not overtly or distortingly intrude himself, upon the scene. Though he is profoundly involved in the scene, Dickens is Dickens, and Pecksniff is Pecksniff.

It is worth pausing here to consider one or two striking features that Pecksniff's pursuit of Mary shares with Hugh's pursuit of Dolly.

The former pursuit ends with the great head of the "flabby-faced" "monster" Pecksniff leaning over the petrified maiden and beginning to nibble her pretty little fingers. But this is the very image (shorn of its localizing details) that is repeated four times with Hugh (and four times, vicariously, by Dickens as narrator). Hugh's "great head" twice looms monstrously at the "larder" window, and his great ogre face twice has to be fought off by the terrified Dolly. This frightening image of a great, menacing ogre head looming before one and threatening to devour one alive, or to devour some other helpless innocent or defenseless victim alive, haunted Dickens.

Earlier we examined several of these terrifying cannibalistic scenes of looming ogre heads. In one of those scenes, David Copperfield sees the great ogre head (not the body just the head) of Uriah Heep loom out of the darkness and croak the threat to eat the "ripe pear" Agnes, a threat accompanied by mouthings and swallowings that mime the devouring violation to come. In another of these scenes, the terrifying "Oh, goroo" man, "an ugly old man, with the lower part of his face all covered with a stubbly grey beard," rushes at David, "mouthing as if he were going to tear me in pieces." "I never was so frightened in my life," David tells us, "before or since." All the while this monster, rolling his ghastly head, his "inflamed eyes" "starting out" of that head, proclaims his fierce ogrehood with his horrible "Oh, goroo!" cry, a weird, wild cry that rattles in his throat (*DC*, 13:132–33). This infernal ogre with stubbly beard, working mouth, throaty cry, and bulging red eyes, who is said to have sold himself to the Devil, is named, we are startled to discover, after Dickens himself: his name is "Charley." Dickens, in other words, is once more both innocent victim (for David is profoundly autobiographical) and depraved predator. In the third of these scenes, the terrible, toothy head of the ogre Carker approaches ever closer to Edith Dombey, until, at the assignation in Dijon, it glides toward the dining table and Edith, the toothy head become at last all rapacious mouth and appetite. The roster continues. Quilp's great grimacing ogre head, "smacking" its lips, appearing suddenly before Little Nell; Mr. Venus' blinking ogre head, gulping, swallowing, and

choking, looming eerily out of its steam-filled charnel-house darkness, a ghastly incarnation of charnel-house swallowing; and Magwitch's shaggy ogre head, "licking" its lips, rising suddenly out of
the grave to threaten and terrify Pip (Magwitch is both shameful
father and uncouth alter ego to Pip), then rising once more, rising
out of the misty marshes to bite and snap and tear at its food like
the sharp-toothed head of a ravenous dog—these three devouring
heads are three more evocations of this abiding nightmare vision.[49]

These recurring images of a great ogre head with a terrifying ogre
mouth looming suddenly toward one go back to Dickens' childhood—perhaps, to his infancy. In "A Christmas Tree," an essay that
Dickens wrote in 1859 for *Household Words,* he recalls some of his
earliest memories—"my youngest Christmas recollections," he calls
them—mostly frightening memories of toys, persons, games,
scenes, and episodes that would seem harmless enough, even delightful, to adult perceptions, but which nevertheless scarified the
emerging sensibility of the little child. One of those early memories
concerned a Christmas toy, an "infernal snuff-box":

> Out of [this infernal snuff-box] there sprang a demoniacal Counsellor in
> a black gown, with an obnoxious head of hair, and a red cloth mouth,
> wide open, who was not to be endured on any terms, but could not be
> put away either; for he used suddenly, in a highly magnified state, to fly
> out of Mammoth Snuff-boxes in dreams, when least expected. (*HW*
> 2: 289)

This infernal creature, highly magnified and demoniacal, springing out at one with its great red mouth wide open, haunted Dickens' childhood dreams and his adult imaginings as well. In its
original childhood form, that unendurable nightmare is strongly directive. Its images and associations are freighted with unspoken but
unmistakable meaning. The image of a wide-open red mouth (a
bloodstained mouth?) is not only "infernal," "demoniacal," and
"not to be endured," as Dickens insists (why?), but—and this helps
to answer the "why?"—cannibalistic. The cannibalistic implications
are confirmed not only by the terrifying wide-open mouth itself—
the chief feature in this infernal and demoniacal nightmare—but by

a whole series of linked associations of which the unendurable wide-open mouth is the quintessential prototype.

Later in "A Christmas Tree," for example, Dickens conjures up the childhood image, "dreadfully interesting," of throngs of double-headed giants who stride along "dragging knights and ladies home for dinner by the hair of their heads" (*HW* 2: 290). These throngs of cannibalistic giants are followed by memories of Little Red Ridinghood in the forest (we recall peckish Mr. Pecksniff in the forest with Mary, and Hugh emerging from the forest to attack Dolly) and of the "cruelty and treachery of that dissembling Wolf who ate [Little Red Ridinghood's] grandmother, without making any impression on his appetite, and then ate [Little Red Ridinghood], after making that ferocious joke about his teeth" (*HW* 2: 291). (Hugh, it will be remembered, just before his depredations on Dolly, tells us that he is " 'as ravenous as a hungry wolf' "; likewise, when Carker thinks of Florence, his countenance takes on the ferocious lineaments of a devouring wolf: "Wolf's face that it was then, with even the hot tongue revealing itself through the stretched mouth.") Dickens' cannibalistic allusions in "A Christmas Tree" continue. He follows his references to those "dreadfully interesting" giants who drag their human dinners home and to that fierce cannibalistic wolf of *Little Red Ridinghood* who jokes savagely and then eats grandmother and granddaughter alike, with allusions to *The Arabian Nights* and remembrances of some of the cannibalistic monsters who emerged from those fabled pages. We are told, for example, about "the awful lady, who was a ghoule," and "could only peck [at her rice] by grains, because of her nightly feasts in the burial-place" (*HW* 2: 291). (We think once more of another cannibalistic peck—of the devouring peck of the peckish Pecksniff.)

These intertwined cannibalistic images and associations, all taken from "A Christmas Tree," shed a backward light on the opening cannibalistic image of that essay, the image of the looming ogre head with its wide-open red mouth coming toward one. This terrifying image, nightmare of Dickens' childhood, haunted his early and late dreams and early and late imaginings. Those imaginings, in turn, went into—sometimes became part of—his later fictions.

Variations and transformations of that gaping mouth and ogre head inform some of Dickens' most memorable and frightening fictional scenes. But such variations and transformations are no simple matter. For Dickens often became that demoniacal ogre head, playing the role of the terrifying devourer as well as the terrified devoured. Nor does the ogre head exist in isolation. This emotion-laden cannibalistic image, emerging like King Charles' head out of the dark corners and shadowy depths of earliest childhood, sometimes blends with or reinforces, sometimes counterpoints or contrasts with, other generative but at times also conflicted cannibalistic images from earliest childhood, images such as suckling a mother in love or devouring her in hate, images that are a part of—often a painful, fearful part of—Dickens' artistic enablement and artistic impulse.

But to return to *Martin Chuzzlewit,* not to the delicious Mary Graham and her outrageous (but artistically sublime) nibbler, Mr. Pecksniff, but to a more equivocal case in which, as with the luscious Dolly and her hungry assailant, the larder-plundering ogre, Hugh, Dickens' own contradictory emotions once more intrude into his creation in discordant ways. In the following scene with Ruth Pinch and her brother, Tom, Dickens' emotions, inappropriate in context, overwhelm that relationship, just as they overwhelmed the scene with Dolly and Hugh. Owing to those inappropriate emotions, Ruth emerges as an even more anomalous tidbit of delicious female pulchritude than the tempting morsel Dolly. (In order to convey Dickens' inner vision, I adopt here, as I have occasionally throughout these paragraphs on irresistible young females, Dickens' mouthwatering imagery and mouthwatering point of view.) Ruth is preparing a meat pudding for her sexless brother, Tom. Her food-making here is no accident, and the mouthwatering appetite with which she is observed is not Tom's (poor neutered soul) but Dickens'—a confusion that distorts the scene. After fetching all the ingredients for the pudding, Ruth puts on her apron:

> And being one of those little women to whom an apron is a most becoming little vanity, it took an immense time to arrange; having to be

carefully smoothed down beneath—Oh, heaven, what a wicked little stomacher!—and to be gathered up into little plaits by the strings before it could be tied, and to be tapped, rebuked, and wheedled, at the pockets, before it would set right, which at last it did, and when it did—but never mind; this is a sober chronicle; Oh, never mind! And then there were her cuffs to be tucked up, for fear of flour; and she had a little ring to pull off her finger, which wouldn't come off (foolish little ring!); and during the whole of these preparations she looked demurely every now and then at Tom, from under her dark eye-lashes, as if they were all a part of the pudding, and indispensable to its composition. (*MC*, 39:451–52)

They *are* "all a part of the pudding, and indispensable to its composition." The chief ingredient in this dainty meat pudding, we can be sure, is Ruth, just as the chief ingredients in Captain Murderer's meat pies were his rosy, pie-making brides. But, as with the ogre-larder scene in *Barnaby Rudge,* something has gone wrong here. Unlike most of Dickens' cannibal-tinged scenes, this scene (from an early novel, like the *Barnaby Rudge* scene) is self-indulgent and embarrassing. The inappropriateness of Ruth's coquettishness, the unbelievability of Tom's responsiveness, the incongruity of the brother-sister sexuality, but above all the palpitating coyness with which everything is purveyed—all these discordances serve to emphasize that Dickens' personal emotions (emotions, in this instance, that are primarily rooted in his unresolved feelings toward his sister Fanny who, like his mother, both nurtured and betrayed him—or so he felt), those personal emotions, in context unsuitable emotions, have here overwhelmed his aesthetic control.[50] The meat-pudding vignette violates our concepts of Ruth and Tom: it is false to Ruth's sisterly asexuality, and it is false to Tom's neutered soulfulness, defining character traits, in each instance, that have been assiduously cultivated throughout the novel. Significantly, Dickens pruned this scene of some of its more cloying excesses in later editions. The jarring notes in this vignette are another sign, here in an even more artistically damaging manifestation than the excesses of the *Barnaby Rudge* scene, of the profound connections that linked cannibalistic tropes, equivocal sexuality, and the sources of Dickens' imagination.

XV

In *The Battle of Life* we come upon a very different sort of cannibalistic motif, but one no less rooted in Dickens' beginnings and no less controlling in its shaping power. In that stillborn novelette the central metaphor organizing the framework (but not the substance) of the book is the notion of the living battening on the dead. Dickens conveys this notion quite literally. The chief site of the book is an ancient battlefield. Upon this bloodstained field, life's immemorial cycles occur and reoccur. The living, whether they know it or not, literally feed upon the dead:

> If the host slain upon the field, could have been for a moment reanimated in the forms in which they fell, each upon the spot that was the bed of his untimely death, gashed and ghastly soldiers would have stared in, hundreds deep, at household door and window; and would have risen on the hearths of quiet homes; and would have been the garnered store of barns and granaries; and would have started up between the cradled infant and its nurse; and would have floated with the stream, and whirled round on the mill, and crowded the orchard, and burdened the meadow, and piled the rickyard high with dying men. (*BL*, 9–10)

The rich crops harvested from these fertile fields and burdened orchards spring from the decayed remains of the vast hosts of the dead. Dickens does not shrink from making this notion, artfully suggested in the above passage, graphically and gruesomely explicit in other passages. A bit earlier he had emphasized, in a way that no one could mistake or distance, the revolting relationship between dead bodies and fertile harvests:

> There were deep green patches in the growing corn at first, that people looked at awfully. Year after year they re-appeared; and it was known that underneath those fertile spots, heaps of men and horses lay buried, indiscriminately, enriching the ground. The husbandmen who ploughed those places, shrunk from the great worms abounding there; and the sheaves they yielded, were, for many a long year, called the Battle Sheaves. (*BL*, 7)

scene of that day's work and that night's death and suffering! Many a lonely moon was bright upon the

battle-ground, and many a star kept mournful watch upon it, and many a wind from every quarter of the earth blew over it, before the traces of the fight were worn away.

67. *The Battle of Life:* The Burdened Field

"War." Wood engraving (1846) after a drawing by Clarkson Stanfield. From *The Battle of Life* (1846).

(The illustration that accompanies the harvest passage shows a group of farm workers pausing in their harvesting to drink and refresh themselves in a laden field; the earlier counterpart illustration accompanying the battlefield passage shows the identical field strewn with dead bodies.)

This notion of the living feeding, in effect, on the dead (a refined, time-distanced version of the *Terrific Register's* "THE DEAD DEVOURED BY THE LIVING!") is elaborated in the remainder of the framework. One day the living will join those vast hosts of the dead and will become fodder for generations yet to be born. Then a new crop of men and women will occupy those houses, till those fields, and supply the whirling mill. The connection here with the Dedlock version of this theme, analyzed earlier, is clear; the connection with yet another version in *Edwin Drood,* will be analyzed below. (Dickens wrote the Dedlock version—a much darker rendition of this motif—six years after completing *The Battle of Life;* he wrote the *Edwin Drood* version, another dark rendition, twenty-four years after *The Battle of Life.*) Surprisingly (and instructively), the theme also appears in James Joyce's "The Dead," often with strikingly similar images and juxtapositions. But Joyce was no Dickens, and Dickens no Joyce. The way in which each of these writers conceived the theme, the very vision each had of the idea itself—Joyce renders the motif through myriads of religious associations while Dickens conveys it through thronging cannibalistic suggestions—demonstrates how different, in the midst of kinship and similitude, their outlooks and imaginations were; though it is only fair to add that a very Dickensian sort of cannibalistic imagery emerges strongly in *Ulysses,* especially with Bloom.

The framework of *The Battle of Life* is a meditation. The brief excerpts just quoted, representative samples of the entire framework, provide, like the framework itself, cosmic views of how the present is connected to the past; how, all unconsciously, it takes its sustenance from the past; and how, in the very act of becoming part of the past, it is consumed in turn. The quoted passages, like the entire framework, juxtapose conflict (the battle) with continuity

had marvelled at them as a baby. If the host slain upon the field, could have been for a moment

reanimated in the forms in which they fell, each upon the spot that was the bed of his untimely death, gashed and ghastly soldiers would have stared in, hundreds deep, at household door

68. *The Battle of Life:* The Abundant Harvest

Note that the area depicted in this scene is identical to the area depicted in the battlefield scene (see figure 67). As these illustrations, following Dickens' text, emphasize, the abundant harvest is a product of the burdened field. The living are literally battening on the dead, an idea given dramatic immediacy in this illustration by the drinking and eating harvesters. "Peace." Wood engraving (1846) after a drawing by Clarkson Stanfield. From *The Battle of Life* (1846).

(the regenerative powers of life). Cannibalism, the central image conveying these meanings, is generalized and intellectualized and poeticized here. Yet, even here, traces of Dickens' more habitual usages persist. The "infant and its nurse," that quintessential image for Dickens of felicity and ferocity, emerges once more, like an old blessing or an old curse, from the dim, cannibal-haunted mists of his childhood conditioning. It is as though the mere flow of cannibalistic associations was enough to call forth, quite forcefully yet unbidden, the old, contradictory, emotion-laden image of infant and nurse.

The central idea of the framework of *The Battle of Life*, the idea of taking sustenance from the dead, occurs over and over in Dickens, and in many guises. We see it yet again, but more briefly—more elegiacally and mutedly, as well—in "The City of the Absent," an essay describing the ancient walled City, the commercial and historical heart of London, in its deserted aspect on Saturday evenings after business hours, especially in the summer, or on solitary Sundays in summer. In a long meditative paragraph, Dickens tells us how, on a quiet Saturday evening in the summer of 1862, as he wandered alone through the empty City in the fading light of the fading summer day, he suddenly came upon an old couple reaping a strange harvest in a tiny City churchyard (probably the churchyard of St. Mary-at-Hill): "Gravely among the graves, they made hay, all alone by themselves. They looked like Time and his wife. There was but the one rake between them, and they both had hold of it in a pastorally-loving manner . . . They used the rake with a measured action, drawing the scanty crop towards them; and so I was fain to leave them under three yards and a half of darkening sky, gravely making hay among the graves, all alone by themselves" (*AYR* 9: 494; later in *UT*).

Once more we meet the old image, now no longer in the person of the greedy devourer of putrifying graveyard bodies, or the savage, escaped man-eater of Van Dieman's Land, or the voracious, chewing mothers of the Morgue, or the relentless, ratlike predators of the Vholes tribe, or the hungry harvesters of the fruitful battlefield, but

69. Time and His Wife: "Gravely Making Hay Among the Graves"

"Time And His Wife." Wood engraving (1868) after a drawing by G. P. Pin-
well for the Illustrated Library and Charles Dickens Editions of *The
Uncommercial Traveller.* These editions were produced with Dickens' authori-
zation and under his supervision.

241

in the persons of Time and his wife "gravely making hay among the graves." Yet in this seeming diversity there is unity. All these versions of the old familiar image, and all the other versions we have met, whether ferocious or meditative, grotesque or sublime, tragic or comic, convey the same message, at once universal and inescapable, of man's grim feeding and man's grim end. Earth to earth and dust to dust, they tell us; or, to use Dickens' ordinary, yet extraordinary, workaday similitude, like Time and his wife in the deserted City graveyard, we all, lowly vassals of time, make hay of the grass which is flesh, and in the course of time, at the fading of the day, we become that graveyard hay, garner for those who reap after us.

Churches and graveyards frequently evoked in Dickens these dark cannibalistic thoughts. In the environs of the dead, so Dickens seemed to feel, we confront our destiny most directly. We are all participants in an ineluctable communion, a communion fraught with oneness and with dread. Surrounded by tombs in an ancient tomblike church or gazing at graves in an unkempt city churchyard, Dickens' Christian beliefs whispered brotherhood, community, and continuity; his cannibalistic imaginings whispered revulsion, sickness, and mortality. The more insistent and personalized those cannibalistic imaginings were, the more somber and revolting the recursive aftermath.

Think of some of the beliefs and imaginings we have just surveyed. The battlefield graveyard of *The Battle of Life* (all life is a metaphorical battlefield, Dickens is saying in the story proper) produces not only death but renewal and abundance. Other graveyard messages are drearier. The mouldering dust of the Dedlock church and Dedlock tombs, an exudate of living and dead Dedlocks ingested by Dedlocks and congregants alike, is a baleful distillation of what is yet to come for living Dedlocks and living congregants. What is yet to come for them, as the heedless Dedlock feeding on the living and the dead portends, is death in its bleakest incarnations—a living death (paralysis for Sir Leicester Dedlock), for example, and a retributive death (death at the gate of the fetid city graveyard for Lady Dedlock). The graveyard images, fraught with cannibalistic implications, dissolve, reshape, and recur. In "The City of the Absent," the old man, Old Time himself, steadily reaping the scanty grass of the churchyard tombs, reminds us once more, now in a more distanced and universal image, of our sole destiny: that in time we too will be reaped like grass (indeed, our mouldering bodies will become grass), fodder for the future.

In another late essay, "City of London Churches," Dickens takes up the image of graveyard reaping and feeding yet again, now in a more direct, avowedly cannibalistic, and therefore more disturbing form. The episode takes place on a Sunday morning. Entering an old City church (probably St. James's Garlickhithe off Upper Thames Street), Dickens is confronted by, or rather finds there, dismal images of dust, decay, and death. The church tower is "mouldy"; the bell-puller (death's tolling summoner), "a whity-brown man, whose clothes were once black; a man with flue on him, and cobweb," is ringing time's ancient knell; the church itself is "dim"; the font "has the dust of desuetude thick upon it"; the altar is "rickety"; the Commandments are "damp"; the organ is "hoarse" and "rusty"; the prayer books are "pale" and "faded" (*AYR* 3: 86; later in *UT*). This dust and decrepitude, outward signs of inward rot, are a fitting prelude to the emergence of the presiding feature of this mouldering London church. That feature emerges slowly, quietly. As the service begins, Dickens is overcome by a terrible awareness:

> I . . . find, to my astonishment, that I have been, and still am, taking a strong kind of invisible snuff, up my nose, into my eyes, and down my throat. I wink, sneeze, and cough. The clerk sneezes; the clergyman winks; the unseen organist sneezes and coughs (and probably winks); all our little party wink, sneeze, and cough. The snuff seems to be made of the decay of matting, wood, cloth, stone, iron, earth, and something else.

What is that something else?

> Is the something else, the decay of dead citizens in the vaults below? As sure as Death it is! Not only in the cold damp February day, do we cough and sneeze dead citizens all through the service, but dead citizens have

got into the very bellows of the organ, and half choked the same. We stamp our feet, to warm them, and dead citizens arise in heavy clouds. Dead citizens stick upon the walls, and lie pulverised on the sounding-board over the clergyman's head, and, when a gust of air comes, tumble down upon him. (*AYR* 3: 86)

As Dickens' complicity in and awareness of this gruesome communion grow, so do his responses. He begins to react in profoundly physical ways. He is "so nauseated" by his realization of what he is ingesting, so sickened by this feeding on "dead citizens," that he cannot pay attention to anything that comes thereafter (*AYR* 3: 86). As in the many Morgue episodes discussed earlier, the hallucination of eating corpses, a hallucination ever lurking in Dickens' consciousness, evokes nausea and revulsion. But ingesting the sickening dust of ancient compatriots and fellow sufferers does more than produce a passing wave of nausea: the experience etches on Dickens' consciousness a sickening cannibalistic memory of the occasion, yet another emotion-fraught souvenir of time that festers and gestates and generates, and that cannot be erased.

Dickens continued his survey of City of London churches for about a year, a survey that began with his visit to this tomblike but representative church in the heart of the ancient City. That first visit presaged what was to come. He found that every church he entered throughout that year was pervaded by the "invisible snuff" of "dead citizens," a mortal essence, a gruesome repast, a flavor "sure as Death" (*AYR* 3: 86).

But it was not simply City of London churches or English country churches that evoked fantasies in Dickens of eating dead bodies; other churches, foreign churches, French-Flemish churches and Mediterranean churches (to cite only two examples) evoked images of ghoulish feeding as well.[51] "In the French-Flemish Country," Dickens describes the diminutive chapels, shrines, crosses, and saints that abound at roadside corners, in hollow trees, and on the tops of poles in the French-Flemish countryside, a region that he is now (in the dramatic situation of the essay) traveling through. The essay describes a pause in this rambling journey (most likely made in February 1863) as Dickens wends his slow, stop-filled way toward his hideaway at Condette outside of Boulogne, and probably to a sojourn with Ellen Ternan.[52] During that pause in his trip, as he wanders about a French-Flemish town, he sees yet another small shrine, this one outside a church. He gazes at the shrine and its surrounding churchyard tombs, and as he does so, cannibalistic visions throng through his mind. The cannibalistic associations engendered by the churchyard shrine are more direct and more grotesquely gruesome than those evoked by the solemn churchyard haymaking of "The City of the Absent," or the sinister "snuff" ingestion of "City of London Churches," or the mouldy "taste" of the "dead and buried" Dedlocks in the Dedlock church in *Bleak House*. Now, wandering alone through a foreign town, the sights and thoughts that confront him, sights and thoughts of bones, shrines, tombs, and dead bodies, evoke more savage images:

> Not that we are deficient in such decoration [as small shrines, religious statues, etc.] in the town here, for, over at the church yonder, outside the building, is a scenic representation of the Crucifixion, built up with old bricks and stones, and made out with painted canvas and wooden figures: the whole surmounting the dusty skull of some holy personage (perhaps), shut up behind a little ashey iron grate, as if it were originally put there to be cooked, and the fire had long gone out. (*AYR* 10: 61)

But this was not the onset of Dickens' cannibalistic musings. Just before he wrote this passage, his mind had filled with muted, half-formed cannibalistic associations, associations that rose up unbidden even now as he was writing—some months after the fact of the trip—associations that had become entwined with the day, the scene, the circumstances, and the emotions of that vanished French-Flemish journey. In the same paragraph as the skull-cooking passage, just before he wrote about that grim *memento mori* and the crucifixion and its clustering figures, he had spoken of harvesting and reaping (shades of *The Battle of Life* or of Old Time and his wife making hay!) and then had gone on to say that the harvested ricks he had seen in the French-Flemish country were better constructed than elsewhere—"round swelling peg-top ricks, well thatched: not a shapeless brown heap, like the toast out of a Giant's toast-and-water, pinned to the earth with one of the skewers out of his kitchen" (*AYR* 10: 61). We know only too well what Dickens associated with Giants' food and Giants' kitchens. Knowing such associations, it does not surprise us that he immediately goes on to talk about eggs, chickens, parents of chickens—he uses the word *parents*—and then drumsticks of chickens, and that he follows this series with his cannibalistic disquisition on crucifixions, dusty skulls, ashy grates, macabre cooking, and fires grown cold.

Nor is it surprising, in view of these images crowding one upon the other—images of Giants' kitchens, parents, offspring, dead bodies, food, and eating—that Dickens follows the skull-cooking passage (still in the same paragraph) with images of a poor peasant couple who are inadequate parents to their exploited, laboring child. The images are still cannibalistic, but now they have circled back more directly to Dickens' own childhood and to blacking-factory thoughts, grim nightmare thoughts of slaving and being devoured alive, a "poor little drudge," a mere "little labouring hind," a "small Cain" ("except that I had never done harm to any one"), an innocent little lamb savaged by a predatory world (F, 25; *DC*, 11:111; F, 27). The scene Dickens is now envisioning in this French-Flemish country is stark and savage. Blacking-factory thoughts and feelings color—or, rather, continue to color—what he summons up and what he describes.

The inadequate parents in this new-old French-Flemish nightmare are weavers. They bend over their loom, "while the child, working too, turns a little hand-wheel put upon the ground to suit its height" (*AYR* 10: 61). This French-Flemish child, another laboring hind condemned to drudging labor by its impoverished parents, is enslaved by the insatiable loom. The loom in that tiny dwelling is "an unconscionable monster" who asserts "himself" as "the bread-winner," and who tyrannizes over the meager household, ruling, demanding, and aggrandizing (*AYR* 10: 61). The monster loom, like a voracious latter-day giant, swallows up the household. His menacing neediness, his insatiable demands—these are Dickens' anthropomorphizing designations—give the loom primacy over all those who tend and serve him.

He dominates the house and its inhabitants, "straddling over the children's straw beds, cramping the family in space and air," making "tyrannical" demands to be tended and fed—tended and fed, in the last analysis, by the sacrificed lives of those who wait on him, most notably (and most pitifully) by the sacrificed life of the exploited, laboring child (*AYR* 10: 61). The insatiable loom, in short, gobbles up these human lives. But the monster loom, like some lesser giant, must pay tribute to his mighty kin, his great monster lords. Those monster lords, who demand their "tributary" portion, are the "ugly mills and factories" rising "in an abrupt bare way" out of the sluiced field and claiming their stream of human victims in the old tyrannical way (*AYR* 10: 61). So the child-devouring monster, if not a blacking factory, is a blackening factory after all.

In passages such as these, which blur and blend and meander from association to association like consciousness itself, we see once more the ebb and flow of Dickens' mind in its obsessive cannibalistic phases, and we also see once more his wonderfully free yet profoundly determined and profoundly repetitive imaging[53]: his old association, for example, of harvesting and reaping with cannibalistic feeding (the harvested hayricks and the Giant's kitchen); or yet again, his juxtaposition of corpse-eating (skull-cooking) with devouring parents and devoured or devouring children (exploited children, innocent yet somehow guilty, and consigned in their unaccountable innocence and guilt to monstrous servitude, to blacking-factory or loom-tending hells). In such passages the rich creativity of Dickens' mind and some of the dark secret forces that helped shape that extraordinary creativity, mingle and coalesce and reappear in an almost primordial flux—at once dreamlike, personal, and private, yet real, universal, and uniquely public. Dickens understood this aspect of his creativity. He knew that his stressful past was part of his curse—and part of his gift. He also knew that the dead past is not dead, that it impinges on the living present and shapes its inmost nature.

XVI

In *Edwin Drood*, Dickens' last novel, death-haunted and death-stilled, the living and the dead are no less intimately juxtaposed than they are in *The Battle of Life*, or "The City of the Absent," or "City of London Churches," or "In the French-Flemish Country," but now that juxtaposition is part of the design and execution of the entire work, its outmost seeming and its inmost meaning. In the cold crypts and vaults of ancient Cloisterham Cathedral, the dead moulder ceaselessly, and ceaselessly they become incorporated into the living.

The most obvious example of this absorption occurs with Stony Durdles. He not only makes the dead his food and drink—for he is a stonemason, a dealer in tombstones and monuments, a warder of the nether world of crypt, tomb, and vault, and thus takes his sustenance from the world of the dead—but he breathes the substance of the dead, is dusted by their corporeal remains, and works and dines and sleeps in their domain. Stony Durdles is "covered from head to foot with old mortar, lime, and stone grit" (*ED*, 5:30), and he often complains of his cold, crypt abode. Think, he says on one occasion, " 'what the bitterness [of the cold] is to Durdles, down in the crypt among the earthy damps there, and the dead breath of the old 'uns' " (*ED*, 4:26)—the "old 'uns" being Durdles' familiar term for his dead compatriots long since turned to dust in their ancient graves. (That dust—the dust of the "old 'uns"—is the chief ingredient in the "dead breath" that Durdles constantly breathes.) Durdles ingests—dines on—the "old 'uns," and not just occupationally (when working down in the crypt) or economically (not just when taking his sustenance from the dead). Durdles carries his dinner wherever he goes, but, like Gabriel Grub, the ghoulish gravedigger of *Pickwick* (see figure 70), Durdles often eats his meals

70. The Gravedigger Gabriel Grub, Guzzling on Tombs, Has a Nightmare Vision

In Dickens' first novel, *The Pickwick Papers,* he depicted a surly and drunken haunter of graves who, like Durdles more than thirty years later (in Dickens' last novel, *Edwin Drood*), lives by death, eats and drinks on tombs, and is tormented at night by goblins of the nether world. To cite just one ghoulish detail from the earlier work, a typical touch, as Gabriel Grub digs a grave on Christmas Eve, he takes comfort in the thought that he is helping to prepare "A rich, juicy meal for the worms to eat." Gabriel's subsequent late-night adventures, however, unlike Durdles', are part of a straightforward dream-vision fable. Etching by Hablot Knight Browne ("Phiz") for Number X, Chapter XXVIII (December 1836) of *The Pickwick Papers.*

perched on top of his quarry, that is, on top of that which sustains him. Dickens makes a point of showing us this. He depicts Durdles, quite unmistakably and quite pointedly, "sitting on all manner of tombstones to dine" (*ED*, 4:25). Durdles, clearly, not only lives *by* death but *on* death—and this actually as well as metaphorically: like his many literary and graphic prototypes (see figure 71), Durdles literally and figuratively dines on death. By means of such tropes, comments, and embodiments, and by much more in the same vein, Dickens shows us, beyond any gainsaying or mistaking, that Durdles is the living warder and consumer of the dead. At times, however, Dickens suggests Durdles' nature by direct statement rather than by implication. "Durdles," he tells us on one such occasion, "is always prowling among old graves and ruins, like a Ghoule" (*ED*, 12:89).

Stony Durdles, the dusty and disreputable Ghoul of Cloisterham, is only the most obvious feeder on the dead. John (or "Jack") Jasper, the melodious choirmaster of Cloisterham, who fresh from an opium den sings sweetly of the wicked man, and who spends a night with Durdles exploring the dusty mysteries of the mouldering crypts, busies himself murderously with the living and the dead. Quilplike, he hopes to enjoy thereby his version of a reluctant Little Nell (or his version of other ogre-threatened Dickensian sylphs, his version of Dolly Varden or Mary Graham, say), his "rosy, cosy" rose bud, with her "little pink gloves, like rose-leaves, and . . . her little pink fingers [raised] to her rosy lips" (lips Jasper always gazes at with rapt longing)—the delectable bonbon, Rosa Bud (*MHC* 1: *OCS*, 9:137; *ED*, 3:17). Rosa feels the breath of death overwhelming her whenever Jasper comes near her: she faints or she flees.

Rosa's fear of Jasper, and the cannibalistic imagery that helps convey that primal fear, are underscored and intensified not simply by Jasper's hungry longing and her own terrified reaction but by the actions and responses of others, by the reactions of Edwin, for example. Edwin has good reason to fear the solicitous ogre Jasper, but his fear is intermittent, and it usually exists subliminally or unconsciously. This is not surprising, for Jasper's motives are often hidden and subtle—hidden, at times, even from his own unwavering gaze.

71. "We Live by Death"

Durdles, sitting on tombstones to dine, recapitulates (in a more subtle and ramifying way) what Rowlandson depicts in this drawing. In Rowlandson's sketch, a convivial group of celebrants, sitting in a graveyard, perched on tombs, surrounded by coffins, skulls, and bones, reap the bounty of their ghoulish occupations. A lawyer brandishes a last will and testament, while a gravedigger drinks, a verger smokes, and a clergyman clutches his pot of liquor; the latter two functionaries, fat, jovial, and self-contented, sit comfortably on a tomb that bears the inscription "We Live by Death." Meanwhile, in the distance, the driver of a hearse waves his hat in a brotherly salute and a sign on the church proclaims, "Dye All." *The Churchyard Debate*. Drawing (1816) by Thomas Rowlandson. Huntington Library, San Marino, California.

Yet the outward signs of Jasper's inner appetites often emerge. His hungry designs on Edwin, his complicated cannibalistic love-hate relationship with him (like Dickens' cannibalistic love-hate relationship with his mother) is evidenced not only in Jasper's intense actions and reactions whenever he is with Edwin, but in the extraordinary way he looks at him. As Edwin ("the young fellow," Dickens calls him here) takes off his "coat, hat, gloves, and so forth"—his disrobing is made indeterminate by the "so forth"—the older man "looks on intently" (*ED*, 2:6). It may seem at this point—speaking of "inner appetites" and "hungry designs"—that too much is being read into this intent look and, furthermore, that the parallel drawn between Jasper's complicated love-hate relationship with Edwin and Dickens' complicated love-hate relationship with his mother is farfetched. But this crucial scene is strange and directive (indeed, its very strangeness serves to direct us), and Dickens will soon emphasize and extend the details just isolated.

The scene, as a matter of fact, is fundamental. Dickens is introducing us here to the Jasper-Edwin relationship; this is the first time we see Jasper and Edwin together. As the scene opens, Jasper is waiting in his gatehouse residence for Edwin's arrival. When Edwin enters, Jasper "catches" the "young fellow in his arms," and exclaims, "'My dear Edwin!'" (*ED*, 2:6). Edwin responds with a similar greeting. "'My dear Jack!'" he says. "'So glad to see you!'" Initially, Dickens calls Edwin a "young fellow," but almost immediately he begins to call him a "boy" as well (Jasper also calls Edwin a "boy"), and thereafter the terms "young fellow" and "boy" are repeatedly applied to Edwin (*ED*, 2:6, 7ff.). By these and similar means, Jasper, Edwin's seemingly sedate and judicious uncle, who "looks older than he is" (*ED*, 2:6), is made to appear a generation older than his boyish and impulsive nephew. (It comes as something of a shock to find that Jasper is twenty-six, Edwin twenty.)

But the relationship being depicted in this introductory scene, though it suggests a parent-child relationship, is not that of a father to a son but of a mother to a son. This anomaly emerges at once. Immediately after Jasper embraces Edwin, he says: "'Get off your greatcoat, bright boy, and sit down here in your own corner. Your feet are not wet? Pull your boots off. Do pull your boots off'" (*ED*, 2:6). Jasper, in this incarnation, is a hovering mother (and, as we shall see in a moment, a devouring one); Edwin is an overprotected and diminished son. With the barest hint of exasperation and irritation, Edwin replies to Jasper's fussing and mothering: "'My dear Jack, I am as dry as a bone. Don't moddley-coddley . . . I like anything better than being moddley-coddleyed'" (*ED*, 2:6). (Note here also the reference to "bone," a reference that will shortly take on sinister meaning.) It is at this point that Edwin, having refused to divest himself of his boots, divests himself of his coat, hat, gloves, and "so forth"; and it is at this point that Jasper, devouring mother of Edwin and devouring lover of Rosa, watches "the young fellow" "intently."

Jasper's intent look, as Dickens is careful to let us know, is no ordinary look. Dwelling on the specialness of Jasper's look—it has hypnotic as well as cannibalistic implications—Dickens once more emphasizes its intensity, and then he proceeds to characterize its peculiar qualities and importance: "Once for all, a look of intentness and intensity—a look of hungry, exacting, watchful, and yet devoted affection—is always, now and ever afterwards, on the Jasper face whenever the Jasper face is addressed in this direction" (*ED*, 2:6). (Note the ambiguity and attention-getting awkwardness of the twice-used locution "the Jasper face," a locution that suggests a hard, cold, pitiless mask, a stonelike mask.) Strong and striking and repetitive though this description is, Dickens does not leave the matter here. He goes on to tell us that the "intense," "watchful," "affectionate," "hungry" look—the concentrated look of a ravenous animal stalking the prey it loves and also devours—is present whenever "the Jasper face" is turned toward Edwin. "And," says Dickens, further underlining and elaborating what he has just underlined and elaborated so forcefully, "whenever it is so addressed, it is never, on this occasion or on any other, dividedly addressed; it is always concentrated" (*ED*, 2:6).

Perhaps the most chilling evocation of that intense devouring look comes at the conclusion of Chapter 5. Edwin lies asleep in his "sleeping chamber," "calm and untroubled," and Jasper ascends an inner staircase to look at him (*ED*, 5:32). A moment later Jasper stands over the calm, unconscious young fellow, "looking down upon him." Jasper stands there, opium pipe in hand, looking and looking at the sleeping Edwin "with a fixed and deep attention" (*ED*, 5:32). The scene is simple, direct, chilling. We realize with mounting horror the implications of what we are viewing. Edwin, asleep, is like a dead man, a corpse, and Jasper is looking at him as he always looks—we were told in the early pages of the book of the special and invariable nature of that "intense," "devoted," "hungry" gaze—in other words, Jasper is looking at Edwin once more with a long, lingering, devouring look of love and rapacity. The scene foreshadows what is to come. Edwin will become a corpse; Jasper will devour him.

What are we to make of these strange half-ferocious, half-loving scenes (in the first scene a mother coddles her careless boy, in the second scene a mother looks in on her sleeping child—I underline for the moment only the benign aspects of each scene), and what are we to make of Jasper's strange half-motherly, half-cannibalistic interest in Edwin? Clearly, these strange scenes and Jasper's equivocal responses testify once more to the obsessive force that the mother-cannibal image held for Dickens (we remember the life-long series of mother-cannibal figures who appear in his reports, essays, letters, novels, and recollections, in his childhood reading, coroner's inquest appearances, Morgue visits, night walks, character creations, and set-piece scenes). Jasper's equivocal responses are additional signs of how that mother-cannibal figure haunted Dickens, a haunting that is highlighted once more by the fact that here in *Drood* he casts over two young men the anomalous image of mother and son, and not simply of an ordinary mother and son, but of a "devoted" and "affectionate" mother who is also "exacting" and "hungry," and who devours—that is, eventually murders and then metaphorically consumes (casts into the hellish lime pit)—the object of her love. Given the suggestions and reverberations that hover

over these scenes, given their ultimate origins in Dickens' distant past, it is easy to understand why Dickens, at the very outset of his novel, placed so much emphasis on Jasper's intense equivocal look of devoted and hungry affection.

That hungry look, its many analogues, and its many concordant and discordant implications haunt the consciousness (all unknowingly, of course) of Jasper's would-be prey. His intended victims feel his malign influence, but they respond to rather than understand their fears. When Edwin tells Rosa, "'I am a little afraid of Jack,'" Rosa instantly cries out, turns white, and clasps her hands (*ED*, 13:102). Edwin, disconcerted momentarily by her response, teases her by paraphrasing the best-known line from *Bluebeard*. "'Why, sister Rosa, sister Rosa,'" he says, "'what do you see from the turret?'" (*ED*, 13:102). Rosa does not answer this question, but we see from the turret what Rosa intuits and Edwin, despite his prescient fear, hardly suspects. For Edwin's unthinking raillery conveys Jasper's true nature and Rosa's dire peril. Unwittingly, but most fittingly, Edwin has associated Rosa with the doomed, terror-stricken wife of Bluebeard, last in a long procession of doomed wives, who is about to be murdered (and knows she is about to be murdered) by her implacable husband.

But there is another, more sinister, implication in this frightening foreshadowing. From early childhood Dickens associated the story of *Bluebeard* with the story of "Captain Murderer." The savage protagonist of "Captain Murderer," however, is no ordinary Bluebeard; he is a Bluebeard who not only murders but also eats his wives. (Dickens himself calls Captain Murderer a version of Bluebeard: "This wretch [Captain Murderer] must have been an offshoot of the Blue Beard family" [("Nurse's Stories"), *AYR* 3: 518].) So, for Dickens, the threat in this scene from *Edwin Drood* is not simply murderous but cannibalistic, and though this threat is momentary and distanced—for Edwin and for Rosa—it is real and fearfully palpable: we are given a horrific forecasting glimpse of Jasper's murderous and cannibalistic ferocity.

Cannibalism for Dickens was always a paradigm of supreme degradation and inhumanity. He associated it with the most bestial murders, the most depraved aggressions, the most revolting assimilations, the most profane and gruesome deaths. When unsoftened by humor, undistanced by metaphor, or unmitigated by other screening strategies, it emerges in Dickens' writings as ravening human ferocity, as waking nightmare itself.

Like Edwin's submerged but well-founded fear, Rosa's peril is dire. She intuitively knows that she will be eaten alive by the frightening ogre Jasper, close kin to Bluebeard and Captain Murderer. Dickens surrounds Jasper with scores of similar cannibalistic hints and touches. By such means, by hints, allusions, and associations, Dickens enlarges and mythologizes Jasper's threat, and by such means, and by a multitude of concordant strategies, he turns Jasper into the chief focus of darkness in the novel: a smooth and crafty manipulator and devourer. (Jasper—or at least one half of him, the dark, submerged half—intends, as the looks and fears and hints we have just surveyed portend, to devour Edwin too, and not simply metaphorically. One gruesome portion of Jasper's diabolic plan is to feed Edwin's body to the all-consuming lime pit, there to have the body—perhaps still alive—eaten into nothingness.) But Jasper, public choirist and secret devourer, is only the first demon among many demons. Like Durdles and Deputy—two lesser monsters, who are sinned against as well as sinning—and like all the other graveyard creatures of Cloisterham, haunters of tombs and traffickers in corpses, Jasper, frequenter of opium dens and connoisseur of cathedral crypts, sups at Death's table.

As a matter of fact, Jasper, Durdles, and Deputy are only egregious examples of a universal corruption. All the inhabitants of Cloisterham, indeed, all the inhabitants of the surrounding countryside, participate in this corruption. One sign of their fallen state is their unremitting cannibalism. Yet, for the most part, the citizens of Cloisterham are unwitting man-eaters; they rarely examine—indeed they hardly know—what they do or who they are. They live in a cloistered city and lead cloistered lives, but they cloister (that is protect and veil, seclude and confine) more than the sleepy tranquil-

ity that seems to pervade their daily routines. For Cloisterham is
not simply a city of dreaming spires and heavenly choirs, of drowsy
"bygone time" and "oppressive respectability" (*ED*, 3:12); it is a
city of cloistered, that is, of hidden lusts and hidden evil, of subterranean urges, subterranean appetites, and dim subterranean
tombs—cloisterings of a darker sort. And Cloisterham—based
quite literally on Dickens' boyhood and manhood city of Rochester—is also, quite literally, a city of ghouls and ogres:

> An ancient city, Cloisterham, and no meet dwelling-place for any one
> with hankerings after the noisy world. A monotonous, silent city, deriving
> an earthy flavor throughout, from its cathedral crypt, and so abounding
> in vestiges of monastic graves, that the Cloisterham children grow small
> salad in the dust of abbots and abbesses, and make dirt-pies of nuns and
> friars; while every ploughman in its outlying fields renders to once puis-
> sant Lord Treasurers, Archbishops, Bishops, and such-like, the attention
> which the Ogre in the story-book desired to render to his unbidden visi-
> tor, and grinds their bones to make his bread. (*ED*, 3:12; see figure 72)

All Cloisterham eats this gruesome bread, partaking of a profane
communion. Dickens is usually less explicit than this. He hints and
suggests rather than declares. *Edwin Drood*, like all his middle and
late novels, is dense with covert signs and hidden portents, but
forthright passages such as this also abound, and they are intended
to alert and guide our awareness. They make us sensitive to more
muted implications. Guided by such awareness, we recognize and
interpret the more subtle hints that throng the pages of the novel
and help reinforce and enlarge its meaning. The bone-grinding passage and its many echoes and variations make clear, for example,
that the corruption Dickens is describing, a corruption reified by
images of ogreish feeding, is so insidious and so encompassing that
it taints the entire social order. The earthy flavor of Cloisterham Cathedral, the earthy flavor of Cloisterham bread, is the earthy flavor
of the Cloisterham community, of their—and our (as Dickens sees
it)—mortality. Indeed, Cloisterham Cathedral itself is anthropo-
morphosed into a devouring cannibal. On one occasion, as Mr.

72. Rochester Cathedral: The Earthy Crypt

The "earthy flavor" of the thirteenth-century crypt and of the entire cathedral—a "flavor" that Dickens fashioned in *Edwin Drood* into a richly connotative leitmotif—resulted from the fact that the earthen floor of the crypt (not paved during Dickens' lifetime) exhaled its mouldering breath into every nook and cranny of the unheated and often damp cathedral. "Rochester Cathedral: View of the Crypt." Engraving after a drawing by Hablot Knight Browne. From *Winkles's Cathedrals* (1835–36).

Grewgious passes the great western folding door of the cathedral, a door which is just then opened wide for airing the building, he has a startling reaction: "'Dear me,' said Mr. Grewgious, peeping in, 'it's like looking down the throat of Old Time'" (*ED*, 9:63; see figure 73). Time, of course, will devour not only Mr. Grewgious, but all the sons—and daughters—of men.

Cannibalism is a nightmare reduction and enlargement of our appetites and our destiny. Predators in life, we become fodder in death. In *Edwin Drood*, as in *The Battle of Life, Bleak House,* "City of London Churches," "The City of the Absent," and many allied works, Dickens uses the savage trope of cannibalism as a distillation of our foragings and our final end. Children at their innocent dirt-pie games, ploughmen at their productive and beneficent tilling, become part of this ineluctable process. They become, all unwittingly, bone-grinding ogres and bone-eating cannibals. They thus adumbrate and perpetuate, however dimly (and however mitigated by Dickens' artistic virtuosity and macabre humor), the more terrifying appetites and the more murderous predations of the Jaspers of this world. They also adumbrate our universal complicity and our universal destiny.

As the bone-grinding and Old Time passages suggest, places as well as persons figure in this deathlike banqueting; and, as these passages also suggest, the omnipresent cannibalism that binds children, ploughmen, stonemasons, choirmasters, city officials, and archbishops in a gruesome kinship can be traced to a central source. That source, which imparts its character to all of Cloisterham—imposes its "earthy flavor throughout," as Dickens puts it—derives, ironically, from the "cathedral crypt," the quintessential embodiment, not of spiritual sanctity or blessedness, despite the vast hosts of entombed abbots, abbesses, nuns, friars, bishops, and archbishops that slumber quietly there, but of corrupted and corrupting mortality: the embodiment, in short, of death—of "earthy flavor," "Old Time," and mouldering human dust.

Cloisterham Cathedral—"square-towered," "ancient," "slowly mouldering"—is deceptive and dual in all its multitudinous aspects. Like so much else in Cloisterham, it appears to be and is one thing

73. The Great West Door of Rochester Cathedral
(Cloisterham Cathedral) Opened
Wide for Airing the Building

"'Dear me,' said Mr. Grewgious, peeping in, 'it's like looking down the throat of Old Time.'"—*Edwin Drood.* "Rochester Cathedral (West Door)." Wood engraving by Robert Langton. From Langton, *The Childhood and Youth of Charles Dickens* (1883).

but also is another. Dedicated to the resurrection and eternal life, it is one vast sepulcher of grisly death. It reaches up to light and to heaven, but all the while, deep in its dark depths, it moulders and it festers. Like the old Dedlock church, or the mouldering City of London churches, the still older cathedral is redolent of corpses and decay. The dust and effluvia of the "old 'uns" pervade its atmosphere in damps and chills and vapors that hang heavily in aisle and nave, envelop the altar, and hug the subterranean crypt. All who enter the cathedral's portals, and especially all who enter its dank crypts and hollowly echoing vaults, breathe centuries of rot and decay and with each breath ingest the mouldering bodies of their long-dead fellowmen. Its choirmaster, singing melodiously of life, dreams of opium and of death; its keeper of graves and monuments, dead drunk amidst the sanctified tombs, guzzles his liquor, then sleeps his stony sleep; the cathedral's light is dim, its echoes hollow, its temperature cold, its atmosphere heavy with death and corruption. It is no wonder that this sanctuary of God becomes a sanctuary of murder. It is no wonder, too, that its "earthy flavor" permeates and poisons all the surrounding countryside. Finally, it is no wonder that those who frequent its innermost sanctuary or dwell in its midnight depths feed on death and dissolution. (See figure 74.)

In such encompassing visions as this, cannibalism frequently becomes a shadowy background of daily living and breathing. We are often hardly aware that the cannibalistic theme is there; we respond rather than recognize. The motif fades into atmospheres, dissolves into connotations, dwindles into faintly whispered hints. Blurred, softened, and transformed—now muted, now almost effaced—it murmurs, like a distant chorus or far-off lamentation, of man's dusty appetites and man's dusty end. So transmuted and so effaced, hinting rather than stating, cannibalism becomes another way for Dickens to make tangible his somber meditations on life.

XVII

We have come a long way from nurses' stories and penny periodicals. And yet, have we really traveled so far? With cannibalism, surely,

74. Rochester Cathedral: "Square-Towered"
and "Slowly Mouldering"

This is Rochester Cathedral—"square-towered," "ancient," "slowly moulder-ing"—as Dickens knew it for most of his life. A stopgap wooden spire had been removed from the tower in 1823; the present spire was not erected until early in the twentieth century. In *Edwin Drood*, Cloisterham and Cloisterham Cathedral are patterned closely on Rochester and Rochester Cathedral. "Rochester Cathedral." Drawing (1888) by F. G. Kitton. From Hughes, *A Week's Tramp in Dickens-Land* (1893).

Dickens' end was his beginning. *Edwin Drood, David Copperfield,* and *Our Mutual Friend; Great Expectations, Nicholas Nickleby,* and *Bleak House;* these, and all the other writings we have touched upon—and the many writings, unmentioned here, that might have been summoned in turn—demonstrate what we see so often in Dickens' work: that he has taken the most unlikely anxieties and impositions of his early life and transformed them. The unspeakable rites of cannibalism, fraught with the special dread of his earliest days, became a matrix of art, of bright humor, wild flights of fancy, great structuring metaphors, dark thematic undertones, and penetrating social criticism. But behind the humor, metaphors, and criticism, behind the comic oddity of the "Oh, goroo" man and the measured realism of Gaffer Hexam's ghastly fishing, lurked profound uneasiness and at times profound dread. In the somber depths below such art the dark man of the Morgue floats, and in those same subterranean depths the red-faced man of the London streets enacts his nightly ritual of murdering and eating his mother, sickening symptoms of a fear and a rage that will not disappear. There is nothing mechanical or inevitable in this equation of early scars and subsequent creation. We all have dark corners of the mind that we go back to against our will, but how many of us use such regions to create as Dickens did? We can describe but we cannot fathom the awesome mysteries of creation.

With Dickens, creation was never static. He changed, and he usually grew. We see this everywhere. We see it in the dark shadings of his shaping night side. We see it, most particularly, in his use of cannibalism. With cannibalism he progresses from simple humor to complex criticism, from self-contained allusions to universal themes, from denial to awareness. These developments were not linear or monolithic or total. By the same token, such developments do not diminish his earlier achievements or set them off—set them off entirely, that is—from their later counterparts. It is worth recalling, for example, that in *Holiday Romance,* that *jeu d'esprit* designed for children (though carefully calculated to amuse adults as well), a work written only three years before his death, Dickens pro-

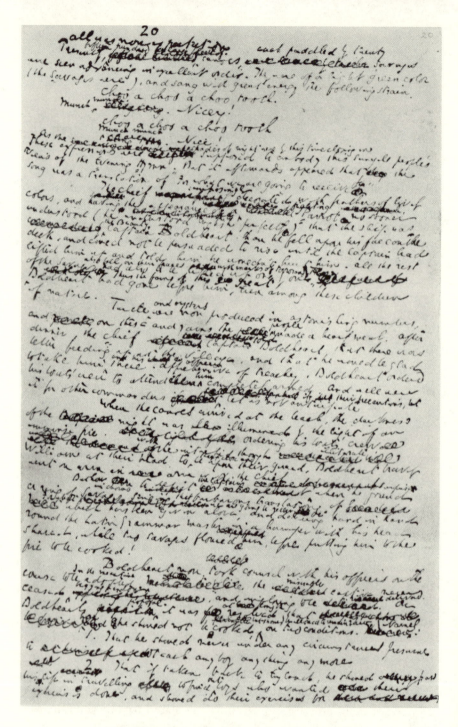

75. The Cannibals Sing of Munching

"Choo" already settled and "muntch" (with a *t*) yet to come, Dickens adds
"munch" (without a *t*) to the cannibals' song: "Munch munch. Nicey!" (See
Part 1, note 54.) Page 20 of the MS (1867) of *Holiday Romance* (1868).
Pierpont Morgan Library, New York.

vides us with the edifying information that William Boozey, the devoted captain of the foretop on Captain Boldheart's becalmed and
beleaguered ship, *The Beauty,* "repeatedly requested to be killed,
and preserved for the Captain's table" (*OYF* 4: *HR,* 3:196). This
burlesque sally, a parody of the literature of voyages and travels, and
of Dickens' rapt and special childhood (and later) interest in that
disaster-filled literature (we recall that the real-life mate of the real-
life *Philip Aubin,* in an episode that Dickens had cited years earlier
in "The Lost Arctic Voyagers," had "exhorted" his crewmates "to
cut a piece out of his thigh, and quench their thirst"), is soon followed by more elaborate invocations of forbidden feasting. A moment or two after Boozey's noble offer, swarms of green-skinned
cannibals paddle gleefully toward the beleaguered *Beauty,* chanting
in the bliss of their anticipation:

> Choo a choo a choo tooth.
>   Muntch, muntch. Nycey!
> Choo a choo a choo tooth.
>   Muntch, muntch. Nyce!
> (*OYF* 4: *HR,* 3:197)

(The fact that Dickens spells "chew" c-h-o-o and "munch" m-u-n-
t-c-h emphasizes the comedy but at the same time, by a species of
inverted disguise, emphasizes the reality of chewing and munching
as well.)[54] And then, lest we distance ourselves too far from the grim
reality lurking beneath the fun, Dickens adds the following passage,
a passage that again combines humor and parody with unmistakable threat:

> As the shades of night were by this time closing in, these expressions were
> supposed to embody this simple people's views of the Evening Hymn.
> But it too soon appeared that the song was a translation of "For what we
> are going to receive," &c. (*OYF* 4: *HR,* 3:197)

These spoofs of cannibalism are followed by other comic accounts
of man-eating, by graphic descriptions, for example, of how the
hapless Latin-grammar master, all shaved and floured, was saved by

the magnanimous Captain Boldheart (despite the fact that Boldheart had long suffered from the Latin-grammar master's persecu-
tions), was saved from being cooked and eaten by the cannibals,
who were even then, at the very moment of rescue, dancing up an
appetite. (Captain Boldheart, after rescuing the Latin-grammar
master—now suitably contrite and begging for mercy—decides
"that he should not be cooked, but should be allowed to remain
raw" [*OYF* 4: *HR,* 3:197].) Boozey's would-be sacrifice, the cannibals' delighted chant, Dickens' irreverent allusion to grace before
meals, the Latin-grammar master's well-deserved comeuppance,
and all that follows are typical: such sallies are irresistibly funny yet
quite graphic and direct. Stripped of their humorous veneer, they
become equivocal and troubling. Yet our overwhelming response is
to laugh. Such renderings hark back to the humor-laced cannibalism of *Pickwick* and *Nickleby* and remind us once again that though
Dickens changed, he was also all of a piece. (In this connection,
it is worth noting that, as the storyteller of *Holiday Romance,* Dickens becomes, in an inverted echo of his own childhood, a benign
Scheherazade, spinning exotic, cannibal-filled tales for listening
children.)

Yet Dickens' later, more central renditions of cannibalism tend to
be increasingly complex, serious, and thematic. This is not to say
that cannibalism ever became the sole or central source of Dickens'
art; nor is it to say that it is the secret key that opens up the true
hermetic meaning of his writings. There is no secret key and there
is no true hermetic meaning. What this long, many-dimensioned
journey through Dickens' life and writings has sought to demonstrate is that cannibalism—something so untoward and unexpected,
so bizarre, repulsive, and fearful—is an important resource in
tracking the early shapings of Dickens' creativity, the growth of his
art, and the meaning of what he wrought. Cannibalism is thus another lens—an important and largely overlooked lens—for seeing
Dickens and for understanding him. This is so because cannibalism
became for Dickens, became in ways that were both conscious and
unconscious, infused with forbidden meaning and forbidden emo-

tion that would not—could not—be suppressed, charged meaning and charged emotion that he had to grapple with and give tongue to, nightmare meaning and nightmare emotion that he had to reconstitute or channel, confront or palliate, acknowledge or transform.

To emphasize these matters is to emphasize the nightmare dimensions and the dark import of Dickens' lifelong obsession with cannibalism; it is also to emphasize the profound night-side necessity, an early-wrought necessity, that helped fuel and drive that obsession. But what of the humor Dickens so often used to convey his awful obsession? Paradoxically, humor helped him progress from the breezy comic cannibalistic asides of such early works as *Pickwick* and *Nickleby* to the profound central cannibal-suffused indictments of *Bleak House* and *Great Expectations, Our Mutual Friend* and *Edwin Drood*, or to the equally profound cannibal-haunted indictments of other later works. Humor made the unbearable bearable. Humor allowed him to speak of impulses he hardly dared to think about, speak to himself and to his large, differentiated, often squeamish audience. As his insight and mastery increased, he sacrificed laughter for demonstration. He could now present cannibalism—that unspeakable crime, that unpardonable sin, that unexpungeable stain—as a metaphor rather than a joke. He had transformed the raw fascination and horror of childhood—the anger and aggression too—into a powerful instrument for alerting and impeaching society. Cannibalism, shaped as in *Bleak House, A Tale of Two Cities, Great Expectations, Our Mutual Friend*, or the other writings discussed in these pages, shaped, that is, to convey Dickens' central message, had become a preeminent way of dramatizing life-threatening aggressions and arraigning a sick social order.

Yet even in Dickens' most uncompromising arraignments there are often sallies of levity and havens of reticence. That this is so is not surprising. For cannibalism, however disciplined and transformed by Dickens' mature art, continued to harbor, for him, elements of unresolved anxiety and unshriven guilt. His responses deepened and became more subtle, but they did not cease to bear the stigmata, however faint or hidden, of his earliest feelings. His twofold response was rooted in that fear and fascination: to feast upon one's brother is so profoundly disturbing, so insidiously enticing, so darkly self-implicating a sin that one must limn it in its awful loathsomeness (thus its synecdochic importance as one of Dickens' ultimate emblems of a depraved society) or disarm its horror with laughter. In both responses, and in all the intermediate combinations, Dickens' voice rarely failed him. He spoke, and spoke again, of the unspeakable. He plumbed the depths of his somber night side. He transformed the unreasoning fears and suppressed aggressions generated by his early experiences—harrowing fears and murderous aggressions, self-implicating fears and self-damning aggressions—into the rich, conflicted achievements of his art. Out of infant wounds and childhood rage, out of "Captain Murderer" revulsions and *Terrific Register* horrors, out of rat-environed banishment and street-pent guilt, out of ghoulish feeding and loathsome appetites, out of midnight fears and unpardonable sins, he fashioned his vision of life's dark complexities.

Out of fear he created strength, out of loathing, silvery laughter.

Part 2
Dickens and Passion

76. Charles Dickens in 1858, Age Forty-Six

Dickens wrote "The Bride's Chamber" in September and October 1857. Engraving after a drawing (1858) by Charles Baugniet.

Dickens and Passion
The Tangled Web

> . . . the secrets of the vast Profound
> Within us, an exploring hand may sound,
> Testing the region of the ice-bound soul,
> Seeking the passage at its northern pole,
> Soft'ning the horrors of its wintry sleep,
> Melting the surface of that "Frozen Deep."
>
> —from Dickens' Prologue to *The Frozen Deep*

I

In late August 1857, at the age of forty-five, Dickens was on the verge of one of the great emotional crises of his life.[1] A few months earlier he had written the last installments of *Little Dorrit,* a dark novel about imprisonment (physical and psychological), pretension, and money. The novel also contained a sad, diminished hero who had been made will-less and self-doubting by a wounding childhood but was redeemed at last by a transcendent love. In 1856, while still in the midst of *Little Dorrit,* and partly as a relief from his solitary writing labors, Dickens decided (as was his custom) to indulge in lavish Twelfth-Night entertainments the following January, and with this end in view he suggested to Wilkie Collins (a literary protégé and *Household Words* confrere) that Collins write a play, with his help, to be founded, in part, on the tragic final Arctic expedition of Sir John Franklin, the drama to be performed during the Twelfth-Night season in the small theater that Dickens had fitted out in his London residence, Tavistock House. The frozen regions and Franklin's expeditions had long fascinated Dickens, and in the event *The Frozen Deep,* as the play came to be called, was so shaped, expanded, cut, and rewritten by Dickens (who also consulted with Collins during the whole process) as to be as much his as Collins'. The play was performed at Tavistock House four times early in January 1857 before small, privately invited audiences of London's literary and artistic élite. As usual, Dickens managed and directed the entire enterprise and acted the principal role, an undertaking that required prodigious expenditures of time and energy. He did not spare himself; on the contrary, he plunged into the task with furious energy and frenetic delight. The outcome was a glorious success and a personal triumph. He was happy.

Dickens completed *Little Dorrit* in May 1857. Bereft of his two-year labors, he felt depressed. He needed excitement and distraction; he also needed a renewed sense of communal involvement and creative fulfillment. When *The Frozen Deep* had been put together, rehearsed, and then performed, there had been, so he felt, that involvement and fulfillment; there had also been a great, largely unsatisfied, clamor for tickets, and intense public interest. Now he was miserable; a restless discontent pervaded his days and nights. Then the unexpected intervened. His old literary comrade Douglas Jerrold died in June 1857. Within days a committee was formed and a fund proposed to aid his now-straitened widow and daughter. Dickens responded at once. He became a charter member of the committee and a mainstay of the drive. For him work and activity had always been antidotes to depression. Here was an occasion ready to his hand. He would banish his discontent, honor an old friend, and serve a good cause by throwing himself into the aid efforts. He would raise a large sum of money for the Jerrold Fund by giving a public benefit reading of *A Christmas Carol* in St. Martin's Hall, London, in June, and then, in July, by giving two or three public benefit performances of *The Frozen Deep* in a London theater.

Dickens set to work immediately. He was soon immersed in his new enterprises. There was much to do. *A Christmas Carol* required painstaking rehearsing and polishing; *The Frozen Deep* required a great deal more. Far from faltering, he reveled in his duties. He was busy now; he felt useful. As manager, joint author, and chief mover of *The Frozen Deep* he was once again coaching the cast, procuring the costumes, supervising the carpenters, overseeing the stage-hands, assembling the props, refining the stage business, rehearsing the company, rewriting lines, undertaking Fund correspondence, and designing the programs. He managed the smallest details and directed the largest effects—and he acted the leading role. He also acted the leading role in the comic afterpiece, a farce by J. B. Buckstone entitled *Uncle John*. (At Tavistock House the afterpiece for most performances had been Mrs. Inchbald's *Animal Magnetism*.)

The plans for the performances were soon enlarged. There were four benefit performances at the Gallery of Illustration in London in July (including a special performance before Queen Victoria), and three at the Free Trade Hall in Manchester in August. The Manchester venue was very large, holding some two thousand persons, and for this large hall it was deemed necessary to replace the women in the cast (for the most part family members and family friends) with professional actresses who could project their voices and their presences in so large a space. Accordingly, after some searching about, Dickens hired, amongst others, Mrs. Frances Ternan and her daughters Maria and Ellen, none of whom he had known personally before (see figure 77).

The Frozen Deep focuses on the Arctic regions (two of the three acts take place there); it also focuses, as Dickens' Prologue to the play makes clear, on the deeps (including the frozen deeps) of a man's soul, deeps that are crucially tested in that harsh environment. Since childhood Dickens had been enthralled by volumes of voyages and travels and by accounts of adventures in the polar regions. He was particularly interested in the Franklin expeditions. He knew Lady Franklin, and in 1854 he had written three articles for *Household Words* on the lost Arctic voyagers and cannibalism, trying to demonstrate, by virtue of his vast reading on that somber subject,

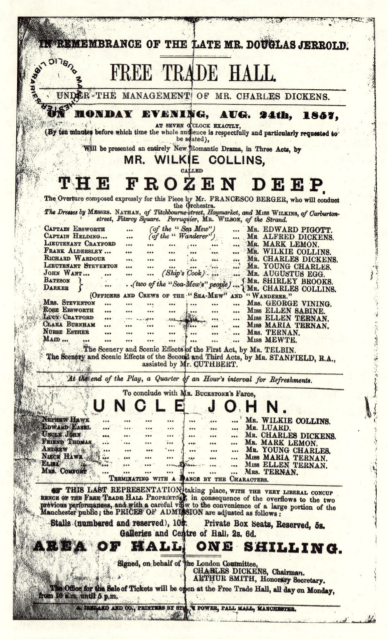

IN REMEMBRANCE OF THE LATE MR. DOUGLAS JERROLD.

FREE TRADE HALL.

UNDER THE MANAGEMENT OF MR. CHARLES DICKENS.

ON MONDAY EVENING, AUG. 24th, 1857,

AT SEVEN O'CLOCK EXACTLY,
(By ten minutes before which time the whole audience is respectfully and particularly requested to be seated),

Will be presented an entirely New Romantic Drama, in Three Acts, by

MR. WILKIE COLLINS,

CALLED

THE FROZEN DEEP.

The Overture composed expressly for this Piece by Mr. FRANCESCO BERGER, who will conduct the Orchestra.

The Dresses by MESSRS. NATHAN, of Titchbourne-street, Haymarket, and MISS WILKINS, of Carburton-street, Fitzroy Square. Perruquier, MR. WILSON, of the Strand.

CAPTAIN EBSWORTH	...	*(of the "Sea Mew")* ...	MR. EDWARD PIGOTT.
CAPTAIN HELDING	...	*(of the "Wanderer")* ...	MR. ALFRED DICKENS.
LIEUTENANT CRAYFORD	...	...	MR. MARK LEMON.
FRANK ALDERSLEY	...	...	MR. WILKIE COLLINS.
RICHARD WARDOUR	...	...	MR. CHARLES DICKENS.
LIEUTENANT STEVENTON	...	...	MR. YOUNG CHARLES.
JOHN WANT	...	*(Ship's Cook)* ...	MR. AUGUSTUS EGG.
BATESON }	...	*(two of the "Sea-Mew's" people)* ... {	MR. SHIRLEY BROOKS.
DARKER }			MR. CHARLES COLLINS.

(OFFICERS AND CREWS OF THE "SEA-MEW" AND "WANDERER."

MRS. STEVENTON	...	...	MRS. GEORGE VINING.
ROSE EBSWORTH	...	...	MISS ELLEN SABINE.
LUCY CRAYFORD	...	...	MISS ELLEN TERNAN.
CLARA BURNHAM	...	...	MISS MARIA TERNAN.
NURSE ESTHER	...	...	MRS. TERNAN.
MAID	...	...	MISS MEWTE.

The Scenery and Scenic Effects of the First Act, by MR. TELBIN.
The Scenery and Scenic Effects of the Second and Third Acts, by MR. STANFIELD, R.A., assisted by Mr. CUTHBERT.

At the end of the Play, a Quarter of an Hour's interval for Refreshments.

To conclude with MR. BUCKSTONE's Farce,

UNCLE JOHN.

NEPHEW HAWK	...	...	MR. WILKIE COLLINS.
EDWARD EARL	...	...	MR. LUARD.
UNCLE JOHN	...	...	MR. CHARLES DICKENS.
FRIEND THOMAS	...	...	MR. MARK LEMON.
ANDREW	...	...	MR. YOUNG CHARLES.
NIECE HAWK	...	...	MISS MARIA TERNAN.
ELIZA	...	...	MISS ELLEN TERNAN.
MRS. COMFORT	...	...	MRS. TERNAN.

TERMINATING WITH A DANCE BY THE CHARACTERS.

☞ THIS LAST REPRESENTATION taking place, WITH THE VERY LIBERAL CONCUR-RENCE OF THE FREE TRADE HALL PROPRIETORS, in consequence of the overflows to the two previous performances, and with a careful view to the convenience of a large portion of the Manchester public; the PRICES OF ADMISSION are adjusted as follows:

Stalls (numbered and reserved), 10s.   Private Box Seats, Reserved, 5s.
Galleries and Centre of Hall, 2s. 6d.

AREA OF HALL, ONE SHILLING.

Signed, on behalf of the London Committee,
CHARLES DICKENS, Chairman.
ARTHUR SMITH, Honorary Secretary.

The Office for the Sale of Tickets will be open at the Free Trade Hall, all day on Monday, from 10 a.m. until 5 p.m.

A. IRELAND AND CO., PRINTERS BY STEAM POWER, PALL MALL, MANCHESTER.

77. Playbill for the Final Performance of *The Frozen Deep* and *Uncle John*, 24 August 1857

This additional (third) Manchester performance concluded the tour and the work of the company. Dickens was now irretrievably in love, though at the moment he may not have realized the irrevocable nature of his commitment. That realization soon gripped him, however. As he put it seven months later, "I have never known a moment's peace or content, since the last night of The Frozen Deep. I do suppose that there never was a man so seized and rended by one spirit." Manchester Central Library, Manchester, England.

that the lost Franklin party could not, as charged, have resorted to that "last resource," as he put it, could not, that is, have succumbed to the dread debasement of cannibalism (*HW* 10: 361).[2] Now the Franklin expedition was again in the news, and now, like the general public, he avidly read each fresh report about the new search party that was being formed for yet another thrust into the frozen north.

The Frozen Deep capitalizes on this topical interest. The Prologue to the play—written and spoken by Dickens—alludes to Franklin. The play itself concentrates on a brave, Franklin-like band of English naval officers and men who have been mapping and exploring the harsh Arctic wastes for more than three years but who are now ice-bound, enfeebled, and perishing. What will become of this band of disciplined Englishmen in their unimaginable ordeal? Will their humanness survive this cruel testing, perhaps even be magnified by it? Or will brute instinct, loosed by the urge to survive, overwhelm all normal constraints? Will they finally come—most brutelike of all—to prey on one another? The play also concentrates on a small group of women in Devon—daughters, wives, sisters, and lovers of the beleaguered men—who eventually, in order to be closer to the rescue efforts, journey north. The lost expedition sickens and dwindles. In a last bid for survival, it despatches a contingent of officers and men southward. Like the doomed Franklin contingent, this group is to make its way as best it can to *terra cognita,* find there (it is hoped) some remote outpost, and bring help to the stranded remnant. The entire conception stirred and excited Dickens; he was moved by its chief constituents: the ice-environed expedition, the waiting women, the desolate solitudes, the soul-testing ordeal.

But what engrossed Dickens most in *The Frozen Deep* was not the awesomeness of vast solitudes or the fortitude of beleaguered men or the heroism of rescue expeditions (though these elements were great attractions for him) but his own moody romantic role. He played the "headstrong and passionate" but now alienated and world-weary Richard Wardour, a rejected suitor, the opponent of the accepted Frank Aldersley (played by Wilkie Collins) (*FD,* 1: 112). Wardour is a complicated protagonist, part Romantic hero, part Victorian self-denier. Haunted and driven, he often voices Dickens' inner turmoils and adopts his outward remedies. Like Dickens, deep just now in a deepening domestic crisis, he cries out despairingly, "The only hopeless wretchedness in this world, is the wretchedness that women cause" (*FD*, 2: 133). Again like Dickens, he soldiers on, and his way of dealing with his "hopeless wretchedness" is eminently Dickensian. "Hard work" is the sovereign remedy (*FD*, 2: 135). Strenuous activity, Wardour tells a friend, "tires the body and rests the mind" (*FD*, 2: 135). Or, as he puts it a little later, all the while furiously chopping up furniture with an axe, "Work, work, work; nothing for it but work!" (*FD*, 2: 136).

Both Wardour and Aldersley become members of the detachment that sets forth on the perilous search for succor. But Wardour, who is stronger and fitter than Aldersley, is bent not upon succor but upon revenge. He isolates his unsuspecting rival (who has no idea that he is a rival) and contrives to journey on alone with him. He dreams resentful dreams of overpowering and killing his nemesis. He waxes stronger as his companion grows weaker. However, it is not Wardour's physical strength but his moral strength, called forth from its frozen hiding place by his abiding love for the girl who rejected him, that triumphs in the end. Reckless and disaffected, hating Aldersley for robbing him of happiness and felicity, Wardour nevertheless now devotes all his energy to helping his exhausted rival across endless miles of Arctic wastes. In the last moments of the play, woefully weakened by his heroic exertions, he delivers the stumbling Aldersley—actually carries him—to the arms of Clara Burnham, their mutual beloved. "Saved, saved for *you!*" he tells her. "I have saved him—I have saved him for *you!*" (*FD*, 3: 158). Wardour saves his once-hated rival, but he himself, all substance spent, dies at the journey's end, a noble sacrifice to a noble renunciation. ("I may rest now—I may sleep at last—the task is done, the struggle is over. . . . My sister, Clara!—Kiss me, sister, kiss me before I die!" [*FD*, 3: 158, 160]).

Dickens abandoned himself to the role. Each night he died upon the stage in the pitying embrace of Clara Burnham. Clara Burnham was played by young Maria Ternan, "a very gentle and good little

78. Dickens Playing Richard Wardour in the Tavistock
House Production of *The Frozen Deep*

"Saved, saved for *you*! . . . I have saved him—I have saved him for *you*! I may
rest now—I may sleep at last . . . My sister, Clara!—Kiss me, sister, kiss me
before I die!" "Private Theatricals at Tavistock House.—Scene from 'The
Frozen Deep.'" *Illustrated London News* (17 January 1857).

girl" who, to continue Dickens' description, had "a very good little pale face, with large black eyes" (5 September 1857). Maria was so overcome by Dickens' rendition of Wardour's death that she could hardly bear to play her part. At the end, as she knelt over the dying Wardour, Dickens describes how "the tears streamed out of her eyes into [Wardour's] mouth, down his beard, all over his rags—down his arms as he held her by the hair. . . . she sobbed as if she were breaking her heart" (5 September 1857). The cast, in a contagion of emotion, wept; and the audience, overcome, sobbed, two thousand strong, in deep-felt sympathy. It was during these moments in Manchester that Dickens conceived the central idea for *A Tale of Two Cities,* an idea embodied less than two years later in the golden-haired Lucie Manette, in her husband, the conventional Charles Darnay, and in her would-be lover, the world-weary, alienated Sydney Carton, who sacrifices himself to save Darnay and bring bliss to his beloved.

The Frozen Deep was a triumph. It raised more than two thousand pounds for the Douglas Jerrold Fund, satisfied Dickens' need to be busy and useful, allowed him to enact a heroic self-immolating role, and inspired his next novel. It also fulfilled deeper needs. "It enables me, as it were," Dickens confessed, "*to write a book in company* instead of in my own solitary room, and to feel its effect coming freshly back upon me from the reader" (8 July 1857). But this was not all. The process of writing, shaping, managing, directing, and acting satisfied, in a most immediate and overwhelming public way, a profound creative hunger—an urge to transcend himself and to transcend the painful imperfections of everyday reality. Earlier, again speaking of *The Frozen Deep,* Dickens had written:

> As to the play itself; when it is made as good as my care can make it, I derive a strange feeling out of it, like writing a book in company; a satisfaction of a most singular kind, which has no exact parallel in my life; a something that I suppose to belong to a labourer in art alone, and which has to me a conviction of its being actual truth without its pain that I never could adequately state if I were to try never so hard. (9 January 1857)

By the end of August the excitements, the busyness, and the applause were over. Back in London, emptiness and dissatisfaction—the "actual truth" and all "its pain"—overwhelmed him once more. Restless and tormented, he yearned for relief. Dickens' emotional state was more than a passing reaction of letdown or pause. He was at a crossroads. He was profoundly unhappy in his domestic life, longing for release. His marriage of twenty-one years, often less than satisfying to him, had latterly become a source of acute misery and discontent. He felt trapped and constrained. How had the beatific visions of his youth been overtaken by the grey reality of his middle age? Now more than ever he saw his own malaise as a version of David Copperfield's discontent in his married bondage to a vapid wife. "Why is it," he wrote to his confidant John Forster in 1855, "that as with poor David, a sense comes always crushing on me now, when I fall into low spirits, as of one happiness I have missed in life, and one friend and companion I have never made?" (F, 639). But by late August 1857, *The Frozen Deep* excitements over, melancholy questioning had become tormenting misery. Now he wrote to Forster:

> Poor Catherine and I are not made for each other, and there is no help for it. It is not only that she makes me uneasy and unhappy, but that I make her so too—and much more so. She is exactly what you know, in the way of being amiable and complying; but we are strangely ill-assorted for the bond there is between us. God knows she would have been a thousand times happier if she had married another kind of man, and that her avoidance of this destiny would have been at least equally good for us both. I am often cut to the heart by thinking what a pity it is, for her own sake, that I ever fell in her way; and if I were sick or disabled tomorrow, I know how sorry she would be, and how deeply grieved myself, to think how we had lost each other. But exactly the same incompatibility would arise, the moment I was well again; and nothing on earth could make her understand me, or suit us to each other. Her temperament will not go with mine. It mattered not so much when we had only ourselves to consider, but reasons have been growing since which make it all but hopeless that we should even try to struggle on. What is now befalling me I have seen steadily coming, ever since the days you remember when

Mary was born; and I know too well that you cannot, and no one can, help me. [August 1857]

These feelings were not simply a reflex of the mounting crescendo of crisis. Almost a year later, with the immediate crisis behind him, Dickens wrote (in the so-called Violated Letter) a virtually identical assessment of his failed relationship with Catherine: "We are, in all respects of character and temperament, wonderfully unsuited to each other. I suppose that no two people, not vicious in themselves, ever were joined together, who had a greater difficulty in understanding one another, or who had less in common" (25 May 1858).

This was written in May 1858, the formal separation agreement already signed and sealed; but in August 1857, just back from Manchester and *The Frozen Deep* intensities, there was a new complication in Dickens' growing misery—and in his restlessness as well. In Manchester, amidst the applause, the noble renunciations, and the heroic feats of romance, Dickens had fallen in love. His beloved was not the large-eyed, pale-faced, brown-haired Maria who had wept so feelingly over Richard Wardour's unrequited love, but her younger sister, the large-eyed, pale-faced, golden-haired Ellen, now eighteen.

Dickens had long been susceptible to pretty, demure girl-women, sweet budding vestals who evoked his deep longing for ideality and his deep impulse to worship and protect. Such girl-women provoked and seduced him. They radiated an adorable archness. He found them innocent, trusting, and indescribably alluring. He created them anew. He cast over them his own conflicted vision of female perfection. His early heroines ring changes on this prototype—think of Rose Maylie, Kate Nickleby, Dolly Varden, Emma Haredale, Madeline Bray, Ruth Pinch, Mary Graham, and all that nymphlike host. His most notable real-life counterpart of this angel-seductress was his adored sister-in-law Mary Hogarth, who had died in his arms in 1837 when she was seventeen and he was twenty-five. In subsequent years he had become infatuated for brief periods with other avatars of this virginal temptress; in 1844 with the eighteen-year-old pianist Christiana Weller, a "spiritual young creature" with "an angel's message in her face . . . that smote me to the heart," a "gentle creature" whom he had introduced, amidst her blushes and confusion, to a large Liverpool audience (28 February 1844; 11 March 1844).

His passion for Ellen seems to have begun in the old protective, self-enchanting way; it was certainly immediate, unpremeditated, and consuming. Its onset had occurred between 17 and 24 August 1857, for that was the entire period of the rehearsals for Manchester and the Manchester performances. (He had met Ellen, along with her sister and mother, a few weeks earlier when he had interviewed all three for the Manchester roles.) Ellen fit Dickens' image of the virginal temptress. She had a low-pitched voice, a vulnerable air, a natural manner, and an alluring, though modestly comported, physicality. (On 19 April 1857, the *Era,* a contemporary periodical, noted that she possessed a "pretty face" and a "well-developed figure.") Dickens was entranced. During this period, and almost certainly for a long time thereafter, no physical union occurred, though the physical was quite obviously powerfully and attractingly there for Dickens from the beginning. (Precisely what occurred then and in the years that followed is, of course, shrouded from our direct gaze.) But in the first rapt flush of love, Dickens saw Ellen as an icon of adorable womanhood, and he saw her physical beauty as an outward and visible sign of an inward purity and grace. He translated his passion, taboo owing to age, marriage, and suitability (he was a national figure and a paterfamilias) to the perfervid realms of romance and fable. Ellen was the immured fairy-tale princess; he was the rescuing chivalric knight. His love would prompt him to deeds of heroism or to ennobling self-immolation. Like Richard Wardour, he would serve his lady or die in the attempt. Here is Dickens writing to an intimate friend, Mrs. Richard Watson, in December 1857, just a few months after falling in love with Ellen:

I am the modern embodiment of the old Enchanters, whose Familiars tore them to pieces. I weary of rest, and have no satisfaction but in fa-

79. Ellen Ternan as a Young Woman

From a photograph. Enthoven Collection, Victoria and Albert Museum, London.

tigue. Realities and idealities are always comparing themselves together before me, and I don't like the Realities except when they are unattainable—*then*, I like them of all things. I wish I had been born in the days of Ogres and Dragon-guarded Castles. I wish an Ogre with seven heads (and no particular evidence of brains in the whole lot of them) had taken the Princess whom I adore—you have no idea how intensely I love her!— to his stronghold on the top of a high series of mountains, and there tied her up by the hair. Nothing would suit me half so well this day, as climbing after her, sword in hand, and either winning her or being killed.— *There's* a state of mind for you, in 1857. (7 December 1857)

This rhapsody out-Wardours Wardour, both in fervor and in derring-do, but the hero of *The Frozen Deep,* transformed in this fantasy from noble, renunciatory rescuer to indomitable fairy-tale champion, was not the only role that Dickens played in Manchester and not the only role he later transformed. He played Uncle John (in the afterpiece of the same name), an old man who helps rear Eliza Comfort, a beautiful young neighbor and protégée, falls in love with her, and then, when she turns nineteen (he is sixty), undertakes to marry her; the farce imbroglio that follows (pointing up the impropriety of such a union) occurs two hours before they are to be married. The marriage, in fact, never takes place. Instead, Eliza becomes betrothed to Edward Easel, a twenty-five-year-old artist, and Uncle John marries Eliza's mother, Mrs. Comfort. In *The Frozen Deep* Ellen had played Lucy Crayford, a trusted, supportive, understanding ingénue who had forsworn love because she was in love with a married man. (In Dickens' next novel, *A Tale of Two Cities,* there is another Lucy—Lucie Manette—and the hero forswears love because he is in love with a married woman—Lucie.) In *Uncle John,* Ellen, pretty and provocative with her golden hair and soulful eyes, played directly opposite Dickens: she was the beautiful young protégée whom Dickens (in the person of Uncle John) had nurtured, shaped ("directed her disposition" is Uncle John's phrase), educated, fallen in love with, and now wished to marry (*UJ,* 1: 12).

Uncle John himself is a bundle of contradictions and delusions. He is all youthful energy, ardor, and impetuosity (or so he likes to think), but his companions constantly emphasize his age. "Cease alluding to my age," he tells them. "I'm a mere boy" (*UJ*, 1: 21). His companions persist in their opposition. They ignore his injunctions and his avowals, and they condemn his unseemly love for a nineteen-year-old girl. When that love is thwarted, Uncle John feels—much as stronghold-scaling, ogre-confronting, winning-or-dying Dickens after him—like "dancing about like a demon, knocking every body down that came in my way, cutting *your* throat, and blowing out *my* brains" (*UJ*, 2: 35). But in farce, all's well that ends well, and *Uncle John* quickly ends on a note of happiness and self-congratulation. In the final speech of this trifling entertainment, Uncle John, having renounced his unsuitable love for a young girl who "loves him as a father," asks, "Hav'nt I acted like a hero?" (*UJ*, 1: 9; 2: 43). For Dickens, who went pell-mell from the sublime, tear-filled self-immolation of Richard Wardour to the ludicrous, laughter-filled posturing of Uncle John, the answer, perhaps, was yes. (One wonders if Dickens realized that Uncle John's "heroic" renunciation of a forbidden love—for Eliza is not only young but in love with another—is a grotesque parody of Richard Wardour's similar renunciation.) In any case, the imperatives of life often differ from the conventions of art, and life was now about to assert its ineluctable hegemony. But the human mind is duplicitous and resourceful. That imperious hegemony, undeniable in life, can be denied, or inflated, or divided and subdivided in art, and Dickens, in his art, shortly gave a different expression to those stage passions and stage renunciations—passions and renunciations so suddenly and so disturbingly made real in his own life. The heightened situations and the forbidden relationships that emerged in *The Frozen Deep* and *Uncle John,* together with still other reverberations from those plays and from the fortuitous conjunctions of everyday life, were refashioned (along with much else) in "The Bride's Chamber," a tormented, self-revealing work that Dickens began to write a month after Manchester and only four days (probably fewer than four days) after he had seen Ellen again.

But to glance a few weeks beyond "The Bride's Chamber" for a moment in order to trace an important continuity, those heightened situations and forbidden relationships were also refashioned in the next imaginative work that Dickens undertook after finishing "The Bride's Chamber" and *The Lazy Tour of Two Idle Apprentices* (*The Lazy Tour*, a travel series, incorporated "The Bride's Chamber"). The new work, written a month after "The Bride's Chamber" and *The Lazy Tour*, was his contribution to *The Perils of Certain English Prisoners*, the Extra Christmas Number of *Household Words* for 1857. Dickens' contribution (Dickens wrote the long opening and concluding sections, Collins the shorter middle section) is another expression of Dickens' emotional state during this period and another manifestation of an imaginative and emotional continuity that extends from *The Frozen Deep* and *Uncle John* to *The Lazy Tour* and "The Bride's Chamber" to *The Perils of Certain English Prisoners* and finally, less than a year and a half later, to *A Tale of Two Cities*.

In Dickens' contribution to *The Perils of Certain English Prisoners* "a very beautiful young English lady," a beleaguered and imperiled angel, is loved by a man who is debarred from pursuing her (in this case, owing to his lowly station) but who nobly serves, champions, and protects his beloved—his "Lady," he denominates her (*PEP*, 1:3; 1:1; 3:36). He serves his "Lady" with mute, chivalric, self-sacrificing passion, and then, having saved her from malignant savagery, he nobly gives her up—another renunciation—to a suitable (that is, genteel) lover, revealing his sanctified love for his "Lady"—revealing it to her—many years later, at the close of his life. The full emotional significance of this donnée (obviously a repeated donnée), already clear in its main outlines, will become clearer shortly.

But to return to Dickens, Ellen, Manchester, and *Uncle John*, what are we to make of this chance coming together and its extraordinary consequences? The spectacle of a great, masterful middle-aged artist, penetrating anatomist of the human soul, acting in a farce that highlighted the folly of an old guardian-mentor falling in love with his pretty, soulful-eyed, nineteen-year-old protégée, while all the while he (the artist) was enacting in his own person the very incongruity he was mocking on the stage, this spectacle is so farcically Dickensian that one can hardly believe Dickens did not invent it, much less fail to see its dire parallels or its presiding farce and folly. But Dickens, whatever his insight—and what he was soon to do, and moreover to write, seems to signify that his insight was painfully acute—was now far beyond farce and folly. Darker and more tragic forces were gripping and impelling him.

I I

The first great outward manifestation of those tragic forces had domestic and literary consequences, the chief literary consequence being "The Bride's Chamber." ("The Bride's Chamber" is my name for a wild, self-contained segment of *The Lazy Tour of Two Idle Apprentices,* a segment entirely by Dickens and written at the very culmination of his domestic crisis. I have named this untitled segment "The Bride's Chamber" in acknowledgement of Dickens' repeated use of that phrase as a keynote in the wild inset story that is the chief feature of the segment. As the inset story unfolds, this seemingly ordinary phrase—"the Bride's Chamber"—soon takes on its thematic and ironic importance, an importance that Dickens further accentuates by capitalizing the phrase each time he uses it. In other words, "The Bride's Chamber" seems to have been Dickens' own choice for the title of his story, though the format of *The Lazy Tour* precluded him from giving that title, or any title, to the segment or the story.) But to return for a moment to *The Lazy Tour. The Lazy Tour* appeared anonymously in *Household Words* in five installments. This collaborative effort by Dickens and Wilkie Collins was not collected in Dickens' lifetime, has never been edited, and has not been reliably attributed as to its parts and subparts. Despite this murky history, however, letters from Dickens and other evidence make clear that, among much else, the whole of the fourth weekly installment of *The Lazy Tour,* that is, the whole of "The Bride's Chamber," which contains the wild inset story of "The Bride's Chamber" proper, is by Dickens.[3]

But "The Bride's Chamber" and its shattering domestic correlatives were still a few weeks off. Now, late in August 1857, just home from Manchester, alienated from his wife, enamored of Ellen, unable to work, at loose ends with himself and with the world, Dickens groped about for something to do. To Wilkie Collins, his collaborator and fellow actor in *The Frozen Deep* and a mainstay on his weekly magazine, *Household Words,* he wrote:

> Partly in the grim despair and restlessness of this subsidence from excitement, and partly for the sake of Household Words, I want to cast about whether you and I can go anywhere—take any tour—see anything—whereon we could write something together. . . . We want something for Household Words, and I want to escape from myself. (29 August 1857)

And then he added despairingly: "My blankness is inconceivable—indescribable—my misery amazing."

A plan, conceived by Dickens, finally emerged. He and Collins would wander for ten or twelve days through picturesque villages and remote fastnesses in out-of-the-way regions of Cumberland and would write a series of five travel pieces for the five October issues of *Household Words.* They would adopt as their noms de plume the names of the protagonists (Francis Goodchild and Thomas Idle) in Hogarth's *Industry and Idleness* (Hogarth was a great favorite of Dickens), and they would observe and write as they traveled.[4] Dickens would be Francis Goodchild, the energetic, industrious apprentice, whose way of idling in *The Lazy Tour* is to bustle and to do; Collins would be Thomas Idle, the lazy, slothful apprentice, whose way of idling is to rest and to dream. They would call the series *The Lazy Tour of Two Idle Apprentices.* They would banter and dramatize each other in their fictional guises (guises based for the most part on reality); describe people, places, and local color; recount their adventures; interpolate a fanciful tale or two; and throw over the whole the coloring of humor, satire, comment, and imaginative insight. This interlude of sauntering and work, Dickens felt, would help save him. He needed saving. A few days before setting off for Cumberland, he wrote to his brother-in-law Henry Austin: "I am

80. Wilkie Collins in 1853, Age Twenty-Nine

From a painting by Charles Allston Collins. Fitzwilliam Museum, Cambridge, England. Seven years after painting this portrait, Charles Collins, Wilkie's brother, married Dickens' younger daughter, Kate.

horribly used up after the Jerrold business. Low spirits, low pulse, low voice, intense reaction. If I were not like Mr. Micawber, 'falling back for a spring' on Monday, I think I should slink into a corner and cry" (2 September 1857).

Dickens and Collins left for Cumberland on Monday, 7 September 1857, arriving in Carlisle by evening. Before they left, Dickens had enlarged their itinerary and their time on the road. They would make their way down and across England to Doncaster, arriving there for Race Week and the famous St. Leger. Doncaster was hardly a picturesque out-of-the-way retreat, and during Race Week it was a veritable Saturnalia of drunkenness and license, an occasion and an ambiance that Dickens abhorred. Furthermore, it would take special pains to get there. The rail connections between the Cumberland coast and Doncaster were indirect and time-consuming; among other things, the journey, though not long in distance, would necessitate an overnight stop in Leeds. But Dickens' real reason for traveling to Doncaster had little to do with Leeds—or with racing, betting, or Saturnalias. He had a more personal incentive. The Ternans would be there, acting in the local Theatre Royal. Francis Goodchild, slaying ogres and dragons, could watch over and champion his adorable princess.

That Ellen's presence in Doncaster was Dickens' reason for going there is made clear by passages omitted from published versions of letters he wrote from Doncaster to W. H. Wills, the subeditor of *Household Words*. "But Lord bless you," he hinted provocatively in one letter, "the strongest parts of your present correspondent's heart are made up of weaknesses, and he just come to be here at all (if you know it) along of his Richard Wardour! Guess *that* riddle, Mr. Wills!" (18 September 1857, Huntington Library MS). A few days later, the provocative Wardour hints were given more precise and more corporeal substance: "I am going to take the little— riddle—into the country this morning; and I answer your letter briefly, before starting. . . . So let the riddle and the riddler go their own wild way, and no harm come of it!" (20 September 1857, Huntington Library MS).

Dickens did go his own wild way, and harm did come of it. How wild and infatuated that way was at the moment may be glimpsed in a passage he wrote two weeks later in his Doncaster section of *The Lazy Tour*, a passage that seems to be an enraptured remembrance of accompanying Ellen to the St. Leger. Dickens had hired a large open carriage drawn by a pair of horses for the St. Leger and for the Cup Day races. He could therefore invite guests, and he and his guests could view the races from the comfort and protection of a roomy open conveyance. Francis Goodchild also views the St. Leger from the privileged vantage of a large open carriage, a "dusty barouche" (*HW* 16: *LT*, 5:412). Goodchild is privileged, but his heart is a "desert" (*HW*, 16: *LT*, 5:412). But now, at the St. Leger, his desert blooms. The cause of this transformation is a wondrous female. He swoons over the adorable creature. She is irresistible and haloed. He waxes rhapsodic:

> "O little lilac gloves! And O winning little bonnet, making in conjunction with her golden hair quite a Glory in the sunlight round the pretty head, why anything in the world but you and me! Why may not this day's running—of horses, to all the rest: of precious sands of life to me—be prolonged through an everlasting autumn-sunshine, without a sunset!" (*HW* 16: *LT*, 5:412)

The rhapsody continues with Goodchild calling upon the "Slave of the Lamp, or Ring," the "Friendly Devil on Two Sticks," and the "Genii in the desert" to "enchant" the scene and allow him, seated so blissfully in a carriage at the St. Leger, to remain in loving rapture by the side of "the little lilac gloves, the winning little bonnet, and . . . the golden hair . . . for ever" (*HW* 16: *LT*, 5:412). The fairy-tale imagery here is no mere rhetorical device but a reflection of Dickens' metamorphosed passion. This imagery surrounds Ellen in the early days of his passion—a passion that had sprung up so unexpectedly only weeks before and that was still echoing in rhapsodic cadences and fairy-tale images ("the Princess whom I adore—" and so on) three months later in the letter to Mrs. Watson already quoted.

81. Celebrants on Race Day

"O little lilac gloves! And O winning little bonnet . . . why anything in the world but you and me!" Detail from *Derby Day*. Oil painting (1858) by William Powell Frith. Tate Gallery, London.

As a matter of fact, that passion and its fervent expression continued unabated in the succeeding months. On a cold, rainy April day
in 1858, more than three months after writing to Mrs. Watson and
almost eight months after meeting Ellen, Dickens visited Hampton
Court, apparently in Ellen's company. As with the St. Leger episode,
he immediately made the visit the occasion for a written tribute,
this time in an essay. He entitled the essay "Please to Leave Your
Umbrella," the title arising from the fact that he was required to
leave his umbrella in the entrance hall (even as one is today) before
proceeding through the palace. He sent the piece to press as soon
as he had finished it, and it appeared in *Household Words* on 1 May.
Though a visit to Hampton Court was the occasion for the piece,
and though Dickens briefly sketches the visit and the palace, his real
subject is the way in which individuals are prevailed upon to abdi-
cate their independent taste, judgment, morals, and perceptions in
the face of established convention and official opinion.

Hampton Court and the request to leave his umbrella (which
stands symbolically for leaving one's independent judgment behind
in the face of authority) are thus merely springboards for Dickens'
polemic; Hampton Court itself (aside from strategic and exposi-
tional preliminaries) is dealt with in a few sentences. Yet this acerbic
essay on independent judgment versus received opinion has an altogether incongruous dimension. It is infused with his passion for Ellen, a passion that seems to intrude, willy-nilly, into the essay. The
personal occasion is all glowing love and rapture; the journalistic
purpose all satire and attack. (Though there is, perhaps, an unfor-
mulated connection between the two impulses. In choosing as the
subject of his essay the need to exalt independent judgment over
received opinion, Dickens was, perhaps, unconsciously justifying his
own conduct in relation to his wife, to Ellen, and even to his present
blissful but socially suspect—and therefore socially equivocal—visit
to Hampton Court with Ellen.)

Dickens' rapture, flaunted before the world yet concealed from
the world as well (Ellen, of course, if she read the piece—as she
probably did—would have recognized the occasion and the trib-

82. Scene, Hampton Court Palace;
Subject, Dickens in Love

"I [and 'my little reason'] made a visit the other day to the Palace at Hampton
Court." *Hampton Court Palace*. Engraving (c. 1825) by Henry Bryan Ziegler.

ute),[5] informs the opening, the ending, and the lingering invocation of the essay. His opening is both direct and indirect. It reveals his true feeling toward his companion but then screens the exact nature and context of that feeling. He manages this sleight of pen by denominating Ellen his "little reason," just as seven months earlier, in a similar strategy of enigmatic hinting, he had referred to her, in the letter already mentioned, as his "little riddle." The "little reason" strategy (like the "little riddle" strategy) not only screens Ellen's personhood but allows Dickens to refer to her as "it" rather than "she." So screened and so protected, Dickens could share with his public glimpses of his real life and his dream life with Ellen, and he could do so even as he and Ellen went "their own wild way." Here, for example, is the opening paragraph of "Please to Leave Your Umbrella": "I made a visit the other day to the Palace at Hampton Court. I may have had my little reason for being in the best of humours with the Palace at Hampton Court; but that little reason is neither here (ah! I wish it were here!) nor there" (*HW* 17:457).

This opening is curious in a number of ways. Dickens asserts that the chief subject of the paragraph is "neither here . . . nor there," but instead of canceling this pointless paragraph, he lets it stand. The paragraph, of course, is not pointless. As his parenthetical play on words makes clear, the paragraph is a tribute to his "little reason." Though not germane to the subject of his essay, the paragraph (for Dickens, at least) is all-important. After all, is not deep-felt rapture more important than slavishly admired palaces, slavishly admired furnishings, and slavishly admired public officials? He also asserts that he has a "little reason" for being in the "best of humours with . . . Hampton Court," but then goes on to attack Hampton Court most savagely: he is really, it seems, in the worst of humors with Hampton Court. Both contradictions emphasize the disjunction between his personal emotion and the polemical occasion, between his private passion and his public task.

After a brief interval, Dickens proceeds, as in his St. Leger rhapsody six months earlier, to invoke the mundane present, forever transformed for him from the bleak and ordinary to the ideal by the

83. The Autonomous Blisses of Passion:
The Palace at Hampton Court

"I wonder . . . whether, with this little reason in my bosom, I should ever want to get out of these . . . interminable suites of rooms, and return to noise and bustle!" The Cartoon Gallery, Hampton Court. From a photograph, c. 1950 or earlier.

presence of his fairy-tale beloved; he also goes on, again as in his St. Leger rhapsody, to conjure up an ideal present eternally transmuted—once more by his beloved—into an endless now of everlasting enchantment. Summoning up Sterne's Yorick (the Yorick of *A Sentimental Journey*) and addressing him rather than the real companion by his side, he gives full rein to his rhapsody:

> "I wonder," said I, in the manner of the Sentimental Journeyer, "I wonder, Yorick, whether, with this little reason in my bosom, I should ever want to get out of these same interminable suites of rooms, and return to noise and bustle! It seems to me that I could stay here very well until the grisly phantom on the pale horse came at a gallop up the staircase, seeking me. My little reason should make of these queer dingy closet-rooms, these little corner chimney-pieces tier above tier, this old blue china of squat shapes, these dreary old state bedsteads with attenuated posts, nay, dear Yorick," said I, stretching forth my hand towards a stagnant pool of blacking in a frame, "should make, even of these very works of art, an encompassing universe of beauty and happiness. The fountain in the staid red and white courtyard without (for we had turned that angle of the building), would never fall too monotonously on my ear, the four chilled sparrows now fluttering on the brink of its basin would never chirp a wish for change of weather, no bargeman on the rain-speckled river; no wayfarer rain-belated under the leafless trees in the park, would ever come into my fancy as examining in despair those swollen clouds, and vainly peering for a ray of sunshine. I and my little reason, Yorick, would keep house here, all our lives, in perfect contentment; and when we died, our ghosts should make of this dull Palace the first building ever haunted happily!" (*HW* 17: 457)

As with the St. Leger occasion, ordinary reality metamorphoses into extraordinary bliss, a perfection that Dickens yearns to possess forever. The "dusty barouche" of Doncaster becomes the "dull Palace" of Hampton Court, a place so transformed by Ellen's magical presence that it blossoms into "an encompassing universe of beauty and happiness." Dickens avows that he and his "little reason" will "keep house" there for the rest of their lives and then, still together after death, will haunt the palace "happily" for all eternity.

Dickens shifts from this ecstatic vision to his journalistic task and

84. The Transforming Power of Passion: Hampton
Court's "Dingy" Closet-Rooms, "Little Corner"
Chimney-Pieces, and "Squat" China Become
Vessels of "Beauty and Happiness"

"My little reason should make of these queer dingy closet-rooms, these little
corner chimney-pieces tier above tier, this old blue china of squat shapes . . .
an encompassing universe of beauty and happiness." A "Closet-Room,"
Hampton Court. From a photograph (1987) by the author.

his fierce polemical attack; but in the final sentence of "Please to Leave Your Umbrella" he returns once more to his "little reason" and to the rapture of his fairy-tale dreams: "I gave back my ticket, and got back my Umbrella, and then I and my little reason went dreaming away under its shelter through the fast-falling spring rain, which had a sound in it that day like the rustle of the coming summer" (*HW* 17: 459).

The St. Leger and Hampton Court episodes are crucial for a number of reasons. First, these two excursions, so different in setting, time, and occasion, yet so similar—even identical—in emotional content, convey the character of Dickens' infatuation with Ellen at this time: his passion and his fairy-tale yearning. Second, they show how sustained and consuming, over a period of many months (exceedingly difficult months for him), that intense fusion of ardor and wishful transcendence was. (At the time of the Hampton Court piece—some eight months after meeting Ellen—Dickens was wracked by accumulating stress: among other things, he was making plans, amidst much contrary advice, to commence his first public readings for profit, and he was negotiating, amidst much contention and anguish, the formal separation agreement with his wife.) Finally, these two public celebrations of being with Ellen demonstrate in dramatic fashion Dickens' strange—and exceedingly dangerous—impulsion to share with his readers his most personal raptures and longings, at once revealing and concealing the emotional weather of his inner life. It is as though Dickens found it impossible to keep totally private the joy he felt in Ellen's presence. This compulsion, offspring of passion and a deep inner necessity, will appear again in "The Bride's Chamber."

Yet despite these barings of his inner life there is a whole world of related emotions that he excluded from the St. Leger and Hampton Court revelations. Fairy tales and romances (to continue with the fervent similitudes that Dickens chose to use) deal with knights and golden-haired princesses and deeds of derring-do and magical fulfillments, but they also deal with fierce ogres and wicked guardians, foul murders and savage onslaughts, nightmare hauntings and supernatural retributions. The St. Leger and Hampton Court episodes concentrate on impassioned love and fairy-tale yearning; they contain no hint of that other fairy-tale world, a world as large and as intense as the world of blissful fulfillments, a world of hate and murderous aggression, of profound sin and profound guilt. Yet these emotions, though absent from the St. Leger and Hampton Court passages, and also largely absent from the factual narrative of *The Lazy Tour*, were also at the heart of what Dickens was feeling and thinking at this time, and they too, though suppressed elsewhere in his writings of this period, make their potent way into *The Lazy Tour*. They emerge in, indeed they permeate, "The Bride's Chamber" (the fourth installment of *The Lazy Tour*); they do more: they help generate, control, and then resolve—or perhaps it would be better to say conclude—that tormented fable of cosmic sin and eternal guilt.

Dickens wrote "The Bride's Chamber" at Gad's Hill Place late in September and early in October 1857, immediately upon returning from Doncaster. (Early in October, having come up to Tavistock House briefly and being "very much put-out" [he was already warring with his wife and with the Hogarths], he had got out of bed at two in the morning—"After all," he thought, "it would be better to be up and doing something, than lying here"—and walked down to Gad's Hill Place, a tramp through the "dead night," the grey dawn, and the early morning, of more than thirty miles [7 December 1857, to Mrs. Watson].) Back at Gad's Hill Place, his mind was filled with fervent visions of a lilac-gloved, halo-headed Ellen, radiant and glorified in the autumn sunshine. Two weeks later (just a week after completing "The Bride's Chamber"), in the St. Leger scenes of *The Lazy Tour*, he committed this vision to paper, a vision that contained no hint of the self-laceration and self-condemnation that also gripped him at this time. But these guilty emotions, dark counterparts to his dreams of felicity, haunted his days and tormented his nights. They throng in frightening intensifications through all the pages of "The Bride's Chamber," written, or rather completed, a week or so before the St. Leger scenes, written in the green seclusion of his bay-windowed study in his new residence, Gad's Hill Place, written in isolation—physical isolation, at least— away from wife, away from Ellen, away from the Hogarths, away from the tangled enmeshments of the busy world, but written in an emotional turmoil of yearning, misery, passion, and guilt. (The lover in the story Dickens was even then writing in his bay-windowed study gazes from his leafy perch through the bay window of the Bride's Chamber; he gazes through that leaf-enfringed bay window as Dickens was now gazing through the leaf-enfringed bay window of his study; he gazes at the yearned for beloved he can never possess.)

Dickens' passion for Ellen was thus (to simplify his divided response) his sin and his salvation. As sin, his guilt and torment (as "The Bride's Chamber" demonstrates) were fathomless. As salvation, his rapture and fervor (as the St. Leger and Hampton Court interludes illustrate) were manifestations of wishful faith, commitments to the possibility of an ideality beyond—perhaps even in—this fallen, strife-torn world. In the latter incarnations, Ellen, idealized and etherealized, was, for Dickens, a fairy-tale embodiment of the heart's desire, an innocent personification of promised bliss. This supernal vision of a bright angel-companion helped sustain Dickens in his turmoil and allowed him (along with work and furious activity) to weather this difficult period. As in Doncaster in September, so in Hampton Court in April: he hugged this radiant vision—his "little riddle" become now his "little reason"—close. Walking with his "little reason" in the cold spring rain it was possible, even amidst the glooms and chills and desecrations of Hampton Court, to put aside the burdens of fathomless guilt and dream of an endless summer.

III

Dickens was always intense, brimming with a concentrated almost demonic, energy. Whatever he gave himself to do or feel he did or felt with all his heart and all his might. He gave himself to writing,

85. Gad's Hill Place: Dickens Wrote "The Bride's Chamber" in the Bay-Windowed Room on the Ground Floor Right

"Gad's Hill Place." Wood engraving (1890) by Robert Langton. From Langton, *The Childhood and Youth of Charles Dickens* (1912).

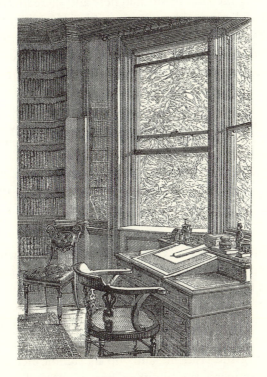

86. Gad's Hill Place: The Interior of the Bay-Windowed Room and Dickens' Writing Desk

Note that Dickens wrote looking through a leaf-enfringed bay window. "The Study at Gadshill." Wood engraving (c. 1873) by L. Liddell. From Forster, *The Life of Charles Dickens*, Vol. III (1874).

acting, mountain climbing, and loving with fervor and abandon. When, in *The Lazy Tour,* in a passage by Dickens, Wilkie Collins (in the person of Thomas Idle) sings *Annie Laurie* and affirms that he would, in Dickens' paraphrase, "lay him doon and dee," Dickens (in the person of Francis Goodchild) is aghast. "'What an ass that fellow was!'" he says. "'I'd get me oop and peetch into somebody'" (*HW* 16: *LT,* 1:313). When Collins replies that he wouldn't take the trouble, Dickens tells him, "'It's no trouble . . . to fall in love.'" Dickens then has Collins voice his own unheeded warning to himself: "'It's trouble enough to fall out of it, once you're in it'" (*HW* 16: *LT,* 1:313). A moment later Goodchild-Dickens confirms that he is in love, a confession reaffirmed here and there in *The Lazy Tour* by an occasional apostrophe or a deep "lover's sigh" (*HW* 16: *LT,* 1:313; 3:367). In another passage, also by Dickens (it is also another of the rare narrative segments in which he reveals that there is a dark reckless Wardour side to his passionate nature), he has Idle say:

> "You do nothing like another man. Where another fellow would fall into a footbath of action or emotion, you fall into a mine. Where any other fellow would be a painted butterfly, you are a fiery dragon. Where another man would stake a sixpence, you stake your existence. If you were to go up in a balloon, you would make for Heaven; and if you were to dive into the depths of the earth, nothing short of the other place would content you. What a fellow you are, Francis!" (*HW* 16: BC, 385)

Goodchild laughs, but Dickens has Idle end the exchange with an ominous rejoinder: "'A man who can do nothing by halves appears to me to be a fearful man'" (*HW* 16: BC, 385). The implications of this rejoinder are intensified by the next scene, a disturbing scene that gives some hint of how compelled and driven Dickens felt at this time. He has just come back from visiting an insane asylum. After describing the visit, he sums up its significance in a somber analogy. He compares the plight of one of the asylum's purblind, compulsive inmates to his own plight and to the plight of all mankind.[6] Like the insane man, he is baffled and driven, a poor, blind, searching creature.

At Doncaster we are given additional glimpses of Goodchild's fearful side, and of his dragon-quelling and ogre-slaying proclivities as well. The demonstration occurs at the theater. Dickens (Goodchild) had gone to the theater to see his adored princess and her mother and sister perform. He describes the scene that greeted him. Even now, writing more than two weeks later, he can barely control his fury. The theater is a bedlam; the racing audience rowdy and unruly. The chief offender at the performance, the monstrous ogre who must be slain by the furious knight, is a drunken young "gentleman born" sitting directly behind Dickens—"a something . . . more depraved, more foolish, more ignorant, more unable to believe in any noble or good thing of any kind, than the stupidest Bosjesman" (*HW* 16: *LT*, 5:412). Members of the audience have been putting "vile constructions" on "innocent phrases" in the play and applauding them in a "Satyr-like manner," and "it" (the young man), "addled with drink," "drawls its slang criticisms" and utters remarks "so horrible" that Dickens is outraged that the pure ears of the women on the stage—"good as its own sisters, or its own mother"—will be polluted by this poisonous filth (*HW* 16: *LT*, 5:412). Dickens can hardly contain himself; his language blazes with passion and contempt. He is inflamed with a "burning ardour to fling it [the young man] into the pit," but is saved from the need to act out his heroic resolve and display that "burning ardour" when "the thing . . . drops its downy chin upon its scarf, and slobbers itself asleep" (*HW* 16: *LT*, 5:412).

Dickens arrived in Doncaster on Monday the 14th of September; the great St. Leger (with Dickens, accompanied by Ellen, in attendance) was run on Wednesday the 16th; the episode with the Ternans at the theater (he attended the theater on several occasions) took place on Thursday the 17th; the final day of racing, Cup Day, with Dickens again in attendance, was on Friday the 18th; the excursion into the country with Ellen occurred on Sunday the 20th; the return to Gad's Hill Place (the house he had recently bought in Kent) took place on the 22nd or 23rd. By the time of his return to Gad's Hill he had completed all of his contributions to the first three segments of *The Lazy Tour;* by the 26th, probably earlier—that is, four days (probably fewer than four days) after leaving Doncaster and Ellen—he was working on the fourth part, "The Bride's Chamber"; by 2 October he had completed it. Before, during, and after writing "The Bride's Chamber," though outwardly calm and productive, he was inwardly anguished and torn. A week or so before leaving on his "lazy" tour he had written Forster the letter complaining that "Poor Catherine and I are not made for each other." Then, a few days later, just two days before departing on his futile attempt to "escape from myself," he had responded to Forster's reply:

> You are not so tolerant as perhaps you might be of the wayward and unsettled feeling which is part (I suppose) of the tenure on which one holds an imaginative life, and which I have, as you ought to know well, often only kept down by riding over it like a dragoon—but let that go by. I make no maudlin complaint. . . . But the years have not made it easier to bear for either of us; and, for her sake as well as mine, the wish will force itself upon me that something might be done. I know too well it is impossible. (5 September 1857)

This was written on 5 September. The resigned misery that Dickens expresses here, like the "hopeless wretchedness" that Wardour had voiced earlier, stemmed, like Wardour's misery, from a failed love—in Dickens' case from a failed marriage that now embittered his life and trammeled his spirit. He was undergoing in his own life what he had undergone in heightened form three weeks earlier through Wardour's baffled life. In Manchester, however, there was relief: through Wardour he had transformed defeated love into self-immolating heroism; he had experienced "actual truth without its pain." Now, his Wardour triumphs behind him, there was no relief: he was experiencing actual truth with all its grinding pain. Left to himself, he turned in upon himself. What he found was chilling. Confronting the doleful "secrets of the vast Profound within," disturbing the "wintry sleep" of "that 'Frozen Deep,'" he had discovered a desolate void. Some deep pulse of his inner being urged him to respond; he must act or perish. The lazy tour was one response;

Doncaster ecstasies were another. By the time he had returned from his fairy-tale week with lilac-gloved, halo-headed Ellen, resignation and desolation had given way to passion and frenzy. He was beside himself; he was driven and compelled. He was once more seeking to blot out pain and thought through action. He was now out-Wardouring Wardour, out-Goodchilding Goodchild. Late in September or early in October, he wrote to Forster:

> Too late to say, put the curb on, and don't rush at hills—the wrong man to say it to. I have now no relief but in action. I am become incapable of rest. I am quite confident I should rust, break, and die, if I spared myself. Much better to die, doing. What I am in that way, nature made me first, and my way of life has of late, alas! confirmed. I must accept the draw-back—since it is one—with the powers I have; and I must hold upon the tenure prescribed to me. (Late September or early October 1857)

In the next week or so, as Dickens finished "The Bride's Chamber," went over its proofs, and wrote his portions of the Doncaster segment, the fifth and final segment of *The Lazy Tour*—the segment that waxed rhapsodic over lilac gloves and golden hair—he pondered a momentous decision. In the course of the last few weeks he had begun to think of ways of escaping from his dilemma. At the end of September, just before beginning "The Bride's Chamber" (that is, just before beginning the fourth segment of *The Lazy Tour*), he had concluded the third segment of the series by expressing what a relief it would be to "eat Bride-cake without the trouble of being married, or of knowing anybody in that ridiculous dilemma" (*HW* 16: *LT*, 3:367). By 11 October, "The Bride's Chamber" proofs corrected—just thirteen days, in fact, before he sent that tormented cry out into the busy world—he reached his decision. He would no longer accept his own dictum of a month earlier that it was "impossible" that "something might be done." The secret "wish" that would "force itself" upon him would now become a reality. Writing from Gad's Hill Place to Anne Cornelius, a trusted servant who had remained in London at Tavistock House, his primary residence, he ordered her to have the sleeping arrangement in the master bed-

87. Lancaster Castle and Its Approaches as They Appeared During Dickens' Visit in 1857

The immediate approaches to the castle were altered subsequent to Dickens' visit (for example, the houses in the right foreground were removed), but the castle itself is virtually unchanged. In Dickens' day, as today, the castle contained courtrooms, a prison, and the grim, unfeeling walls of Hanging Corner—features that helped shape what Dickens was about to write. *Lancaster Castle*. Engraving (c. 1825) after a drawing by William Westall.

room suite there changed. He would henceforth sleep in his old dressing room, using the bathroom as his washing room as well as a bathroom. The entry from his dressing room to the bedroom where he and Catherine had formerly slept would be walled off. The entry was to be "fitted with plain white deal shelves, and closed in with a plain light deal door, painted white" (11 October 1857). He had, he continued, already ordered bedding and a small iron bedstead for his new bedchamber; bedding and bedstead would be arriving before he returned to London to resume his residence there.

With this long-pondered decision, Dickens' twenty-one-year marriage came to an end, though it took many months of anguished contention and formal negotiation before a legal separation between Dickens and his wife was finally worked out.[7] The chilling act of walling up the bedchamber, and the symbolic separation and immurement that act so adamantly enforced, was in stark contrast to the deeds he envisioned when he thought of Ellen: smashing barriers, sword in hand, and rescuing the adored princess. For halo-headed Ellen he would scale mountains, slay dragons, slaughter ogres, breach strongholds. He would win the angel-princess or die in the attempt. No closing off or wall erecting here.

IV

When Dickens sat down to write "The Bride's Chamber" in late September and early October, 1857, the events, emotions, and problems we have just surveyed were thronging his mind. But his mind was also filled with the sights and scenes of his recent trip; the story had to evoke that trip. Accordingly, Dickens decided to associate "The Bride's Chamber" with Lancaster Castle and the old King's Arms, Lancaster. Or perhaps the reverse was true: perhaps memories of his visit to Lancaster Castle (where he had relived the chilling history of a hard man named "Hardman," a cruel husband who had been hanged at Lancaster Castle two weeks earlier, hanged at Hanging Corner, hanged on the very spot where Dickens had stood, hanged for murdering his unwanted wife, a wife named "Ellen"), perhaps memories of this castle visit, so guilt-inducing and guilt-entangled for Dickens at that fateful moment of analogous crisis in his own life (see Part 2, note 10), perhaps these memories and memories of his stay at the venerable King's Arms evoked the first faint lineaments of the story. In any case, the Lancaster visit contributed importantly to his imaginings. It introduced a surcharged occasion and a picturesque setting; it brought together an emotion-freighted tangle of persons, situations, and events: a tangle of doomed marriages, cruel husbands, murders, hangings, ghosts, damning secrets, and an array of consonant associations.

Dickens and Collins arrived at the King's Arms, Lancaster, on Saturday afternoon, 12 September 1857, occupying two bedrooms and a sitting room. (They left Lancaster late Sunday night.) The old inn, as Dickens described it in a letter written from the King's Arms, had formerly been "a very remarkable old house . . . with genuine old rooms and an uncommonly quaint staircase" (12 September 1857). The old house, the most atmospheric and picturesque part of the hotel, had been built in 1625 as a private residence. Its front façade, an imposing wall of large old-fashioned bay windows, stood three stories tall. Dickens occupied a large state bedroom in the old portion with two enormous red four-posters in it. This room, bay-windowed and overlooking the street, contained, in addition to the four-posters, an array of complementary furnishings and art works, all redolent of the past. The room and all its contents evoked the past, evoked long-vanished days, long-vanished occupants, and long-vanished events. Many of the rooms in the Jacobean house were rich with similar furnishings: dark woods, great old oaken beds, costly tapestries, curious carvings, fine paintings, rare needlework, antique furniture, and other venerable treasures.[8] All were rich with ancient associations. One room in the King's Arms, says Dickens in "The Bride's Chamber," or, deliberately obfuscating the matter, one room "in some other old house in that old town," is the focal point of the story (*HW* 16: BC, 387).

Whether Dickens, while in Lancaster, heard a version, or even some fragments, of the story he was about to tell is not clear, though

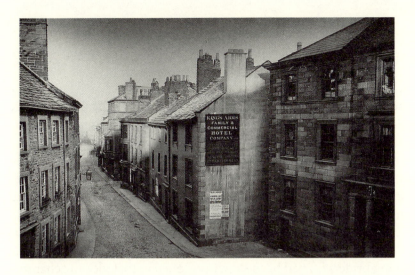

88. The King's Arms, Lancaster: "A Good Old Inn"

Dickens stayed in the oldest and most atmospheric part of the inn, the bay-windowed section at the far end. This section, built in 1625, had originally been a fine old private residence. Photograph 1877–79, shortly before the old King's Arms was demolished and a new King's Arms built in its place. Lancaster City Museum, Lancaster, England.

89. The King's Arms, Lancaster: "A Fine Old House"

"'I have heard there is a good old Inn at Lancaster, established in a fine old house.'" The King's Arms shown from the perspective of the "fine old house," that is, from the bay-windowed section of the inn. The King's Arms, Lancaster. Lantern slide, 1877–79. Lancaster City Museum, Lancaster, England.

there is no direct evidence that he did and a great deal of evidence (direct and indirect) that he did not. There is, however, some after-the-fact hearsay. According to F. G. Kitton (whose account was later embroidered by Walter Dexter, B. W. Matz, and others), the room in question, called the "Bridal Chamber," was located at the King's Arms and contained a famous bed of black oak. This imposing bed and ancient chamber, so the fully elaborated hearsay version went, were the subjects of a romantic legend dating back to the years when the house had been a private dwelling. The legend told of a young bride who had been slowly poisoned in that gloomy chamber and of her cruel husband-murderer who was later executed at nearby Lancaster Castle, a legend that Dickens, who became friendly with the landlord, and visited Lancaster Castle (which then housed—as it does now—criminal courts and a prison), "doubt-less" heard from his lips or from some other local source (or, con-trary to the hearsay account, probably conjured out of a different array of sources and associations—see the opening paragraph of this subsection, Dickens' own statements quoted below in Part 2, and Part 2, note 10), and a legend that was memorialized at the King's Arms—so continues the hearsay version—by the nightly serving of bridecake (Kitton, *Minor Writings,* 136; Matz, *Inns,* 230–32; Dex-ter, *England,* 229).

But there is other, more contemporary, evidence concerning the supposed local legend. The landlord of the King's Arms, Joseph Sly, also testified (though indirectly) on this subject. Sly was neither modest nor reticent; indeed he was a publicity seeker and a skillful promoter. He gave names to several of his suites and later issued a printed guide to his inn, including descriptions of its named rooms (one of which was called "Dickens' Room"), but he made no claim to a room called the "Bridal Chamber" or to any legendary or ro-mantic happenings associated with his inn, and he did not connect the bridecake he served each night with a story or an event—omis-sions that cast grave doubt on the hearsay account. Sly did, however (in various versions of his printed guide), trumpet the connection between the King's Arms, Dickens, and the tale that Dickens located there—but never in such a way as to verify the tale or to take credit for anything that went into it—which again casts doubt on the hearsay account.[9]

As a matter of fact, there is direct evidence concerning these questions, some of it contributed by Dickens himself. In the framework of "The Bride's Chamber," at the very end of the overall narrative, Dickens remarks that the inset story was a farrago of things experienced, felt, and pondered while in Lancaster; to quote his conclusive statement on the subject, the inset story was not a retelling of a legend that he had heard but a compound of "Bride-cake, and fragments, newly arranged, of things seen and thought about in the day" (*HW* 16: BC, 393). "The Bride's Chamber," in other words, was a product of the sights, stresses, memories, and yearnings that surrounded that tormented Lancaster sojourn. Furthermore, later that year, in a letter (3 December 1857) written long after the story had appeared in *Household Words,* replying to Sly's praise of "The Bride's Chamber" and its King's Arms setting, Dickens made no mention of local legends or local storytellers (no mention of Sly or any other storyteller), and he made no mention either of historical events connected with the King's Arms. On the contrary, he indicated that "The Bride's Chamber" and its associations were products of his own imagination. "It was very agreeable to me," Dickens wrote Sly, "to know that you were gratified in my having associated a little fancy with your excellent house."

This conclusive statement was subsequently echoed and affirmed by Sly. In 1866, in a long promotional supplement to his pamphlet on Dickens and the King's Arms, a supplement that covered many matters besides Dickens and his visit, Sly (or his agent), speaking of Dickens, wrote: "The author imagines a Bridal Chamber in the Hotel" (*BBC*, 32). Note the word *imagines,* a word that reaffirms the fictional nature of Dickens' "little fancy." Here again, in a contemporary firsthand account written when either Sly or Dickens could have contradicted the assertion if either had wished to do so (Sly, as publisher, promoter, and financial underwriter of the supplement, could have excised or corrected the statement before publication had he considered it false), the imaginary nature of the Bride's Chamber is affirmed once more.

Dickens' imagination was gripped and stimulated by Sly's "excellent house." The atmospheric old inn and the hospitality of its friendly landlord became entwined with an array of concordant and discordant emotions—intense, warring emotions of which Sly could have had no inkling, emotions which ultimately gave birth to that tormented "little fancy," "The Bride's Chamber." The genial landlord accentuated those emotions and became part of that little fancy. Sly was proud of his ancient, antique-filled hostelry, and proud also of his distinguished guest. He personally greeted Dickens, ushered him to his rooms, and then devised and presided over a lavish dinner for Dickens and Collins, topping the feast with the fabled confection, an enormous bridecake which he placed at the center of the table. "We always have it here, sir," he explained to Dickens, "custom of the house" (12 September 1857). When Dickens sat down to write "The Bride's Chamber" two weeks later, old houses, accommodating landlords, romantic surroundings, brideless bridecakes, unwanted wives, longed-for princesses, heartless husbands, murderous impulses, castle hangings, and guilty reproaches were contending in his mind.

"The Bride's Chamber" is an autonomous work of art, but while it asserts it autonomy independent of its origins, it also reflects the strange array of fact and feeling, precept and passion, that presided over its birth. Those elements appear in "The Bride's Chamber" in conjoined yet discrete form. By a species of double or triple vision that is aided by the complex narrative structure (a structure that includes Dickens, Goodchild, the ghostly narrator of the inset story, and the characters themselves), Dickens was able to be both judge and judged, murderer and savior, observer and participant. He was able, in other words, to separate and dramatize, to enlarge, act out, and in part to relieve, the contending impulses that were rending and tormenting him. To use his own phrase, he could approach the "actual truth without its pain." How conscious Dickens was of the detailed relevance of "The Bride's Chamber" to his own acute di-

90. Joseph Sly, Landlord of the King's Arms, Lancaster

In a letter (12 September 1857) written from Lancaster, Dickens described how Joseph Sly, the landlord of the King's Arms, "presided over the serving of the dinner." That memorable dinner, a lavish feast, had as its most striking feature an "enormous bride-cake"—a brideless bridecake—a bridecake that was placed at the center of the dining table. "'We always have it here, sir,' said the landlord, 'custom of the house.'" From a photograph in the author's possession.

lemma is difficult to tell, but that he was aware of some of the primary connections between story and dilemma is quite clear, as internal and external evidence amply demonstrate.

The chief incidents of "The Bride's Chamber" are quickly told. Francis Goodchild (Dickens) and Thomas Idle (Collins) arrive at the King's Arms, Lancaster, at six in the evening. They are received in the somber entrance hall by "half-a-dozen noiseless old men in black, all dressed exactly alike," cadaverous old men who weirdly "glide" up the dark mahogany staircase, an old mysterious staircase that gravely beckons just beyond the entrance hall. The six old men glide up that somber staircase with the two travelers and with the landlord and a waiter (*HW* 16: BC, 386). As the landlord and waiter proceed toward the sitting room assigned to Goodchild and Idle, the six noiseless old men in black disappear. The next day Goodchild-Dickens is brimming with energy and curiosity. Leaving his injured companion behind—Collins had sprained his ankle—Goodchild explores the inn, the town, the castle (the latter only a block or two from the King's Arms), the County Lunatic Asylum (much farther away), and the countryside. When he returns to the inn at the end of the day, he tells the lethargic Idle of his adventures, especially of his visit to the insane asylum. (He does not mention, however—nor does Dickens mention elsewhere in *The Lazy Tour*—that the insane asylum contained wards for the criminally insane.)

That evening, after dinner, the two companions set to work once more on the *Lazy Tour*, writing steadily for two or three hours, then breaking off to drink and smoke. They grow drowsy. Goodchild, consulting his watch, says it is "One," upon which one of the old men in black appears before them. The night turns cold; Goodchild shivers. The old man, his eyes glowing like "two spots of fire," fixes Goodchild with his gaze (*HW* 16: BC, 387). Two threads of fire stretch from the old man's eyes to Goodchild's, and Goodchild feels compelled to look and listen. They converse. When Goodchild asks the old man if condemned criminals, when hanged outside the nearby castle, are hanged facing the castle, the old man not only answers the question affirmatively, but tells Goodchild what it is like

91. The King's Arms, Lancaster:
Old Entrance Hall and Staircase

Dickens described the King's Arms as "a genuine old house . . . teeming with old carvings, and beams, and panels," and having a "sombre handsome old [entrance] hall" and an "excellent old staircase . . . cut off from it by a curious fence-work of old oak." "Entrance Hall and Ancient Stair Case." Wood engraving (c. 1860) from a promotional pamphlet for the King's Arms Hotel, Lancaster. Gimbel Collection, Beinecke Rare Book and Manuscript Library, Yale University, New Haven, Connecticut.

to be hanged as one stares at the cold unfeeling stones of the castle wall. He describes how the stone wall shimmies, the body throbs, the earth quivers and quakes, how the fire rushes forth and the castle springs into the air as one tumbles into eternity.[10] Goodchild is aghast; he beings to sweat. The ominous signs and portents continue. Finally the old man, who has now gained total ascendency over the mesmerized Goodchild, says, " 'I must tell it to you.' " A moment later he commences: " 'You know she was a Bride' " (*HW* 16: BC, 387). Thomas Idle, through all these preliminaries, has been deep in a sleeplike trance and he continues in that trance as the old man recounts his terrific story to the raptly listening Goodchild.

That wild story—the story of the Bride's Chamber—concerns a suitor who has been put aside by his chosen one for a man with money. His would-be intended marries the man with money, and the suitor smolders with anger. Ten or twelve years later the man with money dies, leaving his wife a fortune and a child, a young, large-eyed, white-clad, flaxen-haired girl. The rejected suitor, hard and vengeful, craving "compensation in Money" for his rejection and humiliation, courts the woman again, dancing attendance upon her every capricious whim; but he is again thwarted in his intention to marry her when she suddenly dies (*HW* 16: BC, 387). But the rejected suitor, now twice denied, has his way. He forges the dead woman's signature to a false document that leaves her entire fortune to her ten-year-old daughter but also makes him the daughter's guardian. This fraud accomplished, he begins his devil's work. He isolates and molds his pliant young ward into a weak, submissive, supplicating wraith. He teaches her to cringe before him; he makes her a supine instrument of his vindictive will. On her twenty-first birthday, he marries this self-abnegating, white-clad wreck. He takes her to the Bride's Chamber, immures her there, and orders her to write out and sign an instrument leaving everything to him in the event of her death. She meekly obeys, executes the document, and implores his mercy and forgiveness. She will do anything he wants, she tells him, if only he will forgive her. But this obdurate Bluebeard, document in hand, is now done with his grovelling bride.

92. The Heartless Husband Commands His Submissive Wife, "Now, Die! I Have Done With You. . . . Die! . . . Die! . . . Die!"

"She had been quiet in the corner of the paneling where she had sunk down; and he had left her, and had gone back with his folded arms and his knitted forehead to his chair." This illustration for "The Bride's Chamber" (here reproduced for the first time) appeared in 1875 (five years after Dickens' death) in a pirated American edition of *The Lazy Tour* published in New York by John Wurtele Lovell under the following rubric: *The Dickens-Collins Christmas Stories, Comprising No Thoroughfare and The Two Idle Apprentices.* (*The Lazy Tour of Two Idle Apprentices* was not a Christmas story, did not appear at Christmastime, and had nothing to do with Christmas.) The Lovell volume contained two illustrations, a frontispiece for *No Thoroughfare* and a frontispiece for *The Lazy Tour.* The latter frontispiece depicted the scene from "The Bride's Chamber" reproduced above. Only two other illustrations for "The Bride's Chamber" seem to exist (only one of these for the inset story). The two illustrations in question—feeble efforts by Arthur Layard—appeared in the first authorized English edition to collect *The Lazy Tour,* a volume published in 1890, more than thirty years after the original appearance of the series in *Household Words.* (See Part 2, note 3.) "The Miser and His Victim.— 'Die! Die!'" Wood engraving signed in the block WLO (Wurtele Lovell?). From *The Dickens-Collins Christmas Stories* (1875).

317

He utters a single contemptuous command: "Die!" (*HW* 16: BC, 389). In the ensuing weeks and months, there in the gloomy Bride's Chamber, he endlessly reiterates his dreadful order: "Die!" "Die!" "Die!" He is implacable; he scorns her pitiful pleading; he wills her into nothingness, into death. Day after day, night after night, he sits in the somber Bride's Chamber, a stern inimical figure of death, whispering, intoning, looking the word, "Die!" When the deed is done, when his compliant bride, sprawled on the floor of the Bride's Chamber, has finally become a "blank nothing," he is content (*HW* 16: BC, 389). At last, after long years, he has compensated himself with money.

But one evening, in the walled garden of his purloined domain, shortly before he is about to dispose of the white-clad bride's—now his—"accursed house," a house that always seems to be "waiting for him like a tomb," he sees a young man clinging to the branches of a tree that faces onto the bay window of the Bride's Chamber (*HW* 16: BC, 389). The young man confronts him, tells him that he has often climbed the tree, gazed into the Bride's Chamber, talked with its white-clad inhabitant, received a tress of her hair, and come to love her. The young man is filled with anguish and grief. Proclaiming his love, he calls the older man, "Murderer!" (*HW* 16: BC, 390). He vows to expose him. The furious husband, in a spasm of rage, throws a billhook at the tree-climbing lover. The sharp blade, following a "red curve" from his hand to the youth's head, finds it preordained mark (*HW* 16: BC, 390). It cleaves the young man's skull and remains there, stuck fast in his head. The husband buries the youth's slender body, billhook in its head, beneath the Bride's Chamber tree. But now the scheming monster is trapped. In a moment of passion he has jeopardized a lifetime's manipulation. He is wracked by fears and suspicions. He dare not leave the old house, so full of whispers and secrets; he dare not turn his back upon the magically expressive tree, so redolent of the tree-climbing suitor lying at its foot. The gloomy house, a part of his long-contemplated "compensation," is now his living tomb. He is a self-ordained prisoner, fearful, watchful, haunted, unable to enjoy the

93. Hanging Corner, Lancaster Castle: "'Your Face Is Turned . . . to the Castle Wall. . . . You See Its Stones Expanding and Contracting Violently'"

The window of the Drop Room opened like a door. Prisoners sentenced to death walked directly through the window onto the scaffold and were hanged facing the cold, unfeeling stones of the castle wall (see Part 2, note 10). Dickens visited the Drop Room and Hanging Corner shortly before writing "The Bride's Chamber." Though the pitlike area in the lower foreground was present in Dickens' day, the iron railings were not. Hanging Corner, Lancaster Castle. Photograph (1987) by the author.

wealth he has schemed so many years to obtain. Ten more years go by, ten long, somber, isolated years, immured in the sepulchral house; and then, during a terrible thunderstorm, lighting strikes the Bride's Chamber tree and cleaves it in two. Scientists come to inspect the riven tree. They dig round its base and discover the young lover's body there with the billhook in its riven skull.

The murderer-husband, now an old man, is taken, tried, sentenced to death, and hanged facing the castle wall. That noiseless old man in black, the teller of the tale—he of the "troubled" throat, the "swollen" face, the nose "hitched up on one side"—is the murderer himself, hanged one hundred years ago, hanged facing the castle wall (*HW* 16: BC, 387). Each night he haunts the Bride's Chamber, and each night he is haunted in turn by the beseeching, white-clad bride and the lovelorn young man, a billhook in his head. The old man's torment is endless, his suffering constantly renewed. One month a year, the month when he was hanged, he suffers additional torments with each sounding of the tolling bell, becoming two noiseless old men in black when the bell tolls two; three old men in black when it tolls three; until, at twelve midnight, twelve old men in black wait for their execution and then, in twelvefold agony, swing out to their horrible deaths before Lancaster Castle, their faces turned to the castle wall.

Endless doom and endless dole. As the old man in black cries, "Woe!" "Woe!" "Woe!" Goodchild breaks free from his immobilizing gaze, catches up the sleeping Idle, and rushes down the dark staircase with him (*HW* 16: BC, 393). Idle, bewildered and ruffled, protests this sudden manhandling, scoffs at Goodchild's wild words about old men, insists, in contradiction to Goodchild's claim that he (Idle) had been asleep, that on the contrary, he had never shut an eye, and charges instead that Goodchild has been dreaming. Goodchild denies this accusation, affirms the plain, unarguable fact that the sitting room is real, the inn is real, the dark staircase is real, and the old men in black are real. He will write down the truth and print it—which he has just now done.

94. The Ancient Staircase in the King's Arms: Dark and Darkly Haunted for Dickens

When Dickens arrived at the King's Arms, he was impressed by this "excellent old staircase," an "uncommonly quaint staircase," a staircase built in 1625. Very soon, that somber staircase, "a certain grave mystery lurking in the depths of [its] old mahogany panels," took on symbolic import for him, somber import associated with his own dark dilemma at that moment of crisis and guilt in his life. When, two weeks after ascending and descending this dark staircase, he began to write "The Bride's Chamber" (his wild expressionistic fictional embodiment of his crisis and guilt), this ancient staircase loomed forebodingly in his imaginings. At the beginning of the story, as Goodchild-Dickens ascends this fateful staircase (fateful by now for him), he has his first disturbing encounter with the noiseless old men in black, at this point six old men in black, and at the end of the story, as he rushes down this dark staircase in a panic of anguish and fear, rushes down amidst cries of "Woe! Woe! Woe!," he tries to escape from his terrifying vision, again a vision of old men in black—now twelve old men in black, all hanged—a vision that embodies his yearning and anger, that embodies also the dread consequences of such forbidden yearning and anger, consequences that always accompany (so Dickens tells himself in "The Bride's Chamber") unbridled passion and attendant sin. "Staircase In The King's Arms." Wood engraving. *Illustrated London News* (25 July 1868). The *Illustrated London News,* in the article on Lancaster that accompanied this engraving, devotes considerable space to the King's Arms, the staircase, Dickens' visit, and the "thrilling story" of "The Bride's Chamber."

V

The relevance of "The Bride's Chamber" to Dickens' immediate predicament and contending emotions is striking. The criminal teller of the inset story bears a double load of guilt. At the outset of his central tale he is a masterful middle-aged man who manipulates an impressionable young girl. Eleven years later he is a cruel husband who wishes to dispose of a compliant, unwanted wife. He is thus an avatar of Dickens' most self-accusatory and guilty feelings toward Ellen and toward Catherine. But Dickens is also the tree-climbing suitor come to rescue the immured princess or die in the attempt (here Dickens enacts his romantic vision of himself as ogre-slaying fairy-tale hero). But these clear-cut roles are not so simple as they at first seem. How are we to view the bride?—as pitiful wife or dazzling princess? And how are we to view the illicit tree-climbing suitor? He is, after all (at the end, at least), in forbidden pursuit of a betrothed and then a married woman. (Here he is similar to Richard Wardour and Edward Easel, and later to Sydney Carton.)

In the case of Dickens, his forbidden pursuit was also barred by marriage: Dickens the middle-aged married man was illicitly pursuing Ellen the young unmarried girl. (Dickens, in this phase of the story, was similar, in age and unsuitability, though not in marital status, to Uncle John.) In "The Bride's Chamber" the middle-aged man murders (in effect) the compliant wife and then murders the ardent suitor. Neither murder gains him his desired relief or his desired freedom. In the end he is haunted forever by the ghosts of those he has wronged; he must fruitlessly seek to expiate his sins through all eternity, forever telling his story, like the Ancient Mariner or the Wandering Jew, to those who need to hear it. In "The Bride's Chamber," taking the work in its entirety, it is Dickens (in the person of Goodchild) who needs to hear the story. And by a species of legerdemain, the story is told only to him; Collins throughout the telling is in a sleeplike trance. Dickens, in effect, is telling the story to himself.

In "The Bride's Chamber" Dickens seems to have seen no way out of his domestic dilemma. To put aside ("murder") his wife would not allow him to win the princess: he was too old, too much the exemplary paterfamilias, too much the adored public figure to carry off Ellen Ternan and live happily ever after. Furthermore, like arrogant old Uncle John, and like the cruel middle-aged guardian of "The Bride's Chamber," Dickens had been using his overwhelming power and mentorlike position to enmesh—enmesh emotionally and sexually—a trusting and vulnerable young girl. He knew this. However innocent his intentions with respect to Ellen, he must have felt, at some level at least (as his reticence and riddling in his letters to Wills attest), deep uneasiness and guilt. It is notable that in "The Bride's Chamber" the middle-aged man (one avatar of Dickens) puts an end to—murders—the romantic lover (another avatar of Dickens). The young lover, though eligible (in the first part of the story, at least), can never win his goal. He can only cry out, in the moment before his death, "'I loved her! . . . Murderer, I loved her!'" (*HW* 16: BC, 390). The dream of felicity, Dickens seems to be saying to himself, is only a dream. Whether he turns to his wife or his princess or his ineffable dream, he feels thwarted, sinful, guilty, a haunted, self-convicted, self-condemned murderer—a cruel Hardmanlike murderer—unable to shrive himself. How cruel and Hardmanlike Dickens felt when he sat down to write "The Bride's Chamber" is given added dimension when one realizes that in the story, as in the Hardman case, the cruel husband sits in the room with his unwanted wife, sits there hour after hour, day after day, sits there and watches coldly, inimically, inflexibly as the wretched wife he is heartlessly propelling into nothingness slowly and miserably dies. The punishment is the same in "The Bride's Chamber" as in the Hardman case too: hanging—hanging facing the grim unfeeling stones of Lancaster Castle wall (see Part 2, note 10).

But art, though related to life, is not life. "The Bride's Chamber," however bleak its burden, however futile its alternatives, seems to have helped Dickens vent his feelings and reach a decision. The door would shut on his married life; he would pursue and win the princess. In the long run, art seems to have been a truer index of the future than Dickens' real-life plans. Though he put his wife aside and, after a fashion, won the princess, he also paid "The Bride's Chamber" price. The separation scarred his later life; and the liaison, shrouded in secrecy and guilt, did not bring him the bliss of marrying the princess and living happily ever after.

The emotional relevance of "The Bride's Chamber" to Dickens' dilemma in the summer and fall of 1857 is multidimensional and profound, but beyond such emotional connections, and beyond the more external Hardmanesque echoes and similitudes, the story had other deep autobiographical undertones, undertones of a more literal kind that Dickens was surely aware of. Fair-haired Ellen, like her darker-haired and darker-eyed sister Maria, had, in Dickens' description, a "pale face, with large . . . eyes" (5 September 1857), and these few features—fair hair, pale face, and large eyes—are virtually the only physical attributes vouchsafed the bride in "The Bride's Chamber." Fair hair, pale face, and large eyes become a motif, the physical correlatives of the blighted bride. We see her with "her flaxen hair all wild about her face, and her large eyes staring"; we see her again when the spots of ink on her white dress "made her face look whiter and her eyes look larger"; and we see her for the last time "a white wreck of hair, and dress, and wild eyes" (*HW* 16: BC, 388, 389). It is as though Dickens was haunted by the image of a vulnerable, supplicatory, white-clad female with fair hair, pale face, and large eyes. That Dickens was haunted there can be no doubt. "I have never known," he wrote a few months later, "a moment's peace or content, since the last night of The Frozen Deep. I do suppose that there never was a man so seized and rended by one spirit" (21 March 1858).

The ghost of Catherine, too, emerges in the portrait of the bride, this time as an unwanted wife. Catherine, now forty-two and growing fat, was not fair-haired and pale-complected like Ellen, but she did have large eyes. More important, she was a yielding and compliant wife. Dickens' ascendancy over Ellen was that of a famous, worldly, masterful middle-aged man over an inexperienced teen-

aged girl; his ascendancy over Catherine was that of an intense, mer-
curial, dominating personality over a submissive and complying
one. "Complying" is the key word. Dickens himself used the word
to describe Catherine in the very letter in which he set forth their
incompatibility: "She is exactly what you know, in the way of being
amiable and complying; but we are strangely ill-assorted for the
bond there is between us." In "The Bride's Chamber," submission
and compliance are the chief features of the unwanted wife's will-
less subordination. She is soft and impressionable (Dickens also
complains of Catherine's pliant "weakness"), and by the time the
vulnerable young ward has become a submissive woman and has
married her scheming guardian, she has but one refrain to sound in
her relationship with her contemptuous husband: "'Look kindly on
me, and be merciful to me! I beg your pardon. I will do anything
you wish, if you will only forgive me!'" (*HW* 16: BC, 388). The
inimical husband is not mollified. "That," he says, "had become the
poor fool's constant song: 'I beg your pardon,' and 'Forgive me!'"
(*HW* 16: BC, 388).

The abnegation depicted here goes far beyond Catherine's subservience and self-effacement, yet one senses that Dickens was looking deep into his own heart when he shadowed forth the compliant
wife's submission and the obdurate husband's refusal to forgive his
wife for being what she is or, perhaps even more to the point, for
being what he has made her. (In this connection it is worth recalling
that in *Uncle John* and "The Bride's Chamber" the dominating
husband-mentor molds—indeed creates—the character of his compliant bride; to use Uncle John's complacently arrogant phrase concerning his bride to be, he "directed her disposition.") One also
glimpses an extreme rendering of Dickens' profound unhappiness
when he has the unloving husband in "The Bride's Chamber" say
of the unwanted wife: "She was not worth hating; he felt nothing
but contempt for her. But, she had long been in the way, and he
had long been weary" (*HW* 16: BC, 388). Finally, when the inimical
husband tells the unwanted wife to die, we can hardly fail to see this
wish as Dickens willing Catherine away. That Dickens regards the

95. Catherine Dickens c. 1857, Age Forty-Two

From a photograph taken about the time that Dickens met Ellen Ternan and wrote "The Bride's Chamber." Huntington Library, San Marino, California.

unwanted wife's destruction—and his own terrible wish ("the wish will force itself upon me that something might be done")—as a murderous act and an unpardonable sin is made clear by the eternal penalty he imposes on the obdurate Hardman-like man who willed his wife into nothingness.

All these emotional similitudes and accusatory self-revelations are hidden enough to one not privy to the inmost secrets of Dickens' private life. But the mysteries of the human mind and the paradoxical perversities of human needs are beyond fathoming. Dickens often felt some strange compulsion to boldly reveal to all the world what he knew would remain concealed to all but himself—or to all but himself and one or two others (witness the concealed, yet blatant and dangerous, self-revelation in "Please to Leave Your Umbrella," for example). And so, the adored princess, who is also the unwanted wife, is given a name—she is the only character in the inset story proper to bear a name. That isolated name, sounding with such singularity in the story, could hardly be more plainly identifying or more plainly revelatory to the handful of cognoscenti—or more blandly ordinary and meaningless to all the multitudinous rest. The name, of course, is "Ellen." To name the rejected wife/adored princess Ellen (Hardman's Ellen notwithstanding) was an indiscreet or, to be more exact, a reckless act. (Think, for example, of Catherine reading the story, or of Ellen.) The name Ellen must have been, for Dickens, a magic sign or sacred amulet, a cherished talisman, a secret banner he could wave for all to see but none—or virtually none—to know.

But this is not the end of the matter; Dickens compounds his secret signaling. In the outer framework of the inset story, not in the inset story proper, one other character—a shadowy character long since consigned to limbo in the story, a character who many years before had been in the position of listener, as Dickens and Collins now are—that Dickens-like doppelgänger character is given a name. And of all the possible names that Dickens might have summoned up, what name does he finally call forth? He calls forth an equivocal name. It is at once ordinary and special, open and hidden, another name for all to see but none to really know—know, that is, in its secret emotional relevance for Dickens. That half-disguised, half-flaunted name, which Dickens now mingles eternally with the emotion-charged name of "Ellen" (emotion-charged for him), that self-reflexive and self-echoing name is "Dick."

Dickens intended the echo. His attention to names, to their secret resonances and their magical import, was abiding. Names had the power to evoke and control, to shape and to summon forth— or so he felt. Names always fascinated and provoked him; he was extraordinarily sensitive to their sounds, their associations, their implications. In his working notes and in his manuscripts he often made lists of trial names for his characters, usually working intricate variations on a dominant theme until he hit upon the exact combination of sounds and suggestions that fit the character he had in mind. In his book of memoranda he recorded long lists of odd or strange or evocative names, names that struck his fancy, names gleaned from newspapers, reports, pamphlets, and other everyday sources, names preserved for possible future use in his fiction, a use (the names occasionally modified by a touch here or there) that frequently came to pass.

Names haunted Dickens' consciousness. He often invested them with deep emotional significance and power, and with lifelong resonance. Sometimes that resonance (as with the name "Ellen" or "Maria") had profoundly personal origins. Listen to his confession to Maria Beadnell, a confession made more than twenty years after he had courted her and been tormented by her long, painful rejection of him, of how the name "Maria" affected him then and ever after: "I have never heard anybody addressed by your name, or spoken of by your name, without a start. The sound of it has always filled me with a kind of pity and respect for the deep truth that I had, in my silly hobbledehoyhood, to bestow upon one creature who represented the whole world to me" (15 February 1855).

But to return to Dickens' new talisman, the magical sound and magical evocation "Ellen." The name Ellen, reverberant now with a different and more tormented "pity," "respect," and "deep truth," attendance on her, and submitted himself to her whims. She wreaked upon him every whim she had, or could invent. He bore it. And the more he bore, the more he wanted compensation in Money, and the more he was resolved to have it.

"But, lo! Before he got it, she cheated him. In one of her imperious states, she froze, and never thawed again. She put her hands to her head one night, uttered a cry, stiffened, lay in that attitude certain hours, and died. And he had got no compensation from her in Money, yet. Blight and Murrain on her! Not a penny.

"He had hated her throughout that second pursuit,—and had longed for retaliation on her. He now counterfeited her signature to an instrument, leaving all she had to leave, to her daughter—ten years old then—to whom the property passed absolutely, and appointing himself the daughter's Guardian. When He slid it under the pillow of the bed on which she lay, He bent down in the deaf ear of Death, and whispered: 'Mistress Pride, I have determined a long time that, dead or alive, you must make me compensation in Money.'

"So, now there were only two left. Which two were, He, and the fair flaxen-haired, large-eyed foolish daughter, who afterwards became the Bride.

"He put her to school. In a secret, dark, oppressive, ancient house, he put her to school with a watchful and unscrupulous woman. 'My worthy lady,' he said, 'here is a mind to be formed; will you help me to form it?' She accepted the trust. For which she, too, wanted compensation in Money, and had it.

"The girl was formed in the fear of him, and in the conviction, that there was no escape from him. She was taught, from the first, to regard him as her future husband—the man who must marry her—the destiny that overshadowed her—the appointed certainty that could never be evaded. The poor fool was soft white wax in their hands, and took the impression that they put upon her. It hardened with time. It became a part of herself. Inseparable from herself, and only to be torn away from her, by tearing life away from her.

"Eleven years she lived in the dark house and its gloomy garden. He was jealous of the very light and air getting to her, and they kept her close. He stopped the wide chimneys, shaded the little windows, left the strong-stemmed ivy to wander where it would over the house-front, the moss to accumulate on the untrimmed fruit-trees in the red-walled garden, the weeds to over-run its green and yellow walks. He surrounded her with images of sorrow and desolation. He caused her to be filled with fears of the place and of the stories that were told of it, and then on pretext of correcting them, to be left in it in solitude, or made to shrink about it in the dark. When her mind was most depressed and fullest of terrors, then, he would come out of one of the hiding-places from which he overlooked her, and present himself as her sole resource.

"Thus, by being from her childhood the one embodiment her life presented to her of power to coërce and power to relieve, power to bind and power to loose, the ascendency over her weakness was secured. She was twenty-one years and twenty-one days old, when he brought her home to the gloomy house, his half-witted, frightened, and submissive Bride of three weeks.

"He had dismissed the governess by that time—what he had left to do, he could best do alone—and they came back, upon a rainy night, to the scene of her long preparation. She turned to him upon the threshold, as the rain was dripping from the porch, and said:

"'O sir, it is the Death-watch ticking for me!'

"'Well!' he answered. 'And if it were?'

"'O sir!' she returned to him, 'look kindly on me, and be merciful to me! I beg your pardon. I will do anything you wish, if you will only forgive me!'

"That had become the poor fool's constant song: 'I beg your pardon,' and 'Forgive me!'

"She was not worth hating; he felt nothing but contempt for her. But, she had long been in the way, and he had long been weary, and the work was near its end, and had to be worked out.

"'You fool,' he said. 'Go up the stairs!'

"She obeyed very quickly, murmuring, 'I will do anything you wish!' When he came into the Bride's Chamber, having been a little retarded by the heavy fastenings of the great door (for they were alone in the house, and he had arranged that the people who attended on them should come and go in the day), he found her withdrawn to the furthest corner, and there standing pressed against the paneling as if she would have shrunk through it: her flaxen hair all wild about her face, and her large eyes staring at him in vague terror.

"'What are you afraid of? Come and sit down by me.'

"'I will do anything you wish. I beg your pardon, sir. Forgive me!' Her monotonous tune as usual.

"'Ellen, here is a writing that you must write out to-morrow, in your own hand. You may as well be seen by others, busily engaged upon it. When you have written it all fairly, and corrected all mistakes, call in any two people there may be about the house, and sign your name to it before them. Then, put it in your bosom to keep it safe, and when I sit here again to-morrow night, give it to me.'

"'I will do it all, with the greatest care. I will do anything you wish.'

"'Don't shake and tremble, then.'

---

96. "The Bride's Chamber" and a Singular Name Appear in *Household Words*

The rejected wife/adored princess is given a name, and the name is "Ellen."
Household Words, XVI (24 October 1857), 388.

would stand alone, then and ever after, not only in the innermost sanctum of "The Bride's Chamber," but in Dickens' writings. "Ellen" would be sacrosanct. He had never used the name in his fiction before, and he would never use it again.

VI

There is more to "The Bride's Chamber" than emotional autobiography and topical allusiveness. There is a strong generative infusion of folklore, fairy tales, and Gothic romance. Through all the fall and winter of 1857–58 Dickens often found himself dreaming wild ogre-beheading and dragon-slaying dreams of immured princesses, mountain-scaling heroes, and sword-brandishing rescuers. This transformation of real-life perils and yearnings into fairy-tale fervencies was the habit of a lifetime. From childhood on Dickens had immersed himself in the wild, sign-filled literature of the invisible world: in portents and wonders, spells and ghosts, magical rescues and dire retributions. And from childhood on he had colored the real world with the hues and tints of romance. But this puts the matter too mechanically. He often saw the world through the wonder-filled eyes of childhood. The streets of London, for instance, were (in one aspect at least) an *Arabian Nights* bazaar filled with people, places, and fulfillments that were, at one and the same time, minutely realistic and workaday, and wildly visionary. Here is Dickens, in a *Household Words* essay, "Gone Astray" (1853), rendering this phenomenon in its direct childhood intensity:

> The City was to me a vast emporium of precious stones and metals, casks and bales, honour and generosity, foreign fruits and spices. Every merchant and banker was a compound of Mr. Fitz-Warren and Sinbad the Sailor. . . . Glyn and Halifax had personally undergone great hardships in the valley of diamonds. Baring Brothers had seen Rocs' eggs and travelled with caravans. Rothschild had sat in the Bazaar at Bagdad with rich stuffs for sale; and a veiled lady from the Sultan's harem, riding a donkey, had fallen in love with him. (*HW* 7: 555)

"The Bride's Chamber," though rooted in the realistic, partakes of this visionary transcendence. The story is intensely real—think, for a moment, of such unmistakably real elements as the King's Arms Inn, Lancaster Castle, and the Lancaster Lunatic Asylum— but the tale is also a veritable mosaic of storybook literature and motifs. The framework, for example—not the Goodchild-Idle framework but the framework of the inset story—draws heavily on legendary and literary lore, primarily on the motifs of the Wandering Jew and the Ancient Mariner, with a strong infusion of the Gothic romance and the supernatural ghost story. Like the Wandering Jew and the Ancient Mariner, the narrator is old beyond mere mortality, and like them he is doomed to tell his dread tale through all eternity. Like the Ancient Mariner, he picks the person who must hear his monitory story: it is Dickens, not Collins, who has need of his awful warning. (Dickens, who knew "The Rime of the Ancient Mariner" well and often referred to it, would have been conscious of this application of the story to himself.)[11] Again, like the Ancient Mariner, the ancient teller of the tale holds his listener with his "glittering eye"—in "The Bride's Chamber," with "threads of fire" that "stretch from the old man's eyes to his own, and there attach themselves" (*HW* 16: BC, 387). And, like the Wedding Guest in the "Ancient Mariner," Goodchild, who "had the strongest sensation upon him of being forced to look at the old man along those two fiery films, from that moment," cannot choose but hear (*HW* 16: BC, 387). Other portions of the framework, the duplication of the old man with the striking hours, the cycling recurrences, the verbal repetitions, the magical numbers, the haunting of the scene of the crime, come from the more general stock of folklore and the supernatural. The fact that the narrator is a hanged man, that he frequently touches his neck, that he has a hitched-up nostril, and that he exhibits many similar signs of his terrific fate, are variations on favorite devices of the Gothic ghost story, though Dickens' rendering of those motifs—for example, the sensation of being hanged— is infinitely superior to the general run of such renditions. The end result is no mere assemblage of stock scraps and pieces. Dickens adds, shapes, re-creates, and transforms.

Dickens called "The Bride's Chamber" "a very odd story, with a wild, picturesque fancy in it"; he also called it a "grim" story, "a bit of Diablerie" (2 October 1857; 4 October 1857). The picturesque fancy and the grim diablerie bring forth different aspects of Dickens' current dilemma, but these aspects are harmonized by the fairy-tale energy that undergirds them both. That energy is more pervasive and more diffuse in the story proper than in the framework. In the story proper it is also more original and compelling; it incorporates Dickens' most passionate yearnings and guilty self-accusations.

The story proper embodies many familiar fairy-tale themes and devices. We quickly notice these storybook cues, and we respond, both consciously and unconsciously, to their richness of association and implication. We respond to the narrator's repeated curse with its strangely archaic and unmistakably Biblical overtones: "Blight and Murrain on her!" (*HW* 16: BC, 388). We respond also to his other fablelike repetitions: to his formulaic insistence, echoed throughout the story, on having "compensation in Money," and to his constantly reiterated injunction to his unwanted wife, the terrible imperative, "Die!" (*HW* 16: BC, 388, 389). We respond no less to the unloved wife's endlessly repeated and endlessly reiterated pleas: "I will do anything you wish," "I beg your pardon," "Forgive me!" (*HW* 16: BC, 388).

These ritualistic refrains are undergirded by fairy-tale scenes and fairy-tale imagery. We have met versions of those scenes and images before. We understand the mythic implications of the tree-climbing suitor, his peeping through the window, his speaking to the immured maiden, his obtaining the token tress of hair, his attacking the evil schemer, his dying his terrible, skull-cleft death. We understand his magical as well as his physical presence in the enchanted tree, and we understand the vernal and the deathlike signs that emanate from that tree after he has been murdered at its foot. Those signs, ever changing with the cycling seasons, ever remain the same. They preach one message, a message of grievous sin and unexpungeable guilt; they cry out for retribution: the leafy branches swinging with the young man's ghostly presence; the dropped leaves mounding on his grave; the bare, accusatory, threatening boughs, endlessly repeating his challenging blow; the blood-contaminated sap rising each spring to incriminate and accuse; the riven tree trunk, riven like the young man's skull. It is at the foot of this fateful tree, so expressive of good and evil, that the murdered youth lies buried. And it is through this selfsame tree that the wicked man is punished. For the lightning bolt cleaves the tree as the young man's skull was cleft, a condign intervention that breaches the wall and brings justice at last to that ruined garden and ruined house. We are obviously, here, in a magical world, a world in which each falling leaf, each glimmer of light, each gust of wind testifies in due degree to the beneficent natural order of the universe and to the dire consequences of violating that harmonious order.

Added to this reverberating symbolism are penetrating psychological insights. "The Bride's Chamber" is a compressed sketch of the willful destruction of a human ego; it is also a condensed study of the havoc that destruction wreaks in the soul of the willful destroyer. We see how the young girl—mere putty in the hands of the masterful older man—is shaped into a submissive instrument of his will; but we also see how the aggressive shaper, impiously assuming the role of God, destroys his own humanity in the process and forgoes the possibility of any peace or joy. For Dickens, the wanton manipulation of one human being by another was an unpardonable sin, a sin he depicts often in his writings. Think, for example, of *Great Expectations* and doomed Miss Havisham. In fashioning Estella to be an instrument of revenge, Miss Havisham turns herself into a light-shunning witch. She immures herself, a ghastly embodiment of death in life, and she perishes at last a victim of her own self-immolating entombment.[12]

Miss Havisham's fate is fitting, but nowhere does Dickens depict the unpardonable sin of egregious manipulation with such elemental concision and fablelike directness as in "The Bride's Chamber," and nowhere does he exact a bleaker retribution. The wages of such sinful dominion over others are unassuageable guilt and murderous self-destruction. Dickens makes this clear on every level of the story. From a realistic and psychological point of view, the whisperings of the accusatory tree are simply the projections of the narrator's fear-

ful guilt, while the actions that undo him are his impulsive yet compulsive act of murder (an act of murder that comes after long,
calculated, self-controlled years of carefully executing an earlier
act of annihilation—a cruel murder that is no murder), his fearful
and hastily improvised entombment of his victim, and his subsequent fear-engendered and guilt-engendered self-immolating
self-entombment. The lightning bolt is no chance event. In the
shorthand of fable, it is an ineluctable working-out. The masterful
manipulator of others—really destroyer of others (for a manipulator
who extends his control over others to its utmost verge *is* a destroyer, that is, a murderer)—can have no relief and no escape.
Dickens shows us this. He shows us that the cruel, vindictive narrator has become a prisoner of his inner needs and passions; he is now
enslaved by the imperious necessity—a self-created necessity—that
grips and shackles him. The dread nature of his bondage is emphasized by his ultimate fate. That fate could hardly be more unrelenting or terrible. Its chief features are a self-entombed immurement
(in this the narrator is a precursor of Miss Havisham), a ghastly, endlessly reexperienced death, and an eternal consignment to ghost-
haunted damnation. Dickens fuses the verisimilitude of compressed
psychological insight and the rich showing forth of fable. The result
is a whole in which every element—every season, every imprecation,
every gesture—takes on accreting and reverberant meaning.

Only the inset story has this richness and power. The story framework, fine though it is, and interlaced as it is with weird, compelling
fancies, seems distanced and contrived when compared to the incan-
descent central tale. The framework is a product of wit (it contains
a good deal of gallows humor) and of deft craftsmanship; the inset
story is a product of passionate imaginative involvement. The difference is a reflection of Dickens' psychological state. The inset story
embodied the most intense emotions of his inner conflict. Through
the story, through its expressionistic roles and emotional enlargements, he was able to indulge his most passionate longings and
forbidden urges and, at the same time, bear witness to their self-
reflexive destructiveness. But the inset story, and "The Bride's

Chamber" as a whole, is much more than personal release. In plumbing his own turbulent emotions Dickens was plumbing deep universal impulses. "The Bride's Chamber" is anchored in the universal. It is, above all, a primal fable of unbridled love, hate, violence, and guilt.

This fusion of the personal and the universal was not part of a preconceived plan. Dickens was not seeking—at least not consciously—to analyze his psychological state and then turn self-analysis into myth. Though he was aware of connections between the story and his psychological state—the story, though rooted in fact, even in topicality (even in Hardmanesque topicality), emerged from that psychological state—he was not attempting to give a history of that state. Indeed, the power of the story (and its truth) comes from its expressionistic exaggeration, not from its autobiographical or topical verisimilitude. In this sense the story is truer to Dickens' inner life than any faithful rendering of outward events could have been. Furthermore, the vehicle for allowing that inner passion such full expression—perhaps the only vehicle that could sanction such full expression—was the vehicle of folklore, fantasy, and fairy-tale fulfillment. It is the masterly fusion of passion and vehicle (content and form), a fusion that transcended the blandishments of mere happenstance or the impositions of mere propinquity, that makes the central story of "The Bride's Chamber" so powerfully affecting.

VII

Yet happenstance and decades of slow gestation also played roles in "The Bride's Chamber." When Dickens was a young boy, he often saw a strange, eccentric, white-clad woman wandering the precincts of Berners Street, Oxford Street. He was told, or imagined—so he wrote years later in "Where We Stopped Growing"—that this white-clad woman had been jilted by a wealthy man, and that since that time she had wandered those crowded London streets in her bridal dress, impelled by the sustaining delusion that she was on her way to church to marry her rich suitor (*HW* 6: 362–63). Dickens tells us that this ghastly White Woman was one of the unforgettable images of his childhood, an image that always retained its childhood force and implication for him. By a stroke of chance (the kind of chance that Dickens loved to marvel at), it was also an image that was reinforced several years later in an unexpected manner. When Dickens was nineteen he probably saw Charles Mathews play the role of Miss Mildew, a daft, white-clad ghost of the London streets, the protagonist of a sketch written by Mathews and based upon the wretched Berners Street White Woman of Dickens' childhood. Mathews' sketch, like Dickens' vision of his childhood White Woman, involved marriage, jilting, money, white-clad supplication, and deluded expectations. Dickens, who admired Mathews enormously, who always went to see him whenever he played, and memorized and acted out many of his roles, would not have forgotten this strange dramatic reappearance of the weird White Woman of his childhood.[13]

Counterparts of that childhood White Woman, always appearing as weird, bereft white-clad brides, continued to recur and evolve. In 1850—Dickens was now thirty-eight, famous, and in the midst of writing the autobiographical *David Copperfield*—he reprinted in his monthly journal of current events, the *Household Narrative* (a companion periodical to his weekly miscellany, *Household Words*), a paragraph from the *Examiner* (then edited by his intimate friend John Forster) about a wealthy old London recluse named Martha Joachim who had died late in January 1850 all alone in her York Buildings residence. Her history, reprinted in the *Household Narrative* under the rubric "*Wealthy and Eccentric Lady*," was filled with violence and storybook occurrences. Her father had been murdered and robbed in Regent's Park when she was a young woman; his murderer was eventually caught, convicted through incriminating evidence, and hanged. Years later a suitor of Martha Joachim, whom her mother had rejected, shot himself while sitting on the sofa next to his unattainable beloved and she was "covered with his brains" (*HN* 1: 10). From that moment she lost her reason, and from the time of her mother's death, eighteen long years before her own, she had dressed in white, immured herself in her York Buildings residence, and never ventured out into the daylight. Her house was environed by a walled garden; when tax collectors or other officials sought admission, they had to scale the garden wall (see figure 97).

When Dickens first read about Martha Joachim in the *Examiner* he must have been stunned, and when, several months later, he pondered her history once more, now in the pages of his own journal[14]—he probably suggested that the story (taken, with some excisions, verbatim from the *Examiner*) be included in the *Household Narrative*—he must have marveled yet again, not simply because Martha Joachim was another wild version of the unforgotten Berners Street White Woman of his childhood, or because she was another real-life counterpart to the weird White Women who had peopled the Gothic literature of his childhood (Monk Lewis' white-veiled Bleeding Nun, for example, who haunts her walled imprisoning castle home "robed" all "in white" and exacts a ghastly bloodstained vengeance ["The Bleeding Nun"]; or Lewis' Fair Imogine, another castle dweller, who, "arrayed in her bridal apparel of white," dances to damnation with the gruesome skeleton specter of her jilted lover ["Alonzo the Brave and Fair Imogine"]; or Lewis' tale of Ellen, castles, jilting, and revenge, and of the Grim White Woman, a cannibalistic, shroud-wrapped "female in white," a pale cadaverous instrument of revenge, who feasts on her victims, "feasts on [their] blood" ["The Grim White Woman"]—three favorites, lurid White Woman favorites, Monk Lewis favorites, of the young Dickens), but Dickens, on reperusing Martha Joachim's history in his own *Household Narrative*, must have marveled yet again because for eleven years he had lived—he still lived—just a few hundred yards from York Buildings and its veritable White Woman, just a few hundred yards from a blighted, death-environed, self-incarcerated White Woman, a bloodstained White Woman sealed up in her living tomb. In other words, for eleven years Dickens had been living just a few hundred yards from where Martha Joachim had festered day after day, night after night, year after year in her dark London majority refuses to make one; Baron Rolfe, Baron Parke, and Chief Justice Wilde, dissented from the doctrine that the minority can bind the majority. The judgment of the majority of the bench was, that the judgment of the court below (the Queen's Bench) must be affirmed. So the monition of the Ecclesiastical Court to make a rate is now of operative force.

At the Middlesex Sessions, held at Clerkenwell, on the 22nd, William Anderson, a sharp-looking boy, aged fourteen, was indicted for *Robbery*. At about mid-day, on the 10th, he entered the shop of Mr. Cooper, baker, at Stepney, and asked Mrs. Cooper, who was serving behind the counter, for a halfpenny-worth of bread, at the same time laying down a penny. As she was about to give him the difference, he threw a handful of pepper in her eyes; and, jumping upon the counter, proceeded to help himself to the contents of the till, but becoming alarmed, he retreated, having got but threepence into his possession. Mr. Cooper pursued, and having overtaken him in Suffolk Street, he very coolly turned round, and presenting Mr. Cooper with the threepence, said, "It's only threepence, so it's not worth running for, and I gives in; but you wouldn't have nabbed me if it had been more!" He was then handed over to a policeman. But two days before this transaction, the prisoner had been liberated from Ilford gaol; where he had been imprisoned for highway robbery. He, and three others, having stopped a chaise on a turnpike-road; and one of them, not the prisoner, fired a pistol at the driver. They robbed the chaise and made off. The judge said this case presented a most extraordinary instance of juvenile depravity; and sentenced the culprit to imprisonment with hard labour for six months.

At the Mansion House, on the 28th, Alderman Humphery expounded a point in *Omnibus Law*, when a conductor of a Camberwell omnibus was summoned for having refused to admit a gentleman as a passenger into his omnibus. A few days before, at a quarter before five, the complainant went to the door of the omnibus, being desirous to be driven as far as Walworth, and requested the conductor to allow him to enter. The evening was extremely wet, but the conductor refused to admit the applicant, and excused himself upon the ground that all the seats were engaged, at the same time that there was abundance of room in the vehicle. The complainant represented the unfairness of the refusal, and determined to have the decision of a magistrate upon the subject. A gentleman who regularly takes a seat in the defendant's omnibus stated that the defendant was expected by his regular "whole of the way" customers to keep seats for them, especially in wet weather, during which alone the passengers to Walworth or the Elephant and Castle were disposed to ride. The conductor stated he considered himself bound to reserve seats for his regular "whole of the way" customers, and had acted accordingly. The Alderman admitted the reasonableness of the defence, but the law was positive on the subject. No seat could be reserved so as to prevent any applicant being refused admission into the omnibus. No penalty was inflicted.

An inquest was held on the 29th, on Martha Joachim, a *Wealthy and Eccentric Lady*, late of 27, York-buildings, Marylebone, aged 62. The jury proceeded to view the body, but had to beat a sudden retreat, until a bulldog, belonging to deceased, and which savagely attacked them, was secured. It was shown in evidence that on the 1st of June, 1808, her father, an officer in the Life Guards, was murdered and robbed in the Regent's Park. A reward of 300*l.* was offered for the murderer, who was apprehended with the property upon him, and executed. In 1825, a suitor of the deceased, whom her mother rejected, shot himself while sitting on the sofa with her, and she was covered with his brains. From that instant she lost her reason. Since her mother's death, eighteen years ago, she had led the life of a recluse, dressed in white, and never going out. A charwoman occasionally brought her what supplied her wants. Her only companions were the bull-dog, which she nursed like a child, and two cats. Her house was filled with images of soldiers in lead, which she called her "body-guards." When the collectors called for their taxes, they had to cross the garden-wall to gain admission. One morning she was found dead in her

bed; and a surgeon who was called in, said she had died of bronchitis, and might have recovered with proper medical aid. The jury returned a verdict to that effect.

In the Insolvent Debtors' Court on the 29th, Capt. Robert Talbot, of the Royal Artillery, having applied for his *Discharge*, the application was opposed by counsel on behalf of John Jeffreys. Jeffreys was the racket-keeper of the regiment, and Captain Talbot its treasurer; Jeffreys sued his Captain in the County Court for 5*l.* arrears of salary, and obtained judgment; thereupon he was dismissed from his appointment, and "forcibly ejected therefrom" by Captain Talbot and some other members of the regiment. He brought an action for the assault; and it came on for trial at the Maidstone Assizes, but was compromised on the advice of the Judge, by an admitted verdict for nominal damages only enough to carry costs; six counsel had been engaged. It appeared that Capt. Talbot's debts amounted to 700*l.*; 600*li* in respect of his own costs and those of Jeffreys. Not being in possession of funds to pay this amount, he sought the benefit of this Court, almost exclusively, if not solely, for the purpose of relieving himself from the costs attendant on keeping up the legal ball with Jeffreys; and he admitted the arrest on which he was in custody was a friendly one, made with the above object. The Commissioner felt doubts as to receiving such a petition, and dismissed it after consulting with the Chief Commissioner.

At the Marylebone Police Office on the 30th, J. Gammage, master of a National School at Paddington, was charged with having *Cruelly Ill-used* a William Taylor, one of his pupils, a delicate little boy, 10 years of age. The witnesses examined proved the boy had been severely caned for a breach of school discipline, that large wheals, from one of which blood flowed, were produced on his shoulders and sides. In reply it was alleged that the boy had behaved with great impropriety while in attendance on a lecture in the school, and required correction, and also that he was generally unruly; and a number of testimonials from clergymen, which set forth that the defendant was a man much respected, firm of purpose, and kind towards his pupils, were produced. The Rev. Mr. Boone spoke in the highest terms of the defendant, whose salary had recently, in consequence of his valuable services, been raised. The magistrate considered that the chastisement was of much too severe a nature, and inflicted a penalty of 40*s.* The amount was paid by the Rev. W. Boone, who considered it a very hard case.

NARRATIVE OF ACCIDENT AND DISASTER.

Accounts have been received of the *Loss of the Transport, Richard Dart*, with a lamentable loss of life. She left Gravesend on the 5th of April last year, for Auckland; besides the crew, there was a detachment of twenty-eight sappers and miners, under the command of Lieutenant Liddell, Dr. Fitton with his wife and child, Dr. Gale, Mr. Kelly, four soldiers' wives, and nine children. South of the Cape of Good Hope bad weather was experienced, and on the 19th of June the ship struck on the north side of Prince Edward's Islands. The waves ran terrifically high; the boats were filled and torn from the quarter, and the sea swept away forty-seven of the passengers and crew. Of these, the chief mate alone contrived to reach the rocks. The commander, four seamen, an apprentice, and four of the soldiers, took refuge in the mainmast rigging; and the wreck having been driven broadside to the shore, the mainmast went by the board, falling fortunately upon the rock, and the survivors crawled along the spar to the shore. The night was intensely cold, and there were frequent falls of snow; the sufferings of the unfortunate men were consequently most severe. They found on the shore a few blankets which had been washed from the wreck; but they were unable to obtain any provisions beyond a bird. In the course of six or seven days they determined on exploring the island. One of the soldiers perished from the intensity of the cold and the want of proper nourishment, and after rambling about the island for no

---

97. The Mysteries of Creation: A Constellation of Images and Motifs Grows

Martha Joachim enters Dickens' new periodical: "The Bride's Chamber" and *Great Expectations* come closer to being born. Other vignettes in this strangely influential issue of the *Household Narrative* haunted Dickens' consciousness; such vignettes helped shape Jo's interrogation in *Bleak House* and Miss Havisham's fiery immolation in *Great Expectations* (to cite only two additional examples). From the *Household Narrative of Current Events*, I (January 1850), 10.

dungeon-home. The unexpected impingement of this real-life White Woman romance and its Gothic overtones upon his own everyday life, and the strange way it re-sounded old chords, would have stirred Dickens' imagination.

Dickens' imagination had always been preternaturally sensitive to the wonder and mystery of everyday life. He extracted extraordinary meaning from the ordinary, and he imbued the ordinary with extraordinary meaning. In *Bleak House,* that vast epic of everyday life, he had made the wonder of the commonplace a central feature of the book. "In Bleak House," he wrote in the Preface, "I have purposely dwelt upon the romantic side of familiar things" (*BH,* x). He might have said the same about most of his writings. Now, at his very doorstep, he had been presented with a stunning embodiment—moreover, a White Woman embodiment—of wild romance dwelling mutely behind the ordinary façade of the familiar. For eleven years he had passed and repassed Martha Joachim's walled, isolated residence; for eleven years he had gone about the busy rounds of his active life, while Martha Joachim, clad in white, had sat in the gloom of her York Buildings fortress, cut off from all the world.

The weird, blighted history of Martha Joachim reinforced old icons. It gave added reality and relevance to the image of the jilted, eccentric, wealthy, demented, white-clad bride (or would-be bride), the unforgotten specter of his childhood and youth. It also introduced into the old array of associations darker, more violent elements: robbery, murder, execution, and lifelong immurement. And it introduced a new, highly evocative setting as well: a sealed-off mansion, a surrounding garden, and a strong imprisoning wall.

Yet when Dickens sat down to write "The Bride's Chamber" in 1857, this array of images and associations was nothing more than that, an array of loosely connected, strangely recurrent bits and pieces that Dickens found memorable or picturesque or evocative. The bits and pieces were bizarre fragments of anarchic life, not moving embodiments of revelatory meaning. That transformation took place in "The Bride's Chamber." In "The Bride's Chamber" we have all the salient features of the White Woman constellation; indeed, those features are at the very center of the story. We have jilting, marriage for money, and a rich, pitiful white-clad bride; we also have robbery, murder, retribution, and hanging; finally, we have an immured female, an isolated and isolating mansion, a wall-enclosed garden, and wall-scaling visitors. These rudimentary givens, colored by childhood romance and speculation, reinforced by youthful recurrences and adult extensions, overlaid with the intense passion of Dickens' immediate emotional predicament, mediated by the transforming vision of his fabling imagination, became the generative matter of "The Bride's Chamber."

In "The Bride's Chamber" the unwanted lover becomes an unwanted wife; the solitary recluse, a solitary captive-recluse; the self-murdered suitor, an other-murdered champion (though still self-murdered from a psychological point of view); the mercenary hints, a mercenary mania; the ordinary residence, an extraordinary mansion; the natural garden, a supernatural arbor; the commonplace wall, a fairy-tale enclosure; the conniving man, a Satanic persecutor. Obviously, the stray bits and pieces of the White Woman constellation have been reordered, reshaped, and brought into meaningful conjunction. But a bald summary of the reshaping fails to convey the heart of the matter: the way in which these transformations radiate and enforce meaning. Martha Joachim's isolated residence and walled garden have become more than house and garden; they have become emblems of the human ruin and desolation that reign within. The realistic core remains, a bedrock of literal fact, but that selfsame core is now charged with implication and significance. Sometimes that significance is hidden and hermetic. Note in the following passage, for example, how Dickens chooses eleven years—the exact time that he had lived near white-clad Martha Joachim and her dark house—as the period during which white-clad Ellen had lived (or rather died) under her guardian's tutelage in her dark house. (The additional ten years before the guardian-husband's discovery and punishment bring the period of his hegemony to twenty-one years—the exact term, to the moment of writing, that

Dickens had lived with his wife.) Such carefully calculated undertones are secret and personal; but for the most part the meanings that Dickens evokes—reverberant, ramifying meanings—are open and universal. Here is how he describes the "dark house" of "The Bride's Chamber," a house dark with human evil and with death:

> Eleven years she lived in the dark house and its gloomy garden. He was jealous of the very light and air getting to her, and they kept her close. He stopped the wide chimneys, shaded the little windows, left the strong-stemmed ivy to wander where it would over the house-front, the moss to accumulate on the untrimmed fruit-trees in the red-walled garden, the weeds to over-run its green and yellow walks. He surrounded her with images of sorrow and desolation. (*HW* 16: BC, 388)

In this passage, house and garden, though still described with precise realism, have become more than house and garden, more even than Martha Joachim's gloomy house and garden: they have become physical correlatives of Ellen's wicked neglect. Ellen, the setting now tells us in reinforcing clusters of images and tropes, is confined, blocked, shaded, uncared for, uncultivated. She is a sorrowful ruin, a weed-grown garden, the monstrous product of her mentor's blighting will. The transformation that Dickens works here he works throughout the story. A great centripetal force has been moving through the flotsam and jetsam of experience. It has brought order to the chance entanglements of life—to old memories, a recent hanging, immediate emotions—and shaped them into something akin to but quite different from, and infinitely more meaningful than, that which they once were. This is no mere mechanical process. At the heart of the synthesis is a central transforming vision. Dickens is imbuing these tangled bits and pieces with the iridescence of his fable and with his own dark vision of life's stern denials and diminishments, a vision colored by his baffled predicament at that moment in 1857. Everywhere he looks he finds the same somber message: in the midst of life we are in death.

This meaningful fusion of the remote past and the surrounding present, of shaping traumas and fleeting inconsequences, is wonder-provoking enough, but the fusion which took place in "The Bride's Chamber" did not end with the grim story that Dickens wrote in September and October 1857. Three years later the curious nexus of eccentricity, immurement, aggression, and passion that was ignited into meaning by "The Bride's Chamber" became a central focus of *Great Expectations*. Indeed, but for "The Bride's Chamber," *Great Expectations* could scarcely have been. This is so not because the same givens went into the two works (though they did) but because the transformation of those givens into a particular pattern of deep reflexive meanings—a pattern that would become crucial to *Great Expectations*—took place in "The Bride's Chamber." In *Great Expectations* that pattern emerges in the Pip-Miss Havisham-Satis House-Estella-Money-Magwitch conjunction of the novel. In *Great Expectations,* as in "The Bride's Chamber," one finds a blighted bride in white; a damning money nexus; a passionate, impossible love; a decaying, isolated, and isolating mansion; a ruined, wall-enclosed, desolate garden; an atmosphere of crime and murder; and the deadly sin of fashioning another human being to be an instrument of revenge. The consanguinity of the two works is much closer than this bare outline would suggest, for in each work Dickens surrounds the figure of the blighted white-clad bride with an atmosphere of decay, imprisonment, manipulation, and money-generated corruption. In *Great Expectations,* as in "The Bride's Chamber," the sin of valuing money more than human beings pervades and integrates the story. But the pecuniary similarities go further. In both works the destructive forces are set in motion when a projected marriage is broken off for monetary considerations. And again, in both works the injured parties destroy themselves and all those around them in their attempts to assuage their injuries by monetary means. These fundamental similarities are buttressed by many more detailed correspondences: echoes of phrasings, recurrences of omens, repetitions of images, and the like. (On this score, early omens and images of hanging in *Great Expectations* [*AYR* 4: *GE,* 8:269] suggest that Dickens originally intended that Miss Havisham—like Edward Hardman and the protagonist of "The Bride's Chamber"—would die by hanging.)

Great Expectations, of course, is more than an enlarged version of "The Bride's Chamber." There is much in *Great Expectations* that bears no relationship to "The Bride's Chamber," and the generative elements that the two works do share are elaborated in the novel in different and much more detailed ways than in the story. The bride-cake featured at the King's Arms, for example, figures centrally in *Great Expectations* but only peripherally—that is, only in the frame-work—of "The Bride's Chamber." But, paradoxically, such differences only serve to highlight similarities. Disparities that seem at first to preach of separateness testify at last to kinship and connection. It is the sad, foredoomed, symbolic, candlelit bridecake, standing night after night at the center of a brideless table at the King's Arms, that gripped Dickens' imagination. That image haunts "The Bride's Chamber" and *Great Expectations.* In both works the candlelit bridecake, glimmering in the gloom, is a token of barren-ness, despair, and death. In both it is also a token of a foredoomed marriage, a marriage that cannot or should not be, and of the devas-tation that flows from such deep perversions of the moral order. It is no accident that the bridecake in "The Bride's Chamber" is "bil-ious and indigestible" (though the rest of the dinner is "admir-able"), and it is no accident that the bridecake in *Great Expectations* is a mass of festering corruption (*HW* 16: BC, 386).

How could it be otherwise? Think for a minute of what marriage, so mockingly epitomized by the brideless bridecake, meant to Dick-ens (marriage meant misery, guilt, and thralldom) at that tormented moment at the King's Arms in September 1857—the moment when the bridecake image and its clustering associations burned into his consciousness. That candlelit image, profoundly meaning-ful and profoundly conditioned, imbued with personal anguish and despair, imbued also with the chance associations of that memorable time and place, lingered forever in his mind. Later permutations of that image, however varied, however different or transformed—

protean offspring of imagination and art—are permutations still. This deep reflexiveness serves to demonstrate once more that the joining that took place in 1857, first in the King's Arms and then in "The Bride's Chamber," created for Dickens a new synthesis, a synthesis that continued to haunt him.

That new synthesis teases our understanding. What is the significance of this coming together? What is the significance of this tangled web of events and emotions and associations that slowly became "The Bride's Chamber"? And what is the significance of the reemergence of that tangled web three years later in *Great Expectations?* The potency of that coming together, the generative fusion it helped produce and then reproduce, tells us how crucial that coming together was. Knowing what went into that coming together, in turn, can bring us closer to the shrouded regions—indeed, can bring us into the shrouded regions—that veil the mysteries of creation. We can see how early encounters (the Berners Street White Woman), later recurrences and increments (white-clad Martha Joachim's walled garden, imprisoning house, and self-murdered suitor), Gothic childhood reading (Monk Lewis' doomed, white-robed female ghosts), and multitudes of other linkages—some reinforcing, some extending, the products of chance or circumstance—can form a gradually enlarging web of specially sensitive and profoundly evocative associations. We can also see how a very different array of generative associations, more localized in time and totally different in origins and effects, can come together, the result of a seemingly random series of juxtapositions. Think for a moment of the juxtapositions of August, September, and October 1857: of Dickens playing the role, before sobbing thousands, of a doomed, disaffected, rescuing lover, then immediately playing the contrasting role of an old, manipulative guardian-suitor; of his falling in love at forty-five with a pliant, teen-aged girl that he cannot have and should not woo, then enacting with her, at the very same time, a monitory stage version of that forbidden love; of his wishing to rid himself of his amiable and complying wife, of his cold, hard opposition to her, then reading newspaper reports of the chilling crime of a harsh, inimical wife-killer; of his dreaming romantic fairy-tale dreams of scaling a castle stronghold, slaying ogres and dragons, and rescuing an immured princess, then visiting a fortress-castle where a marriage-weary wife-killer had just been hanged facing a castle wall; of his meeting secretly with his adored princess, then walling off his unwanted wife; of his eating bridecake in an ancient, legend-haunted house, then conjuring up guilt-filled fantasies concerning a fabled Bride's Chamber. The exact process—the ultimate process—whereby Dickens fused his domestic skeletons and fairy-tale dreams with the old Lancaster inn, the crazy Berners Street White Woman, the immured wall-encircled Martha Joachim, the hanged wife-killer Edward Hardman, and all the rest, we can never know. That this fusion took place, that what emerged transcended all its constituents, that it generated meaning and insight where there had been no meaning and insight, that it became "The Bride's Chamber," and that it later contributed crucially to *Great Expectations*—this we do know.

VIII

As a matter of fact, we know even more. "The Bride's Chamber" and the real-life events that surrounded it also contributed to other novels, and "The Bride's Chamber" shaped *Great Expectations* in additional ways as well. In fact, every novel that Dickens wrote after "The Bride's Chamber"—*A Tale of Two Cities, Great Expectations, Our Mutual Friend,* and *Edwin Drood*—contains a central character made miserable by, usually destroyed by, a consuming passion. In Dickens' work prior to "The Bride's Chamber," passion—passion of a man for a woman—is depicted in conventional guise. Feeling, language, psychology, perceptions, events—all the elements that go into that depiction—are filtered through conventions that distance them, sanitize them, channel them, codify them. Anguish, destructiveness, obsession, ecstasy, transcendence are excised or cauterized, or they are treated in formulaic ways, or made superficial, or asserted rather than convincingly depicted. Consider, for example, Nicholas

Nickleby's love for Madeline Bray. One can hardly remember who the heroine is, what she looks like, or what she says. She has no realized personality, and her love relationship with Nicholas is not only passionless but contentless. Her high-flown romance with Nicholas is conveyed almost entirely by Nicholas himself, and primarily through his sounding speeches, histrionic gestures, and rhetorical declarations. It is a stage romance; it is taken directly from the theater (Nicholas saves Madeline from having to marry a loathsome old miser). It is an exercise in convention, not a reflection of lived experience and real emotion.

One sees this strategy of evasion whenever Dickens grapples with passion. In the climactic moment of Nicholas' rescue of his beloved, Dickens uses the word *passion,* but, characteristically, he is referring not to the passion of Nicholas' love but to the passion of his righteous anger. Nicholas expresses his passion for Madeline by surrogate means: he defends her sanctified purity and repulses the sexual evil that threatens her. The rhetoric of rescue, meant to embody Nicholas' virtuous passion, is an unwitting parody on Dickens' part, or rather an uncritical acceptance by him, of romantic heroics and stilted theatrical clichés. Dickens translates the wild intensity of passion into the safe banality of shopworn fustian: " 'Stand off!' cried Nicholas, letting loose all the violent passion he had restrained till now, 'if this is what I scarcely dare to hope it is, you are caught, villains, in your own toils' " (*NN,* 54:542–43).

Phiz's rendering of this scene ("Nicholas congratulates Arthur Gride on his Wedding Morning") emphasizes, as Dickens apparently desired that it should (for he supervised and approved all illustrations), the blatant staginess of the emotions and relationships being depicted. The illustration, like the scene itself, is an epitome of histrionic composition, histrionic expression, histrionic postures, and histrionic gestures. Phiz's tableau features heroic love triumphant. Madeline faints, Kate ministers to her, an elderly woman weeps, while Nicholas, tall, stalwart, and righteously accusatory, holding Madeline's limp hand, confronts the villains, who, thwarted at the very moment of their triumph, shrink back in their wedding

98. Histrionic Passion in the Early Novels

Nicholas Nickleby saves Madeline Bray from the connubial clutches of the miser Arthur Gride. "Nicholas congratulates Arthur Gride on his Wedding Morning." Etching by Hablot Knight Browne ("Phiz") for Number XVII, Chapter LIV (August 1839) of *Nicholas Nickleby*.

347

finery, astonished and confounded. Significantly, Madeline is unconscious. Though Nicholas holds her hand, their contact (given
Madeline's unconscious state) has been purged of the slightest hint
of unseemly physicality—or meaningful passion.

What is true of Nicholas' love for Madeline Bray is true of love in
all the early novels: such love may be constant or spiritual or arch or
ennobling or foolish or unrequited or self-sacrificing or secret or
heroic, but it is never passionate—passionate, that is, in a deeply felt
and believable way. In *Oliver Twist*, Rose Fleming's, or, to use the
name she goes by, Rose Maylie's love for Harry Maylie is a duplicate
of Nicholas' love for Madeline Bray: again, it is pale, anemic, sub-
stanceless, conventional (this time we cannot remember the male
lover's name or role). The relationship lacks the slightest hint of
physicality or personality, much less passion; it is all bloodless spirituality and disembodied harmony, a union redolent of heaven rather
than earth. *Martin Chuzzlewit* is more of the same. Martin's love for
Mary Graham is as pure and etherealized as the loves of angels; it
contains no hint of the sublunary world. One can easily see how
emasculated this love is if one turns to the escapades of the outrageous Pecksniff. His drunken amorousness, while remote from love
and passion, is at least real and believable, as well as being wonderfully funny and deliciously ironic. But Pecksniff is of-the-earth
earthy; he hypocritically mouths what Martin (in love) unconvinc-
ingly professes.[15]

Love in the early novels, in short, is devoid of realized passion.
In its higher flights—that is, with heroes and heroines—love is a
romantic stereotype shorn of psychological engagement or robust
physicality. In the middle novels, those after *Chuzzlewit* but before
"The Bride's Chamber," there is an increase in depth of characterization, psychological acuity, and symbolic implication, but passion
is still a territory left largely unexplored. Though Florence Dombey
is a more complex heroine than Rose Maylie or Madeline Bray or
Mary Graham (her love for her father and for her brother is, in each
instance, crucial, and is carefully and meaningfully explored), her
love for Walter Gay and his love for her fall into the old mold of

disembodied romance. At the very end of the book Florence marries, has children, and lives happily ever after, but this is a function of the plot and the symbolic working out of the novel, not of her relationship with Walter Gay—that remains as remote and distant as ever.

Much the same can be said for *Bleak House* and the love of Allan Woodcourt and Esther Summerson. Again, the reasons for Esther's behavior, for her self-effacement and self-denial, are worked out intricately and subtly, but her relationship with Allan Woodcourt has no more passion in it—and less emotional interaction in it—than her relationship with her guardian, John Jarndyce. Dickens depicts Esther's feelings for her guardian and her lack of passion for him with great art, but Dickens only tells us that Allan and Esther love one another: he does not show us the actuality of their love, much less their passion.

Arthur Clennam and Little Dorrit are two more disenfranchised lovers. In each case we are given masterful psychological portraits of grievous emotional damage. We understand, in other words, why each acts as he or she does. We understand, moreover, why their union lacks the passionate ecstasy of less damaged spirits, and it is fitting that Dickens should depict their love in muted tints and convey it in a minor key. After all, Arthur Clennam, for reasons that Dickens depicts wonderfully well, has been emasculated and made will-less. It is a miracle that the seed of love should flourish in him at all, while Amy Dorrit has been forced (but more subtly so) to make a like sacrifice: she can only be herself when she serves others rather than herself. Yet the love they do profess at the end, while infinitely better realized than the love of Nicholas and Madeline or the love of Martin and Mary, is still conventional and contained; passion spins no plots.

One might surmise that Dickens shied away from depicting passion in sanctified unions (for most of the instances we have dealt with so far concern heroes and heroines) but not in instances of unrequited or villainous love; however, such is not the case. Lord Frederick Verisopht's interest in Kate Nickleby may have something to do with self-gratification, titillation, amusement, even desire, but it has nothing to do with love or passion. Carker's interest in Edith Dombey, like Uriah Heep's interest in Agnes Wickfield a year or so later, certainly has a sexual dimension, but his real motivation (like Uriah's) is power and dominance. Carker vents his hostility through power—power over Rob the Grinder, power over Carker Jr., power over Edith, power over Dombey, power over all those beneath him and power over all those he has had to serve with such galling subservience. Sexuality for Carker is a weapon. His sexual interest in Edith, as Dickens makes clear, has to do with lust, conquest, and possession, with cannibalistic voracity and cannibalistic incorporation; it has nothing to do with love or passion. Edith, for her part, in running off with Carker, is striking out at Dombey through Carker. Though she feels Carker's power and is aware of his sexual potency, she loathes rather than adores him.

Steerforth's liaison with Emily is a similar instance. Spoiled, willful, self-indulgent, hostile toward his mother and exploitive of women in general, Steerforth regards Emily as a plaything or a diversion. He will love her and leave her, as he loved and left Rosa Dartle. Emily is simply a toy he will not deny himself—for a term. Again, real love and real passion have nothing to do with his interest in her. Nor does Emily feel passion for Steerforth. Steerforth is her means of translation to the glittering realms of wealth, travel, and adventure, realms she has always yearned for but has never felt she could reach. She is dazzled by that prospect, and Steerforth is the embodiment of that prospect. Passion and love do not impel her. Nor does passion enter into her feelings for Ham. Her relationship with Ham, to whom she is betrothed, is one of convenience. She knows that he is good, and eminently available, but she does not love him. He does love her, with a simple, steadfast, inarticulate love, too low-key for passion.

Passion does occasionally crop up in unsuspected places; but it is passion displaced or transmuted or otherwise co-opted and made safe by that sea change. Think, for example, of the passion of Toots for Florence Dombey. Toots is so simple-minded, his passion so innocent and ludicrous, his expression of it so delicate and naive (he tells us, for instance, that he is "'perfectly sore with loving'" Florence, or that "'If I could be dyed black, and made Miss Dombey's slave, I should consider it a compliment,'" or that he has become so thin with loving her that "'If you could see my legs when I take my boots off, you'd form some idea of what unrequited affection is'" [*DS*, 32:329; 39:387; 48:480]), that we think of his obsession as a delightful eccentricity rather than the profound emotion of all-consuming love. Dickens wants us to view Toots' passion in this way, for though he is wonderfully sympathetic to Toots' simple goodness, he too regards Toots' passion as a charming foible rather than a serious emotion.

Young John Chivery's passion for Little Dorrit is a similar case. Like Toots, he is gentle and good-hearted, and like Toots he is given a foible that allows Dickens (and the reader) to discount his passion. In Chivery's case, his foible is self-dramatizing sentimentality. He wallows in his sentiment. He is most content when, after some major rebuff to his love—such as Little Dorrit's rejection of his threatened proposal of marriage—he can compose imaginary epitaphs parading his woe. On the occasion of his rejection by Little Dorrit, for example, after deciding he will be buried in Saint George's Churchyard, he conjures up the following inscription for his tombstone:

> Here lie the mortal remains of JOHN CHIVERY, Never anything worth mentioning, Who died about the end of the year one thousand eight hundred and twenty-six, Of a broken heart, Requesting with his last breath that the word AMY might be inscribed over his ashes, Which was accordingly directed to be done, By his afflicted Parents. (*LD*, 1: 18:160)

Young John's passion is real but his foible is comic, and so we do not have to take his passion seriously. There are other, similar, portraits. Mr. Guppy's high-flown but fair-weather passion for Esther Summerson in *Bleak House* ("'Would that I could make Thee the subject of that vow, before the shrine!'" [*BH*, 9:88]) is yet another instance.

99. Mr. Guppy's Passion for Esther Summerson

"In Re Guppy. Extraordinary proceedings." Etching by Hablot Knight Browne ("Phiz") for Number III, Chapter IX (May 1852) of *Bleak House*.

The pre–"Bride's Chamber" work in which Dickens focuses most directly on passion is *David Copperfield*, and here, as Dickens himself attests, he is depicting, often quite directly, his own experiences. There is much of Maria Beadnell, his first great love, and much of Kate, his wife, in Dora, just as there is much of Fanny Dickens, his sister, and Mary Hogarth, his sister-in-law (both idealized and spiritualized) in the sisterly angel, Agnes. David's love for Dora is passion incarnate—but passion that has been shorn of all, or virtually all, its wildness and physicality. (We are given a few glancing hints of sexual interplay. One such hint occurs in the scene in which Dora sits on David's lap and half beguiles him out of his resolve to reprove her—"quite delighted me in spite of myself"—by talking baby talk to him and drawing frowns on his forehead with her pencil, "putting it to her rosy lips to make it mark blacker" [*DC,* 44:450].) David's love, rosy lips and all, is depicted with the utmost charm, lightness, and ideality. It is also depicted with gentle humor and sympathetic mockery. Passion is translated into a daze of romantic and chivalric excess. David swoons and moons over his Dora. The period of infatuation—before the disillusionment of marriage and living together sets in—is presented in a rosy glow of fairy-tale wishes, fairy-tale dreams, and fairy-tale tropes. David's passion (and Dickens' as well—or that part of it that he chose to reveal here) has been etherealized, translated to the realm of seraphic romance. We are charmed by this airy rendition of the summerdawn of love; we smile at a passion so beguiling, foolish, and innocent (see figure 100).

Dickens was not blind to the darker side of passion. He chose here to ignore, or at least to efface, that side and to present its destructive effects through suggestion, symbolism (often cannibalistic suggestion and symbolism), and, most of all, through the aftermath, through the grey limping reality that replaces David's infatuation.[16] Dickens does present darker counterparts to David and Dora, lovers such as Steerforth and Emily, for example, but the reality of passion—dark or rosy-hued—is, except for an occasional oblique hint, deliberately excluded from such presentations. There is, however, one exception, or partial exception, to this rule. That exception is

100. The Summerdawn of Love: David Falls into Captivity

"I fall into captivity." Etching by Hablot Knight Browne ("Phiz") for Number IX, Chapter XXVI (January 1850) of *David Copperfield*.

Rosa Dartle, the dependent distant connection, older than Steerforth, who comes to live in the Steerforth household as a companion to Mrs. Steerforth.

Rosa and Steerforth soon become precocious lovers. On Rosa's part there is real passion; of that there can be no doubt. On both parts the affair is tempestuous; of that there can be no doubt either. In one fit of rage, Steerforth, still a mere boy, throws a hammer at Rosa, scarring her permanently with his infernal brand, a crooked scar across her mouth that flares and starts forth whenever her pent-up passions are aroused. In a rehearsal of things to come, Steerforth eventually leaves his passionate mistress for fresher pastures and fresher faces. She continues to live with Steerforth's mother in the Steerforth mansion, her love turned into hate, her passion transformed into a seething glow of anger and hostility. She smolders with resentment. She can find no sanctioned release for the thwarted passion that drives and torments her.

We learn the history of Rosa only in retrospect, and then at second hand. But though Dickens does not depict the affair and its passionate course directly, he does depict the scarred aftermath with wonderful insight and art. And he does give us one direct glimpse of that early passion. On the occasion in question, in David's presence, long after Steerforth's affair with Rosa has cooled—indeed, just before he is about to run off with Emily—Steerforth, exerting all his charm and all his old winning wiles (he has been beguiling Rosa all day long), coaxes her to play the harp and sing a song as she had of yore, when they were very young. Softening gradually to his cajoling, captivated in spite of herself, she at last consents. She begins with a strange, mute miming motion but then quickly sits down and plays and sings a wild, enthralling song:

> I don't know what it was, in her touch or voice, that made that song the most unearthly I have ever heard in my life, or can imagine. There was something fearful in the reality of it. It was as if it had never been written, or set to music, but sprung out of the passion within her; which found imperfect utterance in the low sounds of her voice, and crouched again when all was still. I was dumb when she leaned beside the harp again, playing it, but not sounding it, with her right hand. (*DC*, 29:307)

Steerforth gets up, puts his arm about Rosa, and says, "'Come, Rosa, for the future we will love each other very much!'" Rosa strikes him, throws him off "with the fury of a wild cat," and bursts from the room (*DC*, 29:307).

The scene is unforgettable, and it is rich with crucial meanings. For a moment Rosa is back in the time of her early, unalloyed, undisfigured passion for Steerforth (the miming at the beginning and end of the song frames and accentuates this). That early period (she was young and innocent then) was a transcendent "unearthly" time, fashioned "out of the passion within her." But now the "passion within her," which had been re-created for the moment in its old prelapsarian purity, "crouched again"; the passion of love has long since been turned into the passion of hate. Dickens' imagery constantly guides our awareness. Prompted by that imagery, we absorb his central meanings even when we do not conceptualize them: Rosa had been an angel (the singer at the harp) and now she is a devil (the wild cat in a fury).

The portrait of Rosa is richer and deeper than is suggested here. It is made up of innumerable hints, intimations, and implications. An occasional scene such as the one just described, which at last gives us a direct glimpse of the crouching "passion within her," is as close as Dickens comes in the early and middle novels to depicting passion unalloyed. Yet even here he is careful and reticent; he relies largely on a masterful use of symbolism and connotation.

Symbolism and connotation are characteristic of Dickens' art, but total (or virtually total) reticence is not. Dickens was never shy when it came to anatomizing nonsexual passions. His early and middle writings are filled with the histories of men and women caught up in the overwhelming pursuit of some desired object or end. There are abundant examples in Dickens—often quite extraordinary, beautifully realized, examples—of the passion of hate, the passion for power, the passion for money, dominion, possession, revenge, and more. Such examples are worlds away from their low-key counterparts, worlds away, that is, from ordinary emotions and everyday desires; the renderings in question—virtuoso renderings—are of consuming, single-minded compulsions. Think for a moment (limiting ourselves for now to the early and middle novels) of the imperious compulsions—passionate, nonsexual compulsions—that drive so many of Dickens' characters: the all-consuming hatred, for example, exhibited by Heyling (in one of the interpolated stories in *Pickwick*); the insatiable need to dominate and control exhibited by Carker in *Dombey and Son,* or, by way of contrast, the sadistic need to dominate and control exhibited by Quilp in *The Old Curiosity Shop*—Dickens often gives us totally different versions of the same impulse become a mania; the almost autonomous compulsion to annihilate demonstrated by Jonas Chuzzlewit (toward the end of *Martin Chuzzlewit*); the inordinate desire for secret, power-conferring knowledge exhibited by Mr. Tulkinghorn in *Bleak House;* the endless need to torment herself demonstrated by Miss Wade in *Little Dorrit;* the pathological lust for power and ascendency (paradigm for the fascist mentality) highlighted by Simon Tappertit in *Barnaby Rudge;* the blind, self-destructive pursuit of material possession demonstrated by Mr. Dombey in *Dombey and Son;* the crippling obsession for revenge embodied in Mrs. Clennam in *Little Dorrit*—all these examples of needs and desires gone out of control are only a tithe of the instances that might be cited. Furthermore, in many of these examples (especially those from the later novels in this group) Dickens not only exhibits these passions gone amok but analyzes their origins, growth, and culmination, a culmination that often ends in destruction.

These case histories do not end with the early and middle novels but continue, perhaps even increase, in the late novels. What is new in the late novels, the novels after "The Bride's Chamber," are case histories of sexual passion, often dark, rending, sexual passion, passion that cannot be curbed or controlled, passion that inevitably escalates into monomania and compulsion. What is also new is that these case histories of compulsive sexual passion are now featured and highlighted and are examined without the old protections that distance and soften and sanitize. This is not an occasional or a passing phenomenon. In each of the four novels that comes after "The

Bride's Chamber" there is a central character who is caught in a destructive web of sexual passion and sexual obsession.

IX

A Tale of Two Cities, the first of these late novels, is the most equivocal of the instances, for though Sydney Carton is certainly caught up in a web of hopeless love, a web that finally destroys him, his love is presented more in the old than the new way. (In the late novels Dickens continues to treat some of the love interests in the old way, but in each novel he highlights at least one major character gripped and driven by passion.) Except for a single, highly mannered confessional interview with Lucie Manette, Sydney Carton suffers in silence. His love for Lucie—she is seventeen at the opening of the novel, a few years older when Carton declares his love—is his cherished secret, his holy grail. To the world he is a lazy reprobate interested only in dissipation. Yet he has always yearned for love. His inability to consummate a meaningful love has been his great desolating affliction: it robs his life of purpose. As a result, he wastes his potential, or rather, he never cultivates it, and he is filled with cynicism, nihilism, and self-loathing (a portrait tinged for today's reader with a good deal of posturing and a good deal of mawkish self-pity). But when Carton's frustrated passion finally finds an object, that passion saves as well as destroys him. His love for the budlike Lucie (she of the "soft blue eyes" and "golden hair" [*AYR* 1: *TTC,* 2: 20:389; 1: 4:26]—shades of eighteen-year-old, blue-eyed, golden-haired Ellen Ternan, who had played another Lucy, Lucy Crayford in *The Frozen Deep* a year or so earlier) becomes the talisman that allows him to turn aside from his worst self and act in accordance with his best self. In the shorthand of Dickens' symbolism, Carton dies and is reborn; that is, his worst self dies and his best self is reborn. His final act of self-destruction is also an act of redemption, as the famous final words that Dickens imagines he might have spoken attest.

Perhaps the transitional nature of Carton's unrequited passion— that it redeems as well as destroys him, and that his sufferings and blisses are usually treated in the old, high-flown romantic manner—is a function of the book's inception and Dickens' state. *A Tale of Two Cities* was Dickens' first novel after the turmoil that preceded and followed the breakup of his marriage. Given this emotion-fraught context, it is natural that the book should contain some reverberations of his emotional situation and emotional yearnings. And it does. Carton is one version of Dickens. Like Dickens, Carton is a fervent and reverent lover; and, again like Dickens, but for different reasons, he is a forbidden and unworthy suitor. But Carton is not the only avatar of Dickens in the novel; the book also contains less Byronic surrogates. Darnay, who is also Dickens—Darnay and Carton are doubles as well as look-alikes—is the sanctified lover. As in "The Bride's Chamber," by means of such doubling, Dickens could be, at one and the same time, passionate lover and condemned sinner; but, unlike in "The Bride's Chamber," in which he allowed himself only paradigms of destruction, in *A Tale of Two Cities*, by virtue of limning more beneficent visions, he could also achieve blissful fulfillments: he could be—indeed, in *A Tale of Two Cities* he is—sanctified lover and sanctified mate.

These and other emotional parallels, both fulfilling and frustrating, continue throughout the novel. For example, and once more like Dickens, Carton is unable to consummate his love (I assume that Dickens, whatever his ultimate relationship with Ellen, was not her lover at this time). Carton, ineligible as a suitor, suffering nobly, is bereft. Cut off from sanctioned felicity, he yearns for other fulfillments. He longs to demonstrate and redeem his forbidden love through some transcendent act of self-sacrifice. Here again creator and hero merge. Carton's love is forbidden, since Lucie loves, then marries, Darnay; Dickens' love is forbidden, since he is a married lover. As for redeeming one's love through transcendent self-sacrifice, we recall Dickens' impassioned yearning, voiced several months before he created Carton, Darnay, Lucie, and all the rest, for the opportunity to rescue his beloved princess, rescue her against all odds, or die in the attempt—a fulfillment and an attendant death that Dickens allowed himself to experience through Carton.

In view of such repeated emotional parallels and interconnections (one could easily lengthen the list) it is not surprising that Charles Darnay, the sanctified lover, shares Dickens' initials and bears his first name, just as an earlier surrogate, David Copperfield, who Dickens at one point contemplated naming "Charles" (Stone, *Working Notes,* 126–27), bears Dickens' initials in reverse. Nor is it surprising that some of the ennobling renunciations and sacrificial fulfillments one finds in *The Frozen Deep* and *A Tale of Two Cities*—renunciations and fulfillments that Dickens experienced vicariously—one also finds in the interval between *The Frozen Deep* and *A Tale of Two Cities* (that is, late in 1857, shortly after "The Bride's Chamber"), in the brave rescues, mute adorations, and noble forgoings of *The Perils of Certain English Prisoners,* a story that contains a prominent rescuer and rival—a rescuer and rival named Carton, no less—and a story that also contains a disenfranchised narrator-hero (with early associations with the Chatham region and a last name that begins with a D) who secretly nurses a forbidden love that both torments and exalts him.

There are other deep connections between Sydney Carton and Dickens. Dickens tells us in the "Preface" to *A Tale of Two Cities* that Sydney Carton and *A Tale of Two Cities* emerged out of the passionate avowals and renunciations of *The Frozen Deep,* avowals and renunciations that he experienced in his own person night after night. He was Wardour in truth, not just in seeming (*TTC*, [v]). Carton and the novel, in other words, emerged out of a play conceived and partly written by Dickens, out of a central character shaped and acted by Dickens (Ellen Ternan at his side), a character who redeems his love by forgoing it, nobly sacrificing himself to save his hated rival, all for the sake of his beloved. Furthermore, each night Wardour-Dickens' heroic nobility, his goodness and selflessness too, were verified by the emotional support of his responsive audiences, by their heartfelt sobs and their wild applause, balm to the unfulfilled soul of the wife-weary, guilt-tormented, disaffected Dickens. Given such concatenations of origins and aftermaths it is no wonder that Sydney Carton has deep affinities with chivalric longings, noble sentiments, and high romance, and it is no wonder that Dickens allowed him a heroic transcendence. The darker side of Dickens' passion for Ellen Ternan, the pain, destructiveness, and obsession, are in Carton too, but usually mitigated in the romantic, *Frozen Deep* way, a way that also harks back to Dickens' breakup with Maria Beadnell. Ultimately, the two aspects of Carton's being are neither convincingly projected nor effectively joined. We know that under his ennui and world-weariness a despairing self-destructiveness smolders, but these darker elements are affirmed from the outside rather than depicted from the inside. In other words, post–"Bride's Chamber" attributes are rendered in pre–"Bride's Chamber" ways. We are told at various times that Carton is debauched, reckless, disreputable, insolent, careless, drunk, coarse, idle, dissipated, sullen, hang-dog, disagreeable, and profligate. But Dickens pulls back from any real exploration of Carton's reckless self-destructiveness. We see Carton not as a demon-haunted lover but as a noble sacrificer redeemed by love.

Carton's passion and his obsession are surely there, but they are there in safe and conventional guise: they are conveyed through the rarified posturings of high romance. We note at once the outward signs of his chivalric longing. He soon haunts the pavements surrounding Lucie's house, wandering there at night and lingering till the break of day. After about a year, he declares his love. "You have been the last dream of my soul," he tells her. "You kindled me, heap of ashes that I am, into fire" (*AYR* 1: *TTC*, 2: 13:268). He affirms that he is a man "who would give his life, to keep a life you love beside you!" (*AYR* 1: *TTC*, 2: 13:269).[17] Later, when Carton speaks of Lucie, Dickens sometimes capitalizes the "She" or "Her" to emphasize the worshipful reverence of Carton's passion (*AYR* 1: *TTC*, 3: 9:602). Though worshipful and reverent, though high-flown and heroic, his obsession is sexual. On one occasion, after Darnay's imprisonment, when Carton is told that Lucie is anxious and unhappy, but that even in her unhappiness she is "very beautiful," "a long, grieving sound, like a sigh—almost like a sob" breaks forth from Carton's bosom (*AYR* 1: *TTC*, 3: 9:602). Lest the reader fail to detect the import of that sound, its full depth of passion (passion for Lucie's beauty, passion for her unhappiness, passion for the sacrifice of self he will soon make to assure her bliss), a moment later Dickens has Carton put his foot into the fire and leave it there, indifferent to its burning heat (*AYR* 1: *TTC*, 3: 9:602). This gesture affirms Carton's renunciation and world-weariness, his indifference to his own corporeal fate. The gesture is the outward and visible sign that he no longer pays heed to mere bodily concerns; but it is also the outward sign of his inward passion, of the fire that burns within, the fire that elicits the "long, grieving sound, like a sigh— almost like a sob," the fire that animates and consumes him ("You kindled me, heap of ashes that I am, into fire"). The gesture also foretells the future. It shows us that Carton is willing to immolate himself in the burning fire, to sacrifice his physical identity (his physical desire as well) for the sake of the "very beautiful" woman he so passionately loves. Out of the ashes of self-immolation he will kindle the fires of spiritual transfiguration; he will be reborn. ("Recalled to Life," the title of Book 1 of *A Tale of Two Cities,* is a dominant theme of the novel, a theme upon which Dickens works endless variations and reiterations.)

Carton's self-immolation and transfiguration, the climactic signs of his rebirth, are now only hours away. Soon after the fire episode, Carton retraces Lucie's footsteps, just to stand where she has stood. The next morning, the look of love she gives her husband as he is brought into the court "called the healthy blood into [Darnay's] face, brightened his glance, and animated his heart"—and exerted "the same influence exactly" in Carton (*AYR* 1: *TTC*, 3: 9:604). Carton is now about to undergo apotheosis; in sacrificing his worst self, he becomes his best self (he becomes his double, with whom he will soon change clothes and places); in forgoing his love, he gains his love (he reacts to the look of love Lucie gives her husband "exactly" as her husband reacts). A while later he kisses the unconscious Lucie—shades of Nicholas Nickleby and the unconscious Madeline Bray—and murmurs over her body, as over an altar, the pledge he gave long ago to sacrifice his life for "A life you love" (*AYR* 2: *TTC,* 3: 11:22). Carton is now beatified by love. As he goes to his execution he has "the peacefullest man's face ever beheld there." He looks "sublime and prophetic" (*AYR* 2: *TTC*, 3: 15:95). At that transcendent moment he has a vision of the future. He sees Lucie as "an old woman, weeping for me on the anniversary of this day" (*AYR* 2: *TTC*, 3: 15:95). This vision of unfulfilled sexual adoration transformed by sacrifice into spiritual love, sublime exaltation, and everlasting peace ends the novel. It is a far, far better rest that Carton now goes to, so Dickens tells us, than he has ever known.

The trouble with this picture is that it is a wishful vision of sublimation rather than a believable account of transformation. Carton may go to his better rest, but Dickens has not made palpable the misery and unrest from which he ascends or the psychological processes of that ascent. Carton's largeness of soul is evident from the first; his victory is too easy and too assured. We know that he will triumph over the reckless despair he clutches to his bosom, trumpets to the world, but never displays. This is a sanitized picture of desire and reckless abandon, a picture purged of its sin (purged, also, of its reality) and made sublime by the magic wand of self-sacrifice. It is a vision of what Dickens wished for, dreamed of, rather than what he knew to be.

Dickens identified so closely with Carton that he responded to every sounding phrase in Carton's self-pitying rhetoric. In the "Preface" to *A Tale of Two Cities*, Dickens writes that he had a "strong desire" to "embody [the central idea of the story] in my own person" and that throughout the execution of the novel this idea "has had complete possession of me." "I have so far verified what is done and suffered in these pages," he continues, "as that I have certainly done and suffered it all myself" (*TTC*, [v]). Through such heroic role playing, Dickens remade his own flawed passion. He indulged himself with the comforting dream of noble sacrifice and beatific renewal and reveled in the self-assuaging rhetoric of redemptive renunciation. By such means he gilded the corrosive reality that frequently lurks in passion—that lurked in his passion—the reality that produces anguish and anger, the reality that sears and afflicts. This somber reality is present in *A Tale of Two Cities;* the darker vibrations of Dickens' own experiences are there—a love that cannot be exorcised or fulfilled, a love that leads to suffering, degradation, guilt, and destruction—but this reality has been burnished with exalted feeling and sentiment. "The Bride's Chamber" configuration of passion lurks darkly in the unrealized depths of *A Tale of Two Cities,* but it has been ennobled, purified. *The Frozen Deep* configuration prevails. Frustrated love gives rise to rebirth, suffering to heroism, destruction to salvation. It is a consummation devoutly to be wished.

X

By the time of *Great Expectations,* begun a year later, Dickens was willing to confront the enigma of passion without the old pre- "Bride's Chamber" distancings and exclusions and without the sublime sublimations of *A Tale of Two Cities.* The onset of Pip's passion for Estella, like the onset of David Copperfield's passion for Dora (and Dickens' passion for Ellen), is soul-shaking and immediate. But unlike David's passion, which is all rosy daze and ecstatic delight, Pip's passion is coeval with bafflement, yearning, and pain. From the very first instant Estella treats him scornfully, calls him "boy," and orders him about (*AYR* 4: *GE,* 8:266). She tells him disdainfully—in front of Miss Havisham too—that he calls knaves Jacks, has coarse hands, and wears thick boots; he is nothing but a stupid, clumsy, common laboring boy. When Miss Havisham later asks him in private what he thinks of Estella, Pip says she is proud, very insulting, and very pretty. When Miss Havisham then asks him if he is willing to "'never see her again, though she is so pretty,'" Pip is unable to forgo her (*AYR* 4: *GE,* 8:268).

Later, in the courtyard, Estella gives him bread and meat "as insolently as if I were a dog in disgrace" (*AYR* 4: *GE,* 8:268). Pip is so "humiliated, hurt, spurned, offended, angry, sorry" that tears start to his eyes, whereupon Estella looks at him with "quick delight in having been the cause of them" (*AYR* 4: *GE,* 8:268). Estella goes off. Pip cries, twists his hair, and kicks the wall. A little later, in the deserted brewery, he sees her walking before him, never turning around, always out of reach. She finally ascends some stairs and goes out by a gallery "high overhead, as if she were going out into the sky" (*AYR* 4: *GE*, 8:269). The scene is a precursor of Pip's relationship with Estella. She is always out beyond him, always high above him, never looking backward, always out of reach. She is, as her name implies, a star, cold and remote yet ever luring him on. Their first meeting ends when Estella unlocks the gate to let Pip out. He tries to pass out without looking at her, but she touches him "with a taunting hand":

> "Why don't you cry?"
> "Because I don't want to."
> "You do," said she. "You have been crying till you are half blind, and you are near crying again now."
> She laughed contemptuously, pushed me out, and locked the gate upon me. (*AYR* 4: *GE*, 8:269)

The next time they meet, Estella immediately begins to taunt him:

> "Am I pretty?"
> "Yes; I think you are very pretty."
> "Am I insulting?"
> "Not so much so as you were last time," said I.
> "Not so much so?"
> "No."
> She fired when she asked the last question, and she slapped my face with such force as she had, when I answered it.
> "Now?" said she. "You little coarse monster, what do you think of me now?"
> "I shall not tell you."
> "Because you are going to tell, up-stairs. Is that it?"
> "No," said I, "that's not it."
> "Why don't you cry again, you little wretch?"
> "Because I'll never cry for you again," said I. Which was, I suppose, as false a declaration as ever was made; for I was inwardly crying for her

then, and I know what I know of the pain she cost me afterwards. (*AYR* 4: *GE*, 11:314)

These great scenes, so full of insight and complexity, show how Pip's passion, from the very first, masters and torments him. He is the slave of that passion. Swept by emotions he cannot fathom or control, he follows his cold, distant star, crying as he goes. This is a metaphorical way of stating Pip's condition, but it is also the literal truth. He cries on his first encounter with Estella; he is "inwardly crying for her" on the second encounter; and, as for subsequent encounters, "I know what I know of the pain she cost me afterwards." But despite his pain, Pip cannot turn away from Estella. He is compelled by a deep inner necessity. He is caught in his poor labyrinth of blind unreasoning passion. That blind passion is profoundly sexual. Dickens recognizes this, and he makes sure that the aware reader will recognize it too. It is not simply that Estella is able to provoke, taunt, and arouse Pip, or that Pip finds her pretty and feels hurt and spurned by her. Some scenes bristle with an almost primitive sexuality. Toward the end of Pip's second encounter with Estella, he meets Herbert Pocket and fights with him, a fight vaguely associated at its outset with Estella. Estella has been secretly watching the boys fight, and after the fight is over and Pip, the victor, has cleaned himself up and gone to the gate, he finds Estella waiting to let him out:

> There was a bright flush upon her face, as though something had happened to delight her. Instead of going straight to the gate, too, she stepped back into the passage, and beckoned me.
> "Come here! You may kiss me, if you like."
> I kissed her cheek as she turned it to me. I think I would have gone through a great deal to kiss her cheek. But, I felt that the kiss was given to the coarse common boy as a piece of money might have been, and that it was worth nothing. (*AYR* 4: *GE*, 11:318)

The sexuality is there, profoundly there, but it leads to bafflement and unhappiness, not to fulfillment.

The various motifs so artfully commenced in these beginnings are masterfully enhanced and elaborated throughout the novel. We see Pip enacting his ecstatic ritual of commingled passion and pain. He is clear-eyed concerning his fate but powerless to avoid it—indeed, he rushes to embrace it. He tells us how "the air of inaccessibility which [Estella's] beauty and her manner gave her, tormented me in the midst of my delight" (*AYR* 5: *GE*, 29:4). He tells us that he began to adore Estella the first time he saw her and that "I have never left off adoring her" (*AYR* 5: *GE*, 30:26). He explains how he felt when sitting with Estella in an inn: "The room was all in all to me, Estella being in it. I thought that with her I could have been happy there for life. (I was not at all happy there at the time, observe, and I knew it well)" (*AYR* 5: *GE*, 33:51). One recalls Dickens' identical statements in the first flush of his love for Ellen. How, at the St. Leger with Ellen, and later at Hampton Court with her, he felt he "could have been happy there for life"; more than this, how he yearned for those moments to be extended beyond life and prolonged through all eternity. But the St. Leger and Hampton Court rhapsodies, unlike Pip's retrospective analyses, contained no hint of pain—that was reserved, in those first wild days of rapture and torment, for the expressionistic magnifications of "The Bride's Chamber."

In *The Lazy Tour*, in other words, the pain and the bliss are cordoned off from one another. "The Bride's Chamber" is all agony and suffering; the St. Leger interlude, all swooning adoration. Furthermore, in *The Lazy Tour* the two impulses are separated in time and in setting (separated in publication also) as well as in psychological state—again unlike their rendition in *Great Expectations*. "The Bride's Chamber," with its wild, guilt-haunted cry of anger and anguish, was written a week or so before and published one week before its perfervid St. Leger counterpart; indeed, the gloomy torments and emotional purgations of "The Bride's Chamber" probably helped clear the way for that joyous counterpart, the paean of praise of Ellen at the races. That paean of praise, an ode without reserve and without shadow, an ineffable dream-vision embodiment of Dickens' idealized yearning, glorified his young companion, the self-created incarnation, in that grim time of misery and frustration, of his unfulfilled longing. Ellen became an icon as well as a winsome sylph; she became the golden-haired, lilac-gloved, halo-headed personification of his desire for unearthly felicity. There, in that bright Doncaster afternoon, the dark "Bride's Chamber" agonies banished for the moment—there, with Ellen at his side, "with her golden hair [making] quite a Glory in the sunlight round the pretty head," Dickens could dream, as Pip does after him, of perfect fulfillments (*HW* 16: *LT*, 412). And there, "the desert of [his] heart" greening under Ellen's angelic influence, he could, again in anticipation of Pip, wish unabashed for the unattainable, he could wish for eternal bliss: "Why anything in the world but you and me! Why may not this [moment] be prolonged through an everlasting autumn-sunshine, without a sunset!" (*HW* 16: *LT*, 412).

Pip's wish, while equally fervent, is never so unalloyed as this. Time has intervened. *Great Expectations* was written three years after "The Bride's Chamber" cry and the St. Leger rhapsody. In *Great Expectations*, so sad, so inward-looking, so full of sorrowful knowledge, Dickens no longer disassociates passion and pain. Now, the elegiac wisdom of long-pondered experience replacing the tumult of the immediate, he constantly emphasizes the oneness of passion and wretchedness. Yet insight does not mean liberation. Like Dickens, Pip sees; but, like Dickens, he cannot help himself. He is compelled, compelled by the overriding necessity of his passion—a heedless, dolorous, self-wounding passion—to yearn for that which he knows he should not have. Here, for example, is another statement by Pip of his longing for Estella: "And still I stood looking at the house, thinking how happy I should be if I lived there with her, and knowing that I never was happy with her, but always miserable" (*AYR* 5: *GE*, 33:53). Or, yet again, much later: "I never had one hour's happiness in her society, and yet my mind all round the four-and-twenty hours was harping on the happiness of having her with me unto death" (*AYR* 5: *GE*, 38:121).

Pip's knowledge that he is miserable does not reduce his passion or his desire to be with Estella. Despite his clear-eyed insights, he pursues his self-wounding course. Finally, in a transport of ecstatic passion, he confesses his love to Estella:

> "You are part of my existence, part of myself. You have been in every line I have ever read since I first came here, the rough common boy whose poor heart you wounded even then. You have been in every prospect I have ever seen since—on the river, on the sails of the ships, on the marshes, in the clouds, in the light, in the darkness, in the wind, in the woods, in the sea, in the streets. You have been the embodiment of every graceful fancy that my mind has ever become acquainted with. . . . Estella, to the last hour of my life, you cannot choose but remain part of my character, part of the little good in me, part of the evil." (*AYR* 5: *GE*, 44:221)

These are the wild dithyrambs of obsessive love, the fine frenzies of overwrought passion; but perhaps a less extravagant declaration best sums up Pip's condition. In this more thoughtful avowal Pip tells us that despite the "all-powerful" influence and "possession" of passion, "according to my experience, the conventional notion of a lover cannot be always true" (*AYR* 5: *GE*, 29:1). He also tells us that although a lover is possessed, at the very same time, in the midst of his possession, he is—or at least he can be—clear-eyed and insightful, and this confounding paradox "is the clue by which I am to be followed into my poor labyrinth" (*AYR* 5: *GE*, 29:1). One senses it is also the clue (a deep-pondered, confessional clue) by which Dickens is to be followed into his identical labyrinth:

> The unqualified truth is, that when I loved Estella with the love of a man, I loved her because I found her irresistible. Once for all; I knew to my sorrow, often and often, if not always, that I loved her against reason, against promise, against peace, against hope, against happiness, against all discouragement that could be. Once for all; I loved her none the less because I knew it, and it had no more influence in restraining me, than if I had devoutly believed her to be human perfection. (*AYR* 5: *GE*, 29:1)

Think how different Pip's passion is from David Copperfield's rosy ecstasy—yet both protagonists are madly in love, as Dickens wants us to see, with women who can only cause them dole. In

101. Pip Enslaved by Passion

"I held [her hand] and put it to my lips. 'You ridiculous boy,' said Estella, 'will you never take warning? Or do you kiss my hand in the spirit in which I once let you kiss my cheek?' . . .

'If I say yes, may I kiss the cheek again?' . . .

I leaned down, and her calm face was like a statue's. 'Now,' said Estella, gliding away the instant I touched her cheek, 'you are to take care that I have some tea, and you are to take me to Richmond'" (*AYR* 5: *GE*, 35:52).

"'If I Say Yes, May I Kiss The Cheek Again?'" Wood engraving (1861) after a drawing by John McLenan. This illustration (one of thirty-four), specially commissioned for the first American appearance of *Great Expectations,* preceded the English illustrations by almost two years. For more on these matters, and for another example of McLenan's work, see figure 50.

Copperfield Dickens cordons that dole off from David's passion. David's passion is ethereal, delightful, charming; his dole (separate from his passion) is sad, bittersweet, mild. That mild dole, a kind of muted resignation or melancholy, is segregated in time as well as in circumstance. It emerges long after the days of David's rosy ecstasy; it emerges after marriage, after the fading of passion and illusion. Not so in *Great Expectations.* In *Great Expectations* the dole and the passion are one—one from the very beginning, and one all life long. Furthermore, in *Great Expectations* we have no doubt that Pip's passion is profoundly physical: he loves Estella "with the love of a man."

Great Expectations presents through analysis and realistic detail (and in greater depth and scope, of course) what "The Bride's Chamber" presents through wild dithyrambs and expressionistic fabling. In "The Bride's Chamber" the passionate love is acted out by the tree-climbing suitor, and his suit brings him destruction and death. The black perversions of passion (thwarted desire leading to isolation, hate, deformity, violence, and the like) are embodied in the soul-destroying husband; and his passionate excesses—unpardonable sins—bring their inevitable aftermath: destruction, death, and everlasting damnation. Or, to put the matter in slightly different terms, "The Bride's Chamber" conveys through cosmic enlargement what *Great Expectations* conveys through psychological verisimilitude. This does not mean that the two works are identical, simply that they emerged from the same matrix, both in terms of autobiography and imagination.

XI

That matrix, which subsequently contributed so much to Sydney Carton as well as to Pip, still later contributed darker shadings yet to Bradley Headstone (*Our Mutual Friend*) and John Jasper (*Edwin Drood*). Headstone's history often approaches the tragic. Born woefully poor and bereft, he raises himself up in accordance with society's behest, and he achieves this near miracle of transformation through his own useful labors. He is eager, receptive, ambitious, obedient. He disciplines himself. He studies diligently, forgoes all frivolities, pursues his education, and pursues respectability. He decides to become a teacher, throws himself into his work, and rises in his chosen field. He finally becomes a certified schoolmaster, a man to be reckoned with in his little world of pedagogy and learning. He is mindful of his position and his achievement. He leads a life of probity, hard work, and moral rectitude. But he also displays some of the weaknesses of the workful middle-class ethic he has adopted. He is solemn, puritanical, unbending, and self-righteous. He is also serious, and he takes himself seriously. The emotional side of his nature is undeveloped, or rather, is repressed. He has been too busy improving himself and getting ahead to cultivate his feelings. He is like Louisa Gradgrind in *Hard Times,* or, to take a somewhat different, nonfictional example, like John Stuart Mill before his breakdown: a being incomplete and desperately vulnerable because of that incompleteness.

Yet, Bradley Headstone is a decent, useful man, and by society's standards an exemplary man as well. His downfall is brought about by the deadly convergence of his emotional poverty and an overwhelming passion, a passion he is not prepared to deal with. But for that convergence he might have married the adoring schoolmistress Miss Peecher (or some other respectable toiler in the ranks), had a houseful of proper, dutiful children, and been buried with great probity and propriety with a headstone which read: "Here, lamented by his family and friends, lies Bradley Headstone, a decent, worthy laborer in the ranks. Seek, fellow sojourner, to emulate his decorous ways and days." But Headstone's destiny was different. His headstone would have to read: "Here, alone and unlamented, lies Bradley Headstone, a violent, passionate man, the murderer of two and the would-be murderer of three. Take warning, stranger, and avoid his tempestuous ways and days."

Once Headstone meets Lizzie Hexam, he is lost. He is the thrall of passion, a mere bit of flotsam tossed and battered and finally broken by great tidal waves of inexplicable emotion. He has no defenses. His sexual passion, so long repressed and stunted (like all his emotions), now drives him in ways he cannot understand or control. The dark, buried Headstone—dark because so long hidden, dark because deformed by lack of light and cultivation—now overwhelms the old staid Headstone, a creature of rules, restrictions, and decorum. Caught up in that sensual clamor, he now rushes toward destruction. Headstone is a stage beyond Pip. Pip, despite his passion, despite even his rejection by Estella, can fall back on other resources of love, affection, friendship, support. Furthermore, once Pip has died and been reborn—that is, once he has been purged of his false values and has resigned all extravagant hope—he can live a quiet, chastened life. Pip, it should be remembered, is burned and broken. In the end, he does not win his greatest expectation and live happily ever after. Even in the "happier" ending he only visualizes—that is, hopefully foresees—no further parting from Estella; and, in any case, he and Estella are so totally changed and chastened at the end that their union would not be a fulfillment of the old expectations.

Not so Bradley Headstone. Once he has been caught up in the rush of passion he must consummate that passion or die. Unlike Pip, he has no way of living with his dream unconsummated, no emotional resources to fall back upon, no slumbering reserves of humanity to be reawakened and reborn. He has been betrayed by the workful ethic he trusted, an ethic that excluded emotions, fancy, art, playfulness—not to speak of passion—as inconsequential or pernicious. As a result, once Headstone's last chance of satisfying his passion is gone—that is, once he has been rejected by Lizzie—he is doomed.

Dickens paints this portrait stroke by stroke and tint by tint. In the scene in which Headstone proposes to Lizzie, every object, word, and gesture tells of passion long suppressed. The scene takes place in a cramped, claustrophobic, stone-paved city churchyard. In the center of this desolate yard stands a raised island of the dead. This forbidding island of death, enclosed by iron railings, is adorned with drooping tombstones (headstones) mouldering in neglect. As the interview progresses, Lizzie and Headstone go round and round the gritty pavement or pause at the iron bars while Headstone speaks and wrenches at the stone coping of the wall-begirt burial island. He wrenches at that grim stone wall as though he wished—all unconsciously, of course—to join the quiet dead. But before this wrenching thrust toward death, early in the interview, unable to control himself, Headstone had blurted out, "'You are the ruin of me.'" Lizzie had started at the "passionate sound" of those words and at the "passionate action" of his hands.

> "Yes! you are the ruin—the ruin—the ruin—of me. I have no resources in myself, I have no confidence in myself, I have no government of myself when you are near me or in my thoughts. And you are always in my thoughts now. I have never been quit of you since I first saw you. Oh, that was a wretched day for me! That was a wretched, miserable day!" (*OMF,* 2: 15:301)

He speaks in a suffocated way but "always speaking passionately, and, when most emphatic, repeating that former action of his hands, which was like flinging his heart's blood down before her in drops upon the pavement-stones" (*OMF,* 2: 15:302). Headstone's suffocated avowal of his passion reminds us of Miss Havisham's vehement avowal (communicated in a "hurried passionate whisper") of what "real love"—that is, overmastering passion—truly is: "'I'll tell you,' said she, in the same hurried passionate whisper, 'what real love is. It is blind devotion, unquestioning self-humiliation, utter submission, trust and belief against yourself and against the whole world, giving up your whole heart and soul to the smiter—as I did!'" And then death-environed Miss Havisham, self-immured and self-confined, like death-environed Bradley Headstone after her, erupts in an agonized torment and strikes symbolically at an enclosing wall, an enclosing wall of death: "She rose up in the chair, in her shroud of a dress, and struck at the air as if she would as soon have struck herself against the wall and fallen dead" (*AYR* 5: *GE,* 29:4).

Headstone, too, will soon strike at a wall, an unyielding wall of death. As his interview with Lizzie continues, the decorous and repressed schoolmaster, suffocating and barely controlling himself, environed by death, rushing headlong toward death, runs passionately on. He tells Lizzie he is under a spell. "'You draw me to you,'" he says. "'If I were shut up in a strong prison, you would draw me out. I should break through the wall to come to you.'" All the while, with a "wild energy" that is "absolutely terrible," he tears at the coping stone of the burial-ground enclosure, he tears at the cold forbidding wall of death. Continuing to wrench at the stony abode of death, compelled by the furious necessity within him, he rushes on. "'No man knows till the time comes, what depths are within him. To some men it never comes; let them rest and be thankful! To me, you brought it; on me, you forced it; and the bottom of this raging sea,' striking himself upon the breast, 'has been heaved up ever since'" (*OMF*, 2: 15:302).

Lizzie, aghast, tries to stop the torrent, but after a pause, Headstone goes on:

> "I love you. What other men may mean when they use that expression, I cannot tell; what *I* mean is, that I am under the influence of some tremendous attraction which I have resisted in vain, and which overmasters me. You could draw me to fire, you could draw me to water, you could draw me to the gallows, you could draw me to any death, you could draw me to anything I have most avoided, you could draw me to any exposure and disgrace." (*OMF*, 2: 15:303)

When Lizzie refuses him, Headstone strikes the stone wall of the burial island, the enclosing wall of death. The scene seethes with passion and with death. Headstone brings his "clenched hand down upon the stone with a force that laid the knuckles raw and bleeding" and holding out his "smeared hand" as though it held a weapon that had just struck a deadly blow, he says, "'Then I hope that I may never kill him!'" (*OMF*, 2: 15:303–4). Headstone does kill, of course, though he fails in his attempt to murder Wrayburn. He goes to his watery death (he also foreshadows that end in this love scene with Lizzie) clutching Rogue Riderhood, that dark mirror-image of his darker self (Headstone on his way to murder Wrayburn had dressed like Riderhood), clutching Riderhood in a last passionate embrace of self-destruction, murder, and annihilation.

Who would have thought, at the very opening of *Our Mutual Friend,* that this violent, passion-wracked death would be the final end of the staid, decorous schoolmaster, a being so careful and so constrained, the product, indeed the very embodiment, of Victorian values, of puritanical workfulness and diligent respectability? Headstone's exemplary beginning and disgraceful end—a passion-generated, passion-driven end—cause us to pause and to think. We are meant to ponder the cautionary history of the stifled schoolmaster. We are meant to ponder the dark destructiveness of the passionate forces—deeply human forces, eminently natural forces, manifestly universal forces—that lurked unacknowledged and profoundly suppressed in the shrouded recesses of Headstone's unsatisfied soul, forces that were waiting in the "depths . . . within him," forces that became a "raging sea," forces that finally "heaved up" in wild, uncontrollable fury. This, Dickens is saying, is what can happen when we (with the connivance and through the impositions of society) deny our deepest emotions. Those neglected emotions, once evoked, will not be denied; when they do emerge, they will emerge monstrously transformed.

We see this in Bradley Headstone. Despite a lifetime of self-disciplined propriety and inhibited respectability (deeply committed, totally sincere propriety and respectability), Headstone quickly and recklessly descends into savagery, into murderous rampages and ghastly self-slaughter. These are the deadly fruits of repression and emotional deprivation (socially induced and socially enforced repression and deprivation). Headstone is the fearful product of this life-betraying conditioning. We ponder the tragic end of a decent man gripped and compelled by his birthright of passion, a birthright turned death warrant by the fateful complicity of a flawed self and a flawed society.

We are light years away, here, from the charming passion of David in *David Copperfield,* even beyond the tormented passion of Pip in

CAIN × ABEL

GREEN Sc

102. Bradley Headstone Gripped
and Compelled by Passion

"Better To Be Abel Than Cain." Wood engraving after a drawing by Marcus
Stone for Number XVII, Book IV, Chapter VII (September 1865) of *Our
Mutual Friend*.

Great Expectations; we are in the raging, demon-haunted realms of "The Bride's Chamber" with its cosmic passions and cosmic hates, but domesticated now, made real as well as cosmic. We are also in the tempest-tossed realms of passion personally experienced and painfully suffered—experienced and suffered by Dickens—the realms of the "raging sea" and the "depths . . . within," realms that "no man knows till the time comes."

XII

In *Edwin Drood,* passion continues to be depicted in the intense, driven, divided mode of *Our Mutual Friend,* but now, extending and confirming the steadily darkening post-"Bride's Chamber" progression, it is depicted with blacker and more sinister overtones yet. John Jasper, like Bradley Headstone, has two divergent aspects to his character, but unlike Headstone, whose passionate aspect lay long suppressed, Jasper's dual nature is schizophrenic and duplicitous. Under his fair, controlled exterior lurks an intense and ever-present iniquity and violence. His life reflects this duality: serene choirmaster in Cloisterham, sordid opium eater in London; solicitous mentor to his "dear boy," devouring murderer of that same nephew. Often, in one intense look, he is both devoted parent and hungry predator. And often, as in the very opening of the book, he comes directly from the opium den and his fevered opium dreams to sing sweetly in the hallowed precincts of Cloisterham Cathedral, sing sweetly of the wicked man. (He is a precursor here of Stephen Daedalus in *A Portrait of the Artist as a Young Man,* who comes fresh from the stews and dreams and desecrations of Night Town to kneel as a holy acolyte at the feet of the Virgin Mary.)

In his division and duality, Jasper the melodious choirmaster is like much of Cloisterham. For Cloisterham, too, is not what it seems to be: though dreamy and decorous to outward view, it is divided and festering within. (It too hugs close its dark, subterranean midnight secrets.) The very name "Cloisterham," so redolent of ancient holiness, worship, and retirement, evokes this deceptive

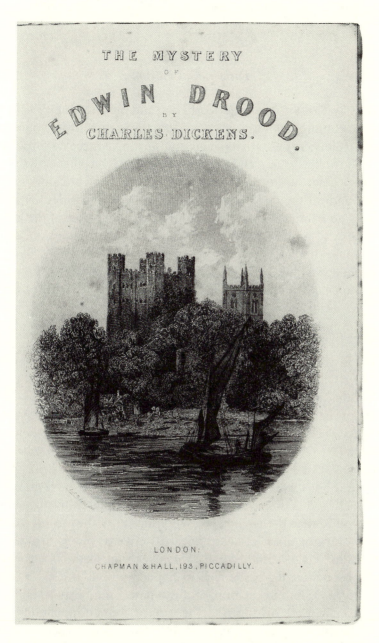

THE MYSTERY
OF
EDWIN DROOD.
BY
CHARLES DICKENS.

LONDON:
CHAPMAN & HALL, 193, PICCADILLY.

103. The Duality of Cloistered Cloisterham: Beneath
Cloisterham's Quiet Beauty and Sheltering Façades
Unbridled Passion and Rampant Evil Flourish

This illustration shows serene, evil-harboring Cloisterham as depicted on the
original vignette title page of *Edwin Drood*. In reality, the vignette (following
Dickens' careful sketching in the novel) is a faithful rendering of Rochester
Castle and Rochester Cathedral, seen here from the Medway. Steel engraving
after a drawing by Luke Fildes. This title page was included with Number VI
(September 1870) of the unfinished novel—the final number.

duality. To cloister is to seclude, shelter, and protect; but it is also to isolate, confine, and conceal. Cloisterham is true to its equivocal name: it cloisters beneath its sheltering surfaces concealed sin as well as public holiness (or seeming public holiness). Deep beneath Cloisterham's quiet beauty and sedate exteriors, beneath the drowsy old spires and sleepy old façades of its cathedrals, castles, chapter houses, academies, homes, and tombs (dwelling places of the living and the dead) evil flourishes: drunkenness, malice, oppression, desecration, murder, and cannibalistic ferocity.[18]

Jasper exemplifies and magnifies this pervasive disjunction between appearance and reality. Deep beneath his sweet singing, civility, friendship, peacemaking, and civic-mindedness (so deep that surely even he is unaware of some of its darkest depths) fires of hatred and violence, and, deepest and hottest of all, fires of intense sexual passion, burn day and night. This passion and these hostilities smolder below the pleasant surface of Jasper's smooth social presence, but they burst into naked flame occasionally, ignited by a range of characters, including Neville, Durdles, Deputy, Sapsea, the Princess Puffer, and Edwin himself (his "dear boy" and beloved nephew).

Jasper's sexual passion focuses wildly, obsessively on Rosa. That passion is both secret and open. It is secret from the busy everyday world; after all, it does not accord with the carefully cultivated image of rectitude that the circumspect choirmaster wishes to project to the world, nor does it accord with his effusive public avowals of friendship and solicitude for Edwin, to whom Rosa is betrothed. But it is open to Rosa; she feels its hypnotic force in Jasper's every gesture, look, and intonation, and ultimately she hears its affirmation from Jasper's own lips, for he cannot contain indefinitely the overwhelming urgency of his passion.[19] That urgent passion can be dissembled, hidden from the outer world, made, for a term, to bide its time, but it cannot be deflected, and it cannot brook any impediment to its ultimate consummation.[20] As with Bradley Headstone, Jasper's passion leads to murder (needless murder, as it turns out), and as with Bradley Headstone (if Dickens had lived to finish his design) it would have led to total self-destruction. This sort of elemental passion—overwhelming, involuntary, unassuaged passion, passion that seizes and possesses—Dickens seems to be saying, cannot be contained and will not be denied. Such passion—often hidden and illicit, always tormented and unrequited—will inevitably exact its dread toll. It will burst forth in violent ways, wounding, maiming, smashing all opposition. But most of all, it will turn on itself. It will destroy all the defenses of the tormented one (he who is possessed), rending the entire fabric of his life, and, at last, destroying life itself.

Even in its earlier stages, for example when Jasper first openly reveals his passion to Rosa, the force of that passion is frightening. Jasper is still in control of himself, but only barely so. The will required to maintain that control, though titanic, is barely sufficient, and it is fast eroding and cracking under the onslaught of his passion. (He will attempt to survive by separating his two selves, his choir self and his opium self, in an almost schizoid manner; but this partly unconscious strategy of self-defense would, most certainly, have collapsed in the end, assuring the totality of his self-destruction.) Jasper's duality and division are aspects of his inmost being. Everything he says and does is rife with doubleness. When Dickens depicts Jasper's wildly emotional yet rigidly controlled interview with Rosa, the interview in which he first openly declares his love, he emphasizes Jasper's tumultuous passion—a compulsive, irresistible passion—but he also emphasizes Jasper's iron self-discipline and consummate dissembling. In other words, Dickens emphasizes Jasper's self-division—his dark, driven self and his bright, dissembling self—and he shows us what it costs Jasper to maintain the fiction (for the benefit of the world at large, at least) of a single, tranquil, virtuous self.

The interview takes place in the garden of the Nun's House. Rosa, deserted for the moment by her companions and unable to avoid the meeting, feels desperate and shudders at the very thought of being along with Jasper. When she enters the garden she sees him leaning on the sundial (one immediately interprets the lady, the garden, the dial, and the tempter) and she feels "compelled" by him as of old (*ED,* 19:148). Yet she shrinks from him, also as of old, withdrawing her hand from his touch. Jasper tells her that Edwin did not love her "'as he should have loved, or as any one in his place would have loved—must have loved!'" (*ED,* 19:148). He calls her "'Dearest Rosa! Charming Rosa!'" (*ED,* 19:149). Restraining himself, and leaning casually against the sundial so that no one looking on would imagine the purpose of his visit or the intensity of his emotions, he calls her "'my beloved'" (*ED,* 19:149). His face when Rosa opposes him sometimes flushes with menace, but his outward demeanor gives the appearance of easy negligence. In this casual attitude he goes on:

> "Rosa, even when my dear boy was affianced to you, I loved you madly; even when I thought his happiness in having you for his wife was certain, I loved you madly; even when I strove to make him more ardently devoted to you, I loved you madly; even when he gave me the picture of your lovely face so carelessly traduced by him, which I feigned to hang always in my sight for his sake, but worshipped in torment for yours, I loved you madly. In the distasteful work of the day, in the wakeful misery of the night, girded by sordid realities, or wandering through Paradises and Hells of visions into which I rushed, carrying your image in my arms, I loved you madly." (*ED,* 19:149)

Dickens then adds: "If anything could make his words more hideous to her than they are in themselves, it would be the contrast between the violence of his look and delivery, and the composure of his assumed attitude" (*ED,* 19:149).

When Rosa flares with anger, Jasper maintains his easy attitude, but his "working features and his convulsive hands" seem "absolutely diabolical" (*ED,* 19:150). "'How beautiful you are!'" he says. "'You are more beautiful in anger than in repose. I don't ask you for your love; give me yourself and your hatred.'" Rosa's face flames; she breathes in choking pants. Jasper tells her that insofar as he can control matters, no "'other admirer shall love you and live'" (*ED,* 19:150). He calls her "'worshipped of my soul!'"; he tells her he

104. Jasper's Duality: Inner Passion, Outer Calm

This illustration appears in a chapter with the evocative and equivocal title "Shadow on the Sun-dial." The title of the illustration, also equivocal, is "Jasper's Sacrifices." Wood engraving after a drawing by Luke Fildes for Number V, Chapter XIX (August 1870) of *Edwin Drood*.

loves her "'more madly now than ever,'" that henceforth he will have "'no object in existence but you only.'" "'My love for you,'" he goes on a moment later, "'is above all other love, and my truth to you is above all other truth. Let me have hope and favor, and I am a forsworn man for your sake.'" She is his "'darling,'" his "'angel,'" he "'could fall down among the vilest ashes and kiss'" her "'dear feet,'" his "'adoration'" of her outweighs an "'inexpiable offence'" (*ED*, 19:151). Speaking with "frightful vehemence," but all the while maintaining a manner so that someone viewing them from the window would think his words to be the "airiest and playfulest," he rushes on: "'There is my past and my present wasted life. There is the desolation of my heart and my soul. There is my peace; there is my despair. Stamp them into the dust, so that you take me, were it even mortally hating me!'" Rosa rushes toward the house. As she is about to enter, Jasper, at her side, speaking in her ear, says "'I love you, love you, love you. If you were to cast me off now—but you will not—you would never be rid of me. No one should come between us. I would pursue you to the death'" (*ED*, 19:152).

What are we to make of such lovemaking, so violent and so frenzied, and why are these elaborate studies of passion run amok absent from Dickens' early and middle novels? One reason has to do with the changing times. The late novels were written in a period when increasing attention was being given to psychology, to the mind's interior workings, to the inner landscape rather than the outward panorama. Dickens' writings reflect these changes. To move from *Pickwick* to *Drood* is, in many ways, to move from a writer looking back toward the eighteenth century to a writer looking forward to the twentieth. Another element is realism. One sees the movement toward realism everywhere: in painting, the decorative arts, poetry, the drama, and elsewhere. In Dickens, one sees it in such outward manifestations as the illustrations to his novels (which he strictly controlled), which move from caricature to representation no less than the substance of the novels themselves, a trend that is reflected as well in the other novels of the period. In part Dickens mirrors these changes; in part he helps create them, though his particular brand of realism, especially in the middle and late novels, is always profoundly interfused with a singular, and very Dickensian, vision of the symbolic and the extrarational. Coupled with the increasing realism is an increasing frankness about every aspect of daily living, and this despite the fact that imposed reticences and restraints were still enormous, as the case of Thomas Hardy, who abruptly terminated his novel-writing career just before the end of the century, largely as the result of intolerable outside pressures and censorships, makes clear.

The movement toward frankness and realism had many guises. To cite one form of change, the one most relevant to our present discussion, titanic passion, cosmic evil, unpardonable sin, moved out of the unrealistic, high-flown realms of ranting melodrama and Gothic romance (the latter form, as a genre, dried up well before the middle of the century) and, transformed rather than effaced— that is, made ordinary and believable—moved into other realms, for example into the realistic novel where it was blended with everyday lives and domestic relevancies, familiar and meaningful territory for the contemporary reader. Such changes occurred in ragged and unpredictable ways; after all, the changing times were always refracted through the vagaries of an individual consciousness. Yet the overall movement was away from Gothic enormities and toward everyday perversities.

Wuthering Heights and *Bleak House,* both neo-Gothic novels of sorts (the former infinitely more Gothic and backward-looking than the latter), are two milestones in one aspect of that evolving journey. In this connection, one should keep in mind that some of the passages quoted in this section, torn from their realistic contexts, resound more loudly than they do in place with echoes of the stage and vibrations of the Gothic. But to return to realism, frankness, and the changing times, these matters—they are only a sample of those that might be pursued—are mentioned here simply in passing. Even without exploring them further, they can serve as reminders that a complicated external world of social forces also impinged on Dickens' life and helped shape his writings. In this respect, of course, he was no different from any other writer.

XIII

But beyond the changes that flowed from (or perhaps with) the changing times, are those that came about by virtue of Dickens' own experiences. In the case of passion, these changes, as one would expect, owe much to his inner life; and even though that inner life is largely veiled, some glimpses behind the veil are possible. It seems clear, for example, that some of Dickens' reticences concerning passion and some of his transformations of its very nature (especially in the early and middle works) go back to situations and relationships in his childhood and early manhood. Take, for instance, to begin with, a matter that might seem remote from passion: brother-sister relationships. Close, intense, passionate brother-sister relationships (whether blood relationships or surrogate unions) abound in Dickens' novels and in his life. In the novels think of Harry and Rose Maylie, Nicholas and Kate Nickleby, Kit Nubbles and Little Nell, Tom and Ruth Pinch, Paul and Florence Dombey, Walter Gay and Florence Dombey, John and Harriet Carker, David Copperfield and Agnes Wickfield, Tom and Louisa Gradgrind, Amy and Tip Dorrit—to cite only a partial list from the early and middle novels. These brother-sister (or surrogate brother-sister) pairs are not products of happenstance, nor are they casual conveniences in long multiplotted novels. Dickens treats them as crucial relationships; in many instances he makes them central to the emotional dynamics of the novel.

In his own life there was an analogous range of crucial sisterly figures. Consider, to begin with, his sister Fanny, who was about fifteen months older than he. She filled a profound emotional void when, a year or two after his birth, their beleaguered mother turned to new offspring and new cares. In the Chatham years especially (the years from five through ten), Dickens turned to Fanny for love, companionship, sharing—even mothering. How special and intense

105. Fanny Dickens c. 1836, Age Twenty-Six

From a pastel drawing by Samuel Laurence. Dickens House Museum, London.

that relationship was (it was shadowed and partly destroyed by the march of events a few years later) may be glimpsed in such works as *A Christmas Carol* where, in an autobiographical section concerning Scrooge's childhood and boyhood, Scrooge's sister—named Fanny, no less—is the only person who remains steadfast and loving after Scrooge (like Dickens himself in his last Chatham school term and in the blacking-warehouse period) has been banished from the family circle and (so Dickens felt in his case too) banished from family love. Another direct image of Fanny as steadfast, all-loving sister—again with many autobiographical associations—appears in *The Haunted Man*.²¹ Redlaw, the haunted man (a reflection, in many outward and inward ways, of Dickens), haunted by betrayed love and betrayed friendship, is succored by his loving sister, who cleaves to him till her early death (Fanny had died only weeks before), a loss that leaves Redlaw alone and tormented by festering memories. Or, to cite just one more instance, again after Fanny's death, Dickens memorialized and fantasized his loving childhood relationship with her in "A Child's Dream of a Star," an idyll of innocent brother-sister closeness and yearning strongly tinged with emotion-fraught sentiment and angel-thronged religiosity.

Fanny was not the only loyal, adoring sister-figure in Dickens' life. Mary Hogarth, his sister-in-law (one of Kate's younger sisters) was another. Mary was innocent and beautiful. She was also sweet, warm, spontaneous, and light-hearted. She became the close, loving companion of Dickens' late bachelor and early married days, and she died suddenly in his arms when she was seventeen and he twenty-five. Dickens was so shattered by this loss that he missed the monthly installments of *Pickwick* and *Oliver Twist*, the only occasion in a lifetime of serial writing that he missed any installments. Mary, the bright, sweet presence of his days and nights, now became the sanctified and idealized angel of his memory.

One can scarcely overemphasize the intensity of Dickens' adoration. "I solemnly believe," he wrote shortly after Mary's death, "that so perfect a creature never breathed. I knew her inmost heart, and her real worth and value. She had not a fault. . . . if ever a mortal

106. Mary Hogarth in 1837, Age Seventeen

From a drawing (c. 1838) by Daniel Maclise based upon a miniature painting by Hablot Knight Browne. The painting was executed in 1837 shortly after Mary's death.

went to Heaven, [she] is there" ([17 May 1837]). On other occasions he spoke of her as "the dear girl whom I loved, after my wife,
more deeply and fervently than anyone on earth," referred to her as
"the gentlest and purest creature that ever shed a light on earth,"
and confessed that since her death, "I have never had her sweetness
and excellence absent from my mind" ([17 May, 26 October
1837]).

The importance of this idealized image, the profound emotion,
yearning, and confusion it held for him, may be glimpsed when one
notices that the language Dickens used twenty-one years later in his
defense of Ellen Ternan ("a young lady for whom I have a great
attachment and regard" [25 May 1858]), language he employed
when he championed her and Georgina Hogarth against the calum-
nious gossip that swirled around them (and him) at the time of the
dissolution of his marriage, echoes the cadences and images that he
wove round Mary when he translated her to heaven. Dickens, it
seems, had desperate need of such supernal visions and immaculate
prototypes. He clung to those celestial visions, or rather, he clung
to the single supernal vision from which those later versions sprang,
reminting the succoring ideality of the original vision over and
over again.

It was such a vision, pure and beatific, that he enshrined in his
mind during the first chaotic year of his needy adoration of Ellen.
"Upon my soul and honor," he wrote of her in that troubled time,
echoing his earlier praise of Mary, "there is not on this earth a more
virtuous and spotless creature than that young lady" (25 May
1858). And then, in phrases that echoed his championing of halo-
headed Ellen against the vile theater crowd in Doncaster six months
earlier ("good as its own sisters, or its own mother"), he continued
his defense of her: "I know her to be innocent and pure, and as
good as my own dear daughters" (25 May 1858). But even these
private avowals, were not sufficient. A few days later, in his single,
ill-advised public defense of Ellen and Georgina against "misrepre-
sentations, most grossly false, most monstrous, and most cruel," he
declared them "innocent" and "dear to my heart" (*UW*, 2: 586)—
two additional sister-daughter angels.

Mary's angel goodness, unlike Ellen's spotless goodness or Georgina's selfless ministering, was never sullied by monstrous accusations or tarnished by corrosive change. Mary had the good fortune to die untouched by time's diminishments. Her radiant perfection, or rather Dickens' radiant idealization of what she was and might have continued to be, contributes importantly to many of his sisterly heroines. She appears, to cite two quick examples only, in angelic Little Nell ("Old wounds bleed afresh," Dickens wrote as he approached Nell's death, "when I only think of the way of doing it: what the actual doing it will be, God knows. . . . Dear Mary died yesterday, when I think of this sad story"), and she appears in angelic Florence Dombey (Dickens wrote on Mary's tombstone, "Young, Beautiful, And Good./ God . . . / Numbered Her With His Angels": so also, when dying Paul looks at his angel-sister Florence—Florence is accompanied by angel imagery—Dickens has Paul think how "young, and good, and beautiful"—the words Dickens put on Mary's tombstone—his angel-sister is) ([?8 January 1841]; *DS*, 14:143). When Mary died, Dickens took a ring from her finger and wore it ever after. He arranged to be buried in her grave. He dreamt of her every night for many months (till he told his wife of his dreams, and they stopped). Over the years, however, he dreamt of her again. On one occasion she appeared to him as the Virgin Mary.

Mary was not the last of Dickens' young, virginal, sisterly companions, nor was she the last of his prototypes (for such companions served as prototypes) for the sweet, budlike angel-heroines who populate his novels. After Mary's death, as though responding to some deeply felt inner need, Dickens drew yet another, still younger sister-figure (another sister-in-law) into his emotional life. Like Mary, Georgina Hogarth was comely and prepossessing. As she emerged into womanhood, she spent more and more time with the Dickens family; and finally, five years after Mary's death, she came to live with the Dickenses permanently. She was then fifteen; Dickens, thirty. She stayed in the Dickens household when her sister, Dickens' wife, departed; and she stayed there, unmarried, till Dickens' death, twenty-eight years after her arrival. Thus, through virtu-

107. Georgina Hogarth c. 1849, Age Twenty-Two

From a painting by Augustus Egg. Photograph, T. W. Tyrrell Collection, Dickens House Museum, London.

ally the whole of his married life—that is, till the coming of Ellen and the departure of Catherine—Dickens had both a sexual wife (the mother of his many children) and a young, adoring, virginal sister circling about him or living with him.

Dickens loved and cherished Georgina for her own sake, but he also associated her with her vanished sister Mary. There are many signs that Dickens, in the early days at least, regarded Georgina as a soft, muted afterglow of the bright angel Mary. One such sign was a letter he wrote to Henry Wadsworth Longfellow. He told Longfellow how much he regretted that Kate's younger sister Georgina, who usually lived with them, had not been there during Longfellow's visit. Then, as though musing to himself, he continued with the following regretful sigh: "There *was* another [sister] when we were first married, but She has been my better Angel six long years" (29 December 1842). (Note the capitalizing of "She," and note the designation, "Angel.") Georgina grew up in the Dickens household; she changed (as Mary would have, too, had she lived) from innocent virginal nymph to ordinary competent mortal. She bustled busily about Dickens' household as Esther Summerson later bustled busily about Bleak House, a steady, useful, loyal presence. She continued to evolve in her role and in Dickens' image of her. She metamorphosed from angel-sister to cheerful housekeeper to trusted maiden aunt and domestic companion. At the time of the breakup of his marriage, Dickens called her the "playmate, nurse, instructress, friend, protectress, adviser and companion" of his children, and he affirmed that she "has a higher claim . . . upon my affection, respect and gratitude than anybody in this world" (25 May 1858).

There is a night side to these sisterly relationships, a side that evoked deep hidden feelings of betrayal and abandonment in Dickens, feelings that magnified still earlier feelings of parental betrayal and abandonment, especially betrayal by his mother (see Part 1, "Dickens and Cannibalism," and Part 3, "Dickens and Necessity"). With the sisterly relationships, these feelings of resentment were deeply buried. When they did emerge, they emerged disguised or displaced, somber impulses of the unconscious calculus of feeling.

108. Charles Dickens, Catherine Dickens,
and Georgina Hogarth

From a drawing (1843) by Daniel Maclise.

This is not surprising. After all, Dickens' feelings were complicated and divided. There was much for him to resent as well as exalt in his loving sisters. Fanny, in this darker scenario, a scenario of emotions rather than self-conscious accusation, abandoned him. She went off to the elegant and expensive Royal Academy of Music while he, exiled and forgotten, a worthless drudge, suffered all alone the rat-infested nightmare of the blacking warehouse. Dickens' soreness at this disparity and his despair at his unaccountable degradation were profound. One Sunday during his blacking-warehouse servitude he went to the Royal Academy of Music to watch Fanny receive a prize. Here is his account of his reaction:

> I could not bear to think of myself—beyond the reach of all such hon-
> ourable emulation and success. The tears ran down my face. I felt as if
> my heart were rent. I prayed, when I went to bed that night, to be lifted
> out of the humiliation and neglect in which I was. I never had suffered
> so much before. (F, 34)

In this intense vignette (recalled by Dickens from the distant, but, in this case, unhealing, mists of time) the culminating incarnation of his humiliation and suffering focuses on—is epitomized by—Fanny's radiant exaltation and his own hellish degradation. Though Dickens does not consciously arraign Fanny, the emotional under-current is clear. In his time of greatest need (so his unconscious indictment went) Fanny had betrayed and then abandoned him; she had ascended blithely to the heaven of the Royal Academy of Music, while he, innocent Cain that he was, had been consigned to the outer darkness of the rat-infested blacking warehouse. She learned and flourished and received prizes, while he, abandoned by all the world, abandoned even by Fanny, was left to fester ignominiously in the lowest depths of hell.

Other sisters or sister surrogates repeated this pattern of betrayal and abandonment. Mary, following Fanny's example, had betrayed and deserted him: she died without a word of warning, leaving him bereft. Georgina also betrayed him: did she not change from inno-cent, adoring helpmate to workaday matron-housekeeper? The sweet, young, all-loving sylph-companion, it appears, was always leaving or eluding him. But Dickens seems to have cordoned off these darker feelings from the bright ideality of the steadfast angel-sister. The angel-sister enshrined the ideal; the betrayals and abandonments that dimmed that ideal were banished, or rather transformed. The suppressed anger that surrounded these betrayals and abandonments (in using the words "betrayals" and "abandonments," I adopt here, as I have in the last paragraph or two, the language of Dickens' emotions), did enter Dickens' writings, but separately from the yearned-for angel-sister. One way that anger entered, as "Dickens and Cannibalism" demonstrates, was through the fearsome magnifications of his dark cannibalistic fantasies, fantasies that threaten sisters as well as mothers.

But to return to Dickens' idealization of his real-life brother-sister relationships, such relationships, purged of their dross, purged also of their coarser realities, supplied the need he felt for intense, close, devoted female companionship unalloyed—or seemingly unalloyed—by egoistic self-interest, divided loyalties, petty carping, or crass sexuality. Such idealized relationships, etherealized re-creations of reality, provide the prototype for one ideal of womanhood he yearned for and also wrote about—a young, innocent, spiritual, adoring (and adored) angel-companion, the insubstantial sylph that haunts his early and middle novels. This angel-companion is in marked contrast to her dangerous counterpart: the pert, flirtatious charmer and seductress. The latter embodiment of womanhood, the nonsisterly temptress, who also haunts Dickens' pages—she is cast in a greater variety of guises and disguises but in fewer numbers than her angel-foil—is the sexual woman. The sexual woman is adorable and bewitching, but in the early and middle works she is not what she later becomes; she is not a *femme fatale*.

What Dickens yearned for most in his own daily life was a woman who combined these attributes; yet the way he defined each image of womanhood made combination impossible, or at least fraught with conflict and discord. To preserve the virginal angel, one must banish the alluring seductress; to embrace the alluring seductress,

109. Georgina Hogarth c. 1870, Age Forty-Three

Portrait based upon a studio photograph. From a photograph, T. W. Tyrrell Collection, Dickens House Museum, London.

one must forgo the virginal angel. After all, one cannot be innocent and knowing, virginal and sexual, ethereal and earthy, angelic and seductive at the same time. This is to make Dickens' dilemma very simple and schematic when in reality it was very complex and shaded, but in his fictions Dickens often projects these polarities—typical Victorian polarities—with startling purity.

In *David Copperfield,* for example, Dora is the alluring seductress, Agnes the sisterly angel. They are doubles, as Dickens takes pains to show us, but doubles who embody antipodal yearnings in David. David satisfies both yearnings, first marrying Dora, then Agnes. But what is noteworthy is that he cannot satisfy both yearnings at once. When he possesses Dora, Agnes can only wait patiently in the wings; and before he can possess Agnes, Dora must die. Dora is body (her name echoes "adorable" and "adoration" in its sexual connotations), while Agnes is soul (her name signifies "chaste" and also "lamb," and, by triple association, chaste lamb of God—St. Agnes was a virgin martyr). The implications conveyed by these names, and by Dickens' many other explicit and implicit signalings, are clear. In the calculus of *Copperfield,* body and soul cannot be combined. But even so, body in these pre–"Bride's Chamber" works rarely means sexual passion. As in *Copperfield,* where David's infatuation with Dora is translated into airy romance and her sexual allure emerges only by implication or in an occasional whispered hint, so also in the other pre–"Bride's Chamber" works: sexual passion is effaced or transformed.

In the intense devotion between brother and sister (or brother and sister surrogates), sexual passion is, by definition, not a consideration, for brother-sister love is (supposedly) free of any sexual taint. This immaculate purity breaks down occasionally, most notably in a bedroom scene in *Hard Times* between Tom and Louisa Gradgrind, but Tom's exploitive love and Louisa's self-wounding love are both products of a perverted starvation of the emotions; their love demonstrates the results of such starvation—it is part of Dickens' arraignment of the warped (and warping) philosophy of fact (*HW* 9: *HT,* 24:457–58). Usually, however, Dickens uses his brother-sister characters to portray a loving closeness and passionate attachment of unalloyed purity and spirituality, a closeness that often shows a selfless sister sacrificing, nobly as Dickens lets us know, to serve a beloved and worthy brother. These intense relationships go far beyond normal brother-sister affection. They are fervent evocations of intimacy and ideality—fantasies, one would think, of sisters Dickens always yearned for, knew briefly, but never could keep. (In real life perfect sisterhood never lasted long: Dickens' sisters and surrogate sisters left him or died or became ordinary workaday mortals.)

In many of the novels, especially the early ones, the brother-sister relationships are more important than the lover relationships. The brother-sister relationships occupy the greater part of the book; the lover relationships (when they occur) often emerge at the very end of the book, as a sort of distanced, low-key reward (so it would seem) for fervent, long-enduring brotherhood or sisterhood. Sometimes the brother, or more often the sister, in a saintly gesture, gives up all thought of marriage in order to serve his or her sibling for life (as with Harriet Carker in *Dombey and Son*); at other times, at the very end of the book, the loyal brother or sister does marry, but the unmarried sibling is then brought to live with the newly married pair and becomes part of an innocent and idyllic *ménage à trois,* a third partner in a permanent union of perfect felicity (as with Tom Pinch in *Martin Chuzzlewit*).

A special problem arises, however, in those fictional instances in which Dickens wishes to transform a brother-sister relationship into a lover relationship. This occurs, for example, with Walter and Florence in *Dombey and Son* and David and Agnes in *David Copperfield*. Both Walter and David in the earlier portions of the novels, are made surrogate brothers—Dickens makes their brotherhood explicit and emphasizes it—so that, when each falls in love with his future wife, he torments himself with self-accusations of disloyal brotherhood. As a matter of fact, owing to his brotherly status, at first each hero is unable to approach his future wife as a lover. How can he profane the radiant spirituality of his brotherly love with the black sin of forbidden—that is, incestuous—sexuality? (Dickens makes this conflict explicit as well.) It is only after each has subdued his brotherhood (a process accompanied by much confusion and by feelings of betrayal) that he can confess his love and consummate it. Yet that later love always perpetuates a brotherly-sisterly aura, an aura that sanctifies and spiritualizes the union. In such unions sexual passion emerges not as something physical and urgent, but (à la Walter and David) as something ineffably harmonious, a quietus of intimacy and spiritual bliss.

A variation of the brother turned lover is the reverse: a lover becomes a brother. Thus, Richard Wardour, the disaffected lover of *The Frozen Deep* (a part played and largely written by Dickens), at the very end of the play, as he dies, transforms his impermissible and tormented sexual love for Clara (who is betrothed to the rival he has saved) into sanctioned brotherly love: "I may rest now—I may sleep at last—the task is done, the struggle is over. . . . My sister, Clara!—Kiss me, sister, kiss me before I die!" (*FD*, 3: 158, 160). Note that Richard Wardour—his rival saved, his sacrifice made, his task done, like Sydney Carton after him, his rival saved, his sacrifice made, and his task done—"may rest now," his "struggle is over." The struggle in each case has been to transform the violence and despair of unrequited sexual passion into the peace and sublimity of selfless spiritual love, represented here by the serene purity and sanctified unselfishness of perfect brother-sister love. Richard Wardour goes to his far, far better rest (he has earned that rest) with a chaste sisterly kiss (he has earned that kiss), just as Sydney Carton goes to his far, far better rest (he too has earned that rest) with a chaste brotherly kiss (he too has earned that kiss), the chasteness of Carton's kiss accentuated by Lucie being unconscious.

If we turn from the rarified realm of the brother-sister-lover configuration in Dickens' life and works (that configuration is suggested here in briefest shorthand only) to his two important early loves—Maria Beadnell and Catherine Hogarth—we can discern other shaping influences on his depiction of passion. Maria Beadnell was the first great romantic love of Dickens' life. He met and fell in love with her when he was eighteen and she close to twenty, and he adored her from then till he broke up with her three years later, no longer able to cope with her manipulation of his affections, her swings in mood and role from flirtatious allure to cold indifference. There is no doubt that Dickens loved Maria to distraction. His dazed adoration of her (without its darker shadows) is depicted, as Dickens himself affirmed in middle age (15 February 1855), in David Copperfield's euphoric courtship of Dora. But Dickens' youthful love letters to Maria demonstrate that, despite his sincerity and total commitment, he was also (quite unconsciously) playing, and often savoring, a banal, self-deceiving, self-dramatizing role. When he wooed her he felt, and acted, and spoke as the impassioned courtier of stage and romance, and when the end came he adopted the stance, the language, and the attributes of the high romantic lover, wearing his heart upon his sleeve, tormented by his lady-love, but nobly true to his troth, and suffering his melancholy fate with undying, though tragic, devotion.

His letters dramatize these roles. His letters are filled with the stilted clichés of lofty literary lovemaking and love breaking, with remarks such as, my feelings for you are "as strong and as good as ever warmed the human heart," and "nothing will ever afford me more real delight than to hear that you the object of my first, and my last love, are happy" (18 March [1833]). There are hosts of similar remarks; such avowals are usually turgid, trite, self-conscious, and self-pitying. He tells Maria that loss of her love has made him "the miserable reckless wretch I am" ([14 May 1833]); he affirms that "I have no hopes to express no wishes to communicate. . . . I have been so long used to inward wretchedness, and real, real, misery that it matters little very little to me what others may think of or what becomes of me" ([14 May 1833]); he declares that "destitute as I am of hope or comfort I have borne much and I dare say can bear more" ([16 May 1833]); and finally, at the very end of the long affair, after saying that he will allow "no feeling of pride no haughty dislike" stand in the way of a self-abasing attempt at reconciliation, he confesses, "I never have loved and I never can love any

110. Maria Beadnell as a Young Woman

From the *Sphere* (20 February 1909). Newspaper Library, British Library, London.

human creature breathing but yourself" ([19 May 1833]). (One catches in such statements something of the tone and mood— sometimes the very phrases—of Sydney Carton, created thirty-five years later.) It is as though Dickens could only express his love and misery in the turgid language and stale formulas of literary romance and stage rhetoric. This is not to say that he did not feel this love deeply—he did, and it had a profound effect upon his life; it is to say that he translated his passion into phrases and formulas that conventionalized his feelings. It was a way of escaping his feelings. It was also a way of triumphing over them. Passion became a role that he played rather than an emotion that mastered and subdued him.

When Dickens met and fell in love with Catherine Hogarth a year and a half later, and then married her little more than a year after that, he was no longer the noble, self-sacrificing literary hero enslaved by love. He loved Catherine truly, deeply, but not in a way that put him at the mercy of her whims and commands. When, shortly after their engagement, she began to display incipient symptoms of the Beadnell syndrome, to be cold to him for some perceived slight or disappointment, he rebuked her (steeled, no doubt, by the Beadnell experience) and told her that if she could not be constant in her love for him they had better part. ("If . . . my society has wearied you, do not trifle with me, using me like any other toy as suits your humour for the moment; but make the acknowledgment to me frankly at once—I shall not forget you lightly, but you will need no second warning" [May 1835].) Catherine tearfully and humbly capitulated.

But it was not simply Dickens' role that had changed, the whole quality of the romance had changed. Dickens was now dominant, and he displayed a certain ultimate reserve or withholding. Yet, despite this, he conducted his courtship in a much more realistic, down-to-earth, playful, and affectionate way. Gone are the stilted glooms and affirmations of the literary lover, in their place are the distracting concerns of everyday life, endearing names, and occasional phrases of baby talk. Dickens, as even the baby talk attests, had matured. He had become more worldly and self-confident; he

111. Catherine Dickens in 1846, Age Thirty-One

Detail from an engraving after a painting (1846) by Daniel Maclise.

had also become—the two changes are not incompatible—more easy and more controlled. He would no longer make himself vulnerable as he had with Maria Beadnell. He would rein himself in. By avoiding violent delights, he would avoid violent ends. These were not considered decisions but instinctive reactions. (Many years later, but before the coming of Ellen, Dickens wrote to Maria: "My entire devotion to you, and the wasted tenderness of those hard years which I have ever since half loved, half dreaded to recall, made so deep an impression on me that I refer to it a habit of suppression which now belongs to me, which I know is no part of my original nature, but which makes me chary of showing my affections, even to my children, except when they are very young" [22 February 1855].)

What all this suggests is that, prior to meeting Ellen Ternan, Dickens had not experienced sexual passion in the way of the late novels; he had not grappled with its wilder or darker manifestations; he had not felt its full power to overwhelm or destroy. Confronted by a recalcitrant love and then by a submissive one, he had in each case pulled back: in the first, transforming his passion into heroic role-playing; in the second, curbing his passion by setting inner and outer limits. On both occasions he had protected himself; he had reined in, displaced, and transformed.

One can see a striking instance of how he transformed (and also screened) his experiences if one glances at his second rendezvous with Maria. Maria had dropped out of his life in 1833. Subsequently she had married and become a mother. Then, in 1855, more than twenty-one years after their parting and little more than two years before the thunderclap of Ellen and "The Bride's Chamber," Maria suddenly wrote to him. Upon receiving her letter, Dickens instantly winged back to the old enchanted days. The mists of what had once been rose before him and engulfed his being. For an interval of weeks he reinvoked his old lost dream of love, but when he did so he viewed that long-vanished dream (or supposedly long-vanished dream) not as disillusioning or destructive or painful but as wonderfully constructive (as, indeed, in many ways it was). In an ecstatic burst of hyperbole, he wrote to Maria:

Whatever of fancy, romance, energy, passion, aspiration and determination belong to me, I never have separated and never shall separate from the hard-hearted little woman—you—whom it is nothing to say I would have died for, with the greatest alacrity! . . . It is a matter of perfect certainty to me that I began to fight my way out of poverty and obscurity, with one perpetual idea of you. . . . The most innocent, the most ardent, and the most disinterested days of my life had you for their Sun . . . and . . . I know that the Dream I lived in did me good, refined my heart, and made me patient and persevering. (15 February 1855)

How should we read this extraordinary avowal? According to Dickens, assessing the experience in retrospect, his first love affair—so frustrating and wounding at the time, so warping and scarring in its lingering aftermath—did him nothing but good.

For a while in the winter of 1855 Dickens believed in this euphoric assessment. Caught up in the bliss of his reawakened rapture, he saw everything in a radiant light. In the interval between Maria's unexpected reincarnation and his first excited remeeting with her, he wrote to her several times. His letters grew more and more ardent. Warmed by the embers of his still-glowing dream so suddenly and so miraculously rekindled, he filled his letters with superlatives or with the soft, melting cadences of an ineffable tenderness. He spoke to Maria of his "old passion." He told her there was "no woman in the world, and there were very few men, who could ever imagine how much" he had loved her (22 February 1855). When she wrote that she had really loved him long ago, he replied that when he "read in the old hand what I never read before," he was overcome with emotion and with "the old tenderness softened to a more sorrowful remembrance" (22 February 1855). To her demurrer that she was now "toothless, fat, old and ugly," he replied, "I don't believe [it]." "Remember," he wrote, concluding a long, fervent letter, "I accept all with my whole soul, and reciprocate all" (22 February 1855). But Maria's sense of what she now was triumphed over Dickens' sense of what she had once been. When they met a few weeks later, he found her fat, foolish, and forty-five, and the reawakened dream of felicity faded in the light of common day. The enchanting

112. Maria Beadnell about the Time of
Her Remeeting with Dickens

From an engraving after a photograph (c. 1855–60).

young Dora of *David Copperfield* became, only months after that disillusioning remeeting, the pathetic middle-aged Flora of his new novel, *Little Dorrit*. Poor deluded Flora! Good-hearted but scatter-brained, she lives in her own (not Clennam's and not Dickens') waking dream.[22]

The point to notice here is that Dickens' initial response to Maria's reappearance was a glowing, virtually unshadowed appraisal of what she had meant to him. Passion, as Dickens recalled and remade it, leads to higher and better things—to noble goals, purity of heart, patience, and perseverence. This strategy of re-creation (largely unconscious but impelled by his strongest yearnings and fears) is a hallmark of Dickens' early and middle treatments of passion. In these early and middle works, the pre–"Bride's Chamber" works, sexual passion is always transformed or screened or displaced—or it is given a conventionalized or a benign habit. It is translated into romantic postures and sounding literary rhetoric (as with Maria in the time of their falling off) or into summerdawn dreams of rosy bliss (as with Maria and Catherine in the earlier stages of their romances) or into warm, sometimes comic, often sentimental, but never impassioned domesticity (as with Catherine); or, greatest transformation of all, for here passion has been purged (or at least overtly purged) of its dross and sexual taint, into the close but innocent fervencies of idealized brother-sister love (as in the examples already detailed).

XIV

The turning point in Dickens' treatment of overwhelming sexual passion came at the time of his infatuation with Ellen, his writing "The Bride's Chamber" (where it is manifest), and the breakup of his marriage. The coming together of the changing times (changing perspectives, mores, interests, reticences) with his own changed ways and being—with his deepening art, darkening outlook, and profound personal experience of passion—produced the matrix out of which his late portraits of sexual passion (invariably tormented passion) grew. After that coming together, and after "The Bride's Chamber," every novel, contains a portrait of tormented passion.

That tangled coming together contributed crucially to "The Bride's Chamber"; it also contributed crucially (along with other interwoven strands) to such post–"Bride's Chamber" novels as *A Tale of Two Cities* and *Great Expectations,* especially to the frustrated passion of Sydney Carton and Pip Pirrip. It may seem, however, that Dickens' last two novels, *Our Mutual Friend* and *Edwin Drood,* with their portraits of murderous passion, of passion totally out of control, are another matter. After all, Dickens did not murder his wife, and his passion was never totally out of control. But this is to draw analogies too literally and superficially. The portraits in *Our Mutual Friend* and *Edwin Drood* hark back (in the first instance, more than six years, in the second, more than twelve) to Dickens' first profound literary expression of guilt-filled passion and wild destruction—hark back, that is, to "The Bride's Chamber" and its more enlarged and expressionistic rendering of dark inner emotions.

The likenesses here are profound, yet there are critical differences as well. In *Our Mutual Friend* and *Edwin Drood* (unlike in "The Bride's Chamber"), the dark emotions are conveyed through the familiar rather than the marvelous; they are conveyed, in other words, through scenes and personages of everyday life, not through ghosts, revelatory lightning bolts, and everlasting torments. But despite this great change, the portraits in the novels are no less overwhelming in their intensity and no less devastating in their destructiveness than the portraits in "The Bride's Chamber." In this respect, "The Bride's Chamber," *Our Mutual Friend,* and *Edwin Drood* are similar rather than different. Dickens achieves this magic through sleight of hand. In *Our Mutual Friend* and *Edwin Drood* the commonplace remains commonplace, but Dickens forces us, as he so often does, to see that familiar reality with eyes that penetrate beneath the mundane surface of things. As in the culminating scene in *Our Mutual Friend* between Lizzie and Headstone, the ordinary gradually becomes extraordinary, the everyday slowly metamorphoses into the cosmic. We are still in the matter-of-fact world of veritable London pavements and veritable London railings, of ordinary London churches and ordinary London graveyards, of everyday love declared and everyday love rejected; but we are also, without realizing it, guided by the presiding symbolism that now emerges from those matter-of-fact places, objects, and interactions (iron bars, prisonlike paving stones, untended tombstones [Headstones], frantic wrenchings at the stony abode of death), back once more in the realm of transcendental signs, titanic emotions, and unpardonable sins—the realm, in short, of universal certitudes and condign punishments. Reality remains reality, but it now transcends reality as well.

There are other differences and similarities between "The Bride's Chamber" and *Our Mutual Friend* and *Edwin Drood*. Despite disparities in genre, length, and dates of composition, all three works, when it comes to their common subject, exhibit a common ontogeny: they depict blind passion escalating into murderous rage and self-destruction. But in *Our Mutual Friend* and *Edwin Drood*, in the spacious amplitude of the novel (and distanced from the traumatic real-life moment of onset), Dickens can be more forthright, both with himself and with his reader. He no longer needs the screen and shorthand of fable and fairy tale to convey his somber message. He can tell his harrowing tale as a matter-of-fact chronicle of ordinary people and everyday life: we, not gods or demons—or, rather, we, both gods and demons—are the workaday subjects he is depicting. The amplitude of the novel also makes other explorations possible. As in *Great Expectations*, Dickens can show the social and psychological origins of the passion he is tracing, and he can develop character and interaction; in short, he can pursue slow shapings and slow unfoldings, explorations impossible in "The Bride's Chamber."

Obviously, then, though Dickens' five late portraits of sexual passion have much in common, they are far from identical. Nor are they incremental stages in a steady progression from inhibited to full expression. "The Bride's Chamber" was a reflex of the very moment of crisis. In terms of Dickens' writing, the dam burst at that moment; but the flood waters, so long contained or channeled, did not all instantly gush forth. Sydney Carton, created almost two years after "The Bride's Chamber," is a transitional figure, owing a good deal to Richard Wardour and *The Frozen Deep* and much to the high gloom and noble despair of Dickens' breakup with Maria Beadnell—that is, owing a good deal to the romantic, conventionalized, pre–"Bride's Chamber" embodiments of passion, though also owing much to the experiences and emotions of 1857 and 1858.

Pip is a full-scale portrait of sexual passion in the later mold, yet it is also the most ordinary or realistic of these later portraits in the sense of dealing with universal experiences and emotions in a mimetic manner; it is also the closest to Dickens' own life history not only in its presentation of passion but in other ways as well. To cite one brief series of examples only, the portrait of Pip is an emotionally faithful rendering of some of the deepest associations and feelings of Dickens' childhood and youth. Dickens' childhood in the Rochester region becomes Pip's childhood in the Rochester region; Dickens' "shameful" blacking-warehouse bondage becomes Pip's "shameful" blacksmith indenturing (note the "black" in both occupations); Dickens' childhood yearning for his lost gentility (lost, he thought, forever) becomes Pip's childhood yearning for a gentlemanlike gentility (as remote from his childhood grasp as a distant star). In the cases of Bradley Headstone and John Jasper, the analogues to Dickens' life, though very real, are much more expressionistic (much more like "The Bride's Chamber" in this respect) but all the more revealing as an index of Dickens' inner life because of their exaggerations and displacements. (These exaggerations and displacements, it should be noted, have no direct connection with the marvelous; though both characters, like both novels—and like all Dickens' novels—draw crucial strength from the extrarational, they are, unlike "The Bride's Chamber," rooted and steeped in the everyday.)

The kinship of *Our Mutual Friend* and *Edwin Drood* with "The Bride's Chamber," *A Tale of Two Cities*, and *Great Expectations*—kinship in passion, that is—is immediately apparent. Headstone and Jasper exhibit the same sudden, overwhelming, irresistible onslaught of passion as do the tree-climbing suitor, Carton, and Pip; they also exhibit the same obsessive love, the same frustration, the same unhappiness, the same dashed hopes. What is different in the portraits of Headstone and Jasper is the driven darkness, the savage violence and destructiveness of their unfulfilled passion. Here the histories of Headstone and Jasper (especially the symbolic dimensions of those somber histories) are not in accord with *A Tale of Two Cities* and *Great Expectations* but with "The Bride's Chamber," with those dark portions of "The Bride's Chamber" that delineate cosmic rage, towering passion, murderous assault, and everlasting guilt.

But how, exactly, are all five of these late portraits of tumultuous passion connected to Dickens' emotional life from 1857 on? Those connections—now hidden, now flaunted, now artfully transformed—emerge over and over again in these portraits, and they hark back, as one would expect, to Dickens' own tumultuous experience of overwhelming passion. Of the early days of Dickens' passion for Ellen Ternan we can glean occasional perfervid glimpses, direct glimpses such as those recorded here earlier. Of the later days we know much less. We do know, however, that the relationship—an intimate relationship of some sort—endured. The early days were filled with ecstasy, tumult, rage, infatuation, joy, guilt, frenzy, despair. Think, for a moment, not only of *The Frozen Deep* and "The Bride's Chamber," but of the despairing letters to Collins, Forster, and others, the ogre-slaying letter to Mrs. Watson, the lilac-gloved, halo-headed angel of *The Lazy Tour*, and the "little secret" of "Please to Leave Your Umbrella." But what of the period long after this—after the separation agreement, after the dislocation of the family, after the breaking of many friendships, after the shattering of business partnerships, after the subsidence of the wildness of early infatuation? What of five or ten years later, long after the summer-dawn of love and unfulfilled longing had given way to the familiar routines and everyday concerns of an established relationship?

With the exception of a few brief, longing declarations in Dickens' American letters to Wills (declarations excised in the published letters) and his solicitous instructions to a servant at the time of the Staplehurst accident, we get no firsthand glimpses of those inner feelings.[23] In other words, the full, ongoing, inmost nature of that established relationship is hidden from our view. But whatever the closeness, the happiness, and the fulfillment of those later years—and clearly (as the American asides and the Staplehurst instructions demonstrate), Dickens continued to be deeply devoted to Ellen and tenderly protective of her in those later years—we can safely assume that there was much that fell short of Dickens' idealized expectations. Like David Copperfield, and like all pursuers of ideal felicity, after Dickens had won his fairy-tale princess he would have come to feel once more that perfect felicity had somehow eluded him. How could it be otherwise? After all, the dream of ideal love is only a dream. Did not Dickens often and often say as much? Does not Pip (this long after the coming of Ellen) reiterate this truth over and over again, reiterate it, but find himself unable to refrain from endlessly pursuing his ideal love and so his ideal torment? And in *David Copperfield* (this long before the coming of Ellen), in a passage that Dickens much later related to his own life, does he not tell us how David, after marrying his adored Dora, finds himself unfulfilled; does he not describe how David comes to feel that there is "one happiness I have missed in life, and one friend and companion I have never made"? (F, 639).

Dickens continued to yearn for that one happiness, that one friend and companion. How could Ellen, how could any mortal, satisfy that celestial dream? The disparity between Dickens' dream of felicity with Ellen and its prosaic workaday fulfillment would have been profoundly disillusioning, and this despite the fact that he knew all along—knew rationally, that is, not emotionally—that the dream was only a dream. But added to such disillusionment and disappointment would be darker burdens yet, burdens, for example, of guilt—guilt surrounding his banishment of poor, supplicating, submissive Catherine, guilt hovering over the equivocal subsequent departures and nondepartures of his children, guilt over old friends he would no longer speak to or who would no longer speak to him, guilt over longtime business partners now become bitter business rivals, guilt over old ways and old days lost forever.

And then there was the direct guilt always associated with Ellen herself. For no matter how much Dickens loved her, how satisfying their relationship was—and there are also hints that this May-December liaison was less than satisfying in some respects—it was always, in the decorous eyes of the watching world, illicit and forbidden. It had to be kept secret from the world. Wherever he went with Ellen, whatever he did with her, had to be hidden or disguised, had to become part, in other words, of a constant charade of pretending and dissembling. In society's eyes, she would be, if the truth ever became known, a palpable sin, and he a palpable sinner. One can only imagine what burdens of daily guilt this situation imposed upon Dickens' later years, what sense of a dark, hidden, double life (after all, he was a preeminent celebrator of hearth, home, and family), what sense of secret sin.[24] He had to adopt such guilt-betraying and guilt-engendering stratagems as using an assumed name ("Mr. Tringham") in his secret life with Ellen, establishing discreet hideaway residences close to her inconspicuous residences in nearby but out-of-the-way suburbs (in Slough, and later in Peckham); seeking out other secluded hideaways (such as Condette in France); constantly referring to her, to Slough, to Peckham, and to other aspects of their hidden life together (even in his diaries or even, on occasion, when communicating with the few close confidants, such as Wills, who were privy to his secret) by laconic initials, code words, code designations, and code phrases, and, on special occasions (such as his trip to America), by an elaborate stratagem of prearranged secret signaling.[25]

Even Dickens' more direct avowals of his feeling for Ellen, even his more candid communications to Wills concerning her—she was, he told Wills, his "Dear Girl," his "Darling"—even such avowals had to be partially veiled (veiled for the most part, at least), had to be uneasily hedged or distanced or attenuated. Such avowals were often compromised in their very formulation, their very utterance, by outward and visible signs—uneasy signs—of lingering inward

113. Dickens' French Hideaway in the Countryside Near Condette

See, in Part 1, "Dickens and Cannibalism," the analysis of Dickens' French-Flemish journey (also Part 1, note 52); see, in the present section (Part 2), the discussion of Dickens' guilt-filled sojourns and associations with Ellen Ternan (also Part 2, note 24). Photograph (1966), Dickens House Museum, London.

guilt. While in the United States Dickens wrote to Ellen frequently, but his letters to her, unlike his letters to others, were not sent openly and directly, but sealed and enclosed in his letters to Wills. The immediate reason for this stratagem was that Ellen was visiting relations on the Continent; but lurking deeply buried in this cumbersome arrangement (for Dickens knew her addresses on the Continent) was an uneasy sense that the correspondence was equivocal and that it should be managed discreetly. (Dickens uses such words to describe Wills' oversight of the correspondence as "care," "exactness," "dispatch," and "protection.") "After this present mail," Dickens writes, "I shall address Nelly's letters to your care, for I do not quite know where she will be. But she will write to you, and instruct you where to forward them. In any interval between your receipt of one or more, and my Dear Girl's so writing to you, keep them by you" (Huntington Library MS: 21 November 1867).

Dickens' subsequent mentions of his enclosures for Ellen are invariably couched in oblique, or guarded, or formulaic language; only the letter just quoted refers to Ellen, or rather "Nelly"—Dickens' pet sobriquet for Ellen—by name. Here are some subsequent references to enclosures for Ellen: "*The enclosed letter to your care as usual*"; "Enclosed is another letter for my dear girl"; "Enclosed is another letter for my dear girl, to your usual care and exactness"; "Enclosed, another letter 'as before'"; "Enclosed, another letter as before, to your protection and dispatch"; "Another letter for my Darling, enclosed"; "'From the same to the same,' enclosed"; "Toujours from the same to the same"; "Another letter from the same to the same"; "Enclosed, another letter to your care. By next Saturday's mail, I will send *the last!*"; "One last letter enclosed" (Huntington Library MSS: 3 December 1867, 6 December 1867, 10 December 1867, 17 December 1867, Christmas Eve 1867, 30 December 1867, 25 February 1868, 28 February 1868, 16 March 1868, 14 April 1868, 17 April 1868). All of these references are omitted from published versions of the letters. Some of the references—and other similar references—are lightly canceled, some more heavily canceled, while still others, sometimes whole paragraphs, are so heavily canceled in black ink (over Dickens' blue ink) as to be readable only through infrared photography.

There are still other references to Ellen in these letters, but they are always safely elided, disguised, or (most often) totally suppressed in published versions of the letters (the published versions were initially controlled by Wills, and then, for many years after Wills' death in 1880, by his family). "I am," Dickens writes in one letter to Wills, "in capital health and voice." This glowing self-appraisal, so serene and unalloyed, ends a sentence and a paragraph in all published versions of Dickens' letter to Wills of 10 December 1867 (from New York); but the original sentence and paragraph go on as follows: "—but my spirits flutter woefully towards a certain place at which you dined one day not long before I left, with the present writer and a third (most drearily missed) person" (Huntington Library MS: 10 December 1867). (Note, once more, the typically indirect nature of Dickens' reference to Ellen.) Or, yet again, two weeks later, here is another suppressed avowal of his longing for Ellen (suppressed, that is, in published versions of the letter), an avowal that evokes once more (but only for Wills' eyes and for Wills' contemplation) the ardor of his commitment to Ellen and the intensity of his yearning for her. Once again she is "woefully" absent, and once more she is "drearily missed": "Enclosed, another letter as before, to your protection and dispatch. I would give £3,000 down (and think it cheap) if you could forward *me*, for four and twenty hours only, instead of the letter" (Huntington Library MS: Christmas Eve 1867). Or again, two months later, the following familiar lament: "You will have seen too (I hope) my dear Patient, and will have achieved in so doing what I would joyfully give a Thousand Guineas to achieve myself at this present moment!" (Huntington Library MS: 21 February 1868; for an explanation of the "Patient" reference, see Part 3, "Dickens and Necessity," note 7).

These equivocal and guilt-laden yearnings, concealments, and circumlocutions (yearnings concealed to all but a favored few and deemed by Dickens and those favored few to be sufficiently scandalous to require rigorous and permanent suppression), these guilt-laden yearnings and dissemblings were part of his daily life, not just while in the United States and thousands of miles away from Ellen, but part of his daily being, part of his waking and breathing, part of his moment-to-moment existence whether together with Ellen or apart. His hidden relationship with Ellen may have been comfortable and full of solace for the most part; their time together may have been rejuvenating, uplifting, even exalted; but that unsanctioned relationship and those clandestine interludes together could not be open and could not be free.

Furthermore, Dickens could not conceal from himself the equivocal nature of their relationship. The radiant aura of sweet innocent adoration that he had cast round Ellen in the first weeks and months of his infatuation eventually faded into the sober light of ordinary day. How could that ideal vision have failed to fade? How could it have remained undimmed by years of ordinary workaday living, let alone by years of dissimulation and guilt? The early image of a pure, immaculate, halo-headed Ellen, kin to that still earlier image of a pure, immaculate, ministering angel (the yearned-for, adoring, and adored sister-daughter-lover figure that he had conjured up from his need-filled re-creations of Fanny, Mary, Georgina, Christiana, and the others) had gradually given way to a darker vision, a double yet undivided vision, at once clear-eyed and self-aware yet full of passionate longing. For Dickens had changed; or at least his insights had changed. He no longer saw himself as disjointed and separate, oscillating from one emotional extreme to another, in one phase a shining fairy-tale champion, in another a dark Satanic monster. Rather, he now saw himself as a more complicated, intermingled, perplexed creature, a creature rife with inward and outward contradictions. He was, at one and the same time, a truth-teller and a dissembler, a patron and an exploiter, a model and a reprobate. Most disturbing of all, he was, again at one and the same time, a blissful lover and a secret sinner, a poor, blind human atom driven and derided by a passion he could not deny and dare not profess— that is, dare not publicly profess. These stressful contradictions, with

Ellen as their most palpable embodiment, were at the center of his emotional life in these latter years. Whatever joy and whatever darkness Ellen brought into his days and nights—and she must have brought great joy and grievous darkness—one thing is certain: the tumultuous events of 1857 and 1858 cut a deep swath across his existence. Everything we know about Dickens tells us this. After that upheaval the world was more somber and more full of painful knowledge.[26]

Some of these night-side feelings flowed into the portraits of Headstone and Jasper.[27] In those fictionalized renderings, these secret inner emotions, driven and divided emotions, are magnified and extended. This is not surprising. After all, it is only natural that the very center of Dickens' emotional life, the innermost feelings of his later years, should enter and color his writings. How had this taken place? How had autumn passion changed his life and shaped his writings? Had it produced the ennobling effects that he attributed to his springtime love for Maria Beadnell? Quite the contrary. What more monitory, what more devastating pattern could he have of debasement rather than ennoblement, of outward seeming hiding inward truth, than his own daily life after 1857? Was not the upright, moral Dickens (truly upright and truly moral) compelled by illicit passion; was he not an emblem of outward rectitude concealing inward sin?

That sense of concealed sin and the profound guilt that flowed from it creeps into his latter-day writings over and over again. Sometimes it emerges in startling ways, ways that, in typical Dickens fashion, reveal the inmost depths, the secret ecstasy or the secret sin, even as those revelations conceal what they reveal. In *Edwin Drood*, when Neville comes under suspicion of being what Jasper in reality is, he tells us that he feels "marked and tainted." " 'I cannot persuade myself,' " he confesses to Mr. Crisparkle, " 'that the eyes of even the stream of strangers I pass in this vast city look at me without suspicion' " (*ED*, 17:134). He thinks of ways of escaping from himself, of assuming another identity. " 'If I could have changed my name,' " he tells Mr. Crisparkle, " 'I would have done so. But as you

114. Ellen Ternan c. 1867, Age Twenty-Eight

This portrait was probably taken a year or two after Dickens had completed *Our Mutual Friend* and a year or two before he began *Edwin Drood;* it probably dates, in other words, from the time that Dickens was writing *George Silverman's Explanation,* another work that, like *Our Mutual Friend* and *Edwin Drood,* bears, in many profound ways, the guilt-filled imprint of his liaison with Ellen Ternan (see Part 3, "Dickens and Necessity"). From a photograph. Enthoven Collection, Victoria and Albert Museum, London.

wisely pointed out to me, I can't do that, for it would look like guilt'" (*ED*, 17:134). Dickens wrote these words, as the ink color of this portion of the manuscript indicates, while staying at Peckham near Ellen, staying there, one should remember, amidst a "stream of strangers" under the "changed . . . name" and changed identity of Mr. Tringham.[28]

What intricacies of secret knowledge, of secret self-awareness and secret self-condemnation, are implicit in this passage? At the very moment he was causing his character to speak of feeling "marked and tainted," of yearning to escape from his everyday identity, and of the guilt implicit in adopting an assumed identity and an assumed name, even in a "vast city," and even when amongst a "stream of strangers," at that very moment Dickens was writing and living in a vast city amongst a stream of strangers under an assumed identity and an assumed name. He was, moreover, doing so in the simulacrum of his guilt, that is, in the quintessential circumstances of what "would look like guilt" to that "stream of strangers"; he was in his Peckham hideaway close to Ellen. Can anyone doubt that he felt "marked and tainted" even as he wrote those Cainlike words?

Ironies and discordancies and self-arraignments such as this must have occurred hundreds and thousands of times in the daily transactions of these latter years. Enamored and enchanted like Pip or Headstone or Jasper, Dickens often felt, again like Pip or Headstone or Jasper, driven to do what he condemned himself for doing. He felt that he was a thrall of passion, of iron necessity, a thrall compelled to live and act and dissemble in a multitude of secret ways; but he also felt the deep shame and wickedness of leading such a divided life: the public life so open and esteemed, the private life (and here he is most like Headstone and Jasper) so driven, hidden, and disgraceful.[29]

This stern assessment of Dickens' situation magnifies his transgressions of the Victorian social and moral code (transgressions that seem so human and commonplace to us); but Dickens, in one unflinching portion of his soul (and in his imagination), would have magnified those transgressions too. Would he not, profound anatomist of the human soul, often and often have contemplated how he came to be caught in his own dark web, how he came, after so much living and so many victories—scarcely rivaled achievements—to be compelled and driven and searching and dissembling and never satisfied, how he came, in short, to be what he now was? Surely Headstone and Jasper, in some profound ways, are probing explorations and nightmare exaggerations of the darkest portions of Dickens' own inner life in these last years.

Think once more of the tormented Headstone, avatar of the unsuspected darkness within. Who and what is this somber creature, this stricken, passion-tossed offspring of Dickens' latter-day imagination? He is certainly not what he seems to be. What could be more unsuspected and untoward than Headstone's riven doubleness? And what could be a more devastating commentary on Dickens' own hidden doubleness? This decent, respected schoolmaster, decent and respected to outward view, but inwardly the passionate pursuer of a young reluctant love, is a man disguised to the world and, at the end, disguised for murder's sake (for her sake) in the lowly trappings of a bargeman, the coarse costume of his dark alter ego, the veritable garment of his hidden self. Or, yet again, Dickens' secret double life is given nightmare exaggeration in Jasper's secret double life. What could be more hidden and untoward than Jasper's riven doubleness? And what could be more revelatory of Dickens' hidden feelings? This decent, respected choirmaster, decent and respected to outward view, but inwardly the passionate pursuer of a young reluctant love (he will murder for her), is a man, when we first meet him, soon to sing sweetly in the sanctified cathedral, but sprawled now (demon shadow of his choir self) upon a ramshackle bed in Princess Puffer's hellish opium den—a shocking duality that is the essence of his existence. These nightmare similitudes, enlarged and extended versions of Dickens' own hidden life and guilt-filled doubleness, are reinforced by other parallels. Dickens' sense of the destructiveness of overwhelming single-minded passion, passion that can obliterate wives, friends, businesses, the whole fabric of one's life, and his sense of the grievous sin involved in such headlong pursuit, is not only magnified in Headstone and Jasper but carried to its utmost stretch; that is, it is carried to uttermost destructiveness and primal sin, to murder (murder, in Jasper's case, of his nearest kin, his "dear boy") and to self-annihilation. This is not to say that Dickens saw himself as a hidden monster or a passion-driven murderer, though at times, propelled by guilt, he certainly felt, as much ancillary evidence makes clear, like a pariah-criminal; it is simply to suggest that these latter-day portraits are magnifications of dark forces in his own soul: frightening and abhorrent forces that he had come to recognize and to acknowledge; compelling and destructive forces that he had seen unloosed; imperious and malignant forces that he had bent to and had brooded over in his later years.

These night-side forces were not the whole Dickens or even the primary Dickens. Dickens continued to exult in rollicking humor, absurdity, and playfulness; he continued to be concerned with social reform, social improvement, education, and good works; he continued to celebrate simple virtues, quiet goodness, and redemptive love; he continued to be life-affirming and compassionate. All these characteristics were at the center of his life and art. But the dark strand that was woven through his life from his earliest days—the strand of early disorder, blacking-warehouse servitude, parental resentment (especially of his mother), baffled teen-aged love, lingering manhood shame and anger, and latter-day passion, dissembling, and guilt—that dark strand is there too, a somber thread, dusky and disturbing, but obscured for the most part by brighter strands and richer colors. The genial, warm, sympathetic Dickens predominates, but the other Dickens—the driven passionate Dickens who is the subject of this section, who is the subject, in one way or another, of the entire book—that Dickens is also present, a somber shadow darkening the obscure depths.

That somber shadow or (to change the metaphor) that somber cluster of intertwined forces—compelling forces of sexual passion, frustrated aggression, blind self-destruction, and profound guilt—found their first full fictional rendering in "The Bride's Chamber." There these subterranean forces, lifted to the surface, lifted simulta-

neously to the level of fable and myth, were given cosmic significance. Emotions that Dickens had always curtailed in his writings
were now loosed in a new way. That commingling and that release
paved the way for much that came thereafter. Think once more of
that violent, guilt-filled tale that Dickens wrote in those tumultuous
early fall days of 1857. With its young impassioned tree-climbing
suitor, its old inflexible murderous husband, its vulnerable flaxen-
haired teen-aged heroine-victim (named Ellen); with its driven
characters, titanic rages, unpardonable sins, and everlasting punishments; with its riven skulls and riven trees, riven as Dickens' emotions were riven; with all this and much more, and all applied by
Dickens to himself, for he and only he is told the admonitory tale
and runs, haunted, down the dark staircase—because of all this, and
for additional reasons detailed earlier, "The Bride's Chamber" is a
seminal work. It commingles new themes and urges, or rather,
newly expressed themes and urges, that Dickens would now explore
over and over again. The driven suitor, divided and enslaved, baffled
and tormented by passion, yearning for sexual fulfillment, blind
with stifled rage, propelled into violence, rushing toward self-
destruction, riddled with guilt, would appear like an unquiet ghost
in every novel that came thereafter.

XV

Paradoxically, it is both strange and natural that this unquiet ghost
should first rise up in "The Bride's Chamber." It is strange when one
thinks of the story's journalistic occasion, swift conception, rapid
rendition, and taut brevity. The story combines local color with
spellbinding diablerie, the latter element a change of pace to fill and
diversify the pages of a travel series. The sauntering occasion, the
insouciant manner, the goal of entertainment—all these seem remote from consuming passion and fathomless guilt. Yet it is natural,
too, that the ghost of Dickens' sudden passion should rise up just
then, natural when one realizes that the story was written at a moment of supreme crisis in Dickens' life. Through the vehicle of the
story he could release (in part he could assuage) a tumult of con-

flicting emotions, emotions that had risen up so swiftly and unaccountably, emotions that had gripped and compelled him, emotions that had become entwined with a vital series of linked associations, some old some new. This passionate moment, and the passionate experiences that lay behind it, allowed—even forced—Dickens to express the emotions that were rending him, an expression that embodied for him a new and newly evocative configuration, a configuration that would reappear hereafter—stigmata of his passion—in all his major works.

"The Bride's Chamber," like any work of art, imposes order and meaning on the random welter of experience—on the author's experience and (once we have internalized the story) on our experience—and on his and our tangled, often conflicting responses to experience. What distinguishes "The Bride's Chamber" is not that it does this but that it does it with such passionate intensity. What also distinguishes the story is the expressionistic vehicle that Dickens fashioned to render that intensity. He forged his vehicle cunningly. Only the cosmic heightenings of the Gothic, the sentient signalings of the fairy tale, and the compressed summations of the short story could express in so brief a compass the wild heights and dark depths of the tumultuous feelings—the night-side feelings—he needed to dramatize. Dickens surely accomplished what he set out to do. Though "The Bride's Chamber" is virtually unknown, its central story is one of the most haunting and chilling tales that he ever wrote, a small, disturbing masterpiece that speaks in fairy-tale tropes of forbidden passion, unpardonable sin, and eternal retribution. These are mighty matters. But what of their unlikely origins? Those origins can only make us wonder at the mysteries of creation. Out of boyhood apparitions and manhood news stories, out of childhood reading and youthful playgoing, out of criminal trials and Hanging Corner visits, out of heroic acting and bridecake dining, out of domestic misery and undomestic euphoria, out of fairy-tale fantasies and murderous impulses—above all, out of ecstatic passion and tormenting guilt—he wove his dark web of life's shadowy entanglements.

That tangled web is a good metaphor for "The Bride's Chamber"

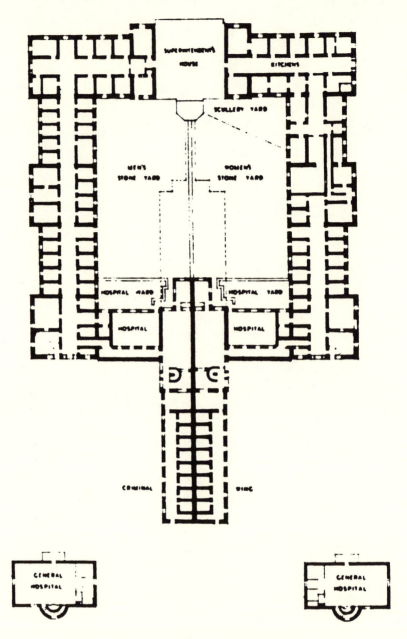

115. Lancaster Lunatic Asylum: Plan of
the Wards Visited by Dickens

"One gallery . . . looked to me about the length of the Long Walk at Windsor." Dickens is referring to the long, uninterrupted ward shown on the left in the above plan, a men's ward, empty when Dickens visited it, except for the "meagre man." The buildings shown here (built in 1816 and 1824) still exist virtually as Dickens saw them, though this core of buildings has been extended. H. E. Davies and H. H. Davies, *Lancaster Mental Hospital: Survey 1939* (Privately Circulated), 4.

426

and for Dickens' art. For in "The Bride's Chamber" Dickens set out, both consciously and unconsciously, to untangle as best he could some of the chaotic threads of image and event, feeling and passion, that were enmeshing him, trace their dim underlying patterns, and weave them anew. As a man he was searching for meaning; as an artist he was creating it. Dickens knew this. He knew that all men, great or lowly, brilliant or dull, sane or insane, must puzzle out, as best they can, life's inscrutable weavings. Perhaps Dickens had this metaphor in mind when he sat down to write "The Bride's Chamber." In the outermost framework, the Goodchild-Idle framework, of the "The Bride's Chamber," Dickens, re-creating his Lancaster experiences, describes the visit he has just paid to the nearby County Lunatic Asylum.[30] As he recalls the visit, his tone changes and he seems to be musing to himself. He sketches the long corridors of blighted men and women, their hopeless faces staring vacantly at one another; but then, as he goes into an otherwise empty ward, another long ward, long as "the Long Walk at Windsor," he notices a "poor little dark-chinned, meagre man, with a perplexed brow and a pensive face, stooping low over the matting on the floor, and picking out with his thumb and fore-finger the course of its fibres" (*HW* 16: BC, 385). All day long the meager man pores compulsively over the matting, oblivious of the larger world. Now the day is waning. The afternoon sun slants through the windows and cell doors, and checkers the long avenue of the empty ward with patches of light and shade. As Dickens and his conductor approach the solitary man, he does not pause in his contemplation. The conductor gently suggests to the poor, perplexed man that he go to his room and read or lie down. The little man thinks for a moment, then answers that he will go and read, and he shuffles off to his tiny cell.

This encounter occupies considerable space in Dickens' narrative framework, and its continuation occupies considerable additional space. The episode seems at first to be an unaccountable digression; one wonders why Dickens dragged the perplexed man and the lunatic asylum into his bantering framework. But then Dickens contin-

116. Lancaster Lunatic Asylum: Interior of the Ward of the "Meagre Man"

"The afternoon sun was slanting in at the large end-window, and there were cross patches of light and shade all down the vista, made by the unseen windows and the open doors of the little sleeping cells on either side. In about the centre of the perspective, under an arch, . . . was the poor little dark-chinned, meagre man." (See Part 2, note 30.) Photograph (1987) by the author.

ues his account of the waning day, the long ward, and the "poor little dark-chinned, meagre man," and we realize that Dickens, in describing the meager man and his tangled web of inscrutable matting, is describing himself, describing the reader, and describing the task he is about to undertake as he begins "The Bride's Chamber":

> I turned my head before we had gone many paces. He had already come out again, and was again poring over the matting, and tracking out its fibres with his thumb and fore-finger. I stopped to look at him, and it came into my mind, that probably the course of those fibres as they plaited in and out, over and under, was the only course of things in the whole wide world that it was left to him to understand—that his darkening intellect had narrowed down to the small cleft of light which showed him, "This piece was twisted this way, went in here, passed under, came out there, was carried on away here to the right where I now put my finger on it, and in this progress of events, the thing was made and came to be here." Then, I wondered whether he looked into the matting, next, to see if it could show him anything of the process through which *he* came to be there, so strangely poring over it. Then, I thought how all of us, GOD help us! in our different ways are poring over our bits of matting, blindly enough, and what confusions and mysteries we make in the pattern. I had a sadder fellow-feeling with the little dark-chinned, meagre man, by that time, and I came away. (*HW* 16: BC, 386)

Part 3
Dickens and Necessity

117. Charles Dickens in 1868, Age Fifty-Six

From a photograph taken in America at the time that *George Silverman's Explanation* (which was first published in the United States) was appearing there. Engraving after a photograph (1868) by Ben Gurney.

Dickens and Necessity
The Long Chain

> Pause you who read this,
> and think for a moment
> of the long chain of iron or gold,
> of thorns or flowers,
> that would never have bound you,
> but for the formation of the first link
> on one memorable day.
>
> —*Great Expectations*

I

How do we become what we are? What are the forces that shape and impel us? These are questions that preoccupied Dickens.[1] At first he gave simple answers—even glib or superficial ones—to these questions. But as his experience of life and his art grew his answers became more probing, and also more tentative. These evolving answers are scattered through his writings, but nowhere does he confront these fundamental questions of human existence more directly or with greater insight than in *George Silverman's Explanation*. This little-known work, familiar primarily to experts, deserves the closest scrutiny.[2] It is the most succinct embodiment in all Dickens' writings of his late art and thought. In particular, it is his most mature grappling with the question of free will and necessity and with a tangle of associated puzzlements. But the story has another, very special importance. It is not only his culminating statement on such issues, but his last; for *George Silverman's Explanation* is the last work of fiction that Dickens completed. It thus offers us an opportunity to examine Dickens' mature art and thought in an unusually concentrated form, and to do so in great depth. It also offers us an opportunity, given its strategic perspective, to take a fresh look at some of Dickens' early and late writings, especially those which raise the issues of free will and necessity, and to reassess those works in the light of that culminating perspective. Finally, it offers us an opportunity to probe some of the night-side perplexities that haunted Dickens' consciousness, perplexities that shaped the inmost nature of his art.

The immediate or commercial origins of *George Silverman's Explanation* are strangely remote from its subject and its message. Indeed, those origins are doubly unusual and doubly ironic, for they are linked closely with the United States and with personal and commercial promotions. Early in 1867, Dickens agreed to write a story for Benjamin Wood, an American entrepreneur, gambler, wheeler-dealer, and member of Congress. This story—which eventually became *George Silverman's Explanation*—was to be published first in the United States, and for this priority Wood was to pay a thousand pounds, a very large sum in those days for first rights to so short a piece, equal today to well over fifty thousand dollars. (The first rights, moreover, would give priority for a very brief interval, for a matter of weeks only.) This agreement eventually fell through, and thereupon Dickens sold first-publication rights, apparently on the same terms, to his good friend, the American publisher James T. Fields of Ticknor and Fields. Ticknor and Fields owned the *Atlantic Monthly,* and Fields published *George Silverman's Explanation* in that periodical (in Volume XXI) in three installments (January, February, and March 1868), thus making the story one of the very few works by Dickens to be published first in the United States.

The appearance of the story in America was specially timed, for during its publication, Dickens was in the United States on a reading tour, and Ticknor and Fields, as planned, used the serialization of the story and the immense publicity surrounding the tour to promote their magazines and their many editions of Dickens' writings and readings. Dickens republished the story in his own weekly magazine *All the Year Round* on 1, 15, and 29 February 1868, while still in the United States. About this time, possibly while Dickens was in the United States, or perhaps during the following year when Fields spent several months in England, Dickens gave him the manuscript of *George Silverman's Explanation*. The story was not reprinted or collected in England or America in Dickens' lifetime.[3]

II

George Silverman's Explanation is a wonderful story—profound, complex, disturbing. It centers its steady gaze on free will versus necessity, but necessity of a particularly personal and inward sort. This inward necessity is a very Dickensian necessity, and it is worth pausing for a moment to consider what that Dickensian necessity was and what it was not. It was not the necessity (supposing that such exists) that determines the fate of nations; nor was it the necessity (again supposing it exists) that determines an individual's fate before or at birth. Though Dickens sometimes toyed with such concepts of necessity in a playful or marveling way, and though he sometimes used such concepts metaphorically or symbolically, such formulations of necessity were repugnant to his sense of individual responsibility and individual soul-making; he rejected a universe of mere mechanistic determinism or crass necessity. As a consequence, though one often finds in Dickens' writings (and in his daily living and thinking) invocations—or seeming invocations—of necessity, usually in a wondering or poetic or symbolic guise, these should not be taken as the proclamations of a philosophical determinist. Such invocations tend to be extempore meditations or effusions—or still slighter bows in the direction of some predetermined pattern in the lives of men and women.

To cite just one example, he could and did speak, in a vein of
bantering wonderment, a vein half-serious half-jocose, of the way in
which momentous events in his life so often occurred on a Friday.
In one literary reflection of this notion, Dickens tells us at the very
outset of *David Copperfield*—in the second sentence, as a matter of
fact—that David, Dickens' surrogate and in many ways his literal
second self, was born, portentously and bodingly, as David makes
clear, on a Friday, the day, as it happens, on which Dickens himself
was born; and when some notable event in Dickens' life did happen
to fall on a Friday, Dickens (or a member of his family) would sometimes exclaim, "Friday! Friday!" (F, 651). In such a context, this
exclamation was a mere bagatelle, an unthreatening (and largely unthinking) affirmation of something much more weighty: the mysterious and meaningful orderings of fate. Such orderings intrigued
and provoked Dickens. They teased his imagination. But that is the
point: for Dickens, the importance of such recurrences was imaginative rather than philosophical. All the family had heard Dickens
expound—expound many times—his theory of the special importance of Fridays in his life. The intertwining of Fridays with Dickens'
destiny had long since become a cherished Dickens myth and a favorite family myth (the kind of playful myth or superstition that
innumerable individuals and families held in Dickens' day and
hold today).

Such Dickensian invocations of a recurrent and patterned necessity, though strenuously proclaimed, were momentary and superficial. More important and serious were Dickens' metaphorical and
symbolic uses of necessity. Thus he sometimes had people in his
fictions meet or cross paths in ways that foreshadowed their future
interrelated destinies. In *Little Dorrit* he did more than this. He
shaped—or really reshaped—the opening in order to accentuate
such comings together and in order to foreshadow (but only dimly
and suggestively) more momentous entanglements to come. That
interweaving, Dickens determined, would be a striking and crucial
feature of the book. In his working notes for the opening of *Little
Dorrit*, Dickens summed up how this idea for a gradual intermesh-

ing—or rather, a gradual reintermeshing—of crossed paths and crossed lives would work and how that working could help organize his novel:

> People to meet and part as travellers do, and the future connexion between them in the story, not to be now shewn to the reader but to be worked out as in life. <u>Try this uncertainty and this not-putting of them together, as a new means of interest</u>. Indicate and carry through this intention. (Stone, *Working Notes*, 270–71)

Dickens' wording of this conception is curious ("uncertainty," "not-putting," etc.). His formulation of the idea shows that his chief interest in this kind of uncertain yet fated recurrence is strategic and artistic rather than philosophical, and in any event, as he executed his design, the idea as a keynote (to use Dickens' term for such central and recurrent motifs) gave way more and more to other organizing and unifying principles, to the keynote of imprisonment, for example (a keynote also strong in the opening), including inner or psychological imprisonment, a different and more congenial kind of necessity for Dickens.

Perhaps the closest Dickens came to depicting a comprehensive, external, ineluctable working of necessity was in *A Tale of Two Cities*. In that novel, the only Dickens novel driven primarily by plot, Dickens wishes to show us how the forces of history, forces long preparing and long evolving, culminate—inevitably culminate—in the cataclysmic events he is depicting. In "Dickens and Cannibalism," in the long section on *A Tale of Two Cities* (pp. 162–98), we saw how these inexorable forces exerted their slow but stern dominion over the lives of men and women. Dickens structured that novel on an intricate pattern of inextricably linked and immutably unfolding external causes and effects, a pattern whose inevitability is emphasized by a tight net of interwoven recurrences, analogies, similitudes, and the like (similitudes often enforced by cannibalistic aggrandizements and cannibalistic retributions), a net that is knitted loop by loop and stitch by stitch. (Some of Dickens' chapter titles emphasize this portentous knitting that entangles us in our destiny, or, to use another metaphor that Dickens employs, some of the titles emphasize the inexorable tide of culminating events that sweeps us to our final end: for example, "Knitting," "Still Knitting," "The Knitting Done," "The Sea Still Rises," "Fire Rises," and "Drawn to the Loadstone Rock." By the same token, Book the Third of *A Tale of Two Cities,* the final section of the novel, is titled "The Track of a Storm.") However, this intricate pattern is not designed to show us the immutability of fate but the inevitable consequences of acts. The initial acts of aggrandizement were not preordained; they were willful acts, acts of systematic squeezing and subjugation repeated and then multiplied over many generations by a greedy and arrogant privileged class, and finally become intolerable to the ravaged and plundered victims.

The drama of *A Tale of Two Cities* ("drama" in the sense of theater is an appropriate word here) is external.[4] The emphasis is on outer events, melodramatic and strongly contrasted outer events which take precedence over all else: over character, over inner motivations, inner compulsions, inner developments, and the like. Character is a reflection of events and of incident; character, in other words, is the sum total of outward acts and happenings. Dickens put the matter quite clearly (though in somewhat different terms from those I have just used) in a letter to Forster:

> I set myself the little task [in *A Tale of Two Cities*] of making a *picturesque* story, rising in every chapter with characters true to nature, but whom the story itself should express, more than they should express themselves, by dialogue. I mean, in other words, that I fancied a story of incident might be written, in place of the odious stuff that *is* written under that pretence, pounding the characters out in its own mortar, and beating their own interests out of them. (25 August 1859)

Six weeks later, responding to Wilkie Collins' demurrers on the way the plot of *A Tale of Two Cities* had been handled, Dickens defended his technique as closer to the "ways of Providence" than Collins' camouflaging and baited method of plotting: "I think the business of art is to lay all that ground carefully, not with the care that conceals itself—to show, by a backward light, what everything has been working to—but only to *suggest*, until the fulfilment comes. These are the ways of Providence, of which ways all art is but a little imitation" (6 October 1859). Later still, in a letter to Bulwer-Lytton, he defended the "accident" of Madame Defarge's death by invoking "divine justice":

> Where the accident is inseparable from the passion and emotion of the character, where it is strictly consistent with the whole design, and arises out of some culminating proceeding on the part of the character which the whole story has led up to, it seems to me to become, as it were, an act of divine justice. . . . This *was* the design, and seemed to be in the fitness of things. (5 June 1860)

The emphasis in these explanations and defenses is upon outward actions which can be justified as conforming to the "ways of Providence," or "divine justice," or "the fitness of things." Dickens' conception, in short, is based upon an idea of moral order, not upon a belief in inflexible determinism.

The one person in *A Tale of Two Cities* who changes, Sydney Carton, changes only to outward view; at the end we see him acting nobly, we do not see the inner springs that bring that change about.[5] Charles Darnay, for his part, is even more of a façade than Sydney Carton; that is, his actions and reactions are even more subservient to a moral ordering and to the exigencies of plot than Carton's. In a scene that could stand as an epitome of Darnay's subservience to such external manipulations, he is taken out of La Force Prison without any action or knowledge on his part, taken out drugged and insensible, a mere puppet dragged this way and that. His unwitting escape from prison, and thus from the toils of history, is quite obviously imposed from without; it is a function of plot and the "fitness of things" (he is saved by Sydney Carton and a fortuitous resemblance, and he is saved—saved arbitrarily by Dickens—because he is virtuous, he is loved by an "angel," and he has renounced allegiance to his class). In short, Dickens allows Darnay to break his links with the past (an act of free will), but he then intervenes to save him from the consequences of that past, from the fate of the St. Evrémondes (Darnay's cruel aristocratic family) and the wrath of history, an intervention that is not only arbitrary but counter to the central sweep of the novel and its most powerful demonstrations. The inevitability of history, in other words, is created by man, not by gods; furthermore, it is an inevitability that, on occasion at least, can be contravened by man—or so Dickens, taking the place of the gods, would have us believe. The inevitable is not inevitable after all—or not, at least, for some favored few. Nor, for that matter, are the sins of the fathers (Darnay's father was an egregious sinner) visited upon their children unto the third and the fourth generation, and this despite the fact that an early possible title for the novel, a title that long preceded the book, had been *The Children of the Fathers.*[6] In this respect *A Tale of Two Cities* is again a most un-Dickensian work; for Dickensian children almost always pay, pay heavily and all life long, for the sins of their fathers—and mothers.

The necessity underscored in this section, then, is not the necessity of outward forces, whether created by gods or man (or whether suspended by gods or Dickens)—though outward forces helped shape the iron necessity examined here—the necessity underscored in this section is a necessity of inward needs and inward compulsions, shacklings of the mind and spirit. We have met this necessity before. In "Dickens and Cannibalism," we examined a circumscribed but very clear example of this inward necessity in Dickens' own life. The instance in question (one of many) was an instance, or rather a series of instances, of compulsive behavior that Dickens himself noticed and remarked upon. Dickens tells us—and the many examples in "Dickens and Cannibalism" give credence to his avowal—that whenever he was in Paris he was "dragged [to the Morgue] by invisible force" (*AYR* 2: 558). This compulsion to visit the Morgue, a strange, conflicted, cannibal-haunted compulsion, touched profound encumbered regions of Dickens' being and had deep emotional significance for him. This significance, and the inward necessity of which it was compounded, a dark, dolorous, night-side necessity, informs many of Dickens' later writings, a fact that is made abundantly clear not only by "Dickens and Cannibalism" but by "Dickens and Passion" as well. That inward necessity, in turn, has profound affinities with the inner compulsions and psychological imprisonments (necessities of an analogous sort) depicted in *Bleak House, Little Dorrit, Great Expectations, Our Mutual Friend,* and other middle and late works—the inner compulsions and psychological imprisonments of such characters as Esther Summerson, Miss Flite, Arthur Clennam, Mrs. Clennam, Little Dorrit, Miss Wade, Miss Havisham, Pip, Bradley Headstone, and many others. But though related, even closely related, to the predetermined behavior exhibited by such characters, the necessity emphasized in this section (and emphasized most devastatingly in *George Silverman's Explanation*) is more tragic than those psychological imprisonments, more inexorable, and more enfeebling; it is also (to return to Dickens himself for a moment) more diseased and more disabling than his most driven behavior, than his many involuntary journeys to the Morgue, for instance. The necessity underscored in this section is insidious and duplicitous. It is more hidden, more enigmatic, and more dismaying—more implacable and more encompassing too—than all Dickens' prior evocations of necessity.

III

George Silverman's Explanation centers its steady gaze on free will versus necessity (inner necessity), but it focuses as well on a number of allied or ancillary issues that also fascinated and perplexed Dickens, issues such as nature versus nurture, chance versus fate, appearance versus reality, innocence versus guilt, intention versus result, withdrawal versus participation, self-hate versus self-love, the individual versus society, and an array of consonant themes. These are deep matters, and *George Silverman's Explanation,* simple and straightforward though it seems to be, is a deep work, a work that provides us with dark, ironic answers, or perhaps it would be better to say, with dark, ironic insights.

The story, stark and unadorned, unfolds like a Greek tragedy.

George Silverman, poor striving human mole, enacts his inevitable fate. Born in a Preston cellar to parents griped and twisted by poverty, George Silverman grows—or rather exists—a mere animal. Immured in the darkness of his cellar den, he is a rude reflex of gross animal needs: he knows hunger, cold, and thirst; he feels misery, and he feels fear. His abusive mother, embittered by poverty, is affronted by this ravenous mite. She constantly tells him he is a worldly little devil, he cares only for his crass creature comforts. The hungry child accepts this damning verdict. He is a monster. Does he not think and act as a beast? Does he not focus exclusively on eating, drinking, and staying warm? He cares only—it is a simple fact—for his own brute survival. His mother's assessment, then, is true; her loathing of him justified. He is worldly; he is a devil.

For five or six years the boy exists in this appalling state of mental and physical deprivation. He rarely ventures forth from his dismal den. He festers in the darkness. He crouches in his cellar lair, a frightened, furtive, fearful, hungry animal. Then, quite suddenly, his mother and father sicken with fever, and within a few days they die. When the young survivor is finally plucked out of his dark den, now literally as well as figuratively a den of death, he can hardly bear the light. He cowers in the squalid street as a staring crowd gathers round him. Fearful of catching the fever, the crowd keeps its distance, watching with horror as the little beast, apparently unconcerned that his parents are newly dead, ravenously eats and drinks. The boy feels the crowd's horror and disgust, but he cannot curb his hunger or his instinct to survive. Surrounded by the condemning crowd, isolated in the inimical street, he goes on eating and drinking.

Brother Verity Hawkyard, a friend of the boy's recently dead grandfather, Brother Parksop, identifies this small diseased bundle of appetites and contagions. The boy is thereupon sequestered, bathed, and clothed, and a few days later he is taken out of the city, into the country, and then up a high hill. Atop that high hill he is delivered to a farmhouse within the precincts of a crumbling old abandoned manor house, the fortlike fastness of Hoghton Towers,

118. Hoghton Towers, Alone and Fortresslike, Atop the High Hill

"We were mounting a steep hill . . . to the old farm-house in the thick stone wall outside the old quadrangle of Hoghton Towers." Note Hoghton Towers, alone and fortresslike, atop the high hill, and note in the far distance the smokestacks of Preston darkening the Lancashire skies. (See Part 3, note 15.) *Houghton Tower.* Engraving (c. 1825).

there to be (in effect) quarantined, and there to begin his rehabilitation. The Hoghton Towers farm people are good to the boy, and he soon responds with the first faint stirrings of human feeling and emotion. The stirrings grow. Wandering alone through the desolate ruins of the old heavily walled manor house, he yearns for something more than food and drink. He resolves that he will no longer be a selfish worldly little devil. He will think of others, sacrificing his own creature satisfactions for their welfare. He will begin by protecting the farm people from possible contagion; he will keep his distance from them. He will protect, most especially, the farmer's pretty young daughter, Sylvia. He holds to his resolve. He rejects Sylvia's offers of friendship and social participation; he sacrifices his own pleasure, his own regular meals and comforts too, to protect her from the dread disease he may be harboring. The little farm community, seeing only his outward conduct rather than his inward intentions, does not judge him as he judges himself. To those about him he seems simply aloof, self-centered, self-absorbed, walled-off, unwilling to respond or participate. Sylvia and her family grow tired of reaching out. They finally let him go his solitary way; he is, they decide, a moody, unsociable little beggar.

When Silverman's Hoghton Towers quarantine period is over, Brother Hawkyard, an elder of a fanatical fundamentalist sect, fetches the boy and brings him home to the fold—home, that is, to the sanctimonious and intolerant world of the Brethren. In that world the boy grows up, and from that world he wins entry to a nearby Foundation school (at no cost to Brother Hawkyard) and begins to make his independent way. He feels no affinity with the holy Brethren and their dire ravings and rantings, and they, in turn, have little love for him. They regard him as selfish and obdurate; he repays his benefactors (so they feel) by turning his back on them. He is, in short, an ingrate and a sinner.

For his part, Silverman feels troubled and guilty. Why is he so misunderstood? Why does he appear to be so selfish and aloof? What ineradicable stain darkens his daily living? Yet despite these troubling aspects of his conduct and his character—or perhaps despite the troubling outward appearance of his conduct and his character—he prospers. Though shy and withdrawn, though fearful of being thought worldly or self-seeking, he perseveres. He does well in school. He toils upward through the non-Brethren world and finally wins a scholarship to Cambridge.

Before leaving for Cambridge, Silverman decides to make amends to Brother Hawkyard and the Brethren for his aloofness, seeming ingratitude, and occasional unvoiced suspicions, so worldly and unworthy, that Brother Hawkyard has appropriated to himself an inheritance from Silverman's grandfather that was to have been held in trust for his young charge. These suspicions are suddenly given substance by the innuendoes of Brother Gimblet. Silverman undertakes to defend his benefactor and, at the same time, to wipe the slate clean of past misperceptions of himself. He will leave a written testimonial that will bear witness to Hawkyard's benevolence and his own thankfulness. He composes the document carefully and feelingly, exalting the altruism and spirituality of his benefactor and acknowledging his own great debt. He delivers the letter directly to Hawkyard, coming upon him and Brother Gimblet at the very moment when Hawkyard is counting out money and agreeing to share with Gimblet the inheritance purloined from Silverman.

Hawkyard's newfound magnanimity toward Gimblet has nothing to do with Christian charity. Gimblet, a mercenary humbug in the Hawkyard mold, has uncovered Hawkyard's perfidy and has threatened to expose his coreligionist unless he divides the spoils. Silverman interrupts this avaricious conspiracy, but he is so intent upon self-purification and self-sacrifice that he fails to divine what is going on. At the next Sunday service of the Brethren, Hawkyard and Gimblet, with Silverman in dutiful attendance, use his confession to harangue the young man before the entire congregation. They castigate his self-serving worldliness—verified by Silverman's own words—and they exalt their selfless benevolence—again verified by Silverman's words. Silverman emerges from the chapel with an aching heart and a weary spirit. In the very moment of his self-sacrificing generosity he has been dishonored and despised, held up to all the world as a monster of deceit and ingratitude.

At Cambridge Silverman keeps to himself. He works hard and

slowly wins his way, but he has a morbid fear of being thought worldly or self-serving. He always hangs back. He lives in the shadows, timid and constrained. He is an observer of life, not a participant. Upon graduation, having taken a good degree, he is ordained an Anglican clergyman and remains at Cambridge for a while. He gains a quiet reputation there for his tutoring and his rectitude. He is finally recommended for a small country living at the bestowal of Lady Fareway, an exploitive, managing woman. Lady Fareway uses and dominates Silverman. She dictates the terms of their relationship, playing on his wounded sensibility. He will not only undertake his clerical duties at a bargain rate (so she informs him), he will also undertake to be her private secretary and to tutor her teen-aged daughter, Adelina; indeed, he will assume the latter burdens free of charge. Silverman, of course, acquiesces. Far be it for him to raise worldly considerations or selfish concerns when asked to shoulder such duties.

Silverman, now thirty, undertakes his new duties modestly, conscientiously. Almost at once he comes to admire and then to love Adelina, and after a year or so, to his great astonishment, he begins to realize that she loves him. Nevertheless, he feels duty bound (a duty compounded of pride and pain) to keep his love secret. Lady Fareway would never approve, and, in any case, he is not worthy of the divine Adelina. But in addition to such weighty considerations, how would their love be understood by others? Adelina will soon be of age and rich in her own right. Will the world not say that he has ignobly used his office to ensnare her heart and thereby gain her fortune? Will he not be seen as a worldly monster bent solely on social advancement and selfish aggrandizement? Silverman is appalled. He will not countenance the appearance, let alone the actuality, of worldliness. He will sacrifice his love and his dream of happiness on the altar of selfless altruism. Silverman, who is now thirty-one, has begun to grow grey, and within a year and a half he becomes white and old. He accentuates this change, and he gradually begins to distance himself from Adelina. He also arranges to have Granville Wharton, another student he is tutoring, spend more and more time with her. Slowly, imperceptibly, he recedes into the shadows, allowing Granville and Adelina to draw closer and closer together. Gradually his two young charges fall in love, and finally they come to him and ask him to marry them. Silverman, like the lovers, realizes that Lady Fareway will disapprove of the marriage: after all, Granville is poor and without worldly prospects. Nevertheless, Silverman, despite his deep, hidden love for Adelina, and despite his knowledge that he will be crossing Lady Fareway, agrees to conduct the secret ceremony. He has achieved his goal; he knows that his two charges truly love one another, and he knows that he has assured their happiness. With aching heart he is ready to complete his sacrifice. No one can now accuse him of sordid self-interest or grasping worldliness.

The themes and impulsions that dominate this segment of *George Silverman's Explanation*, like those that shape other portions of the tale, have profound autobiographical overtones—overtones, in this instance, that illuminate what immediately follows. In particular, the themes and emotions that emerge in this part of the story seem to be associated with Dickens' feelings for Ellen Ternan, his adoration of her and his condemnation of himself for adoring her. They also seem to be associated with his using his "office" as Silverman does; that is, his using his lofty position and his role as revered mentor, guide, and teacher, to attract and influence Ellen and to ensnare her heart. When Dickens wrote *George Silverman's Explanation* he had known Ellen and been in love with her for ten years. He was now fifty-five, older-looking than his years, and increasingly ill—so ill, in fact, that he had just three years left to live. Ellen, who had long since given up the stage and now lived a quiet life of genteel leisure, was twenty-eight. Dickens' relationship with her, as "Dickens and Passion" amply demonstrates, enchanted and dismayed him. His secret life with her, so idyllic and golden in one aspect (an idealized aspect), was also forbidden and disgraceful—or so he felt (see below in Part 3; see also Part 2, "Dickens and Passion," note 24). Beneath the outward rectitude, usefulness, and achievement of his public life, dark, sinful private abysses yawned. Those dark, secret abysses tormented him, yet he seemed unable to give up the golden angel who dwelt in the center of that somber domain (the social order, his domestic plight, and his public position all ordained that she dwell in that shadowy region).

Throughout this period, but especially as Dickens grew older, as he grew more driven, more discontented, and more worn, he must have felt, often and often, the disparities and inequities of his attachment to Ellen as well as the equivocal blisses—the proscribed blisses—of that compelled (and for him) night-side attachment. Among many other disparities, he must have felt—increasingly felt—the disparity of their ages and their circumstances. He must also have felt and often condemned his unfairness in keeping her from her natural life, a life of young love, marriage, open meetings, open comings and goings, recognized social position, children, and the like. George Silverman's sudden white-haired oldness and his renunciation of the divine Adelina allowed Dickens to enact in fiction what he was unable to enact in life. The iron necessity that decrees Silverman's renunciation is the iron necessity that decrees Dickens' inability to renounce. Like Pip, Dickens must love "against reason, against promise, against peace, against hope, against happiness, against all discouragement that could be" (*AYR* 5: *GE,* 29:1). More than that, Dickens must go on loving in the very manner and in the very circumstances that make him feel a grievous, guilty sinner.

Dickens surely felt that he was a grievous, guilty sinner, a driven and compelled sinner. Even as he was writing *George Silverman's Explanation,* he was guiltily enmeshed as George Silverman was guiltily enmeshed, but unlike Silverman, Dickens would not—indeed could not—renounce. On 6 June 1867, while working on *George Silverman's Explanation,* working under an assumed name in his secret Peckham hideaway close to Ellen, Dickens wrote to his subeditor, W. H. Wills. (Wills was one of the very few confidants who had been told about Ellen.) Dickens wrote to Wills on stationery that bore an adored but somehow disgraceful monogram (adored but disgraceful in Dickens' eyes), the guilt-provoking monogram that was an embodiment of his bondage and his sin, the precious monogram, interdicted in its association with him to all the prying world but cherished in that association by him, the monogram that provided, even as he wrote, mute witness to comfortable clandestine meetings, secret ongoing intimacies, and easy domestic sharings; the monogram of his "Darling"—its owner so entwined about his heart and so physically close to him at that equivocal moment as he wrote upon her stationery—the monogram of his "Darling," "ET" (Huntington Library MS, 6 June 1867; see fig. 119).[7]

These latter-day meetings, concealments, yearnings, and dissemblings—guilty meetings, guilty concealments, guilty yearnings, and guilty dissemblings—the center of Dickens' emotional life in these later years, an emotional life so hidden and so full of guilt-provoking stratagems, helped shape Silverman's emotional life, his secret impermissible love (a love so entwined with his intimate "tutorial" meetings with Adelina), and also helped shape Silverman's guilt-provoked renunciation and what immediately follows as the story rapidly concludes. What immediately follows for Silverman is "the crowning of my work" (*GSE*, 9:281). He gives up his secret impermissible love; he gives up his love and at the same time he confirms—he more than confirms—he demonstrates his selfless altruism. He marries the happy pair; he marries his beloved Adelina to the adoring and adored Granville. He publicly and privately purges himself—or so he thinks—of worldliness, dissembling, and guilt.

Now, the newlyweds gone, he must undertake a final duty. He has promised Adelina and Granville that he will break the news of their marriage to Lady Fareway. True to his word, he goes to her and tells her what he has done. She explodes in a paroxysm of fury and strikes him hard upon the cheek. She accuses him of perfidious cunning and calculation. He has performed this marriage for his own enrichment. He has manipulated those who have trusted him and sold his office for selfish gain. She asks him how much he has been paid by Granville for this act of mercenary treachery. Lady Fareway forces Silverman to resign his living. She warns him that she will denounce him to the bishop and to the world.

A great scandal ensues. Silverman is reprimanded and barely es-

119. Close to Ellen in His Peckham Hideaway, Working There on *George Silverman's Explanation* (Working Under a Pseudonym), Dickens Pens a Letter on Stationery Bearing a Forbidden but Adored Monogram

A letter such as this—a letter written on Ellen's stationery—which testifies so secretly but eloquently to the degree of intimacy that now subsisted between Dickens and Ellen, could only be sent to Wills or to the one or two other confidants who were privy to the equivocal and guilt-laden secret of Dickens' later years. This letter, replying to Wills' attempt to dissuade Dickens from embarking on his American reading tour, sets forth Dickens' arguments in favor of that golden quest. The lightly canceled paragraph on the last page, a paragraph omitted in published versions of the letter (Ellen's monogram was also discreetly omitted), speaks to the difficulty of Ellen vis-à-vis the proposed trip: Dickens' reluctance to be separated from her during the six months of his American tour versus his fear that her presence—her presence close to him—would create a scandal. "The Patient," Dickens writes, "I acknowledge to be the gigantic difficulty. But you know I don't like to give in before difficulty, if it can be beaten." (For an explanation of the "Patient" reference, see Part 3, note 7.) The penciled comment at the head of the letter is in Wills' hand. He writes that the letter is a good example of Dickens' "powerful will." Huntington Library, San Marino, California.

capes suspension. His name is tarnished. He moves in disgrace to a new post; there he toils on under a shadow, chastened and diminished. The years circle slowly by. Silverman endures. Sadly, self-effacingly, he wears away his lonely life in a secluded country corner. Now in his sixties (close now to Dickens' age in actuality, not simply in inward and outward seeming), wounded in his inmost soul, looking out at the quiet graveyard that will one day hold his last remains, he takes up his pen to write an explanation of his life. He does so without thought of whether or not his explanation will ever have a reader. He does so for his own sake, for his own long-sought-for relief.

But Silverman will never know relief. His baffled life and baffled dreams will haunt him till his final end. The dark, ironic insights that *George Silverman's Explanation* provides us with—insights that are scarcely touched upon in this brief résumé of the plot—are Dickens' insights (and so, in the course of time, ours), not Silverman's.

IV

We dwell on those doleful insights from the very beginning, though at first, like Silverman himself, we cannot know their dread significance. The strange opening of *George Silverman's Explanation,* for example, immediately evokes the somber perplexities and desolate ironies (spurs to insight) that guide and inform our awareness. The puzzling opening, seemingly capricious and redundant, is daring and to the point. In that opening Silverman tries and tries again to begin his explanation. He cancels his first attempt and starts a second commencement, only to find that his second try is a duplicate of his first. Letting these two abortive efforts stand (an anomaly that he accentuates by making each canceled effort a separate chapter), he begins for a third time, but now realizes he must abandon his initial goal or duplicate his twice-rejected beginning yet again. This recursive tripartite opening seems quirky and baffling, but its very strangeness should make us pause and take notice. It is Dickens' artful way, at the very outset of his perplexing fable, of drawing attention to the "diseased corner" of Silverman's mind (*GSE*, 6:149). The opening—so obvious, yet so cunningly veiled—is a brilliant objectification, rendered in a most compressed and evocative shorthand, of Silverman's central predicament: though he seeks to exert his free will in a virtuous and open manner, he finds himself condemned to repeat a destructive pattern he does not understand and cannot control. Dickens shows us this happening in the unfolding events of Silverman's life, but he embodies it most succinctly and directly in Silverman's first two abortive attempts to begin his explanation. In those attempts Silverman's "intention," to adopt his own word, and his result are at odds; and this, as ever, surprises him (*GSE*, 2:118). This disparity is all the more striking since in both openings Silverman uses the identical formula of words, though he assures us that in his own mind he had employed the words in two very different connections. This small difficulty (which we eventually come to see is not small, but central) encapsulates Silverman's history and his destiny. Each fresh beginning results willy-nilly in the same self-wounding ending. Like an enchanted wanderer in an enchanted land, Silverman ventures along many paths, determined to reach the shining castle glimmering brightly at the top of the high hill; but, try as he will to gain his lofty goal, he circles unerringly to his preordained destination: he emerges battered and bleeding in the dark canyon where he began.

Silverman conveys this reality, but he does not apprehend its circularity or understand its significance. He cannot, as he puts it, explain his explanation. As a matter of fact, after his first two abortive attempts to begin his explanation, he actually begins (at the commencement of the third chapter) by saying that he will no longer directly aim "at how it came to pass" (*GSE*, 3:118). In other words, he abandons the conscious attempt to understand causes and contents himself with a determination to give an account of events.

Nevertheless, Silverman does not expunge the two abortive openings. He will not conceal, as he puts it, any of his "infirmities" (*GSE*, 2:118). The infirmity he reveals to us, however, is not the one he thinks he is revealing, is not, that is, an indecisive propensity for false or unclear starts. His true infirmity, disclosed in spite of his incomprehension, is much more profound and much more damaging: it is a compulsion to repeat the past with every fresh beginning. Silverman does not understand that iron necessity or the matrix that formed it. He offers us his explanation as an apology for his misunderstood life, but we read it as a testament to how he became what he is. Moreover, we read it as an explanation of how we all become what we are—though few of us have been fashioned by so implacable and ironic a fatality as George Silverman.

V

Dickens apparently conceived the idea of *George Silverman's Explanation* in the spring of 1867, but found himself in a Silverman-like dilemma. "It is very curious," he wrote, "that I did not in the least see how to begin [Silverman's] state of mind, until I walked into Hoghton Towers one bright April day" (28 June 1867). This chance conjunction, an engendering conjunction, of the means of beginning Silverman's history and a ruined fortified Lancashire manor house, combined with such additional engendering Hoghton Towers conjunctions as "dark pits of staircase" and "fresh green growth" (*GSE*, 5:122), were to be momentous not only for the opening of the story but for the entire tale (see figure 120).

The tale, or rather the donnée of the tale, the idea for the protagonist's state of mind, haunted Dickens. He had originally intended that idea to be the wellspring of his next novel. "The main idea of the narrator's position towards the other people," he wrote to W. H. Wills, subeditor of his magazine *All the Year Round*, "was the idea I *had* for my next novel in A. Y. R." (28 June 1867). It is not clear why Dickens abandoned the novel format, but what the unwritten novel lost the completed story gained. As a matter of fact, in many ways the story is a miniature novel, witness, for example, its nine chapters. Dickens was pleased with the story. *George Silverman's Explanation* struck him as compelling; he found it deep-probing,

120. Hoghton Towers: "Dark Pits of Staircase" and "Fresh Green Growth"

"It is very curious that I did not in the least see how to begin [Silverman's] state of mind, until I walked into Hoghton Towers one bright April day." What Dickens saw in Hoghton Towers—"dark pits of staircase" and "fresh green growth"—was crucial not only in objectifying Silverman's state of mind but in shaping the genesis and unfolding of the entire story. See text; see also figure 127. Photograph (1987) by the author.

truthful, and fresh. "Upon myself," he wrote, "it has made the strangest impression of reality and originality!! And I feel as if I had read something (by somebody else) which I should never get out of my head!!" (28 June 1867).

George Silverman's Explanation was fresh and original, but it dealt with matters that had long since engrossed Dickens. Those matters can be summed up by the question, how do we come to be what we are? Or, to put the question more narrowly and more in keeping with Dickens' own history, how do we succumb to or transcend powerful early blight? Furthermore, what are the forces that enmesh and impel us? In Dickens' case he had transcended his youthful sojourn in darkness. He had not succumbed to blacking-warehouse servitude or blacking-warehouse neglect. Nor had he succumbed during that period to the sinister blandishments of the unfeeling city streets—tawdry London streets that later metamorphosed into tawdry George Silverman streets—miles of long, busy streets, sometimes rough streets, which he had to tramp each morning and evening, often in the dark, jumbles of mean, crowded streets that he lounged through at noon, taking his scanty solitary meal.

And yet in many ways he had succumbed. All life long he struggled with the guilt and shame of his blacking-warehouse taint. Dickens tells us that even when famous and petted he could not go near the streets associated with his bondage; his old way home through the Borough made him cry after his eldest child could speak (F, 35). But elsewhere he also tells us—he tells us this, too, long after he had become famous and petted—that when he was deeply engaged in writing, he needed busy streets, the "black streets of London, fifteen and twenty miles, many a night," to walk in as an accompaniment and stimulus to his creativity (2 January 1844). City streets, apparently, could be both painful (essential to avoid) and crucially stimulating (essential to seek out). The latter need, the need to charge or rather to recharge his imagination by walking in bustling city streets, was not the reflex of a single time or place. While Dickens was living in Lausanne, Switzerland—this more than two years after his remark about tramping miles and miles "many a night" through the "black streets of London"—he pondered yet again the odd phenomenon that when he was writing he needed busy city streets to walk in. To his great frustration, he found that the sleepy provincial streets of Lausanne did not produce the needful magic-lantern effect, but the bustling city streets of Geneva, always waiting just across the lake, worked the old magic. "It seems," he wrote, "as if [crowded streets] supplied something to my brain, which it cannot bear, when busy [writing], to lose." This strange need, he went on with wonderment, is "a curious fact" (F, 423).

Dickens does not connect this "curious fact" with a striking counterpart fact, a fact which no one but Dickens (and a few mute members of his family) knew at the time he made these statements about his need for busy city streets to walk in. That counterpart fact is very simple, and it is this: that Dickens' induction into walking alone through miles and miles of dark, crowded city streets, walking those miles of streets six dark winter mornings and six dark winter nights each week, had taken place during his servitude at the blacking warehouse; indeed, those somber street journeys were the solitary beginning and the solitary conclusion of each day's servitude, a concomitant and inseparable part of that humiliating bondage. This intense boyhood experience of tramping alone through dark crowded city streets—on the one hand, an engaged and life-thronged experience (looking out entrancedly, at times also fearfully, at the astonishing street-world all about him); on the other hand, a removed and solitary experience (looking inward, alone and hopeless—alone though surrounded by crowds—at the dark, secret, Cainlike desolation filling his being and corroding his soul); and, finally, a humiliating and shame-filled experience (being stared at and pointed to—so he felt—like a freakish curiosity or a repulsive beast)—this emotion-laden and unexpungeable experience of dark, crowded city streets, an experience so diverse, even contradictory, yet so intricately interfused and intertwined even in its contradictions, was to shape Dickens' vision and his art in innumerable ways. It was to help shape, for example, the very essence of *George Silverman's Explanation*—help shape the origins, conflicts, bafflements, disablements, and, above all, the presiding images of that somber and necessitous work.

Many of the "black streets" that Dickens walked through during the blacking-warehouse period were quite literally wicked and dangerous (and filled as well with his own secret pain); but paradoxically, many of those same streets and many of the other streets that he tramped through or lounged in on these enforced street journeys were, as he later acknowledged, diverting and exciting as well as fearful, the source of limitless stimulation and imaginings. So the streets, even the fearful streets, were, somehow, desperately needed; they were, in one aspect at least, anodynes and gifts; they inured him to the present and they nourished his fancy—indeed, they inured him to the present *by* nourishing his fancy.

Dickens' response to the darker side of these street experiences (to cite for the moment just one brief example) is typified by his intense boyhood reaction to the tawdry tangle of Seven Dials, a somber ganglion of streets and rookeries that had "a profound attraction of repulsion" for him (F, 11), a bleak maze of courts and lanes and alleys and warrens that festered malignantly hard by the Chandos Street blacking warehouse. Listen to Dickens' evocation of his boyhood response to Seven Dials: "Good Heaven! . . . what wild visions of prodigies of wickedness, want, and beggary, arose in my mind out of that place!" (F, 11). "Visions" is the key word here: what he saw as he walked those streets, the horrors and the delights—he was even then, though profoundly suffering the experience, also, at the same time, a very different being, an outsider and an observer—both shaped and fed his imagination. At the time, however, suffering engulfed him; the harvest of the streets, an imaginative harvest, was undreamed of, and in any case, except for the immediate play of his fanciful transformations, that undreamed-of harvest was a world away.

The harvest was a world away, but the suffering was here and now, and the suffering lingered—it, too, was part of the harvest. What that experience of city streets, especially in its more threatening aspect, came to mean to Dickens, how angry, humiliated, and haunted

121. The Nightmare but Empowering
Streets of Dickens' Boyhood

In the blacking-warehouse period, Dickens had to tramp through miles of mean streets, often in the dark. These dark journeys, which both harrowed and stimulated him, helped shape his imagination and his art. "Houndsditch." Wood engraving after a drawing by Gustave Doré. From Doré and Jerrold, *London: A Pilgrimage* (1872).

he was by that experience, may again be glimpsed when he writes in the autobiographical fragment how cut off and neglected he felt in those menacing city streets. "I know," he wrote, "that I have lounged about the streets, insufficiently and unsatisfactorily fed. I know that, but for the mercy of God, I might easily have been, for any care that was taken of me, a little robber or a little vagabond" (F, 28). His vision of that time is apocalyptic. Why had he been banished from family and felicity? Why had he been thrust into this dreary workaday hell? What fell crime had he committed to be meted out such Cain-like punishment? He suffered exquisitely and he suffered in silence, but his silence only served to intensify his anguish; he could not reconcile himself to his banishment. How solitary and isolated he felt as the busy world bustled unfeelingly, often threateningly, all around him may be glimpsed again and again in the autobiographical fragment. He was a lowly laboring hind; he had been banished and abandoned: "I certainly had no . . . assistance whatever . . . from Monday morning until Saturday night. No advice, no counsel, no encouragement, no consolation, no support, from any one that I can call to mind, so help me God" (F, 27). In the middle of bustling streets, busy workplaces, and crowded lodgings he was—or at least he felt—an outcast and alone. Given these experiences and these feelings, it is no wonder that vulnerable and neglected children, children such as Oliver Twist and Florence Dombey, flee terror-stricken or wander lost and abandoned in unfeeling city streets; and it is no wonder that the cellar George Silverman, alone and cut off from any human nurturing, prowls furtively through frightening city streets, or, plucked from his cellar den, his parents newly dead, sits isolated and loathed, a crowd-condemned, guilt-ridden, pestilential pariah, eating and drinking like a ravenous devil in the cold inimical city streets.

There were, then, quite obviously, other "curious facts" about streets, more hidden, painful, as well as more saving facts, and above all, more generative facts than those Dickens disclosed (or perhaps even understood) at the time of his Lausanne and earlier remarks, but facts that he fully comprehended and acknowledged (to himself

122. Old Hungerford Market and the
Nightmare of the Past—and Present

"Until old Hungerford-market was pulled down, until old Hungerford-stairs were destroyed, and the very nature of the ground changed, I never had the courage to go back to the place where my servitude began." In this illustration (an idealized view of a decaying region) one can see, just beyond Old Hungerford Market, the commencement of ramshackle Old Hungerford Stairs (stairs that continued down to the river); one can also see, adjacent to and backing on the stairs, the blacking-warehouse building (more run-down than shown here) in which Dickens toiled. (For a closer and more tumble-down view of the blacking warehouse, see figure 128.) "Hungerford Market, Strand." From an engraving (1830) after a drawing by Thomas H. Shepherd.

460

and to Forster) two years later, in his autobiographical fragment. To dwell for another moment on the blacking-warehouse streets, Dickens also acknowledged in his autobiographical fragment—acknowledged, that is, in yet other ways than those already touched upon—that the pain those unfeeling streets epitomized and engendered did not fade from his consciousness. On the contrary, the anguish of those dark streets and that dark time haunted his days and disturbed his nights. In 1849, with the innovative and brilliant *Dombey* already behind him and the triumphant *Copperfield* about to be launched, that unshriven anguish not only troubled his waking consciousness but continued to pursue him in his sleep: "I often forget in my dreams that I have a dear wife and children; even that I am a man; and wander desolately back to that time of my life" (F, 26).

Dickens often wandered back to that time of his life in his dreams, but many years went by before he could prevail upon himself to wander back to the nightmare scenes of his shameful past in his waking person. The very streets, the very approaches, that led to the blacking warehouse were deeply, in some ways unalterably, contaminated: "Until old Hungerford-market [located a few score feet from the blacking warehouse] was pulled down, until old Hungerford-stairs [where the blacking warehouse stood] were destroyed, and the very nature of the ground changed, I never had the courage to go back to the place where my servitude began. I never saw it. I could not endure to go near it" (F, 35). Dickens might well have said of himself, as George Silverman says of himself, that he too had a "diseased corner" of his mind that "winced and shrunk when it was touched, or was even approached" (*GSE*, 6:149). Yet out of such experiences and such wounds, gifts as well as curses, enablements as well as disabilities, can flow. "I know," Dickens wrote, speaking of the blacking-warehouse time and the blacking-warehouse events, "I know how all these things have worked together to make me what I am" (F, 35).

In *George Silverman's Explanation*, Dickens' shameful blacking-warehouse taint becomes Silverman's shameful cellar taint. There is no eradicating that taint. "Some vapor from the Preston cellar cleaves to me," Silverman says truly (*GSE,* 6:145). He says this years after he has become a Cambridge graduate, an ordained clergyman, and a responsible member of society. Like Dickens, though marked by his painful past, Silverman seems to have transcended his past. However, Silverman's cellar vapor did more than cleave to him; it disabled him. How did that disablement come about, and why? Who or what forged the "long chain of iron" that burdened and "bound" him? (*AYR* 4: *GE,* 9:291). And why was Silverman's dolorous chain so heavy and unbreakable? Dickens' answers to these questions and to similar questions—for such questions perplexed and troubled him all his life—changed over the years.

VI

In many of his early works, and in some of his later ones as well, Dickens denied the relationship between early blight and later disability. Oliver Twist, who is steeped from birth in unimaginable depravity, emerges unscathed. Dickens understood the implications of Oliver's immunity. "I wished to show," he tells us in "The Author's Introduction to the Third Edition," "in little Oliver, the principle of Good surviving through every adverse circumstance, and triumphing at last" (*OT,* 1: iii, 3rd ed.). This is another way of saying that some people are so good and so pure that no evil can taint them. But for every Oliver there are—to stay with this early novel for the moment—scores of Fagins, Sikeses, Noah Claypoles, and the like. Apparently Evil (to employ Dickens' capitalization here) is as innate and as impervious to alteration as is "Good." Such immutable polarities are all very well if you happen to be an Oliver, and all very ill if you happen to be a Sikes. Soon, however, Dickens became concerned not simply to show evil characters living in evil circumstances but to emphasize cause and effect. His most condensed embodiments of this fell collaboration appear as deformed young creatures who dramatize society's responsibility and guilt: blighted waifs and monstrous beast-waifs. These blighted creatures—deformed seeds of a fearful gathering yet to come—portend doom for the social order that creates and condones them.

Such warning creatures appear frequently in Dickens. They appear in *A Christmas Carol* quite unadorned as the two dire children, Ignorance and Want. These children, hardly more than allegorical figures in a masquelike demonstration (they are ushered before us by the Ghost of Christmas Present), are "wretched, abject, frightful, hideous, miserable"; they are also "yellow, meagre, ragged, scowling, wolfish" (*CC*, 3:117, 118). "No change, no degradation, no perversion of humanity, in any grade, through all the mysteries of wonderful creation, has monsters half so horrible and dread" (*CC*, 3:118). When Scrooge asks whose children they are, the Ghost of Christmas Present replies:

"They are Man's . . . And they cling to me, appealing from their fathers. This boy is Ignorance. This girl is Want. Beware them both, and all of their degree, but most of all beware this boy, for on his brow I see that written which is Doom, unless the writing be erased." (*CC*, 3:118–19; see figure 123)

A few years later, in another Christmas Book, *The Haunted Man,* Dickens created the full-fledged beast-waif, an even more sinister presentiment of what must inevitably emerge (and what that emergence ultimately portends for society) when infants are treated like beasts. The beast-waif in *The Haunted Man,* though still strongly allegorical, is more central, more realistic, and more thematic than Ignorance and Want. Furthermore, he is more artistically satisfying. Yet Dickens feels compelled toward the end of the story, so intent is he on reaching his reader, to translate his powerful imaging into a bald didactic message. The message, delivered this time by a Phantom rather than a Ghost, is fervent and familiar:

"This," said the Phantom, pointing to the boy, "is the last, completest illustration of a human creature, utterly bereft . . . this wretched mortal from his birth has been abandoned to a worse condition than the beasts, and has, within his knowledge, no one contrast, no humanising touch, see that written which is Doom, unless the writing be erased. Deny it!" cried the Spirit, stretching out its hand towards the city. " Slander those who tell it ye! Admit it for your factious purposes, and make it worse! And bide the end!"

123. *A Christmas Carol:* Ignorance and Want

"No perversion of humanity, in any grade, through all the mysteries of wonderful creation, has monsters half so horrible and dread." Note the lowering factories smoking in the background. Woodcut (1843) after a drawing by John Leech. From *A Christmas Carol* (1843).

to . . . spring up in his hardened breast. All within this desolate creature is barren wilderness. . . . Woe . . . to the nation that shall count its monsters such as this, lying here, by hundreds and by thousands!" (*HM,* 3:141–42; see figure 124)

Figures such as Ignorance and Want or the beast-waif of *The Haunted Man,* rudimentary prototypes of the cellar George Silverman, are a kind of passionate shorthand, allegorical devices designed to educate and move the public concerning an issue about which Dickens felt deeply. For Dickens, offspring of his own early experience of neglect, and heir of the new Romantic sensibility, the victimized child, innocent and vulnerable, was (as he was for Blake) the quintessential emblem of society's transgressions and of the awful harvest those transgressions must one day reap. The thrust here, in its implications for society, is largely sociological. But one must make distinctions between these allegorical figures and certain other portraits in the Christmas Books. The inward or psychological wounds of childhood (and their dire aftermath) are conveyed, not through the wolfish beast-waif of *The Haunted Man,* but through the protagonist of the story, Redlaw—just as in *A Christmas Carol* such wounds and their equally devastating consequences are conveyed, not through the allegorical children Ignorance and Want, but through Scrooge. Clearly, the reiterated lesson Dickens is conveying in these Christmas Books has an inward (psychological) and an outward (sociological) thrust.

Redlaw and Scrooge (to look at the inward thrust for a moment) are walking wounded. But they are saved in the end: their psychological wounds are healed by insight (insight achieved through supernatural intercession) and by subsequent rebirth. Their histories reiterate a familiar sequence of beginnings, consequences, and endings. Both characters undergo childhood wounds that lead to slowly escalating adult pathology. This deepening pathology culminates in a shattering crisis, a hallucinated inward cataclysm that finally produces insight, conversion, and then, at long last, abiding felicity— the latter, redemptive stages of this long pilgrimage achieved quickly and with the aid of preternormal mediation. In other words, to

back again, and interposed his arm to ward off the expected blow.

124. *The Haunted Man:* Redlaw and the Beast-Waif

"Woe . . . to the nation that shall count its monsters such as this, lying here, by hundreds and by thousands!" Wood engraving (1848) after a drawing by John Leech. From *The Haunted Man and the Ghost's Bargain* (1848).

change the terms of reference briefly, Redlaw and Scrooge have free will. Yet their free will is strangely contingent upon outer forces. They are free to change, but only insofar as their will to change is coincident with supernatural intervention. Without that intervention, presumably, they would have lacked the ability—even the desire—to change; they would have continued in their destructive courses.

We see the inexorable working out of those destructive courses; that is, we see the inexorable working out until the fantastic psychological reversals of the latter stages cancel and overturn them. In those latter stages, Dickens indulges himself with wishful consummations. The profound reformations and blissful fulfillments he conjures up are, quite patently, acts of faith and flights of hope, magical representations of the sweet fruits of grace. They are visions of what might be rather than depictions of what is. Such resolutions have a reassuring and a didactic purpose, but they are not simply reflections of Dickens' desire to encourage and teach a perilously remiss public. The portraits of Redlaw and Scrooge have other, more inward-looking and more personal dimensions. Both characters are avatars of Dickens; they are unquiet ghosts of Dickens' haunted past. They are thus, in some ways, Dickens' mechanisms for objectifying contending impulses in himself (Redlaw and his haunted other self engage directly in such soul-searching and soul-making contention); they are also, in part, Dickens' attempt to understand and absolve himself.

In *The Haunted Man*, for example, Redlaw, the haunted man of the title, broods over past sorrows and past wrongs. Those afflictions, somber shadows from his painful past, obsess and torment him, and he wishes he could blot them out of his consciousness. Through the agency of his dark alter ego (his haunted self) he is granted his wish; but such surcease, the story shows us, can only be bought at the expense of one's humanity. This is the lesson that Redlaw must learn: rather than forget such afflictions, he must come to understand their equivocal nature; he must come to accept them as inseparable from all that he values and cherishes in life. Dickens, who wrote *The Haunted Man* a few weeks after his sister Fanny's death (a lingering death that called up a turmoil of conflicting emotions from the most painful part of his past), is, through Redlaw, once again affirming that he too must accept past sufferings and wounds as concomitants of his present joys and powers, his present humanity as well, indeed, as inseparable from them—a doctrine that Dickens believed in and espoused ("I know how all these things have worked together to make me what I am"), but one that somehow failed to cauterize his wounds.[8]

The identification of Redlaw and Scrooge with Dickens is not limited to such shared concerns and similitudes, central though such matters are. In these hortatory works, the close connections—additional connections—between autobiographical facts and fictional fancies confirm such identifications. The life histories of Redlaw and Scrooge parallel crucial configurations in Dickens' own emotional life; they reprise early relationships and occurrences that are versions (as Dickens saw them) of such highly emotional issues as—to adopt Dickens' point of view—his neglectful parents, unaccountable banishment, profound isolation, betrayed love, ministering sister, wounded sensibility, and much more.[9] But there is a crucial difference between these fictional renditions, even when shorn of their emotional distortions, and their real-life culminations, and that crucial difference is this: while Redlaw and Scrooge are shriven and saved, Dickens continued to be haunted. His direct testimony and reiterated actions bear witness to that continued haunting; he could not lay the stressful ghost—he tells us this long after the Christmas Books—of his hurtful past (F, 26, 35). His works testify with equal eloquence to the power of that past. There are many symptoms in his subsequent writings of his continuing perturbation: the unshriven progeny of Redlaw and Scrooge are one indication of his enduring inward or psychological unrest; the steady slaughter of innocents, young and old alike, blameless victims of a corrupt social order, are another symptom, a symptom this time of his enduring outward or social anger. The relevance of all these matters to George Silverman's painful history is manifold, in-

125. *The Haunted Man:* Redlaw-Dickens and His Dark Alter Ego

" 'Thus, . . . I bear within me a Sorrow and a Wrong. Thus I prey upon my-self. Thus, memory is my curse.' " Wood engraving (1848) after a drawing by John Leech. From *The Haunted Man and the Ghost's Bargain* (1848).

469

tricate, and revealing—revealing, most particularly, concerning the evolution of Dickens' thought and the impact of that evolution on his art.

How deeply Dickens felt about these inward and outward matters is conveyed, not simply by the passion with which he rendered them, but by the endless succession of exemplary characters who embody them. One large group of such characters consists of the outward, nonpsychological personifications of Dickens' monitory message. That emblematic category is most succinctly represented by the savage beast-waif and his distant offspring; but allied types, even antipodal (but no less emblematic) types, are part of the same demonstration. An untainted paragon such as Oliver, while robbing vice of some of its power, can throw evil into relief. Other paragons, such as Little Nell (in *The Old Curiosity Shop*), while immune from taint, are not immune to the destructiveness of corruption: pursued by evil, angelic Nell must die. Later characters, also vessels of virtue, children or childlike adults such as Smike (in *Nicholas Nickleby*), Jo (in *Bleak House*), Maggy (in *Little Dorrit*), and Betty Higden (in *Our Mutual Friend*), though maintaining their purity in the midst of depravity, are deeply compromised: they are unwitting martyrs, sacrificial lambs, innocent victims. Here, too, the connection with George Silverman is clear.

A more interesting category, more interesting because composed of more inwardly vulnerable, less immutable beings, contains characters who would have been virtuous but for the taint of a corrupt system. In the middle and late novels, we see such characters degenerate as the poison of a sick social order infects and then claims them. Characters who undergo this transformation include Rob the Grinder (in *Dombey and Son*), Richard Carstone (in *Bleak House*), and Sydney Carton, before his self-immolation and salvation (in *A Tale of Two Cities*). (Walter Gay, the nominal "hero" of *Dombey and Son*, was also to have undergone this slow deterioration until Dickens, in mid-course, decided to save him.) Another engrossing category, again only present in middle and late works, consists of amoral characters who are the end result of the new pragmatic ethic of cold, logical, calculating self-interest. These characters, products of an unfeeling industrial capitalism—they too are deformed by a corrupt social order—include such mercenary creatures as Mr. Filer (in *The Chimes*), Bitzer (in *Hard Times*), and Charley Hexam (in *Our Mutual Friend*).

All the characters dealt with so far are either embodiments of immutable good (or evil), pursuers of false doctrines (who are converted at the end), or products of a defiling social order, although some of the later characters, such as Richard Carstone or Sydney Carton, begin to edge beyond these demarcations. In other words, in none of these characters does Dickens concentrate on soul-making or will-making, a long interior process. These externalized characters lack interior lives, or perhaps it would be better to say that Dickens pays little attention to their interior lives. They are either born the way they are, vessels of goodness or evil, or they are miraculously converted from evil to good, or they are passive victims of outside forces, creatures of the social order. (Sydney Carton, for example, though seemingly corrupt, is essentially good; his innate goodness is made manifest and redeemed by love. But, as we saw in "Dickens and Passion," Dickens never shows us this; that is, he never shows us from within, how Carton comes to be saved.) All the characters discussed so far exhibit the overriding ascendency of nature or of nurture; they do not evoke the perplexities of the intersections of these forces. Or, to put the matter another way, in his earlier writings, Dickens rarely concerned himself with the interplay of free will and necessity. In his later writings, however, this crucial matter—his growing interest in it prompted by the unfolding mysteries of his own complicated history—began to occupy him more and more.

It is no wonder, then, that the characters most closely allied with George Silverman appear in the later novels. Such characters include Arthur Clennam and Miss Wade (in *Little Dorrit*), Pip and Magwitch (in *Great Expectations*), and Bradley Headstone (in *Our Mutual Friend*). Headstone, like Silverman, comes from lowly origins, rises through his own efforts, becomes a valued teacher, and then drifts into a disastrous love affair.[10] Because of his early conditioning, he pursues respectability in the same way that Silverman flees worldliness; and, as with Silverman, his deformed need impels him to a deformed end. Like Silverman, he is profoundly repressed. But the differences between the two men are also great. Headstone's early days are not nearly as brutal as Silverman's, and Headstone is not imprinted so inflexibly with an implacable pattern. Also, Headstone's repressed passion will not be contained. It ultimately explodes, to his own great dole and to the dole of others. Though the originating pathology is similar, the courses of the disease differ. Headstone, though hostage to his birth and the social order, is not so bonded in his destiny; he can exert more conscious control over his life than Silverman. One can imagine many scenarios in Headstone's childhood and youth, even in his manhood, in which he would have escaped his doom. What if he had never met Lizzie, for example; or what if he had fallen in love with Miss Peecher? For Silverman, however, after the first few years, there is no escape.

Magwitch is another character who bears a strong family likeness to George Silverman. Magwitch has an impoverished and brutal childhood, and he is forced into an even more primitive "worldliness" than Silverman: from his earliest days he must steal or starve. Society compounds the deformation by punishing Magwitch for struggling to survive. The inevitable occurs. A helpless transgressor as a child, he becomes a habitual criminal as a youth and a hardened convict as an adult, a coarse, brutish animal rather than a man. He contaminates everything he touches, preying on the society that created him, unconsciously heaping misery and pain on the random "innocents" who cross his path. He is Dickens' familiar beast-waif, come in the fullness of time into his preordained inheritance and wreaking his preordained vengeance, but fleshed out now, made real and believable, no longer a one-dimensional allegorical figure. Yet Dickens, as in the Christmas Books, softens his demonstration. He mitigates the retribution he has Magwitch inflict upon society. Magwitch can be redeemed, or at least partly redeemed. He is partly humanized and partly transformed, first by compassion and finally by love; but, like Miss Havisham, and unlike Pip, he must die: he is too tainted to be reborn. Magwitch harrows Pip and he harrows society, but fittingly, in view of Pip's central role in Magwitch's transformation, he helps transform Pip as well.

Pip, a very different transgressor from Magwitch, also has strong affinities with Silverman. Silverman thus combines attributes that Dickens divided between Magwitch and Pip in *Great Expectations*. (Significantly, and most artfully—most instructively, as well—in *Great Expectations* Magwitch and Pip often serve as alter egos.)[11] Pip's first important self-conscious act, one might call it an existential act, is stunningly contradictory and complex: he steals food and a file for Magwitch. The act is both a crime and a gesture of virtue: he steals in order to feed a starving fellow human being. That equivocal act is coeval with Pip's dawning identity; it is at once his fall, from which all the events in the book flow and, far off, at the very end of the novel, the means of his salvation. Furthermore, that first ambiguous act of sin and virtue is both imposed from without (Pip is a helpless victim) and generated from within (Pip is a self-willing agent). After all, when Magwitch released Pip, the boy could have run home and informed on the escaped convict instead of protecting him and stealing; on the other hand, who can blame the isolated and mistreated seven-year-old child from hugging his fearful secret close and obeying Magwitch, that terrifying utterer of such terrifying cannibalistic threats? Pip, in this dawning moment of his identity (Dickens tells us this is the birth of Pip's identity, the birth of his "first most vivid and broad impression of the identity of things" [*AYR* 4: *GE*, 1:169]), in this dawning moment, Pip is both shaped and shaper. In other words, he is at one and the same time an exemplar of necessity and an embodiment of free will. The similarities with George Silverman are striking.

There are other affinities as well. Pip, as a result of an early concatenation of influences and events, is impelled into a pattern of circularity as surely as Silverman. Poor blind Pip, endlessly yearning for the insubstantial attributes of station and gentility, circles through his "poor labyrinth" as unseeingly as he circles through the lightless rooms of Satis House wheeling Miss Havisham round and round her dark domain (*AYR* 5: *GE*, 29:1). But Pip's early years were less oppressive than Silverman's; Pip was not encoded so narrowly or so searingly. After pain and suffering, after undergoing bitter blows and passing through hellish fires, he can die and be reborn—a consummation not vouchsafed George Silverman.

Arthur Clennam, the diminished hero of *Little Dorrit* and another sad beginner, also ends more happily than Silverman. His early blight, like Silverman's was imposed upon him by strict, obdurate parents. Groomed in a stern religion, "trained by main force," "broken, not bent," exiled as a youth to a distant land (to China, a realm that isolates him physically and alienates him culturally), he returns many years later, a repressed and diminished man, mistrustful of his worth, drifting aimlessly on the tides of time, timid, guilty, self-reproachful (*LD*, 1: 2:15). He has little ego, little identity, little purpose. Gradually, in the course of his exile, in the course of his continuing deprivation and isolation, he has become a thrall of necessity, a sad, fettered prisoner of a long-forming and grievously disabling inward necessity that shackles him in self-diminishment and self-doubt. By the time of his return to England, he has, in effect, no free will. As he himself puts it, quite directly, "I have no will" (*LD*, 1: 2:15). His salvation comes slowly and painfully. He, too, must die and be reborn; he must be imprisoned bodily before he can be free mentally. He is redeemed by love, but only when he has been regenerated sufficiently to allow himself to be loved, a regeneration that poor George Silverman is too damaged to permit himself.

In some ways, the closest precursor of George Silverman is Miss Wade, another character in *Little Dorrit*. In the chapter entitled "The History of a Self Tormentor" she tells us her dread tale (*LD*, 2: 21:500–507). Like Silverman, she has no insight into the true springs of her enslavement; she is free only to will her self-destruction. Again like Silverman, she unconsciously reveals to us the necessity, self-imposed, that constantly undoes her. An orphan who early felt unappreciated and unloved, she soon came to validate these feelings by projecting them into the statements and actions of all those who surrounded her. Gestures of acceptance, acts of kindness, offers of friendship, tokens of affection, protestations of love are invariably seen by her as camouflage for hypocrisy, hostility, and contempt. Hungry for love, she will not let herself be loved. Her sense of the world's perfidy and rejection must be fulfilled over and over again, and she sees to it that her paranoia and her secret sense of unworthiness will be verified by inducing (or inventing) the very conduct she professes to abhor. Her bitterness at her "mortifications" makes her angry, strident, and assertive (*LD*, 2: 21:505). She accumulates fancied insults, hoards her rancor, and expresses her need to love through a series of passionate, possessive, and eventually destructive affairs with young girls and young women. She is, as Dickens puts it, a "self tormentor," endlessly fulfilling her prophecy of woe.

Though the particularities of the compulsions that grip Miss Wade and George Silverman are often different, their etiologies are similar. Owing to early influences and early labeling (the repeated accusations of "worldliness" against Silverman are paralleled by repeated accusations of "an unhappy temper" against Miss Wade [*LD*, 2: 21:502, 503, 507]), both are compelled to embrace and reembrace that which entraps and imprisons them. There are other more local likenesses. Both are intelligent, make their way through their own exertions, become tutors to young people, reject the prospect of love and marriage, and end as they began, imprisoned by their maimed identities.

But there are important differences. We know a great deal about Silverman's earliest days and the grim circumstances that helped make him what he became. On the other hand, Miss Wade's earliest days are not depicted. Although we know she is illegitimate, "orphaned," and living with strangers, and can infer why she became what she is, when we first meet her as a young girl (in her narrative) she already displays the stigmata that entrap her (*LD*, 2: 21:501). Even more important, Miss Wade misinterprets the world about her. She construes kindness, friendship, and love as covert affronts. She generates the nightmare she sees. Silverman's nightmare is often real rather than self-generated. Though his case is more ambiguous and complex than Miss Wade's (also more universal and ironic), such realities as the hellish Preston cellar, the brutal mother, the unimaginable poverty, the fraud and duplicity of Brothers Hawkyard and Gimblet, and the exploitiveness of Lady Fareway are not self-created.

We have dwelt for a while now on characters who have affinities with George Silverman. What do those characters, so ranging in time and so varied in example, tell us? First, they demonstrate how widespread and deep the issues raised by such portraits were for Dickens. Second, they show how Dickens changed in his depiction of such personages, moving from rather simple allegorical beings who carried narrow sociological messages to complicated psychological characters who raised more ambiguous and universal issues. One could easily add other portraits to buttress and enlarge these intertwined demonstrations. Rosa Dartle (*David Copperfield*) is a kind of precursor of Miss Wade, locked forever by chance and circumstance into her passion and her hostility, while Eugene Wrayburn (*Our Mutual Friend*) is a later Arthur Clennam, a personage who combines old compulsions and weaknesses with new social and economic circumstances to produce a modern anomie.[12] But none of the characters or works discussed so far focuses with such clarity as *George Silverman's Explanation* does on the issues set forth at the outset of this section. And none conveys so uncompromising and so ironic a message.

VII

The intricate art of Dickens' opening in *George Silverman's Explanation,* an opening that in a few subtle sentences both embodies and presages Silverman's controlling "infirmity," is astonishing in its virtuosity; it is at once simple and complex. The rich evocation of the opening, in turn, is maintained in what follows, for the entire story is most consummately crafted. We are made privy at once to Silverman's dawning identity. He is literally born in hell, in a dark den beneath the surface of the earth. In the unimaginable poverty of this dank lair, Silverman, like the beast-waif in *The Haunted Man*, grows a mere animal, for no human touch of kindness, grace, or fellow-feeling softens his brutish life. Like the boy Magwitch, bare survival, the dogged, self-centered drive for food, warmth, and shelter, is his sole preoccupation. His state is parlous. As Silverman puts it, speaking quite literally but invoking for us deeper metaphorical resonances as well, "I was in the dark" (*GSE*, 3:119).

That hellish darkness, like Dickens' darkness in the blacking warehouse—the latter dungeon, in its black cellar depths, also a kind of den below the surface of the earth—is intensified by Silverman's mother. The parallels here to Dickens' own emotional development are striking. Dickens' misery and guilt in those early days were compounded by his mother; for, as he wrote with undiminished resentment many years later, she wanted him returned to the blacking warehouse for the sake of his small earnings (F, 35).[13] In some ways, then, Silverman's sense of guilty selfishness mirrors Dickens' sense of guilty selfishness, a guilt engendered (in this context) when Dickens' mother made him feel that he put his own selfish desire to survive (that is, to escape the spiritual and intellectual annihilation of the blacking warehouse) above his family's welfare. He, too, was a worldly little devil. How deeply Dickens resented his mother's treatment of him (especially then, but also before and afterwards), and yet, at the same time, how responsible he felt for that unmotherly treatment—he *must* be a selfish devil, why else would she treat him so cruelly?—may be seen with exceptional clarity in *George Silverman's Explanation*, for there Dickens magnifies both the mother's sinning and the son's assumption of guilt. In this, Silverman is like Pip in his relationship to Mrs. Joe, his sister-mother. Pip's resentment of her, engendered by her emotional and physical abuse of him, is so great and so guilt-producing that when Orlick, Pip's dark alter ego, bludgeons her over the head, Pip feels that he himself has committed the crime—which, no doubt, he often has, in wish-fulfilling ways. Dickens depicts this mother-child pattern over and over again in his writings (in *David Copperfield, Bleak House, Hard Times,* and *Little Dorrit,* as well as in *Great Expectations*), but nowhere does he depict it more starkly than in *George Silverman's Explanation.* There the pattern emerges in its most primal and devastating form.

From earliest childhood Silverman is helpless, hapless, and vulnerable. His mother, goaded by poverty, makes him feel that to want to eat when he is hungry or to seek warmth when he is cold is selfish and despicable, the height of worldliness. Each of Silverman's instinctive impulses to survive is met by his mother with the same refrain: "'O you worldly little devil!'" (*GSE,* 3:119). Silverman soon assumes the mantle of his guilt: he deems himself selfish, worldly, evil—a diseased, repulsive object in his own eyes and in the eyes of others.

His first major interaction with the world confirms this diagnosis. Lifted starving out of the pestilential cave where his parents died, he can, like Plato's stunted cave dweller, "hardly bear the light" (*GSE,* 4:119). His first words are, "'I am hungry and thirsty!'" (*GSE,* 4:119). The assembling spectators are repelled by this creature's single-minded concern for his own bodily wants, and they are horrified by his total lack of feeling for his dead parents. A moment later comes one of the unforgettable scenes of the story. A pestilential Silverman, pelted with camphor and vinegar, sits in the middle of the street, eating and drinking ravenously, while a staring crowd rings him round and smoke from a great vessel of steaming disinfectant rises toward heaven. The scene has the air of a profane rite: the potent substances, the efficacious pelting, the ravenous child, the watching circle, the smoking cauldron, the rising offering. The wary crowd, forming an ever-widening circle round the contagious child, gazes at the munching, guzzling imp "in silent horror" (*GSE,* 4:120). What is this small poisonous creature, harbinger and purveyor of death, that feasts so gluttonously in the crowded city street? What dark birth has been torn so suddenly from its secret midnight womb? "I knew at the time," writes Silverman, recalling his desolate, street-environed state, "I knew at the time they had a horror of me, but I couldn't help it" (*GSE,* 4:120).

126. Elizabeth Dickens, Dickens' Mother,
c. 1830, Age Forty-One

From a painting by John W. Gilbert. Dickens House Museum, London.

By means of this marvelous scene, so simple and profound, Dickens drives home (along with many other richly articulated meanings) a few basic precepts. Silverman is not able to express any sense of love for his parents or grief at their loss because these are human emotions and, like Magwitch at the opening of *Great Expectations,* he has never known such emotions. Bred and reared as a beast, he behaves as a beast. In calling for and then devouring food and drink, he is, like the beast-waif in *The Haunted Man,* or Magwitch at the outset of his life, merely obeying brute instinct; he is trying to survive. The crowd's reaction confirms his mother's and his own verdict: he is a worldly little devil. He is diseased and repulsive. All humanity bears witness to these devastating truths. Silverman, though he acknowledges these truths, is unable to amend his conduct. Huddled in the unlovely street, engulfed by unimaginable darkness, he goes on eating and drinking. Like Magwitch, he wants to live.

Thus ends the first phase of the story; thus ends also the first crucial stage in the formation of Silverman's character. We may take it as an axiom that Silverman will never be able to eradicate the imprint of this ferocious conditioning. Come what may, the darkness of the cellar will always shadow his life. But at this early stage the darkness of the cellar, that is, mere brute instinctive selfishness, is more than a shadow: it is all that he knows and all that he is.

The next stage begins with Silverman's purification and humanization. As with Magwitch, the purification serves at first only to accentuate his contamination—a contamination, as Dickens' rendering makes clear, that includes not simply the danger of contagion posed by the boy, but the cellar mentality that engulfs him. When asked, after a few days in the ward, how he feels, he replies that he feels neither cold nor hunger nor thirst. "That was the whole round of human feelings, as far as I knew, except the pain of being beaten" (*GSE,* 4:120). When he travels through the bleak Preston streets to the Hoghton Towers farmhouse, all he can think of is whether the fare there will be as good as in the ward, and the bed as warm. When he arrives at the farmhouse, he sees everything in terms of his lifelong struggle for survival. The pigeons flying overhead, the cattle, the ducks, the very fowls pecking about the yard, are potential meals; he wishes that they might be killed so that he can be fed. Objects are similarly co-opted. The dairy vessels become "goodly porringers"; their ample dimensions are harbingers of "belly-filling food" (*GSE,* 4:121). The whole universe reflects his sorely straitened vision, a vision of creature appetites and dark, fathomless guilt. He is immersed in guilt. Like a small Caliban, he sees the very shadows cast by passing clouds as nature frowning and shuddering at him. What else should nature do, "small Brute" that he is? (*GSE,* 4:121). When he goes to sleep on his first night in the old farmhouse he feels wolfish and loathsome. His conception of himself, bred in the cellar, confirmed by the world, is now further confirmed. He is a repulsive beast; his appetites are sordid and unnatural; he is set apart from humankind. He stretches out "opposite the narrow mullioned window, in the cold light of the moon, like a young Vampire" (*GSE,* 4:121).

It is a reflection of Dickens' deep faith in the human spirit and his reliance on the power of love to transform and ameliorate that he allows so maimed and deformed a creature as young Silverman to be humanized at all. That humanization begins almost immediately. The medicines of kindness, care, and concern, of healthful living and fair example, work on his spirit and stir his atrophied heart. Like the dread beast-waif in *The Haunted Man,* who responds not as an animal but as a child as soon as the love of Milly touches him, or like the coarse, wolfish Magwitch of the opening pages of *Great Expectations,* who is immediately softened, if ever so slightly, by Pip's human regard for him, Silverman begins to respond in a new way to the world about him. He cries for the first time for a cause that is not physical; he begins to concern himself with the feelings and welfare of others; he thinks of his father and mother with stirrings of understanding and sympathy; and he makes his initial attempts to put the well-being of others above his own.

In the latter effort he succeeds. He sacrifices his own selfish pleasure—his reputation, as it turns out, as well—for Sylvia's sake. He is not a young vampire, a worldly little devil, but a feeling, altruistic human being. So he acts, and so he attempts to regard himself. He acts according to the world's professed code of ethics and unworldliness. He puts Sylvia's welfare—her well-being and her health—above his own creature comforts and satisfactions. He protects her; he forgoes her friendship and companionship in order to protect her; he distances himself from her; he retreats into the dark ruined fastnesses of Hoghton Towers. He sacrifices for her, he sacrifices without explaining what he is doing or why he is doing it, he sacrifices without thought of reward. He is the epitome of idealism, of altruism and unworldliness—so he acts, and so he feels.

The world, of course, does not assess Silverman's behavior as unworldly. Quite the contrary, the more altruistic his conduct, the more he is condemned for worldliness, for egotistical exclusiveness and sullen self-aggrandizement. Yet he feels compelled—compelled then and compelled over the years—to repeat his ritual of self-sacrifice and altruism; he must purge himself of worldliness, of the old cellar taint. This need and these repeated acts color his entire life. Rebuffed at every turn, he becomes timid, withdrawn, unsocial, misunderstood, mistrustful—mistrustful of the world and mistrustful of himself. He develops a morbid concern to eschew even the appearance of worldliness.

It is Silverman's ironic destiny that the more he flees worldliness, the more he embraces it in the eyes of the world. It is also his ironic destiny that he must reenact his flight from worldliness endlessly. He must purge himself of worldliness no matter what the cost in forgone money, friendship, love, happiness, or pleasure. Silverman is imprisoned by his cellar taint. He must live life in the shadows, a shade himself.

Dickens presents these night-side compulsions with great art and richness, and with great subtlety. George Silverman is a classic example of what we would now call neurosis, and *George Silverman's Explanation* is a classic instance of how art sometimes prefigures the insights of other disciplines, and transcends them as well. From a Freudian point of view, Silverman's behavior is unconscious and deeply compulsive. Made to feel as a child that he was selfish and evil, he endlessly sacrifices his own self-interest to advance the welfare of others. But these altruistic acts are powerless to purge him of his early sin. Nevertheless, he repeats and repeats his fruitless ritual, driven and lamed by self-hatred and guilt. Presumably, through analysis he could understand and work through his neurosis and perhaps be made whole again.

Dickens does not take this Freudian view. He is saying something more complicated, more tentative, more mysterious, and more tragic than this.

VIII

Dickens, as our earlier survey made clear, became increasingly interested in the interplay of innate temperament, early conditioning, and social influences—the flux of forces that shapes an individual's destiny. He seems to have regarded early familial conditioning and later social influences as different, or, at the very least, as two functionally distinctive aspects of a whole, hence the invariable tripartite nature of the interplay in his fiction. It is true that some characters, such as Oliver, or Little Nell, or Milly (*The Haunted Man*), are wholly and incorruptibly good, while others, such as Quilp (*The Old Curiosity Shop*), or Carker (*Dombey and Son*), or Orlick (*Great Expectations*), are wholly and irredeemably evil. But as Dickens' art developed, more and more of his protagonists fell in between these polarities. In the most searching later cases—Pip is a good example—the birth of self-consciousness and identity, that is, of awareness and responsibility, is hedged about by conflicting and ambiguous influences, both external and internal, influences that show the individual to be both a free agent and a helpless victim. As we saw with Pip, such an individual is simultaneously a sinner and a virtuous being. He works out his destiny in a field of forces which controls him but which he also controls. Indeed, his original fall or wound is often the means whereby, after long struggle and travail, he redeems himself. The fall in such instances is necessary to the long, arduous process of making the self, and, depending upon the final outcome of that making, to the ultimate redemption (or damnation) of the self, though the redeemed self in these late examples, even in its triumph, is often sadly muted and chastened.

George Silverman's Explanation gives us a darker, more despairing vision of the disorders of the human soul. Dickens seems to be saying that nature, nurture, and society can condemn and imprison an individual no matter how obvious his innocence, how superior his gifts, how real his achievement, how loving his heart, or how virtuous his acts. In this world there is no balm and no surcease for a being as woefully damaged as George Silverman. One must realize that Silverman does not smite his enemy, as Miss Wade does, but turns his other cheek. He lives by the ethical principles of society, not by its selfish practices. He sacrifices his own welfare for the welfare of others. Yet he has no friends, achieves no happiness, knows no fulfillment. Condemned to endless acts of self-effacing virtue, he will never be rewarded, never be released. Only death can free him from his bondage.

How much Silverman's innate nature contributes to the ultimate prison of his personality we can never know. What we do know, and what Dickens takes pains to show us, is that in a corrupt or insensitive society even the best medicines—good food, adequate shelter, liberating education—are powerless to cure grievous early damage.

George Silverman's society is corrupt and insensitive, of that there can be no doubt. There are many signs of this pervasive sickness. Religion, which should be the ethical bench mark of a community, in George Silverman's community has become a corrupting force. When Silverman attempts to perform Christian acts, he is undone by Christian duplicity. The loudest protestations of Christian faith cloak the most virulent exemplars of un-Christian greed and rapacity. The secular world is equally corrupt. The chief embodiment of birth, wealth, influence, and station in the story proves to be as selfish and as sordidly exploitive as the chief embodiments of religion. In a hypocritical and topsy-turvy society, virtuous acts are condemned as worldly while worldly conduct is portrayed as altruistic.

This devastating complicity between private wounds and public flaws is what makes *George Silverman's Explanation* different from, or perhaps it would be better to say more uncompromising than, Dickens' other writings. Silverman is not allowed, like Clennam, to discover love and a reborn will; he is not permitted, like Pip, to find a toilsome way to salvation; he is not vouchsafed, like Magwitch, a redeeming and transforming end. Nor is he like Miss Wade. Miss Wade, though a victim, subsequently creates her own evil. Silverman, a greater victim, subsequently has evil thrust upon him. He does not create the Brother Hawkyards and Lady Fareways of the world.

What then of free will? And what of necessity? Isn't George Silverman able to make choices? Isn't he responsible for his destiny? After all, unlike Jo in *Bleak House,* a suffering sacrificial lamb of God who has no chance whatsoever, who is the helpless victim of an early and then an unremitting deprivation, Silverman is saved from his initial cellar doom and given opportunities to expunge his cellar taint. Furthermore, unlike the totally wasted Smike (*Nicholas Nickleby*), another long-suffering lamb, or the lifelong outlaw Magwitch, Silverman is brought into society and then given the support and training to allow him to succeed in society, a feat that he accomplishes, by outward measure at least. Surely, then, his isolation and unhappiness are self-generated and self-imposed. Surely he has chosen his fate of his own free will.

On this matter Dickens is exceedingly subtle and ambiguous. He has Silverman pursue virtue and suffer because of that pursuit. But Silverman's motives in pursuing virtue are not always pure. He performs virtuous acts not simply for their own sake but also, in part at least, so that others will not perceive him as selfish and materialistic. His desire to appear before the world in virtuous guise sometimes seems more important than virtue itself. This is most apparent when he loves and is loved by Adelina. To deny the promptings of love for the sake of the world's superficial response is neither virtuous nor intelligent. And there is something presumptuous and egotistical, abhorrent and gravely sinful, in manipulating Adelina and Granville as he does, even if that manipulation ultimately brings happiness to the manipulated couple and foreseen misery to himself. In other words, Silverman does exercise his free will. He makes choices; he often makes bad choices; and he sometimes makes bad choices for equivocal motives. He does bring his own doom upon himself. And yet Dickens shows us with absolute clarity that, given his cellar years and his first subsequent shaping experiences, given, that is, the ineluctable coming together of a susceptible nature, a deforming nurture, and a venal society, George Silverman had no choice but to make the choices that he chooses to make.

Like Pip, Silverman chooses his fate, yet he also has his fate imposed upon him. Unlike Pip, however, he is not free to work his way toward salvation; he is too damaged by his dawning years and by his need to accommodate a flawed society. Silverman's fate is tragic. For him, truly, character is fate, but fate is also character.

Why did Dickens return so often to this theme? And why did he provide varying answers to the mystery it embodied? The reason, surely, is not far to seek. He was a Silverman of sorts. He too was blackened by an indelible taint; he too, "small Cain that I was, except that I had never done harm to any one"—to quote his own words (F, 27)—felt himself a pariah and a criminal, profoundly guilty somehow of a crime he had never committed; he too sat in a public place—at the street window of the blacking warehouse—and suffered shaming stares in his disgrace; he too wandered all alone through black, unfeeling city streets; he too was plucked forth unexpectedly from the blacking-warehouse cellar (one of his workplaces was below the surface of the roadway) and found himself, bewildered and oppressed by the suddenness of his liberation, crying, "with a relief so strange that it was like oppression," crying in the old familiar roaring city streets (F, 35); he too hid his early taint and nursed an unaccountable guilt; he too strove to move beyond his shameful cellar days; he too felt those days shaped his destiny ("I know how all these things have worked together to make me what I am"); and he too never exorcised their power to influence and obsess him—witness his direct confession to this effect in his fragment of autobiography, his similar avowals to his confidant John Forster, his many literary "confessions," and this "explanation" written at the end of his life, written in part, as the inks of the manuscript show, in his Peckham hideaway close to Ellen Ternan, written, that is, while he assumed a cellar name and a cellar identity, compelled by some inescapable necessity to live and act and write (in some measure, at least) in guilty contravention of his values and beliefs.[14]

But Dickens was a Silverman only of sorts. Unlike Silverman, he understood and largely escaped his shackles. His life burgeoned. It was filled with action, recognition, money, fame, friends, love, joy, laughter, and creation, as well as cellar shadows, a fulfillment to which the ample world of his writings bears unparalleled witness. He transcended his early sufferings, but he never forgot their import. The shades of what he had been, what he might have become, and what he yet was, always darkened his consciousness.

IX

The art of *George Silverman's Explanation* is everywhere evident. We have already examined those unforgettable scenes, richly imbued with thematic and symbolic meanings, in which a contaminated Silverman, crouching beastlike in a crowded city street, greedily devours food while a ring of staring strangers looks on with revulsion and horror, or in which an animal-like Silverman, obsessed with slaughtering and eating, convinced of his own depravity, stretches out in the cold moonlight like a young vampire. There are many similar scenes. The stark episode at the outset, in which Silverman's mother comes into the cellar and into the story, is a good example. The scene is a marvel of trenchant economy:

> I recollect that, when Mother came down the cellar-steps, I used tremblingly to speculate on her feet having a good or an ill-tempered look,—on her knees,—on her waist,—until finally her face came into view and settled the question. From this it will be seen that I was timid, and that the cellar-steps were steep, and that the doorway was very low. (*GSE*, 3:118–19)

With a few strokes Dickens evokes not simply the cellar steps, the low doorway, and the cowering child, but the whole cellar world. The details and the dramatic situation are so carefully chosen and so pregnant with implication that we do not have to be told at this point of the lair's darkness, dankness, coldness, and meanness, or that it is a festering wen below the hard Lancashire streets. The somber touches evoke the sordid essence of the place: we are thrust instantly into a cramped, claustrophobic world of unspeakable deprivation. What all this means in human terms is also quickly conveyed. The scene is viewed both literally and figuratively from the child's perspective, and the spatial relationship of the protagonists, the child looking up fearfully as the all-powerful adult slowly materializes inch by frightening inch to tower over him once more, tells us all we need to know about what the mother is and what the child feels. The boy trembles and speculates on the fateful omens of feet, knees, and waist, projecting onto these attributes of his mother— the stern, vindictive God of this dark world—his own dire fears and vulnerabilities. The scene, in other words, is powerfully expressionistic, rich with the spare evocativeness of a sure and disciplined art.

This spareness greets us on every hand, a fitting vehicle for the stark tale that is being told. Religion partakes of this universal impoverishment. The bleak picture of religious hypocrisy and fundamentalist fanaticism in *George Silverman's Explanation,* perhaps the most savage of all Dickens' many portraits of such excesses, is mitigated only slightly by a cutting, sardonic humor. Again the desired effects are achieved with a few masterful strokes: Brother Hawkyard's telltale verbal tic of verifying his truthfulness by repeating his lies (his given name, ironically, is Verity); his spiritual messages conveyed in monetary and moneylending imagery; his fitting occupation (he is a drysalter, a dealer in drugs, dyes, and oils); his conspiracy with Brother Gimblet, consummated in a counting-house to the sound of money being told out (the two conspirators "cadaverous in the early gaslight" [*GSE*, 6:148]). These venalities and rapacities, tokens of supposed religious grace, are part of a deep spiritual unloveliness. The outward correlatives of that unloveliness assault our eyes and ears: the "coarse chapel," the "unmusically" delivered prayers, the "bellowed" sermons, the "roared" and "shrieked" hymns, the self-indulgent "rolling . . . on the floor" (*GSE*, 6:148, 149). With such touches—rapid, brief, unadorned—Dickens enforces his deadly attack.

In other contexts Dickens uses brevity and starkness to achieve different effects. He recounts the final illness and death of Silverman's mother and father in a few terse lines:

> For three days Mother lay upon it [the foul heap of litter that served as a bed] without getting up, and then began at times to laugh. If I had ever heard her laugh before, it had been so seldom that the strange sound frightened me. It frightened Father, too, and we took it by turns to give her water. Then she began to move her head from side to side, and sing. After that, she getting no better, Father fell a laughing and a singing, and then there was only I to give them both water, and they both died. (*GSE*, 3:119)

Here economy is a fitting reflection of the starkness and waste of these sad lives; it is also a fitting correlative of the horror of Silverman's predicament and the desolation of his emotional impoverishment. This bare aneuric rendering, coefficient of Silverman's bare aneuric world, confronts us at every turn.

Darkness, another attribute of Silverman's barren world, also confronts us everywhere. The pall of the cellar, somber shadow of an ineradicable taint, settles on every nook and cranny of Silverman's life: on the hellish cavelike den, on the gloomy Lancashire streets, on the ruined Hoghton Towers, on the shadowy Cambridge retreats, on the deep recesses of Silverman's imprisoned will. Many a scene and many a character is sketched with a few strong strokes and a few dark touches. Of the corporeal Lady Fareway we know only that she is handsome, well-preserved, and large, and that she has "a steady glare in her great round dark eyes" (*GSE*, 7:278). Those dark eyes perpetually embarrass and disconcert Silverman. Like his mother, this aggressive dark-eyed mother seems to tower over him, and like his mother, this mother too strikes him in her fury.

As the last parallels indicate, *George Silverman's Explanation* does not rely for its meaning solely on spare sketching and dark toning. Its eloquent structure is a series of repetitions that artfully advance the plot while skillfully objectifying Silverman's reiterated, self-reflexive "infirmity." These central repetitions, which begin with the opening lines, irradiate every interstice of the story; for all the chief actions of the work—all Silverman's dealings with the farmer, Sylvia, Brother Hawkyard, Adelina, Granville, Lady Fareway, and others— come down in the end to a single reduplicated action. After the cellar imprinting, all the episodes originate in the same impulse, take the same course, and come to the same end. This circling and recircling, with its rich freight of analogy and implication, is further enriched by an evocative symbolism that echoes and reechoes throughout the story. The symbolism, natural and organic, a hallmark of Dickens' mature art, gives virtually every setting, object, action, and relationship in the piece added dimension.

Take, for example, the setting of Hoghton Towers.[15] One sees immediately that the ruined mansion, isolated and wall-begirt, is a correlative of Silverman's ruined, isolated, wall-begirt life. But the symbolism is much deeper than this. As Silverman wanders wolflike and diseased amidst the falling ceilings, dropping plaster, walled-up windows, and rotten floors of the forsaken mansion (all sad representations of his fallen and forsaken state), he begins to respond to another world: to the healthy life in the inhabited farmhouse where he sleeps and takes his meals. This dawning response to the first inklings of a human, rather than a bestial, world begins the slow process whereby his "dark soul" becomes human (*GSE*, 5:122). This crucial development, the possibility of new life springing out of ruin and neglect, is prefigured by Silverman's lonely wanderings in the desolate decay of Hoghton Towers. His first dim notion of something beyond Preston cellars and Hoghton ruins occurs when, in the midst of the ruins, he finds an unimaginable world: "down at the bottom of dark pits of staircase, into which the stairs had sunk, green leaves trembled, butterflies fluttered, and bees hummed in and out through the broken doorways; . . . encircling the whole ruin were sweet scents and sights of fresh green growth and ever-

127. The Old Farm Buildings at Hoghton Towers: "Green Leaves Trembled, Butterflies Fluttered, and Bees Hummed In and Out Through the Broken Doorways"

Though the great manor house and its immediate grounds are now restored, some of the adjacent farm buildings, such as these, are still much as they were when Dickens saw them. Photograph (1987) by the author. See also figure 120, "Hoghton Towers: 'Dark Pits of Staircase' and 'Fresh Green Growth,'" an illustration that embodies (as this does) a contrast that helped Dickens begin *George Silverman's Explanation*: the contrast between man-generated neglect and ruin, and nature-generated "fresh green growth and ever-renewing life."

491

renewing life, that I had never dreamed of" (*GSE*, 5:122). He yearns in some broken fashion for that world of "fresh green growth and ever-renewing life"; he wishes to turn away from the old, savage cellar world, a world that he glimpses once more a few moments later when he looks down into the cellar darkness at the bottom of another broken staircase and sees three rats scuffling for some prey. Silverman makes the equation between the scuffling rats and his own cellar condition very plain. When the rats "started and hid themselves, close together in the dark, I thought," he tells us, "of the old life (it had grown old already) in the cellar" (*GSE*, 5:122). How can he rid himself of his own disgusting cellar scuffling? "How not to have a repugnance towards myself as I had towards the rats?" (*GSE*, 5:122).

This episode, so carefully designed and exemplary, so artfully fashioned for its purpose, is, at the same time, profoundly auto-biographical—autobiographical in a strangely juxtaposed and intertwined way. The episode is imbued with the sights and impressions of Dickens' recent visit to Hoghton Towers; but it is also imbued with the surcharged memories of an earlier time and place. The entire scene, down to details of language, imagery, and emotion, harks back more than forty years, back to the blacking warehouse and to the still-fresh anguish of that time and place. The connections between the recent visit and the old experience are startling. Here, for example, to cite one brief passage only from his fragmentary autobiography, written some twenty years before *George Silverman's Explanation,* is how Dickens describes the blacking warehouse itself:

> It was a crazy, tumbledown old house, . . . literally overrun with rats. Its wainscotted rooms and its rotten floors and staircase, and the old grey rats swarming down in the cellars, and the sound of their squeaking and scuffling coming up the stairs at all times, and the dirt and decay of the place, rise up visibly before me, as if I were there again. (F, 25)

Quite obviously, the old blacking-warehouse scene and all its dark freight of graphic details and painful emotions also rose up visibly before Dickens as if he were there again when he tramped through

128. The Blacking Warehouse from the River
at Hungerford Stairs—Low Tide

"It was a crazy, tumbledown old house, . . . literally overrun with rats." *Hungerford Stairs, Westminster.* Lithograph (1822) by George Harley and Denis Dighton. (Dighton drew the figures.) Department of Prints and Drawings, British Museum, London.

129. The Hellish Dungeon Pit and Dark
Nightmare Streets of Tom-all-Alone's

Note how the framework and perspective in this illustration place one within the hellish pit that Dickens evokes in *Bleak House*—a dark, death-haunted, street-environed pit. Note also the hanged figure on the left; the pawnshop, blackened church, and neglected graveyard (rank and disease-breeding) in the background; and the rat in the right foreground. "Tom all alone's." Etching by Hablot Knight Browne ("Phiz") for Number XIV, Chapter XLVI (April 1853) of *Bleak House*. One of the "dark plates."

Hoghton Towers. How could it be otherwise? There, gazing at the old wainscotted rooms, rotten floors, broken staircases, decaying passageways, hellish cellars, and scuffling stairwell-dwelling rats of Hoghton Towers, he saw, eerily transformed yet somehow just the same (even the time of year was the same), the old nightmare of his childhood, with its wainscotted rooms, rotten floors, broken staircases, decaying passageways, hellish cellars, and scuffling stairwell-dwelling rats; and at that moment he finally saw, too, as he tells us, what had baffled him up to that time: "how to begin [Silverman's] state of mind."

A few days later Dickens was back at Gad's Hill Place. Sitting down to write, new-old scenes and new-old pains again rose up visibly before him. Festering Preston cellars, mouldering Hoghton ruins, and blacking-warehouse rot and shame merged into a single vision of ineradicable blight. The recent Preston visit combined with dark rat-infested Hoghton stairwells and old blacking-warehouse miseries to evoke an archetypal (yet distinctively Dickensian) vision not simply of decay and ruin but of hell. As in *Bleak House, Hard Times,* and *Great Expectations,* hell is a dark pit. (In *Bleak House* it is the deep, black nightmare dungeon of Tom-all-Alone's, a rat-infested, disease-ridden, street-environed dungeon-pit; in *Hard Times* it is a murderous black mine pit called, unmistakably, "Old Hell Shaft"; in *Great Expectations* it is a burning limekiln and stone quarry, a dark choking pit in the bowels of the earth.) In *George Silverman's Explanation* the dark pit is more evocative, complex, and surcharged with meaning than these earlier counterparts. The dark pit of *George Silverman's Explanation* is a pit of ruin, misery, and brute instinct, a pit that partakes of what Dickens had recently seen and felt—or refelt: a pit (that is, a hell) compounded of dank Preston cellars, yawning Hoghton stairwells, somber city streets, blacking-warehouse miseries, and voraciously scuffling rats.

Rats are a key association here. Scuffling rats swarming in the dark subterranean depths (rats in the depths, and, in particular, "scuffling" rats in dark, fathomless, stairwell depths, are common to the blacking-warehouse and Hoghton Towers descriptions), had a spe-

cial horror for Dickens. From his earliest days, through the agency
of nightly nurse's stories such as "Chips and the Devil" and by other
reiterated means, he had come as a child (long before the blacking
warehouse) to associate rats with hell, the devil, and voracious feeding on human flesh. It is worth evoking "Chips and the Devil" and
that early rat-filled nightmare once more, but now from a somewhat
different perspective, for that nightmare not only lingered but
evolved. In "Chips and the Devil," as in the blacking warehouse and
in Hoghton Towers, rats swarm and feed in the dark depths. In the
story, however, those cannibalistic rats are doom itself. They gnaw
away in the black hold of the ship and consume its very timbers.
Only Chips, who has long since sold his soul to the devil (the devil,
it will be remembered, takes the form of a speaking rat), can see and
hear the voracious feeding of the rats in the dark depths of the ship,
but when he warns of their furious subterranean ravages, nobody
believes him. The rats finally destroy both ship and crew, and Chips
goes to his horrible rat-ravaged perdition. The rats, in effect, claim
their own. The story ends as the devil, in the guise of a great bloated
speaking rat, sports on Chips' half-eaten body. Rats, in short, especially subterranean rats, rats in the dark depths, were then and ever
after a quintessential, and quintessentially loathsome, embodiment
for Dickens of hell, aggressive malignancy, cannibalism, and early
childhood trauma. And a few years later rats—scuffling cellar rats—
and dark crowded city streets became the embodiment of an even
more terrifying childhood trauma: the trauma of the blacking
warehouse.

. It is hardly surprising, then, that the conjunction of rats and neglected children—or of neglected children (most often street children) become scuffling rats—appears over and over again in
Dickens' writings. Nor is it surprising that this conjunction, which
is nothing more nor less than an especially virulent version (and for
Dickens an especially evocative and reverberant version) of the
street-dwelling beast-waif, is also an emblem of hell, an emblem that
betokens perdition, not only for the neglected children, but for the
society that neglects them. In *Bleak House* the motherless and fa-

130. Rats in the Dark Subterranean Depths

A Victorian ratcatcher working in the black depths of the London sewers. As this illustration demonstrates, rat-haunted images of hell were not simply idiosyncratic figments of Dickens' exotic imaginings; such images were also a hidden but omnipresent part—a dark subterranean part—of everyday London life. "The Rat-Catchers of the Sewers." Engraving after a daguerreotype from the studio of Richard Beard. From Mayhew, *London Labour and the London Poor* (1861).

therless crossing sweep Jo (more waif than beast), who lives in the black depths of Tom-all-Alone's amidst diseases and swarming rats, and then transmits the pestilence of his filthy hell to the affluent purlieus of the middle class (mortally ill, he dutifully sweeps the refuse of the streets from the comfortable path of the complacent middle class; he is, to all intents and purposes, part of that despised refuse), poor, neglected Jo is the chief exemplar in that novel of this dire warning, but the monitory image, linked for Dickens to his own past (a secret street-tainted, street-environed past) but festering in his present as well, casts its dark shadow on other books and other scenes.

That shadow, a nightmare image of children (usually street children) turned into ravenous, destructive, hell-dwelling rats, waxes and wanes. At times the image appears as a central motif, at times as a passing glimpse; more often it appears as a series of reinforcing glimpses. Here, for example, is one glimpse from *Little Dorrit*. This vignette occurs as Little Dorrit, having just walked through Covent Garden and its adjacent streets at midnight, conjures up some of the region's more somber aspects. Dickens emphasizes at the very outset of the vignette that he is viewing all these matters "with Little Dorrit's eyes," but the emotions the images generate soon cause him to view the scene with his own, not Little Dorrit's eyes, and then, carried away by his midnight vision, a dolorous street-pent vision of "miserable children . . . like young rats" (a vision surcharged with special meaning for him), to throw off all pretence of giving us Little Dorrit's point of view and to intrude himself into the scene in a passionate outburst. The passage begins matter-of-factly with Little Dorrit's street-evoked and street-haunted musings, but it soon takes on a life of its own. Little Dorrit summons up

> desolate ideas of Covent Garden, as having all those arches in it, where the miserable children in rags among whom she had just now passed, like young rats, slunk and hid, fed on offal, huddled together for warmth, and were hunted about (look to the rats young and old, all ye Barnacles, for before God they are eating away our foundations, and will bring the roofs on our heads!) (*LD,* 1: 14:120)

131. London's Shame: "Miserable Children . . . Like Young Rats"

Wretched children—neglected, abandoned, hunted, and exploited—swarmed the streets, alleys, and warrens of Victorian London. For Dickens, such children, monstrously transformed by a diabolical society from vessels of innocence into ravening rats, were nightmare portents of society's hellish doom. These illustrations, less apocalyptic than Dickens' infernal visions (these homeless children have not yet been abandoned), testify nevertheless to the ubiquitous reality of this woeful problem in Victorian life. Wood engravings after drawings by Gustave Doré. From Doré and Jerrold, *London: A Pilgrimage* (1872).

Dickens' vision of rats "eating away our foundations" and bringing the roofs down on our heads reminds us of "Chips and the
Devil." In that exemplum the rats eat away the foundations and
bring perdition on the heads of all the crew, that is, on all the members of that self-contained and heedless society. As a matter of fact,
in "Chips and the Devil" the voracious cannibal rats eat more than
the foundations, they devour Chips himself. We contemplate the
apocalyptic meaning of this ferocious message. In "Chips and the
Devil," as in *Little Dorrit*, we are given a nightmare vision, a rat-
environed vision, of the inevitable outcome—the profoundly necessitous, ravaged and ravaging outcome—of such hellish and heedless
engenderings.

Permutations and variations of these linked images and associations and their preordained culminations emerge broadcast in Dickens' writings; when they do emerge, they emerge in the old familiar
patterns, yet patterns that are also ever-changing and ever-new.
Take, for example, yet another version of this childhood- and
boyhood-generated nexus, in this instance a more extended example from *Our Mutual Friend*. In that novel Jenny Wren (her
real name is Fanny Cleaver), a stunted and deformed but clever
twelve-year-old child (twelve was Dickens' age in his deforming
blacking-warehouse days), plays parent to her parent (a recurrent
autobiographical theme in Dickens), in this case parent to her wayward and childish father, the alcoholic Mr. Cleaver (also known as
Mr. Dolls). Jenny often, or rather usually, refers to her father, so
weak, so dependant, so self-indulgent, as a child or a boy—she calls
him " 'my child,' " " 'you bad old boy,' " " 'you disgraceful boy,' "
you " 'wicked child,' " and so on (*OMF*, 2: 2:181, 182; 3: 10:87)—
and she treats him as an errant child as well. Though she loves him,
takes care of him, and latterly supports him, that support is at her
own life's cost and ravaging (she too, like Dickens at her age, is a
lowly "labouring hind" helping to support a feckless parent [F,
23]). At the same time, quite naturally, she feels intense rage toward
the irresponsible child who is her father, a careless creature who,
despite fleeting spasms of remorse, battens shamelessly and unre-

mittingly upon her heart's blood. She has visions of punishing and tormenting him, even of torturing him. She tells Lizzie how she will harrow her sinful child. She will pour " 'boiling liquor bubbling in a saucepan . . . hissing . . . down his throat, and blister it and choke him' " (*OMF*, 2: 2:184).

Her drunken father, in his usual alcoholic daze, is not merely a child, but an imperiled child, especially when he is in the dangerous city streets—and he is always in the streets now. Childlike, he vulnerably wanders the black unfeeling London streets, the very streets that Dickens had wandered as a child. He often wanders (as Dickens had) the streets around Covent Garden, wanders those busy streets and falls prey—weak, drunken pariah that he is—to the foraging urchin street-rats that swarm through those streets (the same scurrying Covent Garden street-rats that had horrified Little Dorrit). Mr. Dolls, Jenny's "wicked child," her "disgraceful boy," lingers in those stressful streets. He sins in those streets, he degenerates in those streets, and he dies in those streets. After his death, as Dickens takes pains to point out, he is paraded through those same unfeeling city streets, not once but twice. Jenny sums up her child-father's street-tainted life: " 'I was obliged to let him go into the streets. And he never did well in the streets . . . How often it happens with children!' " (*OMF*, 4: 9:239).

But long before Mr. Dolls' street-environed death, Jenny Wren foreshadows that wretched end. She vents her anger by conjuring up fitting punishments for her father—or, rather, for the needy, street-contaminated child who is her father, a child who is part comfort to her and part torment, a child she both loves and hates. She envisions ravenous creatures battening upon him as he has battened upon her. She tells her wayward father, whose rampant alcoholism is fast propelling him into his grave (it has already propelled her into interminable work and worry), that she would like to see him thrust into a black hole, a hole we recognize (once more) as the black dungeon-pit of hell. That hellish pit has nightmare denizens and nightmare horrors (we have met those phantasms before also), nightmare visions that well up once again in Dickens' consciousness, angry afflictions from the primordial depths. "'I wish,'" says Jenny to her irresponsible parent, "'I wish you had been poked into cells and black holes, and run over by rats and spiders and beetles. *I* know their tricks and their manners, and they'd have tickled you nicely'" (*OMF*, 2: 2:182).

In that black hole, a rat-infested hell (like the black, rat-infested subterranean depths of the blacking warehouse or the black hold of Chips' rat-infested coffin-ship), the sinful parent, transformed by Dickens into a vulnerable street child (as he himself had been transformed) will meet his ghastly fate. Though Dickens does not make that fate explicit, we know what it will be. In the black depths of that dark pit, he will be eaten alive ("tickled . . . nicely") by the scuffling rats. That these thoughts—thoughts of streets and children and exploitation and hell and rats and cannibalistic ferocity and anger (anger of a child toward an erring parent, a parent who errs while the child is compelled, compelled by the incomprehensible orderings of a stern, unjust necessity, to pay and pay and pay)—that these thoughts were gripping and impelling Dickens is made clear a moment later when Jenny, continuing her tirade against her guilty child-parent, tells him: "'If you were treated as you ought to be . . . you'd be fed upon the skewers of cats' meat;—only the skewers, after the cats had had the meat'" (*OMF*, 2: 2:183). This image of dismembering and skewering and devouring—Jenny's father, in her associative imagining (imagining that associates even as it displaces), will be dismembered and skewered and devoured like the old useless horses that are brutally butchered to provide skewered meat for hungry cats—this savage image evokes more openly than Jenny's usual "wicked-child" scolding the furious cannibalistic ferocity that she directs toward her sinning parent, a cannibalistic ferocity only hinted at (but more than hinted at for Dickens) in the hellish, rat-infested black hole to which Jenny Wren (guided by Dickens) consigns her sinful "child."

Given such recurrent concatenations of associations and reiterations, given the emotional necessity that seems to generate and order them, one can scarcely overestimate the importance of that still

132. The Child as Responsible Parent,
the Parent as "Wicked Child"

This illustration showing Jenny Wren chastising her irresponsible father reifies a repeated theme in Dickens that goes back to his dawning experiences and that appears in his early and late work: the child becomes the responsible (that is, trustworthy and blameworthy) parent; the parent becomes the bad child. But there is more to this inversion than the simple reversal itself. There is bewilderment and displacement and self-condemnation; there is also shame and guilt and anger. Dickens could not reconcile himself to the unfairness of this reversal, nor could he reconcile himself to the pathology that flows from it. Though he acknowledged the reality of life's stern orderings, he could not reconcile himself to those orderings: he could not reconcile himself to a harsh, ineluctable, unjust necessity—a necessity that decrees that the sins of the fathers be visited upon the children, a necessity that ordains that the child must become a burdened and toiling (and somehow guilty) parent, while the parent becomes a dependent and irresponsible child. "The Person Of The House And The Bad Child." Wood engraving after a drawing by Marcus Stone for Number VI, Book II, Chapter II (October 1864) of *Our Mutual Friend*.

later intermingling of old and new: the merging of the rat-infested nightmare of Dickens' childhood and youth (a dire, hellish, cannibalistic nightmare) with the rat-infested ruin of Hoghton Towers. By the same token, one can scarcely overestimate the importance of that melding for *George Silverman's Explanation*. In the same fragment of autobiography in which Dickens described the blacking warehouse and its rotten floors, mouldering staircases, and swarming cellar rats, he also described the psychological impact of that experience on his susceptible boyhood consciousness, how that experience had affected him then, and ever after. "No words," he tells us, writing these lines more than twenty years after the event, "can express the secret agony of my soul . . . I suffered in secret, and . . . I suffered exquisitely . . . How much I suffered, it is, as I have said already, utterly beyond my power to tell. No man's imagination can overstep the reality" (F, 26, 29). Or, yet again, still speaking of what seemed to him an unaccountable banishment to hell, he writes, "My whole nature was so penetrated with . . . grief and humiliation . . . that even now, famous and caressed and happy, I often forget in my dreams that I have a dear wife and children; even that I am a man; and wander desolately back to that time of my life" (F, 26).

Dickens soon went beyond the blacking-warehouse experience, of course—in part he took strength from it (strength of character and strength of artistry)—but, clearly, he never fully lanced its pain or shame or fear, and he never eradicated its insidious ability to shape, and often to darken, his life. Listen to his own words on this score: "Until old Hungerford-market was pulled down, until old Hungerford-stairs were destroyed, and the very nature of the ground [in the vicinity of the blacking warehouse] changed, I never had the courage to go back to the place where my servitude began. I never saw it. I could not endure to go near it." It "reminded me," he continues, in a phrase that could stand as an emblem of George Silverman's ineradicable cellar taint, "of what I was once" (F, 35). The pain "of what I was once"—an exile and a drudge in a rat-infested street-environed hell—was not merely abiding but overwhelming. Retracing the steps of his old way home from the blacking warehouse, a long, lonely way through dark, crowded city streets, "made me cry," he tells us, "after my eldest child could speak" (F, 35). When, a little while after writing the autobiographical fragment, he began the autobiographical *David Copperfield*, the blacking warehouse loomed before him painful and foreboding, a great black shadow darkening his consciousness. As he came to the fourth number of *Copperfield*, the number in which David relives some of Dickens' blacking-warehouse experiences, Dickens wrote on virtually the whole of the left half of the sheet of his working notes for that number, a half usually crowded with queries, decisions, plans, and reminders, only five words: "what I know so well" (Stone, *Working Notes*, 148–49; see figure 133). He needed no guides and no reminders to conjure up his sojourn in hell.

Having descended into the pit of hell—or, in George Silverman's case, having been born there—one is in danger of losing one's soul alive. One can sink into utter darkness and oblivion (as most such unfortunates do) or one can occasionally climb out of—or be rescued from—the gulf. Having been thrust into the pit, Dickens was plucked out, and then, always remembering "what I was once," began his encumbered climb to the heights; having been born in the pit, George Silverman is also plucked forth, and then, always remembering his cellar taint (but too woundedly remembering—here the wound is more curse than gift), also begins his encumbered climb. This is no simple or mechanical process; Dickens examines with great subtlety the intricate play of diverse forces that makes George Silverman what he is, and, by implication, all of us what we are. Furthermore, Dickens transforms that examination from mere autobiographical probing or simple analogy into images and parables of richly ramifying art. Autobiography is the emotional core, but this core is varied, elaborated, and reshaped into a history that is not Dickens but of Dickens, and into a fable that ultimately becomes a paradigm for the human condition.

A great sea change has been at work. In *George Silverman's Explanation* Dickens works this momentous transformation through a multitude of devices, and he continues to work it, among other

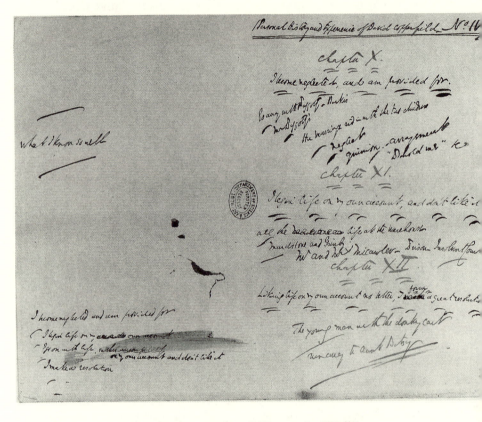

133. "What I Know So Well"

The left, or prospective, halves of Dickens' number plans are usually crowded with leitmotifs, queries, reminders, and the like. Here, in the plan for *David Copperfield* Number IV (August 1849)—the number that incorporates Dickens' blacking-warehouse experiences—virtually the whole left-half space is occupied by the words, "what I know so well." From Stone, *Dickens' Working Notes for His Novels*, 148.

means, by giving every action and nuance of his tale symbolic portent and echoing implication. He also continues to work the transformation by forging the long chain, the long chain of necessity, "the long chain of iron or gold" (*AYR* 4: *GE*, 9:291), the long chain that links past, present, and future, the long chain that binds us—binds Silverman, binds Dickens, and binds Everyman—binds us in our fetters of iron or of gold, and makes us what we are.

X

It is no coincidence, for example, that at the very moment George Silverman looks down into the "dark pits" of staircases and sees the scuffling rats, he also sees the trembling green leaves, the fluttering butterflies, and the vision of "ever-renewing life." And just as the ruined rooms, swarming rats, and other blacking-warehouse associations reminded Dickens of his hidden cellar past, of the shameful reality of "what I was once" (a secret guiltily hidden all his life) or, more importantly, of what he might have become—"a little robber or a little vagabond," as he put it (F, 28)—so the crumbling walls, dark pits of staircases, and scuffling rats of Hoghton Towers goad George Silverman into finding some way to flee his cellar taint, to put behind him the hellish and guilt-engendering nightmare of mere brute scuffling. Or, to frame the matter as George Silverman framed it in a question to his dawning consciousness, "How not to have a repugnance towards myself as I had towards the rats?" (*GSE*, 5:122). Poor, stunted, cellar-dwelling George Silverman; ratlike and self-loathing, he yearns to become a human being.

It is at this point that he resolves to save Sylvia from possible contamination. Silverman's unselfish resolve and his subsequent unselfish act, in which he sacrifices for the first time his own animal appetites and animal self-interest for another's welfare, initiate the green growth within that transforms him from scuffling rat into human being, a transformation the world perceives as sullen selfishness. These complicated developments, again fraught with psychological and autobiographical significance (but now, in the latter case at least, in more submerged ways) are also objectified by the Hoghton Towers setting and Dickens' evocative symbolism.

In human form the fresh green growth that Silverman glimpses at the bottom of the broken staircase is Sylvia. Her very name, Sylvia—she of the forest—allies her with "green leaves," "sweet scents," and "ever-renewing life," and marks her off from the Silverman domain: cellar taints, Preston streets, Hoghton ruins. But the cellar taint will not be eradicated; the flawed world perpetuates, indeed magnifies, what nature and nurture began. When Sylvia invites Silverman into the green realm, that is, when she tries to coax him to join her friends in a joyous celebration of her birthday, his concern to protect her from infection and his need to prove himself unselfish call forth his refusal and initiate what becomes the world's invariable response: "'You are a disagreeable, ill-humored lad,'" Sylvia tells him disdainfully. "'I shall never speak to you again'" (*GSE*, 5:123). Rejected because of his virtuous resolve, Silverman nevertheless maintains his resolve. He puts virtue ahead of felicity, ahead even of his own animal wants. But he pays a price. To save Sylvia from possible infection and purge himself of scuffling ratlike selfishness, he retreats into the shadows; he withdraws into "secret corners of the ruined house" (*GSE*, 5:122); he retreats into the lonely fortress of his scarified mind. He saves her, but he isolates himself. He soon becomes in fullness what here he is in embryo: an outcast from life's feast, mistrustful of who and what he is, misconstrued by the world. Poor, yearning George Silverman. Pure in heart but contaminated in soul, he creates and fulfills his inexorable destiny.

All this is reflected in the Hoghton Towers setting. Resolved to promote Sylvia's welfare, Silverman shuns the lighted farmhouse, the merry music, the dancing feet. His shaded realm is with the wall-begirt ruins. Hostage to the cellar taint, creature of the midnight streets, he can adopt the professed values of the green realm, but never know its "ever-renewing life." He frequents "secret corners" of the ruined house, pushes farther and farther into the fortresslike ruins when the family calls him to meals, remains hidden

134. Hoghton Towers and Its "Secret Corners"

"I withdrew myself . . . into secret corners of the ruined house, and . . . watched." Note the crenellations, a striking fortresslike feature of the front façades of the house. Photograph (1987) by the author.

until Sylvia goes to bed (*GSE*, 5:122). Separate, secret, engirdled by walls, shielded and withdrawn, he watches Sylvia from a distance. Through "dim windows"—Silverman is always looking through windows and doorways at a world he cannot join—he sees that she is "fresh and rosy," and he feels happy (*GSE*, 5:122). On the evening of her festive birthday party he remains outside, a creature of the night. He is one with the dark ruin, the ghostly statue, and the empty quadrangle.[16] He watches, but he does not participate. Out in the dark night, flanked by the dark ruin, companioned by the "lifeless quadrangle, and . . . the mouldering statue," he gazes at the "lighted farm-house windows," all alone (*GSE*, 5:122, 123).

The setting and the images, though totally realistic, are deeply expressive. They are the physical correlatives of Silverman's "infirmity," the harbingers and witnesses of his fate. His inmost being is lifeless, isolated, mouldering, walled-off. He is condemned to be forever in the protective shadows looking on alone. The latter image, an image of shaded apartness, is central to the story, and it recurs in many guises. At Cambridge he lives in a "corner" where the "daylight was sobered" (*GSE*, 7:277). He thinks of himself as "always in the peaceful shade" (*GSE*, 7:277). He dwells in shadows, a shadow himself, set apart, watching, alone. "I can see others in the sunlight; I can see our boats' crews and our athletic young men on the glistening water, or speckled with the moving lights of sunlit leaves; but I myself am always in the shadow looking on. Not unsympathetically,—GOD forbid!—but looking on, alone" (*GSE*, 7:277). In such passages, as throughout *George Silverman's Explanation*, objects, shadows, houses, walls, actions, clothing, windows, relationships—all the manifestations of existence—conspire to accrete and convey meaning.

Yet here again, at the very heart of this artful and seemingly archetypal rendering of isolation and alienation, exists, surprisingly—for outwardly Dickens was the most genial and gregarious of men—a profound autobiographical core. As a boy in Chatham Dickens had frequent bouts of disabling spasms, fever, and sickliness that required him, sometimes for weeks at a time, to rest and watch while

135. Hoghton Towers: "The Lifeless Quadrangle, and . . .
the Mouldering Statue Becoming Visible
to Me Like Its Guardian Ghost"

When Dickens visited Hoghton Towers on 26 April 1867, the manor house
was unoccupied and in a ruinous state, but the mouldering, wall-begirt statue
(now missing) was still there. (See Part 3, notes 15 and 16.) *Hoghton Tower,
Lancashire (Inner Court)*. Engraving (c. 1845).

others played, an affliction, in part nervous, that forced him to turn inward for comfort and to live vicariously in the world of reading and imagination. Furthermore, as Forster tells us, Dickens was never good at cricket, or even at marbles, peg-top, or prisoner's base. "But he had great pleasure in watching the other boys, officers' sons for the most part, at these games, reading while they played" (F, 3). Dickens would sit with a book in some shady spot near Rochester Castle or Rochester Cathedral, sit, usually, in a sheltered nook hard by the cathedral churchyard (the churchyard, filled with melancholy old graves, extended up to the castle in those days—it was Dickens' intention, expressed later in life, to be buried in that boyhood churchyard). Or, even more frequently, he would sit in the shadowy protection of his tiny Chatham room (the window of which, like David Copperfield's window, overlooked a churchyard and its waiting graves), and there, sheltered and hidden, guarded by walls, he would read and he would watch. "The picture always rises in my mind," writes Dickens of one such occasion, or rather of a summation of many such occasions, "of a summer evening, the boys at play in the churchyard, and I sitting on my bed, reading as if for life" (F, 6).

As with Dickens, so with Silverman. *George Silverman's Explanation* ends in the summertime with a sequestered Silverman sitting in his room, looking out the window at the churchyard, "equal resting-place for sound hearts, wounded hearts, and broken hearts" (*GSE*, 9:283), and writing as if for life—that is, writing to explain or justify his life. Isolated and cut off in childhood, Silverman is isolated and cut off in old age. With George Silverman, truly, the child is father of the man. And what of Dickens? Like George Silverman, Dickens sees his childhood self (but only one version of his childhood self) as being always in the shadows, always on the sidelines, always isolated, always looking through windows, always observing, while others live and others play. This is not surprising. Like George Silverman, Dickens felt that he had lost his birthright, lost it through no fault of his own: that he had been cut off in crucial ways from the bright healthy world, that he had languished from

136. Rochester Castle: Shaded and Begirt by Graves,
Dickens Would Sit in the Castle Precincts,
"Reading As If For Life".

Alone, secluded and excluded, begirt by graves, absorbed by the world within yet watching the world without, the boy Dickens would sit in the darkened protection of his tiny room (which overlooked a graveyard) or in some shady spot near Rochester Castle and its adjacent graveyard, "reading as if for life." "Rochester Castle." Wood engraving by Robert Langton after a drawing (1879) by William Hull. From Langton, *The Childhood and Youth of Charles Dickens* (1883).

term to term in darkness, that he had looked longingly through windows at a world he could not join—and all this not only in his sickly childhood days. In the blacking-warehouse period he had walked the busy city streets each morning and each night, walked the streets alone (in winter he walked in darkness), looking in at shopwindows, doorways, casements, and alleys, looking at a bustling world he did not belong to and could not join, and being looked at in turn, looked at with cold scornful stares, looked at by blank unfeeling eyes.

During his childhood and boyhood, this sense of alienation and pariahhood was reinforced, often by recurrent patterns—how meaningful and guilt-producing their recurrence!—that intensified and confirmed his outcast state. One such recurrence, a daily one, became a painful embodiment for him of his baleful outcast state. In the blacking-warehouse period, during the Chandos Street days, he often worked at a street window along with other laboring boys but never feeling one with them, watching the unfettered world go by and, to his great shame, being watched, in turn, by passing strangers—free, untrammeled strangers—watched, and gawked at, and stared at while he toiled on in his shadowy den, an ignominious street show, a wretched emblem of degradation and servitude. This pitiful picture, however exaggerated it seems to be, faithfully reflects Dickens' own assessment of his state at this time: he was cut off, banished, disgraced, a "small Cain," except that he "had never done harm to any one" (F, 27).

In his fragment of autobiography, Dickens emphasizes this later isolation, a reinforcing blacking-warehouse isolation that compounded his earlier, sickly childhood isolation. On the one hand, the blacking-warehouse isolation was a shabby, street-pent isolation (scarifying but empowering); on the other hand, it was a degrading windowed isolation, and he emphasizes in each instance the shame and humiliation he attached to these intertwined isolations. The windowed isolation often took on the same nightmare emotions as the street-environed isolation. This is not surprising. After all, these twin blacking-warehouse isolations were identical in time and inter-

137. "I Saw My Father Coming In at the Door One Day . . . and I Wondered How He Could Bear It"

This illustration shows the street window, very open and very public, at which Dickens worked after the blacking warehouse moved to 3 Chandos Street, Covent Garden. Dickens' humiliation at being (as he felt) an ignominious street show, a degraded Cain-like creature, gazed at and gawked at as he labored at his despised occupation, emerges in his writings in multitudes of direct and indirect ways (see text). These emotion-fraught literary evocations of his pariahhood bear witness (as analogous reiterations do with George Silverman) to the dark festering power of that durance-generated sensitivity, to the tyranny of that "diseased, corner of my mind," as George Silverman puts it, that "winced and shrunk when it was touched, or was even approached." Drawing after a photograph (1911 or earlier) by T. W. Tyrrell. Dickens House Museum, London.

138. John Dickens, Dickens' Father, c. 1830, Age Forty-Four

From a painting by John W. Gilbert. Dickens House Museum, London. When John Dickens quarreled with James Lamert, and Dickens was dismissed from the blacking warehouse (the quarrel centered on Dickens and may have concerned his employment at the window), Dickens' mother took special pains to accommodate the quarrel and, succeeding, insisted that Dickens return to the blacking warehouse. John Dickens refused. He vowed that Dickens "should go back no more, and should go to school."

mingled in emotions. But there were differences as well—differences in emphasis, and in the way Dickens internalized each species of blacking-warehouse isolation. The street isolation engendered special fears and special imaginings (despairing and empowering imaginings); the windowed isolation engendered humiliation. Stationed at the blacking-warehouse window, Dickens not only felt exiled and excluded but sentenced (for what fell crime?) to slavelike public drudgery. At times the humiliation of working in a window for all the world to see seemed unendurable. "We worked, for the light's sake," Dickens writes in his autobiographical fragment, "near the second window as you come from Bedford-street; and we were so brisk at it, that the people used to stop and look in. Sometimes there would be quite a little crowd there. I saw my father coming in at the door one day when we were very busy, and I wondered how he could bear it" (F, 34). Dickens does not add (though the implication and resentment are unmistakable) that he also wondered how he himself could—and did—bear it.

Nor does he add something else. His mother, unlike his father, visited the blacking warehouse frequently (F, 35), but Dickens never wondered how *she* could bear it. His silence on this score is eloquent: he knew that his mother could and did bear it; he knew that she had arranged for his servitude (James Lamert, the manager of the blacking warehouse, was her relative by marriage), and he knew that she, again unlike his father, had strenuously sought to perpetuate his servitude when it finally came to an end (F, 35), to perpetuate, in effect, his banishment and his windowed street-show humiliation. His mother had insisted that he go back to the blacking warehouse; his father had insisted that he go back to school. Given such shapings and such awarenesses, it is not surprising that so many mothers and surrogate mothers in Dickens have ogreish proclivities, nor is it surprising that so many are meted out a dismal fate. By the same token, given the indelible conditioning of his windowed street-show humiliation, it is not surprising that so many of Dickens' characters look longingly out through windows or longingly in through windows at worlds they cannot possess.[17] Finally, it

is not surprising that so many outlawed or alienated characters—
nightmare offspring, in many psychological ways, of Dickens' own
anguished durance in pariahhood—are haunted and enfeebled (like
those hunted Cain-like pariahs Fagin and Sikes at their final har-
rowings) by staring eyes.

George Silverman exhibits this staring and shrinking from being
stared at behavior over and over again. Even before he is humanized
he participates in the portentous ritual of eyes. He occasionally
"slunk" out of his cellar lair, crept through the nearby city streets,
and "glared in at shop-windows," an unimaginable world to him,
glared in like "a mangy young dog or wolf-cub" (*GSE*, 4:121).
Plucked from the cellar, he is surrounded in the busy street by a
crowd of strangers that stare at him "in silent horror" (*GSE*, 4:120).
In the Hoghton ruins he fears that "dead-alive creatures" might
stare at him "with I know not what dreadful eyes, or lack of eyes"
(*GSE*, 5:122). He soon comes to feel that even "the sky stared sorrowfully" at him (*GSE*, 5:122). When the Hoghton ruin is dark,
when the music plays and the children dance, he stares in mute, self-
enforced estrangement at "the lighted farm-house windows," alone,
self-condemned, self-banished, watching from a distance in the dark
(*GSE*, 5:123). He is an outcast; he is always looking in, looking out,
or being looked at. This glaring and staring goes on throughout the
story. It is no wonder, given Silverman's dire conditioning, that half
a lifetime later, the "steady glare" of Lady Fareway's "great round
dark eyes . . . embarrassed" the sensitized clergyman (*GSE*, 7:278).
He is embarrassed because he feels guilty. If he were not guilty, why
would he have suffered as he did? Of the relationship between the
staring world and Silverman's feelings of guilt there can be no
doubt:

> I have written that the sky stared sorrowfully at me. Therein have I
> anticipated the answer. I knew that all these things looked sorrowfully at
> me. That they seemed to sigh or whisper, not without pity for me: "Alas!
> Poor worldly little devil!" (*GSE*, 5:122)

The intricate ritual of eyes in *George Silverman's Explanation*
emerges like a dead-alive ghost out of Dickens own guilty, embar-

rassed, sensitized past. The concealed sorenesses and susceptibilities that rise up when Dickens recalls that distant past (sorenesses and susceptibilities not voiced until many years later) shape, indeed constitute, the hidden, diseased night side—the wounded George Silverman side—of Dickens, a side that had its origins (again as with George Silverman) in a series of repeated and reinforcing experiences that go back to Dickens' earliest days. Many years after those earliest days, long after Dickens had become rich and famous, Thomas Carlyle had glimpses of this region of darkness that lay so deeply buried beneath the burnished surface of Dickens' intense life-affirming engagement with the outer world. Beneath Dickens' "bright and joyful sympathy with everything around him," Carlyle wrote, there were "deeper than all, if one has the eye to see deep enough, dark, fateful, silent elements, tragical to look upon, and hiding, amid dazzling radiances as of the sun, the elements of death itself" (V&A MS, Carlyle to Forster, 16 February 1874).

Dickens recognized these "dark, fateful, silent elements" within himself, "tragical to look upon." *George Silverman's Explanation* is one expression of those silent night-side elements. George Silverman articulates what Dickens profoundly felt. Silverman speaks of "the delicate, perhaps the diseased, corner of my mind, where I winced and shrunk when it was touched, or was even approached" (*GSE*, 6:149). In probing that diseased corner of Silverman's mind, Dickens was also probing the diseased corner of his own mind, the night-side corner that winced and shrunk when it was touched or even approached. He was probing the corner that included his rejecting mother, improvident father, sickly childhood, and desultory boyhood; he was also probing the shameful corner of his mind that concealed the painful black streets and the cruel staring eyes of his secret guilt-filled boyhood humiliation, the corner that hid the rat-haunted nightmare of his blacking-warehouse degradation. He was probing, in other words, those "dark, fateful, silent elements," or rather, the origins of those dark, fateful, silent elements, origins that lay "deeper than all." But Dickens also recognized within himself the "radiances as of the sun"—the radiances, that is, of his own great imaginative gifts—and he understood that the darkness and the radiance were two aspects of a single whole. "I know," he wrote, to quote once more his insightful words about the intermingling of the deathlike and the radiant in his own life, "how all these things have worked together to make me what I am" (F, 35). It was an insight that gave primacy to an attendant struggle (a struggle in which a chastened fulfillment emerges painfully out of disability and defeat), a struggle he articulated in many of his works. It is present most succinctly, almost schematically, in Redlaw in *The Haunted Man,* the first character and the first work to center on this repeated paradigm. It emerges in many later characters and works. It shapes, for example, the early disabilities and the ultimate victories—equivocal victories—of Esther Summerson in *Bleak House* and Arthur Clennam and Amy Dorrit in *Little Dorrit*—all blighted characters who must transcend their early blight. It is also at the center of *Great Expectations.* Like Redlaw, the archetypal Haunted Man (haunted by his sorrowful past), Pip (who is also haunted by his secret past) learns slowly and painfully that the gift he was so unaccountably given as a boy (as it turns out, because of his past) really is a curse; but he also learns that that very same curse is his true gift. It is an insight that emerged from Dickens' hardest experiences, though the full realization of its significance and the ability to conceptualize it came only in maturity, only, that is, after long years of thought and experience, as it also comes to his characters after long hard experience, but only to his middle and late characters.

Yet the nascent origins of the pattern, as Dickens recognized, are coincident with the dawn of consciousness. He usually traces the pattern, the shaping and empowering conjunction of affliction and transcendence, back to a disordered childhood and its earliest memories, in his own case, back to his disturbed, shadowed, but enabling beginnings. To cite only one example of this primordial dialectic, in the very passages in which he describes his early alienation—that is, his early sickliness and enforced seclusion—he also describes his early imaginative nurturing. Primary in that nurturing is his "reading as if for life" (F, 6). The phrase speaks volumes. It connotes the saving nature of that compensatory and life-succoring reading: in a time of isolation and disorder, he read and imagined in order to live (as he repeatedly acknowledged not only in his fragment of autobiography but elsewhere), a process of imagination and compensation that became even more crucial to his survival and, much later, to his triumph (as he also makes clear in his autobiography and elsewhere), when he descended into the still darker shadows and deeper alienation of the blacking warehouse and its aftermath. That process of imagination and compensation did not end with childhood and boyhood, and it was not confined to reading. Later still, years later, as a man and as an artist, did he not continue to imagine? Was he not imagining now, even as he was writing *George Silverman's Explanation,* imagining in order to live? That is, did he not literally imagine in order to earn a living, and did he not literally imagine in order to create himself and understand himself and transcend himself, to make his life meaningful and to fashion himself and his world anew?

We are talking here about some of the formative influences and impulses that shape an artist's gift (or that shape many artists' gifts), the development, especially in certain very great artists, from a variety of causes, of a double and a triple, really a multivalent vision; the ability, or rather the necessity, to be, at one and the same time, insider and outsider, participant and observer, initiate and alien; the need, indeed the fate, to belong and not to belong, to be blessed and cursed (or, more precisely, to be blessed because one is cursed), to be a winner and a loser (that is, to be a winner because one is a loser), the equivocal destiny of being caught between two worlds and two conditions, one yearned for and one fled from, but each necessary to the other—a status and an attendant power that Dickens shared with such very different writers as Shakespeare, Cervantes, Dostoevsky, and Joyce, to name only four.

George Silverman, unlike Dickens, is powerless, robbed rather than enabled by his alienation. Yet he reflects, or rather magnifies, many aspects of Dickens' development. Like the child Dickens, Silverman watches and empathizes but is precluded, or rather precludes himself, from participating. Like the child Dickens, he is always in the shadows looking on while others play and others live—

looking on, as he tells us, "not unsympathetically,—GOD forbid!—but looking on, alone" (*GSE*, 7:277). Yet Dickens was no George Silverman. In outward ways, surely, he succeeded where Silverman failed. For Dickens, early alienation became part of his power as well as part of his pain. Not so for George Silverman. For Silverman early alienation was a wound that warped his personality and disordered his life, a disabling wound, a wound that would not heal.

In *George Silverman's Explanation* Dickens examines that unhealable wound. With profound art and insight, he examines Silverman's wound, and his own wound as well: he examines what he might have become and what, in part, he was.

XI

But *George Silverman's Explanation* is much more than self-analysis. The psychological and autobiographical core of *George Silverman* is not the literal substance of the story (though it often contributes striking literal details to the donnée), but the deep primordial matrix out of which the story was born. In the story itself, the disorder of life becomes the order of art. Disciplined and spare, the story moves swiftly and inexorably toward its preordained conclusion. Though ambiguity and perplexity remain, nothing now is inconsequential or extraneous. Action and setting, gesture and character, all the innumerable nuances of animate nature and inanimate objects, generate and focus meaning.

Names, too, participate in this integrative process and in Dickens' all-encompassing art. Earlier we saw how the given names "Sylvia" and "Verity" became part of the story's meaning. But, as so often in Dickens, these strong central connections are surrounded by less obvious hints. Thus the name Sylvia (Silverman comments, "that was her pretty name" [*GSE*, 5:123]), or Sylvy, as she is also known, not only connects her with the vernal and sylvan regions, with the ever-renewing growth that Silverman glimpses, yearns for, yet can never become part of, but with his own name and his own condition, so similar yet so different—the sounds of "Sylvia" and "Sylvy," we perceive with something of a start, are echoed in "Silverman." Yet the similarity in sound only accentuates the disparity in meaning and implication. "Sylvan" and "Silver," after all, are as different as forest and money.

By the same token, the name Verity not only accentuates the fact that Brother Hawkyard is a liar but becomes the ironic badge of his central hypocrisy. Taken by itself, the name has a forthright Bunyanesque ring to it; or, to emphasize its later associations, it is redolent of puritanical zeal and religious self-righteousness. Brother Verity in the flesh oozes puritanical zeal and religious self-righteousness, but he is no Bunyanesque embodiment of virtue. He is neither a brother to his fellowman nor a truthteller in his moral being. He is a rapacious opportunist whose hypocrisy is equally evident in his personal relations, commercial dealings, public utterances, and religious professions. "Verity" is thus, in the most profound and comprehensive sense, the antithesis of all that Hawkyard is and represents; his name becomes an ironic paradigm for a society sick to the core.

Other given names—Adelina, Granville, Gaston—speak in different but equally eloquent ways of the characters and the values they represent. Such genteel given names not only signal that the characters who bear them are part of a patrician world that is their birthright, a world that Silverman can never enter (his given name is the plebian George), but such names resound as well with more hidden overtones and undertones. Take the name Adelina, for example, a name that stirred deep emotions—hidden, passion-generated emotions—in Dickens. The sounds of the name Adelina work changes on the sounds of the names Ellen and Nelly, Nelly being Dickens' affectionate pet name for Ellen. But in addition to these primary associations, the sounds of the name Adelina also echo the sounds of the names "Estella" and "Bella," the names of the heroines of *Great Expectations* and *Our Mutual Friend*—the heroines, that is, of Dickens' two most recent novels, and heroines who, like Adelina, are (in part, at least) emotional surrogates of Ellen.[18] It is as though, from 1860 on, the sounds of Ellen's (Nelly's) name, and variations

on their enchanting melodies—enchanting for passion-bound
Dickens—reverberated lovingly, hauntingly, unceasingly in his enraptured consciousness: Ellen, Nelly, Estella, Bella, Adelina.[19] And,
just as in life Ellen was secretly adored by Dickens but publicly forbidden him, so also in *George Silverman's Explanation,* Adelina is
secretly adored by Silverman but publicly forbidden him.

The surnames Dickens devises—sometimes transparently open,
sometimes profoundly private, sometimes both—are no less eloquent in their iridescent signalings. If "Verity" disguises Hawkyard's
true moral being, his surname trumpets it forth. He is a hawk, a
rapacious bird of prey (one is reminded of the rapacious Sir Mulberry Hawk in *Nicholas Nickleby*) who feeds ruthlessly on creatures
smaller and weaker than he. The other element of his name—
"yard"—is no less eloquent, containing within it such meanings, all
pertinent to his pervasive materialism, manipulativeness, and aggression, as measuring device, scourging rod, confining enclosure,
animal pen, and business place. (The rear yard of Hawkyard's own
business place, littered with the casks and boxes of his occupation,
is labeled, most appropriately, "Private Way to the Counting-house"
[*GSE*, 6:147].) Brother Gimblet's name also bodies forth his nature.
He is a gimlet, a sharp, twisting instrument for boring, cutting,
screwing, piercing. Brothers Hawkyard and Gimblet personify the
only true brotherhood in the story, a brotherhood based upon a
mutual partnership in criminal fraud, a brotherhood of greed, chica-
nery, and self-interest.

In their rapacious brotherhood, Brothers Hawkyard and Gimblet
prey upon weakness and gullibility wherever they find it, even—or
perhaps especially—when they find it in the sanctified ranks of the
Brotherhood itself. With Brothers Hawkyard and Gimblet, one may
be sure, no trust is sacred, no bond secure. But Brother Parksop was
born to be gulled. His name tells us this. Brother Parksop, Silverman's well-to-do grandfather, who foolishly entrusts Brother
Hawkyard with Silverman's heritage (an inheritance of real estate—
"park" again), proves by that very action that he is both sappy and
a sop.[20] He is weak in insight and in judgment, a moral milksop.

(Doesn't Parksop know that hawks prey in parks? And doesn't he know that yards and parks, though similar, are antithetical?) Brother Parksop's name combines his parklike wealth and parklike exclusivity (he rejects his daughter and the outer world) with his softheaded soppiness. Silverman never receives the Parksop sop that might have translated him (had it come early enough) from cellar to park.[21]

Other names are more equivocal, but all the more revealing once one deciphers their signaling ironies. Lady Fareway's name is a good example. Her seemingly simple name conceals and proclaims her true identity. At first glance the "fare" of her name seems to suggest that she is "fair," that is, evenhanded in her dealings and comely in her aspect (we are told that she is "handsome" [*GSE*, 7:278]). But this outward appearance of fairness conceals her inward exploitiveness. Her "way" (the word here signifies manner, method, and path) is not "fair" but "fare"—the spelling Dickens gives the homonym is indicative: her "way" (manner, method, and path) has to do not with evenhandedness or comeliness but with money and charges, with "fares": not Fairway but Fareway. Furthermore, the "way" of her name is a pun on "weigh." She weighs, that is calculates, her every action. She also weighs one down. The burdens she places on all who serve her, as Silverman and his predecessor know only too well, weigh heavily. Her "way," in short, is to exploit. Her "way," in the language of her name, is to charge a weighty "fare"—again Fareway. Dickens' irony here is most telling, for Lady Fareway, though admirable in the eyes of society, is neither a lady nor fair nor a practitioner of an acceptable way.

The name Silverman is no less equivocal and instructive. Like many of Dickens' names, Silverman's name seems to embody and control his inmost being, and thus his destiny; it seems to be an outward sign of some emergent inward necessity, a necessity that will eventually express and confirm itself, a necessity that links name and named. What are we to make of Silverman's name? Does Silverman connote a worldly man, a man of silver, of money? (That is the way the world perceives him.) Or does it connote a sterling man, a man of high worth, integrity, and purity? (That is the way he portrays himself.) Or does it connote both? Or neither? As a matter of fact, the name Silverman is more complex and paradoxical than even these contradictory connotations suggest. For Silver-man is what Silverman is—all he is—for Brother Hawkyard and Brother Gimblet: a man of silver, silver they can steal. And Silver-man is what Silverman is—all he is—for Lady Fareway: a silver lode to be relentlessly plundered. But silver is also the preeminent metal of betrayal—we recall the archetypal thirty pieces of silver—and Silverman is the very type and emblem of betrayal. He is betrayed not only by Brother Hawkyard, Brother Gimblet, and Lady Fareway, but by himself. He plays Judas to himself, betraying himself for fear that he will be thought worldly—that is, that he will be regarded as a Silver-man.

Silverman's equivocal name, a name glinting with subtleties and contradictions, was meant to provoke and guide us. Dickens, who always gave an almost magical importance to names and naming (see Part 3, notes 18 and 19) was very much aware of the rich suggestiveness inherent in Silverman's name: he chose it because of those ambiguous resonances, and he used those resonances (as was his practice) to evoke and reinforce the profound harmonies and discordances he wished to convey. That this is so may be seen in his formulation of Silverman's name. Dickens originally decided on "Silvermanor" for Silverman's name (the original title of the story, changed in manuscript, was *Mr. Silvermanor's Explanation,* an echo, perhaps, of the ruined manor, Hoghton Towers, that had shown Dickens how to begin his story), and "Mr. Silvermanor," its homonym "Mr. Silvermanner," and its components "Mr. Silver man or," evoke (as "Parksop" also does—Parksop, it will be remembered, is Silverman's maternal grandfather) the counters Dickens is working with in Silverman's case: the yearning for gentility (for the manor and the title "Mr."), the emphasis upon outward show (upon manners and upon "Mr."), and the raising of doubt (of Mr. Silver man or?), with "Silver" in each case also introducing the sterling-worldly ambiguity, that is, also introducing the question of whether Sil-

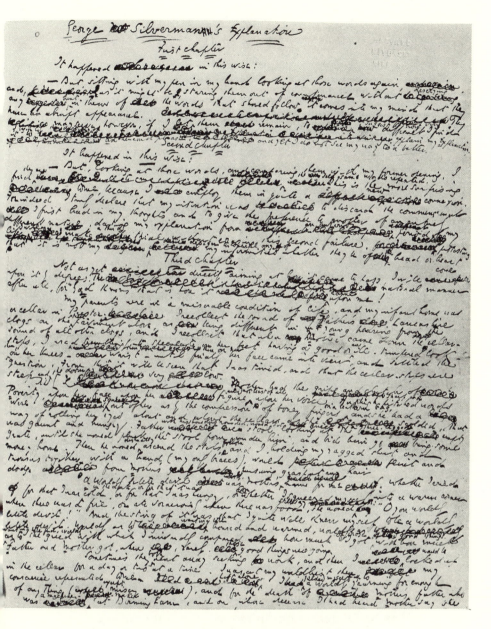

139. First Page of the Manuscript (1867) of
George Silverman's Explanation (1868)

Notice the changes Dickens made in the title, including the change in Silverman's name (see text). Houghton Library, Harvard University, Cambridge, Massachusetts.

verman's deepest impulses are pure or self-serving. In other words, Dickens' original name for George Silverman (Mr. Silvermanor) verifies more openly than his final choice the themes and meanings that emerge everywhere in *George Silverman's Explanation*. Perhaps this is the clue to the change. Perhaps Dickens felt that "George Silverman" was less insistent and directive, and consequently less restrictive, than "Mr. Silvermanor."

"Silverman," after all, is directive enough, and it evokes a wider (and quieter) range of implications than the rejected name. Silverman, for example, also suggests a man greyed-out, insubstantial, a man who is pale, lacking color and vitality. Silverman's hair turns grey at thirty-one, is white at thirty-two, changes that coincide with his renunciation of sex. We always see Silverman in tones of black, grey, and silver. We picture him in the shadows, a colorless shadow himself, timid, subdued, mistrustful—a retiring scholar, a self-effacing clergyman, a faded bachelor—looking on rather than participating, mournful, fearful, alone. His name is as enigmatic as the attributes of his identity. It seems to mirror the equivocal puzzlements of his being: his clouded character, his reflexive fate, his ambiguous reputation. Who and what is he?—worldly devil, sulky loner, misconstrued saint, sacrificial lamb, morbid self-tormentor, compulsive self-betrayer, tragic victim? His name, at once noble and mercenary, glimmering with hints of ostentation and effacement, comprehends these contradictions. But there is no question that he is damaged. As Silverman puts it at the end of the story, emphasizing the metaphorical implications of his name, "my name was tarnished" (*GSE*, 9:283). He says this but he does not understand the deeper meaning of what he has said. For in ways that he cannot fathom, his name comprehends the sad perplexities of his equivocal character and the glinting ironies of his checkered history. Silverman, as Dickens wants us to see—see in the enlarged sense that the insights and the contrarieties of the story make manifest, see as Dickens, looking into his own heart, saw himself—Silverman is a tarnished Silver man.

XII

Dickens' masterful use of names demonstrates once again how deep and carefully wrought was his seemingly simple art. In this stark tale, as in most of Dickens' mature work, every touch tells, every chord reverberates. The muted end rounds out what the broken opening began. The central images recur and accrete, the dominant meanings cohere. Fable and idea fuse seamlessly to enrich and ordain meaning, a perfect, reciprocating whole.

We last see George Silverman writing at the open window. He is an observer still, lingering as always in the protection of a shaded place. What he sees is the churchyard, "equal resting-place," as he puts it, "for sound hearts, wounded hearts, and broken hearts" (*GSE*, 9:283). Silverman's heart is wounded, his spirit lamed. There is nothing that will mend his heart or heal his spirit in this imperfect world. He cannot be made whole, he cannot be released. He will emerge from the shadows only to enter the shadow of death. His life, a kind of death, has been a slow pilgrimage to extinction. The shadow of the cellar has cast its long darkness over all his ways and days, over the Lancashire streets, the Hoghton ruin, the Preston chapel, the Cambridge chambers, the Fareway vicarage, the college-living, the open window—open but offering no escape for him. He writes at the open window, an observer rather than a participant, cut off, as always, from life's abundance and life's felicities; he writes, as he tells us, "for the relief of my own mind" (*GSE*, 9:283).

But he can have no relief. The shadow that darkens all his landscapes and all his prospects lies darkest on his mind, shading his every thought, obscuring now, as it always has, the cruel necessity that compels his servitude. Like passion-driven Pip, he is bound by chains of iron. Like Pip, he could write (if only he had come to Pip's late realization) what a chastened Pip writes of his life, indeed, of all lives: "Pause you who read this, and think for a moment of the long chain of iron or gold, of thorns or flowers, that would never have bound you, but for the formation of the first link on one memorable day" (*AYR* 4: *GE,* 9:291). But Silverman, unlike Pip, has no insight into the long chain that binds him or into his complicity in forging that chain; he cannot write Pip's warning (and freeing) words of self-implicating knowledge. Like Miss Wade, Silverman is a self-tormentor. Self-loathing and self-arraigning, he stifles his natural desires and fashions them into fetters. He blindly hammers out the fate he dreads but also cherishes. Like Arthur Clennam, he is convinced of his primal guilt. He is, he knows, a cellar sinner. Though he seeks to atone for his childhood "sin" by altruistic acts of self-immolation, his self-sacrifices are unavailing. Through those self-sacrifices he subverts the felicity he yearns for, the felicity he can never let himself know. Like Arthur Clennam, he creates his identity by effacing his identity: he has no will. Or rather, he does have will, free will: free will to will what he, of necessity, must unwittingly will. Hence the long chain of iron that binds him; hence the ceaseless repetition that blinds him. Hence the uncomprehending explanation of his opening; hence the uncomprehending explanation of his conclusion.

The conclusion is cosmic and immutable. Necessity controls his pallid days. He tells us that, gradually, the belief widened that he was not guilty of the perfidy laid to his charge. What he does not see, what he can never see, is that guilt—self-imposed guilt, uncleansable guilt—has long since passed a crippling sentence on his life. And so he sits at the open window, a hobbled prisoner still. Dickens takes pains to demonstrate that Silverman's plight is not special or local but universal. Our lives, if we are fortunate, may be less constrained, less shadowed than Silverman's, but we too are shaped by forces we only partly control. The great towering mountains of nature, nurture, and society loom over each one of us, casting long shadows. For each person the shadows are different, but no one lives outside their darkening influence.

Dickens shows us this. He shows us that Silverman's condition is only an extreme instance of the human condition. He also shows us (though only he knew at the time the full personal import of his revelations) that Silverman's condition is a melancholy version of his own condition: he too is haunted and compelled. Dickens shows us this most clearly in the scene in which Silverman prepares to sacrifice all hope of worldly happiness on the altar of selfless virtue. He will prove to all the world, will prove conclusively, at long last, after so many futile attempts, that he is not a "worldly devil." He will do this by performing an altruistic act (for his own future felicity, a dolorous act), an act that he has long contemplated and worked to bring to fruition: he will perform the sacred ceremony that will unite Granville and the divine Adelina in holy matrimony. To calm himself before the ceremony, Silverman walks down to the sea. Here, by this emblem of death and immortality (Dickens often uses the sea this way), Silverman girds himself to effect the crowning renunciation of his life—a renunciation (not in the person of Adelina Fareway but of Ellen Ternan) that Dickens, in his own life, fettered by his own long chain of guilt-encumbered necessity, could not bring himself to make.

This paradox (or seeming paradox)—that Silverman does what Dickens was unable to do—enforces rather than effaces the deep autobiographical relevance of the story and dramatizes its universality as well. *George Silverman's Explanation* is full of such autobiographical inversions, reversals, and seeming contradictions. (It is also full of literal and undisguised autobiography.) It is replete with other meaningful oppositions as well: with tragic ironies and strategic contrasts, the deliberate ironic tension between outward narrative voice and inward defining emotion, for example. These oppositions are at the heart of the story. The story is universal in its application and cosmic, almost detached, in its point of view, but it is also intensely personal and perplexed. Dickens, at one and the same time, is looking out at the great wide world and in at his own secret self. We are all, he finds, driven and trammeled, poor perplexed creatures. Silverman, despite his own special pathology, incorporates the universal and the personal (the personal for Dickens, that is). Silverman embodied for Dickens versions—often heightened or intensified versions—of his inmost self, his secret night-side self. Dickens, unable to renounce, was not different from Silverman but like him. Silverman, driven by guilt, must endlessly renounce (Adelina is the culminating incarnation of his renunciation); Dickens, driven by passion and his inability to renounce, must endlessly suffer guilt (Ellen—"my Darling," he calls her in a phrase that was inked out of one of his letters after his death [30 December 1867, Huntington Library MS], a phrase written while he was thousands of miles away in America, written longingly and secretly at the very moment *George Silverman's Explanation* was poised for launching into the busy world, there to be read, for the most part uncritically and uncomprehendingly, by a vast Dickens-worshipping public— Ellen, "my Darling" Ellen, is the culminating incarnation of Dickens' guilt).

Confronting his own dilemma, Dickens saw no way out: he saw— as *George Silverman's Explanation* repeatedly and devastatingly shows us—no salvation in renunciation (a salvation, or would-be salvation, that he had embraced fervently eight years earlier through Sydney Carton in *A Tale of Two Cities*); and he saw, as his own guilt-haunted latter-day actions show us, no salvation in refusing to renounce (a refusal, and its ultimate toll in misery and self-destruction, that Dickens re-created and then underwent, or rather underwent again, vicariously through such passion-bound, post-Carton surrogates—emotional enlargements of his own headlong pursuit—as Bradley Headstone in *Our Mutual Friend* and John Jasper in *Edwin Drood*). Dickens' refusal to renounce, in any case, was only a sign of his deep inescapable bondage, a sign, in other words, that he was incapable of renouncing. Release from that deep inner bondage, from that compelling inner necessity—the necessity that would not let him renounce, the necessity that drove him in countless other ways—release from that inner necessity will come not during the wrenching turmoil of life (in cosmic terms, a momentary turmoil) but in the calm stasis of death (an unimaginable, an eternal stasis). Our final destiny is the quiet grave, "equal resting-place," as Dickens has Silverman write, "for sound hearts, wounded hearts, and broken hearts" (*GSE*, 9:283). Our comfort is that "life is so short" (*GSE*, 9:282).

George Silverman is profoundly linked to Dickens: he is profoundly linked to Dickens' mother-afflicted childhood, he is profoundly linked to Dickens' blacking-warehouse boyhood, he is profoundly linked to Dickens' Ellen-centered later years, and he is profoundly linked to Dickens' last ponderings (*George Silverman's Explanation* is a summation of Dickens' last ponderings) on life, death, and necessity. But Silverman, whether child or man, and despite his close blood relationship with Dickens as both child and man, is no simple surrogate of Dickens—no simple surrogate as shameful cellar dweller, no simple surrogate as guilty disbarred lover, no simple surrogate as driven self-tormentor. Though the two share much, they differ in much as well. Silverman, unlike Dickens, has no insight into his predicament; he cannot, as he tells us, explain his explanation (*GSE*, 1:118). That insight and that awareness, however comforting or comfortless, however mitigating or intensifying, however empowering or disabling (in many ways that insight combines these contending contrarieties), that perplexed insight is Dickens' insight, not Silverman's. Silverman, without comprehending, must suffer in silence; he can have no catharsis, no relief. He must endlessly reenact and endlessly endure. Shackled—profoundly shackled—by his cellar taint, he must blindly embrace his sad necessitous fate.

Silverman embraces his fate. In the last fleeting moments before he denies himself (and thus confirms himself) once more, he goes out of his dwelling place and walks toward the dawning light. By denying himself he will vindicate himself—so he feels, and so he has ever felt. Before that guilt-driven denial, this time a denial that will culminate in his uniting Granville and Adelina in marriage and thus doom his own hopes for felicity, Silverman, to calm himself, walks down to the shore of the illimitable sea. Communing with himself, about to consummate the supreme renunciation of his life, he stands alone at the rocky verge of the eternal sea. Facing the abiding sea, ready to exalt virtue (or seeming virtue) over the self-indulgent bliss of worldly love, over the self-indulgent bliss of his own secret love (he is not a "worldly devil," after all), poor, hobbled George Silverman contemplates the prospect of his virtuous sacrifice and contemplates also the mystery of existence—of his own existence and universal existence. It is dawn. In this quintessential moment of birth and fresh beginnings, Silverman prepares, all unwittingly, of course, to forge afresh, not fresh beginnings, but his old necessitous fetters, to enact once more his self-imposed ritual, his inescapable ritual, of denial and death. Dickens makes the moment universal, the setting cosmic. Silverman is dwarfed by the ocean, the sky, the shore. He is a mere speck in the vast solitary reaches of space and time. Dickens' language is majestic. He echoes the Bible; he invokes the eternal rhythms of life and death:

> I rose before the sun, to compose myself for the crowning of my work with this end. And my dwelling being near to the sea, I walked down to the rocks on the shore, in order that I might behold the sun rise in his majesty.
> The tranquillity upon the Deep and on the firmament, the orderly withdrawal of the stars, the calm promise of coming day, the rosy suffusion of the sky and waters, the ineffable splendor that then burst forth, attuned my mind afresh after the discords of the night. Methought that all I looked on said to me, and that all I heard in the sea and in the air said to me, "Be comforted, mortal, that thy life is so short. Our preparation for what is to follow has endured, and shall endure, for unimaginable ages." (*GSE,* 9:281–82)

The heavens and the earth continue in their immutable courses, perfect, ordered, beautiful, harmonious. Only man is vexed and troubled, a creature subject to the "discords of the night." In this dark world and wide, man must be content to suffer. His comfort is that "life is so short."

What then, in its bleakest and darkest aspects, is our destiny? What, to pose the question more figuratively, is our night-side destiny, our George Silverman destiny? Our night-side destiny, Dickens tells us in this his last complete formulation of the subject, is to give obeisance (we are compelled to give obeisance) to that which shaped—and shapes—us. We are chained and fettered; we cannot escape the early forgings that determine our fate; we cannot escape the ineluctable necessity of our journey and our mortality; we cannot break the long chain—whether it be a chain of iron or a chain of gold—we cannot break the long chain that binds us. In this short life, so full of discord, we are poor, blind, puny creatures. We are compelled to do that which we must do, that which hobbles and fetters us. We must endure. Enduring, we must forge our inescapable chain, forge it link by link, forge it as we are compelled to forge it, forge it until the moment of death. Having forged our long chain, we can sleep at last. Then death will endure everlastingly.

There is much of Charles Dickens in George Silverman; or perhaps it would be better to say there is much of George Silverman in Dickens—and in every human soul. Was not Dickens, even as he wrote this explanation—George Silverman's explanation and his explanation—was he not bound and compelled? Was he not bound and compelled by mother-centered yearnings (deep unsatisfied yearnings) and mother-centered betrayals (unforgotten and unforgiven betrayals)? Was he not bound and compelled by loathsome cannibalistic fantasies (obsessive fantasies) and terrifying cannibalistic fears (ineradicable fears)? Was he not bound and compelled by blacking-warehouse angers (still-festering angers) and blacking-warehouse stigmas (still-shaming stigmas)? Was he not bound and compelled by other chains and other goads: by guilt-laden autumn passion, soul-searing self-wounding passion, inexplicable, inescapable passion? Was he not bound and compelled by all this and much much more? Finally, was he not bound and compelled by his mortality and his last destiny, the mortality and last destiny of every man? Was he not fast approaching that universal destiny, fast approaching a strange, inconceivable tranquillity (a frozen tranquillity), fast approaching an unimaginable surcease (an extinguishing surcease), fast approaching an incomprehensible condition when he would be sleeping at last? Was he not moving inexorably toward that final extinction, toward that longed-for yet dread "resting-place," an eternal resting place? Was he not approaching ever closer to that all-leveling and all-ceasing resting place, an "equal resting-place," equal

Gads Hill
10ᵗʰ June 1870

140. Sleeping at Last, Dickens in Death: "Equal Resting-Place for Sound Hearts, Wounded Hearts, and Broken Hearts"

This sketch evokes a recurrent image that emerges with increasing force and implication in Dickens' later life and art. That recurrent image, death-haunted and death-focused, is of the night-side Dickens, the George Silverman Dickens, long compelled and long driven, sleeping at last. (*George Silverman's Explanation* ends with that sad self-reflective Dickensian image; it ends with the graveyard, "equal resting-place for sound hearts, wounded hearts, and broken hearts," and it ends with the fettered and compelled narrator writing not for a reader but "for the relief of my own mind"—a relief he can never know except in death.) This moving pencil drawing by Sir John Everett Millais was made at Gad's Hill Place on 10 June 1870, the day after Dickens died. Kate Macready ("Katey") Dickens, Dickens' younger daughter, and a friend of Millais in her own right, was married to Charles Allston Collins, brother of Wilkie Collins. Charles Collins, a writer and painter (see figure 80), was an intimate of the Pre-Raphaelites, including Millais, hence Katey had a twofold connection with Millais. When Dickens died, Katey asked Millais to go down to Gad's Hill and make a drawing of Dickens in death. For an unpublished letter from Millais giving an account of these arrangements, see Part 3, note 22. The letter is in the author's collection; the drawing is in the Dickens House Museum, London.

536

for high and equal for low, equal for rich and equal for poor, equal for blessed and equal for cursed, equal "for sound hearts, wounded hearts, and broken hearts"?[22]

In this dark masterpiece, at once so simple and so deep, Dickens, heeding the sad insistent murmurings of his night side, tells us once more, and now most uncompromisingly, that we are all prisoners, in great or small degree, of forces we did not create and cannot control. If those forces are too cruel and deforming, if society's impositions are too hypocritical and unjust, nothing we do can save us from our damaged fate. Oedipus-like, we will rush towards that fate, each new attempt to escape compelling us to reenact our endlessly enacted doom.

Perfect goodness may be exempt, or may seem to be exempt, from this law. Other virtuous creatures, fortunate in their innate purity, fortunate also in their nurture and their surroundings—fortunate, that is, in being bound by golden rather than iron chains—may escape virtually unencumbered and unscathed. But for the rest of us—the Pips, Clennams, Copperfields, and Wrayburns of life—salvation, if it comes at all, comes only to the chastened and still-hobbled psyche after much suffering and travail. Salvation may come, enablement and achievement may also come, but even then the dark shadows remain, haunting and shading the nethermost depths, shadowing the soul itself and darkening the soul's equivocal salvation, a hard-won, pain-fraught, precarious salvation.

For the George Silvermans of this world there is no hope, no salvation. Consigned to the cellar, imprisoned additionally by society's afflictions and society's false professions, they must forgo life even as they seek—indeed, because they seek—to affirm its highest behests. No act of expiation, no gesture of renunciation, can purge them of their cellar guilt. Yet they must seek that purgation endlessly; they must expiate and renounce. For them, free will is only the freedom to forge their chains and embrace their implacable fate. They do not understand their compulsion or the necessity that controls it. They suffer mutely. Defeated and rebuffed, they grow timid, withdrawn, self-effacing; they become mistrustful of themselves.

They linger in the shadows, under a shadow. They sacrifice themselves. They watch dumbly, uncomplainingly, as life slips slowly past them. They end their days as they began them. They sit at open windows looking out at their final end, waiting for death to release them from life, friendless and alone.

Abbreviations

HM	*The Haunted Man* (1848)
HN	*The Household Narrative of Current Events* (1850–55)
HR	*Holiday Romance* (1868)
HT	*Hard Times* (1854)
HTI	*The Holly-Tree Inn* (1855)
HW	*Household Words* (1850–59)
L	*The Lamplighter, A Farce* (1838)
LD	*Little Dorrit* (1855–57)
LS	"The Lamplighter's Story" (1841)
LT	*The Lazy Tour of Two Idle Apprentices* (1857)
MC	*Martin Chuzzlewit* (1843–44)
MHC	*Master Humphrey's Clock* (1840–41)
MJ	*Mugby Junction* (1866)
MP	*Miscellaneous Papers* (in the National Edition of Dickens' *Works*)
NN	*Nicholas Nickleby* (1838–39)
NT	*No Thoroughfare* (1867)
OCS	*The Old Curiosity Shop* (1840–41)
OED	*The Oxford English Dictionary*
OMF	*Our Mutual Friend* (1864–65)
OT	*Oliver Twist* (1837–38)
OYF	*Our Young Folks*
P	*The Portfolio* (1823–25)
PEP	*The Perils of Certain English Prisoners* (1857)
PI	*Pictures from Italy* (1846)
PNP	*The Pic Nic Papers* (1841)
PP	*The Pickwick Papers* (1836–37)
RP	*Reprinted Pieces* (1858)
S	*The Speeches of Charles Dickens* (1837–70)
SB	*Sketches by Boz* (1836)
TR	*The Terrific Register* (1824–25)
TTC	*A Tale of Two Cities* (1859)
UJ	*Uncle John* (1833)
UT	*The Uncommercial Traveller* (1861; 1868)
UW	*Charles Dickens' Uncollected Writings from "Household Words," 1850–1859*
V&A	The Victoria and Albert Museum, London
WGM	*The Wreck of the "Golden Mary"* (1856)

Notes

Part 1: Dickens and Cannibalism

1. All quotations from Dickens' published letters through 1852 are taken from *The Letters of Charles Dickens,* ed. Madeline House, Graham Storey, Kathleen Tillotson, K. J. Fielding, and Nina Burgis, vols. 1–6, Pilgrim Edition (Oxford, 1965, 1969, 1974, 1977, 1981, and 1988). All other quotations from Dickens' published letters, with three exceptions, are from *The Letters of Charles Dickens,* ed. Walter Dexter, 3 vols., Nonesuch Edition (Bloomsbury, 1938). The exceptions are as follows: letters to Angela Burdett Coutts are from *Letters from Charles Dickens to Angela Burdett-Coutts,* ed. Edgar Johnson (London, 1953); letters to Catherine Hogarth Dickens are from *Mr. & Mrs. Charles Dickens: His Letters to Her,* ed. Walter Dexter (London, 1935); and letters to Mr. and Mrs. Richard Watson are from Franklin P. Rolfe, "More Letters to the Watsons," *Dickensian* 38 (March, June, and September 1942). These sources contain many letters not in the Nonesuch Edition and fuller texts of some letters that do appear there. In order to eliminate unnecessary documentation and to avoid the use of notes that do not add substantive information, the date of a published letter is always incorporated into the text and, if relevant for pursuing the citation, the name of the correspondent as well. This will enable the reader (taking cognizance of the matters set forth at the beginning of this paragraph) to consult the source if he wishes. Quotations from unpublished letters (or from unpublished segments of letters) are cited in the text or in the notes.

All references to Dickens' writings are taken from first editions or, in the case of periodicals, from the periodicals themselves, and are cited in the text. With novels, chapter as well as page (book, also, where relevant) is cited; this method of citation will enable the reader to locate references in any edition of Dickens' writings. Novels that first appeared in periodicals are cited from that source. For abbreviations, see the List of Abbreviations. This list (mostly of major works by Dickens) also contains dates of publication. For fuller bibliographical information concerning these sources and other relevant works, see the Select Bibliography.

Considering the centrality of cannibalistic fantasies and themes in Dickens' life and writings, it is surprising that the subject has gone largely unnoticed. It is also surprising that on those rare occasions when critics have touched upon the subject, they have almost always done so in passing: a brief word or phrase or occasionally a sentence is all that one usually finds. This neglect may be a reflection of the macabre and often repellent nature of the subject itself. It may also be due, in part, to the fact that Dickens frequently cauterized the subject with humor: why dwell portentously on a lighthearted joke or a grotesque flash of characterization? But more likely the neglect is a result of the subtlety and seamlessness of Dickens' art, especially his mature art: we simply pass over his hints and images and muted motifs, responding emotionally rather than recognizing intellectually. In any case, whatever the reasons, little has been written about Dickens and cannibalism.

The following survey lists works that touch upon the subject or that parallel it in meaningful ways. Full bibliographic listings of the works cited below will be found in the Select Bibliography.

Rowland D. McMaster, one of the first to recognize the importance of the *Terrific Register* in Dickens' development, touches lightly on cannibalism in "Dickens and the Horrific" (1958). Cannibalism in this study is one more manifestation, a minor one, of Dickens' preoccupation with the horrific. Other critics approach the subject of Dickens and cannibalism tangentially as they work toward other ends; when this occurs, they usually move away without exploring (usually without even mentioning) cannibalism. Thus, Andrew Sanders, in his informative *Charles Dickens: Resurrectionist* (1982), discusses Resurrection Men, the Morgue, corpses, and the like, but he does so in pursuit of Dickens' views on transcendence and rebirth; cannibalism does not enter the picture or the discussions. By the same token, Albert D. Hutter, in his two valuable articles, "The Novelist as Resurrectionist" (1983) and "Dismemberment and Articulation in *Our Mutual Friend*" (1983), focuses in the first piece on death and its denial, and in the second on dismemberment as a metaphor for social disintegration; but though he deals with the Morgue, dead bodies, burking, and many similar matters (including scenes and characters with strong cannibalistic implications), he does not mention the cannibalistic import of these motifs.

In a similar fashion, Richard A. Lanham, in *"Our Mutual Friend:* The Birds of Prey" (1963), a short but wide-ranging study, sees the central theme of *Our Mutual Friend* as predation, but predation here is primarily a metaphor for exploitation; the words "cannibal" and "cannibalism" never appear in the article. What applies to Lanham's article also applies to Rowland D. McMaster's earlier and similar study, "Birds of Prey: A Study of *Our Mutual Friend*" (1960).

Ian Watt, in "Oral Dickens" (1974), a useful survey of eating and drinking in Dickens, ranges over many works and many occasions, delving into their orality and what that orality signifies, but again without mentioning cannibals and cannibalism. Deborah A. Thomas, in "Dickens and Indigestion: The Deadly Dinners of the Rich" (1983), does mention cannibalism (mainly in an aside concerning the Franklin Expedition), but her article focuses primarily on the "deadly" dining of the unregenerate as compared to the harmonious dining of the pure in heart.

Cannibalism is an issue (since Dickens made it one) for those discussing Dickens and the Franklin Expedition, but such discussions are usually confined to the Franklin controversy itself. The chief works in this category are: Harry Stone, ed., *Charles Dickens' Uncollected Writings from "Household Words"* (1968); James E. Marlow, "The Fate of Sir John Franklin: Three Phases of Response in Victorian Periodicals" (1982), "Sir John Franklin, Mr. Charles Dickens, and the Solitary Monster" (1981), which glances beyond the controversy proper, and, most importantly, "English Cannibalism: Dickens after 1859" (1983), which again surveys the Franklin controversy but also discusses the cannibalistic elements in Dickens' later novels—Marlow views such cannibalism (which he usually sees as economic and objectified as generalized metaphors of predation) as a function of the chasm between classes, for, as he sums up, "that social chasm causes the hunger for security that is English cannibalism" (662); and Ian R. Stone, "'The contents of the kettles': Charles Dickens, John Rae and Cannibalism on the 1845 Franklin Expedition" (1987).

Works that concentrate on the shaping role of cannibalism in Dickens' imaginative writings include three studies by Harry Stone: "Dark Corners of the Mind: Dickens' Childhood Reading" (1963), the first critically oriented exploration of Dickens and cannibalism; "Fairy Tales and Ogres: Dickens' Imagination and *David Copperfield*" (1964), and *Dickens and the Invisible World: Fairy*

Tales, Fantasy, and Novel-Making (1979). Other significant commentaries in this vein, though brief, include John Cary's suggestive two-page discussion in *The Violent Effigy: A Study of Dickens' Imagination* (1973); Anya Taylor's "Devoured Hearts in *Great Expectations*" (1982), an attempt to link cannibalistic images in *Great Expectations* with Pip's lost—that is, "devoured"—heart; and Michael Hollington's scattered but useful mentions in *Dickens and the Grotesque* (1984). Fred Kaplan, in his recent book, *Dickens: A Biography* (1988), alludes to Dickens' cannibalistic fantasies, especially in conjunction with "Chips and the Devil" and the Morgue. These comments, as Kaplan later informed me, were indebted to my lecture on "Dickens and Cannibalism," delivered at the University of California, Santa Cruz, in 1985.

2. For a fuller account of the Franklin controversy and more on Dickens' contributions to *Household Words* concerning it (including some uncollected contributions), see Harry Stone, *Uncollected Writings*, 2: 513–22. For more on the Franklin expedition and its putative cannibalism see Ian R. Stone, " 'The contents of the kettles,' " 7–16. See also the previous note and the next note.

Dickens' library contained many volumes of voyage and travel literature, including many books on Arctic voyages and explorations, and several works by and about Franklin. Dickens also owned an Arctic painting by Clarkson Stanfield of a polar scene from *The Frozen Deep*. (*The Frozen Deep* [1857], a play by Dickens and Wilkie Collins, was inspired by the Franklin expedition. Dickens managed and directed the first two productions of the play; in each production he also played the leading role. See below in this part and at greater length in Part 2, "Dickens and Passion.") In addition to these Franklin connections and his own *Household Words* essays on Franklin and the lost Arctic voyagers, Dickens published other articles on the subject in *Household Words*, including the following: [Frederick Knight Hunt], "A Visit to the Arctic Discovery Ships," *HW* 1 (18 May 1850): 180–82; [John Rae], "Dr. Rae's Report," *HW* 10 (30 December 1854): 457–59—a continuation and conclusion of Dr. Rae's reply to Dickens begun in the third of "The Lost Arctic Voyager" articles; [John Rae], "Sir John Franklin and His Crews," *HW* 11 (3 February 1855): 12–20—a "faithful copy" of Dr. Rae's report to the Hudson's Bay Company. The critical opening paragraph of this article, which precedes the report proper, is almost certainly by Dickens (see Stone, *UW*, 2: 520, n. 4); [Henry Morley], "The Lost English Sailors," *HW* 15 (14 February 1857): 145–47; and [Henry Morley], "Official Patriotism," *HW* 15 (25 April 1857): 385–90. The last two articles, which Dickens commissioned, were written shortly after Dickens had helped write *The Frozen Deep* and had performed in its first production. This was also the period when Lady Franklin was appealing for a new expedition to the Arctic to settle the Franklin controversy. For more on *The Frozen Deep* and its Franklin connections, see below in Part 1. For still more on these matters, and for a great deal more on *The Frozen Deep* and its momentous aftermath, see Part 2, "Dickens and Passion."

There were also other pieces in *Household Words* on cannibals and cannibalism. For example, [Thomas Inman], "Six Years Among Cannibals," *HW* 7 (9 April 1853): 134–38—including a graphic account of killing, dismembering, preparing, and cooking four white men and then eating them, but with the consolatory information that these man-eating natives of the Marquesas Islands, "epicures in cannibalism . . . do not think so much of white men as they do of black. Black men's flesh is greatly preferred to pork" (134); and [William Moy Thomas], "Famine Aboard!" *HW* 17 (16 January 1858): 108–12—a story of shipwreck in which the narrator is attacked by a man who wants to eat him. See also, Part 1, notes 10 and 22.

3. Dickens proved to be quite right in his conviction that Franklin and his main party had not succumbed to cannibalism, a conviction that few authorities held after Dr. Rae's revelations. Subsequent expeditions and researches (ranging from Captain Leopold McClintock's evidence of 1859 to Dr. Owen Beattie's of the 1980s), have demonstrated that Franklin died aboard his ice-bound flagship, the unfortunately named *Erebus* (the other ship, the *Terror*, bore an equally unfortunate name), on 11 June 1847, more than two years after the expedition set sail from England. At the time of Franklin's death and for almost a year thereafter, though there was much privation, suffering, and death in the expedition, there was no cannibalism. It was not until some time after 22 April 1848, when a desperate group of survivors took off in a futile attempt to reach help by pushing overland in a southerly direction—a headlong dash depicted in *The Frozen Deep*—that some of the starving men in that dwindling group began (contrary to Dickens' self-comforting speculations) to eat members of their party as they died.

4. *The Frozen Deep* had profound domestic and sexual implications for Dickens. For a full discussion of these implications, see Part 2, "Dickens and Passion." For more on the Arctic backgrounds of the play, see note 3 above.

5. *The Wreck of the "Golden Mary"* was the Extra Christmas Number of *Household Words* for 1856. The opening, the wreck, the ordeal, and the linking passages were by Dickens; the continuing ordeal and the rescue, by Wilkie

Collins. The middle section of the number consisted of interpolated contributions by Percy Fitzgerald (two), Harriet Parr ("Holme Lee"), Adelaide Anne Procter, and the Rev. James White. See Stone, *Uncollected Writings*, 2: 563–69, 663–66.

In what may have been an unconscious association, Dickens named the captain of the *Golden Mary* (an upright and compassionate man, and Dickens' narrator) "Captain Ravender"—a subliminal combination, perhaps, of "ravenous" and "provender." Other names are more consciously and obviously directive. The chief mate, for example, is named "Steadiman."

Captain Ravender is obsessed by thoughts of cannibalism. He tells us that, as the food supplies dwindled, "I had one momentous point often in my thoughts," namely, that "human beings in the last distress have fed upon each other." He feels that some of the other survivors, especially some of the men, women, and children passengers, may be tormented by "having such a terrific idea to dwell upon in secret"; and in order not to "magnify it until it got to have an awful attraction about it," he tells the survivors the story of Captain Bligh's ordeal, how Bligh (of *Bounty* and mutiny fame), "who was no delicate man," had "solemnly placed it on record . . . that he was sure and certain that under no conceivable circumstances whatever, would that emaciated party who had gone through all the pains of famine, have preyed on one another." After this pronouncement, Dickens has Captain Ravender depict the reaction of his audience: "I cannot describe the visible relief which this spread through the boat, and how the tears stood in every eye" (*WGM,* 9).

6. This episode is dealt with at greater length in Part 3, "Dickens and Necessity." That Dickens' servitude in the blacking warehouse was probably a good deal longer than is usually supposed (more like a year) is argued persuasively by Michael Allen in *Charles Dickens' Childhood,* 101–4.

7. Dickens' nightmare view of rats is reflected in his periodicals as well as his writings. In the course of twenty years, Dickens published in *Household Words* and *All the Year Round* three articles devoted entirely to the subject. These articles add another dimension to our understanding of Dickens' childhood-generated, cannibalism-haunted horror of rats. There is no doubt that the articles reflect his own views. Dickens exerted strict editorial control over his periodicals, insisting that they reflect what he was known to advocate and believe, and he shaped each issue, commissioning, reading, choosing, rejecting, changing, editing, rewriting, adding to, cutting, titling, arranging, and proofing the articles that went into each weekly number. (For a detailed description of Dick-

ens engaged in this weekly process, see Stone, *Uncollected Writings*, 1: 15–16, 29–43.) The three articles devoted to rats are: [Frederick Knight Hunt], "Rats!," *HW* 2 (23 November 1850): 214–16; [Edmund Saul Dixon], "Rat Tales," *HW* 18 (14 August 1858): 211–16; and "Farmer Pincher's Rats," *AYR* 5 (21 September 1861): 611–14.

The first article, "Rats!," is based on a pamphlet entitled *Rat!!! Rat!!! Rat!!!*. The purpose of this pamphlet (and the article, too, though less stridently) was to rouse the nation "to one universal warfare against these midnight marauders and common enemies of mankind" (214).

The second article, "Rat Tales," is longer and far more revealing. Its burden is similar to "Rats!" but its language and incidents are filled with loathing and relish—strange attitudes and strange fare for a family magazine. Rats, says the narrator in "Rat Tales," could "dispute the supremacy [of the world] with man himself" (211). In Montevideo, the streets are "so infested with voracious rats as sometimes to make the way perilous" (211). The rats "will gnash their teeth at you fiercely, like so many wolves . . . and will then make a rush at your legs in a way to make your hair stand on end" (212). The narrator goes on to evoke a real-life version (almost) of "Chips and the Devil." A ship docked in London becomes so infested with rats that soon after it sails the madly multiplying rats begin to dispute control of the ship. "The passengers were obliged, during the night, to sleep with cudgels by the side of their berths, to dispute by force of arms the possession of their mattresses" (212). Then, "one dark night, at twelve o'clock," as the ship is sailing up the river Plata, it strikes fast on some rocks and quickly begins to sink. The rats swim off into the river; the frantic humans rush to the pumps and labor furiously to survive. Exhausted, desperate for water, the imperiled passengers and crew soon find that their last water has been contaminated: "The rats had got in; several of their bodies lay at the bottom [of the water butts]; their hairs thickened the turbid water; and the taste (the sickening taste!) was indescribable" (212). The passengers and crew survive, but barely.

This is not the end of the article. "Rat Tales" goes on to give us other loathsome examples of the ferocity and power of rats. "Rats," we are told, "are eminently ratophagous, which is lucky for us; for, without ratophagy, rats would have devoured all the other living inhabitants of the globe. Not only do nearly-related species devour each other, but individuals of the same race also practise cannibalism. Fathers eat their babes in the nest, to spare them from the pains of teething; children eat their declining parents, to relieve them of the burthen of life, exactly like the Massagetae, the worthy ancestors of the modern Cossacks" (212–13).

This passage is ravenous and cannibalistic enough, but the *pièce de résistance* of "Rat Tales" is an account of a midnight excursion arranged by Brissot-Thivars and undertaken by Balzac, Brissot-Thivars, Dr. Gentil, and a fourth gentleman (E. S. Dixon?), to Montfaucon, just outside of Paris, an excursion to watch a savage spectacle. (Montfaucon was a government slaughtering place for worn-out horses, stray dogs, and the like; Brissot-Thivars was in charge of Montfaucon and also of the sewers of Paris.) The party finally arrives at its destination. The newcomers watch as a large dead horse is dragged into a walled arena. While the four eager witnesses perch on the wall of this grim arena, grates are opened and multitudes of neighborhood rats, attracted by the smell of carrion, swarm into the hellish pit. The scene is nightmarish. The culminating rat-frenzy (like the entire excursion) is not only described at great length but in rich detail and with eager relish. We, along with the four privileged spectators—the whole scene lit by flaming torches—watch the rats begin their voracious work:

> The leaders climbing up the horse's flanks, ripped up its skin from one end to the other, just as a tailor unstitches an old coat to tear it up into rags; and then hundreds, thousands, myriads of rodents streamed in at every aperture, crowding thick and anxiously, like an audience rushing out of a theatre on fire. They scrambled over one another; and their rustling movements, their little shrill whistlings, inaudible at first, produced by their multiplication the hum and murmur of a crowd, in which you could almost fancy you heard the sound of human voices. Life was boiling in this animated mass. It made you shudder to think of what would be your fate were you to fall into the midst of it from your perch on the wall. (215)

Soon the frenzy surges to yet madder levels:

> The Montfaucon rats had opened the horse; and they cut it up, bored it, riddled it through and through, and chopped it into mincemeat—a work of destruction which was hidden from sight a few minutes afterwards, the horse having completely disappeared beneath the hideous brutes, who, hanging on with the voracious precision of leeches to its rounded form, soon offered the spectacle of a magnified horse composed of thousands of living rats . . .
>
> What a clash of arms! The gnashing of their teeth was audible; the sound of the knives and forks reached the ears of the spectators in the boxes. [About a year after Dickens published this, he used the

same savage image to describe the cannibal mob in *A Tale of Two Cities,* a mob dancing in a frenzy, dancing in a "slough of blood and dirt," and "keeping a ferocious time that was like a gnashing of teeth in unison"—see below in Part 1.] Amongst these indefatigable gluttons, there were some as large as a full-grown tom-cat. But what cat could risk an encounter with such adversaries as these? He would have been devoured as easily as a partridge by a fox; he would have been swallowed whole before he reached the ground. (215)

When flaming torches and burning resin are thrown into the writhing heap of rats, they disperse with a wail—"as if a multitude of infants were being murdered" (216)—but the horse that had been there just minutes before is gone; only the stark skeleton remains. Now it is time for dogs, and then men with clubs, to enter the fray. The savage scene becomes an inferno of blood and carnage. The men and dogs attack, then attack again. "The rats, exasperated, despairing, bounded over the backs of the dogs, climbed up the men, ran into their beards and hair, round their necks, between their legs, over their shoulders, panted, whistled, clung together, and bit the sticks with such fury as to leave their teeth in them" (216). Here, surely, the ferocious teeth of "Captain Murderer" and the ravenous man-eating rats of "Chips and the Devil" live again.

"Farmer Pincher's Rats" is no less ferocious, but a bit less gruesome and intense. Farmer Pincher is plagued and besieged by rats: "They fell down the kitchen chimney; they bit the cook's legs and the gardener's fingers; they left their limbs in the traps, and were found calmly drowned in the milkpans. . . . They were such big rats, too, with sloughing tails, yellow teeth, naked feet, and eyes out of which an undying and changeless malice stared with cold cruelty" (612). The rats swarm over the house, devouring everything in their path. "They gnawed the corks in the cellar and they drank the wine; they ate the potatoes, and they gnawed the game in the larder" (612).

Finally, Farmer Pincher counterattacks. He lays siege to the swarming rats by attacking their nests in the nearby haystacks. The rats burst forth from their hiding places:

Old rats, lean rats, fat rats, young rats, meek rats, blind rats, spiteful rats, cantankerous rats that fought in corners and defied dogs and sticks, rats that ran for help into the very pockets and bosoms of the women and children spectators, rats that threw themselves from the roof of the stacks, rats that ran suddenly from the bottom, rats that hid themselves, rats that bravely faced sunshine and glittering steel;

> rats that appeared at the mouths of holes in the straw, looked round
> as if to see how the weather was, did not like the look of things, and
> turned in again; rats of every kidney, of all complexions, and of every
> age, were run down and slain, with sudden shouts, sudden runnings
> together, crushing blows of sticks that seemed all in the air at one
> time, like the daggers that slew Caesar. (613)

The farmer, after mobilizing his men, machinery, and dogs—indeed his whole
community—finally prevails; but he prevails only after threshing the tumbling
and boiling rats "like so much rolling black fruit" (614).

This is the way Dickens purveyed rats to the great squeamish family audience
that read the anonymous articles and stories in his anonymous periodicals—
anonymous, that is, except for the large bold black inscription on each and
every issue: "CONDUCTED BY CHARLES DICKENS."

8. See, for example, the rats in *George Silverman's Explanation,* analyzed in
Part 3, "Dickens and Necessity." See also below in Part 1.

9. For evidence that Dickens, at the age of twelve, bought the weekly issues
of the *Terrific Register,* see below in Part 1. For evidence that, as a child, he
owned a copy of *The Dandies' Ball* (1819), see Stone, *UW,* 2: 413–15. Several
of the illustrations from *The Dandies' Ball* described by Dickens are reproduced in Stone, *Uncollected Writings.* Dickens' essay "First Fruits," in which
he discusses *The Dandies' Ball* and quotes some of its verses from memory, was
a joint effort with George Augustus Sala. The essay appeared in *HW* 5 (15 May
1852): 189–92, and is reprinted in Stone, *UW,* 2: 409–19.

In "First Fruits" (in a section by Dickens) Dickens calls *The Dandies' Ball*
his "first picture-book," says its "legend is impressed" on his "remembrance,"
gives an account of its plot, quotes two stanzas (with slight inaccuracies) from
memory, and states that the place where the ball took place—Great Camomile
Street (a real London Street near Bevis Marks)—became a focus of his imaginings and a place he "entreated" to be taken to (*HW* 5: 190).

Shown here, with a caption quoting Dickens' description of one well-
remembered scene from that well-remembered picture book (the description
appears in "First Fruits"), is the specific page from *The Dandies' Ball* that Dickens was recalling when he referred to "male dandies . . . holding on to bed-
posts to have their stays laced" (*HW* 5: 190). Like all the other pages in this
charming, gently satiric picture book, this page contains one hand-colored engraving and one verse. (There are sixteen engravings all told, all by Robert
Cruikshank.)

Here's the stays from the tailor,

For Mr. Mac Nailor.

Oh, Jeffery ! lace it quite tight.

I'll hold by the post,

That no time may be lost ;

At the Ball I'll outshine all to-night.

---

141. The Picture Books of Childhood: One Picture
"Represented Male Dandies . . . Holding On to
Bed-Posts to Have Their Stays Laced"

"Here's the stays from the tailor." Engraving by Robert Cruikshank. From *The Dandies' Ball; or, High Life in the City* (1819).

10. In addition to his own articles and stories in *Household Words* and *All the Year Round* concerning shipwrecks and disasters at sea, some of which have already been alluded to and others of which will be discussed shortly, Dickens also published in his periodicals many similar articles, stories, and poems by others. The following is a partial list: [Cobbe], "The Man on the Iceberg," *HW* 13 (31 May 1856): 479–80—about a man, either shipwrecked or abandoned, frozen on the side of an iceberg; [Miss Marryatt], "Cast Away," *HW* 19 (5 February 1859): 222–27—a short story concerning shipwreck; [R. H. Horne], "Life and Luggage," *HW* 4 (8 November 1851): 152–56—measures that should be undertaken to minimize loss in shipwreck; [John William King and W. H. Wills], "Lighten the Boat!" *HW* 7 (13 August 1853): 563–64—a poem about a "noble boy" who sacrifices himself by jumping from an over-loaded lifeboat; [W. H. Wills and John Joseph Shillinglaw], "The Preservation of Life from Shipwreck," *HW* 1 (3 August 1850): 452–54; [W. H. Wills], "A Sea-Coroner," *HW* 4 (13 March 1852): 597–98—assessing causes and liabilities in shipwrecks; [Thomas Kibble Harvey], "The Wreck of 'The Arctic,'" *HW* 10 (16 December 1854): 420–21—a poem; and [Henry Morley], "Wrecks at Sea," *HW* 12 (11 August 1855): 36–39. Wills and Morley were members of the *Household Words* staff; Dickens probably commissioned some of the pieces they wrote.

Dickens' fascination with the subject continued unabated in the articles, stories, and poems he commissioned, and otherwise selected and approved, for *All the Year Round.* (*All the Year Round*, the successor to *Household Words*, was, like the latter, not only edited and controlled by Dickens—"Conducted" was Dickens' term for his presiding presence—but majority owned by him.) Here is a partial list of *All the Year Round* pieces devoted to shipwrecks and disasters at sea: [Walter Thornbury], "Old Stories Re-Told: The Wreck of the Halsewell, East Indiaman," *AYR* 17 (6 April 1867): 347–52—Dickens had dwelt upon this shipwreck fourteen years earlier in "The Long Voyage," and he tells us there that the story of this wreck was "familiar to me from my early boyhood" (*HW* 8: 410); [Walter Thornbury], "Old Stories Re-Told: The Wreck of the Medusa," *AYR* 17 (19 January 1867): 77–84—Dickens had discussed the *Medusa* and its cannibalism thirteen years earlier in "The Lost Arctic Voyagers"; [Walter Thornbury], "Old Stories Re-Told: The Loss of the Kent East Indiaman by Fire (1825)," *AYR* 16 (17 November 1866): 444–51. Dickens took an active part in the Thornbury series (which also contained many nonshipwreck pieces), editing the pieces vigorously (as was his custom), adding paragraphs on occasion, suggesting topics, approving others, vetoing still others, and the like. The following excerpt from a letter to Thornbury shows Dickens engaged in the latter roles:

I think the Bottle Conjuror and Berrers Street Hoax too well known. Ditto Daniel Lambert, Miss Biffin and Borolowski. The Wonderful Magazine and the books of celebrated characters have used them up, with the misers.

Wild Boys, yes.

Ice Winters, yes, if compounded of several experiences.

Balloons, I am doubtful about. . . .

A Hurricane and an Earthquake might go together?

A Memorable Inundation, a good subject.

And I very much like the idea of those Abyssinian notes. Pray pursue it. (5 August 1867)

In 1870 Thornbury collected this series of *All the Year Round* pieces and published them as a book entitled, *Old Stories Re-Told*. Dickens owned a presentation copy of this work, a copy dated 4 January 1870.

There were, of course, non-Thornbury shipwreck pieces in *All the Year Round* as well, all of which underwent the usual Dickens scrutiny and approval: "Shipwrecks," *AYR* 3 (21 July 1860): 342–46; "Two Crusoes," *AYR* 16 (6 October 1866): 296–99; "Ten Terrible Days," *AYR* 11 (26 March 1864): 164–68—concerning a shipwreck and fears that "some of the crew . . . might eat the children" (167); "The Wreck of the Pocahontas," *AYR* 19 (28 March 1868): 371–72—a poem; "The Wreck Off Calais: Saturday, October 4, 1866," *AYR*, n.s. 2 (5 June 1869): 12–13—a poem in which the wind howls "like a wild beast" and the "wolfish waves" rage "for human blood."

Dickens' library also contained many books on shipwrecks and disasters at sea, including the following (a partial list): R. A. Davenport, *Narratives of Peril and Suffering,* 2 vols., 1862; W. Gilly, *Narratives of Shipwrecks of the Royal Navy, 1793–1849,* with a Preface by Dr. W. S. Gilly, 1850; Hugh Murray, *Adventures of British Seamen in the Southern Ocean: Shipwreck of the Antelope, and Mutiny of the Bounty,* 1827; Capt. T. Musgrave, *Castaway on the Auckland Isles: A Narrative of the Wreck of the "Grafton" and of the Escape of the Crew after Twenty Months' Suffering,* ed. J. Shillinglaw, 1866—Shillinglaw had earlier contributed a shipwreck article to *Household Words;* Cyrus Redding, *History of Shipwrecks and Disasters at Sea,* 2 vols., 1833; *Shipwrecks and Disasters at Sea; Historical Narratives of the Most Noted Calamities and Providential Deliverances,* 3 vols., 1812; *A Token for Mariners, Containing Many Famous and Wonderful Instances of God's Providence in Sea Dangers and Deliverances,* 1708; *A General Collection of Voyages and Travels, from the Discovery of America to the Nineteenth Century,* ed. Dr. Mavor, 28 vols., 1810; *A Collection of Voyages, Containing Capt. W. Dampier's Voyages Round the World, and those of*

Wafer, Cowley, Sharp, Wood, Roberts, etc., 4 vols., 1729; *Hakluyt Society Publications,* 19 vols., 1847–55. In addition, Dickens' monthly periodical, *The Household Narrative of Current Events* (1850–1855), contained a regular section entitled, "Narrative of Accident and Disaster." This section gave substantial accounts of dozens upon dozens of shipwrecks. One should also remember that there are prominent shipwrecks associated with cannibalism in two of Dickens' all-time favorite fictions: *Robinson Crusoe* and *The Arabian Nights.* Dickens read these works, and other shipwreck works, over and over again. On this score, see below in Part 1; see also Part 1, note 19.

Excluded from this list are Dickens' many books on the Arctic, Arctic explorations, and Arctic expeditions; also excluded are all books by or about Sir John Franklin (see Part 1, note 2). It is worth emphasizing, however, that (as with shipwreck literature) Dickens came upon Arctic and Franklin literature not only in manhood but in childhood, especially in his "greedy" reading, in his Chatham days, of voyage and travel literature, and then, a little later, in his equally greedy reading, during his blacking-warehouse and Wellington House Academy days, of periodicals that specialized in popular and sensational fare. To cite just one example, the *Portfolio* (1823ff.)—a popular periodical, partly improving and partly sensational, that Dickens read each week in these early years—published a substantial review, with extracts (*P* 1: 138–41; 278–80), of Franklin's *Narrative of a Journey to the Shores of the Polar Seas.* This work by Franklin, an account of his polar explorations and ordeals, first appeared in 1823. Many years later Dickens drew upon this account firsthand, an account he had originally sampled as a boy in the *Portfolio.*

11. "A Walk in a Workhouse," *HW* 1 (25 May 1850): 205; "Mr. Booley's View of the Last Lord Mayor's Show," *HW* 2 (30 November 1850): 217; ["Titbull's Alms-Houses"], *AYR* 10 (24 October 1863): 206—later in *UT;* "The Overture," *No Thoroughfare,* Extra Christmas Number of *All the Year Round* for 1867, p. 2—though written in collaboration with Wilkie Collins, the passage and section cited are by Dickens; ["City of London Churches"], *AYR* 3 (5 May 1860): 88—later in *UT;* ["Poor Mercantile Jack"], *AYR* 2 (10 March 1860): 466—later in *UT;* "Capital Punishment," *Daily News* (13 March 1846)—from the second of three letters to the *Daily News* collected with *RP* (National Edition), 416.

12. In an early work, "A Visit to Newgate," written in November 1835 for *Sketches by Boz,* First Series, a condemned man in "*the condemned pew*—a huge black pen," his summoning coffin waiting at his side, becomes one climactic

focus of the sketch and a presiding correlative (in the sketch) of Dickens' most intense horror and fear (*SB* 1: 123). What would it be like, Dickens imagines, to sit next to your own coffin in this mean Newgate prison chapel on the last Sunday of your life, sit there less than twenty-four hours before you are to be hanged, sit there a dead man, and join in the responses of your own burial service? What would it be like to listen to the sermon admonishing your fellow prisoners to take warning from your ghastly fate? And what would it be like to know that "between the gallows and the knife" (*SB* 1: 124)—that is, between being hanged and then anatomized—no remnant of your corporeal being would remain?

That Dickens conjured up this gruesome nightmare vision is all the more extraordinary because on his visit to Newgate in November 1835 he did not see, nor could he have seen, a waiting coffin in the condemned pew: the practice of forcing a condemned prisoner to confront his fate in this sadistic way had been abolished at Newgate some years before. Yet the enormity of having to confront one's own death and the rude final receptacle of one's dead body in this frightful manner so scarified Dickens' imagination (and so fascinated him) that he felt compelled to drag the extinct practice into his sketch, using the horror he generated (a compelled, self-tormenting horror) as an occasion to urge further reform: "Let us hope that the increased spirit of civilization and humanity which abolished this frightful and degrading custom, may extend itself to other usages equally barbarous" (*SB* 1: 124–25). See Part 2, "Dickens and Passion," note 10; see also Part 1, note 40.

That the connection of "A Visit to Newgate" and "The Idle Apprentice Executed at Tyburn" is not simply incidental or confined to the condemned felon and his waiting coffin is demonstrated by the fact that the long nightmare fantasy Dickens summoned up in "A Visit to Newgate" for his condemned prisoner's last hours, a fantasy of the prisoner's thoughts and feelings during those final ebbing moments of his life, strikingly parallels (even in minute details) the long nightmare fantasy that John Trusler created for the last hours of the condemned Thomas Idle as a letterpress accompaniment for "The Idle Apprentice Executed at Tyburn," the penultimate plate of *Industry and Idleness*. Trusler's narrative, or rather Trusler's entire series of narratives, which consisted of fictional and moralizing accompaniments for each plate in Hogarth's storytelling series (the narratives appeared originally in Trusler's *Hogarth Moralized* [1768]), were later reprinted (or adapted) over and over again in editions of Hogarth's collected works, usually as letterpress explanations to accompany each plate in turn.

How close to Dickens' everyday awareness and association the whole story of *Industry and Idleness* was may be further gauged by the fact that in September and October 1857, in a time of great crisis and anxiety for Dickens, he chose to associate the framework and contents of the five-part *Lazy Tour of Two Idle Apprentices*—a framework and contents he was then experiencing as well as writing—with Francis Goodchild (the industrious apprentice) and Thomas Idle (the idle apprentice), personas he chose for himself and Wilkie Collins, and personas that are taken from *Industry and Idleness*. (*The Lazy Tour of Two Idle Apprentices* is discussed at length in Part 2, "Dickens and Passion.")

Another striking instance of Dickens' association of public executions with cannibalism occurred in 1846, two years before he wrote his cannibal-haunted impressions of "The Idle Apprentice Executed at Tyburn." In 1846, in *Pictures from Italy*, Dickens described a public execution he had witnessed in Rome shortly before committing it to paper. At this execution, as in "The Idle Apprentice Executed at Tyburn," a "pastry-merchant divided his attention between the scaffold and his customers" (*PI*, "Rome," 203). But soon (again as in Dickens' version of "The Idle Apprentice Executed at Tyburn") this hawker of food and his eager brethren became consumers rather than purveyors. When the condemned felon was at last brought out to the hungry crowd, the "pastry-merchants resigned all thoughts of business, for the moment, and abandoning themselves wholly to pleasure, got good situations in the crowd" (*PI*, "Rome," 205). Clearly, these enterprising food merchants, part of the hungry crowd, take their sustenance from the soon-dead prisoner—both in business (earning through the prisoner's execution their food and drink) and in pleasure (devouring the prisoner's gory butchering with uncommercial relish).

The condemned man in this Roman spectacle is soon beheaded. The executioner, holding the bloody head by the hair, walks with it round the scaffold, displaying it to the staring crowd, and then sets it upon a pole in front for "the flies to settle on" (*PI*, "Rome," 206). Dickens goes on to describe the severed head, the headless body, the blood-enmired scaffold, and the jostling crowd (well-worked, as in Hogarth, by pickpockets—they, too, are hungry, and they, too, flies of a more ferocious sort, batten, in effect, upon the dead body). "It was," Dickens sums up, "an ugly, filthy, careless, sickening spectacle; meaning nothing but butchery." Dickens concludes this savage, blood-steeped vignette with an image of the knife of the guillotine being cleansed of its flesh and tissue and blood, and with the executioner, a fearsome and ghoulish predator, having procured his meat and drink (he, too, is a hungry devourer who lives upon corpses and blood), retreating "to his lair" (*PI*, "Rome," 207). (Later Dickens used these bloody scenes and devouring images in the mob and guillotine scenes of *A Tale of Two Cities,* scenes replete with frenzied butchery and ferocious cannibalism—see below in Part 1.)

13. When Dickens' library was offered for sale after his death, no collected edition of Hogarth's works and no unframed collection of his engravings (as distinct from the framed collection that was offered for sale) were included. That the library contained no collected edition of Hogarth is extraordinary, but one should remember that many books Dickens is known to have owned did not appear in the sale catalogue of his library. (As a matter of fact, the framed collection of Hogarth engravings was withdrawn before the sale; the collection—or at least a portion of it—came into the possession of Dickens' eldest son, Charles Dickens, Jr., and subsequently some engravings passed to Edmund Yates.) That Dickens owned a collected edition of Hogarth's works (or at least knew such an edition exceedingly well) is attested to by the fact (to cite just two pieces of evidence) that he refers to engravings that were not in his collection as offered for sale, and that in "A Visit to Newgate," an early sketch, he drew heavily on the letterpress for *Industry and Idleness*, most particularly on the Trusler letterpress for "The Idle Apprentice Executed at Tyburn." (See, in this connection, note 12 above.) The sale catalogue of Dickens' library did contain a 1726 edition of Butler's *Hudibras* with the Hogarth engravings and a biographical sketch of Hogarth, the latter in Walter Thornbury's *British Artists* (2 vols., 1861). For more on Dickens' library and the books he actually owned and read, see the following note.

14. Dickens' many references to Swift, and the context of those references, especially the context of his numerous references to *Gulliver's Travels*, make it clear that his knowledge of Swift went back to his early days. What is less clear, however, is precisely how precocious that early introduction was. But whatever the exact date of Dickens' introduction to Swift, and more particularly to "A Modest Proposal," there is no question but that the rhetorical strategy of that work impressed Dickens and lingered in his mind. This is evident from his later use of similar strategies (and in certain instances echoing titles) in his polemical writings. See, for example, "Proposals for Amusing Posterity," *HW* 6 (12 February 1853): 505–7; "Proposals for a National Jest-Book," *HW* 13 (3 May 1856): 361–64; "An Idea of Mine," *HW* 17 (13 March 1858): 289–91; and "Five New Points of Criminal Law," *AYR* 1 (24 September 1859): 517.

Dickens owned two complete sets of Swift's works: Jonathan Swift, *The Works of Jonathan Swift; containing additional Letters, Tracts, and Poems, not hitherto published; with Notes and a Life of the Author, by Walter Scott, Esq.*, 19 vols. (Edinburgh: Archibald Constable and Co., 1814), and the second edition of this set, published in 1824. He also owned a two-volume 1838 French edition of *Gulliver's Travels* with several hundred illustrations by Grandville (including the freer illustrations later omitted in the English edition). In addition, he owned a fourth copy of *Gulliver's Travels*, this copy part of a ten-volume set of *Ballantyne's Novelist's Library*, a series edited by Sir Walter Scott and published in Edinburgh, 1821–24. Finally, he owned a fifth copy of *Gulliver's Travels*, this copy in an 1812 volume entitled *Popular Romances*. (*Popular Romances*, a volume of imaginary voyages and travels edited and introduced by Henry Weber, also contained *Journey to the World under Ground* [by Nicholas Klimius], *The Life and Adventures of Peter Wilkins* [by Robert Paltock], *The Adventures of Robinson Crusoe* [by Daniel Defoe], and *The History of Authomathes* [by John Kirkby].)

That Dickens often went back to Swift, dipping into and rereading his writings, is evident from a letter he wrote to Forster on 18 March 1844, the day after he bought many books, including the 1814 set of Swift, at the sale of Thomas Hill's library. (Hill, a well-known bibliophile, collector, and host, had been Dickens' friend since the *Pickwick* days.) "I have done nothing to-day," Dickens wrote, "but cut the *Swift*, looking into it with a delicious laziness in all manner of delightful places" (F, 174). The 1824 set (which Dickens owned at least as early as 1839—see letter of 21 August 1839 to George Cattermole), but not the Hill set, was in Dickens' library when it was sold in 1870 after his death. This is one of many examples of books Dickens is known to have owned (and in some instances to have cherished and read and reread) not being in his library as catalogued and offered for sale. (In most such instances, unlike the Swift example, Dickens owned no duplicate or alternate titles.) The assumption sometimes made that Dickens did not own, much less read, a book unless it appears in the catalogue of his library is thus a false assumption, and is often demonstrably wrong both as to owning and to reading.

15. For a sampling of such references see *AN*, I, 4:146; *AN*, II, 1:23–24; *PI*, "Through Bologna and Ferrara," 98; *BH*, 2:8; "Where We Stopped Growing," *HW* 6 (1 January 1853): 361; *LD*, II, 24:525.

16. This scene would have had both cannibalistic and other crucial resonances for Dickens. See, in this connection, the discussion later in Part 1 of the scene in which David Copperfield comes upon his mother while she is suckling his usurping brother, a scene of profound significance for David and for Dickens.

17. In his fragmentary autobiography and in *David Copperfield*, Dickens tells us how he lived in the world of his childhood reading for months on end and how he often acted out scenes from that reading, merging his real world

with his fictional world. (See F, 5–6; *DC,* 4:41–42.) For an analysis of how this intense, often enforced and compensatory reading helped shape Dickens' character and imagination, see Part 3, "Dickens and Necessity."

18. Both of these references to the cannibals of *Robinson Crusoe* come from "Nurse's Stories," a cannibal-haunted essay that focuses on childhood and Dickens' early memories. The cannibal allusions are part of a larger series of allusions to *Robinson Crusoe.* After opening the essay with these allusions, Dickens moves on to other, much more extensive and formidable cannibalistic fare, recounting, amongst other horrors, those two ferocious cannibalistic nightmares, "Captain Murderer" and "Chips and the Devil." Elsewhere in the essay, Dickens touches on still other cannibalistic memories and fantasies.

19. There are innumerable examples of Dickens rereading these and other favorite childhood works. To give just one or two instances, we find him saying of *Robinson Crusoe,* "I have been reading it again just now, in the course of my numerous refreshings at those English wells" (F, 611). In a similar way, he writes of *The Arabian Nights,* "[I am] one of the most constant and delighted readers of those Arabian Entertainments . . . that they have ever had, perhaps" (10 May 1856). The first remark was in a letter to John Forster; the second, in a letter to George Meredith. Though not cited here, many of Dickens' other references to *Robinson Crusoe* and *The Arabian Nights* concern cannibalism. Some of those references are cited elsewhere in Part 1. For his rereading of Swift, see above in Part 1; see also Part 1, notes 14 and 15.

20. Later in Part 1 the cannibalistic motifs in *A Tale of Two Cities* are dealt with at length (pp.162–98).

21. Dickens was familiar with this last story (found in folklore versions as well as in street-literature and penny-press versions) long before his *Terrific Register* days. He first heard the tale from his nursemaid, the purveyor of so many frightening cannibalistic tales. Her version, a country version, is essentially the same as the *Terrific Register's* tale of the Parisian barber and pastry-cook of the Rue de la Harpe or, to cite a later London version, the tale of Sweeney Todd, the demon barber of Fleet Street. Dickens gives his version of the story, or rather an account of his nursemaid's version (an account softened and distanced by humor and time), in "The Guest," the first section of *The Holly-Tree Inn,* the Extra Christmas Number of *Household Words* for 1855.

The protagonist of *The Holly-Tree Inn,* snowed up in a country inn, recalls his experiences of inns:

> My first impressions of an Inn, dated from the Nursery; consequently, I went back [in my memory] to the Nursery for a starting-point, and found myself at the knee of a sallow woman with a fishy eye, an aquiline nose, and a green gown, whose speciality was a dismal narrative of a landlord by the roadside, whose visitors unaccountably disappeared for many years, until it was discovered that the pursuit of his life had been to convert them into pies. For the better devotion of himself to this branch of industry, he had constructed a secret door behind the head of the bed; and when the visitor (oppressed with pie), had fallen asleep, this wicked landlord would look softly in with a lamp in one hand and a knife in the other, would cut his throat, and would make him into pies; for which purpose he had coppers underneath a trap-door, always boiling; and rolled out his pastry in the dead of the night. ("The Guest," *HTI,* 4)

Obviously this landlord also has affinities with Captain Murderer. A special touch in *The Holly-Tree Inn* version is that the visitor, before being murdered and made into pies, is "oppressed with pie"; that is, his last meal is a cannibalistic one: he eats the body of an earlier victim who had been made into pies.

22. Many years later, in his own periodicals, Dickens published similar but more authoritative (or seemingly authoritative) accounts of cannibalistic practices. In the 30 November 1861 issue of *All the Year Round,* for example, in an article entitled "Stories of the Black Men," he published anthropological accounts of African tribal practices. These accounts had been culled from lectures delivered in London by Du Chaillu, Burton, and Hutchinson before the Ethnological Society and had just been published in a new volume of the society's *Transactions.* In the *All the Year Round* article, amongst other accounts of cannibalistic practices taken from the *Transactions,* we are given a few vignettes worthy of the *Terrific Register* itself. We are told that "a tribe, living interior to Coriseo, is said to come down to the shore to catch people living near the sea, whose flesh they suppose to have a brinier and choicer flavour" (*AYR* 6: 236). By contrast, "the Pangwe tribe, interior to the Gaboon, as we hang venison or pheasant, bury the dead bodies of their enemies for a week, to give them a gamy flavour before they are eaten" (*AYR* 6: 236). The choicest of these reports, however, combines Gothic horror and macabre humor in a manner not only worthy of the *Terrific Register* but of Dickens himself:

At Bonny, secretly, but within sight of our ships of commerce on the river, cannibal ceremonies are maintained. The horrors of one of which Mr. Hutchinson, concealed in a hut, saw unsuspected, and he says: "I can assure you of a fact in connexion with one of their reprisal executions for cannibal purposes, that occurred during the temporary stay of Mrs. Hutchinson and myself at Bonny. We were stopping on board a palm-oil hulk, when one morning there came to the vessel, for some trading object, the very ju-ju man whom I had seen at his bloody work some time previous. It seems that he had repeated this operation on the day before the visit now recorded; and on Captain Straw, who had charge of the hulk, asking him how he could dare to look in the face of a white lady, who had heard of his eating the head of a man the day before (for I must tell you that the head is a part claimed as a tit-bit by the executioner), he replied with the most imperturbable sang froid, expressive of profound contempt for all the culinary art in the world, 'I no eat him, for my cook done spoil him; he no put nuff pepper on him,' meaning that the sauce had not been to his taste." (*AYR* 6: 235–36)

Dickens knew Du Chaillu and Burton, and he had works by Du Chaillu in his library.

Perhaps the most extraordinary example in Dickens' periodicals of cannibalistic dining occurs in an article he published in *All the Year Round* seven years after "Stories of the Black Men." The article in question was the final installment in a series of twenty-one articles on cooking, food, dining, and similar matters, a series that bore the punning title *Leaves from the Mahogany Tree* and ran from 30 May through 28 November 1868. The substantial final installment, entitled "Leaves from the Mahogany Tree. / (Conclusion.) / Pastry and an Entremet of Great Merit." (*AYR* 20 [28 November 1868]: 582–87), ended with a brief five-paragraph epilogue or *jeu d'esprit*, a curious coda that was set off from the main text not simply by a typographical break but by a separate title as well. The title of the article had promised the reader that the piece would concentrate on pastry and on an "Entremet of Great Merit"; the title of the epilogue (which pertains to the entremet only) gives the reader a sample taste of what he may expect in that promised entremet treat: "An Entremet of Great Merit. / (*The English sailor à la maître d'hôtel, and the / Sea captain au gratin.*)" (586–87).

The humorous but gruesomely graphic squib that follows this provocative subtitle, though certainly about food and dining, seems tacked on to the main text; it also seems a most unaccountable way for a family magazine to conclude a book-length series on cooking and dining. Why leave the reader with this loathsome five-paragraph aftertaste? Why dwell, at the end of a long culinary journey (even if fleetingly and even if amusingly), on murderous onslaughts and revolting dining? As a matter of fact, the brief epilogue seems to be an editorial interpolation. Whether this subversive coda was rewritten or even authored by a member of the *All the Year Round* editorial staff, or whether it was touched by Dickens himself (some portions seem unmistakably Dickensian) or by a combination of editorial hands is not clear. (Editorial additions and changes of this nature were commonplace in *Household Words* and *All the Year Round:* see, on this score, the opening paragraph of note 7 in Part 1; see also the comments at the end of the *Household Words* and *All the Year Round* listings in Part 1, note 28.) Here is the opening paragraph of this strange five-paragraph epilogue (or "Entremet," as the subtitle has it) that ends *Leaves from the Mahogany Tree:*

> A cookery book, the property of the last chef of the King of the Sandwich Islands, has lately fallen into our hands. It is a work of great research, and eminently practical. The first recipe struck us as cynically written, but yet showing degrees of scientific thought hardly to be expected from a cannibal. It is entitled The English Sailor à la Maître d'Hôtel. It begins thus: "Take a shipwrecked sailor, not under three-and-forty, flour him and pepper him. Open him down the back, first carefully removing his head, then baste him——" (586)

After this auspicious beginning, the epilogue goes on to reveal other "secrets of cannibal cooking"—namely, "that the natives prefer the soles of the feet and the fleshier part of the legs and back of young subjects, not by any means preferring the male" (586). Note the striking similarity of this passage to the one from the *Terrific Register* just quoted in the main text. We recall that Dickens had laughed over, trembled over, and marveled over that *Terrific Register* passage—a sensational account of cannibalistic tastes and predilections disguised as "useful knowledge"—forty-three years before he published (and perhaps touched or otherwise refashioned) the epilogue to *Leaves from the Mahogany Tree.* Note also that the passages just quoted from *Leaves from the Mahogany Tree* and the passage from that same source quoted immediately below bear a striking resemblance to the "Captain Boldheart" segment of Dickens' *Holiday Romance.* "Captain Boldheart," a self-contained segment of the four-part *Holiday Romance* (and, like the other parts, a humorous entertainment for children) was filled with cannibals, pirates, shipwrecks, and cannibal victims, the latter poor souls all shaved and floured and waiting to be cooked. Dickens had published this cannibal-haunted spoof of voyage and travel literature and, more particularly, this unsettling burlesque of the rollicking delights of dining on one's fellowmen, in *All the Year Round*. In fact, he had published it there just a month or two before *Leaves from the Mahogany Tree* began to appear in those same pages. (For more on "Captain Boldheart," see below in Part 1.)

The cannibal-fraught epilogue (or "Entremet") that concludes *Leaves from the Mahogany Tree* does not desist. After its introductory gourmet hints and savoury recipes, after its revelations concerning the delicious soles and legs of "young subjects," it continues with other "secrets of cannibal cooking": "Tarry old boatswains are generally boiled down for soup. Captains, if under sixty, are treated with bread-crumbs, plum sauce, and lemon juice. Ship-boys are much relished scolloped, and a baby à la Metternich is said to require only legality to carry its fame to both the North and South Poles" (586).

The squib goes on, and so does the humor; the humor sanctions (or at least buffers) the latent violence and aggression, and it cauterizes (or at least relieves) the latent horror and fear—savage violence and terrifying fear—that lurk just below the surface of these debonair descriptions of preparing, cooking, and eating one's fellowmen. The violence and fear—and the mitigating laughter—continue. In Sumatra, we are told, one tribe "never let a man live beyond seventy-two without eating him" (586). The festive and forthright ritual that launches such seventy-two-year-old patriarchs into eternity is both whimsical and brutal. After an amiable and elaborate ceremony, the geriatric entrée "is sure to be 'treed' by the younger and more hungry men." Following the "treeing," the ritual culminates:

> A whoop is then given, and the whole party collect, and sit round the place in a ring—every man, with his leaf of salt, pepper, and lemon by his side, his knife and fork in his hand, and the leaf of a tallypot palm for a table-cloth spread over his knees. Every one then shouts at the same moment, "Dinner time is come. Good night, Mr.———." The chief mourner runs up the tree, shakes hands with the old party, and drops him down. He is instantly clubbed, and eaten, with "sauce piquante," or "sauce à la bonne femme." Such is the remarkable custom of this very interesting people. (587)

The epilogue concludes by informing us that although cannibalism awakens a "natural repugnance" in man, the urge to eat our fellows does not represent "utter degradation" but a natural "craving for animal food" where such food is scarce. The "Entremet" ends with the comforting but humbling information that human flesh is said by the natives of New Zealand "to almost exactly resemble pork," and that human fare is known to the epicures of that far-off realm "by the agreeable metonym of 'Long Pig'" (587).

In this equivocal summation—a five-paragraph summation vouchsafed to the reader after months of regaling him with more conventional lore of cooking and eating, a summation in a family magazine that certified to all the world, in its heading and on the top of every opening, that it was "CONDUCTED BY CHARLES DICKENS"—in this otherwise anonymous family magazine, and in that culminating summation, all men are not grass, but pork. (For Dickens' frequent conflation of human flesh—especially children's and infants' flesh—with butcher-shop pork, see above, and even more elaborately below, in the main text of Part 1. See also the final paragraph of note 2 in Part 1.)

23. Dickens used this expression—the "attraction of repulsion"—throughout his career. He used it, for example, in his first letter (28 February 1846) to the *Daily News* on capital punishment; he also used it on 18 July 1863 in "The City of the Absent" (*AYR* 9: 493). Forster (paraphrasing Dickens) used it when discussing Dickens' boyhood response to London (F, 11).

For more on "The City of the Absent," a late essay filled with cannibalistic imagery as well as with the attraction of repulsion, see below in Part 1.

24. For a good deal more on medical students, dissecting, supplying bodies and parts of bodies to the medical profession, and the significance of such matters, especially in the 1820s and 1830s, see Part 1, note 40. This grisly commerce in human bodies and the abuses it engendered were sensations of Dickens' boyhood and youth. Such grisly matters and allied matters (such as corpse eating), often shorn of the humor that beguiles us in *Pickwick*, became major motifs in Dickens' middle and later writings. See below in Part 1.

25. These words concerning Oliver's mother—"she was weak and erring"—conclude the novel.

26. The "Old Morgue," the building to which Dickens always found himself "dragged by invisible force," was located on the south side of the Île de la Cité on the very edge of the Seine. More exactly, the Old Morgue, small and squat (see figures 36–38 which depict the exterior and the location of this building), was situated on the Quai du Marché Neuf, that is, between the Pont St. Michel

and the Petit Pont, adjacent to where the Préfecture de Police now stands. On the west side of the building, steps led down from the street level to the Seine. Bodies fished out of the river (or transported on the river) were often brought up those steps; if still unidentified after three days of public display, they were frequently taken down the same steps and sent off to a pauper's burial, or occasionally to medical facilities for dissection. This traffic in corpses often had monetary dimensions. Like Gaffer Hexam in *Our Mutual Friend,* who made a living by fishing bodies from the Thames (see below in Part 1), Gaffer's French counterparts made a living by fishing bodies from the Seine (see figures 52 and 53). French, or more precisely, Parisian, scavengers were paid fifteen francs—a considerable sum then—for each body they brought to the police and then to the Morgue. (London scavengers were paid ten shillings; see Griffiths, *Memorials of Millbank,* 405–6.)

Many of the bodies brought to the Morgue were waterlogged or otherwise disfigured. Disfigured or not, they were displayed seminude on inclined copper-clad slabs behind plate-glass windows. Water taps dripped water on the corpses to retard decomposition, and the clothes of the dead persons were hung above the bodies (see figure 39; also Part 1, note 33). Those seeking missing relatives or friends would come to the Morgue in fear and trepidation, but the place soon came to be one of the celebrated sights of Paris—an establishment to which Parisians flocked (especially on Sundays) as to a titillating diversion or a macabre show, and a place to which foreigners flocked every day of the week as to a notorious yet sobering spectacle, one of the shocking but obligatory sensations of Paris. Dickens' visits to the Morgue were thus by no means unusual. (Robert Browning, for instance—to cite the Morgue visits and ponderings of another eminent Victorian literary figure, a friend of Dickens—memorialized one of his own visits to the Morgue in "Apparent Failure," a poem written in 1863 in a futile attempt to save the Old Morgue from destruction.) But Dickens' impulsions and reactions on such visits, though shaped in part by typical urges, had deeper and darker sources than most such impulsions and reactions—and deeper and darker implications, as well.

The Old Morgue was just a few hundred yards west of the front of Notre Dame (see figure 37). The "obscene little Morgue," as Dickens called it, was built in 1830, replacing older buildings that had been used for the same purpose. (Before that, the site had been occupied by meat dealers and butcher shops.) The Old Morgue was torn down in 1864 as part of Baron Haussmann's remaking of Paris. In March 1864, a new, much larger, more professional Morgue was opened. It was designed by Haussmann and contained, amongst other innovative facilities, an amphitheater for postmortems and for dissecting cadavers. (The Old Morgue had contained a dissecting room, too, but not so elaborate as this.) Like the Old Morgue, the new Morgue was situated on the Seine. It stood on a site adjacent to the eastern end of Notre Dame, just a few hundred yards directly east of where the Old Morgue had stood. The new Morgue was demolished in 1914. Since that time there have been no similar facilities on the Île de la Cité.

27. The date of the inquest and the sex of the infant are given in Carlton, "Dickens in the Jury Box," 65–69.

28. Dickens' interest in the Morgue and, more generally, in bodies, burials, funerals, graves, graveyards, epitaphs, mummies, skeletons, skulls, taxidermy, vampires, werewolves, and the like—an interest that often takes on cannibalistic overtones—was not confined to his own writings. He filled his weekly magazines, *Household Words* and *All the Year Round,* with many articles on these and similar subjects. Here is a partial list of those articles (see, in addition to the articles listed below, Part 1, note 22): [Henry Morley], "Use and Abuse of the Dead," *HW* 17 (3 April 1858): 361–65—including accounts of Burke, Hare, Bishop, Williams, other Burkers and Resurrection Men, and the current illegal traffic in bodies for dissection; [Henry Morley and W. H. Wills], "Funerals in Paris," *HW* 6 (27 November 1852): 257–60—this issue of *Household Words* also contained Dickens' own "Trading in Death" (241–45), an article on the commercialization of the Duke of Wellington's state funeral, a barbaric commercialization that turned a dead body (in Dickens' view of such commerce) into food and drink (some enterprising food merchants turned food into effigies of the Duke—quite literally into food and drink); [Henry G. Wreford], "Village Funerals in Naples," *HW* 5 (20 March 1852): 19–20; [James Hannay], "Graves and Epitaphs," *HW* 6 (16 October 1852): 105–9; [Henry Morley], "Mummy," *HW* 15 (28 February 1857): 196–98—concerning the use of mummified heads and other body parts to make medicines, colors, etc.; [Dudley Costello], "Dead Reckoning at the Morgue," *HW* 8 (1 October 1853): 112–16—the history, governance, physical arrangement, and statistics of the Paris Morgue; [Edmund Ollier], "Vampyres," *HW* 11 (10 February 1855): 39–43—lore and legends of vampires (culled from Voltaire, Sir Walter Scott, and others), including accounts of vampires rising thirstily from graves, despoiling graves, and descriptions of how "every night comes the terrible Shape to your bed-side . . . and sucks your life-blood" (39); [Edmund Ollier], "Wehrwolves," *HW* 15 (25 April 1857); 405–8—werewolf stories, including John Webster's description (in *The Duchess of Malfi*) of how men, transformed

into wolves, "steale forth to churchyards in the dead of night, . . . dig dead bodies up," and devour them (406); [Dudley Costello], "Monsters," *HW* 14 (6 December 1856): 498–504—includes accounts of mythological and legendary creatures who eat human beings; "Burning a Priest," *HW* 13 (22 March 1856): 224–26—funeral rites in Burma; [John Archer Crowe], "Crowns in Lead," *HW* 8 (3 September 1853): 11–12—exhuming, in 1793, bodies and relics of those sepultured in the Abbey of St.-Denis, Paris (in order to retrieve the lead in the sarcophagi for bullets), including descriptions of the bodies: "[Henry of Navarre's] beard, moustache, and hair were perfect; and, as the soldiers standing round looked on in awe at the strange spectacle, one of them drew his sword, and, casting himself down before the body of the victor of the League, lopped off one of his moustaches, and placed it upon his own lip" (11–12). Wills and Morley were members of the *Household Words* staff; Dickens probably commissioned some of the articles they wrote.

Here are some analogous articles from *All the Year Round:* "French Treatment of the Drowned," *AYR* 16 (24 November 1866): 475–76—attempts to revive a drowned man: in a notable scene in *Our Mutual Friend,* Dickens had recently depicted Rogue Riderhood's return to life after drowning; "Death in the Latest Fashion," *AYR* 13 (18 March 1865): 181–83—ostentatious deaths and funerals, "the fancy for 'funeral baked meats,'" and other desecrations; "Wolfish Humanity," *AYR* 15 (19 May 1866): 441–45—a review of *The Book of the Were-Wolves* by Sabine Baring-Gould, including accounts of "men and boys gravely confessing to the were-wolf superstition, telling how they changed their skin at will, then roamed over the country as ravening wolves, slaying and eating children wherever found" (443), also an account of Gilles Garnier, the "murderous cannibal," who "satisfied his craving for food on human flesh" (443), the histories of cannibals and "child-eating men," and the story of M. Bertrand, who is described, in a sentence that seems to have been interpolated or rewritten by Dickens, as "a French gentleman and an officer of singularly amiable disposition and gentle manners, which found expression in his delight at digging up dead bodies and hewing and hacking them to pieces" (444); [Walter Thornbury], "Old Stories Re-Told: Resurrection Men, Burke and Hare," *AYR* 17 (16 March 1867): 282–88—murdering (or disinterring) individuals in order to sell their bodies for dissection; [Walter Thornbury], "Turkish Burial-Grounds," *AYR* 2 (18 February 1860), 400–404—includes the information that the Turks' coffinless graves often crack, "much to the comfort and convenience of the wild dogs" (403); "Buried Above Ground," *AYR* 3 (19 May 1860): 138–40—account of an old sculptor who lives isolated (buried alive) in an ancient tower in Flanders; "Buried Alive," *AYR* 8 (11 October 1862): 107–11—accounts of persons who had been buried alive in salt mines ("every hair had fallen from me, my eyes had disappeared, and my body, from head to foot, was covered with crystals of salt" [109]), or persons who had been buried alive in chalk pits, or in poisoned wells, or in similar untoward tombs—including, in one poisoned-well instance, being thrown into the well with a dead body; "American Cemeteries," *AYR* 6 (30 November 1861): 226–29—many individuals enjoy relaxing and promenading in New York's Greenwood Cemetery "and go home with better relish to their green turtle soup and other 'fixings'" (227); "The Studious Resurrectionist," *AYR* 20 (29 August 1868): 285–88—opens with a reference to "nursing the baby, or killing a pig" (probably Dickens' hand—see, above in Part 1, Dickens' repeated slaughterous coupling of babies and pigs), then goes on to describe excavating an Anglo-Saxon graveyard (the inhabitants of which were killed in "the battle of life" [286]—the latter phrase is the title of a Christmas Book by Dickens), then proceeds to a learned disquisition on the bones and artifacts found in the graves, and ends with a tale about several ghoulish boys who excavate a skull from the local churchyard; "Opening a Barrow," *AYR* 3 (21 July 1860): 346–48—the narrator compares the opening of a Wiltshire tumulus to the "charm" of "the first analytic cut at a Stilton" (346), goes on, while "a monster of a speckled thrush [is] pulling a worm out of the lawn," to speak of waking an "ancient Briton" from his resting place with "pickaxes, spades, and other resurrectionary apparatus," although the Briton's resting place has already "been nibbled away by time" (346, 347)—this image of time nibbling on corpses and on corpselike individuals occurs repeatedly in *Great Expectations* (see below in Part 1), a novel published, like this article, in *All the Year Round,* and a novel that Dickens had just begun to formulate when this article appeared—then the narrator of "Opening a Barrow" goes on to exhume finger bones ("not unlike the mouthpieces of pipes"), ribs, vertebrae, leg bones, teeth, and skulls—enough, all told, to reconstitute six or seven men and women (347); "Sacred to the Memory," *AYR* 15 (30 June 1866): 592–95—attacks the old London churchyards, "death in its most hideous and squalid form—and such as we have known and feared it from our earliest days" (593), advocates "gardens of the dead" which can banish the remembrance "that the very lips which we have kissed, and the hands which we have held in ours, are lying there in the cold wet earth, when the days are dark and the nights are stormy" (595); [Henry Spicer], "Speechless Bones," *AYR* 15 (7 April 1866): 297–300—the opening paragraph reads: "When the worthy tenant of Milcote manor was apprised of the circumstance that about three thousand skeletons were reposing within sixty paces of his house door, it probably did not occur to him that, on

the first day after publication of the news, a similar number of skeletons en-
cased in living flesh would wait upon him to luncheon. Such, however, was the
case, and such the hospitality with which they were received, that, had this
influx of archaeologists continued many days, good Mr. Adkins would have
been as effectually eaten out of house and home, as if the warriors who had so
long maintained this invisible leaguer round the mansion could have resumed
their flesh, and placed him in a condition of actual blockade" (297–98). The
"speechless bones" probably date from 1271 and the Battle (or Massacre) of
Evesham (the defeat of Simon de Montfort, Earl of Leicester, by Prince Edward). Note the similarity of the central idea of the opening paragraph (just
quoted) to the central idea in *The Battle of Life* (see below in Part 1). That
similarity was perhaps the reason "Speechless Bones" appealed to Dickens,
though the opening paragraph was probably written or rewritten by Dickens
or one of his staff. On the latter score, it is worth remembering that touching
the opening or concluding lines of an article, adding an opening or concluding
sentence or two, or making other changes or interpolations elsewhere in an
article, was an editorial brightening or lightening or tightening or enticing that
Dickens (and his staff) frequently indulged in. Incidentally, many, perhaps
most, titles for *Household Words* and *All the Year Round* articles were supplied
or chosen by Dickens.

Dickens also had many books and pamphlets on death, executions, funerals,
graveyards, tombs, bodies, taxidermy, ghouls, vampires, werewolves, cannibals,
and the like in his library. Here is a partial list of these works: E. Gibbon Wake-
field, *Facts Relating to the Punishment of Death in the Metropolis,* 2nd ed.,
1832—contains an "Appendix Concerning Murder for the Sale of the Dead
Body"; J. D. Parry, *Urban Burial: the London Churchyards, with Suggestions for
Joint Parochial Cemeteries in Town and Country,* 1847—a pamphlet on a subject that figures in *Bleak House* (other allied works on this subject are listed
below); *Report on a General Scheme for Extramural Sepulture,* 1850—a pamphlet of 172 pages, with plans; *Walker's Lectures on the Condition of Metropoli-
tan Grave Yards*—a pamphlet containing four series of lectures; *Report on the
Subject of Capital Punishment by a Select Committee of the House of Assembly,
State of New York,* 1841—a pamphlet of 164 pages; J. B. Harrison, *Medical
Aspects of Death,* 1852—Harrison was a surgeon; T. J. Pettigrew, *History of
Egyptian Mummies, and an Account of the Worship and Embalming of the Sacred Animals of the Egyptians, with remains of the funeral ceremonies of different
nations, and observations on the Mummies of the Canary Islands,* illustrated by
George Cruikshank, 1834—in the West, especially in the seventeenth and
eighteenth centuries, powdered mummified remains were often ingested as

medicines; C. Waterton, *Wanderings in South America, with Original Instructions for the Perfect Preservation of Birds, etc. for Cabinets,* 1852; *The Dance of Death, Exhibited in Elegant Engravings on Wood; With a Dissertation on the Several Representations of that Subject, but More Particularly on Those Ascribed to Macaber and Hans Holbein, by F. Douce,* 1833—a book (or rather images) that first impressed Dickens in childhood; Dr. Elliotson, *Human Physiology; with which is Incorporated Part of Blumenbach's Institutiones Physicae,* 5th ed., 1840—with many woodcut illustrations (John Elliotson was a good friend of Dickens); John Foxe, *Acts and Monuments of the Church, Containing the History and Sufferings of the Martyrs,* revised and condensed by Rev. Hobart Seymour, 1838—another work remembered from childhood because of its horrendous illustrations; Charles Mackay, *Memoirs of Extraordinary Popular Delusions and the Madness of Crowds,* 3 vols., illus., 1841—contains many accounts of witchcraft, lycanthropy, and other abominations, including, for example, the following vignette: In 1572 Gilles Garnier, a native of Lyons, "seized upon a little girl, twelve years of age, whom he . . . killed, partly with his teeth . . . ; he trailed her bleeding body along the ground with his teeth into the wood of La Serre, where he ate the greatest portion of her at one meal, and carried the remainder home to his wife; that upon another occasion . . . he devoured a boy thirteen years of age, having previously torn off his leg and thigh with his teeth, and hid them away for breakfast on the morrow"— Dickens knew Mackay well and published many articles by him; Herman Melville, *Typee; Four Months' Residence among the Natives of the Marquesas Islands,* 1847—a fictional account of Melville's actual sojourn amongst cannibals; Sir John Maundevile, *Voiage and Travaile, which Treateth of the Way to Hierusalem, and of Marvayles of Inde, etc.,* ed. J. O. Halliwell, illus., 1839—containing many fanciful stories of cannibalism and cannibalistic practices.

29. There were numerous floating bathing establishments on the Seine, several of them on the Île de la Cité, including a few very close to the Morgue. Whether Dickens went into one of the latter is not certain, but the chances are (based both upon his account of his movements and what was about to occur) that the establishment was close to the Morgue.

Many of the Seine bathing establishments were large and elegant, with many ancillary amenities and facilities, and many attendants. Though portions of the bathing structures were fully enclosed, the central bathing area was usually open to the sky, a kind of large outdoor swimming pool (see figure 41). However, the water in the pools was not spring or specially treated water (there was no way to contain the water), but ordinary river water flowing directly from the Seine. The bather, in other words, was bathing directly in the river, though surrounded by a floating enclosure.

30. Another cannibalistic corpse-eating reference associated with water-bloated bodies and sudden sickness (probably another profoundly conditioned recollection of seeing such bodies in the Morgue) occurs in *A Tale of Two Cities* when Charles Darnay is first locked up in his Paris prison, La Force. Darnay feels that he is entombed and that he and all those about him are already dead. Leaning against the wall of his solitary cell, he looks on as his jailer, "a man with a bloated face," prepares to lock him in. Dickens sketches the scene and sketches also Darnay's death-haunted musings and death-haunted cannibalistic associations:

> There were in the cell, a chair, a table, and a straw mattress. As the gaoler made a general inspection of these objects, and of the four walls, before going out, a wandering fancy wandered through the mind of the prisoner leaning against the wall opposite to him, that this gaoler was so unwholesomely bloated, both in face and person, as to look like a man who had been drowned and filled with water. (*AYR* 1: *TTC*, 3: 1:485)

When the unwholesome corpselike jailer, dealer in death and ghastly embodiment of death, has left, Darnay, still musing "in the same wandering way," thinks, "'Now am I left, as if I were dead.'" Then, looking down at the mattress, he sees that it is crawling with creatures, creatures that feed on bodies. He turns away "with a sick feeling." "'And here,'" he thinks, "'in these crawling creatures is the first condition of the body after death.'"

This episode and its images are also related to the resurrection motifs of the novel (see below in Part 1) and to the cannibalistic countermotifs of the Resurrection Men (men such as Jerry Cruncher). See, in the latter connection, the discussion of Resurrection Men in Part 1, note 40. Later in Part 1 the crucial import of cannibalism in *A Tale of Two Cities* is dealt with at length.

31. Still other ramifications of Dickens' feelings toward his mother are discussed in Part 3, "Dickens and Necessity."

32. This strong tradition that Mrs. Nickleby is, in part, a portrait of Dickens' mother is given added force by a letter, unpublished until 1970, written by Elizabeth Dickens (Dickens' mother)—the only letter by her known to have survived. (See Carlton, "A Friend of Dickens's Boyhood," 8–15). In that letter,

written on 12 April 1851 (twelve days after John Dickens' death), Elizabeth Dickens exhibits the same rambling, free-association, run-on style that Dickens reproduced in Mrs. Nickleby. Though Carlton does not mention this resemblance, the consanguinity is striking. Here is a portion of Elizabeth Dickens' letter:

> On my return here I found your very kind letter, doubly grateful at a moment like the present so replete with kindness I scarcely know how to answer it. In the first place I left home the day after the Funeral with my Daughter Letitia now Mrs Austin who is most comfortably and happily married where I shall remain for the present, her affectionate kindness, and unceasing solicitude during the short weeks of my dear Husband's illness is and has been a great solace to me. After a time I have promised to go to my Son Alfreds who is an Engineer married and settled in Yorkshire, with 3 darling Children always a great source of happiness to me, therefore you see how impossible it would be for me to leave home at present, indeed I could not feel happy at present [away] from those around me, but certainly shall the first opportunity bend my steps towards Southampton.

Compare this run-on performance with Mrs. Nickleby's run-on monologue on roast pig and very little babies (a characteristic example of her speech), quoted earlier (p. 84).

33. For example, yet another instance of Dickens' preoccupation with this constellation of associations (many additional instances could be cited) occurs in "Lying Awake," an essay he wrote in 1852 for *Household Words*. In that essay he re-creates the stream of images and memories, feelings and fantasies, that flowed through his mind one night as he lay in bed unable to sleep. After a while, the ebb and flow of associations, mostly disturbing, grows darker, then darker yet: he thinks of the terrors of childhood; then of an execution he witnessed (the bodies of the hanged murderers, husband and wife, swinging slowly from side to side); then of dangerous public exhibitions; then of a man with his throat cut, dashing, all bloody, toward him; then of a young mother at a pantomime "who falls into fits of laughter when the baby is boiled" (*HW* 6: 147—later in *RP*). This last association, a cannibalistic association which depicts a young mother's joy as a baby is boiled, leads to other cannibalistic associations, to memories of the "detestable Morgue," memories which intrude upon Dickens' consciousness willy-nilly and immediately cause him, in the old conflation that juxtaposes cannibalistic mothers and babies with

corpses and food, to present us with yet another version of that primordial association, a version part ferocious and part fearful that quickly moves from its baby-boiling and baby-eating engenderings to its ghastly corpse-eating fulfillment (a Morgue corpse-eating fulfillment), a fulfillment that engrosses and revolts Dickens. Here is the corpse-food association—that is, the Morgue association (sickening to Dickens)—that follows immediately after the mother and boiled baby association:

> I wish the Morgue in Paris would not come here as I lie awake, with its ghastly beds, and the swollen saturated clothes hanging up, and the water dripping, dripping all day long, upon that other swollen saturated something in the corner, like a heap of crushed over-ripe figs that I have seen in Italy! (*HW* 6: 147)

In typical fashion, in this vignette (generated by a vision of a mother who laughs when a baby is boiled) the "swollen saturated something in the corner"—a revolting bloated corpse—is immediately associated with food, with "over-ripe figs."

In connection with the last quotation, see Part 1, note 26; see also figure 39.

34. Pip's responsibility for his "subsequent crimes," and his accountability for them, and for his other acts, is discussed in Part 3, "Dickens and Necessity."

35. For an analysis of the final scene ("The Reward of Cruelty") in Hogarth's *The Four Stages of Cruelty*, see pp. 35–39. See also figure 18.

On the matter of human spontaneous combustion, *Bleak House*, and Dickens' earliest sources, here is a portion of the *Terrific Register* version of Countess Cesena's greasy end:

> The furniture and tapestry were covered with a moist kind of soot of the colour of ashes, which had penetrated into the drawers, and dirtied the linen. This soot having been conveyed to a neighbouring kitchen, adhered to the walls and utensils. A piece of bread in the cupboard was covered with it, and no dog would touch it. The infectious odour had been communicated to other apartments. (*TR* 2: 340)

In his "Preface" (August 1853) to *Bleak House*, responding to George Henry Lewes' demurrers on the subject of human spontaneous combustion, Dickens refers to the case of Cornelia Bandi, Countess Cesena (I use the *Terrific Register* version of the name—Dickens calls her "the Countess Cornelia de Bandi Cesenate" in the "Preface" [ix] and "the Countess Cornelia Baudi" in the text [329]), a case that had supplied Dickens with the chief details for Krook's sooty demise. He also refers to (but draws more sparingly on) other cases described in the *Terrific Register* article. It is important to realize that Dickens, who much later came upon these cases in other sources, first read these lurid accounts of people spontaneously burning and decomposing in the *Terrific Register,* and that he read these accounts at a most impressionable and haunted time for him, the time of his blacking-warehouse and early Wellington House experiences. It was this emotion-charged introduction to the grisly lore of human spontaneous combustion, an introduction darkened by *Terrific Register* and blacking-warehouse associations, that helped shape Dickens' feelings about the subject, an imaginative set that strongly colored what came thereafter. There is no doubt that Dickens was drawing on these cases in *Bleak House.* Of the Cornelia Bandi case, Dickens writes in his "Preface": "The appearances beyond all rational doubt observed in that case, are the appearances observed in Mr. Krook's case" (ix).

36. That Dickens regarded this kind of ingestion as cannibalistic, and that he was fully aware of those connotations, is both confirmed and elaborated in his later writings. See, for example, below in Part 1, the church-grave-corpse-taste-cannibalism imagery that informs "City of London Churches." In that piece, Dickens, sitting in an ancient London church, gradually becomes aware of the "taste" of the ancient bodies in their graves, and this awareness—an awareness that he is eating corpses—causes him to become sick.

37. Dickens often generalizes in this manner; in many works he uses the metaphor of cannibalism (both in overall and in subsidiary ways) to indict an entire nation or society. This strategy is made startlingly clear in a succinct and exceptionally direct (though humorous) reference in *Martin Chuzzlewit* in which he pillories the whole of American society. The reference occurs when Mrs. Lupin, dismayed that Mark Tapley has gone off to the wilds of America and that she has had no news of him, cries out: "'How could he ever go to America! Why didn't he go to some of those countries which are not quite barbarous; where savages eat each other fairly, and give an equal chance to every one!'" (*MC*, 43:490).

38. That Dickens frequently views the members of society as battening each one on the other, and often uses cannibalistic imagery to express that devouring vision, can be seen very clearly in some of his shorter nonfictional

pieces. The vision emerges with great clarity in such pieces, for in them he is not attempting (as in *Bleak House* and other novels) to orchestrate a vast array of contrapuntal themes, but is seeking to convey a simple theme or a few allied themes by means of a central and relatively simple (or singular) conception.

"Poor Mercantile Jack" is a case in point. In that 1860 essay, Dickens re-creates an all-night police tour that he took through a squalid waterside section of Liverpool. This nautical region of Liverpool battens upon sailors— denominated generically in this essay "Jack"—sailors just home, or briefly in port, or otherwise lingering, or passing through. Dickens depicts how these sailors are exploited wherever they turn. They are greeted everywhere as though with a "taunting chorus," a chorus that embodies their fate: "'Come along, Mercantile Jack! Ill-lodged, ill-fed, ill-used, hocussed, entrapped, antic-ipated, cleaned out'" (*AYR* 2: 462—later in *UT*). Dickens and his party ex-plore dismal courts, blind alleys, and black, labyrinthine lanes. He encounters the loathsome creatures who lie in wait for Jack. He sees these creatures as rapacious witches, ghouls, ogresses, predators, and Fates who hungrily wait for their unsuspecting prey. He also sees them as swarming cannibalistic vermin, human rats ready to devour their defenseless victims.

Dickens ends his essay with a visit to the "cave" of "three weird old women of transcendent ghastliness" who are about to eat, who have a baby with them—the old women are witchlike ogress-mothers—and who stitch, stitch, stitch as he talks to them (*AYR* 2: 466). He denominates these weird old stitching Fates "First Witch," "Second Witch," and "Third Witch." Dickens feels that the three ghastly witches are taking his measurement "as for a charmed winding-sheet" (*AYR* 2: 466). He can hardly bear to remain in their hellish room. As he departs their "abominable" den and its revolting "stench," and as he takes his final look at the "nauseous room" and its earthen floor "into which the refuse scum of an alley trickled," the First Witch gazes at him: "The red marks round her eyes seemed to have already grown larger, and she hungrily and thirstily looked out beyond me into the dark doorway, to see if Jack were there" (*AYR* 2: 466). Fortunately, poor Jack, mere fodder for this hungry ogress, is not there.

Dickens returns to his dwelling place and goes to bed, but his mind keeps "wandering among the vermin I had seen," and afterwards "the same vermin ran all over my sleep" (*AYR* 2: 466). That human vermin, those human water-side rats, scuffling and swarming through hovels, caves, and hellish dens, those rapacious cannibalistic rats (just like the cannibalistic waterside rats of "Chips and the Devil" and the scuffling waterside rats in the hellish blacking ware-house), remained with Dickens that night and ever after, part now of that somber and engendering constellation—an ever-evolving and ever-accreting constellation—of cannibalistic images, associations, and emotions, a constellation that goes back, in its nascent beginnings, to his earliest childhood. Dickens ends "Poor Mercantile Jack" and its nightmare vision of cannibalistic predators with this sentence: "Evermore, when on a breezy day I see Poor Mercantile Jack running into port with a fair wind under all sail, I shall think of the unsleeping host of devourers who never go to bed, and are always in their set traps waiting for him" (*AYR* 2: 466).

Here too, then, Dickens sees grievous exploitation, exploitation at its most ferocious and life-threatening, as cannibalistic rapacity. As in *Bleak House,* and as in so many other works by Dickens, the "unsleeping host of devourers" eat and are eaten.

39. The exchange between Lady Tippins and Mortimer Lightwood begins with a reference to Robinson Crusoe and "the Island," hence the subsequent allusion to Juan Fernández. (Alexander Selkirk, the prototype of Defoe's shipwrecked protagonist, survived for more than four years on Más a Tierra, one of the three islands of the Juan Fernández group.) The exchange with Lady Tippins is one more indication that, for Dickens, *Robinson Crusoe* and cannibalism were inextricably intertwined, thus the series of associations—Robinson Crusoe, Island, savages, cannibals—associations quite typical for Dickens, which culminate in the cannibalistic thrust. See above in Part 1 for a discussion of Dickens, *Robinson Crusoe,* and cannibalism; see also Part 1, note 18.

40. Dickens had long been obsessed with Resurrectionist fantasies, both humorous and horrific. As a matter of fact, frequently those fantasies were an amalgam of humor and horror, the humor serving as a buffer to the horror. Dining on corpses, whether freshly slaughtered or exhumed from graves, whether real case histories or fictional enormities, was a horror that had long fascinated and revolted Dickens. When the grisly exploits of the Resurrectionists, or Burkers as the murdering variety was called—criminals who specialized in illicitly providing bodies for medical dissection—became the sensation of the day (Burke was executed in 1829, but other sensational cases continued into the thirties), those ghoulish exploits evoked a horrified response from the public. For Dickens, this gruesome commerce in bodies engendered profound interest and profound fear. Exhuming freshly buried bodies or murdering passers-by in order to obtain bodies that could be sold—sold to live on, sold for food and drink—became, for Dickens, a type of ghastly modern cannibal-

ism, a cannibalism that merged with his multitudes of cannibalistic associations and cannibalistic fears from childhood on.

This ghoulish way of sustaining oneself—reaping one's livelihood from fresh human carcasses sold for the express purpose of being butchered (that is, anatomized) like prime beef carcasses (I invoke here Dickens' butcher-shop imagery)—had been going on for many years before Burke and Hare came upon the scene. Owing to restrictive laws in the British Isles, all those who had a legitimate need for cadavers—anatomy teachers, surgical specialists, medical researchers, and the like—had to depend upon the illegitimate supply purveyed by a group of most unsavory characters, criminal elements who often exacted blackmail or levied other extortionate charges along with their charge for the body itself. These traffickers in bodies obtained most of their wares by buying corpses from desperate or callous relatives or corrupt functionaries or, most frequently, by body snatching—that is, by stealing newly buried bodies from graves. With the rapid growth of medical science and medical education in the first third of the nineteenth century, the demand for dissectible bodies greatly increased and the price of such bodies rose steadily. By the late twenties and early thirties, this price—ten guineas and more—a princely sum to an ordinary laborer, proved a sore temptation to a number of poor, indigent, or rapacious individuals: here was a ready (though illegal) source of very substantial money.

The notoriety of Burke and Hare resulted from their callousness and rapacity, and most of all, from their murdering on a wholesale scale to obtain suitable, that is, fresh, unmutilated bodies. During their depredations (which lasted less than a year), they murdered sixteen times, luring their victims to Hare's house and then suffocating them there. They were apprehended on Halloween 1828, and when, a few days later, their predations became widely known, the news caused a sensation, not only in Edinburgh, but throughout the British Isles. Intense anger and revulsion combined with intense interest and fear, fear of being "burked" as one went about one's lawful business in city streets. William Hare turned King's evidence and was given immunity; William Burke was hanged on 28 January 1829 before tens of thousands of eager spectators. Burke's sentence provided not only that he be hanged, but that "his body thereafter . . . be delivered to Dr. Alexander Monro, Professor of Anatomy in the University of Edinburgh to be by him publicly dissected and anatomized" (Ball, *The Sack-'Em-Up Men*, 89). On the afternoon following the execution, the public dissection was carried out before an overflowing crowd in the anatomical theater of the university. Those outside the theater, deprived of the spectacle proper, rioted for several hours to establish their right to view the bloody remains. This right gained at last, tens of thousands came to gaze that day and the next, fifty at a time, upon the butchered corpse. Burke's skeleton now hangs in the Anatomical Museum of the University of Edinburgh. (For a graphic rendition, well known to Dickens, of a public dissection of a murderer's body and a public display of murderers' skeletons, see figure 18.)

Dickens was almost seventeen when the Burke-Hare predations took place. Given his susceptibilities, one can be sure that he followed every detail of the case as avidly as the most obsessed of his contemporaries. Almost forty years later, he published an article on Burke and Hare in *All the Year Round:* [Walter Thornbury], "Old Stories Re-Told: Resurrection Men, Burke and Hare," *AYR* 17 (16 March 1867): 282–88. He also published other articles on burking and on Resurrectionists, including earlier articles, *Household Words* articles, on Burke, Hare, Bishop, Williams, and others. See Part 1, note 28.

In the early thirties other cases of burking came to light, including the notorious case of Bishop and Williams in London in 1831 (see figure 29). At the time of these predations Dickens, now nineteen, was working in the very London streets where Bishop and Williams committed their atrocities, and in the very London courts where they were tried. After Bishop and Williams were hanged, their bodies were anatomized at King's College, London. Subsequently, Bishop's skeleton, standing and holding a tanned bit of his own skin, was placed on permanent display in the museum at King's, a warning spectacle for students and for curious passers-by. Dickens may have gazed (more than once) at that warning skeleton and warning skin. King's College, housed in a portion of Somerset House, was part of an area that he had known from childhood on, a precinct close to John Dickens' old haunts and hard by Dickens' current working life, a quarter of London he passed and repassed constantly during these days.

But for Dickens the gruesome lore of the Resurrectionists was not confined to such firsthand associations, or to newspapers, or even to the illustrated Resurrectionist broadsides, chapbooks, and pamphlets that abounded. Well before the time of Bishop and Williams, Burke and Hare, that lore had begun to emerge in literature, and Dickens seems to have been familiar with the chief examples. Here are a few of the better-known works that dwell upon that ghoulish theme, together with a sampling of Dickensian interconnections: David Macbeth Moir ("Delta"), *The Life of Mansie Wauch, Taylor in Dalkeith: Written by Himself* (1828; earlier in *Blackwood's*)—Dickens knew Moir's works well (see his letter to Moir of 6 December 1841); Samuel Warren, *Passages from the Diary of a Late Physician* (1838; earlier in *Blackwood's*)—Dickens was familiar with this novel and refers to it (see his letter to Edward Oliver of June or July 1838); John Wilson ("Christopher North"), *Noctes Ambrosianae* (1843; earlier in *Blackwood's*)—Dickens, who met Wilson in 1841, owned a four-volume set of the *Noctes* and had been reading Wilson at least as early as 1830, that is, at least from the time he was eighteen (see Dickens' British Museum indent, dated 27 June 1830, for Wilson's *Lights and Shadows of Scottish Life*); *Tales from Blackwood*—Dickens owned a twelve-volume set of these tales; Edward Bulwer-Lytton, *Lucretia, or the Children of Night* (1846)— Dickens knew Bulwer well, owned this book, and referred to it; Mrs. Crowe, *Light and Darkness* (1850)—Dickens knew Catherine Crowe, corresponded with her, reviewed one of her books, and published three pieces by her in *Household Words*.

A different reflection of body snatching and body selling was Robert Southey's "The Surgeon's Warning" (1798). Over the years Dickens had owned at least eleven volumes of Southey's prose and poetry (some volumes disappeared from his library in the course of time). Furthermore, Dickens' diaries, letters, speeches, and periodicals show him reading, quoting, publishing, and referring to Southey. (See, for example, *Diary,* 9 February 1839; *Letters,* 31 July 1842; *Speeches,* 28 December 1847; *Household Words,* 1 [11 May 1850], 167.) "The Surgeon's Warning," written during the rising tide of Resurrectionist fears, exploits the public's animosity toward surgeons, anatomists, and the like. The latter professionals, consumers of corpses, were often thought to be in collusion with Resurrection Men, or, at the very least, to turn a blind eye to the nefarious dealings that provided them and their students with fresh bodies for dissection. The poem also exploits the widespread fear that one's own body, after a decent burial, would be snatched from its hallowed grave and became a public commodity, a vile, desecrated, gawked-at carcass; one's sanctified body, in other words, would be sold, then publicly butchered, dismembered, cut into bits, and cast upon an offal heap. Here are two excerpts from Southey's satiric and parodic poem. In the first excerpt, the surgeon, who is dying, is speaking:

> "All kinds of carcasses I have cut up,
>   And now my turn will be;
> But, brothers, I took care of you;
>   So pray take care of me.
>
> "I have made candles of dead men's fat;
>   The Sextons have been my slaves;
> I have bottled babes unborn, and dried
>   Hearts and livers from rifled graves.

"And my Prentices now will surely come
    And carve me bone from bone;
And I, who have rifled the dead man's grave,
    Shall never have rest in my own.

"Bury me in lead when I am dead,
    My brethren, I entreat,
And see the coffin weigh'd, I beg,
    Lest the plumber should be a cheat.

"And let it be solder'd closely down,
    Strong as strong can be, I implore;
And put it in a patent coffin,
    That I may rise no more.

"If they carry me off in the patent coffin,
    Their labour will be in vain;
Let the Undertaker see it bought of the maker,
    Who lives by St. Martin's Lane.

"And bury me in my brother's church,
    For that will safer be;
And, I implore, lock the church door,
    And pray take care of the key.

"And all night long let three stout men
    The vestry watch within;
To each man give a gallon of beer,
    And a keg of Holland's gin;—

"Powder and ball, and blunderbuss,
    To save me if he can,
And eke five guineas if he shoot
    A Resurrection Man.

"And let them watch me for three weeks,
    My wretched corpse to save;
For then I think that I may stink
    Enough to rest in my grave."

The surgeon dies. One of his apprentices, a cohort of the Resurrectionists, raising his offer for the surgeon's body (this in the course of three successive nights) from one guinea to three guineas, finally succeeds in bribing the sexton and the guards. The poem concludes as the eager apprentice and his fellow Resurrection Men proceed with their grisly work:

> They burst the patent coffin first,
>   And they cut through the lead;
> And they laugh'd aloud when they saw the shroud
>   Because they had got at the dead.
>
> And they allow'd the Sexton the shroud,
>   And they put the coffin back;
> And nose and knees they then did squeeze
>   The Surgeon in a sack.
>
> The watchman, as they pass'd along,
>   Full four yards off could smell,
> And a curse bestow'd upon the load
>   So disagreeable.
>
> So they carried the sack a-pick-a-back,
>   And they carved him bone from bone;
> But what became of the Surgeon's soul
>   Was never to mortal known.

Not all the literary lore of body snatching, body selling, dissection, and the like was grim or gruesomely graphic. One of Dickens' early literary friends was Thomas Hood. Dickens met Hood in 1840, but he was familiar with Hood's work long before that: he refers to many of Hood's writings and was lending copies of some of Hood's collected writings to friends in 1839 (see Dickens' letter to George Cattermole, [21 August 1839]). Later, referring to Hood, Dickens declared: "[I] hold his genius in the highest estimation" (26 March 1844); and later still, to help his ailing friend, he contributed a short article to the May 1844 issue of *Hood's Magazine and Comic Miscellany* ("Threatening Letter to Thomas Hood, from an Ancient Gentleman"). The following piece by Hood, a comic and allusive poem, concerns a young woman whose ghost laments to her erstwhile lover that her body was filched from the grave by body snatchers and eventually distributed, piecemeal, to the best-known medical schools, anatomy schools, and anatomists in London (all the allusions to places and persons are authentic, many of the references are freighted with comic or satiric meaning). This Resurrectionist poem, with its London allusions and macabre humor, would have appealed—both when initially published and later reprinted—to Dickens' comic and cannibalistic susceptibilities. It first appeared (in collected and illustrated form) in Hood's *Whims and Oddities: In Prose and Verse,* 2d ser., 1827. Here is the complete poem and the woodcut illustration (by Hood himself) that headed it:

"GIN A BODY MEET A BODY."

MARY'S GHOST.
A Pathetic Ballad.

'Twas in the middle of the night,
     To sleep young William tried;
When Mary's ghost came stealing in,
     And stood at his bed-side.

O William dear! O William dear!
     My rest eternal ceases;
Alas! my everlasting peace
     Is broken into pieces.

I thought the last of all my cares
     Would end with my last minute;
But tho' I went to my long home,
     I didn't stay long in it.

The body-snatchers they have come,
    And made a snatch at me;
It's very hard them kind of men
    Wont let a body be!

You thought that I was buried deep,
    Quite decent like and chary,
But from her grave in Mary-bone,
    They've come and boned your Mary.

The arm that used to take your arm
    Is took to Dr. Vyse;
And both my legs are gone to walk
    The hospital at Guy's.

I vowed that you should have my hand,
    But fate gives us denial;
You'll find it there, at Dr. Bell's,
    In spirits and a phial.

As for my feet, the little feet
    You used to call so pretty,
There's one, I know, in Bedford Row,
    That t'other's in the City.

I can't tell where my head is gone,
    But Doctor Carpue can;
As for my trunk, it's all packed up
    To go by Pickford's van.

I wish you'd go to Mr. P.
    And save me such a ride;
I don't half like the outside place,
    They've took for my inside.

The cock it crows—I must be gone!
    My William, we must part!
But I'll be yours in death, altho'
    Sir Astley has my heart.

Don't go to weep upon my grave,
    And think that there I be;
They haven't left an atom there
    Of my anatomie.

Dickens, quite obviously, was not at a loss for materials—comic, folklore, personal, factual, literary, and, above all, emotional materials—when he created Jerry Cruncher and his Resurrectionist graveyard "fishing" and graveyard dining in *A Tale of Two Cities* (1859).

But Jerry Cruncher was not the first of Dickens' fictional Resurrectionist fantasies. As early as *The Lamplighter* (1838) Dickens introduced Resurrectionists into his fiction, conjuring up nightmare visions of monster-predators and then cauterizing his visions with humor (see Part 1, note 44). But this is only part of the story. Long before *The Lamplighter,* Dickens was summoning up nonfictional Resurrectionist fantasies and lacing them with humor also. An anecdote concerning the youthful Dickens gives an inkling of how closely he could identify with the predations of the Resurrectionists (actually calling himself a Resurrectionist) and how brilliantly he could use humor to transform that fearful identification—all this almost twenty-five years before he created Jerry Cruncher and his graveyard "fishing."

The occasion in question occurred in 1835. Dickens had been writing sketches (later collected in *Sketches by Boz*) for Vincent Dowling, the editor of *Bell's Life in London and Sporting Chronicle*. Dowling's office was in the Strand opposite Tom Goodwin's oyster and refreshment rooms. When visiting Dowling, Dickens would usually stop in at Goodwin's, sometimes apparently to pass the time when Dowling was engaged, a practice that led to the following incident:

> On one occasion, Mr. Dowling, not knowing who had called, desired that the gentleman would leave his name, to be sent over to the office, whereupon young Dickens wrote:

> CHARLES DICKENS,
> *Resurrectionist,*
> *In search of a Subject.*

> Some recent cases of body-snatching had then made the matter a general topic of public discussion, and Goodwin pasted up the strange address-card for the amusement of medical students [the chief consumers of such bodies] who patronized his oysters. It was still upon his wall when "Pickwick" had made Dickens famous, and the old man was never tired of pointing it out to those whom he was pleased to call his "bivalve demolishers!" (Taverner, 17)

In *Pickwick,* just a year or so after this episode at Goodwin's, Dickens created the scene, analyzed earlier, in which the medical students Bob Sawyer and Ben Allen, celebrating Christmas at Dingley Dell, discuss dissecting legs and arms and heads—" 'Nothing like dissecting, to give one an appetite' " (*PP,* 29:309)—while they gorge themselves at the breakfast table.

41. Long before these scenes we come to recognize the affinity between—indeed the identity of—Madame Defarge and the guillotine. One of many manifestations of this terrifying oneness occurs when Charles Darnay is captured and brought before Monsieur—or, more correctly, Citizen—Defarge. When Darnay mentions the word *wife,* Defarge has a strange reaction. "The word 'wife,' " Dickens tells us, "seemed to serve as a gloomy reminder to Citizen Defarge, to say with sudden impatience, 'In the name of that sharp female newly born and called La Guillotine, why did you come to France?' " (*AYR* 1: *TTC,* 3: 1:483)

42. For these and allied matters, see Part 2, "Dickens and Passion."

43. This conflicted emotion sometimes took its toll, however, weakening or blurring a motivation, a character, a verisimilitude, or some other aspect—or aspects—of the work. For some major examples of this weakening in *A Tale of Two Cities,* see Part 2, "Dickens and Passion."

44. Twenty-six years before *Our Mutual Friend* and eight years before *Dombey and Son,* Dickens had produced another, much more traditional and much more Hogarthian—mock Hogarthian—version of Hogarth's quack doctor's studio. In "The Lamplighter's Story" (1838, as an unpublished play entitled *The Lamplighter, A Farce;* 1841, as the published story), Dickens had sent star-crossed lovers to a different sort of quack, a gulling and gulled astrologer (who is also a deluded alchemist). The quack astrologer's studio, gloomy like the studio of Hogarth's quack doctor, contains such grisly displays as a bottled child—in Dickens' version a bottled child with three heads—a skeleton, stuffed crocodiles, stuffed alligators, and a central furnace and crucible (LS: *PNP,* I, 17–19). When Tom Grig, the protagonist of the story, sees the skeleton, labeled "Skeleton of a Gentleman—Prepared by Mr. Mooney"—Mr. Mooney is the quack astrologer—he hopes "that Mr. Mooney might not be in the habit of preparing gentlemen that way without their own consent" (LS: *PNP,* I, 19). This wry comment is Dickens' way of alluding to the fact that Mr. Mooney might be a Resurrection Man or might deal with Resurrection-

ists; that is, he might be in league with individuals who dig up fresh corpses (as Jerry Cruncher does in *A Tale of Two Cities*) or who murder unsuspecting citizens (as Burke and Hare did in Edinburgh, or Bishop and Williams did in London) in order to sell the bodies to the medical profession or, less frequently, to sell the bodies (or the remains of "used" bodies), to weird "preparers" such as Mr. Mooney. Dickens associated this ghoulish traffic in corpses, butchered bodies, and skeletons, with cannibalism. Those who gain their sustenance from this ghastly traffic are quite literally, in Dickens' view, feeding on dead bodies. (For more information on the Resurrectionists and on Resurrectionist literature, see Part 1, note 40.)

When "The Lamplighter's Story" was published as the lead offering in *The Pic Nic Papers* (a three-volume miscellany edited by Dickens), Cruikshank provided an etching of the quack astrologer's studio to serve as a frontispiece. Cruikshank's version of the quack's studio, only vaguely reminiscent of Hogarth's similar studios, dispenses with the bottled baby (in Dickens' version a three-headed bottled baby) but adds a bat and an Egyptian mummy—neither of which had been called for by Dickens—to the props that Dickens had stipulated (in 1834, Cruikshank had illustrated a book on Egyptian mummies; see Part 1, note 28). But Cruikshank's modifications of Dickens' conceptions—especially of Dickens' conceptions of how a quack's studio would be furnished—do not end with deletions and additions. He also distances and deemphasizes other props, including important ones that Dickens had not only stipulated but had commented upon (the skeleton, for example), props that Dickens and Hogarth feature centrally and thematically in their cognate quack-doctor works. In both works, such props emerge menacingly and reprovingly as death-haunted emblems of a quack's ghoulish (even when ludicrous) predations, predations, for the most part, on the helpless and the vulnerable: on the daft, the desperate, the deluded, and the gullible. Dickens' first rendering of those quack-doctor props, created initially in 1838 for the play *The Lamplighter* (three years before Cruikshank was brought in to illustrate "The Lamplighter's Story," and thus three years before Cruikshank created his own idiosyncratic version of Dickens' quack-doctor studio and quack-doctor props), suggests that in 1838 Dickens' conception of a quack's studio was Hogarthian rather than Cruikshankian, but not confined to *Marriage à la Mode*.

Hogarth depicted yet another quack doctor's studio, again with the usual grisly tokens, including a skeleton and a bottled baby, in the eighth of his twelve plates for Samuel Butler's satiric and quixotic mock romance, *Hudibras* ("Hudibras Beats Sidrophel and His Man Whachum"). (Dickens owned a 1726 edition of *Hudibras* that contained the Hogarth engravings.) Sidrophel,

George Cruikshank. fect

143. Cannibals and Quacks: The Quack Doctor as Predatory Astrologer (Cruikshank Modifies the Hogarth-Dickens Vision of the Quack)

"The Philosopher's Stone." Etching by George Cruikshank for "The Lamp-lighter's Story" by Dickens. From *The Pic Nic Papers*, ed. Charles Dickens (1841). See also figure 144.

the charlatan necromancer of Butler's mordant satire, is (in Hogarth's render-ing) an engendering prototype of moony-minded Mr. Mooney—a prototype, in other words, of Dickens' charlatan astrologer and preparer of skeletons (and, as Dickens limns the charlatan, possibly a secret trafficker with Resurrec-tionists). Sidrophel, for his part, partakes of an ancient tradition. With his hov-ering black-magic skeleton, his other macabre props, and his arcane mumbo jumbo, he is the ancient magus declined into charlatanism; he is the quack doctor as gulling and gulled conjuror-sorcerer.

Dickens' debt to Hogarth's outward rendering of Sidrophel's inner nature as quack—that is, as gulling and gulled charlatan—is undergirded by other, more thronging, debts. Hogarth's depiction of Sidrophel's studio—trophy-hung with a dramatic array of looming skeletons, alligators, crocodiles, bottled babies, and flaming cauldrons—is a prototype of Dickens' depiction of a quack's studio in both *The Lamplighter* and "The Lamplighter's Story." As a matter of fact, Dickens' version is closer to Hogarth's version (in *Hudibras*) than it is to Cruikshank's actual illustration of Mr. Mooney's studio. It is also closer to the *Hudibras* version, especially in the prominence given to the pre-siding ghoulish props, than it is to Hogarth's other rendering of a quack's studio, the grisly version in *Marriage à la Mode*. (Compare figures 61, 143, and 144.)

Clearly, Dickens was familiar with, really was imaginatively caught up by, these Hogarthian scenes of nefarious quack doctors and their mumbo-jumbo studios years before Cruikshank was brought in to illustrate the already comp-leted "Lamplighter's Story." It follows, of course, that Dickens was caught up by these Hogarthian scenes at the very least eight years before he embarked on *Dombey and Son* and filled it with hosts of *Marriage à la Mode* analogues. Fi-nally, as *The Lamplighter, A Farce* and "The Lamplighter's Story" both demon-strate, Dickens had long since come to associate quack-doctor scenes (and preeminently those in *Hudibras*—as rendered by Hogarth—and in *Marriage à la Mode*) with predatory charlatanism (ghoulish, necromantic charlatanism) and with predatory cannibalistic motifs. In other words, long before *Dombey and Son* Dickens had responded to and internalized, indeed had magnified, the cannibalistic elements scattered throughout *Marriage à la Mode*.

45. Good Mrs. Brown is also an exact counterpart, both in her own right and in her relationship to her daughter, Alice, to Mrs. Skewton, the shriveled "Cleopatra" of the novel, the ever-so-genteel poseur who sells her daughter, Edith, to Mr. Dombey. In one scene, accompanied by a Phiz illustration ("A Chance Meeting"), the two parents and the two daughters (who are also

144. Cannibals and Quacks: The Quack Doctor
as Predatory Conjuror (Hogarth's
Engendering Vision of the Quack)

"Hudibras Beats Sidrophel and His Man Whachum." Engraving (1726) by William Hogarth for *Hudibras* (1663–80) by Samuel Butler. Plate VIII of twelve engravings. Compare this illustration with figure 61, Hogarth's much later counterpart illustration, the more contemporary (contemporary for Hogarth) "Scene With The Quack" (Plate III of *Marriage à la Mode*).

related) confront one another in such mirror-image ways that few readers would miss the fact (a fact purveyed throughout the novel) that both mothers have prostituted their daughters—Good Mrs. Brown in a manner that society labels as degraded, Mrs. Skewton in a manner that society sanctions and labels as "marrying well." By giving Good Mrs. Brown cannibalistic attributes, Dickens helps us to see that her counterparts, Mr. Dombey and Mrs. Skewton, are also cannibalistic, devouring their children—swallowing them bit by bit (little Paul, remember, was a mere muffin)—to appease their own selfish needs and appetites. By such means, as well as by direct representations, Dickens forces us to confront realities that we do not see or do not wish to see, realities we often disguise by custom, context, class, distance, or sentiment. In his middle and later writings especially, Dickens makes frequent and often brilliant use of such counterpart scenes and characters—not confined, of course, to cannibalism.

46. In this connection, see the discussion earlier in this part, and in Part 2, "Dickens and Passion," of *A Tale of Two Cities* and the Carton-Darnay conjunction. This doppelgänger conjunction joins the sacred and the profane and thereby allows Dickens to experience, at one and the same time, through alter-ego characters he closely identifies with, the otherwise incompatible pleasures of a sanctioned love and a forbidden one. Dickens often used this strategy as a means of undergoing a very self-involved indulgence and condemnation. See, for example, the David Copperfield-Uriah Heep and the Pip-Orlick doublings, both of which fit this pattern, and both of which are discussed earlier in Part 1.

These representative examples from *A Tale of Two Cities, David Copperfield,* and *Great Expectations*—all taken, it should be noted, from middle or late novels—are more elaborate and sophisticated than the Hugh-Dickens conjunction. In the middle and late works Dickens leans less on authorial intrusion (as in *Barnaby Rudge*) and more on dramatic representation and alter-ego counterpointing. In the very late works he also dwells more on divided beings. See, for instance, such self-divided, self-warring characters as Bradley Headstone (*Our Mutual Friend*) and John Jasper (*Edwin Drood*). Both of these characters are (in part) emotional surrogates for Dickens; both are discussed (including their surrogate aspects) in Part 2, "Dickens and Passion." For a more comprehensive discussion of David's alter-ego surrogates in *David Copperfield* and of Pip's in *Great Expectations*, see Stone, *Dickens and the Invisible World*, 193–278, 298–339.

47. For additional perspectives on Mary Hogarth, Dickens' view of her, and her influence on his writings, and for more on the entire subject of Dickens and girl-women, see Part 2, "Dickens and Passion."

48. The *OED* indicates that "peck" (as applied to persons) means "to eat, to feed," also "to bite" or "to eat . . . in a nibbling fashion." "Peckish" is defined as "disposed to 'peck' or eat; somewhat hungry." Both "peck" and "peckish," used in the above senses, were commonplace throughout the nineteenth century.

49. There are many other evocations in Dickens' writings of this frightening ogre head looming menacingly before one. To give two additional examples, Uriah Heep's threatening ogre head (which in manhood looms before David and gives him a glimpse of Uriah in the very act of devouring Agnes like a "ripe pear," a forecast of what is to come) first menaces David, foreshadowing what is to come, on the occasion, many years earlier, when David is introduced to Uriah. (We recall that Uriah, one of David's dark counterparts, is the would-be devourer not only of Agnes but of the entire Wickfield household; Agnes, in turn, is David's wife-to-be.) The meeting takes place in Agnes' house where David has come to live during his schooling. As he approaches the house, he sees Uriah's "cadaverous face appear at a small window on the ground floor" (*DC*, 15:156). Uriah enters the novel, in other words, as a disembodied "cadaverous face." This ghastly death's-head soon begins to haunt and threaten David. The last image that lingers in David's mind when he goes to bed that night—the image ends the chapter—is a nightmare vision of Uriah's disembodied head. Looking out the window of his room, David sees a beam end carved into the likeness of a head, a grotesque gargoyle head that looks at him (so he thinks) sideways. "I fancied," writes David, "it was Uriah Heep got up there somehow, and shut him out in a hurry" (*DC*, 15:160).

Another looming ogre head—or, rather, mouth—appears in "Captain Murderer." The terrible, bride-devouring Captain is all fearful maw. He is thus like Carker and his formidable gleaming teeth, or like the demoniacal snuffbox Counsellor and his wide-open red mouth (on the latter frightening creature see the succeeding pages in the main text). In fact, Captain Murderer's terrifying bride-consuming mouth, like Carker's bride-consuming mouth, is not so much a mouth as two rows of very prominent teeth—in Captain Murderer's case two rows of sharp dagger-like teeth—and these menacing teeth, which are referred to throughout the story and which we see (more than once) being filed sharp by the blacksmith, are the only physical feature that Dickens gives to the ferocious Captain. In other words, Dickens reduces this ogre-cannibal Captain to his physical essence: Captain Murderer *is* two frightening rows of very sharp teeth. This monstrous image, in turn, haunts the story, dominates its nightly repetitions, and scars the forming consciousness of the little child who is listening to the story—that is, Dickens. (For a graphic version of this image of a ferocious devourer of women, a creature with a fearsome, toothy maw and a looming ogre head—a version that Dickens owned—see figure 60.)

50. For more on this matter, on Dickens and his sister Fanny, and on brother-sister relations in general, see Part 2, "Dickens and Passion."

51. For instance, many of the churches of Italy evoked cannibalistic fantasies and horrors in Dickens. In *Pictures from Italy* (1846), a book written fourteen years before "City of London Churches" and seventeen years before "In the French-Flemish Country," there are many examples of church-induced cannibalistic associations, often more direct and ferocious than those just surveyed. Toward the end of *Pictures from Italy*, for instance, Dickens tells us, reviewing, in a kind of reverie, the multitudes of Roman churches he had visited, reviewing (to use his phrase) his "great dream of Roman churches," that one of those churches, St. Stefano Rotondo, "a damp mildewed vault of an old church" in the outskirts of Rome, "will always," when he thinks of Roman churches, "struggle uppermost in my mind" (*PI*, "Rome," 195). And why will this particular Roman "vault" of a church always struggle uppermost in Dickens' mind? Dickens knows exactly why. The church will haunt his memory forever because of the "hideous" paintings which cover its walls:

> These represent the martyrdoms of saints and early Christians; and such a panorama of horror and butchery no man could imagine in his sleep, though he were to eat a whole pig, raw, for supper. Grey-bearded men being boiled, fried, grilled, crimped, singed, eaten by wild beasts, worried by dogs, buried alive, torn asunder by horses, chopped up small with hatchets: women having their breasts torn with iron pincers, their tongues cut out, their ears screwed off, their jaws broken, their bodies stretched upon the rack, or skinned upon the stake, or crackled up and melted in the fire: these are among the mildest subjects. (*PI*, "Rome," 195–96)

Later in his "dream of Roman Churches," Dickens calls up a few unforgettable relics from the myriads he had seen displayed in those hosts of ancient churches. One of those relics—Dickens records only six all told—the last and most prominent of the six and, like the others, one of the handful in all of Rome that remains "apart" and keeps its "separate identity" in his consciousness, is rife with fearful horrors for him. This fearsome relic, another begetter of the kind of unspeakable nightmares that make Dickens think of eating "a whole pig, raw, for supper"—note how he associates this relic and the just-described roastings and butcherings with disgusting, gargantuan eating—this unforgettable relic is "the gridiron of Saint Lawrence, and the stone below it, marked with the frying of his fat and blood" (*PI,* "Rome," 199–200). Such a relic was guaranteed to evoke insistent, loathsome, cannibalistic imaginings in Dickens (gruesomely vivid imaginings), and such a relic was guaranteed to stir up a tumult of warring emotions in his mind and in his heart.

In their earliest manifestations, these unexpungeable church-related nightmare visions, revolting and attracting visions that entwine cannibalism and ferocity with "the martyrdoms of saints and early Christians," went back to childhood, especially to Fox's *Book of Martyrs* and the companion *Lives of the Primitive Martyrs.* Such visions, in other words, were entwined with some of Dickens' earliest fascinations and fears, deeply conflicted fascinations and deeply conflicted fears. For an analysis of some of those fascinations and fears, and for Dickens' profound worship at the shrine of Fox's *Martyrs*—or rather, for his worship at the shrine of the illustrations in Fox's *Martyrs*—and for his later use of these cannibalistic images, see above in Part 1. See also figures 45 and 46. Figure 46, taken from the exact sort of edition of Fox's *Martyrs* that David Copperfield (and presumably Dickens) pored over—that is, taken from a late-eighteenth-century "large quarto edition of Fox's Book of Martyrs"— depicts St. Laurence being roasted on a gridiron, one of the "dismal horrors" that David, like Dickens before him, "fell to devouring" over and over again as a child (*DC,* 10:107).

Perhaps it was Dickens' early emotion-fraught response to this St. Laurence illustration that caused him, years later in Rome, when he finally came to gaze on the putative gridiron itself, to remember that relic—after scores upon scores of competing Roman relics, all equally notable and vouched for, had become insubstantial blurs in his "great dream of Roman Churches"—as the culminating relic of those six Roman relics that remained "apart" and that kept their "separate identity." Perhaps, too, it was that early cannibal-haunted *Book of Martyrs* association, an association so compounded of deep-felt attractions and repulsions, that caused him to view that ancient church-enshrined gridiron in the old Fox's *Martyrs* way, that caused him, in other words, to view the grid-iron—really compelled him to view it—as a dismal nightmare horror haunted by debauched cannibalistic appetites and frightful cannibalistic imaginings. In those nightmare imaginings, Dickens does not spare us or himself. Now, some thirty years after his introduction to the *Martyrs* illustrations, he is once more an eager yet sickened participant in a revolting *Book of Martyrs* barbarity. His "dream of Roman Churches," of savage paintings and savage relics, combines with his rapt childhood *Book of Martyrs* devourings; he summons up St. Laurence being roasted on a gridiron—roasted for what unspeakable feast?—and he summons up "the stone below [the gridiron], marked with the frying of his fat and blood" (*PI,* "Rome," 199–200).

Immediately after Dickens' "great dream of Roman Churches" and its attendant cannibalistic imaginings, he describes (though the new description, really a new subsection set off by a typographic break, seems remote in occasion and character from Roman churches) an execution—a brutal bloody beheading, a cannibalistic beheading (cannibalistic as he re-creates the spectacle for his readers)—a beheading that he "determined to go, and see" (*PI,* "Rome," 202). Obviously, the unspoken retrospective associations that caused Dickens to juxtapose these seemingly disparate, indeed, incongruous subsections—the first on Roman churches, the second on bloody beheadings—were cannibalistic associations. In Dickens' associative imaginings, one section led naturally, even inevitably, to the next.

For an analysis of Dickens' cannibalistic rendering of the beheading, an "ugly, filthy, careless, sickening spectacle; meaning nothing but butchery"— to quote Dickens' angry summation of the event (*PI,* "Rome," 207)—see Part 1, note 12.

52. For additional information on Condette and Dickens' slow, meandering trip from Paris—via Arras, Amiens, and other stops—to the French coast in 1863, and for a possible psychological reason for his cannibalistic musings, see Part 2, "Dickens and Passion," note 24. See also figure 113.

53. The driven and compulsive nature of Dickens' obsession with cannibalism emerges clearly here, as it has many times over in Part 1. "Dickens and Necessity," Part 3 of this book, concentrates on these powerful subterranean elements in Dickens' engendering night side—that is, it concentrates on the driven and determined aspects, the necessitous aspects, of his life and art. Dickens' cannibalism, like his passion, often assumed this driven and necessitous character.

54. As a matter of fact, Dickens' manuscript (see figure 75) shows that he originally spelled "munch" conventionally. But before he even thought of introducing the word "munch" into his story he had a totally different locution—"Eating song"—in lines two and four of the cannibals' song. However, he subsequently crossed out "Eating song" and replaced it in each instance with the phrase "Munch munch." Later still, in proof, he changed each spelling of "munch" to "muntch." The evolution of four repetitions of "munch" to four repetitions of "muntch," took place, therefore, over a period of time and was quite deliberate. On the other hand, the word "choo"—spelled thus— was present in the manuscript from the very beginning. The manuscript of *Holiday Romance* is in the Pierpont Morgan Library, New York.

Part 2: Dickens and Passion

1. Despite the vast range of Dickens criticism, the subject of Dickens and passion (the term "passion" used here as it is used throughout this book—see Preface) has scarcely been addressed. On the other hand, much has been written on Dickens' relationships with women, his marriage, his liaison with Ellen Ternan, his views on love, marriage, domesticity, divorce, and a great deal more; and much has been written on how these experiences and views entered and influenced his writings. The factual basis for these assessments and reassessments emerged over the years, but some of the most startling biographical revelations concerning Dickens' life and relationships appeared soon after his death. The most important source of these revelations was John Forster; the vehicle for conveying the disclosures was his three-volume *The Life of Charles Dickens* (1872–74). Forster's closeness to Dickens and his circle, his access to original documents (many of which have vanished), plus his insight into Dickens' character and mind, made his biography an indispensable quarry for all later commentators. Forster, of course, was reticent about some matters, silent about others, and obfuscatory (or even deliberately misleading) about still others. He was especially reticent about Ellen Ternan and the emotional weather of Dickens' later years. Forster was also ignorant—so it seems, at least—of some important matters that have since come to light. But when all is said in this regard, the surprising thing is how little was added to Forster's accounts and interpretations of Dickens on women and love (or his assessments on many other subjects, for that matter) during the next generation and more. (Perhaps, considering the tenor of the times and the numbers of principals who were still living, this long period of Forsterian orthodoxy is not so surprising after all.)

In any case, it was not until George Gissing, in *Charles Dickens: A Critical Study* (1898), and George Bernard Shaw, in a variety of pronouncements and criticisms at the turn of the century and after (see *Shaw on Dickens*), offered their views on Dickens' attitudes toward women and love that perspectives in this area began to change. In subsequent years important biographical revelations (together with changing values and attitudes) stimulated renewed interest in the subject and provided the foundation for new critical assessments of Dickens' treatment of sexuality.

Books that added substantially to the biographical record concerning Dickens and passion or that used the record for new assessments, or both, include the following (for full bibliographic listings of these works, and for full listings of all other works cited below, see the Select Bibliography): Thomas Wright, *The Life of Charles Dickens* (1935), including Wright's account of Ellen Ternan's "confessions" to Canon Benham (as told to Wright by Benham); Gladys Storey, *Dickens and Daughter* (1939), including Kate Dickens' account (as rendered by Storey) of the Ternan affair, together with much ancillary and additional material and some documentation; Jack Lindsay, *Charles Dickens: A Biographical and Critical Study* (1950), mainly innovative for its free-wheeling critical and psychological interpretations based upon the new biographical revelations; Ada Nisbet, *Dickens and Ellen Ternan* (1952), a well-documented scholarly summary of the evidence in the Ternan affair to that date together with important additional evidence; Edgar Johnson, *Charles Dickens: His Tragedy and Triumph* (1952), a full-scale reexamination of Dickens' life and writings with much new evidence; Felix Aylmer, *Dickens Incognito* (1959), new light on Dickens' hideaways in Slough and Peckham and his secret life in his later years; William J. Carlton, "Dickens's Forgotten Retreat in France" (1966), a different aspect of Dickens' secret life in his later years.

Significant essays and articles, primarily critical, that bear upon the subject include: Edmund Wilson, "Dickens: The Two Scrooges" (1940, 1941), which is important not only for its assessment of Dickens' writings (including, of course, Dickens' depictions of love) in the light of the new biographical evidence that had appeared in the thirties, but also for its profound influence on the criticism that followed; Leonard Manheim, "The Personal History of David Copperfield: A Study in Psychoanalytic Criticism" (1952) and "Floras and Doras: The Women in Dickens' Novels" (1965)—pioneering overlapping articles concentrating on the sexless child-lover-heroine figure in Dickens' novels and the sources of that figure—the articles do not deal with passion, and they scant the later novels; three works by Harry Stone: "Dickens, Browning, and the Mysterious Letter" (1966)—the brother-sister component in Dickens' sexuality; "The Love Pattern in Dickens' Novels" (1970)—repeated sexual patterns in Dickens' writings and their sources; and *Dickens and the Invisible World: Fairy Tales, Fantasy, and Novel-Making* (1979)—the latter book includes, among other pertinent discussions, the first recognition of the biographical importance of "The Bride's Chamber" and the first critical examination of that work; Pamela Hansford Johnson, "The Sexual Life in Dickens's Novels" (1970), a stimulating survey of sexuality and romance in Dickens, touches briefly on later passion (but excludes *Drood* entirely); Sylvia Manning, "Dickens, January, and May" (1975), a good survey of Dickens' recurrent depiction (in early and middle novels) of love between an older man and a child-woman, does not deal with passion; Joel Brattin, "Dickens' Creation of Bradley Headstone" (1985), a study of the changes (many of them revealing) that Dickens made in manuscript and proof in the course of creating Bradley Headstone.

Two full-length books are devoted entirely to love and women in Dickens' life and writings. The first of these, C. G. L. Du Cann's *The Love-Lives of Charles Dickens* (1961), is, unfortunately, unreliable. Impressionistic and opinionated, totally undocumented, it frequently purveys speculation as evidence and interpretation as fact. The second book, Michael Slater's *Dickens and Women* (1983), is far and away the best and most comprehensive treatment of Dickens' relationships with and depictions of women. But Slater's focus (by design, of course) is on women, and Dickens usually delineates passion through men. Thus, though Slater approaches the subject of Dickens and passion, occasionally comments on it, and often deals with its contexts, he does not examine it in depth, and he does not dwell on many of the matters that engross my attention in "Dickens and Passion."

Many other books and articles have something to say about Dickens, women, love, and associated themes, but mostly in ways that reiterate or elaborate the analyses that will be found in the works already cited. In those instances in which these parallel or elaborative works are drawn upon, they are cited in the text or in notes; in other instances, where no direct use of such works has been made but where they are relevant in a general way, they are listed in the Select Bibliography. Still other books and articles touch upon the subjects being pursued here in ways that are remote from the focus of this study; such works are not cited at all.

For an explanation of the method used to cite Dickens' letters, writings, and other primary sources, and for an explanation of abbreviations, bibliographical references, and similar matters, see Part 1, "Dickens and Cannibalism," note 1.

2. For more on this aspect of *The Frozen Deep,* and for more on why Dickens could not abide the thought that English gentlemen had succumbed to the "last resource," see Part 1, "Dickens and Cannibalism."

Dickens' eagerness to give the general public a chance to see *The Frozen Deep* was not simply an outgrowth of its topicality and the renewed interest in the Franklin expedition and its fate. The original Tavistock House production of the play had been an enormous success and a personal triumph, a success and a triumph that the general public had clamored at the time—unavailingly—to see. The *Illustrated London News* for 17 January 1857 (vol. 30, no. 840) had devoted a long adulatory review (pp. 51–52) to the Tavistock House performances; it had also included, accompanying the review, in the feature position across the entire top of page 51, a 6″ × 9″ wood engraving of a scene from the play (see figure 78).

The *Illustrated London News* found Dickens' acting in both *The Frozen Deep* and the afterpiece to be superb. Of Dickens' performance in *The Frozen Deep* the reviewer wrote: "The reader will perceive that Mr. Charles Dickens had in such a character as [Richard Wardour] a part that required the consummate acting of a well-practised performer. Too much praise cannot be bestowed on the artistic interpretation that it received from him. It was a fervid, powerful, and distinct individuality, thoroughly made out in all its details." Of Dickens' performance in *Uncle John* (the afterpiece of the final Tavistock house occasion) the reviewer wrote: "Mr. Dickens, as the vigorous old gentleman of seventy, displayed a new phase of his versatile genius, and proved himself a consummate actor."

Now, six months after the Tavistock House performances, Dickens was prepared, through a revival of *The Frozen Deep,* to respond to a diverse set of public and private yearnings, desires, and discontents: he was prepared to satisfy the public clamor for an opportunity to see *The Frozen Deep,* give a major financial boost to the Jerrold Fund, and submerge his own unbearable restlessness and unhappiness in action and in fervent public role playing—role playing sure to be acclaimed.

3. "The Bride's Chamber," the fourth part of the five-part travel series *The Lazy Tour of Two Idle Apprentices,* appeared in Dickens' weekly magazine, *Household Words,* on 24 October 1857. (The other parts appeared in *Household Words* on 3, 10, 17, and 31 October.) Although *The Lazy Tour,* a joint effort by Dickens and Wilkie Collins, was published (as was customary in *Household Words*) without a byline or other indications of authorship, it is easy to demonstrate that Dickens, in addition to writing other specific segments of

the series, was the author of the entire fourth part. For one thing, Dickens' sole authorship is confirmed by overwhelming internal evidence, and not just internal evidence of the stylistic variety. To cite two nonstylistic examples, only Dickens—not the virtually incapacitated Collins, who earlier had sprained his ankle—clambered up and down through Lancaster Castle and roamed the "immense" grounds and "interminable" corridors of Lancaster Lunatic Asylum (*HW* 16: BC, 385), two places that figure crucially and minutely in the fourth part. (Writing from Lancaster, and describing Collins' condition, Dickens says: "Of course he can never walk out, or see anything of any place" [12 September 1857]. And still later, in another letter, written two days after they had left Lancaster, Dickens tells us that Collins might go to the theater that night, "which will be the first occasion of his going out, except to travel, since the accident" [15 September 1857].) But Dickens' authorship is also confirmed by his own declarations. On 1 October 1857 he sent the printer the greater portion of part four. The next morning, "having stuck to it"—he had been at work on the part for at least a week—he finished the segment and despatched the remainder to the printer, calling his effort (in a letter to Wills), "A very odd story, with a wild, picturesque fancy in it" (2 October 1857). Two days later, he informed Angela Burdett Coutts that the fourth part of *The Lazy Tour* is "by your present correspondent," and that it contains a "grim" tale, "a Short Story—a bit of Diablerie" (4 October 1857). (See also, below, in the main text of Part 2, his letter to Joseph Sly taking credit for the fourth part.) "The Bride's Chamber" was not separately titled. Like all segments in the series, it was headed by the general title, *The Lazy Tour of Two Idle Apprentices,* and then by a subheading. Each subheading was identical to the other subheadings except for its chapter number. Thus the fourth segment (which I have called "The Bride's Chamber") bore the following subheading: "In Five Chapters. Chapter the Fourth."

I have titled the fourth chapter "The Bride's Chamber" because Dickens seems to have had that name in mind when he wrote the inset story—the "bit of Diablerie," as he termed it—that was the chief feature of the segment. That name, "the Bride's Chamber," or rather that phrase, quickly takes on its central significance in the story. For one thing, it appears throughout the story, always capitalized; for another, it seems to have served Dickens as a leitmotif or refrain.

The Lazy Tour was not officially (or unofficially) reprinted in Dickens' lifetime; indeed, it was not officially reprinted until many years after his death. However, at least one confused and pirated version was included in a one-volume collection, now extremely rare, entitled *The Dickens-Collins Christmas Stories,* a collection published in the United States in 1875, five years after

Dickens' death. This volume contained no specific attributions of authorship, and it was very far from the mark, of course, in calling *The Lazy Tour* a Christmas Story. The volume contained two illustrations: one served as a frontispiece for *No Thoroughfare* (the only other work in the collection), and the other served as a frontispiece for *The Lazy Tour.* The latter illustration, depicting a scene in "The Bride's Chamber" section of *The Lazy Tour,* is reproduced above in the main text (see figure 92).

In 1890, twenty years after Dickens' death, *The Lazy Tour of Two Idle Apprentices* was finally officially resurrected. This occurred in a volume, now scarce, issued by Chapman and Hall, the English publishers of most of Dickens' works. (The volume, incidentally, was printed by Charles Dickens and Evans at the Crystal Palace Press, the Charles Dickens in question being Dickens' eldest son.) This volume was illustrated, but only one illustration (a feeble one) depicted a scene from "The Bride's Chamber" proper; that is, only one illustration pertained to the inset story. In addition to *The Lazy Tour,* the volume contained *No Thoroughfare* and *The Perils of Certain English Prisoners.* The latter works were very different in character and format from *The Lazy Tour,* though *The Perils of Certain English Prisoners,* written only weeks after *The Lazy Tour,* did refashion a motif embedded in *The Lazy Tour* (see above in the main text). But unlike *The Lazy Tour* (to continue with the differences), *No Thoroughfare* and *The Perils of Certain English Prisoners* had both been Extra Christmas Numbers of Dickens' periodicals; the former, the Extra Christmas Number of *All the Year Round* for 1867; the latter, of *Household Words* for 1857. All three works did, however, share one attribute: they were collaborative efforts by Dickens and Collins. This fact was affirmed on the title page, which simply listed the titles of the three works and then the byline: "by / Charles Dickens and Wilkie Collins." The designation on the spine was somewhat different. It read: "The / Lazy Tour / of / Two Idle / Apprentices / and other / Stories / Charles / Dickens / and / Wilkie / Collins." (There is a variant binding with a variant inscription on the spine, but the interior texts are the same.) There were no other indications of authorship within or without, and there were no attempts to designate who wrote what. There was, however, a prefatory note that read as follows: "These Stories, which originally appeared in 'Household Words,' are now reprinted in a complete form for the first time." The note was wrong in both its assertions: the stories had not all appeared in *Household Words,* and they were not now reprinted in complete form for the first time. *No Thoroughfare* had appeared in *All the Year Round,* not in *Household Words; The Perils of Certain English Prisoners* had been reprinted complete in *Household Words: Christmas Stories, 1851–1858* (1870); and *No Thorough-*

fare had been reprinted complete in *The Christmas Numbers of All the Year Round* (1867).

The Lazy Tour, on the other hand, had not been officially collected or reprinted until it appeared in the 1890 Chapman and Hall volume. Unhappily, that version, though authorized and copyrighted, is not faithful to the original 1857 *Household Words* text—the only text that Dickens corrected and approved in proof. The 1890 text differs in many small ways from the *Household Words* version, as do subsequent reprints in comprehensive editions of Dickens' Collected Works. Such reprintings are also without specific identifications of authorship; that is, without specific identifications of who wrote what—a tangled subject that is clarified for the first time in this study (clarified, that is, in all matters bearing upon the arguments being pursued here).

The text of *The Lazy Tour* used in this book is the text proofed and corrected by Dickens and published by him in *Household Words*.

4. For Hogarth's profound and many-dimensioned influence on Dickens, see Part 1, "Dickens and Cannibalism."

5. In one instance, at least, Dickens sent Ellen advanced proofs of his writing. About a year after "Please to Leave Your Umbrella" appeared in *Household Words*, Dickens asked Wills (in an unpublished letter at the Huntington Library dated 1 July 1859), to procure from the printer revised proofs of his current work for *All the Year Round* and to post the proofs to Ellen. Dickens' current work for *All the Year Round* was *A Tale of Two Cities*. The 9 July episode of *A Tale of Two Cities* contains Charles Darnay's avowal to Dr. Manette that he loves Lucie; the 16 July episode contains Sydney Carton's interview with Lucie and his declaration of love. Darnay and Carton, of course, are alter egos, and Dickens identified with each: he was the upright and conventional Darnay, and he was the dissolute and reckless Carton. He was, in other words, at one and the same time, the sanctified lover of Lucie and the forbidden lover of Lucie. Lucie, in turn, was, in part, an avatar of Ellen. In sending the love-declaration proofs to Ellen, Dickens was both avowing his love for her and avowing his renunciation of that love.

For more on these matters, and for more on Carton's declaration of love and its significance, see below in Part 2.

6. For a detailed examination of Dickens' growing conviction that many individuals are blindly compelled to enact, indeed to embrace, their own somber, self-inflicted destinies, see Part 3, "Dickens and Necessity."

7. That the viable marriage between Dickens and his wife, already much endangered, ceased with this real and symbolic walling up, and not, as many commentators have related, several months later in 1858, is given added point by other, very different, evidence. With the exception of four brief perfunctory notes subsequent to the legal separation (that is, subsequent to May 1858), there are no letters from Dickens to Catherine after 1856 (see *Mr. & Mrs. Charles Dickens: His Letters to Her,* ed. Walter Dexter). This silence is especially striking because Dickens was out of town and away from Catherine for about a week in August 1857 (in connection with the Manchester performances of *The Frozen Deep*) and for more than two weeks in September 1857 (in conjunction with his wanderings with Collins on behalf of *Household Words* and *The Lazy Tour*). During the latter period Dickens found time to write a good many letters, including a number of lengthy ones to John Forster and several long letters to Georgina Hogarth (Catherine's sister, who was living with the Dickenses), but none to Catherine. Dickens was also away from Catherine on other occasions in the autumn of 1857, staying at Gad's Hill while Catherine was at Tavistock House, for example; but again, no letters to Catherine.

In addition, entries in Dickens' bank account at Coutts & Co. show that he stopped his allowances to Catherine altogether after 17 October 1857. This is in marked contrast to his allowances to Georgina, which he increased substantially beginning 10 December 1857 (see Stokes, "Charles Dickens: A Customer of Coutts & Co., 26).

Dickens wrote "The Bride's Chamber" at the end of September and the beginning of October 1857 (he began the story immediately after his return from Doncaster and his secret week with Ellen), and he published it in *Household Words* on 24 October 1857 (the 24 October issue of *Household Words* actually came out on 21 October). The walling-up letter was dated 11 October. Obviously the stressful period from the end of September to the middle of October (the time during which Dickens wrote and then went over the proofs of "The Bride's Chamber") was the time during which he made his decision to change his relationship with his wife. These crucial weeks marked the real (though not the legal) end of Dickens' marriage. The discontinuance of Catherine's allowance after 17 October is further evidence of how fundamental and irrevocable that larger, multidimensioned, multiconsequenced decision to alter their relationship, a decision made in early autumn 1857, was. It is also further evidence of how all-encompassing and unbreachable was the stark dividing inner wall (counterpart of that real dividing bedroom wall) that Dickens then erected.

8. *Sly's King's Arm & Royal Hotel, Lancaster.* Lancaster: Gazette Office, n.d. This pamphlet gives a descriptive listing of the chief contents of the public areas and the notable rooms, including Dickens' room. In addition, various announcements of the auction of the contents of the King's Arms Hotel list the high points of the furnishings. The most complete source in this matter, however, is the official auction catalogue that was issued when the contents and furnishings of the King's Arms (350 lots, all told) were readied for sale. This catalogue bore the following title: *Catalogue of Rare Objects of Mediæval Decorative Design and Stately Domestic Equipment, Substantial Monuments of Refined Taste and Handicraft of Olden Times, Comprising Noble Carved Canopied Oak Bedsteads, Wardrobes, Trussing Chests, and Coffers; Ambries, Cabinets, Sideboards, Tables, Tudor, Elizabethan, and Jacobean Chairs; Massive Ornamental Brackets, Misereres & Other Sacerdotal Relics; Important Examples of Gobelin Tapestry, ("Goodly Arras of Great Majestie;") Archaic Conventual Needlework of extreme beauty; "China Ware of Porcelain" and Other Fictile Products, Crystal Chandelier, Paintings, Drawings, Prints, Bronzes, Ancient Clocks of curious construction, and Miscellaneous Et Ceteras; Appealing to Noblemen, Gentlemen, Curators of Museums, Connoisseurs of Art, and All Interested in Skilled Art-Workmanship of the Past* . . . This substantial catalogue, quarto in size, also proclaims on the title page—at the top of the page, before the portion of the title just quoted—that the King's Arms is " 'The Good Old Inn' of Charles Dickens's, 'Household Words.' " The catalogue proper gives a detailed listing (with descriptions) of all the items that were auctioned. The auction took place on the premises of the King's Arms on 11 and 12 April 1877. The only recorded copy of the auction catalogue is in the Lancaster Central Library, Lancaster, England.

9. Sometime after Dickens' stay at the King's Arms, probably in the 1860s and possibly as late as 1866, Joseph Sly issued a pamphlet associating Dickens with his hotel. In an introductory note to one version of the pamphlet (the 1866 Gimbel version) Sly wrote: "The reader is perhaps aware that Mr. Charles Dickens and his friend Mr. Wilkie Collins, in the year 1857 visited Lancaster, and during their sojourn, stopped at Mr. Sly's, King's Arms Hotel." The wrapper and the title page again emphasized this connection, the title page, for example, reading in part, "Extracts from Household Words, Relating to Mr. C. Dickens' Visit to Lancaster." The extracts (often inaccurate), which Sly titled *The Bride and Bridal Chamber,* were primarily from "The Bride's Chamber." The pamphlet also contained an engraving (see figure 91) depicting "the som-

bre handsome old [entrance] hall" and adjoining "excellent old staircase, with a gallery or upper staircase, cut off from it by a curious fence-work of old oak, or of the old Honduras Mahogany wood" (to quote Dickens' descriptions of these features in "The Bride's Chamber") (*HW* 16: BC, 386).

Sly's pamphlet seems to have been issued as a promotional device in the 1860s; it also seems to have been reissued from time to time (apparently in a variety of formats and with a variety of inserts) in the late sixties and on into the seventies until early 1877. As one might expect, the pamphlet is now very rare. Only five copies are recorded: one, dated 1866, which contains substantial extracts from "The Bride's Chamber," is in the Gimbel Collection at Yale University; a second copy (which dates from the 1870s and dispenses with most of "The Bride's Chamber" extracts and with long supplements concerning the inn, Mr. Sly, distinguished visitors, and similar matters) is in the British Library. The latter pamphlet is a much condensed version of the primary portions of the earlier pamphlet but with a substantial addition (constituting the bulk of the pamphlet) about the hotel itself (see Part 2, note 8). The third pamphlet, also from the 1870s but earlier than the British Library copy, is in the Lancaster Central Library, Lancaster, England. This copy is similar to the British Library version but lacks a one-page preliminary blurb (an extract from Ruskin concerning the King's Arms), and four pages of additional blurbs, testimonials, and ads at the end. In addition, the back wrapper of the Lancaster Library copy differs from that in the British Library copy. The Lancaster City Museum, Lancaster, England, owns two copies of the Sly pamphlet. The first, dated 1866, is bound in a cream silk printed wrapper. This copy, an early version, is identical in text and format to the Gimbel copy. The second copy, issued c. 1866, but much larger in page size and radically different in format and printing, concentrates on the Dickens extracts, the latter being identical to the 1866 extracts.

Sly sold the King's Arms, auctioned the contents of the hotel, and retired from business in 1877. The inn was demolished in 1879, and on the site a new building, the present Royal King's Arms Hotel, Lancaster, was erected.

10. When Dickens visited Lancaster Castle in September 1857 he found that much of it was being used as a prison and much was given over to courtrooms, an arrangement that continues to the present day. But for Dickens the castle also had more memorable uses and more gruesome features. There was, for example, the Drop Room, the room into which condemned prisoners were brought just before they were to be hanged. As the prisoners entered this chamber they would see, on a wide windowsill a few feet away, their own rude

coffins waiting grimly for them. In the presence of those waiting coffins they would prepare themselves for death. Passing their coffins, the doomed prisoners would leave the Drop Room through a large window hinged like a door—a door that ushered them directly onto the gallows platform. On that platform, at "Hanging Corner," facing the castle wall just adjacent to the Drop Room (not facing the Drop Room itself—see figure 93), they would be hanged before the watching multitudes. This ghastly spectacle finally over, the bodies of the hanged would be brought back into the castle through a small window just below the Drop Room (see figure 93), then returned directly to the Drop Room though a trapdoor in its floor, and thence to their coffins. (The Drop Room, now a jury room, is to this day unchanged in its chief features.) Given Dickens' profound interest in prisons, prisoners, murderers, executions, the psychology of the condemned, and the like, one can imagine the impression these scenes and their fearsome associations would have made on his mind (see, in this connection, Part 1, "Dickens and Cannibalism," note 12). One can also imagine his sensations when he looked through the Drop Room door at the very stones, so cold and drab and unfeeling, that so many men and women had looked at in the last moments before they died. (Even today the window-door of the Drop Room is opened for special visitors. As one approaches that fateful verge one can hardly fail to reenact those final steps and glimpse that final view.) How Dickens reacted to this experience—this was his first visit to Lancaster and its castle—is reflected graphically in "The Bride's Chamber." There the sensation of being hanged facing the castle wall is described in apocalyptic terms by the haunted murderer and forms one of the memorable and recurrent set pieces of the story.

Dickens' immediate and subsequent responses to the Drop Room and its gruesome launchings, that is, his imagining and then re-creating the tumultuous sensation of being hanged facing that castle wall, were surely intensified by the fact that public executions were still going on in England; indeed, they were still going on in that very room and against that grimly weathered wall. This fact would not have been a remote abstraction for Dickens in any circumstances. He had long been fascinated and horrified by the very idea of executions, and he had long considered public executions a barbarous spectacle, a spectacle that degraded the beholder. (See Part 1, "Dickens and Cannibalism," including notes 12, 13, and 40.) His writings repeatedly display his intense interest in prisons, prisoners, crime, capital punishment, and the like, and they also display his extraordinary ability to identify with the criminal, especially with the murderer. As Dickens evoked the psychology of the murderer, he not only imagined, he underwent what the murderer, often in the very act of committing the murder, underwent. He also underwent the tumultuous aftermath: the fear and obsession, the hallucinated flight, and on a number of memorable occasions, the trapped, or the imprisoned and condemned murderer living his last fleeting hours and then suffering his ordained doom.

Dickens was knowledgeable on matters of crime and punishment. He owned and read many works on the subject, knew and consulted over the years with a host of police officials and prison administrators, frequently visited criminal haunts, reformatories, prisons, and the like, and wrote essays on a whole range of matters concerning crime and punishment. But the circumstances as Dickens visited Lancaster Castle, entered the Drop Room, and confronted the cold unfeeling stones of Hanging Corner were not ordinary circumstances, and his responses (always darkened and surcharged with emotion when shaded by the prison house) were special even for him.

One Edward Hardman of Chorley—the name "Hardman" seems straight out of Dickens!—was hanged for murder at Hanging Corner, hanged facing those cold unfeeling stones (the very stones that Dickens was now looking at); Hardman was hanged there on 29 August 1857, just two weeks before Dickens' visit. This grisly event had been something of a sensation. Hangings were now comparatively rare at Lancaster Castle. (Lancaster was the county seat of Lancashire, hence Lancaster, or, to be more precise, Lancaster Castle, was the venue for all non-urban Lancashire trials, and Hanging Corner, Lancaster Castle, for all resultant hangings.) The last hanging at the castle had taken place four years earlier; the next would not take place for another eight years. Dickens' guide would surely have informed him of the recent spectacle, probably even conveyed some eyewitness details of Hardman's crime and execution—all of which (together with Dickens' tormented, self-condemning mood at that moment) would have made the visit—fraught for him, as all such occasions were, with momentous significance—even more memorable and charged with emotion than usual.

But the story of the visit and its ramifications does not end—or begin— here. The significance of the visit, its impact on Dickens, its shaping power, and the interweavings of chance and circumstances that surrounded the visit (interweavings mediated by Dickens' imagination), give us additional insights into his mind and art. To begin with, Dickens almost certainly knew a great deal about Hardman's crime before he ever thought of visiting the Lancaster region and Lancaster Castle, and that knowledge would have struck strange answering chords and evoked profound revulsions and condemnations in his own heart, a heart grievously torn and burdened all through this period, and especially at that moment as he stood in the fateful Drop Room.

That moment in the death-haunted Drop Room, a somber moment in

Dickens' very unlazy "lazy tour" (a tour undertaken "to escape from myself"), was a moment of contending emotions and warring impulses, a moment of turmoil, animosity, yearning, and anticipation. Above all, it was a moment of guilt—guilt as he thought of the past, guilt as he pondered the future, guilt as he contemplated Hanging Corner and the stony consequences of grievous sin. Those guilty feelings were not new, and they were not diminishing. In those waning summer days he was becoming increasingly restless and miserable, increasingly baffled and torn. He was pulled this way and that, hesitating on the brink of a momentous decision. He was fleeing from his domestic misery; he was rushing toward his yearned-for bliss. Only three weeks earlier he had fallen in love with the adorable Ellen Ternan; only one day more and he would be with her again. He would spend a whole glorious week (a secret week) in her transforming presence. As he looked about the Drop Room, as he gazed through its dread window-door, the bleak bafflements and beatific anticipations that thronged his mind and besieged his heart must have blended with (or contended with) other emotion-filled dilemmas, kindred dilemmas that baffled and tormented him: How to be released from his unhappy marriage? How to be rid of his unwanted wife?

As Dickens lingered in the Drop Room, these and similar perplexities, perplexities always contending now in the inmost reaches of his mind, mingled with the scene before him, the scene of Hardman's execution. That scene, in turn, evoked somber thoughts, self-implicating and self-arraigning thoughts, of Hardman and his crime. A long account of Hardman's trial, an account that detailed the background and circumstances of the crime, had appeared in the London *Times* (a newspaper Dickens read regularly) just one month earlier, on 10 August 1857; that is, the account had appeared in the *Times* two days after Hardman's trial and sentencing and nineteen days before his execution at Hanging Corner. (An even longer and more detailed account of most of the testimony had appeared in the weekly local newspaper, the *Lancaster Guardian,* on 8 August 1857. The continuation and conclusion of this exhaustive account, including the summations, the charge to the jury, the verdict, and the sentencing, appeared in the next issue of the *Lancaster Guardian* [15 August 1857].)

Hardman, as the London *Times* reported, was convicted of poisoning his young wife, poisoning her deliberately, methodically, agonizingly, over a period of ten days. Vomiting and purging, vomiting and purging (vomiting, no matter what she ate, a ghastly telltale yellow), the poor woman, hollow-eyed and aching, ever more exhausted and depleted, finally died, her cold, antagonistic murderer-husband watching callously at her side. She was soon buried, but as a result of accusations of foul play, her body was exhumed only eleven days after her burial. The authorities thereupon undertook an intensive autopsy and a full-scale inquest. The autopsy established that there was widespread and un-usual inflammation of the esophagus, stomach, duodenum, and rectum, in-flammation symptomatic of irritant poisoning. A chemical analysis of the intestines detected some arsenic and much more antimony, two poisons—es-pecially the latter—that accorded with the dead woman's pathology and illness, and poisons that Hardman was known to have bought shortly before the crime and to have substituted for her prescribed medicines.

This murderous culmination of a seemingly ordinary marriage was not the vindictive aftermath of an aberrant or an enraged moment, nor was it the cal-culated outcome of a few seething weeks or even months. The marriage, a mismatch from the beginning, had been filled with conflict and recrimination. The union had produced one child, but the infant (only six months old at the time of her mother's murder), far from being a focus of mutuality and reconciliation for the warring parents, had become an added source of bitter contention. That contention was chronic. The marriage, always shaky, had col-lapsed for a term three months after it began: the bride had gone home to her father. The patched-up union, unsatisfying and stressful, did not last long. Hardman murdered his wife two years and two months after he had married her.

One of the motives for the murder was money. Hardman boasted to a fellow prisoner that he had collected £11 from no less then four burial clubs upon his wife's death. After this disclosure, Hardman told his prisoner-confidant, whether regretfully or magnanimously or out of a sense of his own rectitude is not clear, "that if he had let her live two months more he should have got 8*l.* more." (Five years earlier, in "Trading in Death" [*HW* 6 (27 November 1852)], Dickens had written that such burial clubs, "by presenting a new class of temptations to the wickedest natures among [the members], led to a new class of mercenary murders, so abominable in their iniquity, that language can-not stigmatize them with sufficient severity" [241].) Another motive Hardman had for murdering his wife was more central and more weighty. He longed to be released from his irksome marriage bonds. His wife (so he felt) was a weari-some drag, a burdensome impediment. Worse: she was "a great blubbering devil." He had already picked a successor. After his wife's death, he invited the new object of his desire to "hang her bonnet up in his house." Dickens, who yearned to be rid of his own tearful wife (yearned "that something might be done"), would have guiltily identified with the callous Hardman (would have identified with Hardman's new-found interest in another woman as well), yet, at the same time, he would have sternly approved of (and somehow shared in) Hardman's deserved sentence. The whole world approved of that sentence. The jury, after hearing two days of testimony, deliberated only twenty minutes before finding Hardman guilty.

Dickens, wife-weary and self-condemned, reading the *Times* account, would have undergone in his own person what Hardman had undergone when the judge placed the black cap on his head and told the doomed prisoner, "You have been convicted . . . of the crime of wilful murder—of the murder of your own wife—a murder committed under circumstances of the most painful kind." Dickens, who often wished in the summer of 1857 that his wife might cease to be, would also have felt, felt in his guilty empathy (in his heart of hearts was he any better than a Hardman?), what Hardman felt when the judge, profoundly moved by the solemn occasion (so the *Times* reported), told the condemned man, told him with grave admonitions and somber injunctions, to prepare for his death ("Your days are numbered," he had said). Then the judge, after outlining other dread details of Hardman's fate, told the doomed prisoner what his final end would be: "You [will] be taken . . . to the place of execution"—to Hanging Corner—"there to be hanged by the neck until you are dead." The black-capped judge, who was "deeply affected during the passing of the sentence," now fell silent. Hardman "trembled" and "turned very pale." (Two years later, in *Hunted Down* [1859], Dickens would write— again from firsthand knowledge, and again in conjunction with a prison visit, though of years before—a story about another callous prisoner, this time the rake, dandy, artist, litterateur, and forger Thomas Griffiths Wainewright ["James Weathercock"], who poisoned, among others, young women relatives for the sake of the insurance he had induced them to take out.)

Dickens, as we noted, read the London *Times* regularly, and he read with special interest and discernment—lifelong interest and discernment—accounts of criminal trials and histories, accounts that filled the *Times* and filled other newspapers and periodicals that he regularly read. (In his own monthly periodical, the *Household Narrative of Current Events* [1850–55], he included a major section in each issue entitled "Narrative of Law and Crime.") Dickens would have encountered the *Times* report of Hardman's grim history and dread fate immediately after interviewing and hiring the Ternans, and just before traveling with them to Manchester, there to act, and then act again, the high romance of *The Frozen Deep* and the tempestuous farce of *Uncle John*. As Dickens threw himself into the plays, as he acted, along with Ellen, roles that portrayed forbidden love, murderous impulses, and foolish infatuation, roles that awakened answering echoes—wild murderous echoes, ecstatic loving echoes—in his own burdened heart, another strange echo (Dickens would have thought it a fated echo) would have mingled with that confusion: the young wife Hardman had murdered (so the *Times* had informed him) had been named the name of names, had been named, of all the multitudinous names in the wide wide world, the magical name of "Ellen."

The sacrosanct but equivocal name of Ellen (a name increasingly imbued for Dickens with forbidden emotions) and the bleak history of the cruel wife-murderer Hardman (callous disposer of an unwanted wife) were repeatedly intruding into Dickens' thoughts in those fateful August days. Moreover, those fragments of different worlds, in most ways antipodal worlds—the ineffable world of fervent love, and the sordid world of murderous hate—were intruding into his thoughts in disturbing conjunction. These unconnected, or seemingly unconnected, aspects of his life—the enchanting teen-aged Ellen, the unwanted middle-aged wife, the constant thoughts (wife-annihilating thoughts) "that something might be done"—were somehow merged and brutally transformed in Hardman's murder of his wife, his murder of the "blubbering" Ellen, a callous cold-blooded murder (how vividly Dickens must have imagined and then vicariously experienced it!) that now began to haunt his days and disturb his nights.

The murder and its strange conjunctions seemed to pursue Dickens. Five days after he read the *Times* account of Hardman's trial and sentencing, he would have read the shorter (but supplementary and reinforcing) *Examiner* account of the ghastly Hardman case. (Dickens read the *Examiner,* a liberal weekly newspaper, assiduously; he had, as a matter of fact, often contributed to its pages, pages edited until recently by his confidant John Forster.) On 15 August 1857, just two days before Dickens began rehearsing intensively with Ellen, just five days before he departed with her for Manchester, and just two weeks before Hardman's execution, the *Examiner* reported the Hardman case under a headline that would have evoked—once more evoked—dark fantasies and guilty reactions in Dickens. The headline, stark and simple, generic and inclusive, would have been for Dickens like the toll of a mournful bell, a deep fearful inner bell: "MURDER OF A WIFE." The opening sentence of the article would have enlarged and reinforced the guilt-inducing associations of the headline. For Dickens the sentence would have once more linked (however subliminally or subterraneously) his yearning to be rid of his wife with thoughts of Ellen and of murder. The sentence read in part: "E. Hardman . . . was indicted for the wilful murder of Ellen, his wife." The final sentence rounded out what the somber opening began. It matter-of-factly enunciated the fate of Hardman and (by implication) the fate of all wife-annihilating transgressors: "The prisoner was convicted and sentenced to death."

Less than a month later Dickens was in Lancaster, staying at the King's Arms, just a few hundred yards from Lancaster Castle, the site of Hardman's imprisonment, trial, and execution. On the day of Dickens' arrival, the still-current issue of the weekly *Lancaster Guardian* (5 September 1857) would have confronted him with a large, bold, riveting headline that would have brought back a myriad of conflicting emotions and associations: "EXECUTION OF EDWARD HARDMAN." Dickens, a rapid and omniverous reader, and a snapper-up of local news, local color, and local sensations (even when he was not emotionally involved or looking for *Household Words* copy), almost certainly read this detailed newspaper account of Hardman's nearby hanging. (As a matter of fact, in his letter of 12 September 1857 from Lancaster, Dickens tells us that throughout his tour, he read the local newspapers.)

In the Lancaster newspaper article recounting Hardman's execution, amidst much detail certain to have made an indelible impression upon Dickens (a stunning impression, given his emotional and domestic predicament), he would have read how, at noon, on Saturday, 29 August 1857, as the castle bell tolled its dread summons, Edward Hardman, in the custody of William Calcraft, the executioner, emerged through the Drop Room window-door and walked onto the gallows platform. An immense crowd of more than eight thousand eager spectators was waiting to see the pitiless wife-killer—the killer of the blameless Ellen—meet his gruesome fate. Hardman, who had "previously stated that he did not intend to look at the crowd," closed his eyes, and under the guidance of Calcraft, finally reached his appointed place under the waiting noose and turned his face to the castle wall.

The night before, for the first time, Hardman's demeanor had become "faltering, and there was evident shrinking from his doom." Now, as the castle bell tolled his doom, "Hardman's face was ashen pale; his nerve was evidently gone." Calcraft positioned him under the beam and then adjusted the noose. A moment later, Hardman was alone on the platform, and in another instant the bolt was withdrawn. "The sharp crash of the falling platform" sent "an audible shudder through the crowd, and with but a faint struggle, Edward Hardman yielded up the life." Many "of the spectators seemed awe-stricken by the spectacle." The lifeless body, dangling limply above the gazing crowd, "remained suspended for about an hour." That night, at midnight, Hardman's body was buried opposite the Drop Room, under the churchyard wall (a site within the precincts of the castle and the prison), a location just a few score feet from Hanging Corner where the callous wife-killer had faced the castle wall and met his terrible fate. As the black coffin, engulfed by midnight darkness, was about to be lowered into the waiting earth, a crowd of jostling onlookers pelted the rude black box with stones, believing in their anger and their suspicion that the coffin was empty.

Now Dickens himself was standing in Lancaster Castle, inspecting the selfsame spot where Hardman's coffin had rested two weeks earlier, looking at the dread window-door, so ordinary yet so momentous, that had ushered the wife-killer onto the scaffold, gazing at the very stones in the castle wall that the wretched prisoner had gazed at with his last tormented mortal glimpse. Standing in the Drop Room, besieged by a tumult of specially charged inner emotions and specially charged outward scenes and associations, besieged also by a confused array of emotion-freighted similitudes, Dickens must have felt profoundly implicated and deeply disturbed by what he saw and what he felt. Considering how guilt-provoking that concatenation of scenes and similitudes must have been for him, it is not surprising that two weeks later, when he sat down to summon up his Lancaster sojourn for *The Lazy Tour* and to write a story set in Lancaster, a story that became "The Bride's Chamber," Lancaster Inns, Lancaster Castles, dismal bridecakes, unwanted wives, passionate yearning, money-motivated murders, hard inimical husbands, slowly murdered wives, exhumed bodies, wall-environed executions, everlasting damnation, and the talismanic name of "Ellen" (so laden for him at that moment with associations of guilt and passion, murder and hangings) rose once more before him like grim accusatory ghosts and then, elaborated and transformed, became enshrined forever in "The Bride's Chamber." (For a summary and then an in-depth discussion of "The Bride's Chamber" that make clear how these elements became part of the chilling, self-condemning story that Dickens then conjured up, see immediately below in the main text of Part 2.)

One other detail. Dickens apparently did not know (or perhaps chose to ignore the fact, though this is less likely) that executions at Hanging Corner did not commence until 1800; prior to that time they had taken place away from the castle on Lancaster Moor, an area usually referred to as Gallows Moor. Since the hanging in "The Bride's Chamber" was said to have occurred in 1757—that is, a hundred years before the present moment in 1857 when the tale is told—the execution, had it been a historical fact, would not have taken place against the castle wall.

11. For evidence of Dickens' familiarity with "The Rime of the Ancient Mariner," see *MHC* 2: *OCS,* 44:37; *DC,* 43:447; and his letters of 10 November

1855 and 28 September 1861, to cite only four instances. In some of these references he emphasizes the same details he emphasized in "The Bride's Chamber." For example, in yet another letter (22 July [1840]), speaking of a young woman "for whom I have conceived a horrible aversion," he writes: "She is the Ancient Mariner of young ladies. She 'holds me with her glittering eye', and I cannot turn away."

12. For a more extensive analysis of Miss Havisham and her sin, see Part 1, "Dickens and Cannibalism."

13. On Dickens' admiration for Mathews, his habitual attendance at his performances, and his memorization of his roles, see F, 59–60, 380, where Forster quotes Dickens' own testimony.

14. Although the account of Martha Joachim in the *Household Narrative of Current Events* appeared in the January 1850 issue, that issue was published after the end of April 1850, the date when the *Household Narrative* actually commenced publication. After that commencement, the issues for January, February, and March 1850 were also offered to the public so that the volume, which was promised at the end of each year as a record of that year (or which subscribers could bind up from their own monthly copies), would cover the whole of 1850. Thus the *Examiner* account of Martha Joachim must have remained fresh in Dickens' mind for several months before he published it in the *Household Narrative*. See Stone, *UW*, 1: 97–99.

15. For the more aggressive and frightening (though still humorous) components of Pecksniff's amorousness, see Part 1, "Dickens and Cannibalism."

16. The discontents of David's marriage to Dora and the cannibalistic aspects of those discontents are analyzed in Part 1, "Dickens and Cannibalism."

17. Dickens sent Ellen Ternan advanced proofs of this scene, in which a renunciatory and self-disparaging Carton declares his secret passion for Lucie; see Part 2, note 5.

18. For an analysis of the pervasiveness and malignancy of this evil, and for a more elaborate discussion of the profound duality of Cloisterham, including Cloisterham's cannibalistic malignancy, see Part 1, "Dickens and Cannibalism."

19. Jasper's consuming passion and the aggressive component of his relations with Rosa, Edwin, and others are often conveyed through cannibalistic
images and associations. For an analysis of Jasper's cannibalism and an examination of some of the other cannibalistic resonances of the novel, see Part 1,
"Dickens and Cannibalism."

20. Although Dickens depicts such passion with great subtlety and psychological acuity, he is essentially following commonplace, or at least popular,
medical thinking. In Buchan's *Domestic Medicine,* a widely used home medical
adviser—its heyday was the 1770s through the 1820s but many families consulted the work well into the Victorian period—and a book Dickens occasionally mentions in his writings (several times in *Little Dorrit,* for example), we
find the following comments on love and passion:

> Love is perhaps the strongest of all the passions; at least, when it
> becomes violent, it is less subject to the controul either of the under-
> standing or will, than any of the rest. . . . We would . . . advise every
> one, before he tampers with this passion, to consider well the proba-
> bility of his being able to obtain the object of his wishes. When that
> is not likely, he should avoid every occasion of increasing it. He ought
> immediately to flee the company of the beloved object . . . There is
> no passion with which people are so ready to tamper as love, al-
> though none is more dangerous. . . . There is no jesting with this
> passion. When love is got to a certain height, it admits of no other
> cure but the possession of its object, which in this case ought always,
> if possible, to be obtained. (Buchan, *Domestic Medicine,* 119–20)

Buchan's remarks are relevant to Dickens' depiction of Bradley Headstone (see
above in Part 2) as well as Jasper.

21. The autobiographical associations that involve Fanny and the many
other crucial autobiographical elements that emerge in this inward-looking
Christmas Book are explored in detail in the following works: Stone, "Dickens'
Artistry and *The Haunted Man,*" 492–505; and Stone, *Dickens and the Invis-
ible World,* 132–45. See also Glancy, "Dickens at Work on *The Haunted
Man,*" 65–85.

22. In 1855, to Maria's assertion that she was "toothless, fat, old and ugly,"
Dickens had replied, "I don't believe [it]." But two years later, he could avow
directly (no longer simply by fictional transformation) that the ineffable Dora

was no longer beautiful. On 10 August 1857, he inscribed a set of his books as follows: "To James E. Roney, my old friend and companion in some of the Copperfield days (when Dora was beautiful), with my faithful regard" (see Carlton, "A Companion of the Copperfield Days," 7). Dickens' inscription hints at his mood of loss and disillusionment (note the past tense of "was beautiful") at that critical and vulnerable moment, for he wrote the inscription a few days before going to Manchester to play in *The Frozen Deep* and *Uncle John* with the Ternans, that is, a few days before his mood of loss and disillusionment was swept away by a new embodiment of womanly beauty, and before plunging into a new—but very different and much more devastating—turmoil of ecstatic love.

23. For useful presentations, in context, of these declarations and instructions, see Nisbet, *Dickens and Ellen Ternan*, 24–25, 52–56, and Johnson, *Charles Dickens*, 2: 1018–20, 1076, 1078. See also, Slater, *Dickens and Women*, 209–10. Nisbet was the first to decipher and publish most of the suppressed passages in Dickens' American letters to Wills. Some additional passages are published here for the first time.

24. This sense of profound guilt and sin (provoked by loving and beguiling a beautiful young woman) is evident not simply in his writings but occasionally in his daily living. On 31 January 1863, Dickens attended a performance of *Faust* at the Paris Opera. In a letter (19 February 1863) to William Charles Macready, the great tragic actor and manager, Dickens gives an account of the *Faust* production and describe how Mephistopheles was "surrounded by an infernal red atmosphere of his own" and Marguerite by "a pale blue mournful light. The two never blending." But after Marguerite takes the jewels—that is, after she indicates that she will yield to the persuasive and all-powerful Faust and so to her damnation—the light changes, the flowers fade, the leaves droop, and "mournful shadows overhang her chamber window, which was innocently bright and gay at first." "I couldn't bear it," Dickens continues, "and gave in completely." In a letter about the same performance written more than two weeks earlier to Georgina Hogarth, written, as a matter of fact, the day after the performance and a few days before departing for a "little perfectly quiet tour . . . touching the sea at Boulogne" (1 February 1863, to Mamie Dickens)—a tour that included stays in Arras, Amiens, and probably in Hazebrouck and other places, and then a sojourn in Condette or, more strictly speaking, in Hardelot, his French hideaway six miles from Boulogne, apparently with Ellen—he tells us why "he gave in completely" to the performance

of *Faust*. "I could hardly bear the thing," he wrote; "it affected me so, and sounded in my ears so like a mournful echo of things that lie in my own heart" (1 February 1863). Note that Dickens, who twice in his remarks on *Faust* associated the word *mournful* with impending damnation, here associates *mournful* with his own secret inner self, with "a mournful echo of things that lie in my own heart"; note also his ambiguous and evocative use of the word *lie*. In one aspect, then, an aspect hidden deep in his "own heart," Dickens apparently saw himself as a Faustian embodiment of darkness, beguiling and damning an innocent young woman.

For more information on Condette and the Hardelot hideaway, see Carlton, "Dickens's Forgotten Retreat in France," 69–86. For Dickens' somber cannibalistic musings—mournful, guilt-filled musings—as he made his slow, wintry way (a Faustian way, as he conceived it) from Paris to Condette and to young, innocent, Marguerite-like Ellen, see Part 1, "Dickens and Cannibalism."

In a footnote referring to Dickens' comments on *Faust,* Johnson points out that in the original three-volume edition of Dickens' letters edited in 1880–82 by Mamie Dickens and Georgina Hogarth, the words "and sounded in my ears so like a mournful echo of things that lie in my own heart" were excised from the text (Johnson, *Charles Dickens,* 2: lxxxv, n. 87). Johnson, who quotes the sentence in unexpurgated form, might have added that the offending confession was omitted from all subsequent editions of the letters as well, including the Nonesuch Edition. The original letter is now in the Huntington Library, San Marino, California.

25. On these and related matters, see: Aylmer, *Dickens Incognito, passim;* Reid, "Mr. Tringham of Slough," 164–65; Longley, "Dickens Incognito," 88–91; Longley, "Letter to the Editor," 56. See also Part 2, note 23.

Katharine Longley has shown ("Dickens Incognito") that Dickens probably chose the name "Tringham" as a result of a conflation of that name as it appears in Thomas Hood's seriocomic "A Tale of a Trumpet" (1840)—a long poem about a deaf old gossip who lived in "the prattling, tattling village of Tringham," bought an ear trumpet from a guileful devil-peddler, then repeated the local scandal (which she could now hear) until "the parish of Tringham was all in a flame," and was finally drowned as a witch—with the reemergence of the name "Tringham" later in Dickens' life (in the early sixties) in the person of Mrs. Mary Tringham, a woman who kept a tobacconist's shop. This shop, which had a sign above the door bearing the name "Tringham," was hard by Dickens' *All the Year Round* offices. Thus "Tringham" was a name he saw constantly in those early and mid-Ternan years and a name freighted with special meaning for him. Longley concludes that for Dickens "the name 'Tringham' was consciously associated with scandal—and also with unjust condemnation" (90).

In his own latter-day adoption of a pseudonymous name, Dickens combined the surname "Tringham" with the Christian names "Charles" or "John," both latter given names part of his veritable full name—Charles John Huffam Dickens. This real-life example of the meaningful intricacies and hidden resonances lurking in his deliberate naming not only accords with Dickens' practice in his fiction, but confirms his impulse in stressful and conflicted personal matters (an impulse discussed above and below in this section, and at greater length in Part 3, "Dickens and Necessity") to, at one and the same time, reveal and conceal, condemn and defend, and to do so through his naming as well as through multitudes of other devices.

For Dickens' early knowledge and appreciation of Thomas Hood's writings and for his friendship with Hood, see Part 1, "Dickens and Cannibalism," note 40. Dickens' personal connection with "A Tale of a Trumpet" and his recollection of the poem and its mentions of Tringham may well have been strengthened (though Longley does not mention this fact) by an allusion in the poem to the underworld of *Oliver Twist:*

> The smallest urchin whose tongue could tang,
> Shock'd the Dame with a volley of slang,
> Fit for Fagin's juvenile gang.

Fagin and his juvenile gang had ceased to utter their lowlife slang (in *Bentley's Miscellany*) just a year before Hood published "A Tale of a Trumpet." The allusion to Fagin and his gang was therefore fresh and topical and would have been widely understood. "A Tale of a Trumpet" first appeared in the *New Monthly Magazine*. Dickens probably read the poem on its first appearance; it later became part of his library in collected form. That the poem lingered evocatively in Dickens' consciousness is suggested as well by another unremarked but startling fact: one of the fiercest of the savage women in Tringham is named "Madam Laffarge." (See the discussion, Part 1, "Dickens and Cannibalism," of Madam Laffarge's latter-day namesake and counterpart, the fierce and savage Madame Defarge of *A Tale of Two Cities.*)

26. Many observers, from Forster and Carlyle to Fechter, Payn, and Longfellow, could be summoned to bear witness to this somber aspect of Dickens' latter-day life. One lesser-known observer, a striking and very different witness, was Annie Fields, the young wife of the American publisher James T. Fields.

She met Dickens in June 1859, about a year after Dickens' formal separation from his wife. In 1859 and 1860 the Fields were on a leisurely postmarriage tour through Britain and the Continent, and Annie, like her husband (who was to emerge as Dickens' chief American publisher during these latter years), soon became Dickens' dear friend. At the time of their meeting, Annie Fields had just turned twenty-five (she was five years older than Ellen Ternan); Dickens was forty-seven, Fields forty-two. During the next decade, the friendship between Annie Fields and Dickens continued and deepened. In 1867–68, while Dickens was on his long arduous American reading tour, he lived for some time in the Fields' Boston home. (Fields had played an important role in convincing Dickens to come to the United States.) On other occasions during the tour, the Fields accompanied Dickens on his reading circuits. A year later, in 1869, the Fields were again sojourning in England. Twice during this stay they were houseguests at Gad's Hill Place, Dickens' home in Kent—on the first occasion, for eight days in June; on the second, for three days in October (this last stay shortly before the Fields returned to the United States). In May 1869, during the first few weeks of the Fields' stay in England, Dickens had taken hotel rooms in London for himself and for Mamie and Georgina (Katey was married and already living in London), so that they could all be near the Fields and show them about. The Fields, in short, were very special and very privileged friends. (They were among the few, for example, who knew—knew from Dickens—that he had a close relationship with Ellen Ternan, though the exact nature of what Dickens told them about Ellen is not clear.)

Annie Fields was an extraordinarily sensitive and perceptive observer, her customary sensitivity and perceptiveness made even more acute in Dickens' case by her fascination with him, by her increasingly passionate attachment to him (an attachment that reached its zenith during Dickens' American reading tour), and by the intimacy of their friendship, an intimacy shared by her husband. Dickens, the Fields agreed, was charismatic, a bringer of light and joy. His outward presence, Annie Fields wrote in her diary after visiting with Dickens in October 1869, was "so cheery and kindly" that it changed "the very aspect of the day" (Curry, 46). This was Dickens' customary presence, a genial and transforming presence—the "Great Enchanter," she called him. But she had long since detected darkness and deep sorrow beneath the exuberant surface of Dickens' sunny playfulness. As early as 6 May 1860, she had confided to her diary: "A shadow has fallen on that house [Tavistock House, Dickens' London home at that time—she was later to say the same of Gad's Hill Place], making Dickens seem rather the man of labor and of sorrowful thought than the soul of gaiety we find in all he writes" (Curry, 5). She was to repeat this diagnosis with increasing force in the ensuing years. Nine years later (10 June

1869), for example, after describing how Dickens sustained the conversation with his sallies and liveliness, and how he "laughed merrily," she went on: "it is wonderful the fun and flow of spirits C. D. has for he is a sad man. Sleepless nights come too often, oftener than they ever would to a free heart. But the sorrows of such a nature are many and must often seem more than he can bear" (Curry, 44). Other diary entries give us similar glimpses of Annie Fields' sad perception—a perception that somber, night-side shadows, shadows that drove and harrowed Dickens, lurked unexpectedly in the concealed reaches of his inmost being. After Dickens' death, those somber elements in his makeup continued to haunt her. Remembering his hidden sadness and his inner torment—this a month after his death—she was comforted by the thought "that he is no longer in a world which held so much pain for him." Then, seven weeks later (30 August 1870), she wrote: "I am grateful to think of him at rest" (Curry, 56, 58).

For additional perspectives on this hidden self-torment in Dickens, its sources and its creative correlatives, see Part 3, "Dickens and Necessity"; see also Part 3, note 22 and figure 140.

27. Another portrait in another late work that exhibits some of these feelings (though with a different focus) is George Silverman, in *George Silverman's Explanation*. For a discussion of the implications of this portrait, including its relationship to Dickens' liaison with Ellen Ternan, see Part 3, "Dickens and Necessity."

28. For more on the ink colors and allied matters, see Forsyte, "The Sapsea Fragment—Fragment of What?," 14–16. See also Batterson, "The Manuscript and Text of Dickens's 'George Silverman's Explanation,'" 473–76.

29. This stressful tangle of contending feelings and emotions, a tangle that entwines and interconnects adoration, compulsion, dissembling, self-division, sinfulness, and profound guilt, recurs in other late works by Dickens. It recurs, for example, in *George Silverman's Explanation,* Dickens' last completed fiction. For an analysis of these elements as they appear in that somber story, and for an analysis of their conjunction there with Ellen Ternan and other shaping forces, a conjunction that casts new light on the old mutating paradigm of these conflicted forces, see Part 3, "Dickens and Necessity."

30. This asylum is now part of the Lancaster Moor Hospital, a large mental illness institution on a parklike estate that at present encompasses 372 acres of

gently rolling, partly wooded countryside. Dickens' overall impression of the asylum was strongly positive: "'An immense place, . . . admirable offices, very good arrangements, very good attendants; altogether a remarkable place'" (*HW* 16: BC, 385). The structures Dickens visited were built in 1816. They still exist, and though they have been added to and modified over the years, the buildings and wards he describes remain substantially as they were when he saw them. To dwell for a moment on the chief interior changes, the fiber floor matting that so engrossed the "meagre man" has been replaced by linoleum, the long central corridor is now interrupted at midpoint by a series of partitioning doors, while the tiny rooms, like the corridor itself, have been provided with lowered ceilings, a modification that partially reduces the natural light that Dickens found so striking. Yet the chief characteristics of the ward—its windows, its arches, its doors, its "cells," its afternoon sun, and its "cross patches of light and shade"—are still very much as they were when Dickens saw them. (See figure 116. This photograph shows the main corridor of the ward—"cells," arches, and all—lit by the afternoon sun.)

At the time of Dickens' visit (as now), the scheme and administration of the institution were advanced and enlightened, and Dickens, in his re-creation of the scene, pays tribute to this fact. The inmates of the near empty ward that he sketches so memorably would have been relaxing in the adjacent yard or (in some instances) tending the nearby grounds and gardens. The wards Dickens described are still in use, many of the small rooms still occupied, but the building is currently being phased out as a residence for patients. (See figures 115 and 116.)

Part 3: Dickens and Necessity

1. Despite the fact that these questions preoccupied Dickens, little attention has been given to them, especially from the perspective of his considered views on such matters. This is not to say that the questions do not come up. Critics and commentators, in the course of their pursuit of some other aspect of Dickens' thought or art, have sometimes touched upon what he seems to be saying about destiny or fate, but such reflections are usually asides that are not pursued; and, in any case, are almost always limited to a particular character or event. This reluctance to concentrate on a matter that Dickens so often concentrated on is probably a reflection of the difficulty of the task, a reflection, that is, of the seemingly inconsistent and even contradictory nature of what Dickens had to say about necessity. But though Dickens did not think consis-

tently or systematically about necessity, he thought deep and long about the subject. As he entered his middle and then his later years, he pondered more and more about those bleak, inescapable, compelling forces (to take for a moment his darkest latter-day formulations of the matter) that make us what we are. The hesitations and inconsistencies in his thinking about the subject—he frequently juxtaposes positive and negative ideas—remain, but at the same time ever more prominent patterns that incorporate his gloomier thoughts on the subject emerge and grow stronger, looming patterns that evolve and darken.

In order to trace these evolving patterns of thought, this study ranges over Dickens' early, middle, and late writings; but it gives special attention to his last completed statement on the subject—an exceedingly important statement—the little-considered *George Silverman's Explanation*. The roster of studies devoted to *George Silverman's Explanation* is short; indeed, the studies themselves are equally short (most are three to seven pages). Few of them—they are all listed below—touch upon necessity. Few touch upon another crucial factor closely connected with necessity as it emerges from the story: the profound connections between story and author. Very little has been written about the autobiographical matrix of *George Silverman's Explanation,* yet that intricate, many-dimensioned matrix is an indispensable aid in interpreting the story; by the same token, very little has been written about how that generative matrix and its earlier formulations in counterpart works caused Dickens to focus ever more darkly and ever more obsessively on necessity.

Here are the studies devoted to *George Silverman's Explanation* (for full bibliographic listings of these works, see the Select Bibliography): M. K. Bradby, "An Explanation of *George Silverman's Explanation*" (1940)—the first article to concentrate on the story, a brief examination "in the light of Freudian psychology"; Harry Stone, "Dickens's Tragic Universe: 'George Silverman's Explanation'" (1958)—the first substantial analysis of the story and the first to emphasize necessity; Barry D. Bart, "'George Silverman's Explanation'" (1964)—a brief but perceptive piece viewing the story in the context of Dickens' abandonment of the ethic of renunciation; Dudley Flamm, "The Prosecutor Within: Dickens's Final Explanation" (1970)—a short insightful article examining the narrative technique and the confessional mode as ways of understanding the story; Deborah A. Thomas, "The Equivocal Explanation of Dickens' George Silverman" (1974)—a short, useful analysis of the equivocal and ambiguous elements in the story; Michael A. Ullman, "Where George Stopped Growing: Dickens's 'George Silverman's Explanation'" (1979)—a well-presented recapitulation of largely earlier views; Richard F. Batterson,

"The Manuscript and Text of Dickens's 'George Silverman's Explanation'" (1979)—a concise bibliographic description of the manuscript and text.

For an explanation of the method used to cite Dickens' letters, writings, and other primary sources, and for an explanation of abbreviations, bibliographical references, and similar matters, see Part 1, "Dickens and Cannibalism," note 1. See also Part 3, note 3.

2. The work has not only been neglected but frequently traduced, usually in an aside or passing reference. J. Cuming Walters, writing in the *Dickensian* in 1930, found *George Silverman's Explanation* to be "as worthless as it is depressing," a "dull and stupid work." "I should like," he continues, "to cast it on the rubbish heap" (*Dickensian* 26: 285). George Saintsbury, Andrew Lang, and Philip Collins, to cite three very different but representative commentators who have mentioned the work over the years, have found it, respectively, "almost worthless," containing "nothing of interest," and "poor" (George Saintsbury, "Dickens," *Cambridge History of English Literature*, 15 vols. [Cambridge: Cambridge University Press, 1907–27], 13: 334; Andrew Lang, ed., *The Works of Charles Dickens*, 36 vols. [London: Chapman & Hall, 1897–1908], 25: xiii; Collins, *Dickens and Education*, 229).

Dickens, however, had a very different estimation of his piece. His strongly positive feeling about it is not only on record in his own words (see below in the main text of Part 3) but is attested to by other witnesses. Percy Fitzgerald, after observing that *George Silverman's Explanation* is "a very remarkable story . . . which has attracted little attention," tells us that Dickens "sent me the proof-sheets in advance, with an evident sense of satisfaction in his work" (Fitzgerald, *Life*, 1: 59). Dickens, as will become clear shortly, was not only satisfied with *George Silverman's Explanation* but struck by its originality and its haunting truth.

3. *George Silverman's Explanation* was first reprinted in the United States in 1870, shortly after Dickens' death. The reprinting was produced in Boston under the auspices of Fields, Osgood, & Co., the successor, in 1869, to Ticknor and Fields. (James T. Fields, the "Fields" of both companies, was a good friend of Dickens; see Part 2, "Dickens and Passion," note 26. During the last ten years of Dickens' life, Fields was the chief authorized publisher of Dickens' works in the United States.) Fields, Osgood, & Co. published *George Silverman's Explanation* as part of a miscellaneous volume of Dickens' writings, a volume that had as its central feature Dickens' last uncompleted novel. This miscellaneous volume appeared under the following rubric: *The Mystery of Ed-*

win Drood and Some Uncollected Pieces, the uncollected pieces being *George Silverman's Explanation, Holiday Romance, Sketches of Young Couples, New Uncommercial Samples,* and *The Will of Charles Dickens. George Silverman's Explanation* was first reprinted in Great Britain in 1875 by Chapman and Hall, Dickens' official publishers. At that time Chapman and Hall incorporated the story into the Collected Works. The first separate edition, a pirated version in the form of a fifty-three-page pamphlet, was issued by the Southern Publishing Company, Limited (Brighton and London) in 1879. The first separate book edition (edited, introduced, and annotated by Harry Stone and illustrated by Irving Block) was published by the Santa Susana Press (Northridge, California) in a limited edition of 325 copies in 1984.

All quotations from *George Silverman's Explanation* are taken from its original appearance in the *Atlantic Monthly.* The *Atlantic Monthly* text, carefully proofed and corrected by Dickens, was sent on to Ticknor and Fields before Dickens' departure for the United States. The *All the Year Round* version of the story and the posthumous Chapman and Hall version (the latter inauthentic redaction providing the text for most later reprintings) differ in many small ways (the Chapman and Hall version especially) from the original *Atlantic Monthly* text.

4. "Drama" is an appropriate word here, not only because Dickens conceived the novel in dramatic terms (that is, as a drama of plot and incident), but because he was exceedingly anxious to have the book staged, an unusual desire for him. He proposed and then strongly urged a French production, writing to his friend, the French actor-manager François Joseph Philoclès (Charles) Regnier, on the subject; he even contemplated going to Paris to rehearse the company (15 October and 16 November 1859). His desire for such a production was partly because of the theatricality of the book's conception and execution (the central idea had come to him in 1857 while playing a Carton-like role in *The Frozen Deep*—see Part 2, "Dickens and Passion"), but partly also because some of his earliest ideas for *A Tale of Two Cities* connected the unborn novel with conventions of the French drama. In 1855, in his *Book of Memoranda,* he had written: "How as to a story in two periods—with a lapse of time between, like a French Drama?" (Kaplan, 5). *A Tale of Two Cities,* of course, is a story in two periods (and two cities) and has a lapse of five years between Book the First and Book the Second.

When Dickens' idea for a French dramatization of *A Tale of Two Cities* proved politically impossible, he agreed, again unusually for him (for he thought most dramatizations of his writings were wretched parodies), to oversee an English version in order, in effect, to make the result less awful than the usual (unauthorized) staging of his works. Quite obviously, he realized how theatrical *A Tale of Two Cities* was, and he wished to exert some influence over at least one of the inevitable dramatizations, finally devoting more than two weeks of concentrated effort to the production of an authorized version at the Lyceum Theatre, London, under Madame Celeste. (Tom Taylor wrote the dramatization; Madame Celeste acted Madame Defarge.) Almost two years later, still taken with the theatricality of his novel, he wrote, "I must say that I like my Carton, and I have a faint idea sometimes that if I had acted him, I could have done something with his life and death" (17 November 1861).

For Dickens to have acted Carton's life and death would have been for Dickens to transcend himself, to transcend the confining limitations of intractable reality. Carton, of course, was profoundly linked to Dickens; among other deep bonds, he was a projection of some of Dickens' inmost yearnings and emotions concerning halo-headed, unobtainable Ellen Ternan. For Dickens to have acted Carton on the stage, then, would be to achieve—and nightly reachieve—a vicarious and very special fulfillment, a fulfillment that would be simultaneously personal and public, that would enshrine nightly self-sacrifice—heroic self-sacrifice—and nightly ennoblement. (See Part 2, "Dickens and Passion.")

Dickens never did act "my Carton." But he was absolutely right about the theatricality of *A Tale of Two Cities. The Only Way,* a much later dramatic version of the novel—one of many—became the most successful of all the dramatizations of Dickens' works, holding the boards well into the twentieth century. (On the stage history of *A Tale of Two Cities,* see Fitz-Gerald, *Dickens and the Drama,* 269–85.)

5. This matter is treated more fully in Part 2, "Dickens and Passion."

6. Kaplan, *Book of Memoranda,* 6.

7. For much more on these and allied matters, especially on Dickens' latter-day relationship with Ellen, see Part 2, "Dickens and Passion."

Published versions of Dickens' letters to Wills (and to others) usually indicate the stationery on which they were written. All published versions of Dickens' letter to Wills of 6 June 1867, however, omit the fact that it was written on Ellen's monogrammed stationery. Furthermore, crossed-out but readable passages in this letter—passages referring to Ellen—are neither transcribed nor noted. For a photograph of the first and last pages of this letter, including the

"ET" monogram (a bold monogram in red), see figure 119. The lightly canceled passage on the last page of this letter (see illustration), a passage omitted
in all published versions, refers to a difficulty vis-à-vis Ellen, or more specifically, vis-à-vis Ellen and the American tour, a difficulty or rather a dilemma that
now confronted Dickens.

On the one hand, the dilemma concerned his reluctance to be separated
from Ellen during the six months of his American tour; on the other hand, it
concerned his fear that her presence in his company, even during a portion of
the tour, would cause a scandal. "The Patient," Dickens wrote as he argued
the case for making the American tour, "I acknowledge to be the gigantic
difficulty. But you know I don't like to give in before difficulty, if it can be
beaten." After arriving in America and consulting with friends, Dickens cabled
Wills a brief message. That message (by a prearranged code that had a special
meaning for Ellen) indicated that she was not to join him (see Nisbet, 54).
Dickens' reference to Ellen as "the Patient" goes back in its origins to the
Staplehurst railway accident of 9 June 1865, and to the fact that Ellen, like
Dickens, was badly shaken up in that devastating and deadly disaster, a trauma
that left lingering aftereffects. See, for a similar "Patient" reference, Dickens'
later allusion (later, that is, than the "ET" letter) to Ellen as "my dear Patient"
in his letter to Wills of 21 February 1868 from Providence, Rhode Island, a
letter, or rather a suppressed passage from the letter, quoted above in Part 2,
"Dickens and Passion." In the years following Staplehurst, both before and
after the two references just noted, there are other allusions to Ellen as the
"Patient." The "Darling" reference ("my Darling," Dickens wrote, referring
to Ellen) also comes from a censored passage in a letter to Wills, a letter written
from the United States on 30 December 1867. For more on the occasion of
the latter letter, see above in Part 2, "Dickens and Passion" and below in the
main text of the present section. All of the letters referred to in this note are in
the Huntington Library, San Marino, California.

8. For more on Dickens' complex relationship with his sister Fanny see Part
2, "Dickens and Passion."

9. For a detailed demonstration of these connections, see Stone, *Dickens
and the Invisible World,* 119–26, 132–41.

10. For an analysis of this love affair, its shaping impulsions and emotional
significances, see Part 2, "Dickens and Passion."

11. See Stone, *Dickens and the Invisible World*, 325–32.

12. Rosa Dartle's self-wounding, self-imprisoning passion—a fierce, compulsive passion—is analyzed in Part 2, "Dickens and Passion."

13. This episode and other crucial aspects of Dickens' relationship with his mother (aspects not analyzed in this section) are discussed in Part 1, "Dickens and Cannibalism."

14. For a fuller discussion of Dickens' hideaway, his relationship with Ellen, his assumed name, his sense of sin, his feelings of guilt, and his perception of being driven and compelled by forces he could not control, see Part 2, "Dickens and Passion"; see also Part 2, note 24. For more on how Dickens' relationship with Ellen Ternan helped shape *George Silverman's Explanation,* see, in the present part, prior and subsequent discussions of this many-dimensioned matter.

The manuscript of *George Silverman's Explanation* is in the Houghton Library, Harvard University. For additional information on the *Silverman* manuscript, see Forsyte, "Sapsea Fragment," 16; see also Batterson, "Manuscript and Text," 473–76.

15. Hoghton Towers (or, more properly, Hoghton Tower) stands on top of a hill in the Lancashire countryside between Preston and Blackburn. The present structure, one of a long series, was rebuilt in 1565. In its heyday, this sixteenth-century fortified manor house saw much history and was visited by many notables, including James I in 1617. According to tradition, it was at Hoghton Towers that James I knighted the loin of beef—known thereafter as "sirloin." The house was the ancient seat of the Hoghton family, but in the late eighteenth and early nineteenth centuries it slowly decayed, then was abandoned, and finally fell into ruin. When Dickens visited the manor on 26 April 1867, it was unoccupied and disintegrating. In contrast, however, a farmhouse and farm buildings, part of the Hoghton estate and adjacent to the mansion proper, were occupied, and chickens and cows roamed the precincts where courtiers once had dallied. Dickens saw the manor house at the nadir of its history; and as he roamed its decaying rooms and gazed at its collapsed ceilings, gaping windows, ruined staircases, and rat-infested stairwells, visions of the ruined rat-infested blacking warehouse of his boyhood, glimmerings of the central idea for his new novel-cum-story, and strategies for beginning and then shadowing forth that tangled tale (which became *George Silverman's Explana-*

tion), mingled in his mind with Preston workers, Preston poverty, Preston cellars, and his own early experiences—all in ways already described.

In his letters and in his story, Dickens always calls the manor house "Hoghton Towers," a designation followed throughout in this book (both in the text and the notes) in order to avoid confusion. However, despite a variety of spellings in the past (some of these variant spellings appear in illustration titles—when those titles are quoted—and as bibliographical documentation in the illustration captions), the house is currently known, and was usually known in Dickens' day, as "Hoghton Tower." Hoghton Towers (to continue with Dickens' version of the name) was restored in the late nineteenth century and is now open to the public on a limited basis, though its location, about a mile off a byroad between Preston and Blackburn, and its lack of ballyhooed collections or widely publicized features, has kept it from being as well-known or as heavily frequented as it deserves to be.

Dickens visited Hoghton Towers by chance. On 25 April 1867, while on a reading tour, he stopped overnight at Preston, having given a public reading there earlier that evening. His next reading on the tour was to be at Blackburn the following night. Being a great walker, and the next day being bright and beautiful, he decided to proceed from Preston to Blackburn on foot, a distance of eleven or twelve miles, mostly through Preston streets, then amongst outlying factories and mills, and finally through fields and rolling hills. His walking companion was George Dolby, a pleasant comrade and his tour manager. When the two sojourners had gone five or six miles toward Blackburn, they saw an old melancholy fortress-mansion looming off in the distance on a high hill, inquired what the place was, and decided to turn out of their way and investigate, since Dickens, as it turned out, knew something of the castlelike residence and its history.

That knowledge may have come through his old friend and distant connection by marriage, George Cattermole. More than twenty-five years earlier, Cattermole had coillustrated (with Hablot Knight Browne) *The Old Curiosity Shop* and *Barnaby Rudge*, and he had later taken part in a number of Dickens' amateur theatricals. Dickens admired Cattermole's work. He owned three watercolor drawings by him: "Sintram and His Companions," "Little Nell's Home," and "Little Nell's Grave." He also helped the Cattermoles in their financial difficulties before and after Cattermole's death. Cattermole was familiar with Hoghton Towers, but his association with that hilltop pile was not limited to familiarity. He had painted Hoghton Towers, memorializing the royal occasion that is the manor's chief claim to fame. Cattermole's painting, which Dickens almost certainly knew, depicts James I, attended by his large retinue of nobles, soldiers, and functionaries, and escorted by Sir Richard Hoghton, 1st Baronet, being welcomed by the Hoghton household and the neighboring gentry into Hoghton Towers, whose front elevations form a striking part of the painting. In other words, the Hoghton Towers elevations and the visit of James I were probably visually familiar to Dickens, and his desire to know what really lay behind those strangely familiar battlemented elevations—he probably had vague visions of dim passageways, echoing halls, ancient chambers, and fabled glories as he stood at the bottom of the hill—may have piqued his curiosity, stirred his imagination, and caused him to want to explore the ancient manor.

In any case, here is Cattermole's richly colored painting of Hoghton Towers:

145. *Visit of James I to Hoghton Tower, 1617*

Oil painting (c. 1850) by George Cattermole. Hoghton Tower Preservation Trust.

But as Dickens and Dolby trudged toward the castellated heights, there were no processions, no festivities, and no glories. When they finally arrived at the outskirts of the abandoned mansion, they found themselves in the midst of the manor farm, a group of formidable stone structures that included an ancient barn and a number of rambling farm buildings. These buildings, all just outside and to the left of the main gate and house but built of the same stone as the main house and harmonizing with it, abutted the old winding road the two men had been toiling up (a road now superseded by a long straight ascent to the main gate). Coming upon the tenant farmer who occupied the farmhouse and worked the manor fields—the farmer was the only authority, or apparent authority, visible—they sought and were given permission to explore the mouldering manor house at their leisure. As Dickens roamed through the ruined rooms and weed-grown courtyards, he was stirred and excited by the old splendor, the sad decay, and the new green growth springing up in the midst of so much blight. Wandering slowly through the melancholy, rat-infested wreck—whose precincts even today are plagued by rats—the key images and ideas of *George Silverman's Explanation* began to emerge in his mind. (See Dolby's brief account of their walk: Dolby, 77–78).

16. At the center of the inner quadrangle or courtyard there was a statue of William III. This statue, still present during Dickens' visit, is now in the United States, but the prominent pedestal on which it stood remains in its original position. See figure 135. This illustration shows the inner courtyard as it appeared (including statue, pedestal, and enclosing buildings) in the middle of the nineteenth century.

17. The young lover in "The Bride's Chamber" also gazes longingly through a window at a beloved he cannot possess. See Part 2, "Dickens and Passion."

The street window that Dickens worked at was not at the Hungerford Stairs warehouse but at the Chandos Street warehouse (see figure 137). On the other hand, the association of the blacking warehouse with subterranean, rat-infested depths belongs to the Hungerford Stairs warehouse (see figure 128). The blacking warehouse moved from 30 Hungerford Stairs, Strand, to 3 Chandos Street, Covent Garden, some months after Dickens went to work in the blacking factory.

18. For the close emotional connections—engendering connections—between Ellen and Estella, see Part 2, "Dickens and Passion." Similar emotional connections, though more subtle and more oblique, relate Ellen and Bella.

19. Furthermore, in *Edwin Drood,* the only novel written after *George Silverman's Explanation,* the name "Helena" (another combination of those enchanted sounds) continues this emotion-charged echoing, an echoing that

is amplified by Helena's last name, "Landless," which echoes Ellen's middle name, "Lawless." For more on names and naming, see the discussion in Part 2, "Dickens and Passion," of the importance Dickens attached to names; see, in the same passage, Dickens' comments on Maria Beadnell's name, and how, ever after meeting her, the mere sound of the name "Maria" overwhelmed him with emotion. So also, we may be sure, with the names "Ellen" and "Nelly" and their haunting (haunting for Dickens) fictional reverberations.

20. "Sappy"—that is, "foolish"—was a familiar Victorian locution. See, in this connection, the *OED*.

21. Brother Parksop, a Birmingham machine-maker, is Silverman's maternal grandfather, a man of substance and property. But all is not well with the Parksops and the Silvermans. Silverman's Parksop mother is resentful of her prosperous father. She feels that her father, who owns "a whole courtful of houses" (*GSE*, 3:119), has deprived her of her birthright—hence their cellar poverty. Silverman, for his part, yearns for his grandfather's death. He hopes (so runs his "worldly" dream) that one day he will ascend from the cellar through his grandfather's demise and his own subsequent inheritance, an inheritance that comes to pass but that is purloined by Hawkyard.

There are strong autobiographical overtones here. Dickens' maternal grandfather, Charles Barrow, was also a man of substance and property. He was an important official in the Navy Pay Office (Chief Conductor of Moneys in Town), handled large sums of money, headed a staff of subordinates, and occupied a suite of rooms in the Pay Office headquarters at Somerset House. He was a person whose income, influence, and prospects assured his children and their children a comfortable life. But in 1810, two years before Dickens was born, Charles Barrow—Dickens was named after him—fled England a dishonored man. The Admiralty had discovered that he had been embezzling money for seven years. (He did it, he said, to maintain his large family.) He now owed the government £5,689 3s 3d, a huge sum, much too much for Barrow to repay on his salary of £350 per year; hence his false promises of restitution, followed shortly after by his flight. He lived very briefly (and surreptitiously) in the Brighton lodgings of Mrs. Elizabeth Roylance, a friend of the family (Dickens, who years later lived in London with Mrs. Roylance for a few months in the blacking-warehouse days, would subsequently depict her in *Dombey and Son* as the ogress and child-queller Mrs. Pipchin). After Barrow's brief clandestine sojourn in Brighton, he continued his flight to the Isle of Man (the latter territory was beyond the jurisdiction of British authority). He never returned to his native land, dying in the Isle of Man in 1826, when Dickens was fourteen. Thus, during the whole period of Dickens' degradation and greatest need, that is, from the time he left Chatham, began his slow descent into the blacking warehouse, and then toiled on there, his notorious grandfather was leading a life of some comfort and serenity in the nearby Isle of Man. (Barrow, who settled in Douglas, the capital of the Isle of Man, and owned a house there, was a respected member of that substantial community. He gave music lessons, tuned pianos, had a musical instrument business, played the organ at the fashionable nearby St. George's Church—where he was later buried—and also owned and ran a circulating library. See Carlton, "Links with Dickens in the Isle of Man," 43.)

In the Dickens family the shameful history of Charles Barrow was a source of discord and (for John Dickens) an emblem of foolishness, weakness, and selfishness. John Dickens, who always needed money, frequently reminded his wife that her genteel but fugitive father had deprived them of their birthright. For her part, Elizabeth Dickens, dunned by the creditors and insistent tradesmen that John Dickens' improvidence brought down upon the family (she bore the brunt of their wrath), bemoaned the tranquil days of her lost affluence and often recalled the vanished glories of her genteel past. (Many of these attitudes and goings-on were re-created by Dickens from a more comic perspective—more comic, that is, than in *George Silverman's Explanation*—in *David Copperfield*, mostly through the agency of the Micawbers.)

Dickens, who had listened to this tale of lost gentility and a lost birthright for years, and who often lived through the attendant crises provoked by lack of money, no doubt occasionally heard speculations concerning his grandfather's health and his grandfather's fortune, and no doubt (like his family) occasionally envisioned his grandfather's death, a subsequent golden bequest, and his and his family's release from bondage—dreams that never came to pass. These dreams (on Dickens' part) must have been most intense during the first half of 1824 when he was toiling in the blacking warehouse six days a week, totally cut off from family and friends. At that time, bewildered, afflicted, and resentful, he felt doubly and trebly deprived, a "small Cain," as he put it. (He must be wicked and accursed. Why else his woeful lot?) He was a pariah; his state hopeless. Forgotten by his rich embezzling grandfather (in *George Silverman's Explanation*, Hawkyard plays the role of rich larcenist and violator of his fiduciary and parental trust), neglected by his preoccupied parents, Dickens drudged on alone in the bleak decay of the rat-infested blacking warehouse, an innocent victim (so he felt), consigned to hell (consigned, in the iconography of *George Silverman's Explanation*, to the dark cellar depths), not knowing if he would ever be released, yearning, like George Silverman, desperately at times, at times vindictively, for some death-generated windfall or miraculous deliverance.

Some of these feelings and some of the feelings he attached to his grandfather, feelings associated with golden releases, shameful larcenies, and dashed hopes, may have been called up once more at that moment in 1867, not simply by the Hoghton Towers setting and its blacking-warehouse associations, but by the fact that, as he wandered through the blackened Preston streets and then through the ruined, rat-infested Hoghton Towers rooms, he was in the region of the Isle of Man, his grandfather's bright (so, in the blacking-warehouse days, it had seemed to him), beckoning, but unshared sanctuary, the focus of so many futile dreams and painful memories of long ago.

22. In his latter days, Dickens had begun to dwell ever more steadily and ever more sorrowfully on his mortality, on mortality in general, and on the dark ineluctable mysteries of life and death. *Edwin Drood,* Dickens' letters, his comments to his friends, comments by his friends, and other evidence testify to this latter-day preoccupation no less than *George Silverman's Explanation.* (See also, on the score of this latter-day preoccupation, Part 2, "Dickens and Passion," note 26.) Here, to cite one instance only, is a striking second-party testimonial, an end-of-life testimonial, to that night-side preoccupation. On the evening of 4 June 1870, less than four days before Dickens was fatally stricken, he had sat through the night talking until dawn with his daughter Kate Macready ("Katey") Collins, who had come down to Gad's Hill Place for a brief visit. Dickens spoke in sad, muted, elegiac ways of matters she had rarely heard him dwell upon. He talked about his own life, talked about his past, talked in a manner that she found deeply disturbing; he talked "as though his life were over and there was nothing left" (Kate Dickens Perugini, "'Edwin Drood,' and the Last Days of Charles Dickens," 652–54). Late the next morning, troubled by her long, sad conversation with her father and unable to sleep, Katey returned apprehensively to London. When Dickens was stricken early in the evening on 8 June—stricken in the dining room—Katey hurried down to Gad's Hill, and when her father died scarcely twenty-four hours later, still in the dining room (he had been unconscious on a couch there all the while), she summoned her good friend John Everett Millais to make a last memorial sketch of her famous father, sleeping at last. (See figure 140.)

Sixteen years later, Frederic G. Kitton, who was then compiling his *Charles Dickens by Pen and Pencil,* wrote to Millais asking him for his reminiscences of Dickens and for permission to reproduce the sketch Millais had made of him in death. In the following unpublished letter (now in the author's collection), Millais replied to Kitton's request. (Charles Collins died in 1873. In 1874, Katey married Charles Edward Perugini [Carlo Perugini], the Anglo-Italian painter.):

> 2, Palace Gate,
> Kensington.
>
> 22 June 86
>
> Dear Sir,
>   Although I frequently met Charles Dickens I cannot say I was one of his intimate friends. I must therefore decline to say anything about him. There are many alive who knew him well and you sh^d apply to them. You are quite welcome to publish the sketch I made after death if you have Mrs Peruginis permission. She is a very old friend of mine and when her Father died she asked me to go down to Gads Hill and make a drawing of him
>
> Y^rs truly
> J E Millais.

Millais gave Katey the sketch a few days after making it, sending the drawing down to Gad's Hill on 16 June 1870 via Charles Collins, Katey's husband. Katey wrote Millais the same day to express her appreciation, saying in part:

> It is quite impossible to describe the effect [your drawing] has had upon us. No one but yourself, I think, could have so perfectly understood the beauty and pathos of his dear face as it lay on that little bed in the dining-room, and no one but a man with genius bright as his own could have so reproduced that face as to make us feel now, when we look at it, that he is still with us in the house. Thank you, dear Mr. Millais, for giving it to me. There is nothing in the world I have, or can ever have, that I shall value half as much. I think you know this, although I can find so few words to tell you how grateful I am. (J. G. Millais, *Life*, 2: 30–33)

Select Bibliography

Dickens' novels, Christmas Books, plays, and similar works are not listed in this bibliography. All such works are cited from first editions. A list of these works, together with their dates of first publication, will be found in the List of Abbreviations. For further information on these and other primary citations, see Part 1, "Dickens and Cannibalism," note 1.

Abrams, M. H. *The Mirror and the Lamp: Romantic Theory and the Critical Tradition*. New York: W. W. Norton, 1958.
————. *Natural Supernaturalism: Tradition and Revolution in Romantic Literature*. New York: W. W. Norton, 1971.
Adrian, Arthur A. *Dickens and the Parent-Child Relationship*. Athens, Ohio: Ohio University Press, 1984.
————. *Georgina Hogarth and the Dickens Circle*. London: Oxford University Press, 1957.
Allen, Michael. *Charles Dickens' Childhood*. London: Macmillan Press, 1988.
Altick, Richard D. *The English Common Reader: A Social History of the Mass Reading Public, 1800–1900*. Chicago: University of Chicago Press, 1957.
————. *Paintings from Books: Art and Literature in Britain, 1760–1900*. Columbus, Ohio: Ohio State University Press, 1985.
————. *The Shows of London*. Cambridge, Massachusetts: Harvard University Press, 1978.

Arabian Nights, The. See *Thousand and One Nights . . . , The*

Ashley, Robert. *Wilkie Collins.* London: Arthur Barker, 1952.

Auerbach, Erich. *Mimesis: The Representation of Reality in Western Literature.* Trans. Willard Trask. New York: Doubleday, 1957.

Avery, Gillian, with the assistance of Angela Bull. *Nineteenth Century Children: Heroes and Heroines in English Children's Stories, 1780–1900.* London: Hodder and Stoughton, 1965.

Axton, William F. *Circle of Fire: Dickens' Vision and Style and the Popular Victorian Theater.* Lexington, Kentucky: University of Kentucky Press, 1966.

Aylmer, Felix. *Dickens Incognito.* London: Rupert Hart-Davis, 1959.

Ball, James Moores. *The Sack-'Em-Up Men: An Account of the Rise and Fall of the Modern Resurrectionists.* Edinburgh: Oliver and Boyd, 1928.

Barnard, Robert. *Imagery and Theme in the Novels of Dickens.* New York: Humanities Press, 1974.

Bart, Barry D. "'George Silverman's Explanation.'" *Dickensian* 60 (January 1964): 48–51.

Basch, Françoise. *Relative Creatures: Victorian Women in Society and the Novel.* Trans. Anthony Rudolf. London: Allen Lane, 1974.

Batterson, Richard F. "The Manuscript and Text of Dickens's 'George Silverman's Explanation.'" *Papers of the Bibliographical Society of America,* 73 (1979): 473–76.

Beattie, Owen, and John Geiger. *Frozen in Time: The Fate of the Franklin Expedition.* London: Bloomsbury, 1987.

Berger, Francesco. *Reminiscences, Impressions and Anecdotes.* London: Sampson Low, Marston & Co., 1913.

Bettelheim, Bruno. *The Uses of Enchantment: The Meaning and Importance of Fairy Tales.* New York: Alfred A. Knopf, 1976.

Bloch, Dorothy. *"So the Witch Won't Eat Me": Fantasy and the Child's Fear of Infanticide.* Boston: Houghton Mifflin, 1978.

Blount, Trevor. "The Graveyard Satire of *Bleak House* in the Context of 1850." *Review of English Studies* 14 (November 1963): 370–78.

Booth, Michael. *English Melodrama.* London: H. Jenkins, 1965.

Bowen, W. H. *Charles Dickens and His Family: A Sympathetic Study.* Cambridge: W. Heffer & Sons, [1956].

Bradby, M. K. "An Explanation of *George Silverman's Explanation.*" *Dickensian* 36 (Winter 1939–40): 13–18.

Brannan, Robert Louis. *See* Dickens, Charles, and Wilkie Collins. *The Frozen Deep.*

Brattin, Joel. "Dickens' Creation of Bradley Headstone." *Dickens Studies Annual,* 14 (1985): 147–65.

Bredsdorff, Elias. *Hans Andersen and Charles Dickens: A Friendship and Its Dissolution.* Cambridge: W. Heffer and Sons, 1956.

Brice, A. W. *See* Fielding, K. J., and A. W. Brice.

Briggs, Katharine M. "The Folklore of Charles Dickens." *Journal of the Folklore Institute* 7 (June 1970): 3–20.

Buchan, William, M.D. *Domestic Medicine: Or, a Treatise on the Prevention and Cure of Diseases by Regimen and Simple Medicines.* 16th ed. London: A. Strahan, T. Cadell, Jr., and W. Davies, 1798.

Buchanan-Brown, John. *Phiz! Illustrator of Dickens' World.* New York: Charles Scribner's Sons, 1978.

Buckley, Jerome. *Season of Youth: The "Bildungsroman" from Dickens to Golding.* Cambridge, Mass.: Harvard University Press, 1974.

Buckstone, J. B. *Uncle John: A Petite Comedy, in Two Acts.* London: John Miller, 1833.

Butt, John. *Pope, Dickens, and Others: Essays and Addresses.* Edinburgh: Edinburgh University Press, 1969.

————, and Kathleen Tillotson. *Dickens at Work.* London: Methuen & Co., 1957.

Calder, Jenni. *Women and Marriage in Victorian Fiction.* New York: Oxford University Press, 1976.

Carey, John. *The Violent Effigy: A Study of Dickens' Imagination.* London: Faber and Faber, 1973.

Carlton, William J. "In the Blacking Warehouse." *Dickensian* 60 (January 1964): 11–16.

————. "A Companion of the Copperfield Days." *Dickensian* 50 (December 1953): 7–16.

————. "The Death of Mary Hogarth—Before and After." *Dickensian* 63 (May 1967): 68–74.

————. "Dickens in the Jury Box." *Dickensian* 52 (March 1956): 65–69.

————. "Dickens's Forgotten Retreat in France." *Dickensian* 62 (May 1966): 69–86.

————. "A Friend of Dickens's Boyhood." *Dickensian* 66 (January 1970): 8–15.

————. "Links with Dickens in the Isle of Man." *Journal of the Manx Museum* 6 (1958): 42–45.

Carlyle, Thomas. *The French Revolution: A History.* 2 vols. London: Chapman & Hall, 1857.

Cassirer, Ernst. *Language and Myth*. Trans. Susanne K. Langer. New York: Harper, 1946.

Catalogue of the . . . Collection of Pictures, . . . Drawings, and Objects of Art . . . See [Dickens, Charles]. *Catalogue of the . . . Collection of Pictures, . . . Drawings, and Objects of Art . . .*

Catalogue of the Library . . . See [Dickens, Charles]. *Catalogue of the Library . . .*

Chancellor, E. Beresford. *Life in Regency and Early Victorian Times*. London: B. T. Batsford, c. 1926.

Chesney, Kellow. *The Victorian Underworld*. London: Temple Smith, 1970.

Christian, Eleanor E. "Recollections of Charles Dickens, His Family and Friends." *Temple Bar Magazine* 82 (April 1888): 481–506.

Clayborough, Arthur. *The Grotesque in English Literature*. Oxford: Clarendon Press, 1965.

Cockshut, A. O. J. *The Imagination of Charles Dickens*. London: Collins, 1961.

Cohen, Jane R. *Charles Dickens and His Original Illustrators*. Columbus: Ohio State University Press, 1980.

Cole, Hubert. *Things for the Surgeon: A History of the Resurrection Men*. London: Heinemann, 1964.

Collins, Philip. *Dickens and Crime*. London: Macmillan & Co., 1962.

———. *Dickens and Education*. London: Macmillan & Co., 1963.

———. "Dickens on Ghosts: An Uncollected Article." *Dickensian* 59 (January 1963): 5–14.

Collins, Wilkie. *See* Dickens, Charles, and Wilkie Collins. *The Frozen Deep;* Dickens, Charles, and Wilkie Collins. *The Lazy Tour . . . ;* Dickens, Charles, and Wilkie Collins. *No Thoroughfare;* Dickens, Charles, and Wilkie Collins. *The Perils of Certain English Prisoners . . . ;* Dickens, Charles, Wilkie Collins, et al. *The Wreck of the "Golden Mary" . . .*

Colman, George, the Younger. *Broad Grins; By George Colman, (the Younger). Comprising, with New Additional Tales in Verse, Those Formerly Published Under the Title of "My Night-Gown and Slippers."* 4th ed. London: T. Cadell and W. Davies, 1809.

Cotsell, Michael. "Mr. Venus Rises from the Counter: Dickens's Taxidermist and His Contribution to *Our Mutual Friend.*" *Dickensian* 80 (Summer 1984): 105–13.

Cox, C. B. "Realism and Fantasy in *David Copperfield.*" *Bulletin of the John Rylands Library* 52 (Spring 1970): 267–83.

Curry, George. *Charles Dickens and Annie Fields*. San Marino, Calif.: Henry E. Huntington Library and Art Gallery, 1988.

Dabney, Ross H. *Love and Property in the Novels of Dickens*. London: Chatto & Windus, 1967.

Daleski, H. M. *Dickens and the Art of Analogy*. London: Faber and Faber, 1970.

Dance of Death, The; From the Original Designs of Hans Holbein. Illustrated with Thirty-Three Plates, Engraved by W. Hollar. With Descriptions in English and French. London: J. Coxhead, 1816.

Darton, F. J. Harvey. *Children's Books in England: Five Centuries of Social Life*. 2nd ed. Cambridge: Cambridge University Press, 1960.

[Davenport, Richard]. *Sketches of Imposture, Deception, and Credulity*. London: Thomas Tegg and Son, 1837.

Davies, H. E., and H. H. Davies. *Lancaster County Mental Hospital: Survey 1939*. Privately circulated, 1940.

Davis, Earle Roscoe. "Charles Dickens and Wilkie Collins." *Municipal University of Wichita Bulletin* 20 (June 1945): 1–26.

———. *The Flint and the Flame: The Artistry of Charles Dickens*. Columbia: University of Missouri Press, 1963.

Davis, Nuel Pharr. *The Life of Wilkie Collins*. Urbana: University of Illinois Press, 1956.

Delattre, Floris. *Dickens et la France: Étude d'une Interaction Littéraire Anglo-Française*. Paris: Librairie Universitaire, 1927.

Deneau, Daniel P. "The Brother-Sister Relationship in *Hard Times*." *Dickensian* 60 (September 1964): 173–77.

Denman, Peter. "Krook's Death and Dickens's Authorities." *Dickensian* 82 (Autumn 1986): 131–41.

DeVries, Duane. *Dickens's Apprentice Years: The Making of a Novelist*. New York: Barnes & Noble Books, 1976.

Dexter, Walter. *The England of Dickens*. London: Cecil Palmer, 1925.

See also Dickens, Charles. *The Letters . . . ;* Dickens, Charles. *Mr. and Mrs. Charles Dickens . . .*

Dickens, Charles, ed. *All the Year Round, A Weekly Journal*. Vols. 1–20; n. s., vols. 1–4. London: Chapman and Hall, 1859–70.

———, ed. *Bentley's Miscellany*. Vols. 1–5. London: Richard Bentley, 1837–39.

———. ["The Bride's Chamber"]. Chapter 4 of *The Lazy Tour of Two Idle Apprentices*. *Household Words* 16 (24 October 1857): 385–93.

———. "Capital Punishment: Three Letters to *The Daily News*." *Daily News* (9, 13, and 16 March 1846); collected with *RP* (National Edition), 403–33.

[———]. *Catalogue of the Beautiful Collection of Modern Pictures, Water-Colour Drawings, and Objects of Art, of Charles Dickens Deceased. . . . Sold by*

Auction . . . on Saturday, July 9, 1870 . . . Ed. J. H. Stonehouse. London: Piccadilly Fountain Press, 1935.

[——]. *Catalogue of the Library of Charles Dickens, Esq. Author of "The Pickwick Papers," Etc. Comprehending His Entire Library as Existing at His Decease.* Ed. J. H. Stonehouse. London: Piccadilly Fountain Press, 1935.

——. *Charles Dickens' Book of Memoranda: A Photographic and Typographic Facsimile of the Notebook Begun in January 1855.* Ed. Fred Kaplan. New York: New York Public Library, 1981.

——. *Charles Dickens as Editor: Being Letters Written by Him to William Henry Wills His Sub-Editor.* Ed. Rudolph C. Lehmann. New York: Sturgis and Walton, 1912.

——. *Charles Dickens' Uncollected Writings from "Household Words," 1850–1859.* Ed. Harry Stone. 2 vols. Bloomington: Indiana University Press, 1968.

——. "A Child's Dream of a Star." *Household Words* 1 (6 April 1850): 25–26. Later in *RP*.

——. "A Christmas Tree." *Household Words* 2 (21 December 1850): 289–95. Later in *RP*, then in *CS* (National Edition).

——. ["The City of the Absent"]. *All the Year Round* 9 (18 July 1863): 493–96. Later in *UT*.

——. ["City of London Churches"]. *All the Year Round* 3 (5 May 1860): 85–89. Later in *UT*.

——. "Cruikshank's 'The Drunkard's Children.'" *Examiner* (8 July 1848); *MP*, 1: 39–43.

——. *Dickens' Working Notes for His Novels.* Ed. Harry Stone. Chicago and London: University of Chicago Press, 1987.

——. ["Dullborough Town"]. *All the Year Round* 3 (30 June 1860): 274–78. Later in *UT*.

——. ["In the French-Flemish Country"]. *All the Year Round* 10 (12 September 1863): 61–65. Later in *UT*.

——, and Wilkie Collins. *The Frozen Deep.* In *Under the Management of Mr. Charles Dickens: His Production of "The Frozen Deep."* Ed. Robert Louis Brannan. Ithaca, N.Y.: Cornell University Press, 1966.

——. *George Silverman's Explanation.* In *The Atlantic Monthly: A Magazine of Literature, Science, Art, and Politics* 21 (January, February, and March 1868): 118–23, 145–49, 277–83.

——. *George Silverman's Explanation.* Ed. Harry Stone. Northridge, Calif.: Santa Susana Press, 1984.

———. *Holiday Romance.* In *Our Young Folks: An Illustrated Magazine for Boys and Girls* 4 (January, March, April, and May 1868): 1–7, 129–36, 193–200, 257–63.

———, et al. *The Holly-Tree Inn.* The Extra Christmas Number of *Household Words* for 1855.

———, ed. *The Household Narrative of Current Events.* Vols. 1–6. London: Office of *Household Words,* 1850–55.

———, ed. *Household Words, A Weekly Journal.* Vols. 1–19. London: Bradbury and Evans, 1850–59.

———. *Hunted Down.* In *The New York Ledger* 15 (20 and 27 August, and 3 September 1859): 5, 5, 5. With seven illustrations.

———. "The Lamplighter's Story." In *The Pic Nic Papers.* Ed. Charles Dickens. 3 vols. London: Henry Colburn, 1841. 1: 1–32.

———, and Wilkie Collins. *The Lazy Tour of Two Idle Apprentices.* In *Household Words* 16 (3, 10, 17, 24, and 31 October 1857): 313–19, 337–49, 361–67, 385–93, 409–16.

———. *The Letters of Charles Dickens.* Ed. Walter Dexter. 3 vols. The Nonesuch Edition. Bloomsbury, London: Nonesuch Press, 1938.

———. *The Letters of Charles Dickens.* Vols. 1–6, 1820–52. Ed. Madeline House, Graham Storey, Kathleen Tillotson, K. J. Fielding, and Nina Burgis. The Pilgrim Edition. Oxford: Clarendon Press, 1965, 1969, 1974, 1977, 1981, 1988.

———. *Letters from Charles Dickens to Angela Burdett-Coutts, 1841–1865.* Ed. Edgar Johnson. London: Jonathan Cape, 1953.

———. "The Long Voyage." *Household Words* 8 (31 December 1853): 409–12. Later in *RP.*

———. "The Lost Arctic Voyagers." *Household Words* 10 (2, 9, and 23 December 1854): 361–65, 385–93, 433–37.

———. "Lying Awake." *Household Words* 6 (30 October 1852): 145–48. Later in *RP.*

———. "More Letters to the Watsons." Ed. Franklin P. Rolfe. *Dickensian* 38 (March, June, and September 1942): 113–23, 161–66, 189–95.

———. "Mr. Booley's View of the Last Lord Mayor's Show." *Household Words* 2 (30 November 1850): 217–19.

———. *Mr. and Mrs. Charles Dickens, His Letters to Her.* Ed. Walter Dexter. London: Constable & Co., 1935.

———. "*The Night Side of Nature; or, Ghosts and Ghost Seers.* By Catherine Crowe." *Examiner* (26 February 1848); *Dickensian* 59 (January 1963): 6–14.

———. ["Night Walks"]. *All the Year Round* 3 (21 July 1860): 348–52. Later in *UT*.

———, and Wilkie Collins. *No Thoroughfare*. The Extra Christmas Number of *All the Year Round* for 1867.

———. ["Nurse's Stories"]. *All the Year Round* 3 (8 September 1860): 517–21. Later in *UT*.

———. "Out of the Season." *Household Words* 13 (28 June 1856): 553–56. Later in *RP*.

———, and Wilkie Collins. *The Perils of Certain English Prisoners, and Their Treasure in Women, Children, Silver, and Jewels*. The Extra Christmas Number of *Household Words* for 1857.

———. "Please to Leave Your Umbrella." *Household Words* 17 (1 May 1858): 457–59.

———. ["Poor Mercantile Jack"]. *All the Year Round* 2 (10 March 1860): 462–66. Later in *UT*.

———. "Railway Dreaming." *Household Words* 13 (10 May 1856): 385–88.

———. ["Refreshments for Travellers"]. *All the Year Round* 2 (24 March 1860): 512–16. Later in *UT*.

———. ["Some Recollections of Mortality"]. *All the Year Round* 9 (16 May 1863): 276–80. Later in *UT*.

———. *The Speeches of Charles Dickens*. Ed. K. J. Fielding. Oxford: Clarendon Press, 1960.

———. ["Titbull's Alms-Houses"]. *All the Year Round* 10 (24 October 1863): 205–10. Later in *UT*.

———. "Trading in Death." *Household Words* 6 (27 November 1852): 241–45.

———. ["Travelling Abroad"]. *All the Year Round* 2 (7 April 1860): 557–62. Later in *UT*.

———. "A Walk in a Workhouse." *Household Words* 1 (25 May 1850): 204–7.

———. "Where We Stopped Growing." *Household Words* 6 (1 January 1853): 361–63.

———. *The Works of Charles Dickens*. Ed. B. W. Matz. 40 vols. The National Edition. London: Chapman and Hall, 1906–08.

———, Wilkie Collins, et al. *The Wreck of the "Golden Mary": Being the Captain's Account of the Loss of the Ship, and the Mate's Account of the Great Deliverance of Her People in an Open Boat at Sea*. The Extra Christmas Number of *Household Words* for 1856.

For titles of novels and Christmas Books cited, and for their dates of publication, *see* List of Abbreviations.

Dickens, Sir Henry Fielding. *Memories of My Father.* London: Victor Gollancz, 1928.

———. *The Recollections of Sir Henry Dickens, K. C.* London: William Heinemann, 1934.

Dickens, Kate. *See* Perugini, Kate Dickens.

Dickens, Mamie. *Charles Dickens.* 2nd ed. London: Cassell & Co., 1889.

———. "Charles Dickens at Home: With Especial Reference to His Relations with Children." *Cornhill Magazine,* n. s. 19 (January 1885): 32–51.

———. *My Father as I Recall Him.* New York: E. P. Dutton & Co., 1900.

Dickens Quarterly. Vols. 1–5. Louisville, Ky.: Dickens Society, 1984–88.

Dickens Studies. Vols. 1–5. Boston: Emerson College, 1965–69.

Dickens Studies Annual. Vols. 1–17. New York: AMS Press, 1970–88.

Dickens Studies Newsletter. Vols. 1–14. Louisville, Ky.: Dickens Society, 1970–83.

Dickensian, The. Vols. 1–84. London: Dickens Fellowship, 1905–88.

Docton, Kenneth. *Lancaster As It Was.* Nelson: Hendon Publishing Co., 1973.

Dolby, George. *Charles Dickens as I Knew Him: The Story of the Reading Tours in Great Britain and America (1866–1870).* London: T. Fisher Unwin, [1885].

Du Cann, C. G. L. *The Love-Lives of Charles Dickens.* London: Frederick Muller, 1961.

Doré, Gustave, and Blanchard Jerrold. *London: A Pilgrimage.* London: Grant & Co., 1872.

Dunn, Richard J. "Dickens and the Tragi-Comic Grotesque," *Studies in the Novel* 1 (Summer 1969): 147–55.

———. "Dickens's Mastery of the Macabre." *Dickens Studies* 1 (January 1965): 33–39.

Dyos, H. J., and Michael Wolff, eds. *The Victorian City: Images and Realities.* 2 vols. London: Routledge and Kegan Paul, 1973.

Dyson, A. E. *The Inimitable Dickens: A Reading of the Novels.* London: Macmillan, 1970.

———. "*The Old Curiosity Shop:* Innocence and the Grotesque." In *Dickens: Modern Judgements.* Ed. A. E. Dyson. London: Macmillan, 1968.

Easson, Angus. "'I, Elizabeth Dickens': Light on John Dickens's Legacy." *Dickensian* 67 (January 1971): 35–40.

———. "John Dickens and the Navy Pay Office." *Dickensian* 70 (January 1974): 35–45.

Eigner, Edwin M. *The Dickens Pantomime*. Berkeley, Los Angeles, London: University of California Press, 1989.

———. *The Metaphysical Novel in England and America: Dickens, Bulwer, Hawthorne, Melville*. Berkeley and Los Angeles: University of California Press, 1978.

Fielding, K. J. *Charles Dickens: A Critical Introduction*. 2nd ed. London: Longmans, 1965.

———, and A. W. Brice. "*Bleak House* and the Graveyard." In *Dickens the Craftsman: Strategies of Presentation*. Ed. Robert B. Partlow, Jr. Carbondale: Southern Illinois University Press, 1970.

———. "Dickens and the Hogarth Scandal." *Nineteenth-Century Fiction* 10 (June 1955): 64–74.

See also Dickens, Charles. *The Letters . . .* ; Dickens, Charles. *The Speeches . . .*

Fields, James T. *Yesterdays with Authors*. Boston and New York: Houghton, Mifflin and Co., 1900. First publ. 1871.

[Fields, Mrs. James T. (Annie)]. *Memories of a Hostess: A Chronicle of Eminent Friendships Drawn Chiefly from the Diaries of Mrs. James T. Fields*. Ed. M. A. DeWolfe Howe. Boston: Atlantic Monthly Press, 1922.

See also Curry, George. *Charles Dickens and Annie Fields*.

Fitzgerald, Percy. *Bozland: Dickens' Places and People*. London: Downey & Co., 1895.

———. *The Life of Charles Dickens as Revealed in His Writings*. 2 vols. London: Chatto & Windus, 1905.

———. *Memories of Charles Dickens*. Bristol: J. W. Arrowsmith, 1913.

Fitz-Gerald, S. J. Adair. *Dickens and the Drama*. London: Chapman & Hall, 1910.

Flamm, Dudley. "The Prosecutor Within: Dickens's Final Explanation." *Dickensian* 66 (January 1970): 16–23.

Ford, George H. *Dickens and His Readers: Aspects of Novel-Criticism Since 1836*. Princeton, N.J.: Princeton University Press, 1955.

———. "Dickens and the Voices of Time." In *Dickens Centennial Essays*. Ed. Ada Nisbet and Blake Nevius. Berkeley and Los Angeles: University of California Press, 1971.

Forster, John. *The Life of Charles Dickens*. Ed. J. W. T. Ley. London: Cecil Palmer, 1928. Originally published in 3 vols., 1872–74.

Forsyte, Charles. "Drood and the Bean-stalk." *Dickensian* 80 (Summer 1984): 74–88.

———. "The Sapsea Fragment—Fragment of What?" *Dickensian* 82 (Spring 1986): 12–26.

Fox, John. *The Book of Martyrs: Containing an Account of the Sufferings and*

Death of the Protestants in the Reign of Queen Mary the First. Revised and Corrected. London: H. Trapp, 1776.

See also *Lives of the Primitive Martyrs . . .*

Frank, Lawrence. *Charles Dickens and the Romantic Self.* Lincoln: University of Nebraska Press, 1984.

―――. "The Intelligibility of Madness in *Our Mutual Friend* and *The Mystery of Edwin Drood.*" *Dickens Studies Annual* 5 (1976): 150–95.

French, A. L. "Beating and Cringing: *Great Expectations.*" *Essays in Criticism* 24 (April 1974): 147–68.

Friedman, Stanley. "The Complex Origins of Pip and Magwitch." *Dickens Studies Annual* 15 (1986): 221–31.

Frye, Northrop. "Dickens and the Comedy of Humors." In *Experience in the Novel.* Ed. Roy Harvey Pearce. New York: Columbia University Press, 1968.

―――. *The Secular Scripture: A Study of the Structure of Romance.* Cambridge, Mass.: Harvard University Press, 1976.

Gadd, W. Laurence. *The Great Expectations Country.* London: Cecil Palmer, 1929.

Gallagher, Catherine. "The Duplicity of Doubling in *A Tale of Two Cities.*" *Dickens Studies Annual* 12 (1983): 125–45.

Gaskell, E. *Dickens and Medicine.* London: Wellcome Institute, 1970.

Geiger, John. *See* Beattie, Owen, and John Geiger.

George, M. Dorothy. *Hogarth to Cruikshank: Social Change in Graphic Satire.* London: Allen Lane The Penguin Press, 1967.

Gibson, Priscilla. "Dickens's Uses of Animism." *Nineteenth-Century Fiction* 7 (March 1953): 283–91.

Gillray, James. *The Works of James Gillray, from the Original Plates, with the Addition of Many Subjects Not Before Collected.* London: Henry G. Bohn, [1851].

Gilly, William O. S. *Narratives of Shipwrecks of the Royal Navy: Between 1793 and 1849.* 2nd ed. rev. London: John W. Parker, 1851.

Gissing, George. *Charles Dickens: A Critical Study.* London: Blackie & Son, 1898.

Glancy, Ruth. "Dickens at Work on *The Haunted Man.*" *Dickens Studies Annual* 15 (1986): 65–85.

Goldfarb, Russell M. *Sexual Repression and Victorian Literature.* Lewisburg, Penna.: Bucknell University Press, 1970.

Gose, Elliott B. *Imagination Indulged: The Irrational in the Nineteenth-Century Novel.* Montreal: McGill-Queen's University Press, 1972.

Griffiths, Arthur. *Memorials of Millbank.* London: Chapman & Hall, 1884.

Grillo, Virgil. *Charles Dickens' "Sketches by Boz": End in the Beginning.* Boulder: Colorado Associated University Press, 1974.

Grob, Shirley. "Dickens and Some Motifs of the Fairy Tale." *Texas Studies in Literature and Language* 5 (Winter 1964): 567–79.

Guerard, Albert J. *The Triumph of the Novel: Dickens, Dostoevsky, Faulkner.* London: Oxford University Press, 1977.

Harbage, Alfred B. *A Kind of Power: The Shakespeare-Dickens Analogy.* Philadelphia: American Philosophical Society, 1975.

Hardy, Barbara. "Dickens and the Passions." In *Dickens Centennial Essays.* Ed. Ada Nisbet and Blake Nevius. Berkeley and Los Angeles: University of California Press, 1971.

———. *The Moral Art of Dickens.* London: Athlone Press, 1970.

Harris, Edwin. *Gad's Hill Place and Charles Dickens.* Rochester: Edwin Harris & Sons, 1910.

Harvey, J. R. *Victorian Novelists and Their Illustrators.* London: Sidgwick & Jackson, 1970.

Hayward, Arthur L. *The Days of Dickens: A Glance at Some Aspects of Early Victorian Life in London.* London: George Routledge & Sons, n.d.

Hill, Draper. *Mr. Gillray the Caricaturist: A Biography.* London: Phaidon Press, 1965.

Hill, Nancy K. *A Reformer's Art: Dickens' Picturesque and Grotesque Imagery.* Athens, Ohio: Ohio University Press, 1981.

[Hindley, Charles]. *Curiosities of Street Literature.* London: Reeves and Turner, 1871.

Hobsbaum, Philip. *A Reader's Guide to Charles Dickens.* London: Thames and Hudson, 1973.

Hogarth, William. *The Complete Works of William Hogarth: In A Series of One Hundred and Fifty Steel Engravings, From the Original Pictures. With An Introductory Essay, By James Hannay; And Descriptive Letterpress, By The Rev. J. Trusler, and E. F. Roberts.* London: London Printing and Publishing Co., [c. 1860].

Holbein, Hans. See *Dance of Death, The.*

Holland, Norman. *The Dynamics of Literary Response.* New York: Oxford University Press, 1968.

Hollingsworth, Keith. *The Newgate Novel 1830–1847.* Detroit: Wayne State University Press, 1963.

Hollington, Michael, *Dickens and the Grotesque.* London: Croom Helm, 1984.

Hornback, Bert G. *"The Hero of My Life": Essays on Dickens.* Athens, Ohio: Ohio University Press, 1981.

————. *"Noah's Arkitecture": A Study of Dickens's Mythology.* Athens, Ohio: Ohio University Press, 1972.

[Hotten, John Camden]. *See* [Taverner, H. T., and John Camden Hotten].

House, Humphry. *The Dickens World.* 2nd ed. London: Oxford University Press, 1950.

House, Madeline. *See* Dickens, Charles. *The Letters . . .*

Hughes, William R. *A Week's Tramp in Dickens-Land: Together with Personal Reminiscences of the "Inimitable Boz" Therein Collected.* 2nd ed., rev. London: Chapman & Hall, 1893.

Hunt, John Dixon. "Dickens and the Traditions of Graphic Satire." In *Encounters: Essays on Literature and the Visual Arts.* Ed. John Dixon Hunt. London: Studio Vista, 1971.

Hunter, Richard A., and Ida Macalpine. "A Note on Dickens's Psychiatric Reading." *Dickensian* 53 (January 1957): 49–51.

Hutter, Albert D. "Dismemberment and Articulation in *Our Mutual Friend.*" *Dickens Studies Annual* 11 (1983): 135–75.

————. "The Novelist as Resurrectionist: Dickens and the Dilemma of Death." *Dickens Studies Annual* 12 (1983): 1–39.

————. "Reconstructive Autobiography: The Experience at Warren's Blacking." *Dickens Studies Annual* 6 (1977): 1–14.

Iser, Wolfgang. *The Implied Reader.* Baltimore: Johns Hopkins University Press, 1974.

Jerrold, Blanchard. *See* Doré, Gustave, and Blanchard Jerrold.

Johnson, E. D. H. *Charles Dickens: An Introduction to His Novels.* New York: Random House, 1969.

Johnson, Edgar. *Charles Dickens. His Tragedy and Triumph.* 2 vols. New York: Simon and Schuster, 1952.

See also Dickens, Charles. *Letters from . . .*

Johnson, Pamela Hansford. "The Sexual Life in Dickens's Novels." In *Dickens 1970: Centenary Essays.* Ed. Michael Slater. London: Chapman & Hall, 1970.

Johnson, William C. "Dickens and Demons: A Comparative Approach." *English Record* 22 (Spring 1972): 33–40.

Kaplan, Fred. *Dickens: A Biography.* New York: William Morrow & Co., 1988.

————. *Dickens and Mesmerism: The Hidden Springs of Fiction.* Princeton, N.J.: Princeton University Press, 1975.

See also Dickens, Charles. *Charles Dickens' Book . . .*

Kayser, Wolfgang. *The Grotesque in Art and Literature.* Trans. Ulrich Weisstein. Bloomington: Indiana University Press, 1963.

Kent, William. *Dickens and Religion.* London: Watts & Co., 1930.

Kincaid, James R. *Dickens and the Rhetoric of Laughter.* Oxford: Clarendon Press, 1971.

Kirkpatrick, Larry. "The Gothic Flame of Charles Dickens." *Victorian Newsletter* 31 (Spring 1967): 20–24.

Kitton, Frederic G. *Charles Dickens by Pen and Pencil: Including Anecdotes and Reminiscences Collected from His Friends and Contemporaries.* 3 vols., including Supplement. London: Frank T. Sabin and John F. Dexter, 1890–92.

————. *The Dickens Country.* London: Adam and Charles Black, 1905.

————. *Dickens and His Illustrators.* London: George Redway, 1899.

————. *The Minor Writings of Charles Dickens: A Bibliography and Sketch.* London: Elliot Stock, 1900.

————. *"Phiz" (Hablot Knight Browne): A Memoir.* London: George Redway, 1882.

Kligerman, Charles, M.D. "The Dream of Charles Dickens." *Journal of the American Psychoanalytic Association* 18 (October 1970): 783–99.

Klingender, Francis Donald, ed. *Hogarth and English Caricature.* London: Transatlantic Arts, 1944.

Knoepflmacher, U. C. *Laughter and Despair: Readings in Ten Novels of the Victorian Era.* Berkeley and Los Angeles: University of California Press, 1971.

Kotzin, Michael. *Dickens and the Fairy Tale.* Bowling Green, Ohio: Bowling Green University Popular Press, 1972.

Kucich, John. *Excess and Restraint in the Novels of Charles Dickens.* Athens, Georgia: University of Georgia Press, 1981.

Laing, R. D. *The Divided Self.* Baltimore: Penguin Books, 1965.

Lane, Lauriat, Jr. "The Devil in *Oliver Twist.*" *Dickensian* 52 (June 1956): 132–36.

————. "Dickens and the Double." *Dickensian* 55 (January 1959): 47–55.

Langton, Robert. *The Childhood and Youth of Charles Dickens: With Retrospective Notes, and Elucidations, from His Books and Letters.* Manchester: Published by the Author, 1883. London: Hutchinson & Co., 1912.

Lanham, Richard A. "*Our Mutual Friend:* The Birds of Prey." *Victorian Newsletter* 24 (Fall 1963): 6–12.

Leavis, F. R., and Q. D. Leavis. *Dickens the Novelist.* London: Chatto & Windus, 1970.

Lehmann, Rudolph C. *See* Dickens, Charles. *Charles Dickens as Editor . . .*

Lesser, Simon O. *Fiction and the Unconscious.* New York: Vintage Books, 1962.

Lettis, Richard. *The Dickens Aesthetic.* New York: AMS Press, 1989.

Lévi-Strauss, Claude. "The Structural Study of Myth." In *European Literary Theory and Practice*. Ed. Vernon W. Gras. New York: Dell Publishing Co., 1973.

Ley, J. W. T. *The Dickens Circle: A Narrative of the Novelist's Friendships*. New York: E. P. Dutton & Co., 1919.

See also Forster, John. *The Life of Charles Dickens*.

Lindsay, Jack. *Charles Dickens: A Biographical and Critical Study*. London: Andrew Dakers, 1950.

Lives of the Primitive Martyrs, from the Birth of Our Blessed Saviour, to the Reign of Mary I, The. With the Life of Mr. John Fox. London: H. Trapp, [c. 1776].

See also Fox, John. *The Book of Martyrs . . .*

Longley, Katharine M. "Dickens Incognito." *Dickensian* 77 (Summer 1981): 88–91.

————. "Letter to the Editor." *Dickensian* 77 (Spring 1981): 56.

Loomis, Chauncey C. "The Arctic Sublime." In *Nature and the Victorian Imagination*. Ed. U. C. Knoepflmacher and G. B. Tennyson. Berkeley and Los Angeles: University of California Press, 1977.

Lucas, John. *The Melancholy Man: A Study of Dickens' Novels*. London: Methuen & Co., 1970.

Lukács, Georg. *The Theory of the Novel*. Cambridge, Mass.: MIT Press, 1971.

Macalpine, Ida. *See* Hunter, Richard A., and Ida Macalpine.

Mackay, Charles. *Memoirs of Extraordinary Popular Delusions and the Madness of Crowds*. 2 vols. London: Office of the National Illustrated Library, 1852.

McMaster, Juliet. *Dickens the Designer*. Totowa, N.J.: Barnes & Noble Books, 1987.

McMaster, Rowland D. "Birds of Prey: A Study of *Our Mutual Friend*." *Dalhousie Review* 40 (Fall 1960): 372–81.

————. "Dickens and the Horrific." *Dalhousie Review* 38 (Spring 1958): 18–28.

————. "Man into Beast in Dickensian Caricature." *University of Toronto Quarterly* 31 (April 1962): 354–61.

Manheim, Leonard F. "Floras and Doras: The Women in Dickens' Novels." *Texas Studies in Literature and Language* 7 (Summer 1965): 181–200.

————. "The Personal History of David Copperfield: A Study in Psychoanalytic Criticism." *American Imago* 9 (April 1952): 21–43.

Manning, John. *Dickens on Education*. Toronto: University of Toronto Press, 1959.

Manning, Sylvia. "Dickens, January, and May." *Dickensian* 71 (Spring 1975): 67–75.

———. *Dickens as Satirist*. New Haven, Conn.: Yale University Press, 1971.

———. "Masking and Self-Revelation: Dickens's Three Autobiograpies." *Dickens Studies Newsletter* 7 (September 1976): 69–75.

Marcus, Steven. *Dickens: From Pickwick to Dombey*. London: Chatto & Windus, 1965.

Marlow, James E. "English Cannibalism: Dickens After 1859." *Studies in English Literature* 23 (Autumn 1983): 647–66.

———. "The Fate of Sir John Franklin: Three Phases of Response in Victorian Periodicals." *Victorian Periodicals Review* 15 (Spring 1982): 3–11.

———. "Sir John Franklin, Mr. Charles Dickens, and the Solitary Monster." *Dickens Studies Newsletter* 12 (December 1981): 97–103.

Marten, Harry P. "The Visual Imaginations of Dickens and Hogarth: Structure and Scene." *Studies in the Novel* 6 (Summer 1974): 145–64.

Matz, B. W. *Dickensian Inns and Taverns*. London: Cecil Palmer, 1922.

See also Dickens, Charles. *The Works*...

Mayhew, Henry. *London Labour and the London Poor*. 4 vols. London: Griffin, Bohn, and Co., 1861–62.

Meckier, Jerome. *Hidden Rivalries in Victorian Fiction: Dickens, Realism, and Revaluation*. Lexington: University Press of Kentucky, 1987.

Meier, Stefanie. *Animation and Mechanization in the Novels of Charles Dickens*. Bern: Francke Verlag, 1982.

Mercier, Louis-Sébastien. *Nouveau Paris*. 6 vols. Paris: Fuchs, 1799.

———. *Le Tableau de Paris*. 12 vols. Amsterdam, 1782–88.

Millais, John Guille. *The Life and Letters of Sir John Everett Millais*. 2 vols. London: Methuen & Co., 1899.

Miller, J. Hillis. *Charles Dickens: The World of His Novels*. Cambridge, Mass.: Harvard University Press, 1958.

Miyoshi, Masao. *The Divided Self*. New York: New York University Press, 1969.

Monod, Sylvère. *Dickens the Novelist*. Norman: University of Oklahoma Press, 1968.

Morley, Henry. *Memoirs of Bartholomew Fair*. New ed. London: Chatto and Windus, 1880. Original ed. 1859.

Nelson, Harland S. *Charles Dickens*. Boston: Twayne Publishers, 1981.

Newsom, Robert. *Dickens on the Romantic Side of Familiar Things: "Bleak House" and the Novel Tradition*. New York: Columbia University Press, 1977.

Nisbet, Ada. *Dickens and Ellen Ternan*. Berkeley and Los Angeles: University of California Press, 1952.

Orwell, George. *Dickens, Dali and Others: Studies in Popular Culture*. New York: Reynal & Hitchcock, 1946.

Parker, David, and Michael Slater. "The Gladys Storey Papers." *Dickensian* 76 (Spring 1980): 3–16.

Patten, Robert L. *Charles Dickens and His Publishers*. Oxford: Clarendon Press, 1978.

Paulson, Ronald. *Hogarth's Graphic Works*. 2 vols. New Haven, Conn.: Yale University Press, 1965.

Payn, James. *Some Literary Recollections*. New ed. London: Smith, Elder, & Co., 1885.

Perugini, Kate Dickens. "'Edwin Drood,' and the Last Days of Charles Dickens. By His Younger Daughter, Kate Perugini." *Pall Mall Magazine* 37 (June 1906): 643–54.

Pope, Norris. *Dickens and Charity*. London: Macmillan Press, 1978.

Portfolio of Entertaining and Instructive Varieties in History, Science, Literature, the Fine Arts, &c. &c. &c., The. Vols. 1–2. London: Duncombe, 1823–24.

Rawlins, Jack P. "Great Expiations: Dickens and the Betrayal of the Child." *Studies in English Literature* 23 (Autumn 1983): 667–83.

Reid, J. C. *The Hidden World of Charles Dickens*. Auckland, N.Z.: University of Auckland, 1962.

———. "Mr. Tringham of Slough." *Dickensian* 64 (September 1968): 164–65.

[Ridley, James]. *The Tales of the Genii*. 2 vols. London: J. Booker et al., 1820.

Riely, John. *Rowlandson Drawings from the Paul Mellon Collection*. New Haven, Conn.: Yale Center for British Art, 1977.

Rogers, Robert. *The Double in Literature*. Detroit: Wayne State University Press, 1970.

Rolfe, Franklin P. *See* Dickens, Charles. "More Letters to the Watsons."

Rudwin, Maxmilian. *The Devil in Legend and Literature*. New York: AMS Press, 1970.

Sanders, Andrew. *Charles Dickens: Resurrectionist*. New York: St. Martin's Press, 1982.

Schlicke, Paul. *Dickens and Popular Entertainment*. London: Allen & Unwin, 1985.

Schwarzbach, F. S. *Dickens and the City*. London: Athlone Press, 1979.

Scott, P. J. M. *Reality and Comic Confidence in Charles Dickens.* London: Macmillan Press, 1979.

Shaw, George Bernard. *Shaw on Dickens.* Ed. Dan H. Lawrence and Martin Quinn. New York: Frederick Ungar Publishing Co., 1985.

Shesgreen, Sean. *Hogarth and the Times-of-the-Day Tradition.* Ithaca, N.Y.: Cornell University Press, 1983.

Shumaker, Wayne. *Literature and the Irrational: A Study in Anthropological Backgrounds.* Englewood Cliffs, N.J.: Prentice-Hall, 1960.

Slater, Michael. *Dickens and Women.* London: J. M. Dent & Sons, 1983.

————. "How Many Nurses Had Charles Dickens? *The Uncommercial Traveller* and Dickensian Biography." *Prose Studies* 10 (December 1987): 250–58. *See also* Parker, David, and Michael Slater.

Sly's King's Arms & Royal Hotel, Lancaster. Lancaster: Gazette Office, n.d.

Smith, Grahame. *Dickens, Money, and Society.* Berkeley and Los Angeles: University of California Press, 1968.

Smith, Sheila. "Anti-Mechanism and the Comic in the Writings of Charles Dickens." *Renaissance and Modern Studies* 3 (October 1959): 131–44.

Southern, Richard. *The Victorian Theatre: A Pictorial Survey.* Newton Abbot, Eng.: David & Charles, 1970.

Speaight, George. *Juvenile Drama: The History of the English Toy Theatre.* London: Macdonald & Co., 1946.

Spence, Gordon. *Charles Dickens as a Familiar Essayist.* Salzburg: Universität Salzburg, 1977.

Spilka, Mark. *Dickens and Kafka: A Mutual Interpretation.* Bloomington: Indiana University Press, 1963.

[Staples, Leslie C., ed.]. "New Letters of Mary Hogarth and Her Sister Catherine." *Dickensian* 63 (May 1967): 75–80.

Stedman, Jane W. "Child-Wives of Dickens." *Dickensian* 59 (May 1963): 112–18.

Steig, Michael. *Dickens and Phiz.* Bloomington: Indiana University Press, 1978.

————. "Structure and the Grotesque in Dickens: *Dombey and Son; Bleak House.*" *Centennial Review* 14 (Summer 1970): 313–31.

Stevenson, Lionel. "Dickens's Dark Novels, 1851–1857." *Sewanee Review* 51 (Summer 1943): 398–409.

Stoehr, Taylor. *Dickens: The Dreamer's Stance.* Ithaca, N.Y.: Cornell University Press, 1965.

Stokes, M. Veronica. "Charles Dickens: A Customer of Coutts & Co." *Dickensian* 68 (January 1972): 17–30.

Stone, Harry. "Dark Corners of the Mind: Dickens' Childhood Reading." *Horn Book Magazine* 39 (June 1963): 306–21.

———. "Dickens' Artistry and *The Haunted Man.*" *South Atlantic Quarterly* 61 (Autumn 1962): 492–505.

———. "Dickens, Browning, and the Mysterious Letter." *Pacific Coast Philology* 1 (April 1966): 42–47.

———. "Dickens and Interior Monologue." *Philological Quarterly* 38 (January 1959): 52–65.

———. *Dickens and the Invisible World: Fairy Tales, Fantasy, and Novel-Making.* Bloomington: Indiana University Press, 1979.

———. "Dickens, Cruikshank, and Fairy Tales." In *George Cruikshank: A Revaluation.* Ed. Robert L. Patten. Princeton, N.J.: Princeton University Library, 1974.

———. "Dickens's Tragic Universe: 'George Silverman's Explanation.'" *Studies in Philology* 55 (January 1958): 86–97.

———. "Fairy Tales and Ogres: Dickens' Imagination and *David Copperfield.*" *Criticism* 6 (Fall 1964): 324–30.

———. "The Genesis of a Novel: *Great Expectations.*" In *Charles Dickens: 1812–1870.* Ed. E. W. F. Tomlin. London: Weidenfeld and Nicolson, 1969.

———. "The Love Pattern in Dickens' Novels." In *Dickens the Craftsman: Strategies of Presentation.* Ed. Robert B. Partlow, Jr. Carbondale: Southern Illinois University Press, 1970.

———. "The Novel as Fairy Tale: Dickens' *Dombey and Son.*" *English Studies* 47 (February 1966): 1–27.

———. "What's in a Name: Fantasy and Calculation in Dickens." *Dickens Studies Annual* 14 (1985): 191–204.

See also Dickens, Charles. *Charles Dickens' Uncollected Writings . . . ;* Dickens, Charles. *Dickens' Working Notes . . . ;* Dickens, Charles. *George Silverman's Explanation.*

Stone, Ian R. "'The contents of the kettles': Charles Dickens, John Rae and Cannibalism on the 1845 Franklin Expedition." *Dickensian* 83 (Spring 1987): 7–16.

Stonehouse, John Harrison. *Green Leaves: New Chapters in the Life of Charles Dickens.* Revised and enlarged ed. London: Piccadilly Fountain Press, 1931. *See also* [Dickens, Charles]. *Catalogue . . .*

Storey, Gladys. *Dickens and Daughter.* London: Frederick Muller, 1939.

Storey, Graham. *Charles Dickens: "Bleak House."* Cambridge: Cambridge University Press, 1987. *See also* Dickens, Charles. *The Letters . . .*

Strange, Kathleen H. "Blacking-Polish." *Dickensian* 75 (Spring 1979): 7–11.

Sucksmith, Harvey Peter. *The Narrative Art of Charles Dickens: The Rhetoric of Sympathy and Irony in His Novels*. Oxford: Clarendon Press, 1970.

Tales of Shipwrecks and Adventures at Sea. London: W. M. Clark, [c. 1850].

[Taverner, H. T., and John Camden Hotten]. *Charles Dickens: The Story of His Life*. New York: Harper & Brothers, 1870.

Taylor, Anya. "Devoured Hearts in *Great Expectations*." *Dickens Studies Newsletter* 13 (September 1982): 65–71.

The Terrific Register; or, Record of Crimes, Judgments, Providences, and Calamities. Vols. 1–2. London: Sherwood, Jones, and Co., 1824–25.

Thomas, Deborah A. "Dickens and Indigestion: The Deadly Dinners of the Rich." *Dickens Studies Newsletter* 14 (March 1983): 7–12.

———. *Dickens and the Short Story*. Philadelphia: University of Pennsylvania Press, 1982.

———. "The Equivocal Explanation of Dickens' George Silverman." *Dickens Studies Annual* 3 (1974): 134–43.

Thomson, David Croal. *The Life and Labours of Hablôt Knight Browne, "Phiz."* London: Chapman and Hall, 1884.

Thousand and One Nights, Commonly Called, in England, The Arabian Nights' Entertainments, The. Trans. Edward William Lane. 3 vols. London: Charles Knight and Co., 1839–41.

Thurin, Susan Schoenbauer. "The Seven Deadly Sins in *Great Expectations*." *Dickens Studies Annual* 15 (1986): 201–20.

Tick, Stanley. "Toward Jaggers." *Dickens Studies Annual* 5 (1976): 133–49.

Tillotson, Kathleen. *Novels of the Eighteen-Forties*. Oxford: Clarendon Press, 1954.

See also Butt, John, and Kathleen Tillotson; Dickens, Charles. *The Letters* . . .

Tomlin, E. W. F., ed. *Charles Dickens 1812–1870: A Centennial Volume*. London: Weidenfeld and Nicolson, 1969.

Trilling, Lionel. "Little Dorrit." *Kenyon Review* 15 (Autumn 1953): 577–90.

Trumble, Alfred. *In Jail with Charles Dickens*. London: Suckling & Galloway, 1896.

Tymms, Ralph. *Doubles in Literary Psychology*. Cambridge: Bowes and Bowes, 1949.

Ullman, Michael A. "Where George Stopped Growing: Dickens's 'George Silverman's Explanation.'" *Ariel* 10 (January 1979): 11–23.

Universal Songster, or Museum of Mirth: Forming the Most Complete, Extensive, and Valuable Collection of Ancient & Modern Songs in the English Language, The. 3 vols. London: Fairburn, 1825–26.

Van Amerongen, J. B. *The Actor in Dickens: A Study of the Histrionic and Dra-*

matic Elements in the Novelist's Life and Works. New York: D. Appleton and Co., 1927.

Varma, Devendra P. *The Gothic Flame: Being a History of the Gothic Novel in England: Its Origins, Efflorescence, Disintegration, and Residuary Influences*. New York: Russell and Russell, 1966.

Wagenknecht, Edward. *Dickens and the Scandalmongers: Essays in Criticism*. Norman: University of Oklahoma Press, 1965.

———. *The Man Charles Dickens: A Victorian Portrait*. New and rev. ed. Norman: University of Oklahoma Press, 1966.

Walder, Dennis. *Dickens and Religion*. London: George Allen & Unwin, 1981.

Walters, J. Cuming. "'Biting' Critics." *Dickensian* 26 (Autumn 1930): 282–85.

Wark, Robert R. *Drawings by Thomas Rowlandson in the Huntington Collection*. San Marino, Calif.: Huntington Library, 1975.

———, ed. *Rowlandson's Drawings for "The English Dance of Death."* San Marino, Calif.: Huntington Library, 1966.

Watt, Ian. "Oral Dickens." *Dickens Studies Annual* 3 (1974): 165–81.

Welsby, Paul A. *Rochester Cathedral in the Time of Charles Dickens*. Rochester, Eng.: Brewster Printing Co., 1976.

Welsh, Alexander. *The City of Dickens*. Oxford: Clarendon Press, 1971.

———. *From Copyright to Copperfield: The Identity of Dickens*. Cambridge, Mass.: Harvard University Press, 1987.

Wilson, A. E. *Penny Plain, Two Pence Coloured: A History of the Juvenile Drama*. London: G. G. Harrap & Co., 1932.

Wilson, Angus. *The World of Charles Dickens*. London: Martin Secker & Warburg, 1970.

Wilson, Edmund. "Dickens: The Two Scrooges." In *The Wound and the Bow*. London: W. H. Allen, 1952. First published (in book version) in 1941.

Winters, Warrington. "Dickens and the Psychology of Dreams." *PMLA* 63 (September 1948): 984–1006.

Wolff, Michael. *See* Dyos, H. J., and Michael Wolff.

Woollcott, Alexander. *Mr. Dickens Goes to the Play*. New York: G. P. Putnam's Sons, 1922.

Worth, George J. *Dickensian Melodrama: A Reading of the Novels*. Lawrence: University of Kansas Publications, 1978.

Wright, Thomas. *The Life of Charles Dickens*. London: Herbert Jenkins, 1935.

Young, G. M., ed. *Early Victorian England: 1830–1865*. 2 vols. London: Oxford University Press, 1934.

Index

Studies in Victorian Life and Literature
Richard D. Altick, Editor